Server+ Certification Bible

Server+
Certification Bible

Trevor Kay

Hungry Minds™

Best-Selling Books • Digital Downloads • e-Books • Answer Networks • e-Newsletters • Branded Web Sites • e-Learning

New York, NY ✦ Cleveland, OH ✦ Indianapolis, IN

Server+ Certification Bible

Published by
Hungry Minds, Inc.
909 Third Avenue
New York, NY 10022
www.hungryminds.com

Library of Congress Control Number: 2001090747

ISBN: 0-7645-4809-3

Printed in the United States of America

10 9 8 7 6 5 4 3 2 1

1P/SQ/QW/QR/IN

Distributed in the United States by Hungry Minds, Inc.

Distributed by CDG Books Canada Inc. for Canada; by Transworld Publishers Limited in the United Kingdom; by IDG Norge Books for Norway; by IDG Sweden Books for Sweden; by IDG Books Australia Publishing Corporation Pty. Ltd. for Australia and New Zealand; by TransQuest Publishers Pte Ltd. for Singapore, Malaysia, Thailand, Indonesia, and Hong Kong; by Gotop Information Inc. for Taiwan; by ICG Muse, Inc. for Japan; by Intersoft for South Africa; by Eyrolles for France; by International Thomson Publishing for Germany, Austria, and Switzerland; by Distribuidora Cuspide for Argentina; by LR International for Brazil; by Galileo Libros for Chile; by Ediciones ZETA S.C.R. Ltda. for Peru; by WS Computer Publishing Corporation, Inc., for the Philippines; by Contemporanea de Ediciones for Venezuela; by Express Computer Distributors for the Caribbean and West Indies; by Micronesia Media Distributor, Inc. for Micronesia; by Chips Computadoras S.A. de C.V. for Mexico; by Editorial Norma de Panama S.A. for Panama; by American Bookshops for Finland.

For general information on Hungry Minds' products and services please contact our Customer Care department within the U.S. at 800-762-2974, outside the U.S. at 317-572-3993 or fax 317-572-4002.

For sales inquiries and reseller information, including discounts, premium and bulk quantity sales, and foreign-language translations, please contact our Customer Care department at 800-434-3422, fax 317-572-4002 or write to Hungry Minds, Inc., Attn: Customer Care Department, 10475 Crosspoint Boulevard, Indianapolis, IN 46256.

For information on licensing foreign or domestic rights, please contact our Sub-Rights Customer Care department at 212-884-5000.

For information on using Hungry Minds' products and services in the classroom or for ordering examination copies, please contact our Educational Sales department at 800-434-2086 or fax 317-572-4005.

For press review copies, author interviews, or other publicity information, please contact our Public Relations department at 650-653-7000 or fax 650-653-7500.

For authorization to photocopy items for corporate, personal, or educational use, please contact Copyright Clearance Center, 222 Rosewood Drive, Danvers, MA 01923, or fax 978-750-4470.

Hungry Minds™ is a trademark of Hungry Minds, Inc.

About the Author

Trevor Kay is a holder of three CompTIA certifications: A+, Network+ and Server+. He is also a Subject Matter Expert (SME) for the development of the Server+ Certification. Born and raised in London, Ontario, Canada, he started his IT career working at a local museum as a desktop publisher. From there he has held many positions, from IT helpdesk, technical support, and network administrator positions for local companies, to having a key roll in the Y2K project of one of the largest financial institutes in Canada. Trevor now is concentrating full-time on technical writing.

Credits

Acquisitions Editor
Katie Feltman

Project Editor
Brian MacDonald

Technical Editor
Joseph J. Byrne, Network+, i-Net+,
MCSE, CNE

Copy Editor
Brian MacDonald

Project Coordinator
Emily Wichlinski

Graphics and Production Specialists
Sean Decker, LeAndra Johnson,
Gabriele McCann, Heather Pope

Quality Control Technicians
Dave Faust, Andy Hollandbeck,
Charles Spencer

Permissions Editor
Laura Moss

Media Development Specialist
Travis Silvers

Media Development Coordinator
Marisa Pearman

Proofreading and Indexing
TECHBOOKS Production Services

To my family and friends, whose continuous support made this book possible.

Preface

Welcome to the *Server+ Certification Bible.* This book is designed to help you acquire the knowledge, skills, and abilities you need to pass CompTIA's Server+ Certification:

✦ **Exam SK0-001:** Server Hardware Specialist

This book is designed to be the only book or course you need to prepare for and pass CompTIA's Server+ Certification exam. The Server+ Certification exam is one of the newest members of CompTIA's certification family.

This book deals with all of the objectives stated by CompTIA for the Server+ exam. You will learn how to deal with advanced PC hardware issues, such as RAID and SCSI, troubleshooting and problem determination, upgrading, configuration, and disaster recovery.

My hope is that you'll find this book the most helpful Server+ Certification product reference you've ever read, and that you'll use it not only to prepare for CompTIA's Server+ Certification exam, but that you'll come back to it again and again as you perform your day-to-day Server hardware technician tasks.

How This Book Is Organized

This book is organized into seven major parts, followed by a robust glossary, an index, and one compact disc.

Here's what you'll find in this book:

Part I: Installation

Part I presents the information needed to plan the installation and verify the installation plan, hardware compatibility, power sources, UPS, and network availability. Part I also presents the information about using EDS best practices, rack mounting, installing UPS, verifying SCSI ID configurations and termination, installing external devices, and verifying power-on via power-on sequence.

Part II: Configuration

Part II covers configuring BIOS/firmware levels, RAID, installing the NOS, external devices, installing NOS updates to design specifications and updating manufacturer-specific drivers. Finally, this part also covers the installation of service tools (SNMP, backup software, system monitoring agents, and event logs), performing a server baseline, and most importantly documenting the configurations.

Part III: Upgrading

Part III is all about upgrading the common components within the server. This part begins with performing a full backup and verifying the backup, adding processors, adding hard drives, increasing memory, upgrading BIOS/firmware, upgrading adapters and system monitoring agents. This part also explains about upgrading service tools and UPS.

Part IV: Proactive Maintenance

Part IV takes a look at one of the most important parts of being a server hardware technician. This part explains how to create a baseline, how to perform regular backups, monitoring backup performance, and what a system snapshot is. This part also goes into detail about monitoring agents and physical housekeeping.

Part V: Security

Part V addresses different kinds of security issues. This part starts off with physical security issues, such as server room access, types of locks, anti-theft devices, backup tape security such as offsite storage, and fire safe. This part also teaches you about environmental issues, learning how to recognize environmental issues, temperature issues, electrical issues and fire safety.

Part VI: Troubleshooting

Part VI is all about troubleshooting server problems. In this part you will learn how to isolate the problem by using your senses, checking hardware, cables, and peripherals. This part also teaches you about software system messages, log files, disk space, and most important checking for viruses. Identifying OS diagnostic tools, selecting the right diagnostic tools, and using vendor resources are also covered. This part ends with information about remote notification for Wake-on-LAN and the right way to document the problem and solution.

Part VII: Disaster Recovery

In this part the importance of having a disaster recovery plan is addressed. This part will take you step by step through the process of creating a disaster recovery plan. You will also learn about different types of disasters including natural disasters, human error, vandalism, and sabotage. This part will also teach you about planning for redundancy and how to insure high availability of common server components. You will also find in this part the different types of backup media, which includes digital linear tape (DLT) and CD-R. The chapter ends with the importance of testing the disaster recovery plan regularly.

CD-ROM

The compact disc included with this book contains some really excellent resources and programs. You'll find a version this book in Adobe PDF format, and a variety of different programs, From LAN monitoring tools to network analyzers, that I hope you will find useful. I hope you will enjoy each and every one of these programs. To find out more about the CD-ROM, please see Appendix D, "What's on the CD-ROM."

How Each Chapter Is Structured

When this book was designed, a lot of thought went into its structure, and particularly into the specific elements that would provide you with the best possible learning and exam preparation experience.

Here are the elements you'll find in each chapter:

+ The complete exam objectives that are covered in the chapter

+ A Chapter Pre-Test to test your knowledge before reading the chapter

+ Clear, concise text on each topic

+ Screen shots and graphics that are worth more than a thousand words

+ A Key Point Summary

+ A comprehensive Study Guide that contains:

  • Exam-style Assessment Questions

  • Scenario problems for you to solve, as appropriate

  • Answers to Chapter Pre-Test questions, Assessment Questions, and Scenarios

How to Use This Book

This book can be used either by individuals working independently or by groups in a formal classroom setting.

For best results, I recommend the following plan of attack as you use this book. First, take the Chapter Pre-Test, then read the chapter and the Key Point Summary.

Use this summary to see if you've really got the key concepts under your belt. If you don't, go back and reread the section(s) you're not clear on. Then do all of the Assessment Questions and Scenarios at the end of the chapter. Remember, the important thing is to master the tasks that are tested by the exams.

The chapters of this book have been designed to be studied sequentially. In other words, it would be best if you complete Chapter 1 before you proceed to Chapter 2. A few chapters could probably stand alone, but all in all, I recommend a sequential approach.

After you've completed your study of the chapters and reviewed the Assessment Questions in the book, use the test engine on the compact disc included with this book to get some experience answering practice questions. The practice questions will help you assess how much you've learned from your study and will also familiarize you with the type of exam questions you'll face when you take the real exam. Once you identify a weak area, you can restudy the corresponding chapters to improve your knowledge and skills in that area.

Prerequisites

Although this book is a comprehensive study and exam preparation guide, it does not start at ground zero. I assume you have networking knowledge or experience equal or greater of the scope required to pass an industry networking certification exam, such as CompTIA's A+ exam or Network+ exam. If you meet this prerequisite, you're ready to begin this book.

If you don't have the networking knowledge or experience, I recommend you use a book such as *A+ Certification For Dummies* (Hungry Minds, Inc.), *Network+ Certification For Dummies* (Hungry Minds, Inc.) or *Networking For Dummies* (Hungry Minds, Inc.) to obtain this knowledge *before* you begin this book.

Conventions Used in This Book

Every book has its own set of conventions, so I'll explain the ones I've used in this book to you right up front.

Icons

You'll see several icons throughout each chapter. There are five different types of icons used in this book. Below are the explanations of each icon:

 **Caution** This icon is used to warn you that something unfortunate could happen if you're not careful. It also points out information that could save you a lot of grief. It's often easier to prevent a tragedy than to fix it afterwards.

 **Cross-Reference** This icon points you to another place in this book for more coverage of a particular topic. It may point you back to a previous chapter where important material has already been covered, or it may point you ahead to let you know that a topic will be covered in more detail later on.

 Exam Tip This icon points out important information or advice for those preparing to take the Server+ certification exam.

 **In the Real World** Sometimes things work differently in the real world than books — or product documentation — say they do. This icon draws your attention to the author's real-world experiences, which will hopefully help you on the job if not on the Server+ certification exam.

 **Objective** This icon points out exactly where an exam objective is covered in a particular chapter, so you can focus your efforts on the areas where you need the most practice.

 **Tip** This icon is used to draw your attention to a little piece of friendly advice, a helpful fact, a shortcut, or a bit of personal experience that might be of use to you.

Acknowledgments

I never grow tired of thanking the many people who make it possible for me to be an author. It's such a great feeling when it's all said and done and I have a huge book like this to share with everyone.

First of all, I owe a huge debt of gratitude to my brother Nigel Kay and to my good friend Kevin Benjamin for the many hours they spent working with me on this project. I don't know how to thank you enough.

Thanks to everyone at Hungry Minds, including Judy Brief, Acquisitions Manager; Katie Feltman, Acquisitions Editor; Brian MacDonald, Senior Project Editor; Kevin Kent, Copyeditor; Joe Byrne, Technical Editor; and to everyone in the Graphics and Production departments for their hard work and dedication to making this book a reality.

And last but not least, thanks to my close friends, Clare Steed, Sharon Cleland, Rob (The Sculpture) Heath, Joe Piotrowski, Dave and Chris Testolin, Jim Esler, and LisaMarie Hernandez, Ricki Fudge, Steve Marino, Ken Dejong, and Lisa Mior, for their tremendous support during this project.

Contents at a Glance

Contents

Part V: Security   321

Installation

Every administrator, at one time or another, will have to deal with the installation of a new server. In some ways, installation is the most difficult phase of implementing a new network. As a project moves closer to reality, the level of detail increases, making tracking and control far more complex and difficult. Sometimes the administrator will have to work late hours and work around the company's normal business hours to install a new server without disrupting the flow of the standard workday.

Installation procedures are important not only in the real world, but also on the Server+ exam. CompTIA focuses 17 percent of the exam on installation. Understanding the importance of pre-installation planning, verifying the installation plan, hardware compatibility, UPS, power sources, space, network availability, and making sure the correct components and cables have been delivered before the installation will all be covered on the exam. In the following chapters, you will understand the importance of these objectives so you can implement a successful installation.

Planning for Installation

EXAM OBJECTIVES

1.1 Conduct pre-installation planning activities

- Plan the installation
- Verify the installation plan
- Verify hardware compatibility with operating system
- Verify power sources, space, UPS, and network availability
- Verify that all correct components and cables have been delivered

CHAPTER PRE-TEST

1. What factors should be taken into consideration when choosing network cabling?

2. Explain the importance of examining the components that have been delivered with a new server.

3. How should servers be organized in a rack to prevent it from tipping?

4. What is the purpose of a firewall server?

5. What hardware is needed to turn a server into a router?

6. What is the purpose of electrical grounding?

7. What is the difference between a RJ-11 and RJ-45 connector?

8. What is the purpose of a server configured as a router?

9. Why should you consult a hardware compatibility list for your OS?

10. Explain the importance of a line conditioner?

✦ Answers to these questions can be found at the end of the chapter. ✦

Pre-installation planning is a critical stage for server installations. Before purchasing server equipment, you must decide on what type of servers will be required, and how much CPU power, memory, and hard disk drive space they will need. Your servers need a home, and a suitable location must be scouted for proper power sources, network availability, and physical and environmental protection. After the equipment has been delivered, it must be checked to ensure that all the proper components have arrived, and that they are of the proper type. This chapter explains how to handle all these elements.

Installation Strategy

Before any server or network installation, you must have a plan in place to ensure that the new servers will meet your specific hardware and service requirements. Some services have dependencies, and knowing how different types of servers interact with each other is integral in pre-installation planning. An assessment of your current and future needs will aid you in this respect. Whether you are adding a server to an existing environment, or creating a brand new server network, you will need a knowledge of the different types of servers and services available.

Installation planning

1.1 Conduct pre-installation planning activities

- Plan the installation
- Verify the Installation plan

Before deciding on your choice of server equipment, you should examine your current needs. They may be as simple as replacing an aging e-mail server, or as complex as installing a large enterprise database server to host a new human resources and accounting package. You may realize that one of your servers is currently running under capacity, and can adequately host the new program or service without impairing its primary function. You may find that with some minor upgrades, such as extra memory, or a new CPU, you can update an existing server to bring it to a level needed to operate the new program or service. If your current server installations do not meet the requirements of present and future needs, you need to plan a new server installation.

Depending on the type of service or function your server will perform, you must carefully check for any prerequisite services that may need to be in place. In order to function properly, a certain server may need access to an available local DNS server to resolve host names. If you do not currently have a DNS server, you must factor that into your planning activities, and know that you will either need to install it on an existing machine if available, or purchase another server to perform that function.

Although you may be only thinking about present concerns, you must consider the possibility of future growth and capacity planning. Depending on the type of application or service you are installing, you must plan for that system to grow, and careful planning must be considered for the amount of CPU, memory, and disk space you will need. A year from now, you may find that the server you purchased is already overloaded, and if upgrading is not an option, you may have to purchase yet another server.

All of these planning concepts must be carefully balanced with the budget available to management. You will have to work within the constraints of certain spending limits, while still maintaining your server plan with respect to current server availability, prerequisite services, current and future needs, and capacity planning.

Before executing your installation plan, you should spend some time to verify and test it. Ideally, this can be done in a lab situation, where you have a small network set up internally that does not connect to your main network. This way, you can test how the certain applications and operating systems will react with different services, without affecting your normal network operations. If you can't do this, the new server can be set up on your own network, but you should perform the tests outside of work hours, to minimize any impact to daily operations. Test how each of your client and server operating systems will communicate with the new server services. Although you will not be using an exact replica of your new equipment, you will get a good idea of how the services that will run on that new server, will communicate and interact with the services and applications on your network.

Exam Tip   For the exam, make sure that you know all of the various server and network device functions, and how they interact with each other.

Types of servers

Before you can plan your installation, you need to know what kind of server will fit your needs. Some of these types of servers can also be performed by dedicated network devices, such as routers or gateways. Many of these types of server services can be combined in one machine. For example, a Web server and an FTP server can reside on the same machine if needed. Combining several services onto one server can greatly reduce your costs, because you do not need a separate server for each service. The following are some of the most common kinds of servers:

✦ **File-and-Print server:** A file-and-print server provides file storage and printing services to clients. When client files are stored on the server, they are centralized in a common place that can be more easily backed up. Print servers enable clients to send a request to a printer. The print requests are queued by the print server for delivery to the final destination printer.

✦ **Mail server:** A server that stores e-mail. Clients connect to the mail server by supplying their mail account information, with which they can send and receive e-mail. The e-mail system may be strictly internal, but it may also send and receive e-mail over the Internet.

✦ **Application server:** An application server is basically a server that acts as a middle tier in a *multi-tiered application.* An application server is often used in a Client/Server architecture, where the client and server computers work together to perform tasks. The server typically handles storage and processing of data, while the client requests these resources from the server for its own use.

✦ **Database server:** A database server stores structured data in a filing system that can be retrieved by multiple users simultaneously. These types of severs should have large amounts of RAM and disk space to be able to store and process the data.

✦ **Backup server:** A backup server is used specifically for backing up system data. The backup server is usually attached to tape unit, and runs the backup applications to store data from your network servers to the tape.

✦ **Fax server:** Combined with special faxing software, and a modem/telephone line connection, a fax server enables clients to fax documents directly from their computer.

✦ **Web server:** A Web server delivers Internet Web pages to client computers. The client runs a Web browser, which makes a request for an HTML web page from the server. The server receives that request, and sends the desired page to the client's Web browser, where it is displayed.

✦ **FTP server:** The File Transfer Protocol (FTP) is a protocol for transferring files. It facilitates these transfers with proper integrity, efficiency, and security. A client computer connects to an FTP server, where they can supply logon credentials, and then be granted access to retrieve files on the server.

✦ **Proxy server:** A proxy server forwards network requests on behalf of another client or server. A proxy server is typically configured to facilitate Internet Web page requests between a client and a Web server. The proxy server can also cache Web data, so that a request for an external Web page can often be taken from the local cache, greatly increasing performance. If the data does not exist locally, the proxy server will go out on the Internet and fulfill the request. Proxy servers are also useful for filtering requests, so that administrators can restrict users from viewing unauthorized Web sites.

✦ **Firewall server:** A firewall acts as a security filter to separate and protect a private network from users of a public network. For example, a company will restrict external users from the Internet from accessing the company's intranet. All network traffic flows through the firewall, and access is granted or denied depending on the filters and rules that are set up by the administrator. Although a firewall can be a dedicated network device, a server can be made into a firewall by installing two or three network interface cards (NICs) and special firewall software. Firewall security is usually set up in three zones: an internal network, an external network, and a Demilitarized Zone (DMZ), which allows users from the Internet to access certain services on the internal network without risking unauthorized access to sensitive internal services. If you are going to use a DMZ network, you will need a third network interface card (NIC) installed on the server. Figure 1-1 shows an example of typical firewall server setup. The mail server and the Web server are in the DMZ, which means they can be accessed from the Internet, but the rest of the workstations are safe behind the firewall.

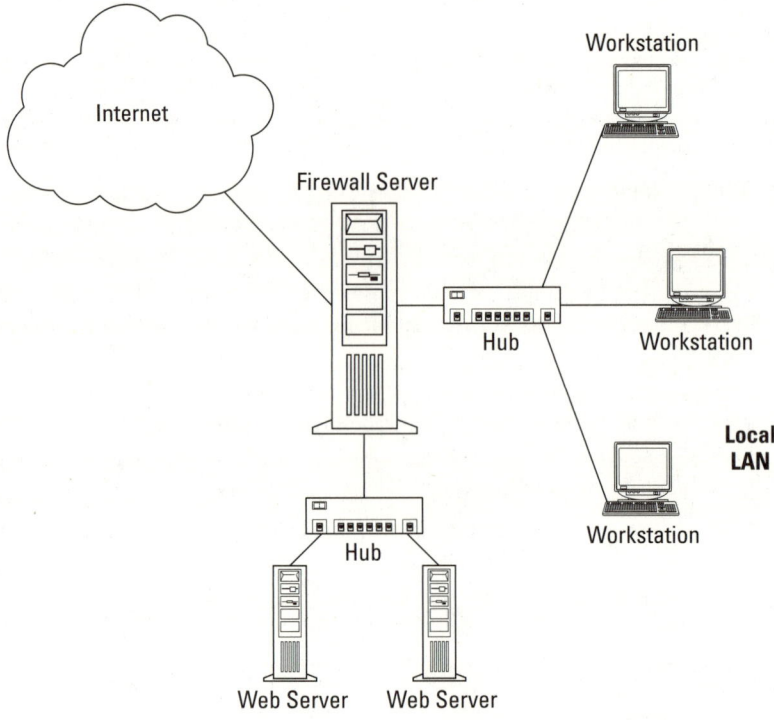

Figure 1-1: A Firewall server separating the Internet from the local LAN and DMZ Internet services

✦ **DHCP server:** A DHCP server runs the Dynamic Host Configuration Protocol, which assigns network IP addresses to clients on the network at start-up. With this configuration, each client workstation does not need to be set up with a static IP address. When the client computer starts, it sends a request to the DHCP server, which assigns the client an IP address.

✦ **DNS server:** A domain name service (DNS) server keeps a database of tables that translate fully qualified Internet domain names to their respective IP address. This enables you to refer to Internet servers by name, such as www.hungryminds.com, rather than by an IP address, such as 38.170.216.15.

✦ **WINS server:** A WINS server is a special Windows NT server that runs the Windows Internet Naming Service (WINS). It enables clients to resolve Windows NetBIOS names to standard Internet domain naming conventions. For example, a computer with the NetBIOS name of `Joe`, would be visible to other clients as `joe.hungryminds.com`.

Exam Tip

For the exam, be careful not to confuse a WINS server and DNS server. The easiest way to remember the difference is that a WINS server is for Windows clients only.

✦ **RAS server:** A Remote Access Server (RAS server) is a Windows NT service that allows users to dial in to the server using a modem or WAN link. Clients connect to the RAS server using a built-in RAS client, or point-to-point protocol (PPP).

✦ **SNA server:** System Network Architecture (SNA) is a set of protocols developed by IBM for mainframe computers. An SNA server acts as a gateway between the client computer and the mainframe computer.

✦ **Gateway server:** Using a combination of hardware and software, a gateway acts as a link between different types of networks. A gateway server must be multihomed, which means it has more than one network card. Each card will be connected to a different network, which are then linked internally. The functions of a gateway server can also be performed by a dedicated network device. See Figure 1-2 for an example of a SNA gateway providing SNA connectivity to a mainframe computer. The AS/400 mainframe uses the Systems Network Architecture (SNA) network model. With the gateway server in place, the workstations can communicate with the mainframe no matter what operating system they're running.

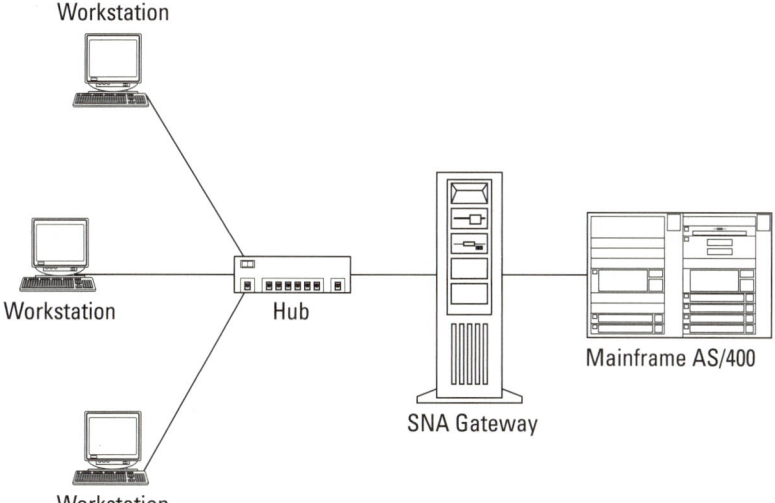

Figure 1-2: An SNA gateway server enables the network clients access to the SNA-based AS/400.

✦ **Router server:** A router can connect any number of Local Area Networks (LANs) by routing network packets to and from these different networks. Routing can also be performed by a dedicated network device. A router contains a *routing table,* which defines the best route for forwarding network information to its respective destinations. A router server must be *multi-homed,* meaning it must have at least two network cards, one on each network. Figure 1-3 shows a server acting as a router. All packets from LAN 1 on the left pass through the router, which forwards them to the appropriate host on LAN 2 on the right. The router also forwards packets from LAN 2 to LAN 1.

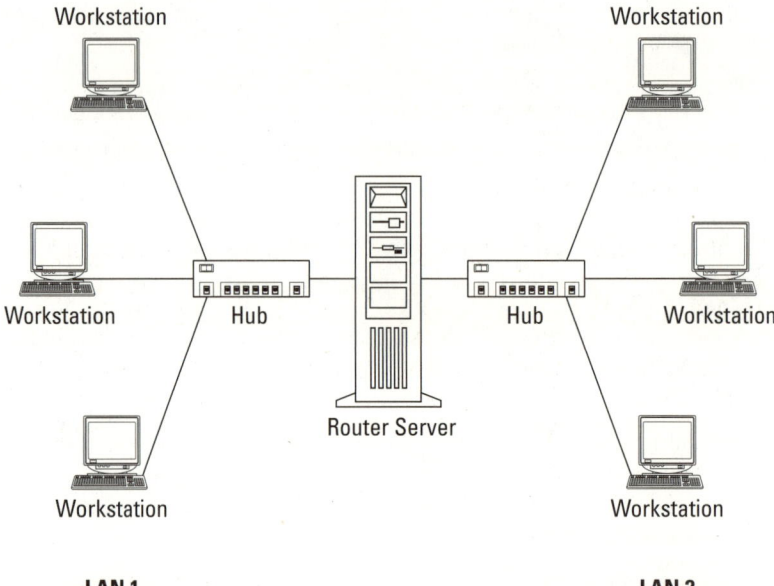

Figure 1-3: A router server transfers packets between the two networks

✦ **Bridge server:** Much like a router, a bridge forwards packets between two dissimilar networks. For example, a bridge can connect an Ethernet network with a Token Ring network. Bridges are protocol-independent, and do not perform any type of special routing functions that would be performed by a router. Figure 1-4 shows an example of a bridge server connecting to different types of networks.

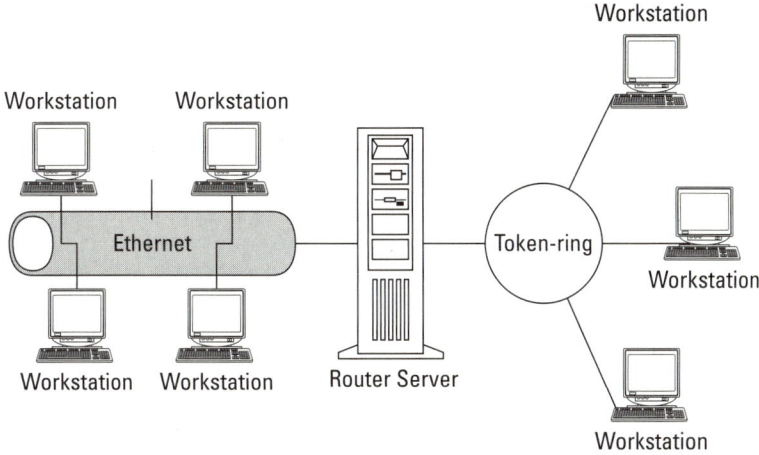

Figure 1-4: A bridge server connects an Ethernet network with a Token Ring Network

Verifying OS Hardware Compatibility

✦ Verify hardware compatibility with operating system

Before ordering any server equipment, you must examine the documentation for your operating system to establish what types of hardware will and will not work with the operating system. Each type of hardware, whether it is the motherboard, memory, disk drives, network cards, or other peripheral cards, must be cross-referenced with the OS hardware compatibility list. If the hardware is not supported by the operating system, it will not work properly, and may even cause the system to fail.

Exam Tip　The most recent information on hardware compatibility will always be found on the OS vendor's Web site.

The hardware compatibility list for each vendor should be included with the OS CD-ROMs, although they could be somewhat out-of-date. The OS CD will only contain information at the time of the initial release of the software. To get the latest versions of the list, go to the OS vendor's Web site.

Verifying Power Sources and UPS Installation

 ✦ Verify power sources, space, UPS, and network availability

Verifying a power source is often the most overlooked aspect of a server installation. You can spend a lot of time and money on planning out a server, such as defining its role, carefully comparing and choosing proper components, hardware compatibility with the OS, the rack size and type, air conditioning, and ventilation. When the server is finally installed, you realize that there is nowhere to plug the server in. Verifying the location of your power source, measuring its quality and consistency, and protecting your equipment with an uninterruptible power supply (UPS) are all vital and important aspects of a server installation.

Location

Before choosing a location for your server and rack, scout out the area and verify that there are existing power outlets in close proximity to the location. Make sure there are enough outlets to power your equipment, including monitors and other peripheral devices such as external tape drives. You should avoid having all your devices on the same electrical circuit. Too many devices on one circuit could affect the consistency of the power flowing to the devices. Some power outlets are color-coded to show which circuit an outlet is on.

 **Caution**   Avoid plugging power strips into the UPS to create more sockets. This will increase the load on the UPS.

Quality

If your server is located in an older building, with outdated electrical subsystems, it is possible that the power you are getting is of very low quality. High deviations in the voltage and amperage could cause problems with modern, highly sensitive electrical equipment. This can cause permanent damage to your components.

Before the servers are installed, you should measure the outlets with a power meter that can accurately assess the quality of your power. If updating the electrical system is not an option, consider the use of a line conditioner, which is a special device that is connected between the power source and the destination that cleans up electrical power to correct any deviances.

Grounding

The primary purpose of electrical grounding is to protect equipment from short-circuiting. A *ground* refers to a path for the overloaded electrical current to dissipate. Ensure that your electrical outlets in your server room are properly grounded. You can check this by examining the outlet to see if it contains a third grounding wire, made for a three-pronged plug. You should also have an electrician test the power outlet. Non-existent or improper grounding can cause great damage to your electrical equipment.

Uninterruptible power supply

Another electrical consideration for a server room is the effect of a power outage. With no type of power backup, your servers will shut down immediately, without a chance to gracefully shut down and save any current information to the storage system. AUPS is a must for any type of server installation. A UPS will supply battery power to servers in the event of a power failure. It will usually keep them up for 10–20 minutes before the battery is depleted, depending on the number of devices it is connected to. This gives you enough time to shut down the system properly.

Most UPS units come with special software that interacts with the operating system of the server. The UPS uses a special signaling cable that is attached to the serial port of the server. In the event of a power failure, the UPS powers the server from battery, and then notifies the OS to shut down the server. This allows the server to be shut down properly without any technician being on site.

Once a UPS is installed, very few people actually test it. Even fewer test the auto shutdown of the server feature. In the case of a real power failure, your current setup might not work properly, so it is a good idea to test these capabilities before relying on them.

UPS systems come in a variety of sizes. They are typically measured using a VA rating, which combines the total voltage multiplied by the amperage. For example, a UPS with a 600VA rating can connect only as many devices as add up to that rating. For example, a server that is rated at 400 VA, and its 14-inch monitor rated at 150 VA would be fine on this UPS. Ensure that your UPS is large enough to handle the combined VA rating of all your equipment. If there is too much load on the UPS, it will not be able to provide any battery power at all during a power failure.

Verifying Rack Space

   ✦ Verify power sources, space, UPS, and network availability

When installing servers, you should have a special server cabinet or *rack* that will hold the equipment. There are many reasons for using a server rack to house your equipment:

✦ **Safety:** The equipment will not be subject to physical abuse and damage by being left out in the open.

✦ **Stability:** When mounted in a proper rack, there is little chance that your server will fall or tip over, compared to having it sit on a table or on the floor.

✦ **Cooling and Ventilation:** Most racks have proper ventilation slots on the doors and sides to allow air to circulate. Some racks also have their own fans, which help circulate the air.

✦ **Security:** Racks are usually lockable, so that no one can tamper with them.

✦ **Manageability:** By using a special keyboard/video/mouse switch, you can control all of the servers in the rack from one console, which can be installed as a pull-out tray.

Exam Tip On the exam, questions on server racks and cabinets usually rely more on common sense for the answer than anything else. Always imagine how you would perform the action in the real world using common sense.

Rack space is measured in Units. 1U is equal to 1.75 inches (4.4 centimeters). Each server or device being installed into the rack will have its own Unit measurement. For example, a medium size server has a rack height of 7U, meaning it is 12.25 inches (30.8 centimeters) tall. Some small servers are only 1U in height. A standard rack height is approximately 42U. You must plan carefully how much rack space you have available for your servers. Remember to include any other devices, such as power strips, keyboard/video/monitor trays, UPS, and also leave some room for expansion. When loading the rack, always use the manufacturer's specifications. If for some reason the specifications are not present, load the devices starting at the bottom from heaviest to the lightest.

Network Cabling and Connectors

✦ Verify power sources, space, UPS, and network availability

There are many different ways in which your server can be connected to the network. Several types of network topologies and cabling exist, each with their own advantages and disadvantages.

Network topologies

Network topology refers to the actual shape of your local area network. The choice of a topology will depend on your business needs, and the environment in which your network will be operating.

Bus

A bus network topology is one in which all of the devices are connected together in linear order by a central cable. A bus topology is most often used by coaxial Ethernet networks. It is perfect for small, office networks, because it is easy and inexpensive to set up. A disadvantage of a bus network is that if any device is disconnected from the network, it will affect the entire bus, and the entire network chain will be disrupted. See Figure 1-5 for an example of bus network topology.

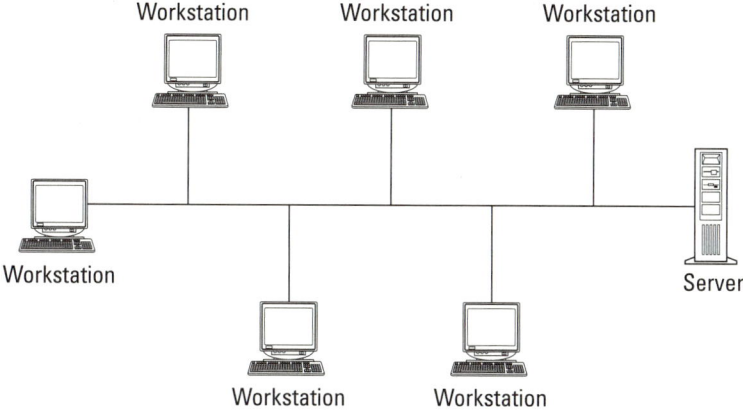

Figure 1-5: A bus topology network

Star

A star network topology is one in which the devices all radiate from a central hub. If one of the network devices fails, it will not bring down the rest of the network. The real point of failure is with the central hub or computer. If it fails, the entire network will be down. A star topology also uses much more network cabling than a bus or ring topology. Star topologies are most often used by twisted-pair Ethernet networks, and support a wide variety of small to large networks. Scc Figure 1-6 for an example of a star topology network.

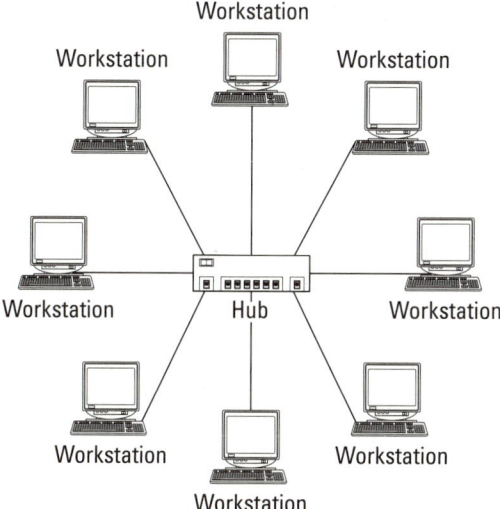

Figure 1-6: A star topology network

Ring

A ring topology network is designed so that all of the network devices are connected together in a ring or loop. Each device is connected to the next device in the
ring. Network information is passed along the ring until it reaches its destination
computer. A ring network is more expensive than a bus or start topology, but they
have the advantage of being able to span large distances. Physical breaks in the ring
cabling or a malfunctioning workstation can take down the entire network, and can
often be time consuming to track down. Token-ring networks use this type of topology. See Figure 1-7 for an example of a ring topology network.

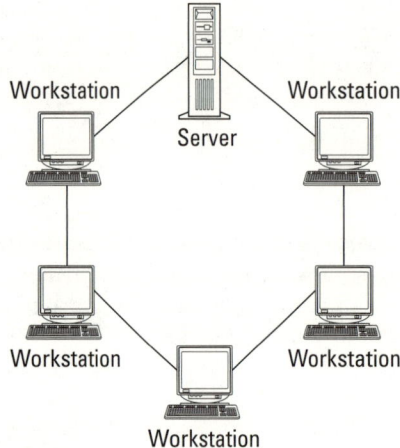

Figure 1-7: A ring topology network

Types of cable

Cabling your network depends on many factors, including network speed, length,
resistance to electrical interference, and cost. Each of the cable types discussed in
the following sections have their own advantages and disadvantages depending on
the type of your server and network installation.

Coaxial

Coaxial cable is one of the earliest types of network cabling. Coaxial cable consists
of a stiff, copper wire conductor, surrounded by a metallic mesh fiber, and then a
thick plastic sheath. The purpose of the plastic is to prevent the cable from being
bent so far that the copper conductor is broken. The metal fiber is used to shield
the wire from electromagnetic interference (EMI), which can interfere with network
communications. Coaxial cable is much more expensive than twisted-pair solutions,
but is cheaper than fiber optic cable. Because of its protective plastic, and EMI
shielding, it is most useful for industrial environments where the cable can be easily susceptible to damage.

There are two major types of coaxial network cabling, Thinnet, and Thicknet:

✦ **Thinnet** (10Base2): Thinnet coaxial cabling is a cabling standard for Ethernet LANs. It uses RG-58 cable, with a maximum distance of 185 meters. The maximum network speed for 10Base2 is 10 MB/s. Due to its cost, Thinnet cabling is usually used in place of Thicknet.

✦ **Thicknet** (10Base5): Thicknet is a larger, thicker type of coaxial cable used in the earliest networks. It uses RG-8 or RG-11 cabling, and can run at 10 MB/s, with a maximum distance of 500 meters.

Twisted-pair

Twisted pair wiring consists of pairs of wires that are twisted together. One wire carries the data, while the other wire acts as a ground and absorbs electrical interference. Twisted pair is used for phone networks and lower-end networks, due to its low cost. There are two different types of twisted pair cabling: unshielded twisted-pair (UTP), and shielded twisted-pair (STP). STP cable uses an extra casing around the wires to further prevent EMI from interrupting network communications. Twisted-pair wiring is the most common network cabling used today, because of its low cost, and the fact that it already exists in most buildings for phone connections. There are several standards for types of twisted pair cabling:

✦ **Category 1:** This cabling is typically used for phone systems, not for data networks.

✦ **Category 2:** Can only support up to 1 MB/s, and should not be used for networks.

✦ **Category 3:** Can support 10 MB/s network speeds.

✦ **Category 4:** Primarily used for 16 MB/s token-ring networks.

✦ **Category 5:** Can support speeds of 100 MB/s. This is the most common type of cabling today.

For most modern network, you will need an absolute minimum of category 5 twisted pair cabling to support 100 MB/s networks. There are a number of different standards for twisted pair cabling:

✦ **10BaseT:** 10BaseT Ethernet networks run at 10 MB/s, and have a maximum segment length of 100 meters.

✦ **100BaseT:** Also referred to as Fast Ethernet, 100BaseT runs at 100 MB/s, and the maximum segment length is 100 meters.

✦ **1000BaseT:** Also referred to as Gigabit Ethernet, 1000BaseT runs at 1 GB/s, and the maximum segment length is 100 meters.

Fiber

Fiber-optic cable uses light to transfer data through glass fibers. A plastic covering protects the cable. Fiber-optic cable is extremely fast and reliable, which also makes it the most expensive of any cabling type. Companies will often build the backbone of their network, which runs between departments and floors, with fiber cabling, and then use twisted-pair to connect the backbone to the workstations and servers.

Fiber cable is split into two different wires, one for transmitting and one for receiving. On the connecting device there will be two connectors, where these wires are connected. The wires must go in the proper connectors, or the transmit and receive feeds will be reversed, and the network will not work.

There are two types of fiber cabling, *single mode* and *multimode*. Single mode fiber has a very narrow internal path that only permits one mode of light through at a time. This provides much greater speeds and distances, but it is expensive compared to multimode fiber. Multimode fiber has a larger core width, so modes of light are reflected more through the pathway, causing lower speeds and higher attenuation resulting in shorter cable lengths.

Connectors

Each type of network cabling requires its own type of connectors and devices to work properly.

✦ **RJ-11:** This connector is used for connecting four- to six-wire connections. It is usually referred to as two-pair wire. It is used for phone cabling.

✦ **RJ-45:** This connector is used to connect eight-wire connections, or four-pair wires. It is widely used for LAN Ethernet networks.

✦ **Attachment Unit Interface (AUI):** An AUI is typically used on coaxial-based network cards. The AUI interface includes a transceiver that connects a coaxial cable with a 15-pin connector.

✦ **BNC connector:** A BNC connector is the type used on the ends of a RG-58 coaxial cable. For bus networks, a BNC T-Connector is used to connect devices to the network, as it has three connections: one for each side of the cable, and one to connect to the device. A BNC barrel connector is used to connect two cables together. BNC connectors are locked into place by a rotating ring.

✦ **Vampire tap:** A vampire tap is used to connect older Thicknet types of networks. The cable is actually pierced and direct contact is made to the core conducting wire. It is usually used in conjunction with a transceiver and an AUI connector.

Exam Tip   Although networking is not the focus of the exam, you should have good general knowledge of the various networking topology, cabling, and connector standards to aid you in troubleshooting questions.

Cable location

A large amount of cabling will be needed to connect your servers to the main switch or router. Running them across the floor is a simple, but bad, alternative. Running the cables along the floor leaves them susceptible to damage from people walking on them, or tripping over them. They should be located either under the floor, above the ceiling, or run along special cable trays on the sides of walls.

Many professional server rooms have false floors, with floor panels that can be easily lifted. Underneath is where most of the cabling is run, usually both power and networking cabling. This is the best solution, as the cabling can be easily accessed if devices need to be disconnected or moved. The cables are also covered and protected from external damage.

Server racks typically come with holes in the top, to enable cable drops to be brought down from the ceiling into the rack, either by themselves, or through a protected conduit. The conduit is usually made of a hard but bendable plastic, so it can be contoured to the environment. The cables are protected from external damage, but if they need to be accessed or rerouted for any reason, accessibility is not easy.

An alternative to running cables right into the ceiling is through the use of cable trays. These are simply brackets that run around the upper perimeter of the room, allowing cable to be protected from external damage, but still accessible for moves and rerouting.

Verifying Components

✦ Verify that all correct components and cables have been delivered

When your new servers are delivered, there is always the possibility that there are parts missing, or incorrect items, that will delay the installation. Be sure to check every component carefully, to ensure that it is the right hardware for your installation, and that it is compatible with other hardware and your network OS.

The following are some things to consider when verifying your server components before installation.

✦ **IDE and SCSI Cables:** Ensure that any IDE and SCSI cables are the proper type for your installation. For IDE systems, make sure that the cable will be able to support all of your devices, and that the peripheral devices have the correct jumper settings for master/slave/cable select abilities as appropriate. Check the vendor's documentation to ensure proper settings.

For SCSI cables, ensure that the connectors on the cables are the right width, and have the same number of pins for your devices. There are quite an array of different SCSI devices and cables, and they can easily be mixed up. Also check that you have received the correct type of SCSI terminators to properly terminate the SCSI bus.

✦ **Peripheral Cards:** Check any additional peripheral cards that were delivered with your server for compatibility with your motherboard. Ensure there are enough slots to connect all of the cards, and check to make sure the cards are made for that particular bus, such as PCI, or ISA.

✦ **Network Adapters:** You should examine the NIC cards to make sure they are the proper model for your network installation. Check that the connectors on the edge of the network card are compatible with your network topology and cabling. Also, check the speed and duplex settings of the card, so that they match your network settings. Some older network cards use jumpers for these settings, but most new NIC cards can be configured through software.

✦ **Software:** Check your network OS CD-ROM to make sure you have the proper version for your type of hardware. Make sure that you have all the proper serial numbers ready for your installation.

✦ **Backup Tapes:** If you are installing a backup server, check the tapes that you have ordered to ensure that they are the right type and size for your tape drive hardware.

Key Point Summary

In this chapter, various types of servers and networks were discussed, to aid in planning a server installation. The importance of verifying hardware compatibility with the network OS was discussed, and various server room issues such as rack space, power sources, and cable location were detailed. Keep the following points in mind for the exam:

✦ The various types of servers perform different network services.

✦ Hardware compatibility should be verified with the network OS vendor's Web site.

✦ Ensure that the power source is of good quality, and has proper grounding.

✦ UPS units should be connected to the server with a serial cable to allow auto-shutdown capabilities.

✦ Server rack space is measured in Units. One Unit is equal to 1.75 inches (4.4 centimeters).

✦ Servers should be installed into a rack with the heaviest device on the bottom.

✦ Know the different network topologies, and their cabling and connector standards.

✦ All components should be verified before installing the server.

✦   ✦   ✦

STUDY GUIDE

The Study Guide section provides you with the opportunity to test your knowledge about pre-installation planning. The Assessment Questions provide practice for the test, and the Scenarios provide practice with real situations. If you get any questions wrong, use the answers to determine the part of the chapter you should review before continuing.

Assessment Questions

1. A technician needs to install a server that will automatically assign IP addresses to devices when they connect to the network. What type of server is required?

    A. DNS server

    B. WINS server

    C. Firewall server

    D. DHCP server

2. A new firewall server has just been delivered. Among the peripheral cards that came with the server were three network interface cards. Why did the server come with so many NIC cards?

    A. To enable the firewall to connect the Internet, the local LAN, and a DMZ

    B. The extra NIC cards were shipping errors

    C. To create redundancy

    D. To increase the total amount of network throughput

3. A technician is looking for the most recent information to verify a new server's hardware compatibility with the OS. What is the best resource for the information?

    A. The OS CD-ROM

    B. The `readme.txt` file

    C. The OS vendor's Web site

    D. The server's installation documentation

4. A technician is installing four new servers into a 42U rack but does not have the manufacturer's specifications on how to load the rack. The servers are a 4U Web server, a 4U FTP server, a 12U file server, and an 8U database server, which is quite heavy due to the amount of disk drives installed. Starting from the bottom, in what order should the servers be placed in the rack?

  A. File, Web, FTP, database

  B. Web, database, FTP, file

  C. FTP, file, database, Web

  D. Database, file, Web, FTP

5. To save on network installation costs, a company wants to use the phone system's UTP cabling already installed in the building, for use in a 10MB local area network. What is the minimum category of twisted-pair cabling that should be used to support networking?

  A. Category 5

  B. Category 3

  C. Category 1

  D. Category 2

6. A customer is complaining that none of the users on the network can connect to an outside Web site. The connection to the Internet seems to be working fine, and the users can connect to the internal intranet Web site. What is the most likely cause of the problem?

  A. The external router is not working properly.

  B. The firewall is blocking FTP access to the Internet.

  C. The proxy server is not working.

  D. The DHCP server is not functioning.

7. A technician is testing a UPS on a new server. When power is disconnected from the UPS, the server runs from the UPS battery for approximately 15 minutes, and then the server is abruptly shut down. The UPS was configured to shut down the server automatically when power is disconnected. What is the most likely cause of the problem?

  A. The UPS software is not configured properly.

  B. The parallel cable between the UPS and the server is missing.

  C. The UPS battery has not been properly charged.

  D. The serial cable between the server and the UPS is missing.

8. A server rack is being moved to a new air-conditioned server room on the second floor of the building. What is the best way to transport the rack to its new location?

    A. Remove the servers, move the rack, and then put the servers back in the rack.

    B. Place the rack on a dolly and roll it carefully to the new location.

    C. Remove the servers, take apart the rack, move the parts, and reassemble the rack in the new location.

    D. Get as many people as possible to help carry the rack to the new location.

9. Two floors of a building are being connected together by a fiber-optic cable. A special fiber-enabled switch is located on each floor. After they are connected together, there does not seem to be any network activity between the floors. What is the most likely cause of the problem?

    A. The fiber cable is multimode.

    B. The cable is defective.

    C. The transmit and receive cables are reversed.

    D. The fiber cable is only single mode fiber.

10. A customer would like to provide access to their new SNA mainframe from their current Windows workstations. What device will be needed to allow connectivity?

    A. bridge

    B. gateway server

    C. router

    D. DNS server

11. A technician is reviewing the hardware compatibility list for the network OS that is being installed on a server. The vendor's Web site lists the current hardware as compatible, but the documentation that came with the OS says the hardware is not compatible. What is the cause of the discrepancy?

    A. The information on the Web site is newer than the documentation.

    B. The `readme.txt` file on the OS CD-ROM is the most reliable

    C. The Web site contains an error.

    D. The information on the Web site is older than the documentation.

12. A new server is being installed to enable Windows machines to resolve NetBIOS names to Internet domain addresses. What type of server is required?

    A. WINS server

    B. DNS server

    C. DHCP server

    D. firewall server

13. A new Ethernet LAN network is being added to a current LAN that is running Token Ring. What type of server or device should be used to connect the two networks?

    A. hub

    B. bridge

    C. firewall

    D. LAN adapter

14. When installing a server, which of the following is the most important when verifying a power source?

    A. proper grounding

    B. proximity to UPS

    C. sufficient VA rating

    D. dual voltage capability

15. A technician is replacing an internal Web server with a new server containing a more powerful CPU and memory. The location of the new server has been verified for proper environmental and power requirements. Which of the following is the next aspect of the server's location to verify before installation?

    A. UPS size

    B. network availability

    C. proxy connections

    D. firewall rules

16. A new RAS server has just been delivered. Parts that came with the server include a 9GB hard drive, video card, network card, and RS-232 cable. The technician notices immediately that a part is missing. What is most likely the missing item?

    A. SCSI card

    B. CD-ROM

C. Sound card

D. Modem

17. A firewall server has been configured to allow only inbound HTTP Web access to an internal Web server, while HTTP, FTP have been enabled for outgoing connections from the internal LAN to the Internet. To prevent inbound HTTP connections from reaching other local LAN devices, what else should be configured?

   A. Proxy

   B. DMZ

   C. DNS

   D. DHCP

18. A 10Base2 network is suffering from frequent network problems. There are 30 workstations hooked together in a bus topology. The server's network card was replaced a week before, as it was deemed to be faulty. What is the most likely cause of the problem?

   A. The new server network card only supports 100 MB/s.

   B. The terminator on the server is loose.

   C. One of the workstations is configured for UTP.

   D. A client workstation is configured for token-ring.

19. A new server has just arrived, which is to be configured as a router. A technician notices that a part is missing from the server. Without it, the server will not perform its proper function. Which of the following is the mostly likely part missing?

   A. ultra SCSI card

   B. second Network card

   C. routing cable

   D. BNC connector

20. A new backup server has just been delivered. It comes with an Ultra2 SCSI card, a DLT7000 tape drive, 40 DAT backup tapes, and an Ultra2 SCSI cable and terminator. Which of these items have been ordered in error?

   A. SCSI card

   B. Terminator

   C. DAT tapes

   D. SCSI cable

Scenarios

1. A customer needs a server solution so that they can serve Web pages, and host an FTP site for the external world, while securing their internal LAN from any outside intrusion. For security purposes, the Web server and FTP services must be installed on their own separate machines. How many servers will be needed, and for what roles should they be configured?

2. Three new servers are being installed into a new server room. What aspects of the server room should be verified before installing the new equipment?

3. A UPS is being connected to a rack containing up to four servers. What considerations must be made when purchasing and installing the UPS?

Answers to Chapter Questions

Chapter pre-test

1. The type of environment will determine how strong and protected your cabling should be from outside influences. Some types of cabling are limited in their lengths, due to signal attenuation. Network speed also depends on the type of cabling used.

2. You must examine all your components, cables, peripheral cards, and connectors, to determine if all the parts are there, and that they are the right type for your installation.

3. The heaviest equipment should be installed at the bottom to stabilize the rack.

4. A firewall server filters incoming network traffic to prevent users from the Internet from accessing private LANs.

5. The server needs to be multihomed, with at least two network cards.

6. Electrical grounding is extremely important in preventing electrical shorts from damaging server equipment. It allows a path for the voltage spike to dissipate.

7. An RJ-11 connector is used for terminating two-pair wiring such as phone lines. RJ-45 connectors terminate four-pair wiring used in twisted pair network cabling.

8. A router server routes network packets to and from different networks.

9. You should consult a hardware compatibility list to verify that your chosen hardware will be supported by the operating system.

10. A line conditioner cleans up noisy, dirty power before it gets to your equipment.

Assessment questions

1. D. A DHCP server will automatically assign addresses to devices connecting to the network. Answer A is incorrect because a DNS server resolves Internet domain names to IP addresses. Answer B is incorrect because a WINS server resolves NetBIOS names to Internet domain names. Answer C is incorrect because a firewall is used to protect internal networks from Internet traffic. For more information, see the "Installation Strategy" section.

2. A. The firewall needs a network card to connect each of the three networks together. Answer B is incorrect because a firewall needs at least two NIC cards to function properly, and a third if you use a DMZ network. Answer C is incorrect because the NIC cards are needed to connect the other networks. Answer D is incorrect because the cards are not being joined together as a team, they are operating separately to connect different networks. For more information, see the "Installation Strategy" section.

3. C. The OS vendor's website will always have the most recent information on hardware compatibility. Answer A is incorrect because the OS CD-ROM will only have information that was available at the time of release. Answer B is incorrect because a `readme.txt` file will only have minor installation information, and will be outdated. Answer D is incorrect because your server hardware documentation will not have OS compatibility information. For more information, see the "Verifying OS Hardware Compatibility" section.

4. D. The heaviest piece of equipment should always be installed at the bottom of the rack to aid in stabilization. Answers A, B, and C are incorrect because they will make the rack top-heavy, and more likely to tip over. For more information, see the "Verifying Rack Space" section.

5. B. To support 10MB networking, the cable should be minimum Category 5 UTP cabling. Answer A is incorrect because Category 5 cabling is the minimum for 100MB capacity. Answer C is incorrect because Category 1 cabling is used for phone lines, and is not suitable for networking. Answer D is incorrect because Category 2 cabling can only support speeds of 1MB, and is not suitable for networks. For more information, see the "Network Cabling and Connectors" section.

6. C. If the proxy server is not working, clients will be unable to contact external Web sites, as the proxy server is responsible for forwarding the requests. Answer A is incorrect because the connection to the Internet is still working. Answer B is incorrect because the clients are using the HTTP protocol to connect to Web sites, not FTP. Answer D is incorrect because DHCP servers are used to assign IP addresses to network devices. For more information, see the "Installation Strategy" section.

7. D. The serial cable connecting the UPS to the server was not connected. Without it, there is no way for the UPS to communicate with the server. Answer A is incorrect because the server software was configured correctly. Answer B is incorrect because a serial cable is used for the connection, not a parallel cable. Answer C is incorrect because the battery operated normally when the power failed. For more information, see the "Verifying Power Sources and UPS Installation" section.

8. **A.** All equipment should be removed from the rack before moving. This prevents tipping, and also makes it easier to move, because it will be lighter. Answer B is incorrect because the server could tip over because of the weight. Answer C is incorrect because taking apart the rack is unnecessary. Answer D is incorrect because it is easier to remove the equipment to make the rack lighter to transport. For more information, see the "Verifying Rack Space" section.

9. **C.** Most likely, the transmit and receive cables were accidentally reversed. Answer A is incorrect because the mode of the fiber in this question was not discussed. Answer B is incorrect because it is rare for a fiber cable to be defective. Answer D is incorrect because the mode of the fiber in this question was not discussed. For more information, see the "Network Cabling and Connectors" section.

10. **B.** A gateway server will be needed to allow the Windows machines access to SNA services. Answer A is incorrect because a bridge will only connect two different networks, it will not provide gateway services. Answer C is incorrect because a router will only route packets between two networks. Answer D is incorrect because a DNS server is used to resolve Internet domain names to IP addresses. For more information, see the "Installation Strategy" section.

11. **A.** The vendor's Web site will always have the most recent information on hardware compatibility. Answer B is incorrect because the `readme.txt` file will not contain the most recent information. Answer C is incorrect because the Web site should have the most recent, accurate information. Answer D is incorrect because the Web site will be more up-to-date than the documentation. For more information, see the "Verifying OS Hardware Compatibility" section.

12. **A.** A WINS server will resolve NetBIOS names to Internet domain names. Answer B is incorrect because a DNS resolves Internet domain names to IP addresses. Answer C is incorrect because a DHCP server assigns IP addresses to the device on the network. Answer D is incorrect because a firewall server is used to protect the internal LAN from external Internet traffic. For more information, see the "Installation Strategy" section.

13. **B.** A bridge connects two different types of networks together. Answer A is incorrect because a hub can only connect two networks of the same types. Answer C is incorrect because a firewall is used to protect the internal LAN from external Internet traffic. Answer D is incorrect because there is no such thing as a LAN adapter. For more information, see the "Installation Strategy" section.

14. **A.** Proper grounding is important in preventing short circuits from harming the equipment. Answer B is incorrect because the proximity to the UPS is not relevant. Answer C is incorrect because the VA refers to the size and capability of the UPS. Answer D is incorrect because dual voltage capabilities are irrelevant in this case. For more information, see the "Verifying Power Sources and UPS Installation" section.

15. B. Network availability is the next most important concern. Answer A is incorrect because the UPS size should be already decided. Answer C is incorrect because there is no need for a proxy for an internal Web server. Answer D is incorrect because firewall rules are irrelevant at this stage of the installation. For more information, see the "Network Cabling and Connectors" section.

16. D. A modem is needed for users to dial in to the Remote Access Server. Answers A, B, and C are incorrect because these devices are not needed for this type of server. For more information, see the "Installation Strategy" section.

17. B. A DMZ should be used to isolate the Web servers from the internal user network. Answer A is incorrect because a proxy server forwards HTTP requests from internal clients to external Websites. Answer C is incorrect because a DNS server resolves Internet Domain names to IP addresses. Answer D is incorrect because a DHCP server assigns IP addresses to devices on the network. For more information, see the "Installation Strategy" section.

18. B. A loose terminator on a bus topology network will result in connectivity problems for the entire network. Answer A is incorrect because the network speed is not an issue. Answer C is incorrect because there should be no UTP devices on a coaxial network. Answer D is incorrect because the network is specifically a 10Base2 Ethernet network, not token ring. For more information, see the " Network Cabling and Connectors" section.

19. B. A router server needs at least two network cards to be able to route between two networks. Answer A is incorrect because a SCSI card is not needed for this configuration. Answer C is incorrect because a routing table is a software-based component. Answer D is incorrect because network termination is irrelevant to the routing function. For more information, see the "Installation Strategy" section.

20. C. The backup tapes ordered should have been DLT tapes. Answers A, B, and D are incorrect because these items were required. For more information, see the "Verifying Components" section.

Scenarios

1. You will need three servers to set up the required environment. To provide Web and FTP services, a server will be needed to perform each function. To secure the internal LAN from the outside world, a firewall server will have to be set up. To fully secure the internal LAN, a DMZ network should be set up, to separate the Web and FTP server on their own LAN. The firewall should have three network cards, one to connect to the outside world, one to connect to the DMZ, and one connected to the internal LAN.

2. The server room should contain adequate air conditioning and ventilation. The power source should be verified to ensure good quality power, and that there are enough outlets to handle the amount of equipment. Network connectivity will have to be verified, including cabling location and cable types.

3. The VA rating of the servers and other equipment that will be connected to the UPS should be calculated, so that the right size of UPS can be purchased. The UPS should come with enough serial cables to be able to attach to all four servers. The network OS of the servers should be configured to automatically shut down in case of a power failure. The UPS should then have its battery fully charged, and then tested to make sure that the battery will take over when power is disconnected, and that the auto-shutdown of the servers works properly.

Setting Up the Environment

1.2 Install hardware using ESD best practices (boards, drives, processors, memory, internal cable, etc.)

- Mount the rack installation
- Cut and crimp network cabling
- Install UPS

CHAPTER PRE-TEST

1. How many wires are in a standard category 5 UTP cable?

2. What must you do to enable the battery in a new UPS?

3. Why should heavy servers be located on the bottom of a rack?

4. What is the purpose of a crossover cable?

5. What is the purpose of a BNC T-connector?

6. What is the purpose of a cable tester?

7. What is the purpose of a serial signal cable on a UPS?

8. Why should you never connect a laser printer to a UPS?

9. What is the purpose of rack stabilization?

10. Why is a straight-through cable used to connect a server to network hub instead of a crossover cable?

✦ Answers to these questions can be found at the end of the chapter. ✦

In this chapter, the installation of your server systems begins. The first step is to install your servers into the rack, keeping in mind the proximity to power sources and network availability. Depending on your equipment, you must cut and crimp network cabling for your new servers, creating different types of cables for different connections. UPS installation and configuration are also discussed.

Server Rack Installation

✦ Mount the rack installation

To keep servers from being physically damaged, and to provide environmental and physical security, the servers must be mounted in a proper rack. There are many different types of racks on the market, from freestanding racks that do not have any doors or sides to specialized server racks that come with locked doors and cooling and ventilation systems. The type of rack or cabinet used depends on your needs and on your budget. There are, however, some general tips for installing servers into a rack mount system.

Preparing the rack for installation

Before installing your servers, there are several key aspects of the rack installation to examine, including power and network availability, and rack stability.

Power sources

Ensure that there are enough power outlets nearby to power your servers and UPS units. Many racks come with their own power strips mounted along the vertical rails of the rack, offering many more outlets than a UPS or regular power bar.

Network availability

Install enough cable runs from your network switch to the rack to connect all of your servers to the network. It is a good idea to add extra cables for future expansion, if you have room to add more servers in your rack.

Depending on your server setup, if you have multiple NIC cards, or NIC cards with more than one network port, you will need more network cable drops. Plan accordingly, as you will need to be able to expand for the future.

Stability

Before installing equipment in the rack, ensure that it is stable on the floor. Most racks have wheels on the bottom that are removable or retractable. When the rack is wheeled into its final position, raise or remove the wheels, and lower any stabilizing legs to hold it firmly in place. Some racks also come with additional stabilizer feet that should be mounted on all four sides of the rack, and then firmly bolted to the floor.

Installing equipment in the rack

Each component needs to have its own rack mounting hardware kit. There are usually no internal brackets or mounting devices that come with the rack. To allow devices to be pulled out of the rack like a drawer, special rails are mounted on either side of the server and connected to similar rails in the rack.

Start by installing the heaviest items first into the bottom of the rack. If you try to install devices from the top, it could cause the rack to become too top-heavy and tip over. Installing heavy servers on the bottom of the rack creates more stabilization. The rack vendor's documentation may have special instructions on where to distribute the weight in their rack, so try to follow these specifications first, but in general, keep the heaviest equipment towards the bottom. Work your way upward, leaving space for other components such as the Keyboard/Video/Mouse (KVM) system.

Keyboard/video/mouse tray

The KVM tray should be installed at a level that you feel most comfortable. If you feel that you will be standing when you are using the keyboard and mouse, you should set the tray at waist-level, with the monitor located right above. If you want to be able to sit at the rack while using the keyboard and mouse, install the tray at a level comfortable for you to use when sitting.

Cabling

All cabling, whether it is power, network, keyboard, or video and mouse, should be bundled together properly, leaving enough slack for movement, and should be tied together with twist ties. This prevents cabling from getting caught in the doors or along the server mounting rails. The amount of cabling for each server can quickly become a nightmare of tangled cables hanging from the rear of the rack, if you don't neatly bundle and tie them together. This also makes it easier to extend servers out the front of the rack, as the cables will not get caught in any moving parts, or be pulled taut and pull the cables from their connecting sockets.

Extending servers

Most racks have the servers mounted on sliding rails, so that they can easily be pulled out of the rack through the front door. This allows you to take the top off the server and perform hardware maintenance without having to take the server out of the rack. Be careful not to extend more than one server at a time, or the shifting weight might cause the rack to tip over.

Exam Tip Install equipment in the rack according to the manufacturer's specifications first. If none are included, the heaviest equipment should go in the bottom of the rack.

Preparing Network Cabling

Although your entire network may already be cabled, within the server room, you will need to create network cables that connect your servers to your network switches and hubs. There are many other special cabling needs within a server room, including being able to connect two servers together, or to chain two hubs or switches together.

Coaxial

As described in Chapter 1, coaxial cable consists of a thin copper wire surrounded by protective, insulated material, to protect it from physical damage, and electromagnetic interference. This is the same type of cable that is used to connect your television or VCR.

The ends of the cables are terminated with BNC connectors, of which there are several types. A *single-end BNC connector* is what is installed on the end of the coaxial cable. On a network card, it is female, while the connector on the cable is male. Because a coaxial cable network is part of a bus topology, the cables can be connected and chained together through different types of BNC connectors. The *BNC T-connector* is in the shape of a letter *T*, which enables you to connect it to a device, and then connect another cable to continue the chain. A *BNC barrel connector* is used to join two coaxial cables together. At the end of the network chain, the cabling must be terminated with a 50-ohm terminator. Without a terminator, the network signal would bounce back onto the Ethernet bus, disrupting network communications.

There are three main ways that a BNC connector can be attached to a cable. It can be bolted on, screwed on, or crimped. The bolt and screw types of connectors are easy to install, as you do not need any special crimping tools to attach the connectors. Generally, when you buy coaxial cable, the connectors are already installed on the ends, and all you need to do is properly connect the BNC barrel and T-connectors as needed, and terminate the end of the chain.

Twisted-pair

A standard network twisted-pair cable contains eight wires. Depending on the type of connection you are trying to achieve, there are a number of different ways these wires can be configured. There are two wires dedicated as transmit, and two for receive. The other wires are not used at all. A hub or switch port is already configured to reverse these wires so that communications can work properly. When a cable is connected to hub, the transmit wires are connected to the receive wires on the hub. At the same time, the receive wires on the cable are connected to the hub's transmit wires. If you are trying to connect one PC to another without a hub or switch, you'll need a crossover cable, which reverses the transmit and receive wires within the cable itself.

Some hubs and switches come with an *uplink port,* which allows a hub to be connected or chained together with another hub through the use of a *straight-through cable*, which is a regular twisted-pair cable without a crossover. Sometimes this port can work both ways, which can be toggled by use of a push switch. However, if the hubs do not have uplink ports, the wires of the standard ports are already reversed, and therefore, you will need a crossover cable to connect both hubs together.

Exam Tip   For the exam, know the specific pin outs of the cables described in the following sections, and know the type of situation for which each one is used.

Straight-through cable

This is the most common type of twisted pair cabling. It connects your server or device to a wall jack or hub to complete the network connection. See Figure 2-1 for a pin-out diagram of a straight-through 10BaseT cable, showing the wires used for both transmit and receive.

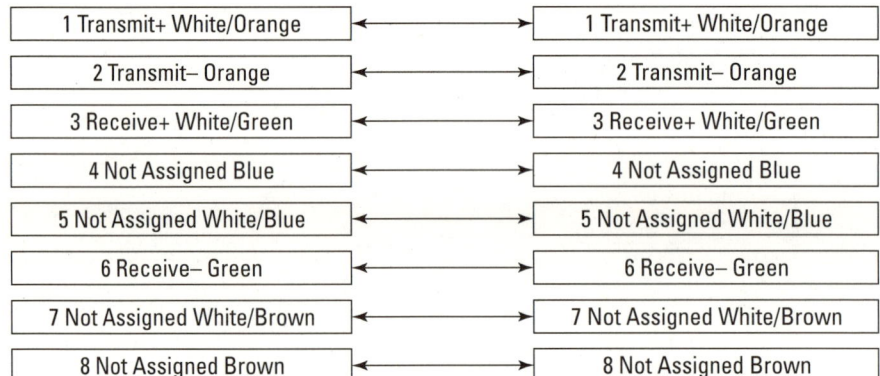

Figure 2-1: A pin-out diagram for a standard straight-through cable

Crossover cable

You need to use a crossover cable when connecting two servers together, or linking two hubs together that do not have special uplink ports. The crossover cable reverses the wires so that the transmit and receive wires are connected together. See Figure 2-2 for a pin-out diagram of a crossover 10BaseT cable.

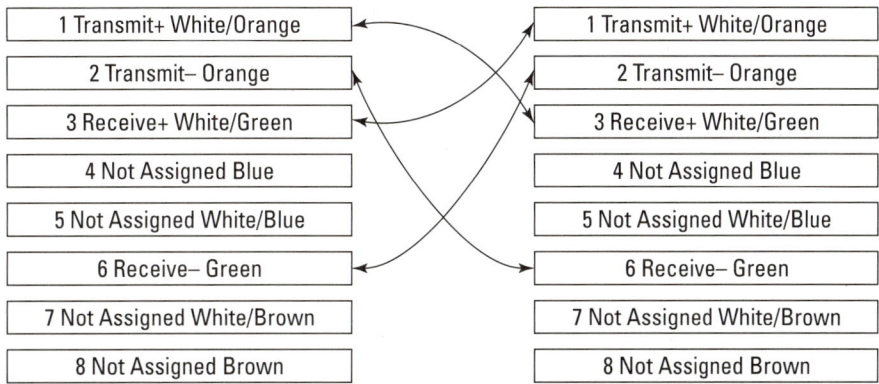

Figure 2-2: A pin-out diagram for a crossover cable showing the crossover of the transmit and receive wires

Rollover cable

A *rollover cable* is a special type of RJ-45 connector where the pins are flipped over so the connector at one end is a complete reverse of the other. This is mainly used for connecting to console ports on network devices for configuration purposes. See Figure 2-3 for a pin-out diagram of a rollover cable.

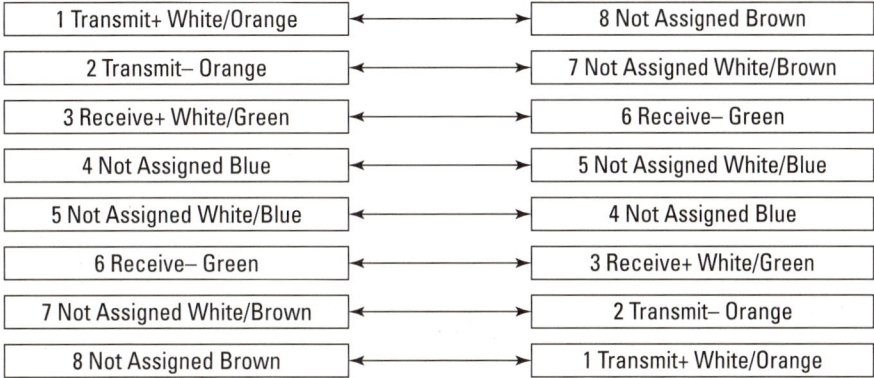

Figure 2-3: A pin-out diagram for a rollover cable

Making the cable

✦ Cut and crimp network cabling

You will probably encounter many situations when you will have to create your own network cables for specific purposes within the server room. With a few simple tools, you can quickly make any type of cable you need:

✦ **Cable:** For most modern networks, you will need minimum Category 5 UTP cabling.

✦ **Connectors:** For UTP cabling, you will need RJ-45 connectors, which look similar to RJ-11 phone connectors, but wider to accommodate 8 wires.

✦ **Cutter:** You will need a good cutting tool to make a nice, even cut in the wires so that the ends line up in a straight line.

✦ **Stripper:** To cut the plastic casing from the cable, you will need a stripper tool, which will make the task much easier. A sharp knife can also be used, but you must be careful not to damage the internal wires.

✦ **Crimper:** This tool clamps and seals the connector onto the wires.

Some inexpensive crimpers do not crimp the cable ends very well, and over time the pins lose their connection. Get yourself a good quality crimper.

The following are some general steps in making a UTP cable.

Making a UTP network cable

1. Strip about two inches of the plastic cover away from the end of the cable, revealing the wires beneath.

2. Spread the wires apart, while holding the base of the wires where the casing was stripped. Now you can separate the color-coded wires into the proper order that you need, depending on the cable. You will have to untwist the cables to do this, but do not untwist them too far, as you will lessen the effectiveness of the cable if you untwist more than half an inch.

3. Once the wires are in the proper order, straighten them out with your fingers Then, using your cutter, make a straight, even cut, about half an inch from the cable casing, to even up the ends of the wires.

4. Now you can slowly guide the wires into the RJ-45 connector, lining up the wires with their identical slots on the connector. Push the cable in until the plastic casing is able to fit inside the jack.

5. Insert the RJ-45 jack into the crimping tool, being careful not to let the wires fall out of the jack. Then clamp the crimper together as tight as possible until

you hear some clicking noises. This is an indication that the crimping is completed.

6. Examine the ends of the jack to make sure all the wires have been crimped into the contacts. If available, test the cable with a special electronic cable tester.

Making a coaxial network cable is much simpler than a UTP cable, because there is only one wire to worry about, and there is no need to worry about color coding or wire twists.

Making a coaxial network cable

1. You will need a special coax cable stripper, because the coaxial cable sheath is very thick, and it may take some patience to strip it with conventional cutters. Strip the end of the cable, leaving about ½ inch of the inner conductor exposed, with ⅛ inch of the inner insulation exposed below that.

2. Place the center pin of the connector over the end of the exposed conductor. It should reach down enough to meet the exposed insulation. Use a special BNC crimper to crimp the connector to the conductor.

3. Slide a small crimp barrel collar onto the to cable, and then the fit the BNC connector onto the end of the cable. Make sure the connection is snug, and that the conductor cable is visible through the end of the connector.

4. Slide the crimp barrel collar back up to fit tightly against the connector. Use the BNC crimper again to crimp the collar onto the cable and connector.

5. Tug the end of the cable to make sure the connector is tightly crimped. Finally, test the connector with a cable tester.

A cable tester is a very helpful tool to have when diagnosing cabling problems. For example, on a UTP cable, they can often tell you which pins are not connected, or if the cable is a standard straight through, or crossover cable.

Installing the UPS

 ✦ Install UPS

Although a UPS is a simple device to operate, there are several steps needed to properly install and configure the UPS for your server, beyond plugging the server into one of the UPS outlets.

There are four main steps to installing a UPS:

1. Charging the battery
2. Connecting the UPS to the server
3. Configuring the UPS software
4. Testing the UPS

Charging the UPS battery

The first step, which is often overlooked, is charging the UPS. Before it can be charged, the battery must be connected. UPS companies are required to ship the UPS with the battery disconnected internally, for safety reasons. The first thing you must do is to open up the UPS and reconnect the cable. Do not plug anything into the UPS while it is performing its initial charge, which can take eight to ten hours.

Exam Tip By law, UPS units must be shipped with the battery disconnected, for safety reasons. It must be connected again when the UPS is unpacked. Many people overlook this, and cannot figure out why a UPS battery will not work when installing for the first time.

Connecting the UPS

UPS units come with serial cables that connect to the serial port of the server it is protecting. This allows the UPS to communicate with the server's network operating system. In the event of a power failure, the UPS will contact the server OS, which will then shut itself down gracefully. This prevents data loss and corruption that can happen if the server is shut down abruptly.

Configuring the UPS software

Within the network OS, you can now configure the UPS software, which will enable you to specify what actions to take in the event of a power failure. You may wish to simply shut down the system, but in the case of a specialized server, such as a critical database server, you will want to be able to run scripts or programs that will safely shut the database down before the rest of the OS is shut down. You should set the shutdown time to begin after at least a few minutes of battery power. If the power failure only lasts less than a minute, there is no need to immediately shut down the server.

You should also set up the program to monitor the current UPS statistics such as current load and current state of input voltage.

Testing the UPS

There are two main scenarios that you should test with your UPS. One test is to make sure the UPS immediately switches to battery in the event of a power failure.

The second test is to ensure that if the power is disconnected, that the UPS signals the server operating system of the power failure, and that auto-shutdown is started.

To test the UPS, simply disconnect it from your power outlet. The UPS should signal a warning sound, to indicate that it is running on battery power. If power to the server is immediately shut off, there is a problem with your battery, or the battery may not be fully charged. Depending on the load on the UPS, and the number of servers it is connected to, the battery run-time might be very short.

If the UPS does not signal the server for auto-shutdown, check the serial cable to make sure it is properly secured to the serial port on both the UPS and the server. Next, you should examine the server configuration to make sure that serial port is enabled and that the UPS is properly configured for auto shutdown.

It is a good idea to test your UPS regularly, at least twice a year, to ensure that the battery is still functioning properly. Make sure to do this during non-production hours in case the test fails.

Caution   Never connect a laser printer to a UPS, as the current surge from the printer when it is first turned on is strong enough to cause damage.

Key Point Summary

In this chapter, several hardware installation concepts were discussed, including installation of the servers into the rack, preparing network cables, and installing and configuring the UPS. Keep the following points in mind for the exam:

✦ Install servers into the rack according to the rack vendor's specifications.

✦ Mount heavier equipment on the bottom of the rack to prevent tipping.

✦ Remove all equipment from a rack before moving it.

✦ Know the pin outs of a regular straight-through and crossover UTP cable, and where they should be used given a scenario of hubs and devices.

✦ Coaxial networks need to be terminated at the end of the network bus.

✦ Connect the UPS internal battery connector after being unpacked.

✦ The UPS should be fully charged for eight to ten hours before use.

✦ To enable server auto-shutdown, a serial signal cable should be connected from the UPS to a serial port on each server.

✦ You need to configure the UPS software on each server's network OS to enable the auto-shutdown features of the UPS.

✦ You should test the UPS regularly to test the state of the battery and the auto shutdown of servers.

✦   ✦   ✦

STUDY GUIDE

The Study Guide section provides you with the opportunity to test your knowledge about setting up the server environment. The Assessment Questions provide practice for the test, and the Scenarios provide practice with real situations. If you get any questions wrong, use the answers to determine the part of the chapter you should review before continuing.

Assessment Questions

1. A technician is creating a cable that will connect a standard network switch port to a network router. What type of cable will be needed to complete the connection?

    A. Straight-through cable

    B. Uplink sable

    C. Crossover cable

    D. Rollover cable

2. A server rack is being moved to a new location on the other side of the building, where a new server room has been constructed. The rack currently holds three servers, but two of them are not used anymore. What is the best process for moving the rack to its new location?

    A. Remove all the servers, move the rack to the new location, and install only the server being used back into the rack.

    B. Remove all the servers, move the rack to the new location, and install all the servers back into the rack.

    C. Put the entire rack onto a dolly and roll it slowly to its new location. Servers are secured so that they will not fall out.

    D. Remove the unused servers. Put the rack onto a dolly, and roll it slowly to its new location.

3. A technician is extending a rack-mounted server that is located near the top of the rack. When the server is fully extended, the rack begins to tip over. What is the most likely cause of the imbalance in the rack?

    A. The rack is too close to the wall.

    B. The rack has no stabilizer feet attached.

C. The server should be located lower on the rack.

D. The rack is on wheels.

4. A technician wants to connect the uplink port on an existing 24-port hub to a new expansion 12-port hub. Which of the following cable and port combinations should be used to properly connect the devices?

   A. Rollover cable from the uplink port of the 24-port hub to the uplink port of the 12-port hub

   B. Crossover cable from the uplink port of the 24-port hub to a standard port on the 12-port hub

   C. Straight-through cable from the uplink port of the 24-port hub to a standard port on the 12-port hub

   D. Uplink cable from the uplink port of the 24-port hub to the uplink port on the 12-port hub

5. A technician is installing four servers with a combined VA rating of 1200. What VA rating should the UPS have to be able to provide battery backup to the servers?

   A. 1500

   B. 1200

   C. 600

   D. 3000

6. A technician is installing four servers into a rack. In what order should the components be mounted into the rack?

   A. Heaviest servers on the top

   B. Heaviest servers on the bottom

   C. Server weight distributed evenly over the rack

   D. According to the rack vendor's documented specifications

7. A server is being connected to a network switch. What type of network cable will be needed to make the connection?

   A. Crossover cable

   B. Straight-through cable

   C. Rollover cable

   D. UTP cable

8. A new server has been connected to a UPS system. The UPS battery has been fully charged and tested. Two weeks later, a power failure caused the UPS to switch over to battery for 20 minutes before the battery ran out and the server lost power. What is the mostly likely cause of the abrupt server shutdown?

    A. The UPS load was too high.

    B. The UPS battery was not charged properly.

    C. The UPS software was not configured.

    D. The server is not compatible with the UPS.

9. A 1500VA-rated UPS is connected to a server and monitor with a combined VA rating of 700. The server needs to print reports on an hourly basis, and a laser printer has been installed beside it. The VA rating of the printer is 400. When the technician plugs the printer into the UPS and turns the printer on, the UPS indicates an overload failure. What is the most likely cause of the problem?

    A. The laser printer is causing an abnormal load on the UPS.

    B. The VA rating of the combined devices is too high for the UPS.

    C. The UPS battery has not been charged.

    D. The printer is incompatible with the UPS.

10. Two network hubs have to be connected together, but neither of them have an uplink port on them. How can the two hubs be connected?

    A. Rollover cable

    B. Straight-through cable

    C. Crossover cable

    D. Uplink cable

11. A technician wants to properly stabilize a server rack. There are currently five servers mounted on the rack. What can be done to make sure the rack will not move or tip over?

    A. Move the heaviest servers to the top of the rack.

    B. Add stabilizer plates to all six sides of the rack.

    C. Add stabilizer plates to the front and back sides of the rack.

    D. Bolt the rack into the floor.

12. A server has just been connected to a new UPS. When the technician pulls the power plug to test the UPS, both the UPS and the server abruptly shut down. What is the most likely cause of the UPS not running from battery?

    A. The server BIOS was not updated.

    B. The UPS software was not installed.

    C. The serial cable to the server was disconnected.

    D. The UPS internal battery cable was not connected.

13. A server with a coaxial Thinnet network card has just been installed. How should the server be connected to the network?

    A. The coaxial cable should be plugged into the coaxial adapter on the network card.

    B. A BNC T-connector should be installed on the network card connector, with one end connected to the network and the other end terminated.

    C. The network cable should be pierced with a vampire tap.

    D. A BNC barrel connector should be connected to the server, with the other end connected to the network.

14. A technician is using a cable tester to test a UTP network cable that is connecting two hubs together . The tester indicates a fault with wires 1, 3, 2, and 6. When the cable is connected to the hubs, it seems to work fine. What is the mostly likely cause of the discrepancy?

    A. The cable was not crimped properly.

    B. The cable is a straight-through cable, and the tester is set for a crossover cable.

    C. The cable is a crossover cable, and the tester is set for a straight-through cable.

    D. The tester should be set to test coaxial cable.

15. A technician has just installed a new UPS to protect two servers from power failure. The battery cable was connected internally, and the serial cables connected to both servers to facilitate auto-shutdown. When the UPS is first turned on, the technician disconnects the power plug to test the UPS. The UPS and servers abruptly shut down. What is the most likely cause of the UPS failure?

    A. The UPS is not compatible with the server OS.

    B. The UPS battery was not charged.

    C. The UPS software has not been installed.

    D. The UPS was not properly grounded.

Scenarios

1. A technician is expanding a 10BaseT LAN by adding two new servers: a mail server and a file server. There is only one unused standard port on the current 24-port server room hub, so a new 24-port hub has been purchased to be added on to the first hub. The new hub does not have an uplink port. How many UTP cables will be needed to connect all of the new devices, and what type of cables should they be?

2. The two new servers in the Scenario #1 have necessitated an upgrade to the UPS, which currently will not handle the load of the extra servers. A new UPS with sufficient capacity for all the servers has been purchased and is ready to be installed. What steps must be taken to properly install and test the new UPS?

3. A technician needs to create a crossover cable to connect two servers together through their network ports. Which wires of a standard UTP cable need to be crossed over to make the cable?

Answers to Chapter Questions

Chapter pre-test

1. A standard category 5 UTP cable has eight wires.

2. The UPS internal battery is disconnected during initial shipping, so you must reconnect it and charge it for the battery to work.

3. If you put heavier severs near the top of the rack, there is a danger that it might tip over because of the weight.

4. A crossover cable is used to connect two server network cards together, or to connect two hubs together through their standard ports.

5. A BNC T-connector enables a coaxial network cable to be attached to a server or workstation, and the network chain can continue or terminate from that point, because the T-connector has three connectors.

6. A cable tester is handy for testing new UTP and coaxial cables that you have made by hand, and also for troubleshooting existing cabling. It will be able to show you cable faults and information on the individual wires.

7. The serial cable is attached to the serial port of a server so that the UPS can send signals to the network OS on the server in the event of a power failure.

8. A laser printer draws a large amount of power, and it may overload your UPS.

9. Adding stabilizer feet or plates to the sides of a rack prevents it from tipping over.

10. The ports on the hub are already configured to cross the transmit and receive wires of the straight-through cable, so a crossover cable is unnecessary.

Assessment questions

1. **C.** A crossover cable will be needed to complete the connection. Answer A is incorrect because a straight-through cable would only be used to connect the standard switch port to a network device. Answer B is incorrect because an uplink cable does not exist. Answer D is incorrect because a rollover cable is used for connecting to console ports. For more information, see the "Crossover cable" section.

2. **A.** All servers should be removed from the rack before moving it. The two unused servers should not be reinstalled. Answer B is incorrect because the unused servers should not be put back into the rack. Answer C is incorrect because the rack should not be transported with equipment still mounted in it. Answer D is incorrect because the rack should not be transported with equipment still mounted in it, even if it is only one server. For more information, see the "Installing equipment in the rack" section.

3. **B.** The stabilizer feet will prevent the rack from tipping over when a server is extended. Answer A is incorrect because this will not cause the rack to tip over. Answer C is incorrect because the cause is the lack of stabilizer feet. Heavier equipment should be located lower in the rack, but stabilizers will prevent this if they are located higher. Answer D is incorrect because the wheels alone would not cause the imbalance, but they should be retracted when the rack is not being moved. For more information, see the "Preparing the rack for installation" section.

4. **C.** The uplink port on the current hub already crosses the cable, so it only needs a standard straight cable to a standard port on the new hub. Answer A is incorrect because a rollover cable is used to connect to a device console port. Answer B is incorrect because there is no need to use a crossover cable on an uplink port. Answer D is incorrect because there is no such thing as an uplink cable. For more information, see the "Twisted pair" section.

5. **A.** The VA rating of the UPS should be greater than the combined VA rating of the devices to adequately power them from battery in the event of a power failure. Answer B is incorrect because the load will be equal to the UPS load capability, and it may not be able to power the servers in the event of a power failure. Answer C is incorrect because this load rating is too low. Answer D is incorrect because this load rating will work, but is not needed for this amount of servers. For more information, see the "Installing the UPS" section.

6. **D.** The documentation for the rack should be consulted for specifications on installing equipment. Answer A is incorrect because a top-heavy rack will tip over too easily. Answer B is incorrect because the documentation should be checked first, but putting the heaviest items on the bottom is safest. Answer C is incorrect because this configuration might not be to the rack's specifications. For more information, see the "Installing equipment in the rack" section.

7. **B.** A standard straight cable is used to connect a device to a standard network port. Answer A is incorrect because a crossover cable is not needed in this case. Answer C is incorrect because a rollover cable is used for connecting to a device's console port. Answer D is incorrect because it does not specify what type of UTP cable. For more information, see the "Twisted pair" section.

8. C. The UPS software was not configured to automatically shut down the server in the event of a power outage. Answer A is incorrect because one server will not overload the UPS. Answer B is incorrect because the battery was working properly. Answer D is incorrect because compatibility is not an issue. For more information, see the "Configuring the UPS software" section.

9. A. You should never connect a laser printer to a UPS, because it draws a considerable load when first started up and could damage the UPS. Answer B is incorrect because the VA rating of the combined devices is below the rating of the UPS. Answer C is incorrect because there is nothing wrong with the battery; the UPS is overloaded. Answer D is incorrect because there are no compatibility issues. For more information, see the "Testing the UPS" section.

10. C. A crossover cable can be used between any standard ports on the two hubs. Answer A is incorrect because a rollover cable is used to connect to device console ports. Answer B is incorrect because a straight cable will not work without an uplink port on one of the hubs. Answer D is incorrect because there is no such thing as an uplink cable. For more information, see the "Crossover cable" section.

11. B. Stabilizer plates can be mounted on all sides of the rack, which prevents it from tipping over. Answer A is incorrect because the heaviest servers should be located on the bottom of the rack. Answer C is incorrect because having stabilizer plates only on the front and back will not prevent the rack from tipping sideways. Answer D is incorrect because bolting the rack to the floor is inefficient and not necessary. For more information, see the "Twisted pair" section.

12. D. When a UPS is first installed, its internal battery must be connected. It is disconnected for shipping safety reasons. Answer A is incorrect because the server BIOS is irrelevant in this issue. Answer B is incorrect because the issue was with the UPS battery. Answer C is incorrect because the serial cable would not have prevented the battery problem. For more information, see the "Charging the UPS battery" section.

13. B. A BNC T-connector is needed to connect the server to the network and terminate the connection. Answer A is incorrect because the network cable needs to be terminated. Answer C is incorrect because a vampire tap is typically used for older Thicknet installations. Answer D is incorrect because a barrel connector will not terminate the network connection. For more information, see the "Coaxial" section.

14. C. The tester is set to test for a straight-through cable, but the cable is a crossover, which is why it shows a fault with the crossed transmit and receive wires. Answer A is incorrect because the cable is working properly. Answer B is incorrect because the cable is a crossover cable. Answer D is incorrect because the tester should be set to test UTP cable. For more information, please see the "Twisted pair" section.

15. B. A new UPS needs time to have its battery charged. Answer A is incorrect because the UPS software compatibility is not relevant to the condition of the battery. Answer C is incorrect because the UPS software is relevant to the condition of the battery. Answer D is incorrect because the problem is with the condition of the battery. For more information, see the "Charging the UPS battery" section.

Scenarios

1. The technician should make three cables, two straight-through cables, and one crossover cable. The straight-through cables are to connect the two servers to the new hub. The crossover cable will be used to connect the two hubs together using a standard network port. A crossover is needed, as the transmit and receive wires on the hub ports are already reversed.

2. Because the new UPS will handle the load of all of the servers combined, the old one can be removed. Disconnect the serial cables connecting the old UPS to the servers, and remove any special UPS software that was installed on the server's network OS. Before connecting the new UPS, open it up and reconnect the battery connector, which was disabled during shipping. Plug the UPS into a power socket, and let it charge for 8 to 10 hours until it is fully charged. Now you can plug the servers into the new UPS and reconnect the serial cables to all of the servers.

   Next, you must install and configure UPS software on each server, to set up how it will behave in the event of a power failure. Each server should be set to automatically shut down gracefully if it is running on battery power.

   Once the servers have been configured, you should now test the UPS. First, pull the UPS power plug from the wall socket, and examine the UPS to make sure it is running on battery power. The UPS should sound an audible alarm to warn you that it is running on battery. Next you should examine the servers to see if auto-shutdown has been initiated after a few minutes.

3. The pin out requirements for a crossover cable are detailed in Figure 2-4. Wires 1 and 3 are crossed over, as are wires 2 and 6. Wires 4, 5, 7, and 8 stay the same.

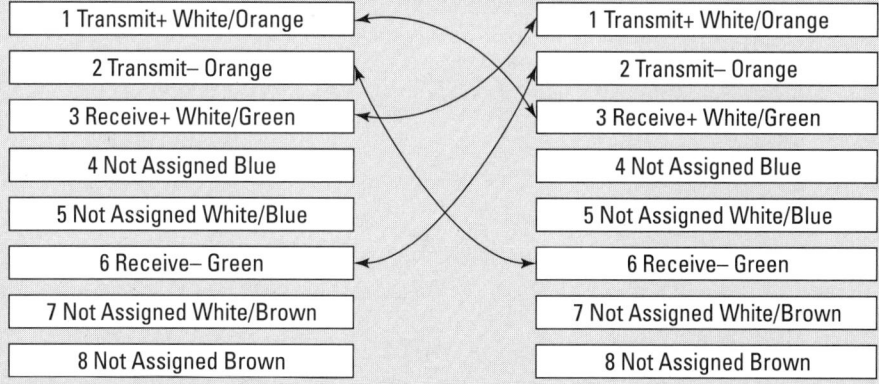

Figure 2-4: A crossover cable pin-out diagram showing the crossover of the transmit and receive wires

Installing Hardware

CHAPTER PRE-TEST

1. Why should BIOS and firmware levels be kept current?

2. Why is the memory checked whenever a server is turned on?

3. What is a KVM switch?

4. What SCSI ID should the SCSI host adapter be assigned to?

5. What is the purpose of a server POST routine?

6. Where is the best place to look up server POST error codes?

7. What is the purpose of protecting devices from ESD?

8. Why should you check your internal cables after installing an internal device?

9. Why should you check POST error codes with the server vendor's documentation and not the BIOS vendor?

10. What is the purpose of an anti-static wrist strap?

✦ Answers to these questions can be found at the end of the chapter. ✦

Once your server installation has been planned, and the environment set, the next step in your installation process is installing your server hardware. This involves more than just installing your main server box into the rack. Other devices such as a second CPU, extra memory, and external devices such as tape drives, modems, and storage systems also need to be installed and configured. Finally, when all the devices and peripherals have been installed and connected, the server system will run a power-on self-test (POST) to verify the integrity of internal components.

This chapter discusses the installation of these internal and external devices, including the importance of electrostatic discharge protection, and ends with a section on the POST process and identifying testing errors.

Installing Hardware

 1.2 Install hardware using ESD best practices (boards, drives, processors, memory, internal cable, etc.)

Installing server hardware components may seem like an easy task, but there are several factors and best practices to keep in mind when adding internal peripherals. The possibility of electrostatic discharge is always an issue, but installing certain components such as memory or another CPU can just as easily cause problems with your server installation.

Installing internal devices

Your server should already come pre-installed from the factory with most of the components you have ordered. Depending on your configuration, there could have been extra items to upgrade generic factory configurations. Extra CPU's, additional memory, redundant power supplies, and special cabling, might have to be installed by the technician.

 When the server has arrived after shipping, it is a good idea to open it up, make sure that all the parts are present, and examine the cables to ensure that they were not dislodged during shipping.

Electrostatic discharge

Electrostatic discharge (ESD) is caused by the release of static buildup between two surfaces. The amount of static discharge can be more than enough to effectively cripple critical computer components. When working with internal server components, you must take steps to prevent ESD from harming server components.

✦ **Use an anti-static area:** Every server room should have a designated area for working on equipment. Make sure to insulate the work area from any type of electrostatic build-up. A workbench with special anti-static padding is excellent, or if you are working in front of a server rack, an anti-static floor mat will do.

✦ **Ground the technician:** To prevent the technician from causing an electrostatic discharge, special anti-static straps can be used, which tie around the technician's wrist, and then connect to a grounded metal surface. This will provide a path for any discharge to dissipate to ground.

✦ **Handle components properly:** Care must be taken when handling and installing components into the server. Components are usually shipped in anti-static bags, which protects them from ESD during shipping. Do not remove them from the anti-bag until you are ready to install them. Before removing the component from its anti-static bag, make sure your grounding wrist strap is properly connected, and touch the server case to discharge any electrostatic build-up in your body.

When handling interface cards, hold them by the edges, or by the faceplate. Do not touch the circuit boards or any chips in the card. If you are replacing another card, remove the original and place it on an anti-static bag or on an anti-static surface.

Exam Tip   Be aware of the various tools and procedures for protecting against ESD.

Expansion boards

You may have extra internal expansion boards that you will have to install before you install the main server. It could be a better video card, NIC card, modem, or SCSI controller. Each component should come in its own anti-static bag, to protect it from ESD damage. Leave the card in the bag until it is time to install it.

Before installing cards, open up the server cover and determine if you have enough slots to install your expansion cards. Each slot has a faceplate that covers an opening in the back of the server chassis. Before you can install a new card, you must remove the faceplate for the slot you want to use. If you have any empty slots, you should cover them up with a faceplate, as this aids in air circulation and internal cooling. The chassis is designed for optimal airflow, and leaving extra holes in it can be detrimental to the cooling process.

Line up the connectors of the expansion board with the slot on the motherboard, and then push it down firmly, using the edges of the card to apply pressure. When the card is fully inserted, all the contacts of the card connector should be fit evenly across the entire slot. Then screw the top of the card faceplate into the chassis to ensure that the card will not be dislodged.

IDE drives

If you have any internal drives to install, such as extra IDE drives or CD-ROM drives, make there is an empty expansion bay for your device. Most servers come with many expansion bays for drives, but if you already have a number of devices installed, especially IDE hard drives, space could be limited. There is a maximum of two IDE devices on each primary and secondary controller. The IDE controllers are built right onto the server motherboard, and control communications between the IDE hard disks and the server bus. Most machines come with two IDE channel controllers to allow up to four IDE devices to be connected. Each device on the controller is set to be either a master, slave, or cable-select device. You need to check the jumpers on the back of the drives to determine their configuration. The configuration of an additional IDE device will depend on your current IDE configuration, and whether there is already a master or slave device on a particular controller.

Configuring IDE drives is discussed in more detail in Chapter 8.

When you install a hard drive, be sure it is properly mounted into a hard drive bay, or a special area on the chassis where the hard drive can be attached using mounting screws. Do not leave any drives unmounted, or sitting on top of other drives. If the server is moved, they might fall inside the case, and pull out wires and cables in the process. Ensure there is enough space between hard drives for proper air circulation. They can get very hot, and if the drives are too close together, they might overheat. Be careful in handling the drives, and be wary of electrostatic discharge, which could harm the drives. Because hard drives are magnetic devices, you should keep them away from any magnetic interference. Do not shake or drop the drive, as it is a mechanical device, and the sensitive drive head components inside can be easily dislodged and broken.

After you have installed the drives, turn on the server and inspect your BIOS configuration for your IDE channels. Modern servers should be able to detect the size and type of the drives automatically, but with older servers, you may need to input the configuration manually. Most hard drives come with their configuration and head, cylinder, and sector information printed on the top of the drive.

If the BIOS fails to detect the drives during the POST routine, check your cabling and jumper settings to ensure they are properly set up as a master, slave, or cable select-setup.

You will need to use your network operating system to set up the new drives to accept and store data. They need to be formatted with a file system particular to the network operating system. If you are installing the server for the first time, the OS will do this automatically, but if you are adding hard drives to a current configuration, you may have to manually set the drives up to be recognized by the operating system.

Most modern servers use SCSI-based storage systems for greater speed and capacity, but on occasion, an IDE drive subsystem might also be implemented for a system partition.

Power supplies

Although servers come by default with one power supply, many servers have the option of running redundant power supplies for increased fault tolerance. If one of the power supplies fails, the other will take over without any interruption in power.

Extra power supplies tend to be modular and hot-plug capable, meaning that you can install or remove a power supply while the system is still on and running. This does not mean that you can remove the power supply if there is only one in the system.

To install a second power supply, first remove the face plate that covers the additional power supply bay. The new power supply will have a connector on one end that will plug into a connector socket within the bay when you insert it. Ensure that the power supply is fit tightly in the connector socket before plugging the power cable in.

You can check the status of a power supply by making the sure the fan is running, and most come with indicator lights showing the status of the power supply. A green light means it is running properly, a red light indicates a failure.

CPU

Your server should already come from the manufacturer with the main CPU already installed in the system. Sometimes, if you have ordered a second CPU for a multi-processor system, it will come in a separate package, and you will have to install it yourself. Take extra care not to expose the CPU to ESD. Always keep the CPU in its anti-static bag until the moment you are about to install it. Examine the extra CPU socket on the motherboard, and compare it to your additional CPU. The CPU should be identical to your existing one, but you must check carefully to make sure it will fit into the socket.

There are many different types of sockets and mechanisms to install CPUs, but typically the CPU is plugged into the socket, and then a special lever is used to push it the rest of the way, while keeping all the pins aligned with the socket holes. Do not force the CPU into the socket, or you risk damaging the tiny pins.

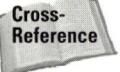

Adding or upgrading CPUs is discussed in more detail in Chapter 7.

Memory

Although your server should come with base memory already installed by the manufacturer, you may have ordered additional memory that needs to be installed before the server is configured. You should take extra care with memory modules, as they are very susceptible to ESD damage. Take care to hold the memory card by its edges, and do not touch the chips on the module. One little static shock can render the memory inoperable.

Depending on the type of memory, there are two main different ways of installing it into the slots on the motherboard. For older SIMM-based modules, insert the memory module into the socket at a 45-degree angle. When the module is fully inserted, push it gently back into an upright vertical position. Special notches on the ends of the module will click into place with special metal clips. See Figure 3-1 for an example of installing SIMM memory.

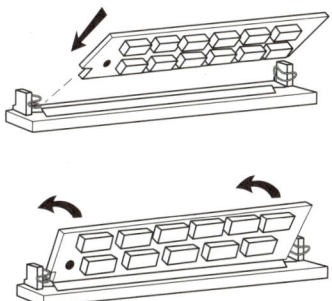

Figure 3-1: How to properly insert a SIMM memory module

With new DIMM-style modules, insert the memory module vertically into the memory slot. To secure it in place, special notches on either end of the module are clipped into place with plastic clips. Slide the module down into the slot, and the push it firmly into the socket until the plastic connectors snap into place. See Figure 3-2 for an example of installing a DIMM memory module.

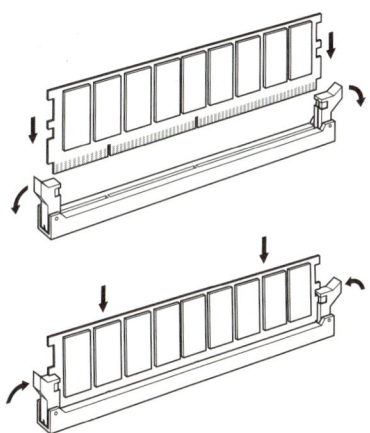

Figure 3-2: How to properly insert a DIMM memory module

When the system is restarted, the BIOS should automatically see the additional memory, which you can verify during the memory-check portion of the server's POST routine. It will verify the memory, and give you the total amount of RAM that is installed. If the additional memory is not reported, or if the POST routine halts with a failure or a beeping noise, the memory may not be properly installed, or it could be the wrong type for your server. Ensure that the memory is compatible with your current system before purchasing memory upgrades.

Adding or upgrading memory is discussed in more detail in Chapter 7.

Internal cables

Before replacing the cover of the server, check all internal cables to make sure they are plugged into the right places and are tightly connected. Some cables and connectors can be worked loose when you are adding and removing components, and constantly unplugging or pulling wires.

Check all the power cables, and ensure that they are tightly plugged into their sockets on each device that requires power. There are usually a large number of power cables in a server, and you should tie-wrap any excess cables not being used, and move them away from the main boards.

IDE cables are notorious for easily coming loose, and should be checked to ensure that the cables are tightly fitted onto both the primary and secondary IDE controller connectors on the motherboard, and onto the proper drives and devices themselves. Remember that the red stripe along the side of an IDE ribbon cable denotes that the wire is pin 1, and should be connected to pin 1 on the device.

You should always check your internal cables after working inside a server chassis, as they can easily be dislodged while moving cables and devices.

Check the internal SCSI cables to ensure tight connections, and that the SCSI bus integrity is preserved by having each device connected in a chain, with proper terminations at each end of the bus.

Installing external devices

✦ Install external devices (e.g. keyboards, monitors, subsystems, modem rack, etc.)

Although installing your external devices and connecting them to the server is a simple task, there are certain things that you should keep in mind when installing devices such as KVM switches, modem racks, and external storage devices.

Keyboards

If you are installing your server into a rack that will house several servers, I recommend that you use a Keyboard/Video/Mouse (KVM) switch to connect all the servers to one keyboard, monitor, and mouse. If you don't, you will have to have separate peripherals for each server, which will take up a lot of space, and will result in a cabling nightmare. The KVM switch has a main port to connect the keyboard, monitor, and mouse to, and several switch ports to connect the cables to each of the servers. Each port contains one 15-pin monitor port, and two PS/2-style ports for the keyboard and mouse. See Figure 3-3 for an example of a KVM switch.

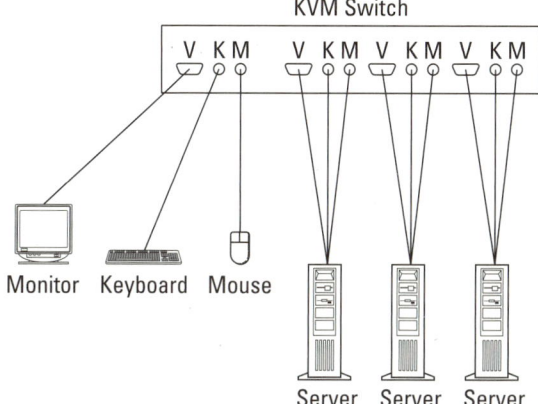

Figure 3-3: A KVM switch connects several servers to one keyboard, monitor and mouse.

You will find that sometimes when using the KVM switch to access the server that the keyboard or the mouse will not work. Most KVM switches come with a reset button that resets all the connections to the switch. Usually this will recover the use of the keyboard and mouse. If this does not work, you may have to reseat the connections and repeat the process.

You should install the keyboard before turning your server on. If there is no keyboard present, the server may sound a warning beep and display a message on the monitor screen and will not boot further. This is to prevent the server from starting up without any way of inputting commands, or shutting the server down safely. Other servers may boot into the operating system anyway, in which case you can sometimes attach a keyboard while the server is loading. This may or may not work, and could cause invalid data to be sent to the keyboard port when it is attached, which could halt the server with a keyboard error. If the connector slips out while the server is up and running, plugging it back in should restore the keyboard, but this does not work all the time.

Monitors

Most servers come with very basic video requirements, with support for basic VGA and SVGA resolutions. The monitor screen will be used rarely, except to troubleshoot problems, or add new software and configurations. Your monitor should also support basic VGA resolutions, and the size of the actual screen should be kept as small as possible, approximately 12 to 14 inches. If you are mounting the monitor in a server rack, it will be impossible to put a larger monitor in there, as it will take up too much space, and may not even fit at all. If the monitor will be sitting on a tray, rather than rack-mounted, ensure that the tray is stable and supportive enough to carry the weight of the monitor.

Peripherals

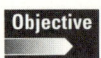 **2.4** Configure external peripherals (UPS, external drive subsystems, etc.)

Your server may also need other peripherals that can be left free-standing or mounted into a rack. Common devices include tape drives, modems and modem racks, and extra storage subsystems and RAID enclosures.

Tape drives

If your tape drive backup system is not internal to your server, you will need to make space available for the tape drive. It must be located in close proximity to the host server, to connect SCSI cables and terminations. It should also be in a position so that the door of the tape drive can be easily accessed to insert and retrieve tapes from the storage device. If it is a rack-mounted tape drive, the same cabling considerations must be kept in mind. Also ensure that there is enough space to eject the tape or open the tape drive door without hitting the rack cabinet door.

If the tape device is the last peripheral on the SCSI bus chain, it must have its second SCSI connector terminated. Check the SCSI host ID of the tape drive to ensure it is unique on the SCSI bus. A conflict with another device can render the system inoperable.

Modems

If your server is being used as a remote access server or fax server, there must be a modem located either internal to the server, or connected to it externally through the use of serial modem cables. Many remote access servers use a bank of modems, to allow many phone lines to be available for dialing in or out. Several modems can be housed within a single rack-mounted device. In either case, the modem system must be close enough to the host server to connect serial modem cables, and in the proper location to provide external phone lines for the modems.

Storage systems

If you have any additional storage devices, such as external RAID enclosures, they should be located close to the host server to provide for connecting SCSI cables. If the device is rack-mountable, this will ensure that it is safe from environmental factors such as physical damage and air pollutants. Hard drives are very easily damaged by excessive physical movement and dust.

UPS

The UPS must be located in close proximity to the servers, and also to the power outlets in the server room. If the UPS is rack-mountable, it is usually mounted on the bottom of rack because of its heavy weight and for easy access to power cables, which usually come from the lower wall or from under the floor. Each server should be connected to the UPS with both a power cable and a serial signal cable for auto shutdown capabilities. Some racks have special power strips mounted onto the rack, which can be safely connected to the UPS, and the devices plug into the power strips. This aids in cable management, as each server on the rack can connect to a power strip outlet closest to it, rather than running all the way down the rack to the UPS itself.

Verifying SCSI IDs and Termination

✦ Verify SCSI ID configuration and termination

When installing SCSI devices, you must pay careful attention to the SCSI IDs of the host adapter and the devices on the SCSI bus. Improper configuration and termination of the SCSI bus may result in unpredictable behavior, and the server might not boot at all. The following are some general rules for configuring SCSI devices.

Exam Tip   For the exam, know what SCSI IDs are usually assigned for the host adapter and the first boot device.

Host adapter

The SCSI *host adapter* facilitates communications between the server system bus and the devices on the SCSI bus. It exchanges commands and information with the devices on the bus, and relays that information to the system bus. The SCSI host adapter should be set to ID 7. This is the highest number on an 8-device bus; the IDs are numbered from 0 to 7. This device number has the highest priority on the SCSI bus, which the host adapter needs to efficiently control the SCSI system.

Verifying device numbers

Each device on the SCSI bus needs to have its own separate ID. There can be no duplications, or else the SCSI host adapters will try to contact both devices at the same time, causing a resource conflict. Any device that you boot from, such as a SCSI hard disk, should be given SCSI ID 0. In older SCSI systems, this was mandatory, but in newer systems, it is not required. It is still a good idea, however, so that the first device seen on the bus will be the boot hard disk.

Device cabling and termination

Ensure that your cables and connectors are of the proper SCSI type, such as Narrow or Wide, and that the number of pins matches the number of pins on your devices. A Narrow SCSI bus uses an 8-bit channel to communicate, and uses a 50-pin connector. A Wide bus uses a 16-bit channel to communicate, and uses a 68-pin connector. Each end of the SCSI bus needs to be terminated, or else the electronic signals will bounce off the end of the bus, and reflect back onto the SCSI channel, disrupting communications. Most host adapters have the ability to automatically terminate its end of the SCSI bus, but another terminator will be needed to terminate the last device on the other side of the chain. There can be no breaks or gaps in the bus chain; each device must connected to another, or terminated. Ensure that the terminator is of the proper type for your SCSI system, and offers the appropriate resistance level for termination.

 SCSI is discussed in more detail in Chapter 8.

BIOS and Firmware Levels

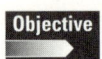 **2.1** Check/upgrade BIOS/firmware levels (system board, RAID, controller, hard drive, etc.)

Many initial server and device installations fail because of improper or conflicting hardware BIOS and firmware levels. You must identify all hardware BIOS and firmware levels, and upgrade them to the latest release. This guarantees that you have the latest internal software for your devices that will support the most current hardware in your setup.

BIOS

BIOS stands for *basic input/output system*. The BIOS is built-in software that contains all the code required to control most of the basic devices and operations, and provides the interface to the underlying hardware of your server for the operating system.

The BIOS is stored in a Read-Only Memory (ROM) chip on your server's motherboard. This ensures that the BIOS will always be available and will not be damaged by power or disk failures. The basic type of chip is called a PROM (Programmable Read-Only Memory) that can be programmed through special software to initially set the code. Once it is there, it cannot be changed. To update the BIOS, the PROM must be physically removed from the device and replaced with a new chip.

Newer firmware chips such as EEPROM (Electrically Erasable Programmable Read-Only Memory) are a special type of PROM that can be erased by exposing it to an electrical charge. EEPROM requires data to be written or erased one byte at a time.

The most recent technology for programming firmware is *flash memory*. Flash memory can write that data to the EEPROM in larger block sizes, which is much faster than a regular PROM. When someone says they are *flashing a BIOS,* they mean they are updating the BIOS flash memory with a new image.

There are three possible sources for a BIOS update: your system vendor (for major brand systems), your motherboard vendor, or your BIOS vendor (if you've already purchased a replacement BIOS chip). Contact the system or motherboard vendor for the flash BIOS file you need to download. Most major system vendors have a database of models and the matching BIOS files.

Exam Tip　Remember that the original manufacturer's Web site is usually the best way to find BIOS and Firmware updates for your particular device or system.

Before downloading a BIOS update, you must check your current BIOS level. You can find this information by booting your server. The first thing to appear on the screen when the system comes up will be your current BIOS information, including its manufacturer and the current version. This way you can verify your BIOS date with the manufacturer's information. If it is out of date, you should obtain the latest BIOS version.

Ensure that you have the correct BIOS for your system. Flashing your BIOS with the wrong image could destroy your BIOS and disable your motherboard. In most cases, you'll download a single compressed file that contains the BIOS image file. Most upgrades involve saving the BIOS upgrade image to a bootable floppy diskette. All you need to do to update the flash BIOS is boot your server with the image floppy and follow the instructions.

Caution　It is extremely important to not power down or reboot the server during a BIOS upgrade. If you do you may render the BIOS inoperable, and you will have to reset it using software or jumpers to a factory-default setting.

Firmware

Firmware is low-level software that programs your hardware. It acts much like BIOS, enabling a device to know its various functions and capabilities and to make them functional. Firmware also coordinates the activities of the hardware during normal operation and contains programming instructions used to perform those operations.

The firmware is separate from your system BIOS, because each device contains its own internal firmware code. The firmware of your device is usually flash-upgradeable as well, and can be updated using the same steps outlined with the BIOS upgrade instructions. Components such as disk drives, disk controllers, SCSI controllers, and RAID controllers need to have their firmware updated to the most recent version to ensure compatibility with other devices in your system.

You can usually check the firmware levels on your devices during your server startup. As your server goes through its power-on self test (POST), it will display the firmware and BIOS information of devices in your system. If it is not listed, you will have to use the diagnostic software that should have come with the device. If you cannot obtain the firmware information, contact the manufacturer for information on how to find your firmware version.

Monitoring the Power-On Sequence

✦ Verify power-on via power-on sequence

When a server is first turned on, it begins a POST (power-on self test) routine. The POST is a built-in diagnostic program residing in the server's BIOS that runs several tests to verify the status of server hardware. It checks the CPU, memory, hard disks, and other peripheral cards and devices for hardware faults. If a fault is detected, it prints an error code to the screen, or sounds an audible beep to warn you of the error. If the hardware failure is fatal, the server will halt at that point, and will not continue its boot sequence. If the error or fault will not harm regular server operations, it is considered a warning, and the server will still boot normally.

Here are the basic steps a server performs when it is first turned on:

1. Power is initialized

2. BIOS is initialized

3. POST tests internal components

4. POST tests external devices

5. Hard drives and RAID systems are initialized

6. Boot device is located and operating system is loaded

Exam Tip   For the exam, know the various stages of the POST process, and in what order components are checked.

Power initialization

When the server is first turned on, the power supplies initialize and their fans begin to spin. Once the power is at an appropriate level, the system is signaled to begin the boot process. The most common problem at this point of the boot process is that there is no power to the system. Check the power LED lights on the front of the server. If they are on, there maybe a problem with the on/off switch, or with the server motherboard itself. If the lights do not indicate power, check all plugs and cables, starting with the connection to the power source, which could be a wall socket, but usually is a UPS. Examine the UPS to ensure that it is working properly, and that its outlets are providing power. Plug in another device to the same outlet to verify power.

If the power supplies are receiving power, and their fans are spinning, turn the server off and check the internal power supply cables to make sure they are properly connected to the motherboard and internal devices. If they are connected properly, there could be a serious fault with the motherboard, in which case you will need to contact the vendor or supplier so that it can be replaced.

BIOS initialization

When the server is first turned on, there will be nothing in memory for the CPU to execute. The CPU will go to a special part of the BIOS ROM to begin processing pre-installed instructions. The first thing you will see on the monitor screen is usually the BIOS logo and information, including vendor information, BIOS version number, and BIOS date. On the same screen, or on the next one, the server or motherboard's manufacturer logo and information will appear. A special function key or key sequence will be indicated to enter the BIOS setup program.

During this BIOS initialization, the BIOS of other devices may be checked as well. The BIOS information of the video card is the most common screen that might appear during this phase.

When the BIOS initialization has finished, the POST routine begins.

Power-on self test

The POST routine is a special hardware diagnostic program that checks all internal and external hardware for faults and proper configuration. The POST performs a system inventory of critical components. If there is a fatal error, the server will not continue to boot. Other messages such as visual or audible warnings may occur during this phase.

Exam Tip For the exam, the key to answering POST-related questions is to know the order of events in which the system is checked. When the POST stops with an error message, you will be able to better pinpoint the cause of the problem.

Internal motherboard components

The BIOS checks all critical internal components first, such as the CPU, cache, and memory. If these components are not working, the server will not boot, and the POST routine will report a fatal error.

✦ **Motherboard:** All components of the motherboard, such as system clocks and timers, cache, BIOS ROM settings, are checked for configuration and functionality. System resource identifiers such as IRQ, DMA, and I/O channels are also checked for conflicts.

✦ **CPU:** The CPU is checked for its type, its speed is calculated, and functionality is tested.

✦ **RAM:** The RAM is examined for its type, compatibility, and total size. A quick memory test is performed, to ensure there are no parts of the memory that do not work.

✦ **Video:** The video controller is checked for proper configuration and functionality.

✦ **Serial/parallel ports:** All serial and parallel ports are checked for proper IRQ settings. Any conflicts will be reported.

✦ **Keyboard:** A check is made to see if a keyboard is attached to the system and functioning. A system can be booted without a keyboard, but it will make it hard for the technician to configure the system with no keyboard.

Storage devices and other external components

After internal motherboard components are verified, the server's storage systems are checked, as are any other peripheral devices such as SCSI bus systems. Depending on the type and arrangement of your storage systems, there are several different tests that take place to verify their configuration and functionality.

For IDE systems, the presence of devices on the primary and secondary controllers are detected and configured.

On SCSI systems, the SCSI controller BIOS begins its own checking routines, and scans the SCSI bus for devices. On the monitor screen, information on the host adapter appears, including the manufacturer and model type, and the BIOS version and date. Then a list of all your devices should appear, including their SCSI IDs and descriptions.

On a SCSI RAID controller, each hard drive is initialized in sequence, and the RAID configuration is initialized. The monitor screen will display what type of RAID arrays are set up, and the size of the logical drives and containers they define. As the controller checks the drives, you can see the lights of the drives turn on in sequence. The light will indicate the condition of the hard drive, with a green light indicating that it is functioning normally, a red light indicating an error fault, and typically an amber light to indicate the array is reconfiguring itself. This condition happens whenever there is a change made to the array, such as an array being created for the first time, or when a failed drive is replaced..

System boot device and operating system

When the storage systems have been verified, the BIOS will look for the drive that has been configured as the boot device. The Master Boot Record (MBR) will be checked on the device, which indicates the location of the operating system to boot. At this point, the operating system boot loader will take over from the BIOS to start the system.

If there is no operating system present, or there is no boot device configured, the server will halt, because it has gone as far as it can go with the boot process. A message will appear indicating that there is no operating system present.

Error indicators

Depending on the type and severity of the server hardware fault, there are different types of error indicator methods.

Audible sights and sounds

There are situations when a fatal error condition can occur before the video system is initialized. Usually, this means a component on the motherboard itself is not functioning. In this case, there is no way for the BIOS to send error messages or codes to the monitor screen. Depending on the maker of the BIOS, a sequence of audible beeps is transmitted through the internal PC speaker and is used to indicate error conditions. Another method is using the system LEDs to show an error code, or to flash in certain sequences.

Tip   If a POST test fails before the video controller is initialized, the problem is most likely with either the power, or the motherboard itself.

The sequence of the visible or audible alerts identifies the component that has failed. You need to consult the manufacturer's documentation to identify the cause of the problem.

Caution   Typically, a motherboard or system manufacturer will modify the BIOS to suit their own needs. Error codes should be checked first with the system or motherboard documentation, rather than those of the original BIOS vendor.

Error messages and codes

If the system gets past the point of video initialization, any error conditions will result in an error message or code appearing on the monitor screen. Some error messages are very specific in their wording, allowing easy identification of the faulty device. Others can be more cryptic, and sometimes might only be an error code of some sort. You need to check the system manufacturer's documentation carefully to identify the fault. You may also need the code for the manufacturer's phone support, in which a technician can remotely troubleshoot the problem using the specific error code.

Exam Tip   Any error codes or messages should be cross-referenced with the manufacturer's documentation to fully identify the problem.

Key Point Summary

In this chapter, the installation of additional internal and external hardware was discussed. ESD best practices were detailed, including several ways to eliminate the possibility of ESD damage in your environment. Finally, the server POST routine was discussed in detail, including possible error scenarios and their causes. Keep the following points in mind for the exam:

✦ Be aware of ESD issues, and how to prevent them, such as anti-static mats, padded work benches, and wrist straps.

✦ Know how to properly install internal and external components.

✦ Know how to check your BIOS and firmware levels, and remember that the best place to get BIOS and firmware updates is from the manufacturer's Web site.

✦ Know the sequence of server startup and POST routines. Depending on where the error occurs, it will help you narrow down the cause.

✦ Each SCSI device needs to have its own unique ID.

✦ The host adapter should be ID 7, and the first boot device should be ID 0.

✦ Ensure that the cables, connectors, and terminators on a SCSI chain are all of the appropriate type for your system.

✦   ✦   ✦

STUDY GUIDE

The Study Guide section provides you with the opportunity to test your knowledge about installing server hardware. The Assessment Questions provide practice for the test, and the Scenarios provide practice with real situations. If you get any questions wrong, use the answers to determine the part of the chapter you should review before continuing.

Assessment Questions

1. A server has just finished its POST routine. There were no errors during the POST, but when it was finished, the message "No Operating System Found" appeared on the monitor screen, and the server halted. What is the most likely cause of the problem?

    A. The CMOS battery has failed.

    B. There is a RAM error.

    C. The network OS has not been installed.

    D. The server's BIOS is missing.

2. A technician is using a KVM switch to access each server in a server rack. On one of the servers, the keyboard and mouse do not seem to be working. What should the technician do first to try to fix the problem?

    A. Press the right mouse button.

    B. Reset the KVM switch.

    C. Reboot the server.

    D. Press the Escape key on the keyboard.

3. Additional memory has just been installed in a server. When the server is turned on, the POST routine reports that the keyboard is missing. What is the most likely cause of the problem?

    A. The technician accidentally knocked the keyboard cable loose when replacing the server cover.

    B. The new memory is conflicting with the keyboard.

    C. There is no keyboard needed for this server.

    D. The BIOS must be flashed.

4. A technician has just removed a NIC card from a server to install a faster one. To prevent the old card from being damaged, what should the technician do to protect the card?

   A. Leave the card on a workbench with anti-static padding.

   B. The card should have been left in an extra slot in the server.

   C. Attach the anti-static wrist strap to the NIC faceplate.

   D. Put the card in an anti-static bag and store in a cabinet.

5. When a server has finished its POST routine, what is the next step in the server startup sequence?

   A. The server will check the RAM.

   B. The server will start the network operating system.

   C. The NIC card BIOS will be checked.

   D. The power supply will be checked.

6. A SCSI host adapter came factory-installed with a SCSI ID of 1. What SCSI ID should the technician set the host adapter to?

   A. 1

   B. 7

   C. 0

   D. 2

7. A technician is installing additional memory into a server. The technician did not perform any proper grounding and ESD prevention measures, and during the installation, a static shock visibly came into contact with the memory. When the server is started, the POST reports a parity error with the memory. What should be done to fix the memory problem?

   A. The memory should be grounded.

   B. The memory should be replaced.

   C. The memory should be reinstalled while the technician is wearing an anti-static wrist strap.

   D. Nothing, the memory is non-parity RAM.

8. Which is *not* a way to prevent electrostatic discharge?

   A. Anti-static floor mats

   B. Anti-static wrist strap

   C. Server room air conditioning

   D. Anti-static component bags

9. During a server's POST routine, the server beeps twice, and then displays an error code with the front LED's. No information was displayed on the monitor screen. What is the best way to troubleshoot the problem?

    A. Check the manufacturer's documentation for the error code.

    B. Check the `readme` file on the network OS CD-ROM.

    C. Run a memory test using diagnostic software.

    D. Reboot the server and see if the problem persists.

10. A server's POST routine halts half-way through the memory check. What is the most likely cause of the problem?

    A. Only one of the memory modules is bad.

    B. The server BIOS does not recognize the memory.

    C. The keyboard is not connected.

    D. One or both memory modules are bad.

11. A technician has just turned on a server. The server does not respond and there are no lights on the server. It is plugged into a UPS, which seems to be functioning normally, and the server power supply is showing a green light. What is the most likely cause of the problem?

    A. The UPS is malfunctioning.

    B. The LEDs are burnt out.

    C. The power button does not work.

    D. The power supply has failed.

12. An external SCSI tape drive has just been connected to a server. When the server is started, the SCSI BIOS reports a resource conflict error. What is the most likely cause of the problem?

    A. The tape drive's SCSI ID is the same as a currently installed device.

    B. The SCSI BIOS does not recognize the tape drive.

    C. The end of the SCSI bus was not terminated.

    D. The SCSI cable has exceeded the accepted length.

13. During a server's POST routine, a fault was found in the server's memory. The server still finishes the POST process and boots the network operating system. What should the technician do next?

    A. Nothing, as the server still boots up.

    B. The server memory should be replaced.

    C. The server should be rebooted.

    D. The BIOS should be flashed, and then the POST should be run again.

14. Which is NOT a step in a server's POST routine?

   A. Memory check

   B. Hard drive check

   C. Network connectivity check

   D. CPU check

15. A new server has arrived from the manufacturer. Most of the original components are pre-installed, but a second CPU and extra memory have also been shipped to be installed in the server. What should NOT be done before the installation?

   A. Remove the CPU and memory from their anti-static bags and lay them out on the floor.

   B. An anti-static wrist strap should be attached to the technician and a grounded object.

   C. A work area should be created with anti-static floor mats.

   D. The CPU and memory should be checked for compatibility with the current system.

16. A technician is installing a new SCSI RAID controller on a server. The system BIOS is not recognizing the card. What can the technician do to fix the problem?

   A. Upgrade the hard disk drive's firmware.

   B. Reboot the server.

   C. Reset the CMOS.

   D. Upgrade the motherboard BIOS.

17. During an upgrade of a server's motherboard BIOS, the power fails in the building and the server will not boot. What can the technician do to fix the problem?

   A. Use a jumper to reset the BIOS to a factory-default setting.

   B. Reboot the server with another BIOS.

   C. Turn off the server for 30 minutes, then reboot.

   D. Recover from backup.

18. After you install a new server, you turn it on for the first time, but the devices on the SCSI bus are not recognized by the system. What is the most likely cause of the problem?

   A. The SCSI bus was not terminated.

   B. The SCSI host adapter was set to ID 7.

C. The first boot device was set to ID 0.

D. One of the SCSI devices has failed.

19. A server has been set up with a SCSI hard drive system. The host adapter has been configured as SCSI ID 7. What SCSI ID should the first boot device be configured with?

   A. 7

   B. 1

   C. 0

   D. 5

20. A technician wants to upgrade a SCSI hard drive to the latest firmware revision. Where is the best place to obtain the latest firmware?

   A. OS CD-ROM

   B. Installation floppy disk

   C. System BIOS manufacturer

   D. Hard drive manufacturer's Web site

Scenarios

1. A new server has just been delivered to the server room. You have been asked to employ ESD best practices while installing and configuring server components. What steps should you take to ensure that the equipment is not accidentally damaged by electrostatic discharge?

2. A server is exhibiting various problems during its startup routine. The POST tests result in errors at various stages of the routine. What are the stages of the POST process, and what components are checked at each stage?

Answers to Chapter Questions

Chapter pre-test

1. You need to keep your BIOS and firmware levels current to ensure the latest software for that device, and also to ensure hardware compatibility with other devices.

2. The memory is checked for faults by the POST routine during system startup.

3. A Keyboard/Video/Mouse (KVM) switch is used to connect a single monitor, keyboard and mouse to several servers.

4. The SCSI host adapter should be set to ID 7 to give it the highest priority.

5. A Power-On Self Test is a set of self-diagnostic tests run automatically by the BIOS at boot time.

6. Any type of POST error codes should be looked up in your server manufacturer's documentation.

7. Electrostatic discharge can cause damage to server components.

8. It is possible that some of them could have been loosened from the sockets as devices were removed and added.

9. Most BIOS settings have been modified by the manufacturer of the server for better compatibility with their hardware.

10. An anti-static wrist strap effectively grounds the technician to discharge any electrostatic buildup.

Assessment questions

1. C. The network operating system has not yet been installed. Answer A is incorrect because the POST routine would not have gotten this far if there was a problem with CMOS. Answer B is incorrect because an error with system RAM would have been detected before this point, and the POST would halt. Answer D is incorrect because the BIOS was present to perform the POST routine. For more information, see the "Monitoring the Power-On Sequence" section.

2. B. Resetting the KVM switch should restore functionality to the keyboard and mouse. Answer A is incorrect because pressing the right-mouse button will not do anything. Answer C is incorrect because rebooting the server might not initially be necessary. Answer D is incorrect because pressing the Escape key will not help if the keyboard is not functioning. For more information, see the "Installing external devices" section.

3. A. The keyboard cable was most likely knocked loose during the installation. Answer B is incorrect because the memory would not conflict with a keyboard. Answer C is incorrect because all servers should have a keyboard installed. Answer D is incorrect because the BIOS does not need to be flashed in this case. For more information, see the "Monitoring the Power-On Sequence" section.

4. D. The card should be put into an anti-static bag to protect it from ESD, and stored safely away. Answer A is incorrect because leaving the card out on a bench leaves it open to physical damage. Answer B is incorrect because the network card should not be left in the server. Answer C is incorrect because the wrist strap is attached to the technician, and the other end attached to ground. For more information, see the "Installing internal devices" section.

5. B. The server will start the network operating system once all the POST tests have finished. Answer A is incorrect because the RAM has already been checked during the POST routine. Answer C is incorrect because a NIC does not usually contain a BIOS. Answer D is incorrect because the power supply is checked at the beginning of POST testing. For more information, see the "Monitoring the Power-On Sequence" section.

6. **B.** The host adapter should be set to ID 7 to give it the highest priority on the SCSI bus. Answer A is incorrect because some other device other than the boot device should have this ID. Answer C is incorrect because ID 0 should be used for the boot device on the SCSI bus. Answer D is incorrect because device 2 should belong to another peripheral on the SCSI bus. For more information, see the "Verifying SCSI IDs and Termination" section.

7. **B.** The memory was damaged by the static shock and should be replaced. Answer A is incorrect because the memory cannot be fixed once it has been damaged by an electrostatic discharge. Answer C is incorrect because the memory is already damaged, and reinstalling it will not repair it. Answer D is incorrect because the message indicates an error and is not relaying information. For more information, see the "Installing internal devices" section.

8. **C.** A server room air conditioning will not help prevent ESD. Answers A, B, and D are incorrect because these are all excellent ways of preventing ESD damage. For more information, see the "Installing internal devices" section.

9. **A.** You need to check the manufacturer's documentation for the error code. Answer B is incorrect because the network OS CD-ROM will not have hardware related information. Answer C is incorrect because the POST routine did not get as far as the memory check test. Answer D is incorrect because the error code is indicating a problem with the server. For more information, see the "Monitoring the Power-On Sequence" section.

10. **D.** This indicates there is a problem with some or all of the RAM modules. Answer A is incorrect because there could be more than one failed memory module. Answer B is incorrect because the memory check had already started, indicating that the memory was recognized by the server. Answer C is incorrect because the POST routine failed during the memory check stage and did not indicate a keyboard error. For more information, see the "Monitoring the Power-On Sequence" section.

11. **C.** The power button is not working properly. Answer A is incorrect because the UPS was said to be functioning normally. Answer B is incorrect because the server would still start up even though the LED's were not functioning. Answer D is incorrect because the power supply light was showing that it was working properly. For more information, see the "Monitoring the Power-On Sequence" section.

12. **A.** The tape drive has been assigned a SCSI ID that already exists. Answer B is incorrect because the rest of the SCSI devices would have been properly identified. Answer C is incorrect because improper termination would not result in a resource conflict. Answer D is incorrect because the SCSI cable length would not result in a resource conflict. For more information, see the "Verifying SCSI IDs and Termination" section.

13. **B.** The memory should be replaced, as it is showing a fault in the POST process. Answer A is incorrect because there is still a problem with the RAM that could affect the network OS performance. Answer C is incorrect because rebooting the server will not fix the problem. Answer D is incorrect because flashing the BIOS will not repair the memory fault. For more information, see the "Monitoring the Power-On Sequence" section.

14. **C.** Network connectivity is not checked during a server's POST routine. Answers A, B, and D are incorrect because these are all steps in a server's POST routine. For more information, see the "Monitoring the Power-On Sequence" section.

15. **A.** The anti-static bags should not be removed until the time when they are to be installed in the server. Answer B is incorrect because this prevents ESD damage to the components. Answer C is incorrect because this will aid in preventing ESD damage to the components. Answer D is incorrect because the components should be checked for compatibility before they are installed. For more information, see the "Installing internal devices" section.

16. **D.** The motherboard BIOS needs to be updated with a new version that will recognize the newer hardware. Answer A is incorrect because the problem is with the system BIOS not recognizing the card, not the other way around. Answer B is incorrect because this will not resolve the problem. Answer C is incorrect because resetting the CMOS will not help in recognizing the device. For more information, see the "BIOS and Firmware Levels" section.

17. **A.** The BIOS cannot be recovered once it has been corrupted. Answer B is incorrect because you cannot use another BIOS image. Answer C is incorrect because rebooting the server will not fix the damaged BIOS. Answer D is incorrect because there is no way to backup and restore a BIOS. For more information, see the "BIOS and Firmware Levels" section.

18. **A.** The SCSI bus will not work properly if it is not terminated. Answer B is incorrect because the host adapter should be using ID 7. Answer C is incorrect because the first boot device should be using ID 0. Answer D is incorrect because the other devices should have been recognized even though one of the others has failed. For more information, see the "Verifying SCSI IDs and Termination" section.

19. **C.** The first boot device should be configured as ID 0. Answer A is incorrect because this ID will conflict with the SCSI host adapter. Answers B and D are incorrect because the boot device should be set to ID 0. For more information, see the "Verifying SCSI IDs and Termination" section.

20. **D.** The hard drive manufacturer's Web site will have the latest firmware version. Answer A is incorrect because the OS CD-ROM will not contain device firmware. Answer B is incorrect because the installation disk will not have the most current firmware version. Answer C is incorrect because the system BIOS manufacturer will not have firmware for the hard drive. For more information, see the "BIOS and Firmware Levels" section.

Scenarios

1. Before unpacking the server, set aside a special work area to start the installation. Use a work bench with proper anti-static padding, or if working from the floor, a special anti-static floor mat can be used. When unpacking the server, leave any extra components in their anti-static bags until the moment you install them. Leaving them out in the open leaves them susceptible to ESD.

   You should attach an anti-static strap to your wrist, with the other end attached to a grounded source, such as the metal casing on the server, or the metal parts of a server rack. Before handling components, you should touch the grounded source to insure that any ESD built up can be discharged.

   Handle the components carefully when you take them from their anti-static bags, and hold them by the edges, without touching electronic parts such as the circuit board or processor chips. If any components are to be removed from the server, put them into anti-static bags and store them in a safe place.

2. When a server is first turned on, the power supplies initialize, and as soon as they are ready, they begin to feed power to the system. The CPU and the RAM will be empty, and information is first read from the BIOS ROM. The BIOS initializes and begins testing internal components. System timers, resource identifiers such as IRQ and DMA, cache, CPU, RAM, are all examples of components that are tested at this time. Then, external devices are tested, such as storage systems and SCSI buses, sometimes by their own BIOS if one exists. At this time hard drives and RAID arrays are verified and initialized. When this is complete, the server looks for the first boot device, where the network operating system boot loader resides, which then takes over the boot process of the OS.

Configuration

After you have installed a new server, the next important step is configuring it. Administrators must have a general understanding of how to properly configure a new network server so it will function properly on the network and not interfere with other servers. An administrator must check, and upgrade if necessary, BIOS and firmware levels, controllers, and hard drives, to name a few.

Most external peripherals (such as UPS and external drive subsystems) must be configured before they will be available. You need to install and configure service tools to monitor the performance of the new server. Finally, performing a server baseline and documenting the configuration is one of the most important procedures a administrator can perform.

Configuring RAID

EXAM OBJECTIVES

2.2 Configure RAID

CHAPTER PRE-TEST

1. What does RAID stand for?

2. Describe the difference between disk mirroring and disk striping.

3. What is parity?

4. Duplexing requires at least _____ disk controllers.

5. What is the difference between hot plug and hot swap?

6. Describe software RAID.

7. What is fail over?

8. Describe the benefits of Fibre Channel technology.

9. Is there fault tolerance in a RAID 0 array?

10. What is a hot spare?

This chapter introduces the concept of RAID (Redundant Array of Inexpensive Disks), and its various implementations for storage systems. RAID technology is an integral part of today's server subsystems. All mission-critical applications and services should incorporate RAID systems for high-capacity storage and high-availability requirements.

The History of RAID

The concept of RAID (Redundant Array of Inexpensive Disks) came about as a solution to the problem of providing high-capacity storage combined with a data availability and redundancy. In the past, hard-disk capacities were limited, and high capacity drives were very expensive. They also offered little, if any, data protection and redundancy. Compounding the problem, CPU processor performance was increasing at an exponential rate, while disk subsystems were quickly falling behind and creating a bottleneck for server performance.

In 1988, three University of California-Berkeley researchers (David Patterson, Randy Katz, and Garth Gibson) established guidelines for the original implementation of RAID, called RAID 1 through RAID 6.

> **Tip** The various RAID configurations are called levels, from 1 to 6. This does not indicate, however, that RAID 5 is inherently better or worse than RAID 1 or 2. Each situation will dictate the appropriate RAID level.

RAID implementations focus on four key areas:

- ✦ **Capacity:** The storage needs of today's networks require high capacity disk systems that are easily scalable. RAID systems allow a number of hard drives to be combined together to create one large "virtual" hard drive, called a *logical drive*.

- ✦ **Reliability:** Any type of mission-critical application or service requires some form of active redundancy and data protection. Using techniques known as *striping* and *parity*, data is spread across a number of hard drives, preventing data loss due to drive failure.

- ✦ **Cost:** Legacy high-capacity disk systems were very expensive. RAID technology uses smaller, less expensive drives to bring down storage costs dramatically.

- ✦ **I/O Speed:** Advances in CPU technology have increased much faster than advances in disk I/O subsystems. RAID arrays provide greater transfer rates to relieve this system bottleneck.

Mirroring and Parity

There are two types of data redundancy available for RAID systems, *mirroring* and *parity*. With mirroring, data is fully replicated on another hard drive of equal size. This method of fault tolerance is very effective, but also very costly, because you need to purchase a separate hard drive for each drive that is to be mirrored.

Parity is a more cost-effective method with which to safeguard data against transmission loss and corruption. The parity information of a RAID array is calculated and stored as an additional piece of data during a write operation to the storage system. This parity data is what enables reconstruction of data in the event of a hard disk failure. It is a method that enables a computer to detect errors in the data being received. More complex versions of parity combine this characteristic with the ability to correct certain errors in the data.

XOR (short for exclusive or) is one method of calculating parity. XOR compares bits and generates a more complex parity value. The advantage of XOR parity is that it enables error detection and correction. Parity RAID levels combine striping and parity calculations to permit data recovery if a disk fails. Parity values are calculated for the data in each stripe on a bit-by-bit basis.

RAID Levels

 **2.2** Configure RAID

In this section, I discuss the most common levels of RAID implementation. Each level of RAID contains its own unique characteristics, strengths, and weaknesses.

RAID 0

The most fundamental storage technique of any RAID system is known as *data striping*. In its most basic implementation, it is known as RAID 0. Data striping is a technique in which data is spread evenly across a number of physical drives to create a larger, logical drive, as shown in Figure 4-1. The data is divided into stripes, which are written across the drive array within a defined block size.

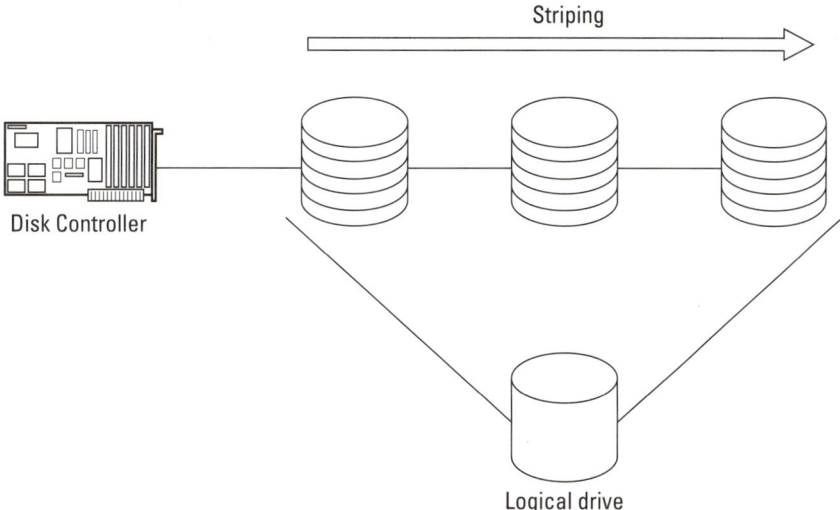

Figure 4-1: RAID 0 array using data striping across all disks

This simple configuration allows for very fast I/O rates, as there is no parity or checksum involved with generic striping. Applications that require mostly sequential reads of data from disks can benefit from disk striping, as the data is read in parallel across all of the drives in the array.

The drawback to this configuration is the lack of data redundancy. Because there is no mechanism for parity, the loss of even one disk in the array results in the loss of the entire data volume. Technically, this lack of redundancy makes RAID 0 not a true RAID system, but it is still considered a low-level implementation of RAID. RAID 0 systems are most often used to store non-critical data and should be paired with a proper tape backup system.

RAID 0 arrays require at least two drives. Additional space can be added to the array simply by adding additional physical disks. Because the total size of the array is the sum of the individual drives, the drives can be different sizes. Most RAID 0 systems even allow the mixing of SCSI and IDE drives.

RAID 1

RAID 1 is the first RAID level with fault tolerance, and is referred to as *disk mirroring*. Disk Mirroring consists of a primary and secondary disk, or groups of identical primary and secondary disks. As data is written to the primary disk, it is duplicated on the secondary disk, as shown in Figure 4-2. If the primary disk fails, the server can be configured to use the mirrored copy on the secondary disk until the primary disk is replaced. The data can then be rebuilt from the surviving drive.

RAID 1 arrays require at least two drives. The secondary drive must be equal to or larger than the primary drive. To increase the total amount of usable storage space, both the primary and secondary drives must be increased equally.

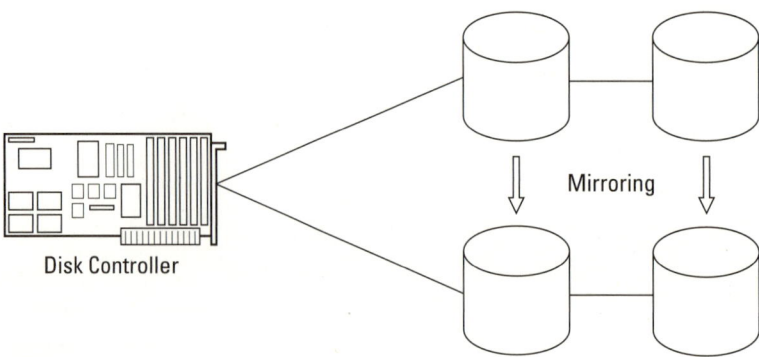

Figure 4-2: RAID 1 array using disk mirroring

Disk mirroring is a very effective method for data redundancy, but it comes at a higher cost because you must have enough disk storage for two complete sets of data. In terms of performance, disk reads are much faster with disk mirroring, because you can read the same data from different drives in parallel. On the other hand, this decreases the speed of disk writes, because the data has to be written twice.

To enhance the fault tolerance of disk mirroring, you can also implement what is known as *disk duplexing*. In a mirrored only system, there is still a point of complete failure at the disk controller level. If the controller fails, the whole system will fail. To prevent this, and add additional protection, a second disk controller is used for the secondary drive, as shown in Figure 4-3. For the slight additional cost, RAID 1 duplexing is preferred over simple disk mirroring.

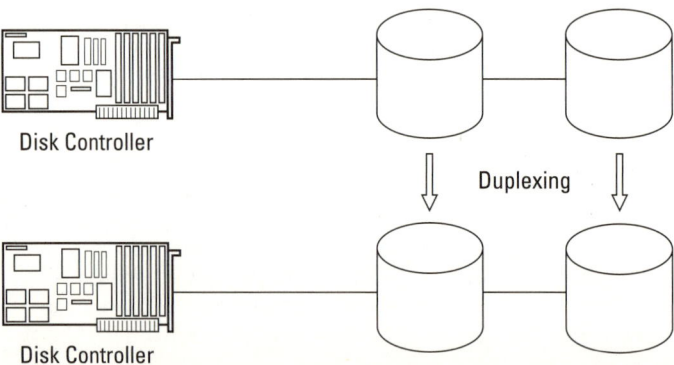

Figure 4-3: RAID 1 array using disk duplexing

RAID 2

RAID 2 performs disk striping at the bit level and uses one or more disks to store parity information. This error-checking and correction method can only be supported by special hard disk drives, and it is rarely supported commercially.

RAID 3

RAID 3 uses a more practical method for fault tolerance than RAID 2. RAID 3 systems use disk striping as their main implementation, with the addition of an extra drive dedicated to storing parity information, as shown in Figure 4-4. If a disk fails, the data is rebuilt across the striped array using the parity information on the extra disk drive.

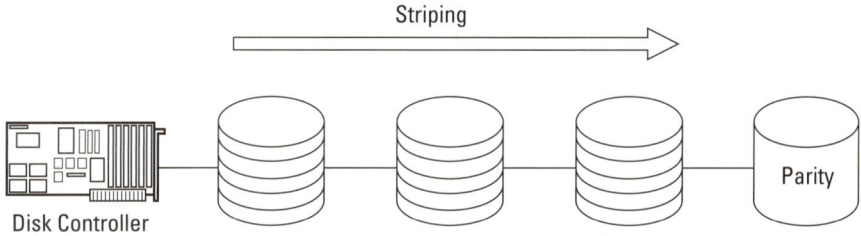

Figure 4-4: RAID 3 array using striping with a parity drive

This parity disk causes some performance issues for a RAID 3 system, especially with writing operations, because this also involves writing parity bit information to the parity drive. The performance of disk reads is about the same as RAID 0, because the parity drive is only accessed if there is an error encountered on the striped drives.

RAID 3 arrays require a minimum of three drives. To increase the total size of the array more drives can be added, but the size of the parity drive must also be increased to match or exceed the physical size of the individual array disks.

RAID 3 is best for applications that require mostly sequential data reads. It would not be suitable for any type of intensive and transactional database applications.

 **In the Real World**   In the real world, there are few implementations of RAID 3, because RAID 5 addresses most of the negative issues of RAID 3, while retaining its strengths.

RAID 4

RAID 4 is very similar to RAID 3, consisting of a number of striped disks and a separate parity disk, but the size of the striping block is larger to accommodate more data. This provides a RAID implementation that is equivalent to RAID 3, but removes the bottlenecks that affected transactional data.

RAID 5

RAID 5 is the mostly widely used RAID implementation today. Its most unique feature, compared to other parity-based RAID solutions such as RAID 3 or 4, is that parity information is distributed across all disk drives, as shown in Figure 4-5. This means that a certain percentage of the total disk space becomes unavailable for user data so that the parity data can be recorded. Typically, the amount of drive space reserved for the parity information is equal to the size of one drive in the array. For example, an array of four 10GB drives would provide roughly 30GB of space for user data while 10GB is reserved for the parity information. A RAID 5 array must contain a minimum of three hard drives.

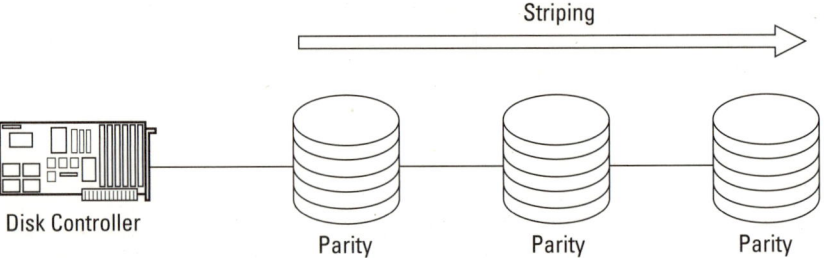

Figure 4-5: RAID 5 array using parity striped over all drives

Although the overhead caused by reading and updating parity information still exists, RAID 5 greatly reduces the bottleneck that a dedicated parity drive can create.

If any one of the drives fails, it can be replaced, and then the data is rebuilt using the parity information that is distributed across the other drives. In addition, the disk subsystem can continue to perform with a failed disk in a RAID 5 array. The lost data is regenerated on the fly from the parity information stored on the remaining drives. Although performance is affected, the data is still available to the users.

RAID 6

RAID 6 is a rarely used implementation that goes a step further than RAID 5 by offering a second level of parity independent from the first and stored on different disks. The result is a very high reliability factor, offset by higher costs for this complex system.

Hybrid RAID Levels

Since the original RAID guidelines, some of the different RAID implementations have been combined to create even more complex and redundant systems.

RAID 0+1

RAID 0+1, also known as RAID 10, combines data striping (RAID 0) with drive mirroring (RAID 1). This creates data striping across a mirrored set of drives, as shown in Figure 4-6.

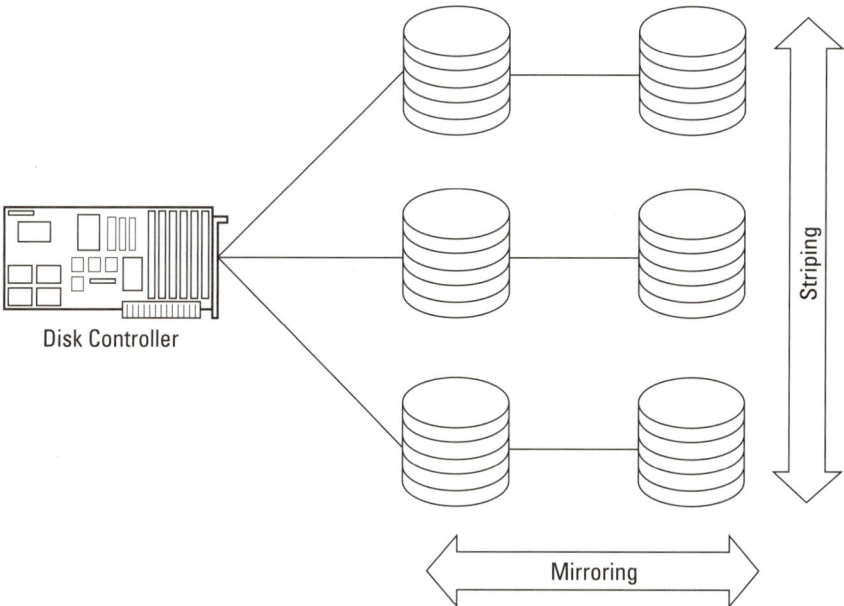

Figure 4-6: RAID 0+1 array using a striped array of mirrors

If a drive fails, data does not have to be regenerated from parity information; it can be regenerated from another disk drive. RAID 0+1 offers a high level of performance and redundancy, because the system will still work if more than one drive fails. The disadvantage of RAID 0+1 is the cost, because its complexity requires a greater minimum number of hard drives than other RAID levels. A RAID 0+1 array requires a minimum of four drives to work, but only two of those are used for data storage. To add more capacity, drives must be also be added in pairs.

RAID 30 and RAID 50

RAID 30 and RAID 50 both combine striping (RAID 0) with parity systems (RAID 3 and RAID 5). The result is a striped array across two parity arrays, as shown in Figure 4-7. These complex RAID systems provide high I/O rates, with excellent data redundancy. The system will still run, even if more than one drive fails in the array. As with other complex, high-level RAID arrays, the disadvantage of such a system is the cost. The minimum number of drives to run RAID 30 or 50 is six.

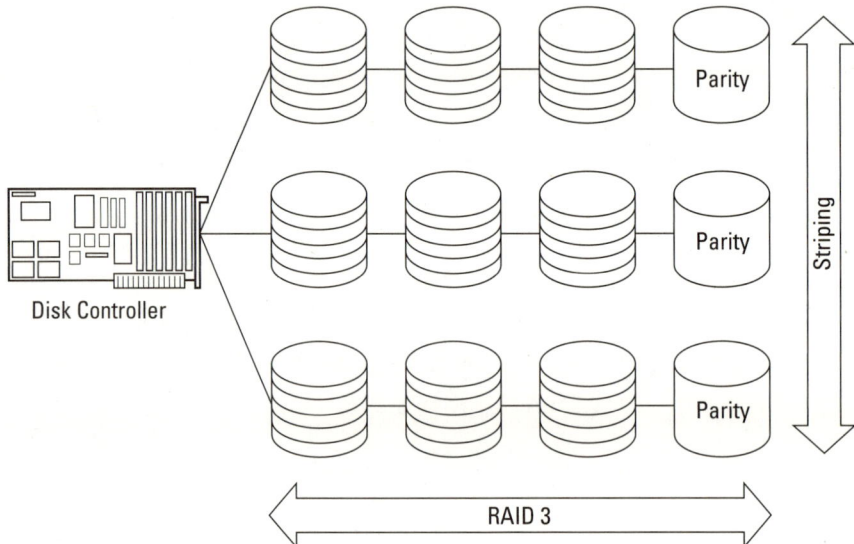

Figure 4-7: RAID 30 array using striping of a RAID 3 array with dedicated parity

As stated at the beginning of this section, each RAID level has advantages and disadvantages. Table 4-1 summarizes and compares the various RAID levels.

Table 4-1
Comparison of RAID Levels

RAID Level	Redundancy	Read performance	Write performance	Rebuilding performance
RAID 0	None	Excellent	Excellent	n/a
RAID 1	Excellent	Excellent	Good	Good
RAID 2	Good	Excellent	Good	Good
RAID 3	Good	Sequential: Good; Transactional: Poor	Sequential: Good; Transactional: Poor	Average
RAID 4	Good	Sequential: Good; Transactional: Good	Sequential: Good; Transactional: Poor	Average
RAID 5	Good	Sequential: Good; Transactional: Good	Average	Poor
RAID 6	Excellent	Good	Poor	Poor
RAID 0+1	Excellent	Good	Average	Good
RAID 30, 50	Excellent	Good	Average	Average

Depending on your business needs and budget, the ratings of each RAID level for certain categories can be misleading. For the average customer, a RAID 5 is more than adequate for someone needing a scalable, fast, and redundant RAID system. Although the rebuilding performance may be slower than other levels, for the average user, this is fine. A business needing a RAID solution for a high-end transactional database system may find that this is not enough, and more complex levels such as RAID 30 or 50 are needed, where redundancy and rebuild performance are more critical.

 Exam Tip You must know the techniques, characteristics, and advantages and disadvantages of each RAID level for the exam.

Hardware RAID and Software RAID

There are many ways of implementing RAID on your servers. Your choices must be balanced by such factors as cost, type of equipment, complexity, data redundancy and availability, and system performance.

Hardware-based RAID systems offer better data protection, availability, and redundancy, but at a higher cost. Software-based RAID systems are much less costly to implement, but put more strain on system performance and offer fewer options for redundancy.

External RAID storage

External RAID systems are separate from the main host server, usually contained in a special enclosure with its own disk controllers. They can be free-standing, or rack-mounted and usually cost more than internal implementations. These systems usually serve as the main storage device in large enterprise environments. Often times, a single server may use multiple external RAID cabinets for storage.

PCI card RAID controllers

Designed to be installed in your host server's expansion slots, these RAID controller systems usually offer the best in cost, scalability, and flexibility. Lower cost cards offer base RAID functionality, while higher priced cards offer added functionality such as caching and high I/O performance. These type of systems can be easily duplexed by adding another card.

Embedded RAID controllers

These RAID systems are embedded right on the system motherboard, and typically offer a subset of the functions that full-blown PCI card RAID controllers use. Embedded RAID controllers usually have some I/O processing capabilities for faster throughput. They offer great functionality and lower cost compared to regular PCI controllers.

RAID BIOS

In the same way that a motherboard has its system BIOS, hardware RAID controllers have a BIOS as well. The controller BIOS is the code that operates the controller and manages the RAID array. Typically, a manufacturer will alter the BIOS code of a RAID controller to add compatibility for new hard disk drives, or to enhance RAID caching and I/O performance. Like your system BIOS, or other device firmware, the RAID BIOS can be flash-updated to the latest version.

Controller caching

The write operations of RAID controllers can be greatly increased with the use of a cache. A *controller cache* enables the controller to store data in its memory before writing the data to disk. This speeds up access to the array, because the controller keeps recently accessed data in the cache. For arrays that use striping and parity, large amounts of data need to be cached as not all the data will fit in one write operation. The best caching performance can be achieved with *write-behind caching*. This popular type of controller writes the actual data to the hard drives after it notifies the host that the data has been written. The danger with this scheme, however, is that a power failure or other interruption can cause the cached data to be lost before it is actually committed to the disk. Another write-cache concept is *write-back caching,* which caches the data to be written but it doesn't notify the host until the data has physically been written to the drives, which is a safer method.

Fibre Channel

With the massive increase in storage requirements of today's networks, and the need for greater speeds in accessing them, the use of separate Storage Area Networks (SAN) is becoming more common. A SAN is a high-speed sub network of shared storage devices. A SAN's architecture works in a way that makes all storage devices available to all servers on a network. Using Fibre Channel technology, these storage systems can be connected with high-speed fiber-optic cable, to allow for very fast speeds (from 100 to 200 MB/s). Because data transfers are routed over a separate network, the bandwidth available to users on the regular enterprise network is much higher.

Software RAID

In small, entry-level systems, it is often most cost effective to employ software RAID for fault tolerance. Network operating systems such as Microsoft Windows offer basic RAID implementations such as RAID 0, RAID 1, or RAID 5. Novell NetWare can only be configured for RAID 1. Although easily the most cost-effective of any RAID solution, it puts considerable strain on your system performance as large amounts of CPU time and memory are used to maintain the system.

Another weakness of some Software RAID levels, with the exception of mirroring, is that the network operating system itself has to be running to enable the array, meaning that the OS cannot boot from the RAID array. A non-RAID partition must be set up for the OS, resulting in slower speed and no data redundancy. With a software mirrored system, the boot drive can be mirrored onto a second drive, but if the primary drive fails, you will need a boot disk to access the second mirrored drive with the boot information.

RAID Disk Concepts

A hard disk is the most mechanical part of your server and the mostly likely to fail over time as a result of wear and tear. In addition to the basic RAID system, there are other systems you can implement to minimize your downtime in the event of a disk crash.

✦ **Hot plug drives:** These special hard drives can be installed and removed from the host system without interrupting its regular operation. This is very important for production servers where downtime often isn't an option.

✦ **Hot swap:** Although similar in concept to hot plug drives, hot swap refers to the ability of the RAID system and the server to recognize when a hot plug drive has been added to or removed from the array and to reconfigure as necessary. For example, if a drive in a RAID 5 array fails, it can be replaced and rebuilt by simply swapping the bad hard drive out for a new one even while the system is still running.

✦ **Hot spare:** The concepts of hot plug and hot swap drives are excellent in theory, but not of much use when you do not have a spare hard drive to fix the problem. A hot spare system allows you to have a live hard drive as part of the RAID system, but it is not included in the array until one of the other drives fail. When an array drive fails, the hot spare is automatically called into service, providing maximum continued performance with minimal human intervention. In most implementations of the hot-spare system, once the failed drive is replaced, the hot-spare drive reverts to its standby status.

✦ **Fail over:** In a mirrored system, when one of the disk drives crashes, the system will automatically use the mirrored drive until the original drive is replaced. Because an exact replica of the data exists on that drive, this fail over process does not interrupt normal operation. The term *fail over* is sometimes also used to describe the recovery process when a RAID system uses an online hot spare.

Exam Tip

Questions concerning hot swap, hot plug, hot spare, and fail over come up frequently on the exam. Be sure you know how each one is implemented on an array, and how it works during a disk failure.

Key Point Summary

This chapter began with a discussion of the importance on maintaining current BIOS and Firmware levels for your system board and devices. The concepts of RAID and its implementation of various levels of fault tolerance were introduced. Various RAID techniques such as data striping, mirroring, duplexing, and parity were described in relation to the RAID level they represented. The advantages of hardware RAID versus software RAID were discussed, along with different types of hardware RAID controllers and disk drives.

✦ Know the different RAID levels and their individual characteristics and configuration:

• RAID 0: Striping without parity

• RAID 1: Disk mirroring without striping

• RAID 3: Striping, with dedicated parity drive

• RAID 5: Striping, with parity striped across drives

• RAID 0+1: Disk mirroring combined with striping

✦ Know the advantages and disadvantages of hardware RAID and software RAID.

✦ Know how the each of these technologies work and how they are applied in a failure situation: hot plug, hot swap, hot spare, and fail over.

✦   ✦   ✦

STUDY GUIDE

The Study Guide section provides you with the opportunity to test your knowledge about installing and configuring RAID arrays. The Assessment Questions provide practice for the test, and the Scenarios provide practice with real situations. If you get any questions wrong, use the answers to determine the part of the chapter you should review before continuing.

Assessment Questions

1. A technician is installing a new SCSI RAID controller on a server. The system BIOS is not recognizing the card. What can the technician do to fix the problem?

   A. Upgrade the hard disk drive's firmware.

   B. Reboot the server.

   C. Flash the SCSI RAID controller's BIOS.

   D. Upgrade the motherboard BIOS.

2. A customer wants to be able to connect an array of 55 hard drives to their two database servers. Which technology should be used for this system?

   A. IDE

   B. Fibre Channel

   C. SCSI

   D. Disk striping

3. A technician is reviewing just-arrived equipment for an installation that requires a duplexed RAID 1 array. The equipment includes a SCSI RAID controller and two 18GB SCSI disk drives with cables. Can the technician proceed with the installation?

   A. No, RAID cannot be performed with SCSI devices.

   B. Yes, RAID 1 uses the two disk drives for mirroring each other.

   C. No, one more SCSI RAID controller is needed.

   D. Yes, all the equipment is correct.

4. A technician has created an array of four 18GB hard drives. One month later, the system is still working fine, but the customer calls to complain that the system shows only 54GB of disk space. What would explain this situation?

    A. One of the disks drives has failed.

    B. The customer is running RAID 0.

    C. One of the logical drives has failed.

    D. The customer is running RAID 5.

5. What happens when hard disk drive fails in a hardware-implemented RAID 1 system?

    A. The server crashes and cannot be recovered.

    B. The system fails over to the mirrored drive.

    C. Nothing; the parity drive takes over from the failed drive.

    D. The duplexed controller repairs the failed hard drive.

6. What aspect of a RAID controller can increase the write performance of an array?

    A. Parity striping

    B. RAID caching

    C. Disk mirroring

    D. BIOS upgrade

7. A customer is running a RAID 3 array with three 9GB drives and one parity drive. The customer needs to expand their system to provide 54GB of disk space. How many more drives do they need?

    A. 3

    B. None

    C. 2

    D. 1

8. A hot spare is configured into a RAID array. What is its purpose?

    A. To have a hard drive to fail over to when the mirror breaks.

    B. If a hard drive fails, you can swap it with this drive.

    C. To provide another RAID disk controller in case the live one fails.

    D. If a hard drive fails, the system will use the installed hot spare in place of the failed drive.

9. Disk striping, with parity distributed over all drives, is an example of what level of RAID array?

    A. RAID 5

    B. RAID 3

    C. RAID 0

    D. RAID 1

10. An embedded RAID controller has what main characteristic?

    A. Another embedded RAID controller can be added to provide redundancy.

    B. It is used for software RAID arrays by the network operating system.

    C. It is external to the main server system.

    D. The RAID controller is built right into the motherboard of the server.

11. Enterprise Storage Area Networks use which type of technology for fast, robust storage access?

    A. IDE

    B. SCSI

    C. Embedded PCI controllers

    D. Fibre Channel

12. A technician visiting a customer site is trying to fix a failed drive in a RAID array. The customer is shocked when the technician pulls the failed drive out and replaces it while the system is still online and live. How did the technician accomplish this?

    A. The drive was a hot spare.

    B. The drive was a hot plug drive.

    C. It was a RAID 5 array.

    D. The server was a non-critical server.

13. Disk mirroring without striping is an example of what RAID array?

    A. RAID 0

    B. RAID 0+1

    C. RAID 1

    D. RAID 3

14. A technician is building a RAID 5 array. The equipment has just arrived, and contains a SCSI RAID controller, four 9GB drives, and SCSI cables. The customer has requested that the disk size be 27GB. Does the technician have enough equipment?

    A. No, an additional disk controller is need.

    B. Yes, all the equipment needed has arrived.

    C. No, an additional 9GB is needed for parity.

    D. Yes, but only enough for a RAID 3 array.

15. A technician is creating a software-based RAID 5 system. The customer requests that the NOS system partition be part of the array. How does the technician do this?

    A. The NOS partition is already part of a RAID 5 system.

    B. By updating the firmware of the RAID controller.

    C. This is not possible with a software-based RAID array.

    D. By mirroring the NOS partition.

16. A customer recently had a hard disk crash on their file server and lost all of their data. They want to add a RAID solution to create fault tolerance for their system. Their server has an old CPU and 64MB of RAM. Which solution will meet their needs?

    A. Create a software RAID array with their network operating system.

    B. Add extra hard disk drives to be used as hot spares.

    C. Add an external RAID storage system running RAID 5.

    D. Use RAID 0.

17. A customer is running a RAID 0 array with six 9GB drives, and one of the disk drives fails. What can the technician do to recover the array?

    A. The technician must restore from a tape backup.

    B. The failed drive can be rebuilt from parity information in the last disk drive.

    C. The failed drive can be rebuilt from the mirrored drive.

    D. The technician can hot swap the failed drive out and use a replacement.

18. Disk striping with parity contained in a separate drive is an example of what level of RAID array?

    A. RAID 3

    B. RAID 1

C. RAID 5

D. RAID 0

19. A customer is running a RAID 1 array with disk duplexing, and the primary RAID controller has failed. What happens to the system?

    A. The controller is rebuilt using parity information.

    B. The controller is swapped with a hot spare RAID controller.

    C. The system immediately fails.

    D. Nothing, the mirrored array becomes active using the secondary RAID controller to service the disk drives.

20. A customer wishes to implement a RAID solution on their server. Because of costs, they wish to use a software-based RAID system. What must be present to implement this system?

    A. An external RAID storage system

    B. Enough CPU power and RAM to power the system

    C. An embedded RAID controller

    D. Hot swap disk drives

Scenarios

This chapter introduced various levels of fault tolerance using RAID arrays. Depending on a customers' needs, there are many different ways in which a fault-tolerant system can be implemented. You must know how each one works, and know what solution should be applied when a disaster happens, such as a disk failure. Given the following scenarios, recommend the RAID level and type of equipment that will needed, or offer a solution to the current RAID system that has had a disk failure.

1. Because of the number of hard disk crashes in the past, your management would like you to develop a fault tolerant system for your company's file server. Your company's users use a lot of disk space, and your system is currently running four 9GB drives in a RAID 0 array, but there is not much disk space left. What system would you recommend to allow for a large disk size plus a good level of fault tolerance?

2. A customer has called to say that one of their hard disks has a red light flashing on it, but the system is still functional and running smoothly. When you visit the customer site, what would be your series of steps to troubleshoot and fix the problem?

3. A database company is currently planning an enterprise-wide server that will be used heavily for transactional data. The management has requested a fast, fault-tolerant system. What system would you recommend and implement?

Answers to Chapter Questions

Chapter pre-test

1. RAID stands for Redundant Array of Inexpensive Disks.

2. Disk *mirroring* refers to the data on a hard disk drive being fully replicated to another drive. Disk *striping* refers to the concept of spreading data over a number of drives.

3. Parity refers to a technique used to store data information that will enable you to rebuild a failed disk drive from other drives.

4. Two. This technique eliminates the single disk controller as a point of failure.

5. *Hot plug* refers to a technology that enables you to add or remove a hard disk drive while the system is still powered on and running. *Hot swap* refers to the ability of the RAID system to recognize the addition or removal of a hot plug drive and rebuild the array information.

6. Software RAID is implemented by the network operating system as a way to create fault tolerance without the need of special hardware.

7. Fail over refers to the technique used by redundant systems to switch to a healthy drive in the event of the failure of another disk drive in the system.

8. Fibre Channel technology uses fiber-optic cable to enable very high speed communications between the hard disks and the controllers in a RAID system. It is usually used in high-end, complex database environments.

9. No. RAID 0 is the technique of striping data over several hard drives without parity information.

10. A hot spare is a hard disk drive in a RAID array that is live, but not used until another disk in the system fails. The RAID system will then use the hot spare to rebuild the data.

Assessment questions

1. **D.** The motherboard BIOS needs to be updated with a new version that will recognize the newer hardware. Answer A is incorrect because upgrading the drive's firmware will not aid the system BIOS in recognizing it. Answer B is incorrect because rebooting the server will not resolve the problem. Answer C is incorrect because flashing the controller BIOS will not aid the system BIOS in recognizing it. For more information, see the "Hardware RAID and Software RAID" section.

2. **B.** A Fibre Channel system is best suited for this complex arrangement. Answer A is incorrect because IDE cannot handle this many hard drives. Answer C is incorrect because Fibre Channel should be used for such a

high-end system. Answer D is incorrect because disk striping refers to a method of RAID implementation, not a hardware technology. For more information, see the "Fibre Channel" section.

3. **C.** Disk duplexing requires at least two hard disk controllers. Answer A is incorrect because RAID can be performed by SCSI drives. Answer B is incorrect because a second controller is needed for duplexing. Answer D is incorrect because there is a controller missing, which is needed to enable duplexing. For more information, see the "RAID Levels" section.

4. **D.** In a RAID 5 array, parity is distributed across all drives, but this takes up the equivalent of one disk drive. Answers A and C are incorrect because the system did not indicate an error condition. Answer B is incorrect because the system is running striping with parity. RAID 0 is striping alone. For more information, see the "RAID Levels" section.

5. **B.** In a RAID 1 array using mirroring, the system will fail over to the mirrored drive, which contains an exact replica of the data. Answer A is incorrect because the RAID 1 system is fault-tolerant and will not crash. Answer C is incorrect because there is no parity involved in RAID 1 mirroring. Answer D is incorrect because a duplex controller does not repair a mirrored drive. For more information, see the "RAID Levels" section.

6. **B.** Caching on the RAID controller will speed up disk writes. Answer A is incorrect because the calculation of parity, and writing data to multiple drives, slows down disk writes. Answer C is incorrect because a mirrored disk array has to write the same data to a separate disk, which decreases performance. Answer D is incorrect because a BIOS upgrade will not affect write performance. For more information, see the "Hardware RAID and Software RAID" section.

7. **A.** Because one drive is used as a parity drive in a RAID 3 array, you need six 9GB drives plus the parity drive to make a total of 54GB of disk space. Answers B, C, and D are incorrect because a total of six drives are needed. For more information, see the "RAID Levels" section.

8. **D.** The hot spare is a live disk in the system, but it is only used when one of the other drives fails. Answer A is incorrect because a mirrored system will continue operating from the surviving mirrored drive. Answer B is incorrect because a hot spare is configured to take over immediately, rather than having to be swapped in. Answer C is incorrect because a hot spare is a disk drive, not a controller. For more information, see the "RAID Disk Concepts" section.

9. **A.** Only RAID 5 performs parity striping. Answer B is incorrect because RAID 3 defines striping with a dedicated parity drive. Answer C is incorrect because RAID 0 defines striping only with no parity. Answer D is incorrect because RAID 1 defines disk mirroring. For more information, see the "RAID Levels" section.

10. **D.** Embedded controllers are built right on the system motherboard. Answer A is incorrect because you cannot add an embedded controller; it is already built into the motherboard. Answer B is incorrect because a RAID controller is a form of hardware RAID, not software. Answer C is incorrect because an external RAID system exists outside of the server. For more information, see the "Hardware RAID and Software RAID" section.

11. **D.** Fibre Channel technology provides high speed access over fiber-optic cable. Answer A is incorrect because IDE is much slower than fiber-optics. Answer B is incorrect because SCSI is slower than fiber-optics. Answer C is incorrect because an embedded PCI controller is dependent on the communications technology used. For more information, see the "Hardware RAID and Software RAID" section.

12. **B.** Hot plug technology enables you to remove and add drives while the system is still powered on and running. Answer A is incorrect because a hot spare does not need to be replaced, it takes over automatically. Answer C is incorrect because the RAID level is not relevant in this case. Answer D is incorrect because you would never pull a non-hot plug hard drive out of a live system, even if it was not critical. For more information, see the "RAID Disk Concepts" section.

13. **C.** RAID 1 mirrors the contents of one hard drive onto another. Answer A is incorrect because RAID 0 defines disk striping only. Answer B is incorrect because RAID 0+1 defines striping a mirrored array. Answer D is incorrect because RAID 3 defines disk striping with a dedicated parity drive. For more information, see the "RAID Levels" section.

14. **B.** Remember that parity is distributed in RAID 5, but it still takes up the equivalent of one drive. Answer A is incorrect because you only need a second controller when performing disk duplexing. Answer C is incorrect because the disk size requested already takes into account the equivalent of one drive for parity. Answer D is incorrect because a RAID 3 array uses the same amount of hard drives as a RAID 5, except the parity is not distributed across all drives. For more information, see the "RAID Levels" section.

15. **C.** The NOS has to enable the array, and therefore the system partition cannot be part of the array. Answer A is incorrect because the OS partition cannot be part of the array. Answer B is incorrect because there is no RAID controller in a software RAID array. Answer D is incorrect because the array was specified as a RAID 5 array. For more information, see the "Hardware RAID and Software RAID" section.

16. **C.** The system does not have enough resources for software RAID. RAID 5 adds the fault tolerance requirement. Answer A is incorrect because the overhead needed for the software RAID array is too large for the system to handle. Answer B is incorrect because adding hot spare drives will not define any type of RAID level. Answer D is incorrect because RAID 0 does not include any fault tolerance. For more information, see the "Hardware RAID and Software RAID" section.

17. A. There is no fault tolerance in a RAID 0 array. Answer B is incorrect because RAID 0 defines disk striping without any fault tolerance. Answer C is incorrect because there is no mirrored drive in a RAID 0 array. Answer D is incorrect because there is no parity information in a RAID 0 array to rebuild the hard drive. For more information, see the "RAID Levels" section.

18. A. RAID 3 uses a disk drive for parity. In RAID 5, parity data is striped across all drives. Answer B is incorrect because RAID 1 defines disk mirroring. Answer C is incorrect because RAID defines data striping with a distributed parity system. Answer D is incorrect because RAID 0 defines disk striping only with no parity. For more information, see the "RAID Levels" section.

19. D. The second disk controller will continue to operate the array if the other controller fails. This removes a single disk controller as a point of failure. Answer A is incorrect because a controller cannot be rebuilt. Answer B is incorrect because only a hard drive can be a hot spare. Answer C is incorrect because the system is duplexed, so the system will not fail, and the secondary controller will take over. For more information, see the "RAID Levels" section.

20. B. Software RAID requires more system resource overhead than a hardware RAID solution. Answer A is incorrect because a software RAID array is implemented by the OS, not by external hardware. Answer C is incorrect because software RAID does not use any type of hardware controller. Answer D is incorrect because hot swap drives will not be used in a software RAID system. For more information, see the "Hardware RAID and Software RAID" section.

Scenarios

1. Because you are running out of disk space, you will need more drives in this system. To create fault tolerance, you will need to implement either a RAID 3 or RAID 5 solution. Consider six or seven 9GB drives, one of which will be used up for parity. Because the system is a file server, and not a transactional database system, read and write performance isn't a large issue, and the higher performance RAID levels are not needed.

2. Your first step in troubleshooting this system is to find out what RAID level it is running. Because the system did not crash, it has some level of fault tolerance. Typically, if there are only two drives in the system, it is a RAID 1 mirroring system. Any system with three drives or more is using a striped RAID system with parity. In either case, if there is no hot spare drive present, all you would have to do is replace the failed disk drive with a new one. If a hot plug system is being used, this can be done while the system is alive and online.

3. Because this is a high-end, transactional database system, read and write I/O performance is a must. A large number of disk drives and strong fault tolerance will also be needed for this enterprise system. If this were a smaller database system, a RAID 0+1 array would be acceptable, but because of its size and the critical nature of the data, a RAID 30 or 50 should be used.

Configuring the Operating System and Network

CHAPTER PRE-TEST

1. Why should a network operating system be installed in its own partition?

2. 205.111.121.5 is an example of what class of TCP/IP address?

3. What should you do after installing a patch or service pack?

4. What file system should you use for a Windows NT installation?

5. What command is used to configure network settings on a Unix server?

6. What is the difference between DNS and WINS?

7. Where is the best place to find the most current patches for your network operating system?

8. What is the purpose of subnetting?

9. What is the difference between a hot fix and a service pack?

10. Why should you back up files before installing any type of patch or update?

✦ Answers to these questions can be found at the end of the chapter. ✦

After you have the server hardware set up and ready, the next step is to install a network operating system (NOS). Depending on your needs, there are several excellent operating systems, each with their own advantages and disadvantages. The major network operating systems include Microsoft Windows NT and 2000, Novell NetWare, IBM's OS/2, and various Unix and Linux distributions. This chapter takes you through the basic installation steps of each network operating system, including disk partitioning, formatting, and basic OS configuration. This chapter also details the process of installing and configuring the network, including a detailed discussion of the most widely used network protocol, TCP/IP. Finally, after you've installed the operating system and configured networking, you must apply various fixes, patches, and service packs to bring the system up-to-date with current bug fixes, security concerns, and new hardware compatibility.

There are five basic steps in setting up any network operating system on a server:

1. **Examine the installation documentation.** You should examine any installation instructions, `readme` files, and last-minute errata before commencing with the install.

2. **Partition and format the disk.** Your hard disks and storage systems must be properly partitioned and formatted for your particular operating system.

3. **Install the OS.** Once the actual installation begins, there will be several pre-installation options that you must set for your particular configuration. When all options have been set, the installation will continue and load all system files to the server from the installation media.

4. **Configure the network.** The final step in the initial setup of your operating system is configuring it for network activity.

5. **Installing Patches and Updates.** After the main install of the operating system, you must update it with all the current fixes, patches, and service packs to bring it to current revision level.

Exam Tip   For the exam, know the basic steps of installing a network operating system, and the order in which to perform them.

Examining the Documentation

Before installing the server operating system, examine the documentation and media that came with the original package. There may be special instructions or documentation errata that apply to your particular hardware and type of configuration. Also check the `readme` file from the installation media. This will contain any last-minute instructions for installation as the operating system went to press. Check the OS vendor's Web site for the most current information on installing your software. Any of the latest drivers, patches, and updates that you might need for installation will be located here.

Configuring the Disk

Before you can begin a network operating system installation, the hard disks and storage systems must be prepared for the install. The first step will be partitioning your disk. Partitioning is a way of splitting up your physical hard disk into smaller sections. This is especially useful for installing multiple operating systems on one computer, but in the case of a network server, which should be running only one operating system, it enables you to separate the system files and user data. This adds security, by keeping users' data and programs away from the core operating system files. It simplifies backups, which can be set to only back up the user data rather than the entire server. If you ever need to upgrade or patch OS core files, the upgrade will not harm the user data partition. Other partitions can also be created for various purposes, such as temporary files, swap files, and system environment files.

Each operating system has its own procedures and utilities for partitioning a disk. The installation boot floppy disk or the boot CD-ROM will come with a partitioning tool. Start the server with the bootable media, and the partitioning tool will begin analyzing the disks. In general, these utilities show you how much of your disk space is currently assigned or not assigned to a partition. Usually, the hard disk will come with one large partition already created, but you can modify this to suit your needs. For example, if your system comes with an 18GB drive, you can assign 4GB to be a separate partition for your system files, and the 14GB can be on another partition to hold user data.

Caution   Be careful not to destroy any utility partitions that might have been installed by your server hardware manufacturer.

Installing the NOS

Objective   **2.3** Install NOS

Depending on your network operating system, there are a variety of ways to install and configure the OS. The following sections provide a brief discussion on each of the major operating systems and their unique installation steps.

Exam Tip   There is no need to memorize each major operating system's installation routines, but you should know some of the special features and commands that are unique to each system.

Microsoft Windows NT/2000

If your server has a CD-ROM installed, and you can configure the CD-ROM drive to be the boot device, you can install the Windows NT operating from a bootable CD-ROM disk. If not, a set of bootable disks is provided to start the installation.

Insert the first boot disk into the floppy drive, or insert the CD into your CD-ROM drive, and then turn on the server. You may need to configure the BIOS settings to boot from the floppy drive or CD-ROM as necessary.

The initial setup screen appears, and the setup program examines and inventories your hardware. You may need to provide driver disks for any special hardware that the NT installation might not have drivers for. After the hard disks have been examined, you will come to the disk configuration screen. Here, you can easily set up the partitions that you need and format them either using the FAT or NTFS file system. Use the FAT file system if you want to remain compatible with any DOS-type partitions and files you have set up. I recommend that you use the NTFS file system, which will allow you to use proper NT security mechanisms to protect your files, and also set up software RAID configurations.

When the disks have been set up, you need to specify the boot drive to which your OS system files will be copied. If you have set aside a partition for the system files, you should put them in that partition. The installation will now begin the process of copying the core operating system files to disk, which could take some time to complete. When this is finished, the server will need to be restarted, and the next level of OS configuration can begin.

When the server restarts, you will be asked to enter such information as the server name, the name of the workgroup or domain, the licensing key, and an initial password for the administrator account. You also need to choose whether the server will be a stand-alone server, a member of a domain, or a domain controller. Windows *domains* are a way of organizing groups of servers and client computers into a common administrative entity. This enables you to control and organize security permissions and network resources from a central point. A *domain controller* is a special Windows NT server that stores all the domain information and authenticates clients to the network so they can access domain resources.

Caution   Be careful when assigning your server role. You cannot switch a member server to a domain controller, or vice-versa, without reinstalling the entire operating system.

When this is finished, the next step is to set up network connectivity. Add the network protocols you will be using, and bind them to your network interface card. Once the server has been restarted again, and network connectivity is verified, the installation is finished.

The final step is to install the latest Service Pack, to ensure that the OS has the most recent patches, bug fixes, and enhancements installed. Microsoft Service Packs and patches are discussed in more detail later in the chapter.

At this time, you must also create your Emergency Rescue Disk. This is a special floppy disk that holds all the configuration and registry information from your Windows server. In the event that your Windows server will not start, or contains corrupted system files, you can use the disk to repair this information. You must keep the ERD up to date whenever you make hardware or software changes. If you try to restore an older configuration, it may not work properly, and may damage the system. You can create the ERD from the command prompt by using the command rdisk.exe.

Novell NetWare

Novell NetWare can be installed either by using a boot diskette or a bootable CD-ROM. The initial setup program creates a small DOS partition on the server. This DOS partition is usually 100 to 500MB in size and contains core system files, including server.exe, the operating system kernel. The NetWare installation automatically allocates the rest of the drive as a NetWare partition. The first NetWare volume of a server is always labeled as SYS. The DOS partition contains the core system files, such as the system kernel, server.exe. When a server is started, these core files in the DOS partition need to be run first, so that the kernel can mount the SYS: volume so that the other device drivers and modules can be loaded. These system files and modules are installed in SYS:SYSTEM. At this point, you are prompted to edit the startup.ncf file so that you can configure the boot-time options that are needed for the server startup. The startup.ncf file is located in the DOS partition, because it needs to load the appropriate hard disk drivers so that the NetWare partition can be accessed and the rest of the operating system loaded.

The installation procedure now loads these disk device drivers, and the server's SYS volume is mounted. At this time, the install routine prompts you to edit the autoexec.ncf file. The autoexec.ncf file resides in the SYS:SYSTEM directory, and contains time zone information and networking information, including the server name and network address. The final line in the autoexec.ncf file is usually a mount command, telling the system which volumes are to be automatically mounted at boot time.

Networking is configured next, as the server installation detects any network boards, and loads the appropriate module for each board. Network protocols can be bound to the network card. Novell NetWare has its own routable protocol called IPX, but to facilitate communications with the Internet, TCP/IP should be used instead of, or in addition to, IPX.

Next, the NDS (Novell Directory Service) is installed, which allows the network's resources to be configured and administered in a logical tree structure.

The next step in the installation includes setting your initial password for the administrator account and setting the license for the server using the license disk.

Finally, you can now install any other services, drivers, programs, and modules that are needed for the server. For example, if you are installing an Internet server, you should load the Web or FTP server modules.

You should download the most recent Support Packs for the core OS files, and also any other software programs and modules. This will bring your server up to date with the latest patches, bug fixes, and enhancements. Novell Support Packs and patches are discussed in more detail later in the chapter.

IBM OS/2

The OS/2 installation begins with starting the server with the Installation Boot Disk. When this procedure is finished, the other OS/2 diskettes 1 and 2 are inserted and loaded in order. At this time, the CD-ROM is needed for the rest of the installation.

After the welcome screen appears, you are offered a choice between two methods of installation, Easy and Advanced installation. Choose Advanced, as this allows you to partition the drives to your own configuration.

Using the `fdisk` utility, you can now partition the drive. If you are creating new partitions, you will have to restart the server again with the installation boot disk. When your partitions have been created, choose the partition where you would like to install OS/2, and mark it as Installable.

You can now format the drive using the OS/2 HPFS (High Performance File System), or FAT. You should choose HPFS if you want to take advantage of OS/2's native file system, which allows you to use larger hard drives (hard drives are limited in size by the FAT file system), and you can also use long file names.

When the basic OS files are installed, the system will restart with a GUI installation tool. Here you can set all your configuration parameters such as language and country settings, configure hardware settings, and network settings.

For the network configuration, use TCP/IP for the network protocol. You will need to setup your IP address, domain name, default gateway, and DNS servers.

When finished, your final step is to download any FixPaks and patches that will be needed to bring the OS up to date with current revisions.

Unix

Because there are so many different types of Unix vendors, I cannot discuss the detailed installation steps for each one. However, most Unix systems are very similar in their basic setup, disk partitioning, and network configuration. Linux is also a Unix-like operating system, and the partitioning and setup procedures are usually the same.

Most Unix OS installation come with a boot disk or CD-ROM. When the system is started from the boot media, the first step is to partition the disk drive to prepare for the installation.

Disk partitioning is performed by using the fdisk utility. With this tool, you can split up the disk into various partitions and format each drive with a specific file system.

The following are some general partitioning tips for Unix systems:

✦ The root partition, indicated by the / symbol, should contain all of the system file directories, such as /sbin, /etc, /bin, and /boot. The /sbin and /bin directories contain several system binaries and commands, while /etc is used to hold all the system configuration files. The /boot directory is sometimes used to hold boot information such as the kernel and related files.

✦ The /usr directory should be set up in its own partition, as it contains all non-critical programs that are run by the users. Because it will grow often in size as programs are added, keeping it in its own separate partition will prevent it from affecting the system file partitions.

✦ The /tmp directory is used for holding temporary files. It greatly fluctuates in size as temporary files are constantly stored and removed. Keeping the /tmp directory in its own partition will prevent it from affecting the system file partitions.

✦ The /var directory is used to store variable information, such as mail and print queues, and system log files. Disk space can quickly run out on this partition, especially on a heavily used mail server. Log files must also be checked for size and rotated at regular intervals.

✦ The /home directory is the directory used to store home directories for the users. Most of the free disk space in a system should be allocated to this partition, to contain the quick growth of user files. This directory should be kept in its own partition, so that disk space issues will not affect the core system files.

✦ Finally, you should make a separate partition for the swap file. The swap file is used to act as virtual memory to augment the system's RAM.

**In the
Real World**
Although you may simplify your installation by putting all of the Unix directories into one partition, separating the major directories into their own partition is an excellent protective and security measure. When user directories are separated from the system files, if the users use up all the free disk space, it will not crash the server.

After the disk has been properly partitioned, the install program will then copy all the operating system files to their respective partitions.

When this phase is finished, you will need to set up your network settings. Unix uses TCP/IP as its default networking protocol. Your machine will need to have a name and an Internet domain that it is part of. Other TCP/IP settings such as default gateway, subnet mask, and DNS servers will need to be set up. All of these configuration settings will be stored in text files in the /etc directory. You may use GUI tools to modify these settings, or edit the text files themselves with a text editor.

Finally, after the network has been setup, you should check the vendor's Web or FTP site to download any system updates, patches, and security fixes for your server.

Configuring and Verifying Network Connectivity

✦ Configure network and verify network connectivity

Before configuring your network connectivity on your server's network operating system, you need to plan what type of network protocols you want to implement. Although many operating systems come with their own proprietary protocols, the use of more widely used standards-based protocols such as TCP/IP would be of greater benefit to your network.

NetBEUI and NetBIOS

Originally created by IBM for its LAN server products, and improved upon by Microsoft, NetBIOS (Network Basic Input Output System) and its advanced version NetBEUI (NetBIOS Extended User Interface), are non-routable protocols used for small, basic local area networks. Non-routable protocols cannot be passed through a router to another network segment, so they are excellent for small, internal local networks. Through the use of a special redirector, NetBIOS and NetBEUI network requests are relayed to servers, while local requests are handled by the local operating system.

NetBIOS uses the SMB (Server Message Block) protocol for resource sharing, while NetBEUI uses broadcasts to relay information. A network *broadcast* means the device sends a message to every other device, advertising its presence on the network. NetBEUI also uses a session service to set up connections between servers for NetBIOS communications.

Because NetBIOS and NetBEUI are non-routable protocols, they are not suited for large networks that require WAN capabilities. Since these protocols generally support peer-to-peer networks, and client/server configurations, there is no need for a central name server.

It is possible to run NetBIOS over TCP/IP networks, but you will require the use of a naming service. For Windows networks, you can use a WINS (Windows Internet Name Service) server to resolve NetBIOS names to Internet names, or a local `LMHOSTS` file, which keeps tables of these name conversions. These are discussed in more detail in the section on TCP/IP.

Novell IPX/SPX

The IPX (Internetwork Packet Exchange) protocol and SPX (Sequenced Packet Exchange), is a protocol suite created by Novell for use in NetWare networks. IPX/SPX is similar to the TCP/IP network protocol, as both provide connection-oriented and connectionless types of communication. A *connection-oriented protocol* maintains a persistent connection between two devices, while sending data along that connection. A *connectionless protocol* does not maintain this connection, making data transfer less reliable, but faster because of there is less network overhead required. IPX is a datagram-based connectionless protocol that operates at a lower level than SPX to address and route packets to their destinations. SPX uses connection-oriented communications to create sessions between network computers.

IPX/SPX is a routable protocol, making it an excellent choice for large LAN/WAN NetWare networks, but to facilitate communications with the Internet, you should use TCP/IP as the primary network protocol.

TCP/IP

TCP/IP (Transmission Control Protocol/Internet Protocol) is the mostly widely used network protocol in the world. TCP/IP has its origins in the 1970s, as various government and university research teams grappled with the problem of interconnecting their dissimilar networks. The TCP/IP protocol was created to facilitate the transport of network packets from one computer to another. In 1983, the TCP/IP protocol was added to the version of Unix created by the University of California at Berkeley. It quickly spread to other universities, and soon became the default protocol for all Unix distributions.

This network, which originally only connected government and educational agencies, soon grew rapidly into what is today known as the Internet, and eventually become the backbone of world network communications.

TCP/IP fundamentals

The TCP/IP protocol is split into parts: TCP (Transmission Control Protocol) and IP (Internet Protocol). TCP is the protocol that creates connections between computers so that packets can be exchanged between them. Because network packets can often be lost during transmission, this protocol provides more reliable connections and data transfer between systems. IP is responsible for addressing and routing packets to their proper destinations. Through the use of special *IP addressing,* a network packet can be routed to any computer throughout the Internet.

TCP/IP addressing

Each device on a TCP/IP network is called a *host*. This can be any type of device, including a server, client PC, printer, router, or any other device that can use the TCP/IP protocol. Each host on a TCP/IP network must have its own unique IP address. This address identifies that host on the network so network packets can be addressed and routed to that host.

TCP/IP network addresses are created using 32-bit values, split into four octets of information, like this: 38.170.216.15. Each *octet* in the IP address represents eight bits of the address, converted to decimal format, and is separated by a decimal. Each address has two parts: one that identifies the network address, and one that defines the host. Which octets define the network address and which define the host address vary, and are defined by *IP classes*.

IP classes are separated into different blocks of addresses. Classes are named Class A through Class E, but only A, B, and C are primarily used for general network addressing. Certain ranges of IP addresses are reserved for special networking functions, such as 127.0.0.0 through 127.255.255.255, which is used for local loopback testing. Other address such as 255 and 0 are used for broadcast messages. Table 5-1 presents some information about classes A, B, and C.

Table 5-1
IP Address Classes

Class	IP Address Range	Octets for Network (N) and Host (H) ID	Total Number of Networks	Total Number of Hosts
A	1-126	N.H.H.H	126	16,777,214
B	128-191	N.N.H.H	16,384	65,534
C	192-223	N.N.N.H	2,097,151	254

An example of a Class B IP address is 162.151.13.57. Because this is a Class B address the first two octets (162.151) define the network address, while the last two (13.57) define the host address. As you can see, the more octets that are assigned to the network address, the fewer total hosts you can have on your network.

If your local network is not connected to the Internet, it is safe to use any IP address and class that you would like. But if you are connecting to the Internet, you cannot use IP addresses that are used anywhere else on the Internet. Typically, your Internet Service Provider (ISP) will assign your company a block of IP addresses to use on the Internet.

Most companies use firewall and proxy servers to enable the local network to use its own IP addresses, while the proxy and firewall provide network address translation (NAT) to mask the internal IP with a valid Internet address. If you have any Internet services running on your servers such as Web, FTP, or e-mail, they will need their own unique external IP address. Figure 5-1 shows an example of using private IP addresses internally, while using a proxy to connect to the Internet. The network uses the Class A address 10.1.2.x internally, and the firewall uses the Class C address 207.210.131.1 for contacting the Internet. As far as any servers on the Internet can tell, all requests from this network come from the 207.210.131.1 address, no matter what the host's address is on the local network.

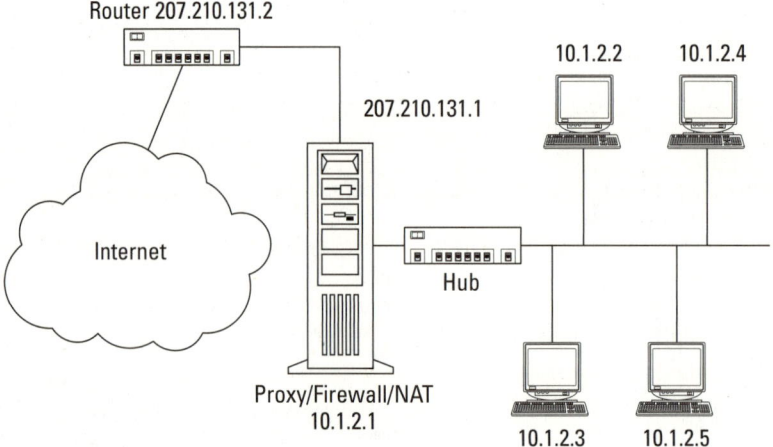

Figure 5-1: A network using internal IP addressing, with NAT addressing providing access to the Internet

Subnets

Each TCP/IP host, in addition to a unique IP address, needs a *subnet mask*. The subnet mask is also a 32-bit value split into 4 octets of information. Subnet masking enables you to break down a single network segment into multiple logical networks, by separating the network and host ID portions of the IP address. Dividing up your network eases administration by making the network more manageable, and can help network data flow and decrease congestion. See Table 5-2 for a list of default subnet masks for different classes of networks.

<table>
<tr><td colspan="2" align="center">Table 5-2
Default Subnet Masks</td></tr>
<tr><td>*IP Address Class*</td><td>*Default Subnet Mask*</td></tr>
<tr><td>Class A 1–126</td><td>255.0.0.0</td></tr>
<tr><td>Class B 128–191</td><td>255.255.0.0</td></tr>
<tr><td>Class C 192–223</td><td>255.255.255.0</td></tr>
</table>

Depending on the number of subnets and hosts you want in your network, there are complex calculations that are needed to determine the proper subnet mask. To simplify the process, see Tables 5-3, 5-4, and 5-5 for a list of subnet mask settings for different classes of networks.

Exam Tip   You don't need to memorize these subnetting tables for the exam, but you should know the general concepts and functions of configuring subnets.

Table 5-3
Subnet Mask Table for a Class A Network

Subnet Mask	Number of Networks	Hosts per Network
255.192.0.0	2	4,194,302
255.224.0.0	6	2,097,150
255.240.0.0	14	1,048,574
255.248.0.0	30	524,286
255.252.0.0	62	262,142
255.254.0.0	126	131,070
255.255.0.0	254	65,534
255.255.128.0	510	32,766
255.255.192.0	1022	16,382
255.255.224.0	2046	8190
255.255.240.0	4094	4094
255.255.248.0	8190	2046
255.255.252.0	16,382	1022
255.255.254.0	32,766	510
255.255.255.0	65,534	254
255.255.255.128	131,070	126
255.255.255.192	262,142	62
255.255.255.224	524,286	30
255.255.255.240	1,048,574	14
255.255.255.248	2,097,150	6
255.255.255.252	4,194,302	2

Table 5-4
Subnet Mask Table for a Class B Network

Subnet Mask	Number of Networks	Hosts per Network
255.255.192.0	2	16,382
255.255.224.0	6	8190
255.255.240.0	14	4094
255.255.248.0	30	2046
255.255.252.0	62	1022
255.255.254.0	126	510
255.255.255.0	254	254
255.255.255.128	510	126
255.255.255.192	1022	62
255.255.255.224	2046	30
255.255.255.240	4094	14
255.255.255.248	8190	6
255.255.255.252	16,382	2

Table 5-5
Subnet Mask Table for a Class C Network

Subnet Mask	Number of Networks	Hosts per Network
255.255.255.192	2	62
255.255.255.224	6	30
255.255.255.240	14	14
255.255.255.248	30	6
255.255.255.252	62	2

DHCP server

Because every host on your network must have a unique address, it can be a daunting task to allocate IP addresses for every device in your network, especially if it is very large. This process is called *static IP addressing*. With static addressing, the IP address that you assign to a device will never change. In large networks this can be very time consuming, and if you ever need to change your IP structure for whatever reason, you will have to reassign addresses to every device on the network.

By using *dynamic addressing,* you can assign IP addresses automatically to devices as they connect to the network. The protocol to facilitate this process is called Dynamic Host Configuration Protocol (DHCP). A DHCP server contains a pool of IP addresses it can draw from to assign them to a device that has just connected to the network. Other TCP/IP properties such as default gateway, DNS servers, and subnet masks can also be assigned automatically.

The client device must be set up to broadcast for a DHCP server. The request is acknowledged by the server, which then sends the device an IP address configuration. The DHCP server uses a lease to assign the address, which means that the lease can expire after a certain period of time, or be used indefinitely. When the lease expires, the same client can renew the lease and continue to use the same IP address.

DNS server

TCP/IP networks communicate with hosts using their IP addresses. Most people find it difficult to memorize all the different IP addresses for the hosts they want to connect to. To make it easier to identify networks, you can use a *domain name* to identify a host. A domain name uses words rather than numbers to identify Internet hosts.

For example, `www.mycompany.com` would be a common name used for a numerical IP address, and is much easier to remember. Internet names are split into various domains depending on their function. For example, government sites all end in with the domain `.gov`, whereas educational institutions use `.edu`. The most common domain is for commercial use, and is called `.com`. The full address is referred to as a Fully Qualified Domain Name (FQDN). For `www.mycompany.com`, the address represents a host, `www`, within the `mycompany.com` domain.

To translate these addresses, a DNS (Domain Name Service) server is required. A DNS server keeps a table of hosts and domains and their corresponding IP addresses. When a host on a network needs to contact another host using its FQDN, the host looks up the corresponding IP address on the DNS server. The Internet has several root DNS servers that store the database of domain names and corresponding IP addresses for all Internet sites. For local area networks, a DNS server will aid you in naming common machines in your environment. For example, `www.mycompany.com` could be a reference to your company's Web server.

WINS server

For Windows networks, the Windows Internet Naming Service (WINS) performs a function similar to DNS. Windows networks use the NetBIOS protocol to identify and locate computers on a network. If you are running NetBIOS over a TCP/IP network, a WINS server will translate NetBIOS names to IP addresses. If you are not using NetBIOS over TCP/IP, you do not need a WINS server.

Exam Tip Do not confuse the function of a DNS server and WINS server. A DNS server maps Internet domain names to IP addresses, and a WINS server maps Windows NetBIOS names to IP addresses.

Verifying network configuration

✦ Verify network connectivity

Each operating system uses its own console commands for checking and verifying network configuration and connectivity. Although the network information can be checked with a graphical administration program, various parameters tend to spread over different menus, making it difficult to get all the information you need.

In addition to the OS-specific commands, there are a few TCP/IP commands that are common among operating systems. The two most important of these are ping and traceroute. The ping command is used to test network connectivity between two devices. The ping command sends a packet of data to the other network device, which sends back a reply. If you get a reply back, you have established network connectivity. If there is no reply, that means the device you are trying to contact, or possibly your own device, is unavailable to the network. The output of the ping command also tells you how much time it took to receive the reply. This a nice general indicator of how congested your connection to the other device is.

To further troubleshoot your connection, and to find the routing path of your connection to another device, you can use the traceroute command. This command will track a network packet from your device to another one. On the way, you can see how many steps or *hops* it takes to get from router to router, until the packet reaches its final destination. When a device is unavailable, this is an excellent troubleshooting tool that can help you trace the network connection to see where along the path you lose your connection.

The following sections list commands that provide key network information for each operating system.

Microsoft Windows NT

For Windows NT servers, you can use the ipconfig command at the server console to get detailed network information on your server. The following is a list of the different parameters and switches you can use to change the type of information displayed from the output of the command.

✦ ipconfig — Used by itself, the command lists your network adapters with each adapter's IP address, gateway, and subnet mask.

✦ ipconfig /all — This command lists all adapters and their settings, including DHCP server and lease information, DNS and WINS servers, type of network card and its MAC address, and the standard IP address, gateway, and subnet mask information.

✦ ipconfig /release — This command releases the address assigned to the network adapter if it is using DHCP. Normally this wouldn't be used on a server, as a server should have a static IP address assigned.

✦ `ipconfig /renew`— This command renews an IP address lease from a DHCP server. This command is used on client PCs to renew a dynamic IP addresses.

✦ `ping`— This command tests the connectivity between two network devices by sending a packet and then receiving a reply back. For example, enter `ping www.hungryminds.com` to test your connection between your device and the Hungry Minds Web site.

✦ `tracert`— This command is the Windows version of the `traceroute` command, which can trace the network connection between two devices, showing the entire path and how long it takes between each network hop to the next router. For example, enter `tracert www.hungryminds.com` to see the route between your device and the Hungry Minds Web site.

Novell NetWare

For Novell NetWare servers, the `inetcfg` command can be used to configure networking and examine your current settings. The command is actually a loadable module, `inetcfg.nlm`. Within the module, you can use a menu-based system to display network information for all of your network cards and make configuration changes. The following commands are available from this module.

✦ `load inetcfg`— This utility is used to configure your network parameters, such as network addressing and other required TCP/IP information.

✦ `config`— This command can be used at the command line to view current network settings.

✦ `load ping`— This command will test the connectivity between two network devices by sending a packet and then receiving a reply back.

✦ `load iptrace`— This command is the NetWare version of the `traceroute` command, which can trace the network connection between two devices, showing the entire path and how long it takes between each network hop to the next router.

✦ `load tcpcon`— This command gives you general information on various TCP/IP statistics on your NetWare server.

Unix

The standard Unix command for obtaining network information is the `ifconfig` command. Without any parameters, `ifconfig` lists the primary network adapters, with their descriptions, MAC address, and IP address information. The `ifconfig` command can also be used to assign IP addresses to network cards. Here is a list of common `ifconfig` parameters and switches.

✦ `ifconfig -a`— This command lists the configuration for all network cards.

✦ `ifconfig -eth0 down`— This command disables the Ethernet 0 interface. This is usually the first network card in the server.

✦ `ifconfig -eth0 up`— This command enables the Ethernet 0 interface

✦ `ifconfig -eth0 192.168.0.5 255.255.255.0` — This command assigns the IP address 192.168.0.5 to the Ethernet 0 interface, and gives it a default subnet mask of 255.255.255.0

✦ `ping` — This command will test the connectivity between two network devices by sending a packet and then receiving a reply back.

✦ `traceroute` — This command can trace the network connection between two devices, showing the entire path and how long it takes between each network hop to the next router.

IBM OS/2

Because it is based on the Unix implementation of TCP/IP, OS/2 also uses the `ifconfig` command to configure network boards, or to retrieve network information. You can also use `ping` and `traceroute` to verify network connectivity. See the previous section on the Unix `ifconfig`, `ping`, and `traceroute` commands.

Exam Tip   For the exam, you should know what command to use on each operating system to display networking information.

Applying Patches and Service Packs

Objective   **2.5** Install NOS updates to design specifications

Network OS vendors frequently release updates, patches, security fixes, and bug fixes to their operating systems. You should always install the latest updates to your NOS before putting the server into production. Since the original release of your operating system, there have most likely been several bug fixes and enhancements. After the initial installation of the system, ensure that every component of the network operating system is patched and updated to its most current level. There are several reasons why these patches, service packs, and fixes should be applied.

Bug fixes

Software will always contain certain bugs or errors, which can harm the regular operation of your NOS. A *bug* is an error in the software code that manifests itself under certain types of conditions. For example, certain combinations of installed software and services might have common components that conflict with each other. Software and OS vendors routinely make available bug fixes to repair these errors. Vendors compile these through the scanning of technical support issues for common error messages that appear during a certain set of conditions. When the bug has been verified, and can be recreated, an update is created to fix that bug. Some software bugs can be very rare, and only affect a few installations that run with complex configurations. Others can be more serious, and affect a large number of installations. Bug fixes for serious errors are made available as soon as available, usually from the vendor's web or FTP site. Minor fixes are often bundled together into one fix, patch, or service pack.

In the Real World   Unless you are experiencing the symptoms of a bug, it is generally not advisable to install every bug fix that is released. Doing so may create a new conflict with your operating system configuration. As the saying goes, if it isn't broken, don't fix it.

Functionality enhancements

After a major, original release of a network operating system, the vendor continues to develop new enhancements to the functionality of services and programs. For example, a vendor might make updates to an internal SNMP-based monitoring application to make it operate more efficiently. The vendor constantly works to enhance and improve various aspects of the operating system, and these are released regularly through the service packs and patches. If a major upgrade to the basic functionality of the OS is created, a new sub-version of the software may be released.

Hardware driver support

Objective   **2.6** Update manufacturer specific drivers

After the original release of the network operating system, support for new hardware devices must be maintained. An NOS will only have support for older or current hardware at the time of its release. To provide compatibility with new hardware released after the operating system, the NOS vendor may include new hardware support drivers with their service packs and patches.

Exam Tip   After the installation of an OS patch or update, certain hardware drivers may fail and will need an updated driver from the vendor.

Security fixes

The security of your network operating system is a major concern. After the original release of an operating system, various security holes and flaws may surface, which may enable outside intruders to compromise your system. Many security holes in modern systems revolve around the use of Web services, which allow outside users access to an internal Web server. If an exploit is found in these services, it could pose a great security risk to your internal network. NOS vendors regularly release security updates and fixes for their systems, and it is very important for you to be aware of any security flaws and the availability of patches to fix them.

In the Real World   It is extremely important to remain up-to-date with the latest fixes for security holes in your server. Without patching them, you run the risk of unauthorized intrusion into your servers.

Types of NOS updates

There are several different ways in which a NOS vendor will release a software update. This will depend on many factors, including the size and nature of the update, its availability, and installation method.

Hot fixes

A *hot fix,* also referred to as a bug fix, is typically a small update of a certain component of the operating system. It usually pertains to only one error condition or issue, which can be fixed updating one or more files. Hot fixes are usually very small, and contain either a single file, which can be executed to install the update, or a file or collection of files that are simply copied over the old version of the files. Major functionality or security issues that are needed immediately are usually released as a hot fix, but they can also be minor or rare issues as well.

Software patches

A *software patch* for a network operating system is usually a collection of various bug fixes and enhancements. Instead of executing just one fix for a problem, as in the case of a hot fix, a patch will usually contain a larger number of files and fixes in one package. These are used to update your system with several minor bug fixes and upgrades. A patch is usually contained in one executable file, which will update the required files all at once.

Service packs

A software *service pack* is a major upgrade or fix to a network operating system. A vendor will typically only release one of two service packs per year, as they contain a very large number of updates. Service packs are a large collection of bug fixes, patches, hardware compatibility updates, security fixes, and functionality upgrades, all rolled into one. Service packs can be incremental or cumulative releases. Incremental service packs must be installed in the order that they are released, as they contain only updates that have been released since the last service pack. For example, you must install service pack one before installing a service pack two. Incremental updates are often numbered by date, or use special revision numbers to identify them, especially on Unix operating systems. Cumulative service packs are ones that contain all the fixes and patches that have ever been released, and automatically contain fixes from earlier service packs. For example, a service pack five will contain its own fixes, including all of those released in earlier service packs. To fully update your system, you will only need to install the latest service pack version.

Major upgrades

Often, a vendor will completely redesign critical components of an operating system. This is considered a major OS upgrade. These upgrades are usually released as subversions of the original operating system. For example, a major upgrade to Novell NetWare 4 is NetWare 4.1. These upgrades contain major changes to the core system since the release of the original, and are typically very large, taking up as many CDs as the original operating system.

Finding updates

There are several ways in which the latest updates, patches, and service packs can be obtained for your network operating system. All NOS vendors keep the most current updates available on their web or FTP sites. This is the first place to check for the most current files that you need. Most small hot fixes and patches can be downloaded over the internet, but some larger service packs, which can often be up 30 to 50MB in size, are not easily downloaded over a slow link.

Vendors make larger service packs and updates available on CD-ROM, which can be ordered for a small fee, or it might come automatically as part of a special service maintenance agreement. Signing up for a software maintenance agreement can save a lot of time having to track down updates for your operating system, as any updates and upgrades are sent to you automatically. The only drawback to CD-ROM updates is that the files might not always be the most current.

Some vendors have implemented special auto-updating features in their network operating systems. This allows you to run a special program that will scan your system for the current levels of programs, patches, and service packs, and compare them to an online database. If a newer update has been released for any of your components, the program will download and install it automatically. By comparing what your system does or does not have with a listing of the all the most recent updates, you will know which programs and services need updating.

Installing a service pack

You must be careful when installing any form of hot fix, bug fix, patch, service pack, or upgrade. Any type of changes to your core operating system files may result in a damaged system if you do not follow the instructions properly. Ensure that the update you have obtained is the proper one for your particular problem. Examine the instructions and `readme` file that came with the update to ensure that you are running the right version of your operating system for the update, and that you have met any system or program dependencies.

Making backups

Before processing with any system update or upgrade, you must back up your system completely. Your system could be damaged if the update is installed improperly, or conflicts with other software in your system. Having a full backup on hand means that you can bring the server back to the exact state it was in before the update was applied.

Many updates and service packs automatically create a system snapshot of files that are going to be replaced, so that if there is an error during the installation, it can revert back to its original state. If the update prompts you if a backup should be made of files before the installation, you should always enable this feature.

Checking disk space

Service pack and OS upgrades can be very large, so you must ensure there is enough disk space to install the update. There should be enough space left on the disk drive to support at least twice the size of the update, because the files have to be uncompressed and then installed into their new location. You must also have enough space to back up the original system files and settings.

Preparing for downtime

Any type of update or upgrade to an operating system component will usually require the server to be restarted for the changes to take effect. If this server is brand new, and has not yet been put into production, this will not be a concern. To update a server that is already in production, you will need to schedule downtime with your users and management. Do not perform the update during production hours, as a problem with the installation could result in the system being down for many hours while you restore it from backup to a previously working state. All users should be logged out of the system during the upgrade.

Installing the update

You must be logged into your server with appropriate permissions to update OS system files. It is best to use the server's administrator or root account to do any type of OS update.

Before installing the update, shut down any services that are not needed during the upgrade. For example, if you are updating the operating system on an e-mail server, you should shut down the e-mail service before the update. This ensures that no system files will be in use during the update. If a file is locked, the installation program will not be able to update that file, and the installation will halt.

Begin the installation of the update as detailed in the installation instructions, and monitor its progress for any warning or error messages. When the installation is finished, you will need to shut down and reboot the server before the update will take effect. The server needs to be restarted, because currently running critical system files will need to be updated during the server startup.

Verifying the update

When the server has been restarted, and the network operating system loaded, you must check to see if the update worked. Check the version number of the OS and its revision or service pack level, which should match the revision number of the update. If you have installed a hot fix to repair a software bug, try to recreate the error you were experiencing. If the error reoccurs, the hot fix might not have installed properly, or your original problem might be something else not related to the hot fix.

It is also important to check any other software or services running on the same server. These programs or services might be dependent on certain critical operating system files that have been changed, which could affect their functionality.

Once you have ensured that everything is running smoothly, the server can be put back into production. It is important to monitor the performance of the server after an upgrade, to examine any functionality or performance issues that may occur because of the update.

Updating major operating systems

Each of the major operating systems use their own procedures and methods for providing and installing OS fixes, patches, updates, and service packs.

Microsoft Windows NT/2000

Microsoft server products make extensive use of the Microsoft Web site for software updates. Most hot fixes, bug fixes, and patches can be easily found and downloaded from the web site. You can troubleshoot various problems through the use of the Microsoft Knowledge Base, which may provide a download to fix the error with a special hot fix or patch. You can launch a special Windows Update program, which examines your system for current software versions and compares them with a database of the most current revisions and updates. The update program can then suggest what updates you should download to bring the OS up to date. These downloads are sorted in order from the most critical updates, which affect security and functionality, to small hot fixes to fix minor bugs.

Microsoft also regularly releases Service Packs, which are cumulative collections of all patches, fixes, and updates since the operating system's release. Because they are cumulative, there is no need to install all the service packs in order; you only need to install the most current service pack. They are available on the Microsoft Web site, www.microsoft.com, but because of their size they are also available on CD-ROM.

To install a Microsoft Service pack, unpack the files to a temporary directory. Run the update.exe file to begin the installation. The install file will ask you if you would like to create a backup of files replaced during the update. You should select this option if you would like to able to back out of the service pack to the previous state if the server is not working properly after the installation. When the installation of the Service Pack is finished, you need to restart the server for the update to take effect.

Novell NetWare

Novell refers to updates of its NetWare operating system as Support Packs. These OS updates are cumulative, so you don't need to install earlier support packs, only the most current one. They are both available on Novell's Web site and in CD-ROM form. Smaller patches and fixes can also be downloaded from the Web site, located at www.novell.com.

Follow the instructions of the support pack carefully. Any dependent services such as GroupWise, or BorderManager, need to be updated with their own support packs when the update is finished. This ensures that each supporting service has the most current updates available.

Support Pack and patch files should be unpacked to the `SYS:` volume, and can be installed using the `nwconfig` command from the server console. In the `nwconfig` menu, select Product Options, and then select Install a Product Not Listed. Choose the location of the unpacked update files and the installation will begin. If you want to be able to back out of the support pack, you should select the option to backup the files that are being replaced. When the installation is complete, you must reboot the server for the update to take effect.

IBM OS/2

OS/2 refers to their system update files as FixPaks. FixPaks exist for both the OS system files and other components, such as networking services. FixPaks are always cumulative, so the latest FixPaks will contain all of the updates from previous FixPaks. You don't need to install them order; you only need the latest FixPak. The latest FixPaks can be downloaded from `www.ibm.com`.

To find out what current levels of OS software you are running, use the `ver /r` command to see the current OS base level and revision level. Using the `syslevel` command will show you all products that are installed, including their revision level. This will aid you in finding the right FixPak for your products.

You need to create special boot disks to install the FixPaks. The disks load the Corrective Services Facility (CSF), also called the FixTool, to install the FixPaks. You must install the CSF separately before you can install a FixPak. FixPak image files are then created on diskettes, which the CSF program uses to install the updates.

Another method used to update OS/2 files is the Remote Service Update (RSU) utility. It enables you to download and install FixPaks using the Web. This method is much easier than having to create separate diskettes for the CSF utility and the FixPak image files, but it does take up more disk space.

After you install a FixPak update, reboot the server so the changes can take effect.

Unix

Each Unix vendor supplies its own patches and fixes through their Web site or through CD-ROM subscriptions. Patches exist for both the core operating system files and the various programs and services installed on the Unix server. Patches come in a variety of formats, some of them as self-executing files, others as source binaries, which must be compiled first to create the installation files. Some Linux distributions use the Red Hat Packet Manager (RPM) system to install and remove software packages.

The main problem with updating Unix systems is that many software packages are dependent on specific software and OS libraries and programs. Changing the version of one program or library might prevent another program or service from working properly. It is very important that each software package, patch, or update is checked for dependencies on different versions and revisions of existing programs.

To install patches and updates, you must be logged in as root on the server console. Although updates to certain programs and services may only require that you restart that service, changes to OS system files will only work if the entire system is rebooted.

Shutting Down the Operating System

 **6.2** Use diagnostic hardware and software tools and utilities

- Perform shut down across the following OS: Microsoft Windows NT/2000, Novell NetWare, UNIX, Linux, IBM OS/2

After you've installed a service pack or update, you need to reboot the server. Normally, you won't need to shut down your network servers, but the following list explains how it's done.

✦ **Windows NT/2000:** Click the Start button and select Shut Down. Choose the Shut Down option to shut the server down completely. If you are installing an update, chose the Restart option to reboot the server.

✦ **Novell NetWare:** Enter the down command to start the shutdown process. When this is finished, you can then type exit to shut the server down completely, or type server.exe to restart the server. If you are installing an update, use the reset server command to reboot the server for the update to take effect. If you are replacing the server.exe file during the update, you should enter the down command and then start server.exe again. Using the command restart server will not update and activate a new server.exe file.

✦ **IBM OS/2:** To shut down the system, you can right-click with the mouse anywhere on the desktop and select the Shutdown command from the menu, or click the corresponding icon from the Launchpad. To reboot the server, type setboot /b at the command line, if you are using the Bootmanager. Otherwise, use setboot /ibd:<drive>, where <drive> is the letter of the drive or partition you wish to boot from.

✦ **Unix:** For most Unix systems, the shutdown command at the console will safely bring the server down. The shutdown command can be passed many different options to perform actions such as sending a warning message to users, or setting a countdown timer.

Key Point Summary

This chapter detailed the major steps of installing a network operating system on to a server. Each of the major operating system's installation steps were discussed, including any special configurations specific to that operating system.

Network configuration and verification was discussed, including sections on the different networking protocols and the tools used to verify the network configuration for each major operating system.

The proper procedures for obtaining and installing the most current service packs and updates for each operating system were discussed.

Keep the following points in mind for the exam:

✦ To install an operating system follow these five general steps:

- Examine the documentation.

- Partitioning and formatting the disk.

- Install the OS files.

- Configure the network functions.

- Install and required patches and updates.

✦ Microsoft Windows NT and 2000 use the NetBIOS and NetBEUI protocols in addition to TCP/IP.

✦ Novell NetWare can use the IPX/SPX protocols, but TCP/IP is recommended for Internet compatibility.

✦ You do not need to know the complex calculations for IP subnetting, but know the general concepts and how they can be applied.

✦ DHCP servers provide dynamic IP addressing.

✦ DNS servers map domain names to IP addresses.

✦ WINS servers translate NetBIOS names to IP addresses.

✦ Each operating system has its own commands for verifying network configuration.

✦ Always back up files before installing a patch or service pack.

✦ When installing a service pack, restart the server to make the update take effect.

✦ Know the shutdown procedures for each type of network operating system.

✦   ✦   ✦

STUDY GUIDE

The Study Guide section provides you with the opportunity to test your knowledge about installing operating systems and patches and network configuration. The Assessment Questions provide practice for the test, and the Scenarios provide practice with real situations. If you get any questions wrong, use the answers to determine the part of the chapter you should review before continuing.

Assessment Questions

1. To facilitate network communications with the Internet, what should the default protocol of a LAN network be?

   A. TCP/IP

   B. IPX

   C. SPX

   D. NetBIOS

2. After the installation of a Windows NT server, a technician begins to set up access and security permissions of files and directories. The operating system will not let the technician perform any type of file security administration. What is the most likely cause of the problem?

   A. The technician is not logged in as administrator.

   B. The installation used the FAT file system.

   C. The installation used the HPFS file system.

   D. The installation used the NTFS file system.

3. During the installation of a Novell Support Pack, the install routine halts halfway through the update and an error message is displayed stating the update cannot continue. What is the most likely cause of the problem?

   A. The support pack is not the most recent version.

   B. The system files were not backed up.

   C. The support pack is corrupted.

   D. The server is out of disk space.

4. A technician is configuring the networking on a Windows NT server. The IP address is set to 10.10.1.5, with a default subnet mask of 10.10.1.255, and a default gateway of 10.10.1.1. When the server is rebooted, the technician cannot ping any other devices on the network. What is the mostly likely cause of the problem?

   A. The gateway address is incorrect.

   B. The IP address conflicts with another machine.

   C. The subnet mask is incorrect.

   D. The server is on a different network segment.

5. A technician has just started an installation of a network operating system by booting the server with a boot disk. What is generally the next step in configuring a new operating system?

   A. Partitioning the disk

   B. Installing the license key

   C. Examining the `readme` file

   D. Configuring the network

6. During the installation of a network operating system, the installer program freezes half way through the procedure. How can the installation be recovered?

   A. Reboot the server

   B. Use an Emergency Rescue Disk

   C. Restart the installation with the boot installation disk

   D. Reinstall the OS in safe mode

7. A technician wants to use the NetBIOS protocol over the TCP/IP protocol for a Windows NT LAN. What service needs to be installed to map NetBIOS names to IP addresses?

   A. WINS server

   B. DNS server

   C. DHCP server

   D. Default gateway

8. A technician has just installed a service pack on a Windows NT server to fix some issues with domain authentication. When the technician retries the operation, it still does work properly. What is the most likely cause of the problem?

   A. The service pack was not the latest version.

   B. The service pack should have been an earlier version.

C. The server was not restarted.

D. The system files were not backed up.

9. A technician wants to examine the DHCP lease information on a Windows based client. The technician types in `ipconfig` from a command prompt, but the only details it shows are the IP address, gateway, and subnet mask. How can the technician obtain the DHCP lease information?

   A. `ipconfig /release`

   B. `ipconfig /renew`

   C. `ifconfig`

   D. `ipconfig /all`

10. A technician is configuring a TCP/IP network for a local LAN. The technician wants to create a number of logical network segments. What should be used to give the required configuration?

    A. Firewall

    B. Proxy server

    C. Subnetting

    D. A default gateway

11. A technician is installing a Novell NetWare server. What network protocol should be bound to the network board to allow access to Internet-based applications?

    A. TCP/IP

    B. IPX

    C. NTFS

    D. NetBIOS

12. A technician tries to `ping` an internal web server called `www.test.com`. There is no response from the server, but it responds to a ping command when the IP address of the server is used instead. What is the most likely cause of the problem?

    A. The server is not listed in the WINS table.

    B. The server is not listed in the DNS table.

    C. The server does not exist in the `LMHOSTS` file.

    D. The subnet mask is not set on the server.

13. An error is made in the `/etc` file system of a new server, and the server will no longer start. What is required to fix the configuration?

    A. OS/2 CD-ROM

    B. Windows emergency rescue disk

    C. NetWare `startup.ncf`

    D. Unix boot disk

14. A network server is being configured with a TCP/IP address. What range of IP addresses can be used to configure the server if it should be a Class C address?

    A. 1.*x.x.x*–126.*x.x.x*

    B. 128.*x.x.x*–191.*x.x.x*

    C. 192.*x.x.x*–223.*x.x.x*

    D. 255.255.255.255

15. What network service should be used to enable a LAN configured with private IP addresses to access the Internet?

    A. Gateway

    B. DHCP server

    C. Firewall

    D. Proxy server

16. A technician is verifying the network configuration of a Windows NT server and types `ifconfig` at the server console prompt. An error message appears stating that the command does not exist. What is the proper command to show the network configuration for this server?

    A. `ifconfig /a`

    B. `ipconfig`

    C. `netcfg`

    D. `nwconfig`

17. A Windows client PC is set to get its IP address automatically from a DHCP server. The client can connect to the network, but it cannot resolve domain names to IP addresses. What is the most likely cause of the problem?

    A. The DHCP server is not set to assign DNS servers.

    B. The DHCP server did not assign the subnet mask.

    C. The DHCP server is not set to assign WINS addresses.

    D. The DHCP server is unavailable.

18. A network operating system was recently updated with a major upgrade package. After the upgrade, the network card fails to work. What should be done to fix the problem?

    A. Get a new driver for the network card compatible with the upgrade OS.

    B. Reinstall the original operating system.

    C. Replace the network card.

    D. Test the network card on another system.

19. A technician is checking the network configuration on a Unix server. What command should be used at the console to obtain the networking information?

    A. `ipconfig`

    B. `ipconfig /a`

    C. `ifconfig`

    D. `inetcfg`

20. An error was made in the configuration of files on an NTFS partition and the server will no longer boot. What is required to recover the server and to fix the error?

    A. OS/2 startup disk

    B. ERD disk

    C. Unix boot disk

    D. NetWare installation disk

Scenarios

1. You are installing Windows NT on a new Web server. The network is using private IP addressing internally, but has a set of ten Class B IP addresses issued by the company's Internet service provider to use for any external servers. What steps should you take to install the server and properly configure the network settings?

2. A Windows network is being configured to support TCP/IP, because several Unix workstations and servers have been added to the network. What new services must you add to the network to enable both the Windows and Unix machines to connect to the network and connect to each other?

Answers to Chapter Questions

Chapter pre-test

1. An NOS should be installed on its own partition separate from user data and programs to prevent users from interfering with system files.

2. 205.111.121.5 is a Class C IP address.

3. You should restart the server after you install any type of patch or system update so that critical system files can be updated and put into production.

4. You should use the NTFS file system instead of FAT, to take advantage of additional security and storage configurations.

5. The `ifconfig` command is used to configure and view network settings on a Unix server.

6. A DNS server is used to convert Internet domain names to IP addresses. A WINS server is used to convert NetBIOS names to IP addresses on a Windows network.

7. For the most current updates, you should go to the OS vendor's Web site.

8. Subnetting is used to divide a network into smaller logical networks.

9. A hot fix is a small update to an operating system that usually only requires the replacement of one or more files. A service pack is a collection of fixes, patches, and upgrades all combined into one large update.

10. Your server should be backed up before installing any type of update, in the event that the update causes the server not to work properly.

Assessment questions

1. **A.** The default network protocol should be TCP/IP. Answers B and C are incorrect because these are NetWare protocols. Answer D is incorrect because NetBIOS is a non-routable protocol, and is only used for local LANs. For more information, see the "Configuring and Verifying Network Connectivity" section.

2. **B.** The file system chosen during the installation was FAT. Only the NTFS file system will allow security permissions to be set on files. Answer A is incorrect because the problem was related to the file systems. Answer C is incorrect because the HPFS file system is used by OS/2. Answer D is incorrect because NTFS would have allowed the operation. For more information, see the "Installing the NOS" section.

3. **D.** The server must have enough disk space to install the support pack. Answer A is incorrect because a support pack does not have to be the most recent version to be successfully installed. Answer B is incorrect because the installation will not halt if a backup is not made of files to be replaced. Answer C is incorrect because a Support Pack would not produce this error message. For more information, see the "Applying Patches and Service Packs" section.

4. C. The subnet mask for this IP address is incorrect. The default subnet mask for a class A network is 255.0.0.0. Answer A is incorrect because the gateway address is correct. Answer B is incorrect because an IP address conflict would have resulted in an error message. Answer D is incorrect because you still should have been able to ping another device. For more information, see the "Configuring and Verifying Network Connectivity" section.

5. A. The next step is to partition the disks to prepare for the installation of operating system files. Answer B is incorrect because the license key installation comes later in the installation process when files are already on the hard drive. Answer C is incorrect because the `readme` file should be checked before the installation is started. Answer D is incorrect because network configuration comes near the end of the installation process. For more information, see the "Installing the NOS" section.

6. C. The installation must be restarted using the boot disk or CD-ROM. Answer A is incorrect because the server will not boot because the installation was not completed. Answer B is incorrect because an ERD disk will not recover an OS that has not been fully installed. Answer D is incorrect because you cannot install an OS in a safe mode. For more information, see the "Installing the NOS" section.

7. A. A WINS server maps NetBIOS names to IP addresses. Answer B is incorrect because a DNS server is used to map Internet domain names to IP addresses. Answer C is incorrect because a DHCP server is used to automatically assign IP addresses to new devices on the network. Answer D is incorrect because a default gateway is a setting for the TCP/IP protocol for proper routing. For more information, see the "Configuring and Verifying Network Connectivity" section.

8. C. The server should be restarted after the installation of a service pack for the update to take effect. Answer A is incorrect because the service pack does not have to be the latest version to fix a particular problem. Answer B is incorrect because service packs are cumulative, and contain all previous updates. Answer D is incorrect because a backup of the files that were updated will not fix the problem. For more information, see the "Applying Patches and Service Packs" section.

9. D. `ipconfig /all` will display all networking information for all network cards. Answers A and B are incorrect because these `ipconfig` commands are used to release and renew DHCP leases, not view DHCP information. Answer C is incorrect because `ifconfig` is used for configuring networking on a Unix machine. For more information, see the "Configuring and Verifying Network Connectivity" section.

10. C. The network needs to use subnetting to create the logical network segments. Answer A is incorrect because a firewall is used to protect an internal LAN from external access from the Internet. Answer B is incorrect because a proxy server is used to forward requests to the Internet on behalf of another client. Answer D is incorrect because a default gateway is used to perform routing functions. For more information, see the "Configuring and Verifying Network Connectivity" section.

11. A. The Internet uses the TCP/IP protocol. Answer B is incorrect because IPX is the Novell NetWare standard protocol. Answer C is incorrect because NTFS is a type of file system used by Windows NT. Answer D is incorrect because NetBIOS is a non-routable protocol used by simple local area networks. For more information, see the "Configuring and Verifying Network Connectivity" section.

12. B. The server does not exist in the DNS table, so the domain name cannot be resolved to the IP address. Answer A is incorrect because a WINS server is used to map NetBIOS names to IP addresses. Answer C is incorrect because the LMHOSTS file is used to map NetBIOS names to IP addresses. Answer D is incorrect because the subnet mask is fine if the technician can ping the IP address. For more information, see the "Configuring and Verifying Network Connectivity" section.

13. D. The `/etc` file system is from a Unix installation. Answer A is incorrect because this should be used for an OS/2 installation. Answer B is incorrect because the Windows ERD disk should be used for an NT server. Answer C is incorrect because the `startup.ncf` file configures boot options for a NetWare server. For more information, see the "Installing the NOS" section.

14. C. A Class C address uses the range of 192–223 as the first octet. Answer A is incorrect because this range is for a Class A address. Answer B is incorrect because this range is used for a Class B address. Answer D is incorrect because this address is used for broadcasts. For more information, see the "Configuring and Verifying Network Connectivity" section.

15. D. A proxy server is used to forward requests on behalf of other clients. The proxy is configured with an external IP to access the Internet. Answer A is incorrect because a gateway is used to route TCP/IP traffic. Answer B is incorrect because a DHCP server is used to automatically assign IP addresses to devices on a network. Answer C is incorrect because a firewall is used to protect an internal LAN from external Internet access. For more information, see the "Configuring and Verifying Network Connectivity" section.

16. B. `ipconfig` will show the network configuration of an NT server. Answer A is incorrect because `ifconfig` is used by Unix servers. Answer C is incorrect because the `netcfg` command does not exist. Answer D is incorrect because `nwconfig` is used to administer a NetWare server. For more information, see the "Configuring and Verifying Network Connectivity" section.

17. A. Without a DNS server set, the client will not be able to connect to a machine using domain names. Answer B is incorrect because the client can connect to the network. Answer C is incorrect because the WINS server maps NetBIOS names to IP addresses. Answer D is incorrect because the client did receive an IP address and connected to the network. For more information, see the "Configuring and Verifying Network Connectivity" section.

18. A. A new driver needs to be loaded for the network card to be compatible with the OS upgrade. Answer B is incorrect because there is no need to reinstall the OS. Answer C is incorrect because there is nothing wrong with the network card. Answer D is incorrect because there is nothing wrong with the network card. For more information, see the "Applying Patches and Service Packs" section.

19. C. The `ifconfig` command is used to configure Unix networking. Answers A and B are incorrect because `ipconfig` is a command used to verify Windows networking configurations. Answer D is incorrect because `inetcfg` is used to configure NetWare networking. For more information, see the "Configuring and Verifying Network Connectivity" section.

20. B. A Windows ERD (Emergency Rescue Disk) will be needed to recover from the error. Answer A is incorrect because an OS/2 startup disk will not fix a Windows NT system. Answer C is incorrect because a Unix boot disk will not a fix a Windows NT system. Answer D is incorrect because a NetWare installation disk will not fix a Windows NT system. For more information, see the "Installing the NOS" section.

Scenarios

1. The first step is in the installation is to examine the documentation and any `readme` files to ensure hardware compatibility and any issues related to installing a Web server.

   Next, you should start the server with the OS install boot disk or CD-ROM. The disk partitions should now be configured and formatted with the NTFS file system, so that enhanced NT security can be used. A separate partition should be made for the Windows NT system files, and another for the Web server files. If external users are accessing this Web site from the Internet, you do not want to take the chance of them possibly being able to access the system files.

   Now you can install the operating system to the system partition that was created in the previous step. When the installation is finished, you need to restart the server. After the server reboots, you need to enter some configuration parameters such as the license key, language settings, and domain/workgroup configuration. Because this server will be used to serve Web pages to external users, it should be configured as a stand-alone server without any domain functions.

   Now you need to configure the network settings. Use the Class B IP addresses issued by your ISP. Because this is a Web server being accessed by external users, it will not be able to use an internal private IP address. Verify the network settings and connectivity by checking the values displayed from the `ipconfig` command. Try to ping another server to ensure connectivity.

   Finally, when the base OS installation is completed, apply the latest service packs and patches to bring the OS system files and related programs up to date.

2. You need to install a DNS server and WINS server on the network. The DNS server will keep a table mapping domain names to IP addresses, so that Unix machines on the network can be referred to by their name rather than an IP address. The WINS server will map Windows NetBIOS names to IP addresses to enable Windows machines to be referred to by their names rather than IP addresses.

Using Services and Monitoring Tools

CHAPTER

6

◆   ◆   ◆   ◆

CHAPTER PRE-TEST

1. What does SNMP stand for?

2. What are four protocol operations used by SNMP?

3. List some typical thresholds in SNMP.

4. What is the monitoring utility that comes with Windows NT called?

5. What is the monitoring utility built into NetWare called?

6. What is the event utility used to view event logs called in Windows NT/2000?

7. What is the event utility used to log events in most versions of Unix?

8. What is the tape backup software called in Windows NT/2000?

9. Briefly describe what a server baseline is.

✦ Answers to these questions can be found at the end of the chapter. ✦

This chapter discusses some of the tools and services that are used in today's server environments. It covers the SNMP protocol, including what it is, and how it is used. I also look at some server monitoring tools with a focus on NT's Performance Monitor utility and Novell's MONITOR utility. It would be almost impossible to look at all the tools available that can perform these tasks because there are so many. However, I suggest that you use a monitoring tool capable of monitoring information from many devices, and multiple server operating systems if your computer environment consists of more than one network operation system. This chapter also discusses event logs, backup software, how to create server baselines, and documenting server configurations.

Using Tools and Services

 2.7 Install service tools (SNMP, backup software, system monitoring agents, events logs, etc)

You have many different tools available for managing your server environment. The good thing is that you have a choice as to which tools you want to use. The bad thing is that it can be hard to pick the right tool. No matter which software tool you choose, make sure it has good documentation, is well-regarded by other computer professionals, and has good vendor support. You do not want to waste your valuable time troubleshooting a program that is designed to help you measure performance, get statistics, and help you to troubleshoot the server environment. It should be simple to use, and the documentation should provide you with the information necessary to accomplish your goals. In this section, I take a look at some tools and services that you will need to use in the server environment. These include SNMP, monitoring agents, event logs, and tape backup software.

Monitoring the network with SNMP

The simple network management protocol (SNMP) is widely used to control network communications devices using TCP/IP. This network management protocol collects statistics from devices on your TCP/IP network, and most network analysis software can interface to SNMP. An SNMP monitor is a very useful tool in an environment that has any degree of complexity. The network device loads the agent that collects information, and forwards the information to a network management console. The devices can also be configured with threshold parameters. When the thresholds are met, an alert message, called a *trap,* is sent to the management console. A management console is an application, running on another computer, where traps are monitored and recorded. You can configure the management console to perform a certain action when the alert message is received. For example, you could have the management software send you an alert via e-mail or pager. Some typical thresholds are the following:

✦ Port malfunctions

✦ Network congestion

✦ Temperature out of range

✦ Packet collisions

✦ Device failures

Exam Tip   SNMP is the primary protocol for managing networks because almost all devices are SNMP-enabled.

There are two versions of SNMP in use as of the writing of this book. SNMP version 1 (SNMPv1), and SNMP version 2 (SNMPv2). Both versions have many things in common, but SNMPv2 offers several enhancements, such as additional protocol operations. SNMPv2 has largely replaced SNMPv1, although you will still find SNMPv1 in use on older devices.

Tip   Standardization of SNMP version 3 (SNMPv3) is now in the works.

An SNMP managed network consists of three key components, managed devices, agents, and network management systems (NMS).

A *managed device* is typically a network node that contains a SNMP agent and resides on a managed network. Managed devices will collect and store management information and make this information available to network management systems.

An *agent* is a software program that resides in a managed device. An agent takes the management information on the devices and translates that information into a form that is compatible with SNMP. For example, on Windows NT/2000 servers the SNMP agent is implemented by starting the SNMP services (`SNMP.exe`).

A *network management system* executes applications that monitor and control managed devices. Network management systems provide the majority of the processing and memory resources required for network management.

The NMS monitors *objects* and *instances*. Managed objects are accessed via a virtual information store referred to as the *Management Information Base* (MIB). An MIB is a collection of information and is organized hierarchically. MIBs are accessed using a network management protocol such as SNMP. Each object type is named by an *object identifier,* which is an administratively assigned name. The object type together with and object instance serves to uniquely identify a specific instance of the object. A text string called the *descriptor* is used to refer to the object type. For example, a list of active TCP circuits in a particular host computer is an object. An object instance is a single active TCP circuit in a particular host computer. Managed objects can either be scalar (defining a single object instance), or tabular (defining multiple, related instances).

SNMP is actually a simple request/response protocol, which means that the NMS issues a request, and the managed devices return responses. This is implemented by using one of four protocol operations (SNMPv2 has a few more protocol operations). The following are the four protocol operations that you need to know for the exam:

✦ **Get:** This operation is used by the NMS to retrieve the values of the object instances from an agent. If the agent that is responding to the Get operation cannot provide values for all object instances in the list, it will not provide any values.

✦ **GetNext:** This operation is used by the NMS to retrieve the value of the next object instance in a list contained in the agent.

✦ **Set:** This operation is used by the NMS to set the values of object instances in an agent.

✦ **Trap:** This operation is used by the agents to inform the NMS of a significant event. A managed device will send a trap to the NMS when certain types of events occur, without the NMS asking for the information.

The following is a list of additional SNMPv2 operations that are not necessary to know for the exam, but should be mentioned.

✦ **GetBulk:** This operation is used by the NMS to retrieve large blocks of data, such as multiple rows in a table. GetBulk will fill a response message with as much of the requested data as it can fit.

✦ **Inform:** This operation enables one NMS to send trap information to another NMS and then receive a response.

The NMS uses these operations to get information from the various SNMP-enabled devices on the network. The NMS sends a request message out on the network. The agent listens for the message, and then sends a response back. The NMS receives the response from the agent. Depending on your network you may be requesting information on hardware, configuration parameters, performance statistics, and so on, that relate to the current operation of the device in question.

Using monitoring tools

You will need to monitor the server's hardware (disk space usage, CPU usage/ utilization), and the primary system processes. You also need to monitor DNS, FTP, SMTP, HTTP, and POP3 services. You also need to keep track of the status messages that are generated by the operating system. To make this process easier, you should try to automate as much of it as possible. The following sections cover two of the most commonly used monitoring tools: Performance Monitor for Windows NT and 2000, and the MONITOR utility for NetWare.

Windows Performance Monitor

The Performance Monitor utility is included in the Windows NT Server and Workstation versions. Performance Monitor is called System Monitor in Windows 2000, and has some improvements over its predecessor but it is relatively the same.

Performance Monitor was created to assist administrators to perform capacity planning. However, it is also used to perform a wide variety of troubleshooting activities, including network troubleshooting. Performance Monitor can show broad or very detailed views of computer performance.

Start Performance Monitory by selecting Start ⇨ Programs ⇨ Administrative Tools ⇨ Performance Monitor. You can use Performance Monitor to view performance statistics for objects on you system or other computers on the network. With Performance Monitor, you can:

✦ View data in charts in real time

✦ Monitor multiple computers simultaneously

✦ Monitor any NT computer in the network

✦ Export data for use in other programs, such as a database

✦ Use alerts to trigger a program or message when a predetermined threshold is met or exceeded

✦ Log data over time from one computer or several

✦ Archive logged data

✦ Save your settings for later recall

Performance Monitor uses *counters* to report on activity, demand, and space used by these objects. Some objects have more than one instance because there may be multiple processors or network cards in the server, or it may be running a program more than once.

The objects represent threads, processes, sections of shared memory, and physical devices. The monitor uses *counters* to measure certain aspects of these objects and reports on activity, load, and resources used by them. Many software vendors add their own counters to Performance Monitor so that you can analyze them as well (SQL and tape backup programs are a couple of examples). Some of the objects you can monitor are:

✦ **Processor:** The hardware that executes program instructions

✦ **Memory:** RAM that stores data

✦ **Physical Disk:** RAID devices or actual hard disks

✦ **Logical Disk:** Disk partitions

✦ **Paging file:** Virtual memory storage

✦ **Cache:** Holds recently used data in memory

✦ **Process:** Typically software or a program that is loaded and running

✦ **Thread:** The portion of a process that uses a processor

✦ **System:** Counters that apply to all system software and hardware

✦ **Redirector:** The file system that redirects requests to servers

Each object can have many counters. For example, some of the counters for the PhysicalDisk object are:

✦ **Avg. Disk Queue Length:** Measures the average number of read and write operations that are waiting to access the hard disk. If this number is high, you may want to consider replacing the hard disk with a faster one.

✦ **% Disk Time:** Measures the percentage of time that the hard disk is performing reads and writes, as opposed to sitting idle. If this number is high (near 100%), you may want to consider a faster disk drive, or a RAID configuration that offers better read/write performance.

✦ **Disk Reads Bytes/sec:** Measures the disk throughput for the disk subsystem. This data is a representation of the disk hardware subsystem's capability to respond to requests for information.

✦ **Disk Reads/sec:** Measures the number of reads that the disk is able to accomplish per second. The changes in this value indicate the amount of random access to the disk. Disk fragmentation can contribute to an increased value in this counter.

✦ **Avg. Disk Bytes/Read:** Measures the average number of bytes transferred in each read of the disk system. This will help you to see if there are more random reads of this disk than there are sequential reads. A smaller value generally indicates more random reads, which may be caused by file fragmentation.

The performance monitor offers four different views to analyze the data that you are capturing. Each view has a uniquely different purpose for analyzing the information. They are as follows:

✦ Chart

✦ Report

✦ Alert

✦ Log

Using the Chart view

The Chart view enables you to monitor the performance of multiple objects and counters simultaneously, in a graphical form. Figure 6-1 is an example of the chart view.

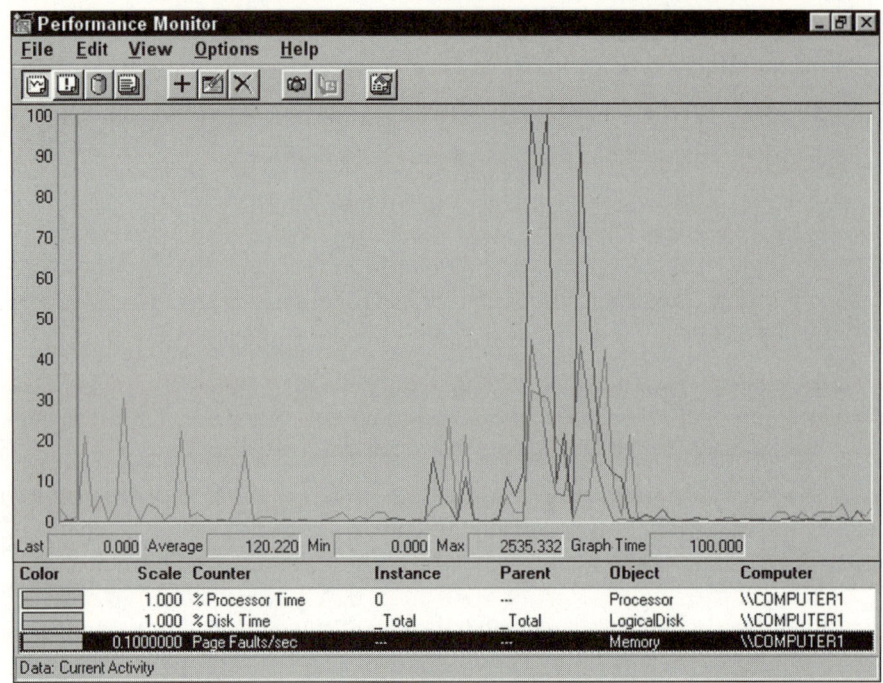

Figure 6-1: Performance Monitor Chart View

Figure 6-1 shows three different counters: % Processor Time, % Disk Time, and Page Faults/sec. Each object is displayed as a colored line in the chart. The vertical line on the left, which is red in the application, shows the progress of the monitoring function. Notice the row beneath the graph that displays real-time statistics on last, average, min, and max values. This row only shows statistics for one counter at a time, but you can select another counter by simply selecting it in the bottom pane of the window.

To add a counter to the chart, follow these steps:

1. Click Edit ⇨ Add To Chart, or click the + symbol on the toolbar. The Add to Chart dialog box appears, as shown in Figure 6-2.

2. Choose the computer you wish to monitor (the default is the one you are running Performance Monitor from).

3. Select the object, then the counter, and finally the instance.

4. Click Add to add the new counter to the chart.

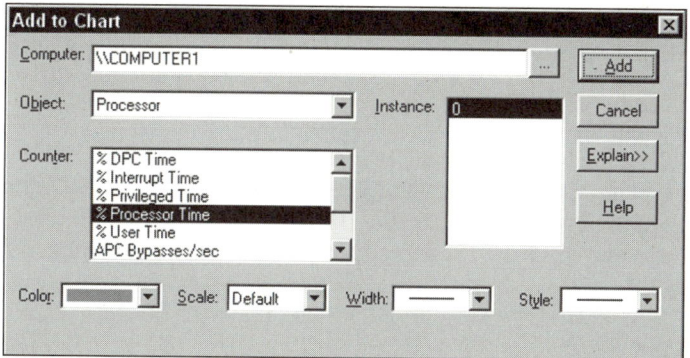

Figure 6-2: Adding a counter to the chart

At the bottom of the dialog box there are several other options to choose from. These options enable you to configure the color, scale, width, and style of the counter. You do not necessarily need to change these as the performance monitor automatically picks the next available color for each counter that you add.

Using the Log view

The Log view records counter information at specific intervals over a period of time. Figure 6-3 shows the Log view.

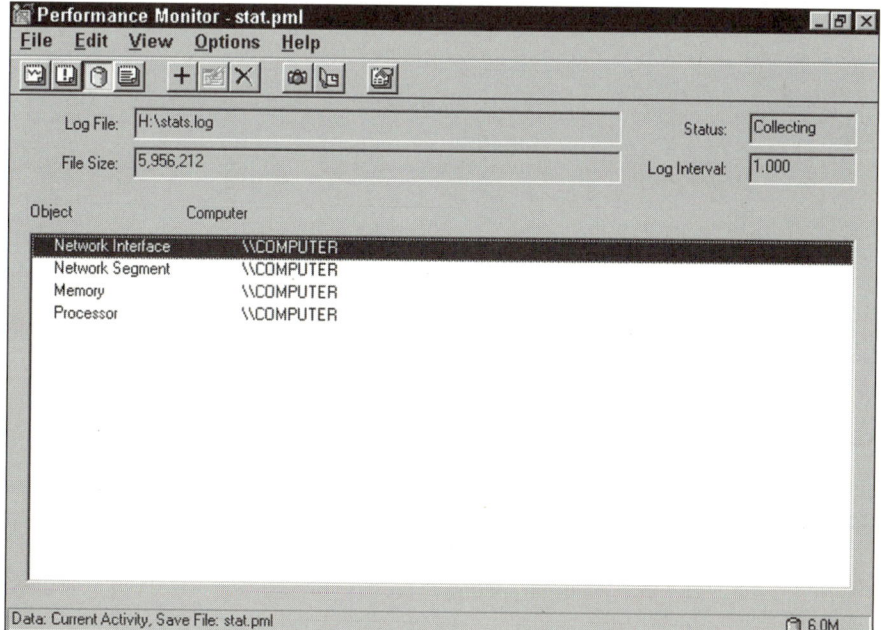

Figure 6-3: Performance Monitor Log view

You can add objects to the view as you can in the Chart view, but you can only select objects, not individual counters. All the counters for that object will be monitored.

Before logging can begin, you must click the log options button at the right of the toolbar. You must specify a directory and file name for the log file. Click the start logging button to log these objects. When you are satisfied that the log has collected enough data, you can stop it from the Options menu and view the data in chart or report view. In the Chart or Report view, click Options ➪ Data From, and select the log file.

Using the Report view

The Report view shows in a text format what the chart shows graphically. The report view lets you display constantly changing counters and instance values for selected objects. The values will appear in columns for each instance of the object. Using Report view, you can print snapshots, export the data, and adjust the report intervals. Figure 6-4 shows the Report view.

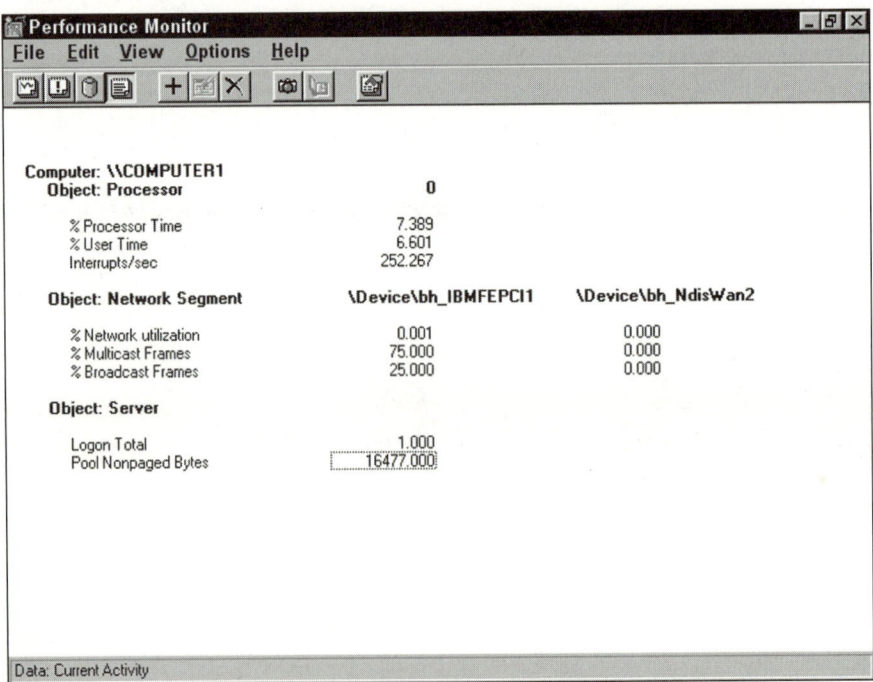

Figure 6-4: Performance Monitor Report View

Using Alerts

The Alert view can be the best part of Performance Monitor. You probably have better things to do than sitting and watching the Chart view, waiting for a problem to occur. Alert view does the watching for you, and can notify you when certain thresholds are reached. Figure 6-5 shows the alert window.

You configure the alert view the same way as the Chart view. However, there is one major difference: you must specify a threshold. You can also tell Performance Monitor to alert you if the data captured is over or under the predefined threshold. You can tell Performance Monitor to run a program for the first time or every time the threshold is met.

Figure 6-6 shows the Alert Options dialog box, which you can access by clicking the right-most button in the toolbar or by clicking Options ➪ Alert from the menu. The Alert Options dialog box allows you to send a network message to a computer or user, log an event in the event viewer's application log, and change the update frequency.

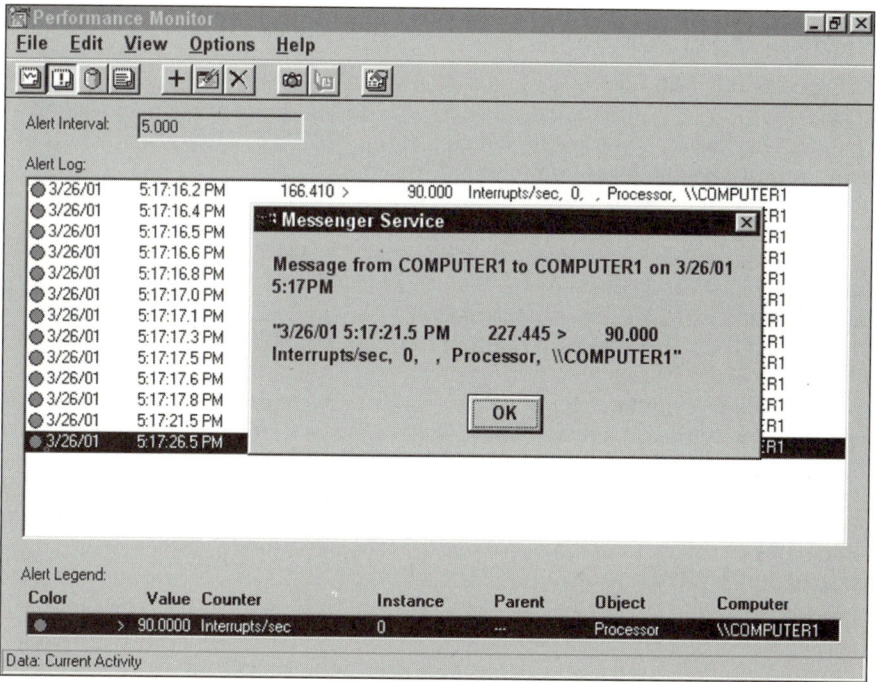

Figure 6-5: Performance Monitor Alert View

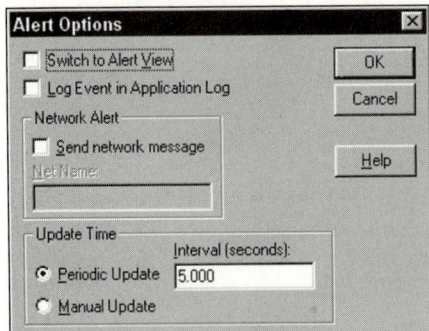

Figure 6-6: Performance Monitor Alert Options dialog box

The Windows Performance Monitor is simple to use, yet sophisticated enough to assist you in monitoring computers in the server environment. It also makes an excellent tool for performing baselines, as well as on-going monitoring.

NetWare MONITOR

The monitoring tool for NetWare is called MONITOR. This tool runs in the NetWare kernel so that it can initiate calls directly to the operating system. However, you can also use the Java-based console for monitoring. To access the MONITOR tool you need to type the following command at the console prompt.

```
[LOAD] [PATH] MONITOR
```

Using the LOAD command tells NetWare that MONITOR is a loadable module, and is only necessary if you have a batch file with the same name. You only need to specify the path if you have moved the tool from its default directory.

In many NetWare environments, administrators leave the MONITOR tool running so that they can access it quickly. There are two ways to toggle to the MONITOR screen if it is already loaded. You can press Alt-Esc to cycle through the console screens until the MONITOR screen appears. Use the bar at the top of the screen for easy navigation. The other option in Novell is to press Ctrl-Esc to pop up a numbered list of available console screens. You then must enter the correct number to display the MONITOR tool.

You can exit the monitor by hitting the Esc key until the exit confirmation box appears, or simply press Alt-F10 and then hit enter to return to the console prompt.

The MONITOR tool's general information screen lists the main performance information and statistics that you will want to look at. This general information screen consists of the following items:

✦ **Utilization:** This is an average of the server's total processing capacity that was used over the last second, expressed as a percentage. The remainder of the time is spent in an idle loop. Things you will want to watch here are:

  • Does utilization reach 100 percent?

  • Does utilization plateau or peak for a few seconds and then subside?

  • How often and when does it peak?

✦ **Server up time:** This is the amount of time that has passed since the server was started last. If you have enabled the auto-restart feature, you can use this field to determine if an error occurred and the server restarted as a result. This information is also useful in detecting power failures.

✦ **Online processors:** This is the number of enabled and online processors. The platform support module (PSM) is loaded from `startup.ncf`, which enables NetWare to use secondary CPUs in a multiprocessing server. All processors are started by default.

✦ **Total cache buffers:** This field shows how many cache buffers are currently available for file caching. The number will drop as more NetWare Loadable Module (NLM) programs are added. The higher the number is, the better performance you will get out of the server.

✦ **Dirty cache buffers:** This field is a representation of buffers that contain data that has changed but has not been written to disk. You may have a bottleneck in the system if this number continuously increases.

✦ **Long term cache hits:** This field represents the cumulative requests for disk blocks that were already in cache. The number is represented as a percentage. This means that if the data requested is already in memory, then the system does not try to read the data from disk. You can use this field to determine overall disk cache use, and if the value falls below 90 percent, you may need to consider buying more RAM. If the value falls below 90 percent, you will see excessive disk thrashes and performance degradation.

✦ **Current disk requests:** This field represents how many read requests are pending. You may have a slow hard disk if this number continuously increases.

✦ **Packet receive buffers:** This field represents how much memory was allocated for storing client requests while the server processes them. The server dynamically allocates more packet receive buffers as needed. Your buffer size ultimately depends on the network adapter.

✦ **Maximum service processes:** This field indicates how many task handlers the server can allocate to service client requests. As the number of client request increases, the server creates more service processes. If the server cannot allocate any more service processes, performance will be negatively impacted.

✦ **Current service processes:** This field represents how many task handlers are currently being used to service client requests. You can use this data to see if the server has enough free task handlers to service client requests. If the number reaches the maximum value, which is set by the Maximum Service Processes parameter, you will need to increase this maximum value. This is found under Available Options ➪ Server Parameters ➪ Communication Parameters.

✦ **Current connections:** This field represents the number of active connections whether they are licensed or not, and whether they are logged in or not.

✦ **Open files:** This field represents the number of files that are currently being accessed by the server, and by other clients. Some files are always in use because the server needs them.

NetWare dynamically allocates resources as they are needed, and if they are not available when requests are received, the operating system waits a specified amount of time to find out if existing resources become available to service the demand. The dynamically allocated services are controlled by three kinds of configurable parameters. They are as follows:

✦ **Maximum Limits:** These control the amount of server resources the operating system can allocate for a particular service.

✦ **Minimum Limits:** These settings enable the operating system to allocate a minimum amount of resources as soon as a request is received. Keep in mind that low minimum limits will slow the growth of a particular service, and high minimum limits will allow rapid growth.

✦ **Wait time limits:** This setting controls how quickly the operating system can allocate a new resource. If a request is made for a resource, and resources become available, no new resources need to be allocated. If they do not become available within the wait time, then new resources will be allocated. The wait time helps to ensure that sudden and sparse peaks of activity do not allocate unneeded resources.

There are many other things you can monitor with the MONITOR utility. You can also perform the following tasks using the utility; however, you are not limited to what is mentioned below.

✦ **Checking disk drives:** Select Storage devices in the Available Options window, and make sure the operating status is marked active for each drive.

✦ **Check free space on disk and volumes:** Do this by selecting Volumes in the Available Options window. The mounted volumes screen lists mounted volumes, their capacity, and the percentage of the volume that is full. Make sure that your SYS volume has at least 20% disk space free, and that all other volumes have at least 10% free. NetWare incorporates the Hot Fix method to ensure that data is stored safely. Data blocks are redirected from faulty blocks on the server's disk to a small portion of disk space set aside as the Hot Fix redirection area. The server will not attempt to store data in the defective blocks once it records the address of the defective block in the Hot Fix redirection area. Approximately two percent of a disk partition's space is reserved as the Hot Fix redirection area.

Using event logs

All server operating systems have event log capabilities and ways to monitor these events. In most versions of Unix, the event log is called `syslog`, while in Windows NT/2000 you would use the Event Viewer utility to view the event log. This section discusses the Windows NT/2000 event log, and how to use it in conjunction with the Unix `syslog` program. You can use the event log utilities separately, but you may find yourself working in an environment with multiple operating systems.

The purpose of the Event Viewer program in Windows NT/2000 is to view events that occur in the server environment (including other servers). When an event occurs, it is logged into the system with a certain degree of severity. The severity levels are as follows:

✦ Information (low severity)

✦ Warning (middle severity)

✦ Error (high severity)

The log entry is time-coded, and the log records the source of the event, the event ID, the user ID, the event category, and the computer name. There are three logs that are managed by the event log service and they are as follows.

✦ **System:** System entries consist of events such as browser service initialization, NIC failures, and so on.

✦ **Security:** Security entries have more to do with the auditing system such as shares, NTFS (the Windows NT proprietary file system), printing, and so on.

✦ **Application:** Application entries consist of events generated form applications such as SQL, backup software, DHCP, and so on.

Each of these log files can be saved in their native `.evt` format or as binary or delimited formats for archive and analysis purposes with a third-party program. For example, you could save the security log in delimited format and import it into almost any database, spreadsheet, or word-processing application.

A good way for dealing with event logs is to archive them and then clear the current log at set intervals. Clearing the logs is necessary because they will eventually reach the maximum storage capability. You can configure the maximum storage capacity with the Event Viewer program. You can also instruct Event Viewer on how to handle the event log when it is full. You can tell it to not log any more events when the log is full, or overwrite events as needed, or overwrite events that have exceeded a certain period of time. However, if you decide to archive and clear the current log, you will not have to worry about this. You will also find that your event logs are much more manageable. The log size that you should set your log files to depends on how busy the server is and how much data you want to store before archiving.

Unfortunately, you can't set Event Viewer to automatically archive the event logs in binary format and clear them as well, at least not without another utility. There are numerous programs out there, either for sale or for free. You may want to take a look at Appmon, which is created by Arcana (`www.arcanadev.com`). This program has a 60 day evaluation version. Appmon is a system and application monitoring tool that provides a centralized point of collection, and distribution of alert and error information.

Some of these programs are command-line utilities that work with the Windows NT task scheduler, and others are GUI-based. If you plan on using a command-line utility, make sure that you set the task scheduler service to automatically start up when NT boots. In Windows NT, you use the `AT` command to schedule jobs, and in Windows 2000, you can use the `AT` command or the Scheduled Tasks program in Control Panel. You can use the task scheduler and the archive program to automatically back up the log file at regular intervals.

Another tool is `dumpel`, which is part of the Windows NT/2000 Resource Kit. This utility will enable you to export any of the event logs in `.evt` format, or as delimited text. Being able to automate dumping files as delimited text gives you the ability to manipulate the files in various programs.

Backing up the server

Backup services are critical to your ability to recover from a disaster, and you must know how to use them properly. The major network operating systems come with backup utilities, which are discussed in this section.

There are also many excellent third party backup programs available for you to choose from. Before you choose one, be sure it is fully capable of backing up from multiple servers and workstations. These programs typically install agent programs on the computers you wish to back up. These agents will increase backup performance immensely, so make sure that you install them on the remote computers.

Cross-Reference   Backing up the server is discussed in more detail in Chapter 19, but these sections discuss the major backup programs.

SMS for NetWare

Storage Management Services (SMS) is a collection of software programs that are created by Novell to provide backup and restore services. The SMS services are actually performed by a collection of components that are independent of the operating system and hardware.

The SMS components include the following:

✦ The Storage management engine (SME) backs up and restores operations. SBACKUP is a basic SME for NetWare 5.

✦ The Storage management data requesters (SMDR) communicates between the backup program and target service agent (TSA) software

✦ The Storage device interface communicates between the SME and the storage devices

✦ Device drivers are used to control the behavior of the storage devices

✦ The Target service agents (TSAs) pass requests and commands between the SME and server database, and prepares the data for the SME

✦ The TSAProxy utility registers the workstation with the host server

Enhanced SBACKUP program enables you to back up SMS targets such as Novell Directory Services (NDS), the file system, or an individual workstation's hard disk.

The Enhanced SBACKUP retrieves and reinstates backup of data. The restore session restores to a location that you can specify. During a storage session, Enhanced SBACKUP reads backup storage media, and the target service agent compares the media data set to the existing hard disk data set.

Windows NT Backup

Windows NT Backup is a graphical utility that enables you to back up and restore the contents of your hard disks and any connected network drives. You can also restore data from tape to the original location, or somewhere else. You can decide to back up data on servers across the network, or you can install a tape drive at each server and back up the data locally.

NT Backup stores the data in the Microsoft Tape Format (MTF). Like most backup programs, NT creates a new backup set on the media each time you perform a new backup, or for that matter, each time you back up a different volume. A backup set is a collection of files, programs, and so on, along with system information on when the backup was done, who has rights to restore it, and other information.

NT 4.0 Backup can accomplish most of your backup needs, but running it manually is really the only practical solution because it does not have a built in scheduling feature. However, Windows 2000 does incorporate the scheduling feature. You are also limited to only backing up NT operating systems. You can, however, use the AT command to schedule a backup. Unfortunately, this is not easy to manage. There are many third party applications that will do the job more effectively, and have several useful backup and restore features.

 Exam Tip The advantage to using backup tools supplied by the operating system vendor is that they are compatible with the operating system.

Novell's SMS backup solution is by far a more sophisticated solution than the NT Backup program. It offers many of the advanced features that you find in a third party program, and offers an all around good solution. However, if you have an NT environment, or mixed environment, I recommend that you seek out a backup program that can handle multiple server operating systems. You should also make sure it is capable of backing up databases such as Oracle, and Microsoft SQL. Veritas BackupExec is an example of such a program. However, there are several others that can also do the job.

Performing a Server Baseline

 Objective 2.8 Perform Server baseline

A *baseline* defines the typical activity of your network servers. Keeping a baseline record of activity on a server lets you determine when activity is normal and when it is not. To create a baseline you should gather statistical information when the server is functioning normally.

 **Cross-Reference** Performing server baselines is also discussed in chapter 10.

For server statistics such as CPU usage, you should create a trend graph that plots information over a period of time. Do not make this time period too short as it may provide false information. If you need to modify the server configuration, make sure you start a new baseline record so that you can compare that to the previous original.

You should use the built-in performance monitors of the operating systems if they are available. Your other option is to purchase a third-party program capable of helping you create a baseline document automatically, or generating server health reports.

Comparing current server performance statistics against performance recorded in your baseline document will enable you to determine how performance is affected by server configuration changes. The comparison will also help you plan for future growth and to justify upgrading to new equipment or software. Most third-party health monitoring utilities enable you to view real-time graphs, or historical trends over hourly, daily, weekly, monthly, and yearly periods.

Another advantage to creating a server baseline is for troubleshooting purposes. If you know what the normal activity is on the server, you will be able to detect and recognize activity that is not normal. This may help you to determine the problem.

The following items should be included in any baseline document:

✦ **CPU utilization:** This will indicate how busy the processor is. Tracking this information will show the load on the server at peak and low times.

✦ **Cache buffers:** Cache buffers greatly increase server performance and enable workstations to access data more quickly, because reading from and writing to memory is way faster than reading from and writing to disk. Low cache buffers can cause very slow performance.

✦ **File reads and writes:** This data will help you to determine if there is a bottle-neck in the server caused by the disk I/O channel.

✦ **Disk utilization:** This is for capacity planning purposes, and for keeping a watch on server storage space. You must ensure that you never let the server run out of disk space, as it could result in a system lockup.

✦ **Running software:** This information will make it easier to spot a problem application when comparing software on different servers. Record how much RAM each application consumes, because if the server happens to get short on memory, you will be able to determine which applications use the most memory.

Documenting the Configuration

 2.9 Document the configuration

It is extremely important to document your server and network configurations. Make sure you keep records on network layout, hardware and software inventory, configurations, repairs, and backup schedules. Having this information will save you a lot of time and effort if you ever need to rebuild or replace parts of the net-work. You should keep a printed version of this documentation, as well as an elec-tronic version. You should also keep an additional copy for off-site storage.

Some items that should be kept in your server configuration documentation include:

✦ BIOS and firmware levels

✦ System board type and information

✦ RAID controller type and configuration

✦ Hard disk information (size, how many, manufacture)

✦ RAID levels and configurations

✦ Disk array configurations

✦ Performance statistics

✦ Network operating system configuration and settings

✦ External devices and their configurations

✦ Any patches or updates added to the operating system and devices

✦ Driver updates

✦ SNMP devices and the configuration of them

✦ Monitoring agents in use and their configurations

✦ Event log utilities

✦ Backup software configuration

Key Point Summary

This chapter focused on some of the tools and services that are available in different server operating systems. The chapter discussed SNMP, monitoring agents, event log analysis, and backup software programs. I also took a look at creating a server baseline for performance issues and troubleshooting, and what you should include in your server configuration document. Keep the following points in mind for the exam:

✦ Simple Network Management Protocol (SNMP) is widely used to control network communications devices using TCP/IP.

✦ Agent configured devices send SNMP traps to a management console.

✦ There are two versions of SNMP: SNMPv1 and SNMPv2.

✦ There are four main protocol operations: Get, GetNext, Set, and Trap.

✦ Monitoring systems enable administrators to monitor their systems effectively and accurately.

✦ Pay special attention to event logs, or system logs, as they provide vital information about your systems.

✦ Good event log systems should be able to send remote notification messages to recipients.

✦ Make sure the backup system you choose is capable of backing up multiple environments and databases.

✦ A server baseline defines the typical activity of your network servers.

✦ It is very important to document your server and network configurations, as it will save you a lot of effort should you need to rebuild or replace equipment.

✦   ✦   ✦

STUDY GUIDE

The Study Guide section provides you with the opportunity to test your knowledge about service tools and monitoring systems. The Assessment Questions provide practice for the test, and the Scenarios provide practice with real situations. If you get any questions wrong, use the answers to determine the part of the chapter you should review before continuing.

Assessment Questions

1. Which protocol is used to perform network management?

    A. SNAP

    B. SMTP

    C. MIB

    D. SNMP

2. In SNMP, what does the agent software do?

    A. Collects data and sends it via e-mail to a predetermined address.

    B. Collects information and forwards it to an NMS.

    C. Collects data and forwards the information to a server operating system.

    D. It simply collects the data, and you must manually seek the information using a NMS.

3. What do you configure on SNMP devices to enable them to send messages to the NMS?

    A. Traps

    B. Alerts

    C. MIBs

    D. PASS

4. What are some typical SNMP thresholds?

    A. Port malfunctions

    B. Network congestion

    C. Packet collisions

    D. Device failures

    E. All of the above

5. What are the two current versions of SNMP called?

    A. SNMPvA and SNMPvB

    B. SNMPv1 and SNMPv2

    C. SNMPv4 and SMPv5

    D. SNMPvC and SNMPvD

6. There are three key components in an SNMP managed network. Based on the list below, which ones are correct?

    I. Managed devices

    II. Thresholds

    III. Agents

    IV. NMS

    A. I and IV only

    B. I, III, and IV only

    C. I, II, and III only

    D. II and III only

7. Which of the following protocol operations is used to retrieve information from an SNMP agent?

    A. Set

    B. GetNext

    C. Get

    D. Trap

8. You decide that you are going to upgrade your third-party monitoring system to the latest version. What conditions should be met before upgrading?

    A. You have confirmed that you are upgrading to the correct version.

    B. You have printed the documentation and read it thoroughly.

    C. You have confirmed that the system requirements are met for the agent.

    D. You have removed all the SNMP traps prior to upgrading.

9. How do you access the Performance Monitor in Windows NT?

    A. Start Menu ⇨ Control Panel ⇨ Performance Monitor

    B. At the command prompt, type **WINPERF**

    C. Start Menu ⇨ Programs ⇨ Administrative Tools

    D. It is located on the desktop

10. How do you load the MONITOR utility in Novell?

    A. Start ⇨ Sys:

    B. At the console prompt, type **MONITOR**.

    C. At the console prompt, type **START MONITOR**.

    D. Choose MONITOR from the Novell Console menu.

11. What is the event log utility used in Windows NT/2000 called?

    A. Event Viewer

    B. Log Viewer

    C. EventReporter

    D. System Log Viewer

12. What is the logging program in Unix that stores system and applications events in log files called?

    A. `eventlog`

    B. `sysevt`

    C. `syslog`

    D. `alrtlog`

13. What is the advantage of using the backup software included in the server operating system?

    A. Compatibility with the operating system environment.

    B. It is cheap.

    C. It has robust features.

    D. The ability to back up multiple operating system environments.

14. When is the best time to take server baseline statistics?

    A. When the server is behaving erratically

    B. When the server is functioning normally

    C. During peak loads

    D. In the morning when everyone logs on to the system

15. What is an import aspect to cover in the server configuration?

    A. Network documentation

    B. Disaster recovery documentation

    C. Documenting the server configuration

    D. RAID levels

Scenarios

1. You are using Windows NT server in you computer environment. Your users are complaining of latency issues on the network. What software tool that comes with NT could you use, and how would you use it effectively?

Answers to Chapter Questions

Chapter pre-test

1. SNMP stands for Simple Network Management Protocol.

2. The four SNMP protocol operations are: Get, GetNext, Set, and Trap.

3. Port malfunctions, network congestion, temperature out of range, packet collisions, and device failures, are all possible SNMP thresholds.

4. Performance Monitor is the monitoring utility in Windows NT.

5. MONITOR is the NetWare monitoring utility.

6. Event Viewer is the Windows NT utility used to view event logs.

7. The `syslog` utility is used to view system logs in Unix.

8. Windows NT Backup is the backup utility that comes with Windows NT.

9. A server baseline defines the typical activity of your network servers.

Assessment questions

1. D. SNMP, the Simple Network Management Protocol, is used to control network communications devices using TCP/IP. The SNMP protocol collects statistics from devices on the TCP/IP networks. Answer A is incorrect because SNAP doesn't stand for anything. Answer B is incorrect because SMTP is the Simple Mail Transfer Protocol. Answer C is incorrect because the MIB is the Management Information Base, which is a component of SNMP. For more information, see the "Monitoring the network with SNMP" section.

2. B. The agent software that is loaded by the devices collects information and forwards the information to a Network Management System (NMS). Answer A is incorrect because the NMS software has e-mail capabilities, not the agent. Answer C is incorrect because the information has to go to an NMS, not the server operating system. Answer D is incorrect because manually seeking the information defeats the purpose of having agents on the devices. For more information, see the "Monitoring the network with SNMP" section.

3. A. Traps are configured on SNMP devices to allow them to send alerts to the NMS. Answers B, C, and D are all incorrect because they are not items that can be configured to send alerts. For more information, see the "Monitoring the network with SNMP" section.

4. E. All of these items are typical SNMP thresholds that traps can be set for. For more information, see the "Monitoring the network with SNMP" section.

5. B. SNMPv1 and SNMPv2 are the current versions of SNMP. SNMPv3 was in the works at the time of writing. For more information, see the "Monitoring the network with SNMP" section.

6. B. Managed devices, agents, and the NMS are the three key components in an SNMP managed network. Thresholds are part of the network, but are configured on the managed devices. For more information, see the "Monitoring the network with SNMP" section.

7. C. The Get operation is used by the NMS to retrieve values of the object instances from an agent. Answer A is incorrect because the Set operation is used to set the value of an instance. Answer B is incorrect because the GetNext operation retrieves the value of the next instance. Answer D is incorrect because the Trap operation sends an event to the NMS. For more information, see the "Monitoring the network with SNMP" section.

8. C. You should make sure that the current version of your operating system is compatible with the latest version of the third-party monitoring system. You may find out that it is intended for the most recent release of your server operating system, or you may be required to have a certain service pack or hot fix installed. Answer A is incorrect because you should ensure that you are not going to upgrade to the wrong version. Answer B is incorrect because this is not a condition that needs to be met before installing the upgrade. This is something that you should do prior to actually installing the original software. Answer D is incorrect because removing all the SNMP traps will only cause you more work as you will have to recreate them. There is no need to remove the traps. For more information, see the "Using monitoring tools" section.

9. C. You can access to the Performance monitor by selecting Start ⇨ Programs ⇨ Administrative Tools, and choosing Performance Monitor from the list. Answer A is incorrect because Performance Monitor is not located in the control panel. Answer B is incorrect because this is a fake command. The correct command to start Performance Monitor from the command prompt is `perfmon`. Answer D is incorrect because there is no shortcut to Performance Monitor on the desktop, unless you have created a shortcut to it. For more information, see the "Windows Performance Monitor" section.

10. B. You just need to type the word MONITOR from the console prompt to start the Novell MONITOR utility. For more information, see the "NetWare MONITOR" section.

11. A. The event log utility used for viewing the logs is called Event Viewer in Windows NT/2000. It can be accessed by selecting Start ⇨ Programs ⇨ Administrative Tools. Answers B and D are incorrect because there are no such Windows utilities. Answer C is incorrect because EventReporter is a third-party utility. For more information, see the "Using event logs" section.

12. C. Syslog is the logging program in most versions of Unix that stores system and applications events in log files. Answers A, B, and D aren't real utilities. Refer to the Event Logs section in this chapter for more information. For more information, see the "Using event logs" section.

13. A. The only real advantage is compatibility with the operating system environment. Answer B is incorrect because some operating system vendors charge an additional fee for including the backup software. Answer C is incorrect because most backup programs that come with the operating system are not as robust as third party programs. Answer D is incorrect because this is false for most operating system backup programs. However, NetWare's backup utility has the ability to backup NT computers. For more information, see the "Backing up the server" section.

14. B. You should always want to perform a baseline operation when the server is performing under normal conditions. All the other answers are incorrect because this would give you false data for your baseline. For more information, see the "Performing a Server Baseline" section.

15. C. Ensuring you have good documentation on your server configurations will make them easier to troubleshoot when problems occur, and easier to recover in the event of a disaster. For more information, see the "Documenting the Configuration" section.

Scenarios

1. Under Windows NT you would use Performance Monitor to analyze your server environment. You could make use of the Chart mode by selecting the proper objects and adding the appropriate counters for real time monitoring. Some of these counters are found under the Network Segment and Network Interface objects. They could include: % Broadcast Frames, % Multicast Frames, % Network Utilization, Packets/sec, and Packets Sent/sec. You would use the Log mode to do some extensive logging over the course of the day, week, and so on. At the end of each day you could export the log files and exam them. You would also configure the Alert mode to notify you automatically if any of the thresholds that you set on the object counters were met. You may want to set thresholds on the %Network Utilization, because this counter should not be consistently higher than 50%.

Upgrading

Upgrading is a constant task when maintaining a network server. You may need to add new processors to handle the increase of new workloads, or new hard drives to increase storage space. Upgrading memory and service tools will be another important part of your job. The most important step before performing any upgrade procedure is to make a full backup of the current system and verify the backup is valid. Some administrators have made the mistake of not verifying the system backup, only to find out the hard way that the backups are bad and cannot be used to restore the system.

This Part focuses on the proper procedures to follow when upgrading a server, and how not to lose any data in the process. More than just servers are covered in these chapters; even uninterruptible power supplies must be upgraded eventually. The chapters in this Part provide you with an overall understanding of upgrading servers and server peripherals. Twelve percent of the exam is dedicated to upgrading, and this Part covers each objective so you will be fully prepared.

Upgrading Motherboard Components

CHAPTER PRE-TEST

1. How does memory caching affect server performance?

2. What does CPU stepping refer to?

3. What is multiprocessing?

4. What is the difference between SRAM and DRAM?

5. How does synchronous RAM differ from asynchronous RAM?

6. How does ECC memory prevent server crashes?

7. How does bus width affect I/O performance?

8. What is an AGP slot?

9. Explain the concept of bus mastering.

10. Describe hot-plug PCI.

✦ Answers to these questions can be found at the end of the chapter. ✦

Upgrading hardware and software on your server is a standard job for a server technician. As user demand begins to outgrow your server resources, you must upgrade the components of your server as required to preserve system performance. Updating the motherboard components of a server can be one of the most complex upgrades to perform, as you are dealing with the core components of the server. This chapter discusses upgrading motherboard components such as the CPU, memory, and BIOS and firmware. Standard upgrading practices are also detailed, including backing up your system, and an upgrade checklist that should be followed when performing any type of hardware or software upgrade.

Exam Tip Although the "Perform upgrade checklist" objective appears several times on the Server+ objectives, it is a general list applicable to all types of server upgrades, and is discussed in this chapter.

Backing up Before Upgrading

Objective

3.1 Perform full backup

- Verify backup

Before you upgrade any components of your system, you must perform a full backup of your current system. Any time an integral piece of your server is changed, whether it is the CPU, memory, or other peripheral, there is the possibility that important data on your server could be corrupted or destroyed. You must always be able to revert to your original configuration with little downtime.

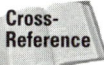

Cross-Reference Detailed procedures for backing up and restoring are covered in Chapter 19.

Perform a full backup of your system to tape or other media, and verify that the backup data is there and available. Do a restore of some test files, and verify that they are available and working after the restore. It is pointless to perform a backup without verifying that it actually worked.

In the Real World Verifying your backups is one of the most important jobs of the server technician. It is no good just to perform a backup, because your backup software might say that the backup was successful, but a hardware problem might cause the tapes to be rendered useless. Do a test restore at least once a month to verify that the backup and restore procedures are working properly.

Central Processing Unit

The CPU (central processing unit) is the main component of the server. It is the brains and intelligence that controls all aspects of server operations. It processes both program instructions and program data. It is no wonder that upgrading CPU power in a server is one of the most common upgrades you can perform to improve server performance. If your Network Operating System and application programs can take advantage of more than one processor, you should definitely implement this strategy.

Exam Tip   For the exam, have a good grasp of the various CPU concepts, especially caching and multiprocessing.

CPU concepts

In order to fully understand how CPU technology works, you should know a number of terms and concepts used to describe their functionality.

Clock frequency

The *clock frequency* of a CPU refers to how often its internal clock "ticks." Each tick represents something being performed in the CPU. The faster the ticking, the faster each instruction is being processed. The clock frequency is measured in Megahertz (MHz).

Cache

As CPU clock speeds increased, fetching data stored in RAM began to create a performance bottleneck. Therefore, a special RAM buffer, or cache, was introduced with the advent of the Intel 80486 processor. This cache memory was built directly onto the CPU and called *Level 1 cache*. Level 1 cache retains the most recently used data, so if the CPU needs that information again, it is readily available rather than having to seek it from the slower system RAM.

Although Level 1 cache greatly increased CPU performance, the amount of data that can be physically stored on the CPU is limited. Therefore, a second cache layer called *Level 2 cache* was created to increase performance even further. Although Level 2 cache is larger, it is slower than level 1 cache because it is located off the CPU between the processor and system RAM. See Figure 7-1 for the relationship between the CPU, Level 1 cache, Level 2 cache, and RAM.

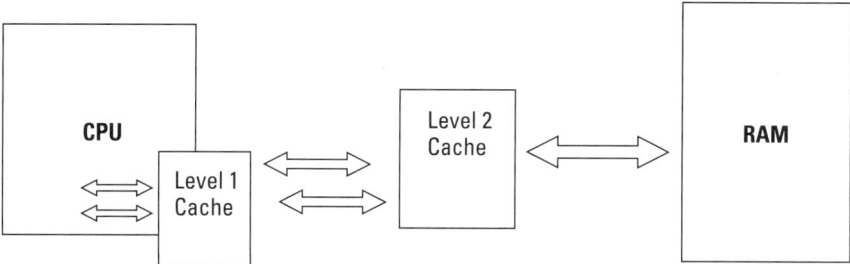

Figure 7-1: The relationship between the CPU, Level 1 and 2 cache, and RAM

Multiprocessing

Multiprocessing simply means a system that has more than one processor. In order for this to work, multiprocessing must be supported by both your hardware and your software. If your operating system does not recognize other processors, it will not use them.

There are two types of multiprocessing: symmetric and asymmetric. Because of its higher performance and efficiency, most modern systems use Symmetric Multi-Processing (SMP). SMP is the ability of the operating system to assign tasks to any of the processors in the system. This enables the operating system to balance the load of the available processors and limit the amount of unused CPU clock cycles.

In asymmetrical processing, certain processors are designated only for certain tasks. Asymmetrical processing is not as efficient at using CPU clock cycles as symmetrical processing. Because specific tasks are assigned to individual CPUs, it is quite possible that one CPU can be nearly idle while other CPUs in the server are running at full capacity.

CPU architectures

You do not need to know the history of CPU architectures for the exam, but the following list of CPU family types is helpful in understanding the progression of CPU technology.

- ✦ **8088:** This was the first Intel chip used in PCs. It was actually less powerful than the 16-bit 8086 chip that came out around the same time, but because of cheaper PC boards that used 8-bit technology, the 8-bit 8088 chip was favored.

- ✦ **8086:** This chip was very similar to the 8088 chip, but utilized a 16-bit bus for greater data bandwidth. Its original clock speed was 4.77MHz, but a later version was released running at 8MHz.

- ✦ **80286:** The next processor leap was to the 80286 processor, which doubled the speed of the earlier 8086 and 8088 processors. It could run up to clock speeds of 20 MHz and address up to 16MB of memory. It also introduced the concept of protected modes. *Protected mode* enables each application to run in its own section of memory without interference from other programs, preventing one from affecting another.

✦ **80386:** The 80386 processor introduced advanced 32-bit operations. With clock speeds of 33MHz, and later released in 40MHz versions, the 80386 again made a giant leap in processor speed. The 386 processor was the first to use full-protected and virtual modes, which paved the way for graphical operating systems like Microsoft Windows A 16-bit SX version came out for lower cost PCs, which was also popular for early portable laptop PCs.

✦ **80486:** Although still running as a 32-bit processor, the 80486 processor boasted faster clock speeds and more efficient instruction handling than its predecessors. The 486 was the first chip to feature caching. In later versions, internal clock doubling and tripling of the processor led to even faster speeds, but because the processor was running faster than the memory bus, the efficiency of the CPU diminished at higher levels. These unprecedented clock speeds introduced a new problem, heat. To combat the heat problems, new heat sink devices were introduced to aid in cooling these processors. Chip vendors AMD and Cyrix gained in popularity at this time with the success of their 486 chip.

✦ **Pentium:** Intel brought in 64-bit-level computing with the Pentium Processor introduced in 1993. Using a superscalar design, the Pentium is capable of executing two instructions per clock cycle. The separate caches and the pipelined floating-point unit increase its performance beyond the *x*86 chips. A floating-point unit, also known as math coprocessor, enables certain applications to perform mathematic calculations faster.

✦ **Pentium Pro:** The Pentium Pro was a dramatic change from the original Pentium. The method for executing instructions changed by translating them into smaller microinstructions and executing these on the internal CPU core. Optimized for 32-bit code, the Pentium Pro includes an on-board Level 2 cache that communicates with the CPU at full processor speed. It can be used in a multiprocessor system with up to four CPU's. (The Pentium and Pentium II can only be used in a dual-CPU system.)

✦ **Pentium II:** Although the Pentium II is an advancement over the Pentium Pro, the Pro still has some features that may make it more advantageous in a server. The Pentium II utilizes an on-board Level 2 cache. The cache and CPU were placed separately on a special SEC (Single Edge Contact) daughterboard that plugs into the motherboard. Unlike the Pentium Pro, the Pentium II only communicates with the cache at half the processor speed. However, architectural changes within the chip minimize these supposed 'downgrades'. In addition, for servers performing multimedia applications, the Pentium II added extra MMX instructions not included on the Pentium Pro.

✦ **Pentium Xeon:** Available for both the Pentium II and Pentium III architectures, the Xeon CPU acts in many ways similar to the Pentium Pro. It contains a very large Level 2 cache that can operate at the same speed as the newer high-clock rate CPU's. Manufactured especially for the server and high-end workstation market, the Xeon's multiprocessor support allows for quad-CPU systems, and even eight CPU multiprocessor systems.

✦ **Pentium III:** The Pentium III is considered a small upgrade from the Pentium II processor. It does boasts higher clock speeds, 70 new MMX instructions for 3D video performance (which means little to server performance), and can run on a 100MHz or 133MHz system bus.

✦ **Pentium 4:** The Pentium 4 is the latest member of the Intel Pentium family. Boasting three times the bandwidth of the Pentium III, the Pentium 4 is a 32-bit processor using a 100MHz system bus. It currently comes in speeds of 1.4 and 1.5 GHz. It also offers the most advanced performance for demanding video and multimedia applications.

Voltage

The voltage level of a CPU chip is an important concept that is often overlooked. The more voltage a CPU uses, the hotter it gets. In pre-486 days, 5 volt CPUs were the normal power rating. In order to keep heat and power consumption down in future processors, designers began to use 3.3 volts. In the most modern CPU architectures, a dual-voltage system has been implemented. Using a voltage regulator, the external CPU voltage is still at 3.3 volts to remain compatible with the motherboard and other components. Internally, the CPU uses less than 3 volts, with various manufacturers using anywhere from 2.0 volts or less to 2.9 volts.

Cooling

In the 386 and earlier CPU architectures, the concept of CPU cooling was not that important, but as the clock speeds of the CPU began to double and quadruple with the 486 family of processors, the need for a cooling mechanism was mandatory. If a CPU chip begins to overheat, it starts to malfunction, and this can result in strange and irregular behavior, including freezes, reboots, and application errors. CPU makers began to include heat sinks and fans on their CPU's to keep them cool. A heat sink is simply a piece of metal, usually aluminum, that is placed on top of the CPU to increase the surface area of the chip and enable heat to dissipate in greater amount through protruding fins projecting out from the top of the heat sink. In all modern processors, and fan is built into the heat sink to increase cooling.

Types of CPU sockets

The type of socket or slot that the CPU plugs into on the motherboard has changed dramatically over the years. The technician must be careful in verifying the proper socket type of CPU before an upgrade. The following is a list of the most common types of CPU sockets and slots.

✦ **Socket 1:** This socket is found on 486 motherboards and supports 486 chips. It contains 169 pins and operates at 5 volts.

✦ **Socket 2:** The next socket from Intel was a minor upgrade from the Socket 1. It has 238 pins and is 5 volt. It supports all the Socket 1 chips and adds support for the Pentium OverDrive.

✦ **Socket 3:** The next Intel socket contains 237 pins and operates at 5 volts, but can also operate at 3.3 volts. This can be switched using a jumper setting on the motherboard. It is backward-compatible with Socket 2 processors.

✦ **Socket 4:** This type of Intel socket was introduced with the Pentium class of machines. The socket has 273 pins, and operates at 5 volts. It supports only the low-end Pentium 60MHz-66MHz and the Overdrive because these chips are the only Pentiums operating at 5 volts.

✦ **Socket 5:** This socket supports the later Pentium machines from 75 MHz to 133 MHz. It has 320 pins and operates at 3.3 volts. Socket 5 has been replaced by the Socket 7.

✦ **Socket 6:** A little-used socket architecture that was made for late 486 models, but with the introduction of the Pentium, was quickly made obsolete.

✦ **Socket 7:** This is the most widely used socket. It contains 321 pins and operates in the 2.5 to 3.3 volt range. It supports most modern Pentium-class, AMD, and Cyrix chips. This type of socket introduced the voltage regulator that makes internal voltages lower than the external 3.3 volt motherboard standard.

✦ **Socket 8:** A socket used for Pentium Pro CPUs, it contains 387 pins and operates at 3.1 to 3.3 volts. It is very large compared to other socket types because the Pentium Pro's onboard Level 2 cache made the chip much larger than others.

✦ **Slot 1:** With the introduction of this new type of slot, Intel moved the CPU socket onto a daughtercard that plugs into the motherboard. This provides faster communication between the processor and Level 2 cache, as the cache module itself was installed on the daughterboard. The CPU can communicate with the cache at half its clock speed. The CPU slot has 242 pins and operates at 2.8 to 3.3 volts.

✦ **Slot 2:** A slot design that was introduced with newer Pentium III chips. The Slot 2 features a wider pin connector than the Slot 1, using 330 pins. In contrast to the Slot 1, the CPU can communicate with the on-board L2 cache at its full clock speed.

✦ **Slot A:** This is a new proprietary slot design AMD is using with the their new Athlon processor. Although similar to Intel's Slot 1, Slot A uses a new bus protocol that increases communication speeds between the CPU and RAM to over 200MHz.

Installing a CPU

3.2 Add Processors

  • On single processor upgrade, verify compatibility

  • Verify N 1 stepping

  • Verify speed and cache matching

  • Perform BIOS upgrade

  • Perform OS upgrade to support multiprocessors

For most modern servers, there are two types of upgrades for the CPU: chip-for-chip upgrade, and daughtercard upgrade. Another method of upgrading a CPU, which is now obsolete and outdated, is the *piggyback method,* where an overdrive CPU is installed on top of an already-installed processor.

Chip-for-chip upgrade

When performing this type of upgrade, you are simply replacing the old CPU with a new one. Most modern boards have a zero-insertion force (ZIF) socket or a Slot 1 socket, where the chip can be easily removed. A ZIF socket has a small lever arm that holds the chip in place when closed. When the lever is raised, the chip pops out for easy removal. Older, low-insertion force (LIF) sockets required the chip to be forced into its socket by hand, increasing the danger of damaging the pins when inserting or removing the chip.

Daughterboard upgrade

A daughterboard upgrade involves installing a new chip on a card that is already plugged into your motherboard. The daughtercard looks very similar to a regular computer expansion card, with a single-edge connector that plugs into special motherboard slot.

Processor upgrade procedures

To upgrade a processor, there are some things you need to verify first. Follow these steps:

Upgrading a processor

1. **Verify compatibility.** Be sure to examine your current CPU and motherboard settings for proper bus speed and architecture, slot size, and proper cooling mechanisms.

2. **Verify stepping and OS compatibility for multiprocessing.** If you are going to install another processor in a multiprocessing system, you must verify that the OS will support such a configuration. Also, carefully check the stepping number of your CPU by physically examining the identifying information on the chip. *Stepping* refers to a revision of a CPU chip, usually to correct a small error in previous version. In a multiprocessing system, the stepping value of the new CPU must be identical to the one already installed to work properly.

3. **Verify the BIOS.** You will have to verify that your current BIOS version supports the CPU that you are about to upgrade., The BIOS will often report an older CPU version after a CPU upgrade, because its internal software does not recognize the new CPU.

4. **Verify the slot or socket.** Examine your current CPU for the type of socket or slot it uses. Your upgrade CPU must have the same number of pins to fit properly.

5. **Remove the old chip.** If there is a fan on top of the old chip, remove it first, but do not disconnect it from the rest of the system, because you will to need to put it back onto your new chip if it does not have its own cooling mechanism.

   If the chip is in an older LIF socket, you will need to use a chip puller tool to gently pry the CPU out of the socket. If your system uses a ZIF socket, simply raise the lever arm and the chip should pop right out of the socket.

6. **Install the new CPU.** For a LIF socket, use caution, as you did when removing the old chip. Line up the pins properly before slowly pushing the CPU down tightly into the socket. For a ZIF socket, align the CPU as before, and then bring down the lever arm to lock the CPU chip in place.

   For a Slot 1 processor, you must align the chip correctly over the slot. The chip will only go in one way. Press the CPU into the slot until the clips connect, securing the CPU into the slot.

7. **Reboot the server.** You can now reboot the server, but you must pay special attention to any error messages you get on the boot screen. Make sure your BIOS reports the name of the new CPU correctly.

Exam Tip   For the exam, remember that for multiprocessor systems, the CPU's should be identical, including the stepping revision number. Also ensure that the OS is updated to support multiprocessing.

System Memory

RAM (Random Access Memory) is the system memory where the server stores running applications and data. Server memory is crucial to server performance, as no amount of CPU power will help a server without enough memory to store its operations. Upgrading the memory of a server is a very common procedure for server technicians. Typically, when new applications are added, they demand more memory from the server. Upgrading memory is just as integral a part of server maintenance as CPU and disk upgrades. There are many different types of memory available, and it is very easy to make a mistake in choosing the RAM for your particular server. The memory types, size, packaging, and supported chip sets are all things you should keep in mind when upgrading server memory.

Basic types of server memory

Your server contains many different types of memory. Some forms of memory are based right on the motherboard, to store static information related to the systems, and other types of memory are dynamic, such as system RAM, which is used to temporarily store information during processing. A detailed knowledge of each type of memory and its purpose, is invaluable when trying to improve the performance of your system.

ROM

Read Only Memory (ROM) is a type of memory that cannot be written to; its information is static. When power is disconnected from your machine, and then reconnected, the information stored in ROM will still be there. ROM is most commonly used in system BIOS chips, as they store information about the computer that does not change. When you first turn on a computer, it reads its system information stored in ROM to be able to boot properly. Most modern computers contain a variant of ROM called EEPROM (Electrically Erasable Programmable ROM), which enables you to make changes to the ROM through special software. Using a *flash BIOS,* the computer's system information can be updated to recognize new hardware and features.

RAM

Random Access Memory (RAM) can be both read and written. This memory is one of the most important contributing factors to the performance of your server. With too little RAM, your server will not be able to run as many applications, large-scale programs may work very poorly, and potential server crashes are likely. RAM is volatile, and when the server is switched off, anything that was in memory will be lost. There are two main types of RAM: SRAM and DRAM.

SRAM

Static RAM continues to hold on to its data without a refresh, as opposed to DRAM (Dynamic RAM), which must be refreshed constantly to retain its information. SRAM is much faster, but more expensive than DRAM, and is typically used for cache memory.

DRAM

Dynamic RAM is constantly refreshed every few milliseconds, hence its dynamic nature. It is used for main system memory because it is much less expensive than SRAM, and the memory modules can fit into a smaller area.

There are several different types of DRAM:

✦ **FPM:** Fast Page Mode RAM was the traditional RAM used in PC's for many years. It came in modules of 2MB to 32MB of RAM. It is considered too slow for fast, modern system memory buses.

✦ **EDO:** Extended Data Out DRAM is slightly faster than FPM RAM. It is similar to FPM RAM, but the timing mechanisms have been changed so that no single access to the memory can begin before the last one has finished. It is, therefore, slightly faster than FPM memory, but still too slow for modern high-speed memory bus requirements.

✦ **ECC:** Error-Correcting Code memory includes special parity operations for testing the accuracy of data as it passes in and out of memory. ECC RAM is used mostly in servers that require high availability. ECC RAM can prevent server crashes caused by memory errors. ECC RAM is slower than other types of RAM because of the overhead involved in calculating parity.

✦ **SDRAM:** Synchronous DRAM differs from earlier types of RAM in that it does not run asynchronously with the system clock. SDRAM is specifically designed to synchronize with the system clock speed of the computer. SDRAM is the most common form of RAM in modern servers, because of its ability to scale to the faster bus speeds of new motherboards.

Another technique that sets SDRAM apart from other memory types is *memory interleaving*. Interleaving is used by high-end motherboards to increase performance. Memory interleaving allows simultaneous access to more than one area of memory. This improves performance because it can access more data in the same amount of time. This type of memory is helpful with large enterprise database and application servers.

✦ **Rambus (RDRAM):** Rambus Direct RAM is a new revolutionary RAM type created by a company named Rambus, partnered with Intel. It contains an intelligent micro-channel memory bus, which can run at a very high clock speed. Although the memory module itself is only 16-bit wide compared to the traditional 64-bit SDRAM module, this allows a much higher clock frequency. Adding more memory channels increases the throughput to even greater levels.

Memory packaging types

Memory can come in a wide variety of different packaging, and has been manufactured with a variety of different numbers of pins. It is very important that you verify the type of memory packaging required by your motherboard before purchasing upgrade memory.

SIMM

Single Inline Memory Modules (SIMM) are the older standard of memory modules. They come in two types, an older 8-bit 30-pin version, and a newer 32-bit 72-pin version. These chips are connected into sockets on the motherboard, which contain clips to keep them in place.

DIMM

Dual Inline Memory Modules (DIMM), used in most modern computer systems, are 64-bit modules and have 168 pins. The term *dual* is used to denote that these modules have two 32-bit paths for a full 64-bits, whereas a SIMM uses a single 32-bit path. They will not work in older motherboard SIMM sockets because of the difference in size. They are the most common form of packaging for SDRAM types of memory. There are three DIMM types: buffered, registered, and unbuffered. Most memory modules are *unbuffered*. *Buffered* modules contain a buffer to isolates the memory from the controller to minimize the load that it sees. *Registered* modules, used in newer Fast RAM modules, contain a register that delays all information transferred to the module by one clock cycle.

Fast RAM

To keep up with the modern fast processors, RAM manufacturers have also had to come up with a RAM solution that can keep up with CPU performance. The following are some of the more advanced types of RAM available today:

✦ **PC100, PC133:** The new Intel chipsets have a 100MHz or 133MHz memory bus. To match these faster bus speeds, you must use PC100 or PC133 memory modules. They use 168-pin DIMM packaging.

✦ **SPD:** Serial Presence Detect (SPD) is a small EEPROM that resides on newer fast RAM DIMMS. When a computer system boots up, it detects the configuration of the memory modules in order to run properly.

✦ **RIMM (Rambus):** RDRAM memory modules are called Rambus Inline Memory Modules (RIMM) and contain 184 pins. Since RDRAM works in channels, any empty sockets have to be filled with a blank memory module called a Continuity Rambus Inline Memory Module (CRIMM).

Installing memory

3.4 Increase memory

- Verify hardware and OS support for capacity increase
- Verify memory is on hardware/vendor compatibility list
- Verify memory compatibility (e.g., speed, brand, capacity, EDI, ECC/non-ECC, SDRAM/RDRAM)
- Verify that server and OS recognize the added memory
- Perform server optimization to make use of additional RAM

Follow these steps to correctly install new memory:

Upgrading memory

1. **Verify compatibility.** As with CPUs, there are many different types of memory and memory sockets, and finding the right memory for your server will usually take some investigation to ensure compatibility.

2. **Verify the memory with the manufacturer and motherboard manual.** Initially, you should confirm with your vendor or the manufacturer of your system the type of RAM that the server uses. Consult the manual for your motherboard to see what type of memory it can handle. You will need to check for memory size, speed, type, and capacity.

3. **Check the memory banks and slots.** Older servers might be using SIMM technology. The SIMM memory slots are organized in banks, and each bank must be full for the system to work properly. The memory must be installed in equal pairs if a bank contains more than one slot. You cannot put 32MB in one slot and leave the other one empty; you must use two 16MB SIMMs. The memory chip is usually inserted into the SIMM slot at a 45-degree angle, and then snapped vertically into place with the clips on the slot's edges.

Newer DIMM slots are separated into single-slot banks, so there is no need to install memory chips by pairs. There are typically three slots labeled DIMM 0, DIMM 1, and DIMM 2. Start with the lower number slot when adding or replacing RAM chips. In a DIMM slot, the memory is inserted vertically, directly into the slot, and secured by two levers on either side of the slot.

4. **Verify the Upgrade.** When you are finished with the memory upgrade, power up the server, and note any error messages that come up during the booting stage. Verify that the amount of RAM listed by the BIOS matches the memory that you have installed. Any discrepancies could mean that one of your memory chips may not be properly seated, or it could be defective.

When running your OS and any applications, be wary of any signs of errors relating to memory. You may have to reconfigure your applications to benefit properly from the added RAM.

Exam Tip   For the exam, most hardware-based RAM questions deal with the type and availability of slots in the motherboard, and compatibility issues.

System Bus Architectures

The communications bus of your server is the all-important link between its various components. The processor, memory, expansion cards, and storage devices talk to each other through one or more system buses.

Exam Tip   Although system bus architectures are not emphasized on the exam, you should know the various architectures, and know the capabilities of the most recent buses such as PCI and AGP.

A bus is a channel through which information flows between devices in your system. A device is able to plug or tap into a system bus, and relay specific information to the other devices on the same bus. The bus itself is simply a common set of wires that connect all the computer devices and chips together. When upgrading any devices on your system board, it is important to know what type of system bus you are running, especially its bus-width, clock speed, and throughput.

In most server architectures there are two main buses that are tightly integrated: the *system bus,* which facilitates communication between the CPU and memory, and the *I/O bus,* which connects the CPU with other devices in the system. The buses are connected by a *bridge,* which is part of the motherboard chipset. Figure 7-2 shows the relationship between these buses and your system components.

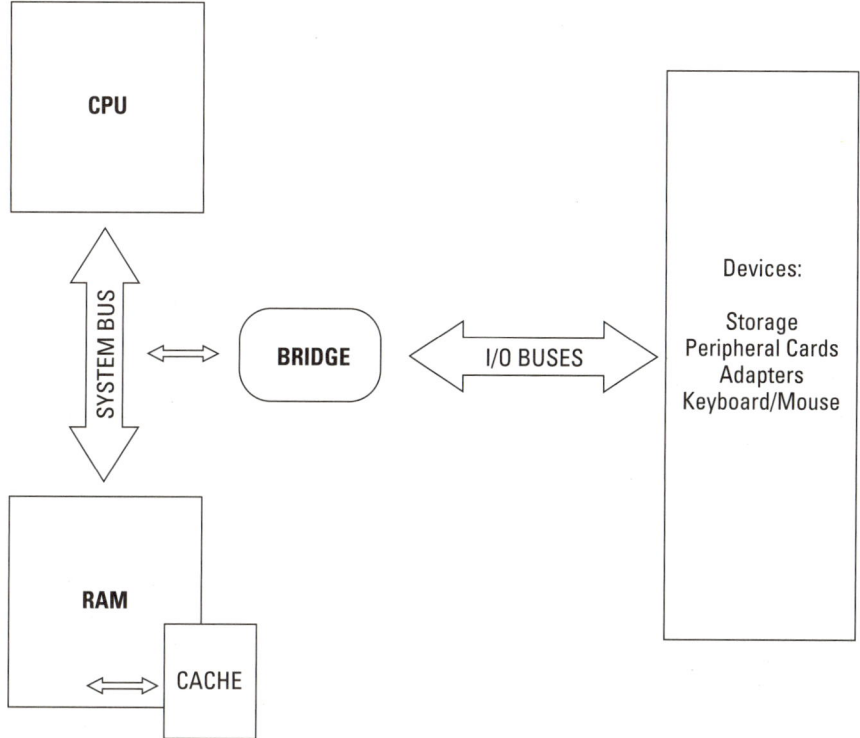

Figure 7-2: Basic system and I/O bus diagram

System bus concepts

The system bus has three main characteristics that define its performance and data-handling capabilities:

✦ **Bus speed:** The speed of the bus reflects how many bits of information can be sent through system. Most buses transmit one bit of data per clock cycle.

✦ **Bus width:** The wider the bus, the more information can flow through it. Older bus widths were 8 and 16-bit, while modern buses use a 64-bit width.

✦ **Bus bandwidth:** Bandwidth refers to the total amount of data that can be transferred on a bus over a certain amount of time. This is typically measured in Megabits per second (Mbps).

The system bus is designed to match a particular CPU. In older computer architectures, the system bus speed closely followed the CPU speed. Bus widths, which determine how much data can travel over the bus, were typically 8- and 16-bit data channels.

In the late 486 and early Pentium models, technology advances enable the CPU internal speed to double its clock frequency, while the system bus retained is own internal clock speed at half the speed. Bus widths were now running at 32-bit.

For many years, the 64-bit Pentium architecture generally relied on 66MHz bus speeds. Recently, in AMD and Pentium III machines, system buses now run either 100MHz or 133 MHz. The new Pentium 4 CPU runs on a 400 MHz system bus.

Table 7-1 summarizes the relationship between the different processors and the buses.

Table 7-1 Bus and Processor Speeds		
CPU	**Bus Width**	**Bus Speed (MHz)**
8088	8-bit	4.77
8086	16-bit	8
80286	16-bit	12
80386	16-bit	16
80486SX-25	32-bit	25
80486DX-33	32-bit	33
80486DX2-50	32-bit	25
80486DX-50	32-bit	50
80486DX2-66	32-bit	33
80486DX4-100	32-bit	40
5X86-133	32-bit	33
Intel Pentium 60	64-bit	60
Intel Pentium 100	64-bit	66
Cyrix 6X86 P133+	64-bit	55
Intel Pentium 166	64-bit	66
Intel Pentium II	64-bit	66
Intel Pentium III	64-bit	100, 133
Pentium 4	64-bit	100×4

I/O buses

As the system bus connects the CPU to RAM, I/O buses connect the CPU to all other components. The I/O buses differ from the system bus in speed. I/O speeds are lower than system bus speeds, as most devices only operate at lower clock speeds. The following are the types of I/O buses.

Legacy I/O buses

The *Industry Standard Architecture* (ISA) bus is the most common of all bus types, and even though its technology is quite old, a 16-bit architecture going back to the early 1980's, most modern PCs and servers still come with a few ISA slots on the motherboard. Older 8-bit and 16-bit peripheral cards still abound today, which typically are serial or modem cards.

The *Micro Channel Architecture* (MCA) bus was created in 1987 by IBM as a rival to the ISA bus. It boasted 32-bit bus width, a bus mastering system for greater bus efficiency, and a plug-and-play system that predated modern plug-and-play technology by many years. Unfortunately, even though MCA was far superior to ISA technology, it was proprietary to IBM, and was not compatible with ISA. These factors led to the discontinuation of MCA.

The *Extended Industry Standard Architecture* (EISA) bus was created as an extension to the ISA standard, although it never became very popular in the PC and server world. EISA was created by other vendors to take the strengths of MCA bus architecture, and make it compatible with ISA. Like MCA, it also featured a 32-bit bus width, plug and play capabilities, and bus mastering. EISA, much like the MCA bus, did not catch on, and was quickly eclipsed by newer, faster bus technologies like VESA local bus, and PCI.

Local bus technologies

As CPU speed began to increase exponentially, a bottleneck developed at the system bus level. The most notable application to be affected by this performance issue was graphical display systems. The amount of information to be conveyed to video card was too great for the slow ISA bus to handle. To increase graphics performance, the idea of a local bus, a bus that was more closely integrated with the processor and memory bus, came into being.

The first local bus technology to become popular was Video Electronics Standard Association (VESA) local bus. The VESA local bus was introduced in 1992; the product of a standards group dedicated to increasing video performance on personal computers. Running as a 32-bit 33MHz bus, VESA was a direct extension of the 486 processor/memory bus. It did not, however, support bus mastering or plug-and-play. It also did not have much relevance with the server market, which did not need advanced video capabilities. Although popular during the 486 era, it was quickly rendered obsolete by the Pentium computer and its PCI local bus.

PCI local bus

The Peripheral Component Interconnect (PCI) local bus was created by Intel in 1993 as a general-purpose local bus that could bring advantages to any device, not just video. PCI local bus uses 32-bit technology, and runs at 33MHz. Newer PCI systems use 64-bit technology and run at 66 MHz. PCI is the highest performance general I/O bus currently used on modern computers. This is because of several factors:

✦ **Burst mode:** The PCI bus can transfer information in a *burst mode,* where a destination device address can be cached so that multiple sets of data can be transmitted in a one connection.

✦ **Bus mastering:** *Bus mastering* is the capability of devices on the PCI bus to take control of the bus to perform data transfers. The design of PCI's bus mastering capability enables multiple devices to take over the bus without locking each other out. The devices also get full bandwidth of the bus while no other devices are using it. The chipset controls the complex interactivity between the local bus and the devices.

✦ **PCI plug-and-play:** Created as a standard by Intel, Microsoft, and other vendors, PCI plug-and-play enables the PCI circuitry to identify system devices, and in conjunction with a plug-and-play operating system, automatically sets the configuration and allocate resources for these devices.

✦ **Interrupts:** The PCI bus uses its own internal interrupt system for handling requests from devices on the bus. These interrupts are mapped to the normal system IRQs used by the operating system.

✦ **Expansion Slots:** Most modern PCs have at least four PCI slots for device cards, while servers often have twice that amount.

✦ **Hierarchical PCI:** For server expandability, a cascaded PCI local bus can be created to allow for more I/O connections and expansion slots. Using a PCI bridge controller, two independent PCI computer buses can be connected together to allow the buses to communicate with each other.

✦ **Peer PCI:** Peer PCI Bus technology was created to alleviate the negative characteristics of having several PCI buses being daisy-chained through a bridge-controller. Multiple Peer PCI buses are directly connected to the host bus, enabling the CPU to access each bus directly. This way, processor/bus bandwidth is more evenly shared between buses, resulting in greater performance. This is very helpful in separating high and low bandwidth traffic on separate PCI buses.

✦ **Hot plug/hot swap PCI:** Hot pluggable PCI is a new technology to enhance standard PCI with hot-plug capability. This hot plug capability enables users to remove and replace PCI cards without removing power from the system. The Operating System must be compatible, and able to detect changes when a PCI card is swapped out.

I2O

Intelligent Input/Output (I2O) is a specification that aims to provide an I/O device driver architecture that is independent of both the specific device being controlled and the host operating system. This offloads system bus I/O activity from the main CPU, greatly increasing server performance. This emerging technology is being used on high-end database and transaction servers where server I/O performance is key to its speed and reliability.

AGP

Accelerated Graphics Port (AGP) is a high performance bus slot, which is based on PCI, but is geared towards the throughput demands of 3D video. Rather than using the PCI bus for graphics data, AGP introduces a dedicated channel so that the graphics controller can directly access main system memory. The AGP bus itself is 32-bit, and runs at twice the system bus speed, which is 66MHz. AGP is ideal for the high-performance workstation and desktop market, but is not a key element for servers, where video performance is rarely an issue.

Upgrading a system's bus is impractical, because it involves replacing the entire motherboard of the server. It is much simpler and more cost-effective to just replace the entire server.

Upgrading BIOS and Firmware

 3.5 Upgrade BIOS/Firmware

As discussed in Chapter 3, your system's BIOS controls the basic functions of your server, and enables your operating system to communicate with the server's hardware. Your BIOS needs to be upgraded just like any other component, and failing to upgrade your BIOS could lead to your system not recognizing new components when you add them.

Updating BIOS and firmware is discussed in more detail in Chapter 3.

BIOS

For new hardware to be properly recognized by your system, you may have to upgrade the BIOS of your motherboard to support the new device. The BIOS controls the communication between the server motherboard and its hardware. If the BIOS does not recognize the device, it will remain disabled. Updating the BIOS enables you to support the most recent hardware devices on your system.

Follow these steps to update the BIOS on your system:

1. **Check the current version.** Examine your current BIOS to check for your current version number. This is usually displayed when the server is first turned on. As the server is powered up, the BIOS manufacturer, and data and version number will quickly flash on the screen before the POST routine begins. You may also be able to check this information in the CMOS information screen.

2. **Obtain latest BIOS release.** The most recent BIOS for your server can be found in a number of places. The first place to check is your server manufacturer's Web site. They will usually have the most recent versions for your particular server. You may also check with the motherboard manufacturer, or the BIOS vendor themselves, but you must be very careful because some server vendors may modify this BIOS for their own hardware.

3. **Upgrade the BIOS.** To upgrade the BIOS, you will need to take your update file and copy it to a bootable floppy disk. You need to use some form of bootable media, because the BIOS is the first component of the server that is used at startup. This process is also called *flashing the BIOS,* because the flash memory of the BIOS will be updated with the new code. Do not interrupt the BIOS upgrade process, because this could damage the BIOS and disable it.

4. **Verify the upgrade.** When the upgrade is finished, restart the server, and check the BIOS version level when the first BIOS information is displayed. If the upgrade was successful, you should see the most recent version. You can check your new hardware device, and check to see if the BIOS will now recognize it.

Firmware

Firmware is special low-level software that resides within your hardware devices to facilitate their functions and communications with the rest of the system. If you are installing or upgrading a device, you should obtain the latest firmware, so that the device software will be up-to-date, to ensure compatibility, and to have the most recent bug fixes. The firmware is stored in special ROM modules that can be flash updated, just like a BIOS.

Follow these steps to update the firmware for your device:

1. **Check the current version.** Examine your firmware to check for the current version number. Some hardware devices will display this information when the server has started and is going through the POST routine. You may also be able to check this information from any special software diagnostic utilities that came with the device.

2. **Obtain latest firmware release.** The most recent firmware for your device can be found at the device manufacturer's Web site.

3. **Upgrade the firmware.** To upgrade the firmware, run the software update that you obtained from the manufacturer. Depending on the type of device, the upgrade may involve using a bootable floppy disk to perform the update. Do not interrupt the upgrade process, because this could damage the device and disable it.

4. **Verify the upgrade.** When the upgrade is finished, restart the server, and check the version level of the device by examining the POST routine, or running the diagnostic software that came with your device. If the upgrade was successful, you should see the most recent version.

Exam Tip For the exam, if a new or upgraded device is not initially recognized by the system, the BIOS or firmware most likely needs to be upgraded to support the new device.

Performing an Upgrade Checklist

✦ Perform upgrade checklist, including: locate/obtain latest test drivers, OS updates, software, etc.; review FAQs, instruction, facts and issues; test and pilot; schedule downtime; implement ESD best practices; confirm that upgrade has been recognized; review and baseline; document upgrade.

Upgrading the components of your server is not just a single act of installing hardware or software. There are a number of steps that must be taken before, during, and after the upgrade, to ensure that it will be successful, and will not interrupt current or future server operations:

✦ **Locate and obtain test drivers:** Before beginning your upgrade, you should ensure that you have the most recent drivers for your device. The driver that comes with the device itself may be obsolete, and you may need to obtain the most recent drivers from the manufacturer for your particular system.

✦ **OS updates:** You must ensure that your OS will be compatible with the new hardware or software by checking for any updates, bug fixes, or service packs that may be needed for your upgrade to be successful. The upgrade you are installing may not have been available at the time the OS was released, and you will need to update the OS to properly recognize and be able to use the upgrade.

✦ **FAQ, instructions, facts, and issues:** Carefully read over the documentation that comes with your upgrades. Examine the installation instructions for any special considerations that might relate to your particular environment. You may find that your device or application is not compatible with the current hardware or software you are using. This will also prepare you for the installation steps, so that you know exactly what has to be done before you attempt the upgrade.

✦ **Test and pilot:** It is preferable to test your new hardware or software in a special test environment or lab. This will give you a chance to monitor how the upgrades will react in your particular environment. You may find that the upgrades conflict with other hardware or software that you are currently using, which you can then resolve before installing the upgrade on your production environment.

✦ **Schedule downtime:** You cannot simply perform the upgrade at any time, because this may affect the services provided to your end users. You must schedule downtime with the users, so that the upgrade can be preformed during off-hours times to minimize impact. It is also important to schedule enough time to allow you to fix any potential problems with the upgrade if the operation does not go as planned.

✦ **Electrostatic Discharge (ESD) issues:** At all times, you must maintain a strict adherence to standard ESD practices such as proper grounding and maintaining a static-free environment. Ensure the proper use of grounding wrist straps, anti-static bags for hardware components, and insulated work areas.

✦ **Confirm Upgrade:** After the upgrade is completed, you must confirm that your new hardware or software is recognized by the system and working properly. For hardware, the server should be able to automatically detect the new device. If not, you may have to examine the device hardware physically to ensure that it is installed properly, and all connections are secure. The device driver may need to be changed or upgraded if the device is not recognized by the operating system.

✦ **Review and baseline:** After the installation of your hardware or software, you will need to review your upgrade, and determine if it was successful in improving performance and functionality of your server. Take a baseline of your server by measuring performance over a specific period of time. Compare your results to the performance of your server before the upgrade, to see if the upgrade is working as you expected.

✦ **Documentation the upgrade:** When you have finished the upgrade, you should carefully document all information and procedures that were performed during the operation, including part type, model number, serial numbers, device settings, software settings, jumpers, and any problems and fixes that were implemented to complete the upgrade.

In the Real World

In many environments, there is no budget for a test lab or pilot stage for an upgrade. If this is the case, you will need to proceed with the upgrade with caution, and plan a back-out strategy in the event that the upgrade is not successful.

Key Point Summary

This chapter introduced the technical specifications of various motherboard components such as CPU, memory, and the system bus. A thorough knowledge of each component and how they relate to each other, is essential to knowing how to prepare and upgrade them. For the exam, keep the following points in mind:

✦ Before any upgrade, you must fully back up your system.

✦ Verify compatibility when upgrading processors, including speed, stepping, and socket slots.

✦ Verify the stepping of CPUs for multiprocessor upgrades.

✦ Verify OS support for multiprocessing.

✦ Upgrade your BIOS, if necessary, to make sure it can recognize new components.

✦ Verify compatibility for memory upgrades, including speed, size, packaging, parity, and BIOS and motherboard support.

✦ After an upgrade, verify that the server has recognized and is using the extra RAM.

✦ Be aware of how system bus architectures affect server performance.

✦   ✦   ✦

STUDY GUIDE

The Study Guide section provides you with the opportunity to test your knowledge about upgrading motherboard components. The Assessment Questions provide practice for the test, and the Scenarios provide practice with real situations. If you get any questions wrong, use the answers to determine the part of the chapter you should review before continuing.

Assessment Questions

1. CPU stepping refers to what aspect of the processor?

   A. Level 1 cache

   B. CPU chip revision number

   C. Level 2 cache

   D. Clock speed

2. A technician receives an additional CPU for a multiprocessor server. What should be verified to confirm that it will work with the other processor?

   A. Voltage

   B. Brand name

   C. Stepping

   D. Speed

3. The Level 2 cache on a Pentium Pro system is located on which part of the server system?

   A. Motherboard

   B. CPU

   C. RAM

   D. Hard disk drive

4. A technician is installing a network operating system on a multiprocessor server. What should be verified before installing the OS?

   A. The OS uses a Level 1 or Level 2 cache.

   B. The OS supports CPU stepping.

    C. The bus speed of the processor is supported.

    D. The OS supports multiprocessors.

5. A customer is reporting that his database server performs slowly. It currently is configured with 512MB of RAM, a Pentium III processor, and a 50GB RAID 5 array. What upgrade can be performed to increase performance of the server?

    A. Add more disk drives.

    B. Add more RAM.

    C. Add another CPU if supported.

    D. Add a Level 2 cache.

6. Symmetrical multi-processing is defined by what characteristic?

    A. Certain tasks are handled by a specific processor.

    B. All tasks are buffered by processor cache.

    C. CPU tasks are distributed between all processors.

    D. Tasks are mirrored in RAM.

7. ECC RAM uses what process to prevent server crashes?

    A. Synchronization with the system clock

    B. Faster memory bus

    C. Level 1 caching

    D. Parity checking

8. The ability of multiple processes to access a certain section of RAM is called what?

    A. Memory interleaving

    B. Caching

    C. Static RAM

    D. Dynamic RAM

9. A technician receives some additional RAM for a memory upgrade to a server. The technician notices that the new RAM has 184 pins, while the current RAM has only 168 pins, and the new RAM won't fit into the memory expansion slot. What is the cause of the discrepancy?

    A. The RAM received was 256MB.

    B. The RAM received was a SIMM module.

    C. The RAM received was an EDO DIMM module.

    D. The RAM received was a Rambus RIMM module.

10. A buffered memory module has what characteristic?

    A. It contains a register that delays incoming data.

    B. It holds data until it can be written to the disk drive.

    C. It helps to minimize the load of information transfer.

    D. It holds data in a secondary cache to speed up processes.

11. A technician has just upgraded a server's RAM from 128MB to 256MB. When the server is rebooted, the BIOS reports that there is only 128MB in the server. What is the cause of this discrepancy?

    A. The BIOS needs to be upgraded.

    B. The new memory is only running at half speed.

    C. The OS does not support the new memory.

    D. Not all of the memory banks have been used.

12. A technician wants to verify that the server's motherboard can handle a new memory upgrade. What is the best source of this information?

    A. The RAM manufacturer

    B. The motherboard manual

    C. The CPU manufacturer

    D. The OS manual

13. A customer wants to add memory to their server. What should the technician do before purchasing additional memory?

    A. Verify the availability of a memory slot

    B. Verify the speed of current memory

    C. Upgrade the BIOS

    D. Upgrade the motherboard

14. A customer reports that a few hours after a CPU upgrade, their server keeps locking up. What could be the possible cause of the problem?

    A. The BIOS needs to be upgraded.

    B. The new CPU is conflicting with RAM.

    C. The CPU fan is not working.

    D. The OS does not support the CPU.

15. After a memory upgrade, a server's OS continues to crash with many application errors. What could be the possible cause of the problem?

    A. The OS does not support the new RAM.

    B. One of the new memory chips is defective.

    C. Parity checking is not enabled on RAM.

    D. The motherboard does not support the new RAM.

16. A technician has upgraded a server with an empty CPU socket with a second CPU for multiprocessing. The customer complains that there has been no difference in server performance. What might cause this?

    A. The O/S does not support multiprocessing.

    B. The new CPU is not fully inserted into the ZIF socket.

    C. The BIOS needs to be upgraded.

    D. The CPU is a different brand name than the original.

17. What must be initially checked before installing a second CPU in a multiprocessor system?

    A. Verify that the motherboard supports the CPU.

    B. Verify that there is enough RAM.

    C. Verify the OS supports multiprocessing.

    D. Verify the CPU stepping with original CPU.

18. The technician receives a new video card for a server, but it won't fit into the existing PCI slot. What is the cause of the problem?

    A. The video card is an AGP card.

    B. The technician is putting it in backwards.

    C. The video card is a 3D card.

    D. Servers can only use ISA video cards.

19. A customer wants to upgrade their Pentium 166MHz MMX system with a new Pentium III processor. What can the technician do to complete the upgrade?

    A. Verify that the new CPU is supported in the BIOS.

    B. Nothing. The new CPU will not work in an older motherboard.

    C. Verify the system bus speed.

    D. Verify the new CPU uses MMX.

20. A technician is upgrading a CPU on a Pentium Pro system. The new CPU, however, will not fit into the old CPU slot. What is the cause of the problem?

   A. The machine does not support multiprocessing.

   B. It is using a Socket 7 slot.

   C. It is using a Socket 8 slot.

   D. The new CPU uses a LIF socket.

Scenarios

1. A customer wants to upgrade their server. It is currently running a dual multiprocessor Pentium Pro system with 256MB of RAM. They want to upgrade the processors to Pentium IIIs, and double the RAM to 512MB. As a technician, what steps would you take to verify that your upgrades will work with the current system?

2. A customer is reporting a problem with their server. A few days before, the CPU was upgraded to a faster processor. They are experiencing frequent lock-ups and system freezes. What steps would you take to diagnose and fix the problem?

Answers to Chapter Questions

Chapter pre-test

1. A cache retains the most recent data accessed by the CPU. When accessed again, the CPU will get the information directly from the cache, which is much faster than RAM or hard disk.

2. CPU stepping refers to the revision number of the CPU chip.

3. Multiprocessing is the ability of your server system to recognize and use more than one CPU.

4. SRAM (Static RAM) will retain its information until the power is disconnected. DRAM (Dynamic RAM) has to be constantly refreshed to retain its contents.

5. Synchronous RAM runs in time with your system clock, while asynchronous RAM runs independently.

6. ECC (Error Checking Code) memory uses parity operations to prevent memory errors that will crash a server.

7. Bus width refers to how many bits are sent across the channel at once. A 64-bit bus can transfer twice as much information as a 32-bit bus.

8. AGP (Accelerated Graphics Port) is a special bus slot that is used for high-performance graphics cards.

9. Bus mastering refers to the ability of a PCI bus to enable any device to take over control and bandwidth of the bus, without locking other devices out.

10. Hot-plug PCI is the ability of the server hardware and software to enable PCI cards to be inserted and removed without powering off the system.

Assessment questions

1. **B.** A step version of a processor is one that contains fixes from the original version. Answer A is incorrect because the Level 1 cache refers to the onboard cache on the CPU. Answer C is incorrect because the Level 2 cache refers to the cache memory that is external to the CPU. Answer D is incorrect because the clock speed refers to the speed at which the CPU executes instructions. For more information, see the "Processor upgrade procedures" section.

2. **C.** All CPUs in a multiprocessor system must have the same stepping version. Answer A is incorrect because the voltage level of the same CPUs will be identical. Answer B is incorrect because the brand name of the dual CPUs should be identical. Answer D is incorrect because the speed of the CPUs is not relevant. For more information, see the "Processor upgrade procedures" section.

3. **B.** The Pentium Pro system has the Level-2 cache located on the CPU. Other systems have the Level-2 cache located on the motherboard, or a daughterboard. Answer A is incorrect because the Level-2 cache of the Pentium Pro is on the CPU itself. Answer C is incorrect because the cache is not part of the RAM. Answer D is incorrect because Level-2 cache is not located on the hard drive. For more information, see the "CPU architectures" section.

4. **D.** Without OS support, the additional CPU will not be used. Answer A is incorrect because the type of cache is not relevant. Answer B is incorrect because stepping refers to the revision number of the CPU itself, and is independent of the operating system. Answer C is incorrect because the bus speed is not relevant. For more information, see the "Multiprocessing" section.

5. **C.** Processing power is most important for transactional database systems. Answer A is incorrect because adding hard drives will only increase disk storage capacity. Answer B is incorrect because the installed RAM is already sufficient for the task. Answer D is incorrect because adding more caching capabilities will not increase performance as much as an additional CPU. For more information, see the "Multiprocessing" section.

6. **C.** In a symmetrical multi-processing system, the CPU tasks are distributed between all processors. Answer A is incorrect because a system where tasks are handled by specific processors is considered an asymmetrical system. Answer B is incorrect because this is already a normal feature of caching. Answer D is incorrect because the RAM does not perform or execute tasks. For more information, see the "Multiprocessing" section.

7. **D.** Parity checking can prevent server crashes by constantly monitoring and correcting memory errors. Answer A is incorrect because clock synchronization is a characteristic of SDRAM. Answer B is incorrect because ECC RAM is actually slower than other types of RAM because of parity calculations. Answer C is incorrect because Level-1 caching takes place on the CPU itself. For more information, see the "DRAM" section.

8. **A.** Interleaving increases server performance because multiple processes can access the same parts of RAM. Answer B is incorrect because caching is a way of speeding up RAM access by storing the most recently used instructions. Answer C is incorrect because static RAM is a type of memory that does not need to be constantly refreshed. Answer D is incorrect because dynamic RAM is a type of memory that needs to be constantly refreshed. For more information, see the "DRAM" section.

9. **D.** It is imperative that memory upgrades be verified with current system specifications, as there are many different types of RAM. Answer A is incorrect because the size of the RAM module is dependent on the number of pins. Answer B is incorrect because a SIMM module uses 30 or 72 pins. Answer C is incorrect because a DIMM module is 168 pins, and would have installed correctly. For more information, see the "Installing memory" section.

10. **C.** Buffered memory holds data so that the RAM is not overloaded. Answer A is incorrect because a buffer does not delay data, which would slow down system throughput. Answer B is incorrect because this is an example of hard drive caching. Answer D is incorrect because this is an example of Level-2 cache. For more information, see the "DIMM" section.

11. **A.** Depending on the type of memory being installed, the BIOS must be upgraded before new RAM can be recognized. Answer B is incorrect because the memory cannot run at half speed. Answer C is incorrect because the memory is not being recognized at the machine's BIOS level, not the OS. Answer D is incorrect because you do not have to fill all of the available memory slots for it to work properly. For more information, see the "Installing memory" section.

12. **B.** The motherboard manual contains all the important information and specifications for any component upgrades. Answer A is incorrect because the RAM manufacturer will not be able to give you information on the motherboard you are using. Answer C is incorrect because the CPU manufacturer will not have information on your motherboard. Answer D is incorrect because the OS manual will not have information on your motherboard. For more information, see the "Installing memory" section.

13. **A.** There must be empty memory slots available, or no RAM can be added. Answer B is incorrect because the speed of the memory is not relevant. Answer C is incorrect because the BIOS may not have to upgraded to recognize the new memory. Answer D is incorrect because there is no reason to upgrade the motherboard to add memory. For more information, see the "Installing memory" section.

14. C. If the CPU fan is not working, the CPU will heat to high temperatures, causing erratic system behavior and failure. Answer A is incorrect because the BIOS does not need to be upgraded in this case, and will not fix the problem. Answer B is incorrect because conflicts between the memory and CPU would not exist. Answer D is incorrect because the server is having problems with the CPU at the system level, not the OS level. For more information, see the "Processor upgrade procedures" section.

15. B. Application errors are often caused by defective memory. Other incompatibility problems would result in the system not booting at all. Answer A is incorrect because the memory problem is at the system level, not the OS level. Answer C is incorrect because there is no way to enable parity checking on non-parity type RAM. Answer D is incorrect because if the motherboard did not support the RAM, it would not be recognized by the system. For more information, see the "Installing memory" section.

16. A. The OS of a server must support multiprocessing for the new processor to provide any benefit. Answer B is incorrect because the second CPU would not be recognized if it were not fully inserted into its slot. Answer C is incorrect because there is no need to upgrade the BIOS in this case. Answer D is incorrect because the CPU manufacturer would not be relevant in this case. For more information, see the "Central Processing Unit" section.

17. D. If there is a discrepancy between CPU versions, multiprocessing will not work. Answer A is incorrect because if you are installing an identical CPU, the motherboard should already support it. Answer B is incorrect because the amount of RAM is not relevant in this case. Answer C is incorrect because you must ensure the CPU will be recognized at the system level before examining compatibility at the OS level. For more information, see the "Multiprocessing" section.

18. A. The card uses the special AGP slot for advanced video cards. Answer B is incorrect because there is no way for the card to be inserted backwards. Answer C is incorrect because the fact that the card supports 3D is not relevant. Answer D is incorrect because servers can use any type of card if there are the slots available to support it. For more information, see the "AGP" section.

19. B. Newer CPU chips will not fit or work in older motherboards. Answer A is incorrect because the BIOS is not relevant in this case. Answer C is incorrect because the system bus speed is not relevant. Answer D is incorrect because the Pentium III chip is already MMX capable. For more information, see the "Types of CPU sockets" section.

20. C. The Pentium Pro uses a unique on-board Level-2 cache that makes the chip very large compared to other Pentium CPU's. Answer A is incorrect because the system in this case is not a multiprocessing system. Answer B is incorrect because a Socket 7 type slot supports 321 pin CPU's, while the Pentium Pro uses 387 pins. Answer D is incorrect because a Pentium Pro socket 8 slot uses only ZIF type CPU's. For more information, see the "Types of CPU sockets" section.

Scenarios

1. The first problem with the customer's request is that their motherboard won't support a simple replacement of the CPUs with Pentium IIIs. The Pentium Pro motherboard has special sockets for the larger Pentium Pro CPUs, which contain an on-board Level-2 cache. The entire system board would have to be replaced.

   The technician would have to inspect the current memory configuration to find out what memory it is currently using, and how many empty slots or banks it has. If it is using DIMM slots, and currently has two 128MB DIMMs, there is only one slot left in which a 256MB DIMM can be installed to bring the memory total to 512MB.

   If the server is using older SIMM technology, it might have four slots of 64MB, which would be full and no more can be added. Considering the motherboard is probably going to be replaced, the SIMM's would all probably have to be replaced anyway.

   Any upgrade should require an update of the system BIOS, to make sure any new components are recognized when they are installed.

2. Because the problems only began since the CPU was upgraded, it would be wise to start with checking the CPU. The BIOS should be checked to make sure it is the latest version and able to support the new CPU.

   The most likely culprit, however, is the CPU fan. If it is not functioning properly, it will quickly overheat, and result in erratic server behavior. Any other CPU related problem would result in the system not functioning at all.

Upgrading Storage Devices

♦   ♦   ♦   ♦

CHAPTER PRE-TEST

1. What are the main differences between IDE and SCSI technology?

2. Describe the purpose of SCA SCSI connections.

3. What are the differences between narrow and wide SCSI?

4. What is the purpose of SCSI termination?

5. Why do certain SCSI technologies have cable length limitations?

6. What is the difference between a physical and a logical drive?

7. What are the differences between Fast SCSI-2 and an Ultra2 SCSI?

8. How many devices are permitted on a SCSI bus?

9. What SCSI device ID is typically the host adapter?

10. What are the differences between single-ended and differential signaling?

✦ Answers to these questions can be found at the end of the chapter. ✦

Upgrading your storage systems is a very common procedure for the server technician. Most often, the server is just simply out of drive space and additional drives are needed. You may have to upgrade an entire disk subsystem to enhance fault tolerance with a redundant RAID system. In this chapter, IDE and SCSI-based disk systems are discussed in detail, with tips on configuration and upgrading. RAID systems upgrades are discussed, as well as making your new disk space available to the operating system.

IDE/ATA Hard Drives

Integrated Drive Electronics (IDE) hard drives, also known as AT Attachment drives (ATA) are the most popular type of hard drives in modern computers. They are fast, and inexpensive compared to their SCSI counterparts. Modern servers, however, typically will use the faster and more flexible SCSI technology, but there are still many servers out there in smaller installations that only need the IDE/ATA interface.

In older computers, the hard drive had to be connected with the computer's motherboard through a separate hard drive controller. The name Integrated Drive Electronics refers to the fact that the hard drive controller logic is built right on to the hard drive itself. These 16-bit drives were then connected to the ISA bus of the computer by means of a cable. Up to two drives could be chained together on the same channel without any data interference.

With advances in technology and bus speeds, modern systems are equipped with hard drive controller logic built right into the motherboard chipset, with drives that are plugged directly into the PC bus.

IDE/ATA standards

✦ Verify that drives are appropriate type

The common characteristics of all IDE technology are the fact that you can have two drives per IDE channel, and the connection width is 16 bits. The standard has gone through many different versions, which are described as follows:

- ✦ **ATA-1:** The original ATA (ATA-1) standard defined these characteristics:

    - **Programmed I/O (PIO):** Enables the CPU and hardware to regulate data traffic between the hard disk and the computer system.

    - **Support for two devices:** Permits a single channel on the computer to use up to two devices, defined as *master* and *slave*.

    - **DMA Modes:** Direct Memory Access modes, which improve on the Programmed I/O technology by enabling the hard drive and system memory to talk directly to each other, effectively bypassing the CPU.

✦ **ATA-2:** The ATA-2 standard combined the technology of various manufacturers' efforts to improve upon the original ATA standard. Other names include Enhanced IDE (EIDE), Fast ATA, or Fast ATA-2. The characteristics of ATA-2 include:

  • **Faster DMA and Programmed I/O modes:** Provides improved performance.

  • **Logical Block Addressing (LBA) mode:** An advanced technique to address hard drive sectors, instead of the older method of manually defining the number of cylinders, heads, and sectors within the BIOS of the system.

  • **Block transferring:** The ability to perform multiple operations over a single interrupt.

✦ **ATA-3:** ATA-3 is a revision of the ATA-2 standard, adding features such as enhanced security and reliability, but little in the way of performance improvements.

Caution

ATA-3 is not the same as ATA-33, a much later standard that refers to its 33MB/s transfer speed.

✦ **Ultra ATA/33:** The AT Attachment Packet Interface (ATAPI) protocol was created to allow non-hard disk devices to also use the IDE channel on a computer system. Using a special ATAPI driver that is loaded into system memory, devices such as CD-ROMS, tape drives, optical drives, can plug into the IDE interface, and also be configured as master or slave, by themselves, or in conjunction with a hard drive.

The AT and ATAPI command sets and protocols were combined to created Ultra ATA/33, also called ATA/ATAPI-4. Its characteristics include:

  • **Ultra DMA (UDMA):** This advanced DMA technique essentially doubled the speed of data transfer clocking, increasing throughput from 16.7 MB/s to 33 MB/s. This also introduced a new 80-conductor IDE cable, to support reliability with the faster speeds.

  • **CRC (Cyclical Redundancy Checking):** Error checking and redundancy are introduced, using CRC type error correction.

✦ **Ultra ATA/66:** Also known as the ATA/ATAPI-5 standard, it features faster UDMA modes that allow up to 66 MB/s data transfer. The special 80-conductor IDE cable, which was optional with ATA-33, is mandatory for ATA-66.

✦ **Ultra ATA/100:** ATA-100, also known as ATA/ATAPI-6, is an emerging standard that brings data transfer speeds to 100 MB/s, among other improvements to LBA support for extremely large hard drives.

Table 8-1 summarizes the important points of the IDE/ATA standards.

Table 8-1
IDE/ATA Standards

IDE Standard	I/O Modes	Speed	Features
ATA-1	PIO	8.3 MB/s	Original standard
ATA-2	PIO, DMA	16.6 MB /s	Block transfers, LBA modes
ATA-3	PIO, DMA	16.6 MB/s	Enhanced security and reliability
Ultra ATA-33	PIO, DMA, UDMA	33 MB/s	Ultra DMA, 80-conductor cable
Ultra ATA-66	PIO, DMA, UDMA	66 MB/s	80-conductor cable mandatory
Ultra ATA-100	PIO, DMA, UDMA	100 MB/s	Faster transfer speeds

Exam Tip   You should not need to memorize the specifics of various IDE standards and technologies for the exam. Most servers run SCSI systems because of its excellent performance and RAID capabilities, and IDE is used mostly on desktop computers. But watch for questions on IDE cabling and configuration scenarios.

IDE configuration

✦ For ATA/IDE drives, confirm cabling, master/slave and potential cross-brand compatibility

An IDE channel can support up to two devices. To differentiate between the devices, and to facilitate communications between them, one drive is configured as the master drive, the other as the slave. Typically, the boot drive is configured to be the master, as it is first in the IDE channel. There is no performance issue between the two, the names are merely designations of order rather than importance. It is often easier to think of master and slave as Drive 0 and Drive 1.

There are, however, some rules to follow when configuring the master and slave designations for IDE hard drives. With two devices present, one must be configured to be the master and the other the slave. You cannot have two masters or two slaves, as this will typically result in a boot failure, because the system will not be able to properly identify the boot disk drive. It is also advisable to keep high-performance devices on a separate channel from a lower-performance device. For example, if you have a hard drive as master on one channel, and a CD-ROM drive as master on the second channel, a second hard drive should be added as a slave to the first hard drive, because they operate at the same speed. If the second hard drive was installed as a slave on the second channel, the CD-ROM activity may decrease the performance of the drive.

Some systems also have a third option, called *cable select,* where the master and slave are configured using a special cable with specific connectors for each drive.

Exam Tip Be aware that the best place to find information on IDE/ATA drive jumper configurations is from the manufacturer's documentation or Web site. Often this information is not printed on the hard drive itself.

The device used to configure each drive is called a *jumper,* a small connector that fits over two pins on the hard drive. The jumper makes a connection between those two pins, to signal the configuration for the hard drive. Although each manufacturer has their own sets of pins on the hard drive for these configurations (typically six to ten pins), most pin configurations are generally the same. Usually, the jumper settings for the hard drive are printed right on the case. If not, you will have to use the manual that came with the drive, or consult the manufacturer's website. Figure 8-1 shows typical jumper settings. On most drives, MA is the setting for master, SL is the setting for slave, and CS is the setting for cable select.

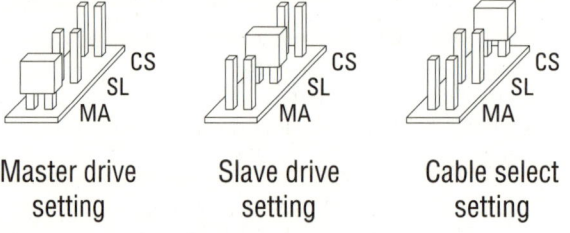

Master drive setting   Slave drive setting   Cable select setting

Figure 8-1: Typical jumper settings for IDE master/slave/cable select configurations

In the Real World Check the documentation carefully for proper jumper positions. Although most configurations are standard, various manufacturers have slightly different positions for the pins and jumpers. The most common error in configuring IDE drives is mixing up the jumper settings.

To set the drive as the master, use a jumper to join the two pins that are labeled Master or MA. Some drives are factory-set as the master drive by default, and there is no need for any jumper at all. If there is only one IDE drive in your system, this may be the case, although some manufacturers also use another jumper setting called Single Drive to designate one single master drive.

To set the drive as the slave, use a jumper to join the two pins that are labeled Slave, or SA.

To use the cable select feature, use the jumper to join the pins marked Cable Select or CS. You will then need a special IDE cable made for cable select configurations. It differs slightly from the older standard 40-conductor connector, using a special signaling to designate the master and slave drive connector. Most newer 80-conductor cables support cable select by default.

Exam Tip   On the exam, watch for scenarios relating to master/slave/cable select misconfigurations.

The master drive should be attached to the end connector of the cable, and the slave goes on the middle connector. The connectors are usually labeled to help you identify where the master and slave drives go, as seen in Figure 8-2.

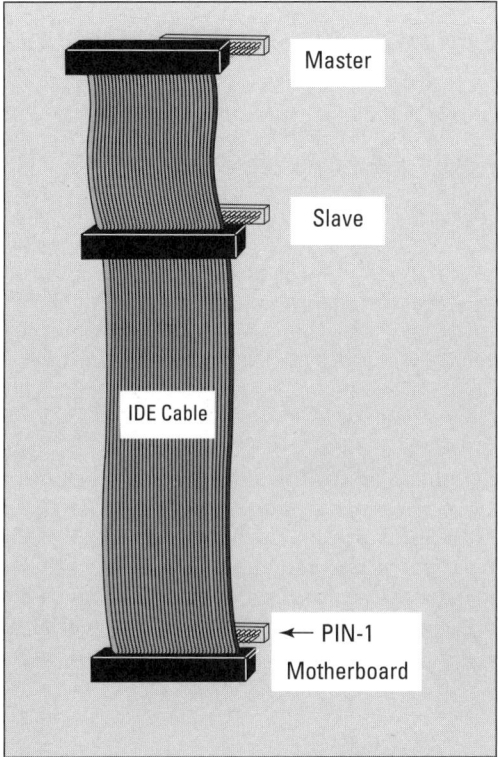

Figure 8-2: Proper setup for two hard drives with a cable-select configuration

IDE cabling

The original 40-conductor standard cable has been used for IDE devices for a very long time. It is commonly called a *ribbon cable,* because the wires are laid out in parallel fashion. The red stripe along the side of the cable is considered to be pin 1, and must be connected to the pin 1 of the IDE device. Although most cables and connectors are keyed, showing which way to connect the cable, some do not, and you must be careful not to reverse the cable or it may damage your hard drives. Because of its slower speeds, and little protection from electromagnetic interference, most modern systems use the newer 80-conductor IDE cables.

The 80-conductor IDE cable was created in conjunction with the introduction of the ATA-33 (ATA/ATAPI4) interface. Although it was optional for the 33MB/s IDE systems, the 80-conductor cable is mandatory for faster UDMA modes supporting 66MB/s and 100MB/s. These cables are automatically configured for cable select operations.

Another new addition to the 80-conductor cable is color-coded connectors, to help in installing the right connector to the right component:

✦ **Black:** This connector goes to the master drive, or to the only drive if it is a single-drive system.

✦ **Gray:** This cable is connected to the slave drive if one is installed.

✦ **Blue:** This cable is connected to the IDE channel connector on the motherboard.

Caution   80-conductor does not mean that the cable has 80 pins. The cable actually still only has 40 pins like the standard IDE cable for compatibility. The extra 40 wires are grounded to help eliminate electrical interference.

SCSI Disk Systems

Although IDE/ATA systems are often compared to SCSI systems because both are hard drive and peripheral interfaces, SCSI (Small Computer Systems Interface) is technically an advanced system bus built for high performance, and has greater intelligence for system data flow. Although SCSI is much more expensive that IDE/ATA, SCSI is preferred in server installations for its robust performance and flexible expansion options. Many devices can be chained together on a SCSI bus, which is required for large disk space installations and fault-tolerant RAID systems.

SCSI standards and technologies

Objective   ✦ Verify that drives are appropriate type

There is a lot of confusion concerning SCSI standards because of the different types of SCSI technology available, and increasing the confusion is the amount of vendor-specific implementations of SCSI systems. The standards discussed in this section, SCSI-1, SCSI-2, and SCSI-3, are the three basic SCSI standards and descriptions of their various implementations.

SCSI terminology

Before discussing the current SCSI standards, you need to know the definitions of certain features and technologies so that you can measure the devices between different SCSI versions.

✦ **Clock speed:** The clock speed of the SCSI bus, measured in MHz.

✦ **Bus speed:** The speed of the SCSI bus, measured in MB/s.

✦ **Bus width:** The width of the SCSI bus. Narrow SCSI is 8-bit, Wide SCSI is 16-bit.

✦ **Signaling:** The type of voltage signaling used to trigger events. The three types are Single Ended (SE), Low-Voltage Differential (LVD), and High Voltage Differential (HVD).

✦ **Termination:** Describes the various types of terminators needed on the SCSI bus. Termination of a SCSI bus is critical to block signal reflection noise.

✦ **Cable type and length:** Different SCSI technologies require certain cable types and lengths.

✦ **Devices supported:** The number of devices allowed at one time on the SCSI bus chain.

SCSI-1

Although now obsolete, SCSI-1 is the original standard, approved by ANSI (American National Standards Institute) in 1986. The characteristics of SCSI-1 include a narrow 8-bit bus width, a 5 MHz clock speed allowing 5 MB/s transfers, single-ended signaling, and passive termination.

With *single-ended signaling,* the voltage level used for triggering events is either a positive voltage for an on condition, or a zero voltage for an off condition. The problem with SE signaling is that the higher the clock speed rate, the shorter the SCSI cables connecting the devices on the bus must be, or signal degradation and corruption occurs. As advances were made in clocking speeds, cable lengths became increasingly too short to use effectively. An alternative to single-ended signaling is called *differential.* This technology uses two wires for voltage signaling, but the signal of an on or off condition is measured by the difference between the two voltages. This proves much more reliable than single-ended signaling, but because of its overhead of high voltages, and its incompatibility with single-ended devices, most signaling in the early SCSI devices is single-ended.

Termination is provided by passive terminators, which are nothing more than simple resistors to terminate the SCSI bus. Up to 8 devices can be used on the SCSI bus chain. SCSI-1 devices are seen only on much older systems.

SCSI-2

SCSI-2 technology was created fairly quickly to improve upon the basic SCSI-1 system. The bus speed was doubled from 5MB/s to 10MB/s. SCSI-2 also introduced the concept of Wide SCSI, which doubled the width of SCSI bus from 8-bits to 16-bits.

Cable termination became active rather than passive, enabling cables to use voltage regulation components to increase efficiency. The number of devices that could be chained together on the SCSI bus increased to 16 from 8.

The following implementations of SCSI technology are based on the SCSI-2 standard:

✦ **Fast SCSI:** Fast SCSI refers to devices with a doubled clock speed of 10 MHz on the narrow 8-bit bus with an effective transfer rate of 10 MB/s.

✦ **Wide SCSI:** The 16-bit bus width provides twice the amount of data at the original clock speed of 5MHz to double transfer rates to 10 MB/s.

✦ **Fast Wide SCSI:** Combining the features of Fast and Wide SCSI, this type of SCSI system used the 10 MHz clock speed, and the wide 16-bit bus width to create transfer rates of 20 MB/s.

SCSI-3

Current SCSI-3 standards encompass many different names and technologies.

The SCSI-3 standard included faster clock speeds. Internal clock speeds were increased to 20, 40, and 80 MHz. The SCSI-3 standard also incorporates Low Voltage Differential (LVD) signaling. The original differential method (also called High Voltage Differential) uses two wires for triggering voltages. The system would take the difference in the voltage levels of the two wires to use for signaling. However, the voltages used were very high, which caused the system to be very expensive compared to single-ended technology. Incompatibility issues with single-ended systems also harmed its adoption and, therefore, was rarely used. Low voltage differential LVD uses the same concept as HVD, with much lower signaling voltages and remains compatible with older single-ended devices. SCSI-3 devices also use *multimode operations*, which means they can work on both single-ended and LVD systems.

The following are the many current versions of the SCSI-3 standard:

✦ **Ultra SCSI:** Ultra SCSI, also called Fast-20 SCSI, uses 20 MHz clock speeds on the narrow 8-bit bus, giving a throughout of 20 MB/s.

✦ **Wide Ultra SCSI:** Wide Ultra SCSI, also known as Fast-20 Wide SCSI, and Ultra Wide SCSI, uses a 20 MHz clock speed on the wide 16-bit bus, enabling a throughput of 40 MB/s.

✦ **Ultra2 SCSI:** The next generation of SCSI-3 standard devices doubled the clock speed again to 40 MHz, which is why these are also known as Fast-40 SCSI. Ultra2 SCSI runs on an 8-bit bus, allowing a transfer rate of 40 MB/s. It did not prove very popular in the marketplace because of the low bus width, and generally was passed over in favor of the Wide Ultra2 SCSI technology.

✦ **Wide Ultra2 SCSI:** Also known as Fast-40 Wide SCSI, it uses 40 MHz clocking rate over a wide 16-bit bus, allowing transfer rates of 80 MB/s.

✦ **Ultra3 SCSI:** Also known as Fast-80 SCSI, Ultra3 SCSI has also been called Wide Ultra3 SCSI because the default bus width for the Ultra3 is 16-bits, and 8-bit technology has been discontinued. The clock speed runs at 80 MHz, effectively giving data transfer rates of up to 160 MB/s. Other names for the Ultra3 SCSI, and which contain their own various subsets of the SCSI-3 standard, include Ultra 160, Ultra 160m, and Ultra 160+.

Table 8-2 summarizes the various statistics for SCSI implementations.

Table 8-2
Comparison of Different SCSI Technologies

SCSI Type	SCSI Standard	Bus Clocking Speed (MHz)	Bus Width (Bits)	Transfer Speed (MB/s)	Signaling Method
SCSI	SCSI-1	5	8	5	SE/HVD
Wide SCSI	SCSI-2	5	16	10	SE/HVD
Fast SCSI	SCSI-2	10	8	10	SE/HVD
Fast Wide SCSI	SCSI-2	10	16	20	SE/HVD
Ultra SCSI	SCSI-3	20	8	20	SE/HVD
Wide Ultra SCSI	SCSI-3	20	16	40	SE/HVD
Ultra2 SCSI	SCSI-3	40	8	40	LVD/HVD
Wide Ultra2 SCSI	SCSI-3	40	16	80	LVD/HVD
Ultra3 SCSI	SCSI-3	80	16	160	LVD

Cables, connectors, and termination

✦ Confirm termination and cabling

Each SCSI technology has its own special characteristics such as clocking speed, bus width, signaling, and termination. Each type also has its own different cabling and connector requirements.

SCSI-1 50-pin (narrow) connectors

SCSI-1 devices use a 50-pin "D" connector, or a 50-pin Centronics type of connector. The D-shaped connector is named for the shape of the shell that surrounds the pins. It is also called a DB-50, and resembles the type of connectors used on printer cables. The Centronics connector, which is named after the type of printer that used this type of connector for a parallel interface, does not actually have pins, but 50 flat contacts. Two latches on either side of the connector lock it into place. Internally, SCSI-1 devices use a rectangular connector of 50 pins, split into two 25-pin rows.

SCSI-2 high density 50 and 68-pin (wide) connectors

The high-density wide connectors are very similar to the D-shaped connectors used by SCSI-1 devices, but they are much smaller, with the pins closer together. They also use latches similar to the Centronics connector, but the latches in this case are pushed together before inserting the connector and before it is locked into place. The 68-pin versions are also referred to as Wide connectors.

For internal cabling, SCSI-2 devices use high-density 50-pin or 68-pin wide connectors.

SCSI-3 68-pin Centronics connector (VHDCI)

The Very High Density Cable Interconnect (VHDCI) resembles the large 50-Pin Centronics connector. These connectors use 68 contacts, which sit very close to each other. Its size makes it much easier to plug two cables into the back of a host adapter.

SCA adapters

For most modern servers that run RAID systems with many SCSI hard disks, the connectors used are Single Connector Attachment (SCA) adapters. These special connections feed all signaling and power through one connector that plugs right into the hard drive without any cabling. This is most important for hot swapping drives. Regular SCSI connections do not allow this critical capability. The SCA connector utilizes 80 pins in a D-shell Centronics-type connector. The server will usually consist of a SCSI backplane, which contains several of these connectors attached together by a common interface so that each hard drive bay is part of the backplane and controlled by one SCSI controller.

Cable lengths

The advantages of differential signaling over single-ended devices are very apparent when comparing the required cable lengths at faster speeds. The error rate for single-ended signaling over multiple devices and longer cable lengths increases dramatically. Therefore, the faster the bus on a single-ended system, the shorter the cable length must be for it to work properly.

For a simple 5 MHz bus speed system, the cable length restriction is 6m, while for differential signaling at the same speed, the length can be 25m. When the speed is doubled to 10 MHz, the single-ended system can only use a maximum of 3m for cable length, while differential remains at 25m. Double the speed again, to 20 MHz, and the maximum cable length for single-ended devices is only 1.5m, while differential can have a maximum length of 25m. Table 8-3 lists the various specifications for the different SCSI standards.

Table 8-3 SCSI Cables Configurations			
SCSI Type	**Contacts/Pins**	**Cabling Length (SE, meters)**	**Cabling Length (meters)**
SCSI	50	6	25 HVD
Wide SCSI	68	6	25 HVD
Fast SCSI	50	3	25 HVD
Fast Wide SCSI	68	3	25 HVD
Ultra SCSI	50	3	25 HVD
Wide Ultra SCSI	68	3	25 HVD
Ultra2 SCSI	50		12 LVD, 25 HVD
Wide Ultra2 SCSI	68		12 LVD, 25 HVD
Ultra3 SCSI	68		25 LVD

Termination

✦ Confirm termination and cabling

The SCSI bus must be terminated to provide a way of stopping cable signals from reflecting from the end of the bus back onto the wire and possibly conflicting with other live data. Terminators must be connected to the end of the SCSI bus, at the end of the chain of devices. Some SCSI cables have terminators built into them, but usually a separate physical terminator is needed. SCSI host adapters usually have built-in termination that can be set on or off depending on where it physically resides on the bus. Some terminators have a light that indicates if they are working properly.

Older SCSI-1 devices used simple passive termination, which simply uses resistors to stop the signal from reflecting back onto the bus. Faster speed single-ended devices used active termination, which added voltage regulators to the resistors to more efficiently terminate signals.

SCSI-2 and SCSI-3 devices need terminators based on the type of signaling being used. LVD and HVD devices need terminators specific to each type.

SCSI configuration

Configuring the SCSI bus can be somewhat complex, involving items such as the host adapter settings, bus settings, and SCSI ID's. Each of these items is essential in installing and configuring the SCSI bus system.

Host adapters

The SCSI *host adapter* facilitates communications between the PC bus and the devices on the SCSI bus. You must choose a host adapter that will be compatible with the SCSI technology you wish to use. Host adapters are backward-compatible, so that older devices will still be able to be used with your system. Most importantly, your host adapter must be electrically compatible with your devices. You cannot mix HVD types of devices on the same bus with single-ended or LVD type devices. Single-ended and LVD devices are electrically compatible, but your devices must support multimode operations. The only problem is that the bus will only run as fast as your slowest device. LVD modes will only work if all the devices are LVD. If there is a single-ended device on the same bus, it will knock down your transfer speeds and also cause cabling limitations. Newer host adapters alleviate this problem by using special segments on the same SCSI channel to separate the devices, or even run a separate SCSI channel for devices running on a different mode.

The connectors on a host adapter are another factor in choosing the right card. Because it supports both internal and external devices, there are connectors for both on the internal side of the card and the external outer edge of the card. If you need to support both narrow and wide SCSI devices, make sure your host adapters come with connectors for both on the same card.

Most modern SCSI host adapters have their own BIOS that can be configured with special software. Before any new installation, you should update the SCSI BIOS to the latest version to ensure support for newer SCSI hard drives and their various modes of operations and commands.

Exam Tip   Pay careful attention to the type of host adapter in SCSI configuration questions.

Device bus

As I stated earlier in the chapter, the SCSI system is configured as a bus topology. Devices are chained together from one end to the other and terminated at each end. If there are extra connectors that are not being used, the termination should still be at the end of the cable. Terminating your cable with other connectors left open can lead to signaling problems.

Original 8-bit SCSI devices could have up to 8 devices on the bus. The wide 16-bit versions can have up to 16 devices. Because single-ended devices are subject to electrical interference, the signaling type used and the maximum cable length for the bus also limit the number of devices. Reducing the number of devices on the bus can effectively lengthen the amount of cable you can use.

Tip   The host adapter itself is considered a bus device, so the actual number of devices on a narrow SCSI bus is 7, and a wide system supports up to 15.

Device IDs

Each device on a SCSI bus must have its own separate ID number. This way, the system can allocate control of the bus to a specific device. The numbers also give a priority level for the devices, with higher device IDs having greater priority than lower numbers. This is why the SCSI host adapter itself is usually designated as device 7. The first boot device, which is usually the hard drive your system boots from, should be set to SCSI ID 0. When the SCSI bus is first initialized, it will start scanning the ID numbers starting at 0. This way your boot device will be recognized first. This is not to be confused with the priority of IDs, which sets the order to see which device has precedence over the bus during regular communications.

Caution   Some older SCSI host adapters will not permit a system to start if the boot hard drive is not assigned as ID 0.

On host adapters that support multiple segments, host IDs must remain unique across the segments so that no two devices have the same ID.

To set the device ID, the oldest SCSI devices used jumpers on the card to configure the ID. Later devices used a small button that would cycle through the various ID numbers when pressed. Modern systems are usually configured using software. SCA-capable servers automatically allocate device IDs, to facilitate hot swapping and auto configuration for RAID arrays.

Installing SCSI drives

Objective   ✦ Replace existing drives

To install a basic internal SCSI drive, power off the server and then open the server chassis cover. If you are initially removing a drive to be replaced, find the original drive on the SCSI chain and remove the SCSI and power cables. Remove any mounting screws that may be present, take the hard drive out, and put it safely into an anti-static bag for storage. Examine the new hard drive for any jumpers or mechanisms that enable you to set the SCSI ID. If you are replacing a drive, it is easiest to assign the new drive the ID of the original; this ensures that there will be no device ID conflicts. Carefully mount the new hard drive in place, and reconnect the cabling. Depending on the type of device, you may need special adapters, especially if you are installing a narrow device on a wide SCSI bus, or vice-versa. If the device is located at the end of the SCSI bus chain, you may need to use a SCSI terminator. Ensure that the termination is appropriate for the device and bus. When completed, replace the server chassis cover and turn on the server. The SCSI host adapter card should show the new device during the SCSI bus initialization. If it does not appear, check the cabling, device ID, and termination to make sure everything is configured and connected properly.

In servers that contain special hot-plug SCA connector bays for SCSI hard drives, the steps are much simpler. The drives are installed in special bays, in which the hard drive slides in and locks in place with the internal connector. These hard drives typically come with levers or handles that are used to release and insert the hard drives into the bays. Depending on the type of system you are running, you may be able to perform this installation while the system is still running, if the server supports hot-plug drives. If not, you should turn the system off to prevent damage to components. If you are replacing a drive, you can pull the handle of the original drive and slide it out of the drive bay. Put the hard drive into an anti-static bag for storage. To insert the new drive, simply extend the handle, push the hard drive into the bay, carefully lining it up with the connector slot, and when it is fully inside the bay, push the handle back to lock the drive into place.

SCSI configuration and upgrading issues

Most SCSI issues regarding upgrading and adding devices center around the mixing of different SCSI devices on the same bus. The most efficient way to mix narrow and wide SCSI devices on the same bus is to use a host adapter that supports segmentation. This way, each segment will have its own cabling and termination that will not conflict with each other. Using different SCSI types on the same bus channel is possible, but you need to use cable adapters that will facilitate connections between 50-pin devices and 68-pin wide devices. Make sure these special cables support termination, so that wide-to-narrow adapters will terminate the extra wide connections. Also keep in mind that your devices will run only as fast as the bus they run on. For example, if you added an Ultra3 SCSI disk drive to an Ultra2 bus, the Ultra3 drive will only run at Ultra2 speeds. Termination is also an important issue when mixing SCSI devices. The SCSI bus must be always terminated by a device that is compatible with that bus. For example, you cannot install and terminate a narrow 8-bit device at the end of a wide 16-bit bus. The terminating device must be the same technology as the bus itself. It is fine for the 8-bit device to appear in the middle of the bus.

Exam Tip   On the exam, be prepared for questions concerning the mixing of various SCSI types.

Upgrading SCSI RAID Systems

Objective   ✦ Upgrade mass storage

✦ Add drives to array

Adding disk space to a RAID array is a very common upgrade for a server technician to perform. It is typically much easier than upgrading a regular SCSI system because of the auto-configuration capabilities of SCSI RAID controllers and their device chains. Typical SCSI configuration parameters such as device ID allocation and bus termination are all performed by the RAID system.

The first step in upgrading any RAID system is updating the BIOS on your SCSI RAID controller. If you have to add new devices, they might not be supported by your current setup, which might be out of date. Obtain the latest BIOS for your controller and install it before going ahead with any upgrades. This ensures that you will not have any compatibility issues with new equipment.

The next step is to examine your current system and see how many drive expansion slots you have remaining. If you have none left, you may be forced to either buy a new external RAID tower, which can be very expensive, or you will have to replace the drives in your current array with drives of a larger size. The drawback to this scenario is that your entire array will be have to backed up and restored to the new system when it is reconfigured.

If you do have slots available, you should obtain hard drives that are of the same make and same size as your current ones. For example, adding an 18GB drive to a RAID 5 array using 9GB drives will result in the new array using only 50 percent of your new 18 GB drive. Using the same hard drive manufacturer will ensure that you will not have any compatibility issues with other manufacturers' equipment.

Once you have verified the availability of slots, you can then install the drives into the array. If your system uses hot-plug technology, you can plug the hard drives into the array while the server is still running, without having to turn it off. If not, you will need to shut down the server before you install the drives, especially if you need to open up the server chassis to install internal SCSI drives.

To enable the RAID array to detect the new disks, it must support array expansion, or else you will have to manually destroy the array and recreate it, which means you will have to back up your data and restore it to the new array when it is configured. Most RAID systems come with their own utilities to resize arrays on the fly, without having to remove the current array. Arrays are grouped together into *containers,* which represent a logical unit of part of the array of disks. For example, in a server with nine 9 GB drives, you can allocate four to one RAID 5 array, while grouping the other five in their own RAID array. This will create two logical drives, or containers. This will appear to the operating system as two separate drives. When you are finished setting up your arrays, the new partitions should become available to you within your operating system.

Exam Tip   On the exam, read questions carefully to distinguish between logical and physical drive issues.

Configuring the OS to Recognize New Hard Disks

  ✦ Integrate into storage solution and make it available to the operating system

Once you have installed your additional hard drives, you will not be able to benefit from the added space until you have made it visible to the operating system.

This is accomplished using a disk partitioning utility, such as `fdisk`, which is used in both Microsoft Windows and Unix systems. It will take the disk space and splice it into different partitions, which can then be formatted with a particular file system.

Formatting the drive creates a file system that is recognizable to the host operating system. From there, you can assign a particular drive letter or mount point depending on your operating system.

Key Point Summary

This chapter discussed various storage techniques, and how to properly configure and upgrade them. Technologies such as IDE/ATA and SCSI were discussed in detail and compared so that you can make an informed decision on storage for a new server installation. Keep the following points in mind for the exam:

✦ Double check jumper positions and configuration by referring to the manufacturer's documentation or Website.

✦ If you have two devices on an IDE channel, make sure one is configured as the master and the other the slave.

✦ In cable-select systems, make sure the hard drives are jumpered as cable select, and ensure that the master and slave drives are hooked up to the proper connectors. The master typically goes on the end connector, while the slave is attached to the middle connector.

✦ Make sure that the Pin 1 on the IDE cable goes to the proper Pin 1 on the connector. Pin 1 is identified by the red stripe on an individual cable wire.

✦ Know the differences between the many different SCSI standards and features, including their limitations such as number of devices, cable length, connectors, bus speed, device ID's, and compatibility with other SCSI systems.

✦ Know in general terms how to make new hard drive space available for RAID arrays and operating systems.

✦   ✦   ✦

STUDY GUIDE

The Study Guide section provides you with the opportunity to test your knowledge about upgrading hard disks. The Assessment Questions provide practice for the test, and the Scenarios provide practice with real situations. If you get any questions wrong, use the answers to determine the part of the chapter you should review before continuing.

Assessment Questions

1. When a server first boots up, a message appears after the POST results stating "3 Logical Drives Found." The system is using a RAID 5 array with six 9GB drives. What does this message indicate?

    A. Three of the drives have failed.

    B. The system is actually using RAID 1.

    C. The RAID array is configured into three separate logical containers.

    D. Only 27GB will be available to the OS.

2. The initial boot drive on an older SCSI bus should have what device ID?

    A. 0

    B. 1

    C. 15

    D. 7

3. A new server has just been installed. The server has built-in SCSI SCA connectors, and it has with four 18GB hard drives with 40-pin connectors. Has all the proper equipment been ordered for this server?

    A. No, SCA requires 80-pin hard drives.

    B. Yes, all the proper equipment is present.

    C. No, an adapter cable will be needed.

    D. No, the hard drives will need termination.

4. A technician wants to add a Wide Ultra2 SCSI drive to a Fast SCSI system. What will the technician need to perform this task?

   A. The current configuration will not work.

   B. SCA connectors are needed.

   C. A special Ultra2 terminator is needed.

   D. A wide-to-narrow adapter is needed.

5. A server with an existing IDE/ATA hard drive is being expanded with an additional drive. After the installation, the server is powered on, but does not boot after the POST routine. What is the mostly likely cause of the problem?

   A. The second drive is configured as a master.

   B. The second drive is configured as a slave.

   C. The second drive is missing a terminator.

   D. The system is configured with cable select.

6. A customer has called to complain that they have noticed a green light on one of the SCSI terminators. What does this indicate?

   A. The terminator is not working properly.

   B. It indicates a narrow SCSI system.

   C. It indicates a wide SCSI system.

   D. The system is fine. The light indicates the terminator is working properly.

7. A new server has just been installed, but it will not boot up properly. The server consists of two IDE/ATA drives, configured to use cable select for its settings. What is the most likely cause of the problem?

   A. The cable is not terminated properly.

   B. The jumpers on the drives are not set correctly.

   C. The drives are in the wrong positions on the cable.

   D. One of the drives has failed.

8. A technician is installing a narrow SCSI tape drive device onto an Ultra Wide SCSI bus system. The bus is using 68-pin high-density connectors. What will the technician need to connect the tape drive?

   A. A 50-pin to 68-pin adapter

   B. Nothing, the current configuration will work fine.

   C. A terminator for the tape drive

   D. An 80-pin to 68-pin adapter

9. A technician is installing a new IDE/ATA hard drive into a server that already contains an IDE/ATA hard drive on the primary IDE controller, and a CD-ROM drive on the secondary IDE controller. What is the best way to connect the new hard drive?

    A. There is no room for another device.

    B. Configure the drive as cable select on the secondary IDE controller.

    C. Configure the drive as a master on the primary IDE controller.

    D. Configure the drive as a slave on the primary IDE controller.

10. A technician is adding an Ultra3 device to a system that already contains four Wide Ultra2 devices. Is the configuration possible?

    A. Yes, with the addition of a 68-pin adapter.

    B. Yes, the configuration will work.

    C. No, the Ultra3 device is not backward-compatible.

    D. No, the bus has already reached its device limit.

11. What cable length limitations are there on a Wide Ultra2 SCSI bus?

    A. 6m with LVD signaling, 12m with HVD

    B. 12m with LVD signaling, 25m with HVD

    C. 25m with SE signaling, 25m with HVD

    D. 3m with LVD signaling, 25m with HVD

12. A server is not booting up properly. It is configured with two IDE/ATA hard drives configured as master and slave. What is the most likely cause of the problem?

    A. The IDE cable is loose.

    B. The master and slave drives should be reversed.

    C. The terminator is missing.

    D. The second hard drive should be on the secondary IDE channel.

13. A technician is investigating freezing problems on a SCSI bus. All the cabling, connectors, and termination seem to be in order. What is the most likely cause of the problem?

    A. The host adapter is set to device ID 7.

    B. The bus is mixing both narrow and wide devices.

    C. The system has exceeded the acceptable cable length.

    D. Two devices have the same device ID.

14. A RAID system is being upgraded with extra hard drives. The system is hot swap capable, and can automatically configure the drives. What must be done to make the extra hard drive space available to the operating system?

    A. Nothing, the allocation is automatic.

    B. The RAID configuration utility must be used to allocate the extra space.

    C. Logical drives must be created within the operating system.

    D. The BIOS must be updated to recognize the change.

15. An ATAPI CD-ROM has been added to an IDE/ATA system, which is currently configured with one 9GB drive on the primary IDE controller. The CD-ROM is installed on the secondary IDE controller. When the system is started, the CD-ROM is not functional. What is the most likely cause of the problem?

    A. A CD-ROM driver has not been loaded.

    B. The CD-ROM should have been installed as a slave on the primary IDE controller.

    C. The CD-ROM should have been installed as a master on the primary IDE controller.

    D. The CD-ROM should be configured as a cable-select slave on the secondary IDE controller.

16. A narrow Ultra2 SCSI hard drive with a throughput of 40MB/s is being added to a Wide Ultra2 SCSI bus with a throughput of 80MB/s. What is the effective transfer speed of the Ultra2 drive?

    A. 40 MB/s

    B. 80 MB/s

    C. 160 MB/s

    D. 20 MB/s

17. A technician is installing a server that uses two ATA-66 drives. The drives came with color-coded 80-conductor cables. What is the color-coding for?

    A. To signify that they are for use with ATA-66.

    B. To signify where the master and slave drives should be located on the cable.

    C. The color is to show where Pin1 on the cable is.

    D. The colors show where the cable is terminated.

18. A customer is complaining because they feel that their new Ultra3 SCSI hard drive is not working to its full potential. It is connected to an Ultra2 host adapter. What is most likely causing the performance problem?

    A. The cable lengths are too long, causing performance lag.

    B. The Ultra3 will only work at the same speed as the bus itself.

    C. One of the terminators is faulty.

    D. The Ultra3 card is defective.

19. The red stripe on the edge of an IDE/ATA cable identifies what feature?

    A. The cable supports cable select.

    B. The cable is a UDMA cable.

    C. The wire that should be connected to Pin 1 on the hard drive.

    D. The cable is self-terminating.

20. SCA connectors on a SCSI system are most important for what feature?

    A. Auto-configuration

    B. No power connections

    C. Hot swap drives

    D. All of the above

Scenarios

1. A technician is installing a new server, consisting of two ATA-33 hard drives and a CD-ROM drive. The server has a primary and secondary IDE controller. What is the best configuration for the devices?

2. A technician has just put together a Wide Ultra2 SCSI system consisting of a host adapter, an internal SCSI tape drive, and 4 Wide Ultra2 hard drives. When powered on, the server will not boot properly. The system bus cabling is currently this configuration:

Host adapter → hard drive 1 → hard drive 2 → terminator → hard drive 3 → hard drive 4 → hard drive 5 → tape drive

Why does the system not boot, and how can it be fixed?

3. A customer has asked that a new database server be installed using a SCSI hard drive system, and it must support fault tolerance. What kind of recommendations can you make for the installation?

Answers to Chapter Questions

Chapter pre-test

1. IDE is less expensive, simpler, offers good performance, leaves little room for expansion, and is best implemented for desktop environments. SCSI is more expensive, offers excellent performance, can be used in RAID systems, is easier to expand, and is best suited for high-end server environments.

2. SCA connections within a SCSI server allows several hard drives to be plugged right into a SCSI backplane. This feature is useful for RAID arrays and hot plug capabilities.

3. Narrow SCSI uses an 8-bit bus width. Wide SCSI uses a 16-bit bus width.

4. Termination prevents electrical signals from reflecting back from the end of the bus and causing data disruption.

5. Cable length is dependant on the type of electrical signaling and the number of devices on the bus. An electrical signal loses quality as it travels a longer distance.

6. A physical drive is an actual single piece of hardware. A logical drive can encompass a number of drives to create partitions of larger sizes.

7. Fast SCSI refers to the doubling of the speed of SCSI-2 standard devices to 10 MB/s. Ultra2 refers to devices within the SCSI-3 standard with speeds of 40 MB/s.

8. Typically, 8 devices for narrow SCSI, and 16 devices for wide SCSI.

9. The host adapter is usually device 7 to give it the highest priority on the SCSI chain.

10. Single-ended signaling refers to using a voltage to indicate an on condition, and using zero voltage to indicate an off condition. Differential signaling uses the difference between two voltages to determine the condition.

Assessment questions

1. **C.** The message is informative, not a warning. Answer A is incorrect because there is no error condition. Answer B is incorrect because this is a RAID 5 system. Answer D is incorrect because a RAID 5 array with six 9GB will result in 45 GB of available disk space. For more information, see the "Upgrading SCSI RAID Systems" section.

2. **A.** Older SCSI systems will not boot unless the drive is set to ID 0. Newer SCSI technology has eliminated this condition. For more information, see the "Device IDs" section.

3. A. SCA adapters require 80-connector drives. Answer C is incorrect because you adapt a regular hard drive to an SCA interface. Answer D is incorrect because the built-in SCSI backplane takes care of termination issues. For more information, see the "SCA adapters" section.

4. D. Fast SCSI has a narrow bus width. Answer A is incorrect, because this configuration will work with an adapter. Answer B is incorrect because SCA connectors are built into a server backplane. Answer C is incorrect, because there is no need for a special terminator. For more information, see the "SCSI-2" section.

5. A. The factory default settings on most hard drives configure it as a master, and two masters in one machine will cause it not to boot. Answer B is incorrect, because this configuration would have worked. Answer C is incorrect, because IDE/ATA systems do not need terminators. Answer D is incorrect because the system would have used the cable select feature to identify the drives on the cable. For more information, see the "IDE configuration" section.

6. D. The lights indicate a proper termination. Answer A is incorrect, because the SCSI system would not work with improper termination. Answers B and C are incorrect because narrow and wide refer to bus widths. For more information, see the "Termination" section.

7. C. The master is usually at the end of the cable, while the slave drive is in the middle. If cable-select drives are placed in the wrong positions, the server will not boot. Answer A is incorrect because there is no termination in IDE/ATA systems. Answer B is incorrect, because the jumpers usually aren't needed in cable select. Answer D is incorrect, because the other drive should still be working if the other failed, unless it was the boot drive. For more information, see the "IDE configuration" section.

8. A. The adapter will enable the narrow device to connect to the wide bus. Answer B is incorrect because the current configuration will not work. Answer C is incorrect, although it might be necessary if the device is at the end of the bus. Answer D is incorrect, because 80-pin connections are usually associated with SCA connectors. For more information, see the "Cables, connectors, and termination" section.

9. D. The new hard drive can be the second device on the primary controller. Answer A is incorrect, because there is room for one more device on each controller. Answer B is incorrect, because you should not connect a CD-ROM with your hard drive, and it is not using cable select. Answer C is incorrect, because the original hard drive is already configured as the master. For more information, see the "IDE configuration" section.

10. B. The configuration will work, although the Ultra3 device will only operate at Ultra2 speed. Answer A is incorrect, because no adapter is needed. Answer C is incorrect, because newer SCSI devices are usually backwards compatible. Answer D is incorrect, because the limit for a wide SCSI system is 16 devices. For more information, see the "SCSI configuration and upgrading issues" section.

11. B. LVD signaling will work with 25m if there are only two devices on the bus. For more information, see the "Cable lengths" section.

12. A. The drives are configured correctly, so it is most likely a bad or loose cable. Answer B is incorrect, because the drives are not using cable select. Answer C is incorrect, because IDE/ATA drives do not require termination. Answer D is incorrect, because the drive doesn't have to be on the secondary IDE channel. For more information, see the "IDE configuration" section.

13. D. Most intermittent problems on a SCSI bus come from conflicting device ID's. Answer A is incorrect, because ID 7 is the normal ID for a host adapter. Answer B is incorrect, because mixing devices will work if the proper adapters and termination are used. Answer C is incorrect because the cabling was mentioned to be in order, without exceeding proper lengths. For more information, see the "Device IDs" section.

14. B. Typically, you have to configure the RAID array to allocate the space to your logical containers. Answer A is incorrect, because you have to configure the extra space. Answer C is incorrect, although it could be a later step in the process. Answer D is incorrect, because the BIOS has nothing to do with the disk space allocation. For more information, see the "Upgrading SCSI RAID Systems" section.

15. A. The CD-ROM still needs an ATAPI driver to run. Answers B and C are incorrect, because it is best to keep the slower CD-ROM on its own channel separate from the hard drives. Answer D is incorrect because the CD-ROM drive is the only device on that controller and, therefore, does not require cable select. For more information, see the "IDE/ATA standards" section.

16. A. The drive will still only run at its current speed. A faster bus will not increase the speed of the device. For more information, see the "SCSI configuration and upgrading issues" section.

17. B. Newer cable select systems color-code the connectors on the IDE cable to more easily show where the master and slave drives go. Answer A is incorrect, because the colors do not identify the device type. Answer C is incorrect, because the red stripe along the edge of the cable signifies pin 1. Answer D is incorrect, because there is no termination on an IDE/ATA system. For more information, see the "IDE configuration" section.

18. B. The device will only run as fast as the host SCSI system. Answers A, C, and D are incorrect, because the system would probably not work at all under any of these conditions. For more information, see the "SCSI configuration and upgrading issues" section.

19. C. The red stripe identifies which part of the cable to connect to pin 1 on the motherboard and on the device. Answer A is incorrect, because special cable select connections have different colors for master and slave. Answer B is incorrect, because it does not identify UDMA. Answer D is incorrect, because

IDE/ATA systems do not need to be terminated. For more information, see the "IDE cabling" section.

20. D. SCA connectors enable the hard drives to be plugged right into the system backplane without the need for configuring device IDs or installing separate power cables for each device and support RAID technologies with hot swap capabilities. For more information, see the "SCA adapters" section.

Scenarios

1. The two hard drives should be kept together on the same IDE controller. Mixing them with a slower device such as the CD-ROM might cause performance issues. The first hard drive should be configured as the master, and the second hard drive configured as the slave. Alternatively, you can use the cable select on both drives if you have a compatible cable and install the hard drives on the proper connectors. The CD-ROM can be installed as a master on the secondary IDE channel.

2. The terminator after hard drive 2 is disrupting the bus. Termination should only be at the ends of the SCSI bus. In this case, the host adapter probably has built-in termination, so the middle terminator can be removed and placed at the end of the bus after the tape drive.

3. The best solution would be a server that contains a built-in RAID controller and SCA hard drive connections. This allows a fault tolerant RAID system using multiple hard drives to be created, with the ability to use hot plug/hot swap capabilities in the event of a single drive failure. There should also be enough hard drive slots to provide for future expansion.

Upgrading Cards and Peripherals

CHAPTER PRE-TEST

1. Why is it important for system devices to have different IRQs?

2. Describe adaptive fault tolerance.

3. How is fast Ethernet different from standard Ethernet?

4. What should always be upgraded before upgrading or adding a device?

5. What is the purpose of a DMA channel?

6. What type of slot is used for high-end video adapters?

7. At what speeds do Gigabit Ethernet adapters run?

8. Why would you upgrade a tape drive on a server?

9. What is the purpose of adapter teaming?

10. What does the VA rating of a UPS refer to?

✦ Answers to these questions can be found at the end of the chapter. ✦

Processors, hard drives, and memory are the most important elements of your system that you need to upgrade, and these procedures are covered in Chapters 7 and 8. Your server also contains many other peripherals and internal and external devices that you will need to upgrade. Without proper preparation, and careful consideration of the various characteristics and resources that a peripheral will use, a simple upgrade can quickly turn into a large nightmare. This is no different with software upgrades, whose dependencies will have to be upgraded at the same time to ensure they will work properly after the upgrade.

In this chapter, various internal and external peripherals are discussed, including tips for upgrading, and solutions to common problems that you may encounter. Software items such as monitoring tools, and vendor diagnostic partitions and utilities are also discussed.

System Resources

✦ Verify appropriate system resources (e.g., expansion slots, IRQ, DMA, etc.)

To function properly, devices and peripherals must be able to communicate directly with system resources such as the CPU, memory, and disk drives. To facilitate this process, and ensure that a device can talk to these resources when needed, the computer assigns certain lines and channels for that particular device to operate on. This enables the devices to appropriately share the computer's resources. The three main ways that are used are Interrupt request lines (IRQ), Input/Output addresses, and Direct Memory Access (DMA) channels. Most modern servers rely on PCI plug-and-play technology to allocate resources for peripheral devices.

Exam Tip On the exam, pay careful attention to questions that deal with device conflicts, as the symptoms of the problem might indicate a different solution.

IRQ

Interrupt request lines are used so that a particular device can directly communicate with the CPU. To do this, the device must first be able to divert the CPU's attention to it. This process is called an *interrupt*. The name accurately describes its use, as the device will actually interrupt the CPU to allocate a resource to it. IRQs are assigned by numbers, 0 to 15. There are two interrupt controllers that handle these IRQs. The first controller handles 0 through 7, the second controller 8 through 15. Interrupts 2 and 9 are used to cascade from the first controller to the second controller. Each device is assigned its own IRQ to use. There cannot be more than one device using the same interrupt, or a conflict will occur, and confuse the processor, and the device will not function properly. Some devices actually share IRQs, such as serial COM ports. The IRQ of a device can usually be set by two ways. On older peripheral cards, you could set the device settings right on the card with special jumpers. On newer device cards, this is all done through software, either through the special configuration software that comes with the device, or through the network OS itself. To resolve an IRQ conflict, you will have to examine the IRQs of your current devices to find the conflict. This can usually be done through the OS, and some OSs will actually notify you of the conflict and tell you which devices are involved. Find an IRQ that is not in use by any other device, and configure the new device to use that setting. You must ensure that the IRQ is not in use by any internal systems in the server. The computer industry has a standard set of IRQ settings to use, summarized in Table 9-1.

In the Real World   IRQ conflicts are very common, especially between sound, video, and network cards, as they often use the same IRQ numbers.

Table 9-1
Standard Interrupts and Device Assignments

IRQ	Device Assignment	Typical Uses
0	System timer	-
1	Keyboard	-
2	Cascade for IRQs 8–15, redirected to IRQ 9	Modems, COM 3, COM 4 serial ports
3	Serial port (COM 2)	COM 4 serial port, modem, sound card, network card
4	Serial port (COM 1)	COM 3 serial port, modem, sound card, network card
5	Parallel port (LPT 2)	Sound card, network card
6	Floppy controller	-
7	Parallel port (LPT 1)	Sound card, network card, other peripherals
8	Real-time clock	-
9	Unassigned (redirected from IRQ 2)	Sound card, network card, SCSI adapter, other peripherals
10	Unassigned	Sound card, network card, SCSI adapter, other peripherals
11	Unassigned	Video card, sound card, network card, SCSI adapter, other peripherals
12	Mouse	Video card, sound card, network card, SCSI adapter, other peripherals

IRQ	Device Assignment	Typical Uses
13	Math co-processor	-
14	Hard disk controller (primary IDE)	SCSI adapter
15	Hard disk controller (secondary IDE)	SCSI adapter, network card

I/O addresses

Input/Output addresses represent special locations in system memory that are reserved for a particular device. As information is passed back and forth between the peripheral device and the CPU, the I/O address is a common place for this information to reside. I/O address ranges can be of various sizes depending on the type of device. As with IRQs, I/O addresses must be unique for each device. I/O addresses can be examined and modified the same way as IRQs, by setting jumpers on the card itself, or by using software configuration. Listed in Table 9-2 is a list of the most frequently used I/O addresses and the devices that use them. I/O addresses are represented in hexadecimal format.

Table 9-2 Summary of Common I/O Addresses and Devices	
I/O Address Range (Hexadecimal)	**Device**
1F0–1F8	Hard drive controller
200–20F	Game controller
201	Game I/O
278–27F	Parallel port (LPT 2)
2F8–2FF	Serial port (COM 2)
320–32F	Hard drive controller
378–37F	Parallel port (LPT 1)
3B0–3BF	Graphics adapter (mono)
3D0–3DF	Graphics adapter (color)
3F0–3F7	Floppy controller
3F8–3FF	Serial port (COM 1)

Direct Memory Access

DMA channels are used to facilitate the transfer of data from a peripheral device directly to system memory. This way, information transfer is faster and more efficient by not having to get to system memory through the CPU. There are eight DMA channels numbered 0 through 7. DMA channels 0 through 3 are on the first DMA controller, and 5 through 7 are on the second DMA controller. DMA channel 4 is used for cascading the channels from the first to the second controller. DMA channels are often used most by sound and network cards. Conflicts can occur because only one device can use a DMA channel at a time. You can resolve a DMA conflict in the same way as IRQ and I/O address conflicts, by using physical jumpers on the device card itself, or through software configuration.

PCI plug-and-play

The concept of plug-and-play was created by Microsoft, Intel, and other hardware vendors to create a way of allocating device resources automatically using both hardware and software. For plug-and-play to work, it must be supported by the peripheral device, the OS, and the system BIOS. Due to the complexity of server systems, plug-and-play is usually not appropriate for configuring devices on a server.

Expansion slots

Before you upgrade any peripheral component, the first thing to examine on your server is if you have any expansion slots left. Most modern servers come with a large number of PCI slots, often more than ten, to support as many devices as you need. With most servers proving on-board devices that are installed right on the motherboard, such as video, network, and SCSI controllers, you are usually not limited with the number of expansion slots that you can use.

Upgrading Network Interface Cards

 3.6 Upgrade adapters (e.g., NIC's, SCSI cards, RAID, etc.)

A Network Interface Card (NIC) connects your server to the network. Its function is to interface network connectivity to your system bus. There are several characteristics of network cards that must be taken into account when choosing a type of card for installation or upgrade.

 More detailed information on Network protocol standards and cabling can be found in Chapter 1.

Protocols

There are a variety of network protocols and standards to choose from for your network infrastructure. If you are installing for the first time, or you are upgrading the networking environment and need to upgrade your NIC cards, you need to know about these different protocols before buying equipment.

✦ **Ethernet:** Ethernet networks use CSMA/CD (Carrier Sense Multiple Access/Collision Detection) to regulate network data flow. Ethernet packets are sent out onto the network, and if they detect another packet, the network will wait a certain amount of time before retransmitting the packet. On large networks, this can cause network congestion and slow the network down. Ethernet can run over a variety of different cables such as coaxial (10Base2), UTP (10BaseT), and Fiber (10BaseFL). It can support speeds up to 10 Mbps.

✦ **Fast Ethernet:** Fast Ethernet offers great speed improvements to standard Ethernet by running at speeds up to 100 Mbps. Fast Ethernet is usually run over a twisted pair or fiber-optic cable. 100BaseTX provides full duplex operations using only two pairs of wires. 100BaseT4 uses all four pairs for transmitting and receiving data, but only supports half-duplex operations. You must use at minimum Category 5 UTP cable to support 100 Mbps. 100BaseFX is fast Ethernet on fiber optic cable.

✦ **Gigabit Ethernet:** Gigabit Ethernet networks can run at speeds up to 1000 Mbps over twisted pair and fiber cabling. Because gigabit Ethernet can run over Category 5 UTP cabling, it is much easier to upgrade from Fast Ethernet networks, rather than switching to fiber. Twisted pair cabling is called 1000BaseT, while fiber is referred to as 1000BaseFX.

✦ **Token ring:** Token ring adapters use a data token that is passed around the network, which is organized in a ring topology. Whenever a device has the token, it can transmit on to the network. In order to connect to a Token ring network, you need a Token ring NIC card.

System bus issues

Even on today's fast PCI buses, newer Gigabit Ethernet cards are able to transmit and receive data faster than the system bus, causing a bottleneck. Most installed servers use a 32-bit wide bus running at 33MHz. Most gigabit Ethernet cards contain on-board memory buffers to stop any data overruns. When upgrading to a Gigabit Ethernet NIC card, take the system bus speed into consideration.

In the Real World New PCI bus technology, currently in development, will provide a 64-bit bus running at 33 and 66MHz speeds that will get over this bottleneck.

Cabling

Your network card must support the type of network cabling you are using. Some network cards have interfaces for different cable types on one card.

✦ **Unshielded Twisted Pair (UTP):** UTP is the most common type of network cabling because of its low cost-to-performance ratio. It consists of four pairs of twisted wires that are attached to an RJ-45 connector. The network card has an RJ-45 jack on its outside edge to facilitate the cable. Twisted pair also comes in a shielded version, which is rarely used because of its higher costs. 10 Mbps twisted pair is called 10BaseT. 100 Mbps twisted pair is referred to as 100BaseT. UTP cables also come in the different categories, which define the speed of transmissions they can run. For example, the most common UTP cable type today is Category 5, which will allow 100 Mbps speeds.

✦ **Coaxial:** Coaxial network cable is not as common as UTP, because of its higher cost, but its more rugged construction is better suited for more extreme environments such as manufacturing. Coaxial cable is also referred to as 10Base2 for 10 Mbps speeds, or 100Base2 for 100 Mbps. Devices are connected together in a chain, and the ends of the cable are terminated with 50-ohm terminators. If the server is at the end of the coaxial chain, it must have a T-connector to connect both the server and the terminator. The actual connector is called a BNC connector.

✦ **Fiber optic:** Fiber optic cable, which sends the signals using light, is only used for the most high-end servers needing large bandwidth requirements. Fiber cables typically contain two strands of glass, one for sending and one for receiving, which connect to the NIC card. You must also know if the fiber cabling is multimode or single mode fiber. Single mode allows for longer distances of cable because the light doesn't reflect inside of the cable, but multimode is used more often because it is less expensive.

Speed

Older NIC cards only supported 10 Mbps network speed. Newer cards are usually 100 Mbps or Gigabit Ethernet using 1 Gbps speeds. You must select a speed that is compatible with your network speed and cabling. For example, to run 100Mbps you need a minimum of category 5 UTP cabling. Many NIC cards can run at multiple speeds, and can automatically sense the maximum network speed and adjust itself accordingly. There are indicator lights on the edge of the NIC card that show what speed it is running at.

Duplexing

Your NIC card should support both *full* and *half duplex* operations. Half duplex communications are when the card can only transmit or receive at the same time; it can't perform both operations simultaneously. Full duplex means that it can both transmit and receive data at the same time. A half duplex connection shares the transmit and receive operations over one line, so Ethernet connections will be fighting for the same pathway, causing packet collisions. In a full duplex connection, the transmit and receive operations are performed on separate wires, removing any chance of collisions and speeding up the connection. A 100 Mbps connection running half-duplex will not be running at full efficiency, and speeds will be lower. You may need to support half duplex operations, if that is the only setting your Ethernet switches or hubs will handle. There is usually an indicator light on the edge of the NIC card that will show what duplex the card is running at. Most NICs can automatically negotiate duplexing.

Exam Tip   For the exam, watch for questions that deal with different types of NIC cards, cabling, speed, and duplex settings. You should know how they interact with each other and what issues they might cause.

Adaptive teaming

A network card can be a critical point of failure for a server. Most servers only have one connection to the network, and if that connection is lost, the entire server is disconnected from the network. This happens often, as a network cable could be loose or defective, or the switch or hub that connects the server to the network could fail. Network activity failures are probably more common than any type of hardware failure such as disks or software OS errors. Network servers can be fault-tolerant, and can be given more bandwidth, with the addition of more network cards. A group of network cards can be brought together in a team by sharing one network address. This is called *adaptive teaming*. If one of the adapters fails, another one will take over. Network load balancing can also be configured with adaptive teams, to combine the bandwidth of all the cards to create one large channel.

Adaptive fault tolerance

By adding additional network cards to a server, you can create a fault-tolerant networking system. If one of the NIC cards fails, or if it's connection to the network is interrupted for any reason, such as a bad or loose cable, or bad switch port, the other NIC card will take over. You do not need the an identical NIC card to the first one, although it may increase compatibility if you choose the same brand and model. It can even be a different speed, such as a server with a primary network connection on a Gigabit Ethernet card and the backup connection on a 100 Mbps card. This way, you still have a reliable connection without the extra expense of another Gigabit Ethernet NIC and compatible switch. It is important for backup purposes to connect your second network card to a different Ethernet hub or switch than the first one. This eliminates the switch as a point of failure for the server.

To configure two network cards in an adaptive fault-tolerant setup, the adapter team is assigned a single address to act as the primary network address. In the event of a NIC failure, the other network card will take over immediately.

Adaptive load balancing

In addition to adding levels of network fault tolerance to your server, additional network cards can also be linked together to form a higher bandwidth connection.

This is called *adaptive load balancing*. Up to eight 100 Mbps adapters can be linked to increase bandwidth up to 800 Mbps. If Gigabit Ethernet links are being used, it could increase bandwidth to 8 Gbps.

Caution   Although outgoing traffic is spread over all of the NIC cards, incoming traffic will only come through one card at its own speed. For example, outgoing traffic on a four 100 Mbps adapter team will have a speed of 400 Mbps. Incoming traffic will only be running at 100 Mbps .

The team of adapters is assigned one network address, and the distribution of network load between the adapters is automatic. See Figure 9-1 for an example of a server with multiple NIC cards.

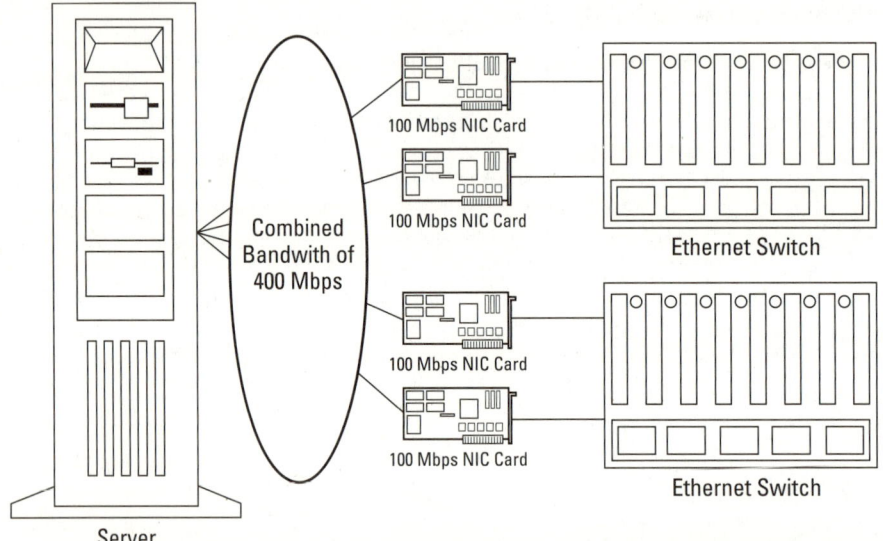

Figure 9-1: Server with four NIC cards using adaptive teaming for fault tolerance and combined bandwidth

Installing a network card

Since network cards are just like any other peripheral device card, installation and replacement is very simple. Some servers have embedded network cards, which are built right onto the motherboard, and cannot be replaced or upgraded. To install or replace a network card, you must open up the server chassis cover and locate the slot where your network card is placed. Before touching any of the components, ensure that you have protected yourself from electrostatic discharge by properly grounding yourself. Unscrew the card from the slot holder, and carefully pull the card out of the slot. It may be tight, so remember to only hold the card by its edges and gently rock it out of position. Never hold onto the card by the middle, as you may damage the electronic components on the card when trying to force it out of the slot.

When installing the card, only hold it by its edges, and line up the edge connectors on the card with the slot on the motherboard. Gently push it down until it is fully plugged in, and then screw in the edge metal plate to the server chassis to secure it into place. Replace the cover on the server and then turn it on.

You will need to first update the driver for the new card in your network OS, as it may not appear to be installed when you start the system. When the driver is installed, check your IRQ, I/O address, and DMA settings to ensure that they do not conflict with another device. After the system has recognized the card, you must configure it with a network address for your particular network. Try some network tests to establish connectivity.

Upgrading Peripheral Cards

 **3.7** Upgrade peripheral devices, internal and external

You can upgrade many different peripheral devices on your server, from important devices such as SCSI adapters, to less important ones such as video and sound cards. There are many different characteristics and settings that you must check before performing an upgrade, including bus compatibility, system resource settings, and expansion slot availability. Many of these settings are discussed in the first section of this chapter.

SCSI adapters

If you are currently running a server with IDE/ATA drives, there are many excellent reasons to upgrade to SCSI technology. SCSI is much faster than IDE/ATA systems, which is very important for today's high-end servers. SCSI can support many more devices than IDE/ATA, which means you can also have room for expansion to add more hard drives. SCSI can give you more options for fault tolerance, including support for RAID.

You may already be running a SCSI system, but one that is fairly old. The newest Ultra 160 SCSI systems have speeds of up to 160 Mbps, compared to an Ultra2 SCSI system which has speeds of 80 Mbps.

Host adapters

Upgrading your SCSI host adapter can be somewhat difficult depending on the types of SCSI devices you have connected to the server. You must ensure that your new host adapter is compatible with your current devices, and also has the proper type of connectors to support the cabling of them. If you are using both IDE/ATA hard drives and SCSI hard drives in your system, your BIOS will have to support SCSI boot options if you want to boot the system from a hard drive on the SCSI chain.

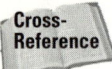

See Chapter 8 for a more detailed look at SCSI standards, protocols, cabling, and connectors.

Before upgrading your SCSI host adapter, make sure that your server BIOS is updated to the most recent version. This ensures that your systems BIOS will properly recognize the card after it has been installed.

Remember to make sure that the host adapter's SCSI ID is set to 7. This makes it the highest-priority device. The host adapter can be anywhere on the SCSI chain, but be sure that the SCSI bus is properly terminated on each end.

RAID controller

Upgrading or installing a new SCSI RAID controller can be a difficult experience, as you will have to back up your entire server before the upgrade. When the controller is replaced, all of the data on the current arrays will be deleted. The RAID array settings will have to be reconfigured, and then the data must be restored back to the server.

Before upgrading the controller, make sure your server BIOS is flashed to the latest version to ensure that it will support the new device. When re-installing the OS, you will need a new controller driver for the RAID card, which will need to be installed during the setup phase.

Video cards

Most modern servers come with a video card installed right on the motherboard. The reason for this is that video performance is not an issue with server installations. The only time you should be using the display is when you are at the server console configuring the server, troubleshooting a problem, or installing or upgrading hardware and software.

It is best to leave the default VGA screen resolution on the server. Changing the video resolution or monitor refresh rates can result in a blank screen, which makes it close to impossible to reverse the problem through regular methods, as you cannot see what you are doing. Some operating systems will let you test the resolution before you actually enable it, giving you a chance to see if the configuration will work. If you happen to restart a server into a non-standard video mode, certain operating systems enable you to force the server into VGA mode at boot time so you can fix your configuration.

Some newer operating systems such as NetWare 5 only allow a minimum of SVGA for the video resolution. This is fine, as long as you do not try to configure higher resolutions that may not be supported.

If you need to use a different or more powerful video card, try to use an Accelerated Graphics Port (AGP) card. The Accelerated Graphics Port is a special expansion slot made for video adapters. This way, you will not use up a valuable PCI slot, or run into resource conflicts with other PCI devices.

Sound cards

Although sound cards are very rare on a server, because there is generally no need for one, there are some things to keep in mind if installing a sound card on your server.

Be careful of the I/O port, IRQ, and DMA resources that the sound card will use. Network and SCSI cards are often configured with the same resources that sound cards use. This will cause a resource conflict, and could possibly disable your SCSI hard drive bus, resulting in a system that will not boot. In the case of a network card conflict, the server will not be able to communicate with the network.

If you don't need a sound card on the server, don't install one. You run the risk of resource conflicts, and taking up an expansion slot on your server that could be used for more important devices.

Exam Tip   For the exam, remember that video and sound card performance are non-critical items in a server configuration.

Tape drives

A common reason for upgrading a tape drive is that your current tape backup system cannot fully back up your current data requirements in a reasonable amount of time. User data tends to grow rapidly, and this extends the time it takes to perform full backups of the system. If the backup schedule begins to extend into normal business hours, it could cause performance issues on your network. Depending on the capacity of your current tapes, it might take several DAT tapes to complete one backup. You should then consider upgrading to a DLT drive to greatly increase the capacity of your tapes and to speed up your backups.

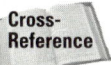

Cross-Reference   See Chapter 19 for a more detailed look at tape standards and capacities.

Upgrading an external tape device is fairly simple. It is most likely a SCSI tape drive, so take note of the current SCSI ID it is using. You should configure your new drive with the same ID, or an unassigned one. You can then simply shut down your server, replace the tape drive with the new one, set the SCSI ID, make sure it is terminated properly if at the end of the SCSI chain, and then turn on the server. The SCSI configuration should be automatic, but you will have to load a new driver for your device in the OS.

Upgrading an internal tape drive is a bit trickier, because you have to open up the case and remove the tape drive from the drive bay, but the other steps remain the same. Be sure to set the SCSI ID to the same number as the original drive, or an unassigned one.

Upgrading UPS

 3.10 Upgrade UPS

There are several factors in the decision to upgrade an Uninterruptible Power Supply system. There could be too many devices plugged into one UPS, causing a large power load. In the event of a power failure, the UPS might not have enough battery power to keep all the systems running for more than a minute, which may not be enough time to shut down the systems gracefully. You might simply have too many servers, and not enough outlets on your UPS systems to handle them. They can be plugged into regular outlets, or surge protectors, but in the event of a power failure, the system will be shut down cold, possibly causing disk and system failures.

 More information about UPS systems can be found in Chapter 2.

UPS units come in various sizes and designated run times, so you should examine your equipment to find out how much of a load you are going to use. The typical unit of measurement for UPS sizes is its VA (Volts/Amps) rating. To calculate the VA rating of a device, multiply the number of volts and amps it uses. This information is usually located on the back or bottom of the device by the serial number. Add up the VA rating of all your devices, and this will give you the approximate VA rating for the UPS you should purchase. You should get a UPS with a VA rating greater than your current VA total, to allow for expansion and proper load and battery usage.

 The VA rating of a UPS should be much greater than the VA rating of your combined devices, to properly handle the load and to give you extra battery time in the event of a power failure.

UPS batteries

UPS batteries do wear out over time, typically in three to five years. Plan on replacing your UPS battery every few years to maintain optimum performance. It is also much cheaper to replace a battery than the entire UPS.

UPS software

When installing new or upgraded UPS systems, you should also upgrade the special UPS software for your particular operating system to the latest version. This ensures that you have the latest drivers and UPS monitoring programs to monitor the health of your UPS, and to configure it to automatically shutdown the file server in the event of a power failure.

Upgrading Diagnostic Tools and Utilities

 3.9 Upgrade service tools (e.g., diagnostic tools, EISA configuration, diagnostic partition, SSU, etc.)

Many manufacturers install a small diagnostic partition on your boot drive. These utilities are helpful in configuring the server hardware and other low-level devices. These utilities are typically used for hard drive partitioning, RAID configuration, and hardware diagnostic programs to detect hardware errors.

More advanced system setup utilities (SSU) can offer advanced capabilities to assign system resources to certain devices, set boot parameters, view hardware server logs, and even obtain serial and model numbers of internal parts in case they ever need replacing.

Upgrading the diagnostic partition enables you to take advantage of new hardware monitoring utilities and have support for new devices.

Most upgrades will come on a bootable floppy disk, or CD-ROM. You have to reboot your server, because the software has to write to the special diagnostic partition that is only available during boot. Do not interrupt the upgrade, or turn off the server while it is updating the partition. Doing so might destroy that partition, and possibly render your server inoperable.

If you reformat your entire server hard drive, to install a new OS for example, the diagnostic can be partition removed. The diagnostic partition can be reinstalled, but only if you do it before all the hard drive partitions are defined. The server will run fine without the diagnostic partition, but you will be missing important hardware utilities and monitoring agents that are there to make your job easier.

Upgrading System Monitoring Tools

 **3.8** Upgrade system monitoring agents

At the OS level, your server contains many tools for monitoring software and hardware performance. Monitoring protocols like SNMP or vendor-specific tools often need to be upgraded to the latest version to support new hardware and software.

Upgrading the monitoring tools and client agents is fairly simple, but often a dependant protocol such as SNMP will need to be upgraded as well, to support new management information bases (MIB). Doing this may require a reboot of the server, so you should perform this upgrade during non-business hours to minimize user impact. You should make a copy of your current threshold settings for your monitoring programs, in case they are overwritten in the upgrade. It can take many hours to get every setting back to its original value if you do not have a copy. You should also make copies of any historic data, or reports, in case they are accidentally removed.

Exam Tip   For any software program that depends on other protocols or services, be sure to upgrade the corresponding protocols and services to their latest versions to ensure compatibility.

Key Point Summary

In this chapter, tips and technical notes for installing and upgrading peripheral devices were discussed, as well as how to update system diagnostic partitions and monitoring utilities. Keep the following points in mind for the exam:

✦ IRQ, I/O port address, and DMA settings should be unique for each peripheral device, or a system conflict will occur causing those devices not to work properly.

✦ Typical protocols for network cards are Ethernet, Fast Ethernet, Gigabit Ethernet, and Token-ring. Common cable types are coaxial, unshielded twisted pair, and fiber optic.

✦ Full duplex cards can transmit and receive at the same time, whereas half-duplex cards can only transmit or receive at any one time.

✦ Several network cards can be teamed together to increase fault tolerance or for load balancing.

✦ Upgrade the system BIOS when installing new SCSI host and RAID adapters to ensure compatibility with the system.

✦ Video cards and sound cards are not important devices in a server.

✦ UPS batteries should be replaced every three to five years.

✦ If a server is upgraded with a new UPS, also upgrade its software monitoring program to facilitate automatic shutdown in the event of a power failure.

✦ Formatting hard drives and disk arrays can destroy a vendor's special diagnostic utility partition.

✦ When updating server monitoring programs, also upgrade their dependent protocols and services such as SNMP.

✦   ✦   ✦

STUDY GUIDE

The Study Guide section provides you with the opportunity to test your knowledge about upgrading peripherals. The Assessment Questions provide practice for the test, and the Scenarios provide practice with real situations. If you get any questions wrong, use the answers to determine the part of the chapter you should review before continuing.

Assessment Questions

1. A technician has installed a new network card in a server. Other peripherals on the server include a SCSI tape drive, an on-board sound card, and an AGP video card. When the server is booted, it reports an IRQ conflict with the network card that disables it. What is the most likely cause of the problem?

   A. Sound card

   B. Video card

   C. Tape drive

   D. System BIOS

2. A technician has replaced a server NIC that was running at full-duplex 10 Mbps with a new one that is dual speed 10/100 Mbps. After installation, and successfully loading a new network driver, the card still does not communicate with the network, although the link light is on. What is the most likely cause of the problem?

   A. The network cable is unplugged.

   B. The new network card is set for half-duplex.

   C. The network cable is defective.

   D. The network isn't configured for dual speed.

3. A customer has a server setup with two NIC cards set for adaptive fault tolerance. A network switch failure causes the server to lose its connection to the network. Why did the fault-tolerant configuration not work?

   A. The network cards have the same IRQ.

   B. The network cards were configured with the same IP address.

   C. You need at least four NIC cards for adaptive fault tolerance.

   D. The two network cards were plugged into the same Ethernet switch.

4. A SCSI host adapter has been removed and upgraded with an Ultra2 SCSI host adapter. When the system is booted, the system does not see the SCSI bus. What is the most likely cause of the problem?

    A. The BIOS needs to be updated with a newer version.

    B. The host adapter ID was not set to 7.

    C. The SCSI bus was not terminated properly.

    D. The host adapter is conflicting with another device.

5. A technician has upgraded some SNMP-based system monitoring tools. When the monitoring program is restarted, it fails to receive any trap messages from devices. What is the most likely cause of the problem?

    A. The SNMP service was not restarted.

    B. The updated monitoring tools are not compatible with the OS.

    C. The SNMP protocol needs to be updated to the latest version.

    D. The monitoring program's trap settings need to be reconfigured.

6. A technician has taken a decommissioned server and formatted all the hard drives so that they can be repartitioned. When the technician tries to run the vendor's hard drive configuration utility, the program cannot be found. What is the most likely cause of the problem?

    A. The program is run from a boot floppy disk.

    B. The system diagnostic partition was erased by the formatting of the hard drives.

    C. The BIOS needs to be updated.

    D. The OS has to be installed first.

7. A technician is setting up a new server with four network cards to be configured with adaptive load balancing. The customer is hoping to achieve network speeds of 800 Mbps for a busy database server. Will the current configuration work as planned?

    A. Yes, the configuration will work as planned.

    B. Yes, the configuration will work, if the adapters are teamed.

    C. No, the current setup will only run at 200 Mbps network speed.

    D. No, the current setup will only run at 400 Mbps network speed.

8. A server has recently had its UPS upgraded to a 1200 VA rated UPS. During a recent power outage, the server ran for twenty minutes before the UPS battery ran out. The server came down cold, and some data was corrupted. Why was the server not shut down properly by the UPS?

   A. The UPS monitoring program was not upgraded.

   B. The system BIOS was not upgraded.

   C. The UPS BIOS was not upgraded.

   D. The UPS does not support line conditioning.

9. A server with eight 100 Mbps NIC cards configured in an adaptive load balancing team should effectively work at what speed?

   A. 80 Mbps

   B. 1600 Mbps

   C. 400 Mbps

   D. 800 Mbps

10. A technician has replaced an older SCSI RAID controller with a new Wide Ultra2 SCSI RAID controller. After the arrays are reconfigured and the operating system is installed, the technician finds that all the server data has been erased. What should have the technician have done to avoid the problem?

   A. Updated the system's BIOS to recognize the RAID card.

   B. Backed up the data and restored it after the upgrade.

   C. Configured RAID 5 striping.

   D. Updated the server's diagnostic system partition.

11. A customer has misconfigured the video card on a server with a non-standard video resolution. The settings cannot be changed back because the monitor is blank. What can be done to fix the problem?

   A. Replace the monitor with a different one.

   B. Install a different video adapter card.

   C. Reboot the OS into VGA mode.

   D. Reboot the server.

12. A technician has discovered that a new network card that was installed in a server is conflicting with the sound card. There are no more free IRQs that can be assigned. How can the technician fix the problem?

A. Install a network card from a different vendor.

B. Reboot the server, and it will auto-configure itself.

C. Configure the network card to use DMA instead.

D. Remove the sound card.

13. A technician has added a SCSI tape drive to a server that already contains four Ultra2 SCSI hard drives. When the system is booted, it does not see the new tape drive, and one of the hard drives is not visible. What is the most likely cause of the problem?

A. The tape drive's IRQ is conflicting with another device.

B. The tape drive and one of the hard drives have the same SCSI ID.

C. The SCSI bus was not terminated properly.

D. The tape driver has not been loaded.

14. A technician has upgraded a server's NIC card from a 10 Mbps card to a 100 Mbps card. The company uses category 3 UTP cabling, with RJ-45 connectors. When the server is rebooted, the network card does not connect to the network. What is the most likely cause of the problem?

A. The cabling must be category 5 to support 100 Mbps.

B. The connectors should be RG-59.

C. The network cable is defective.

D. The Ethernet switch only supports 10/100 network cards.

15. A technician has configured two networks cards as an adaptive team. They have been given two separate IP addresses. When the server networking is started, the adapter teaming does not work properly. What is the most likely cause of the problem?

A. The NIC cards are from different vendors.

B. The adapter team should have its own single IP address.

C. The network cards do not support teaming.

D. The NIC cards are set to half-duplex.

16. A technician has installed a new fiber optic NIC card in a high-end server. The card supports multimode operations and Gigabit Ethernet. When the server is connected to the network, the card does not work. What is the most likely cause of the problem?

    A. The network cable is defective.

    B. The NIC needs to be teamed with another fiber card.

    C. The network only supports full duplex communications.

    D. The network cabling only runs single mode fiber.

17. How often should your UPS batteries be replaced?

    A. Every month

    B. Every year

    C. Every three to five years

    D. Every ten years

18. Why is it important to have fault-tolerant network adapters connected to separate Ethernet switches?

    A. To support both full and half duplex.

    B. If one of the switches fails, the server will still have a network connection.

    C. To support adapter load balancing.

    D. To support adapter teaming.

19. A technician has discovered that a new video card has a conflicting I/O address with a network card in a server. What can be done to eliminate the conflict?

    A. Change the video card's DMA address.

    B. Reboot the server to automatically configure with plug-and-play.

    C. Change the IRQ of the network card.

    D. Change the I/O address of the video card.

20. A server is having network performance issues. When the technician checks the lights on the network card, which is a dual-speed 10/100 NIC card, the indicator light is showing that the card is running at 10 Mbps when it should be running at 100 Mbps. What is the most likely cause of the problem?

    A. The network cable is defective.

    B. The switch that the server is plugged into is only running at 10 Mbps.

    C. The server BIOS does not support dual-speed NIC cards.

    D. The indicator lights are reversed.

Scenarios

1. A customer wants a new Web server set up to use network adaptive teaming, fault tolerance, and load balancing. They would like the server to run at least 400 Mbps network speed, and have redundancy at the Ethernet switch level. How should the networking of the server be set up?

2. Your server's system utility partition is out of date, and needs to be upgraded. You have also received an upgrade to your SNMP monitoring system. What steps should you take to upgrade these various components?

Answers to Chapter Questions

Chapter pre-test

1. When two devices use the same interrupt, a conflict will occur, because the devices both try to communicate with the CPU at the same time. As a result, neither device will work properly.

2. In adaptive fault tolerance, additional network cards are added to a server, so that if the main network link goes down, another NIC will take over.

3. Fast Ethernet is a faster Ethernet standard that supports 100 Mbps network speeds.

4. Before any device is installed or upgraded, the system BIOS should be flashed to the latest version to ensure compatibility with the new device.

5. A DMA channel enables a device to communicate with system memory directly, effectively bypassing the CPU.

6. Most modern video adapters use an accelerated graphics port (AGP).

7. Gigabit Ethernet adapters run at 1000 Mbps (1 Gbps).

8. To take advantage of faster, higher-capacity tape drives such as DLT technology.

9. With adapter teaming, multiple NIC cards can be assigned together in teams to be used as a fault-tolerant system and for load balancing.

10. VA ratings refer to the multiplied value of a devices voltage and amperage. The total VA rating of a UPS is the total device load it can handle.

Assessment questions

1. **A.** It is most likely the sound card that is causing the conflict. Answer B is incorrect because the video is running on an AGP slot without conflicting resources. Answer C is incorrect because the tape is using SCSI bus resources. Answer D is incorrect because nothing should conflict with the system BIOS. For more information, see the "Interrupt request lines" section.

2. B. The new network card should have been set to full duplex mode. Answers A and C are incorrect because the link light would not be on if the cable was unplugged or defective. Answer D is incorrect because there is no configuration to be made for dual-speed connectivity. For more information, see the "Duplexing" section.

3. D. The switch is a point of failure. The second card should have been plugged into a different switch. Answer A is incorrect because the cards would not have worked at all if they IRQ was the same. Answer B is incorrect because an adapter team should be configured with the same IP address. Answer C is incorrect because you only need a minimum of two cards for adaptive fault tolerance. For more information, see the "Adaptive teaming" section.

4. A. The BIOS needs to be updated to recognize the new SCSI device. Answer B is incorrect because the host adapter does not have to be ID 7, although it is preferred. Answer C is incorrect because the termination is not the most likely failure, although it is possible. Answer D is incorrect because the device would have been recognized, but would not have worked properly. For more information, see the "Host adapters" section.

5. C. The monitoring program needs SNMP to run, and because it was a newer version, the SNMP protocol should have also been upgraded to the latest version. Answer A is incorrect because the SNMP protocol did not have to be stopped for the upgrade. Answer B is incorrect because the program was already compatible with the OS, and the program was upgraded, not replaced with a different one. Answer D is incorrect because the program's configuration should not have been altered by the upgrade. For more information, see the "Upgrading System Monitoring Tools" section.

6. B. When the hard drives were erased, the system partition was destroyed. Answer A is incorrect because the system partition can be installed from the boot floppy, but not run. Answer C is incorrect because updating the BIOS would not save the partition. Answer D is incorrect because an OS install will not recover the missing partition. For more information, see the "Upgrading Diagnostic Tools and Utilities" section.

7. D. Four 100 Mbps adapters teamed together for load balancing will have a combined speed of 400 Mbps. Answer A is incorrect because the configuration will not work as listed. Answer B is incorrect because even though the adapters are teamed, the speed will still not be 800 Mbps. Answer C is incorrect because the speed will be 400 Mbps. For more information, see the "Adaptive teaming" section.

8. A. The UPS monitoring program was not upgraded to coincide with the new UPS. Answer B is incorrect because the UPS would not work at all if there were a device compatibility problem. Answer C is incorrect because the UPS does not have a BIOS that can be upgraded. Answer D is incorrect because line conditioning has nothing to do with automatic server shutdown. For more information, see the "Upgrading UPS" section.

9. D. The adapters' effective speed will be their respective bandwidths added together, which in this case is $8 \times 100 = 800$ Mbps. For more information, see the "Adaptive teaming" section.

10. B. When reconfiguring a RAID array for a new adapter, all the data on the disks is lost. Answer A is incorrect because the RAID card was already recognized by the system. Answer C is incorrect because the original data will still be lost. Answer D is incorrect because the server diagnostic partition is separate from the server's data. For more information, see the "RAID controllers" section.

11. C. The OS should be rebooted using VGA mode, and then the settings can be changed back to normal. Answer A is incorrect because changing the monitor will not affect the incorrect video resolution. Answer B is incorrect because installing a new adapter will not fix the problem. Answer D is incorrect because rebooting the server will not fix the resolution settings. For more information, see the "Video cards" section.

12. D. Remove the sound card, because it is not needed on the server. Answer A is incorrect because a different network would use the same address, which is the only one left. Answer B is incorrect because the server will not auto-configure the devices. Answer C is incorrect because DMA is used in conjunction with IRQs, not instead of it. For more information, see the "Sound Cards" section.

13. B. The two devices are configured with the same SCSI ID, causing the problems. Answer A is incorrect because the SCSI device will not be using an IRQ. Answer C is incorrect because the SCSI bus would not work at all if the termination was improperly configured. Answer D is wrong, as the conflict still exists between the hard drive and the tape drive. Loading a driver would not fix the problem. For more information, see the "Tape Drives" section.

14. A. You need a minimum for Category 5 UTP cabling to support 100 Mbps. Answer B is incorrect because RG-59 connectors are used with coaxial network cable. Answer C is incorrect because the problem is with the type of cable itself. Answer D is incorrect because the network can support both speeds, not just a dual-speed NIC card. For more information, see the "Speed" section.

15. B. The adapter team needs to be assigned its own IP address. Answer A is incorrect because it does not matter if the network cards are from different vendors. Answer C is incorrect because any two cards can be teamed together. Answer D is incorrect because the duplex setting does not impact the teaming operation. For more information, see the "Adaptive teaming" section.

16. D. The card must be running the same mode as the fiber network. Answer A is incorrect because the actual physical cable is not the issue. Answer B is incorrect because a fiber card does not have to be teamed with another to run properly. Answer C is incorrect because the duplex setting is not the issue causing the problem. For more information, see the "Cabling" section.

17. C. The battery should be replaced every three to five years, because it loses its charge over time. For more information, see the "Upgrading UPS" section.

18. B. This removes the Ethernet switch as a point of failure. Answer A is incorrect because the question has nothing to do with duplex settings. Answer C is incorrect because load balancing is supported by multiple NIC cards, not multiple switches. Answer D is incorrect because cards in an adaptive teaming setup can be set to the same Ethernet switch if desired. For more information, see the "Adaptive teaming" section.

19. D. Change the I/O address of the video card to an unassigned port address. Answer A is incorrect because the conflict is with the I/O port, not the DMA channel. Answer B is incorrect because plug-and-play will not resolve the conflict. Answer C is incorrect because the conflict is with the I/O address, not the IRQ. For more information, see the "I/O address" section.

20. B. The Ethernet switch only supports 10 Mbps, which the NIC auto-detected. Answer A is incorrect because the server would not be working at all if the cable was defective. Answer C is incorrect because the BIOS has nothing to do with duplex or speed settings. Answer D is incorrect because the lights are not reversed. For more information, see the "Upgrading Network Interface Cards" section.

Scenarios

1. To run the server at 400 Mbps using adaptive teaming and load balancing, you will need four 100 Mbps Ethernet NICS. Within the operating system, the four cards should be configured as a team adapter, with a single IP address. The cards should also be configured to fail over if one of the NIC cards fails. Ideally, to create redundancy at the switch level, you should have each of the four NIC cards connected to a separate switch. If you do not have that many switches, you should have at least one of the network cards attached to a separate switch. This way, if one of the switches fails, the server will still be serviced by from the other switches.

2. To update the system partition, you will have to obtain the latest version of the system partition for your hardware from the vendor's Web site. The file is usually extracted to a boot floppy disk, which you can boot your server from, and it will automatically update the partition. Do not interrupt the upgrade, or switch off the power, as this could corrupt the system partition and it will have to be reinstalled.

Before upgrading the SNMP monitoring system, you should make sure your version of the SNMP protocol is the most recent one, to maintain compatibility with the new monitoring program features and changes to the SNMP client agents. Take note of your current SNMP configuration and trap settings. They can sometimes be overwritten during the upgrade process. Proceed with the upgrade, reboot the server, and then check to see if the server is receiving trap messages and verify that the monitoring program is working properly.

Proactive
Maintenance

◆   ◆   ◆   ◆

◆   ◆   ◆   ◆

To ensure the integrity of the computer systems, an administrator must perform proactive maintenance. Physical housekeeping, analyzing baseline statistics, and monitoring the overall performance of the systems are just a few proactive maintenance steps. Finding a problem before it becomes an issue is one of the most important steps when maintaining a server environment. If a particular problem is not caught before the problem affects the network, the company may experience a few hours of downtime before the problem is fixed.

The chapters in this Part go into detail about the steps an administrator must know to prevent a disaster before it happens. Establishing remote notification is also discussed. The ability to be informed remotely if a server has gone down at a remote location can help prevent prolonged downtime.

Monitoring Performance

◆   ◆   ◆   ◆

EXAM OBJECTIVES

4.1 Perform regular backup

4.2 Create a baseline and compare performance

CHAPTER PRE-TEST

1. What is a server baseline?

2. What elements of the server should you monitor when performing a server baseline?

3. What is the main reason for performing a regular backup?

4. What areas of system performance are affected by performing a backup?

5. What backup jobs can affect performance?

6. List some common backup storage technologies.

7. What are some elements to include when documenting performance?

8. What is meant by performing a snapshot?

9. Define *threshold*.

10. What is the first step to take when evaluating performance?

✦ Answers to these questions can be found at the end of the chapter. ✦

Many system administrators do reactive performance monitoring instead of proactive performance monitoring. Reactive performance monitoring is when you need to analyze performance data because of some pressing problem, whereas proactive performance monitoring is a controlled form of monitoring that enables you to anticipate problems before they actually occur. Proactive maintenance is a key part of any properly-run computer environment, and is essential to ensure integrity of the computer systems. Monitoring performance is also vital to proactive maintenance. To do this properly, you need to capture some baseline performance statistics for your systems when they are running under normal conditions, so that you have a good reference point to which you can compare other measurements. Once you have the baseline, you can periodically monitor your systems over the course of a week, and compare the results of this with the baseline, and to determine any variances in the day-to-day data. This chapter discusses the many aspects of proactive performance monitoring.

Performing Regular Backups

4.1 Perform regular backup

The primary purpose for performing regular system backups is to provide a disaster recovery solution for network servers and services. The backup system also enables you to provide file restoration for user files and software files that are stored on the network servers. You should back up all your servers every night. You should perform a full backup of every file once a week, and daily incremental/differential backups throughout the week. If you do not have a lot of data to back up, or your company has invested in backup hardware and media capable of backing up large amounts of data, you should do a full backup every night, if possible.

Be sure to keep records about the backup system. You should have a document that lists the backup procedures, storage locations, data being backed up, where it is backed up from, and so on.

Procedures for using backups for disaster recovery are discussed in detail in Chapter 19.

Backup performance

Backup performance can be affected by many factors that may not be related to the backup hardware and software. Most backup software applications designed for server environments offer high performance and robust data protection solutions. They are usually designed to work in complex hardware, software, and network environments. Keep in mind that tuning a network server takes a lot of time, patience, and understanding of the server environment. Tuning the backup application to give better backup performance also requires an understanding of the backup software and hardware used.

Backup software can make high demands on system resources and processors. This is necessary because the backup task is both complicated and essential. Some areas that are directly affected by system backups are:

✦ CPU

✦ Memory

✦ Network

✦ Disk subsystem

The purpose of a backup is to get as much data from the server systems through the hardware infrastructure and onto the backup media as quickly as possible. Unfortunately, backup hardware and media performance does not always keep up with the server environment that they need to protect. This is usually a result of the server or network environment growing more rapidly than backup hardware upgrades. You may be forced to make the existing hardware perform a little bit faster, last a little longer, and make use of different media rotation schemes to ensure that all the data can be backed up. As you optimize backup performance, you should not decrease performance with other operations on the servers. The best way to optimize performance is to plan to upgrade your data protection requirements prior to upgrading the server environment. Anticipating network growth, and getting the equipment ahead of time, is one way to ensure that you can get a little chunk of the budget for backup systems.

When performing a backup, the following factors affect performance:

✦ **Data backup:** Backups copy information from the server hard disk and store it on the backup media. During this process, data is written to the media in sequential pattern, which results in fairly fast performance, but is still a drain on system resources.

✦ **Restore:** The restore process is the reverse of the backup operation. The backed up data is retrieved from the backup media and copied back to its original or redirected location. Restore jobs take longer than the original backup process because of the search and retrieval processes that are necessary to perform the restore operations.

✦ **Verify:** Verification is usually a function of the backup media device and software. The backup software checks and confirms that the file being copied from the hard drive is exactly the same as the one on the backup media. To do this, the backup software will issue and record *checksums* for the data that is copied to the backup media. Checksums are essentially mathematical validations for the data on the backup media. Checksums are recalculated during all read operations and are compared to the original. This process requires a lot of system usage and directly impacts the backup performance. However, the verification is very important to ensuring the integrity of the data.

Improving backup performance

You have several different choices for backup hardware, and your choice can affect the performance of your system. Carefully consider your current and future needs for the backup system. Keep in mind that most backup hardware is relatively slow when compared to today's hard drives. The following are some of the common storage technologies:

✦ **Travan:** This is an older and slower technology that is still in use. This technology does not always support hardware compression options. The media drives are slower than current higher-speed systems, and require frequent retensioning. A 3.2GB Travan data cartridge costs about $29.99, and a 20GB data cartridge is roughly $10.00 more.

✦ **DAT:** Digital Audio Tape is available in several formats including DDS, DDS2, DDS3, and DDS4. DDS4 tapes can store over 100GB of data, and the technology is considered to be high performance, reliable, and fast because of excellent throughput and fast file access. A 4GB DDS-1 data cartridge costs approximately $3.59, and a DDS-4 data cartridge costs approximately $30.00.

✦ **DLT:** Digital Linear Tape systems are very fast, and are fairly expensive as well. This is a very popular and reliable technology. A 30GB DLT III cartridge costs approximately $40.00, and a DLT IV 40/70/80GB data cartridge costs approximately $70.00.

✦ **AIT:** Advanced Intelligent Tape is Sony's latest innovation in fast-access, high-density tape recording technology. AIT can store large amounts of data and retrieve information quickly. AIT tapes have Sony's Memory In Cassette (MIC) architecture. The MIC consists of a memory chip built into the data cartridge that holds the system's log and other user-definable information. AIT systems are very fast, but can be very expensive as well. They offer incredibly high performance because of excellent throughput and fast file access. A 25GB AIT cartridge costs approximately $60.00, and a 50GB data cartridge costs approximately $90.00.

Your hardware choices other than the backup media can also affect backup performance. Some of the more important are as follows:

✦ **SCSI controllers:** You should use hardware that is compatible with both the server operating system and the backup software application. Most backup hardware should be compatible with most backup software. Having a faster controller does not always result in faster performance; in fact it can actually cause serious performance issues by causing SCSI bus timeouts. Using a backup drive that is capable of 80MB per minute, and a SCSI controller capable of 160MB per second results in a conceivable throughput of 12,800MB per minute. This can often be too much for the backup drive media and devices to handle, and will most likely result in SCSI bus timeouts. A SCSI bus timeout occurs when either the SCSI controller or the SCSI device detects that a command has not been responded to within a specific time period. Commands are normally issued by the SCSI controller, which then waits for a response from the device being addressed. If no response is detected, the controller may reset the bus to reinitiate communication. Disk drives will normally recover very well from SCSI bus timeouts and resets, but tape drives have greater difficulty in doing so. Most backups systems are purchased as a package that may include the recommended SCSI controller and cabling.

✦ **Mirroring:** This data protection method already comes at an increased performance cost, and the media backup system will only add to its performance degradation. Reading data from a mirrored drive takes longer compared to a non-mirrored drive.

✦ **Server types:** Choosing the right server can sometimes be a daunting task, whether you use mainstream manufacturers or some relatively unknowns. When building a system, ensure that you use hardware of high quality and is on the hardware compatibility list of your server operating system.

✦ **Server roles:** If your server is being used as an e-mail server, proxy server, and virus defense server, it may not be a wise idea to overload it with backup software and hardware. Servers that already have resource-intensive roles should not be used for creating backups.

✦ **RAM:** If you do not have enough memory, you will suffer performance losses. Having memory available to the backup software and other applications will increase the overall system performance, including backups.

✦ **Network:** Ensure you are making use of the Fast Ethernet cabling, switches, and NICs on your network. Ideally, you should ensure that the NICs in the servers are set to 100-MB full duplex, and that you configure the ports in the switches to be the same. This will not only ensure that your backups from remote servers are faster, but it will also increase the overall performance of your network.

Record it

When you perform a full backup of all data, record how long the backup took, and how long the verify took. If possible, perform a complete restore of the data to judge its performance, but this is usually not possible. To measure restore performance time, you can take a large chunk of data (2GB is a good baseline), and restore it to some empty space on the local server. Be sure to record your timings, and then you can estimate the amount of time it would take to do a full restore of all the data to all the systems.

Creating a Baseline

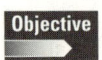 **4.2** Create a baseline and compare performance

As discussed in Chapter 6, a baseline defines the typical activity of your network servers. Keeping a baseline document of activity on a server lets you determine what activity is normal and what is not. To create a baseline, you should gather statistical information when the server is functioning normally. Then you can apply a load to the system such as transferring files, running programs, backing up and restoring data, and so on. While you are placing the load on the system, you would take the same measurements as you took during the original baseline. When performing a baseline, you should ensure that you measure performance data from the processor, memory, network, and disk. For example, you would want to monitor the following statistics to get a basic baseline.

✦ **Pages per second:** This value represents the number of times the operating system has to page to disk to resolve a memory reference. The more paging that occurs, the worse the system performance. When this value is at or above 10, then there could be a problem. Check the paging file to make sure it is large enough, and you may need to consider adding more memory.

✦ **Available bytes:** This value refers to the amount of free bytes of virtual memory that the computer has. If the value is consistently under 4MB, you may have to add more RAM. However, check your particular operating system's documentation for specific details.

✦ **Committed bytes:** This value is the amount of virtual memory that has been committed. Committed memory needs to have hard disk storage to back it up, or else it must never be written to disk. Make sure that the committed bytes do not exceed the amount of available bytes, or your memory resources may be overextended.

✦ **Percent processor time:** This value refers to the percentage of the elapsed time that the processor is busy executing a thread. This counter is discussed several times throughout this chapter. If the counter is near 100 percent, you may have a bottleneck.

✦ **Interrupts per second:** This counter points to the number of device interrupts the processor is experiencing. If the value is consistently above 4,000, you may have an I/O device that is generating too many interrupts.

✦ **Disk time:** This counter measures the percentage of elapsed time the disk is busy servicing read or write requests. On most systems, this value should be less than 70 percent.

✦ **Current disk queue length:** This counter returns the number of outstanding requests for service from the disk.

✦ **Average disk bytes per read:** This counter indicates the average number of bytes in a single read operation.

✦ **Average disk seconds per read:** This counter indicates how long it takes to retrieve data.

✦ **Disk reads per second:** This counter indicates how many reads occur per second.

✦ **Percent of network utilization:** This counter returns the percentage of network bandwidth in use on that particular network segment. Watch for values that exceed 50%.

✦ **Percent of broadcast frames:** This counter returns the percentage of network bandwidth that is made up of broadcast messages.

Documenting these performance counters for your baseline will tell you how the server works under controlled and optimal situations. When you add a load to the system and take the same measurements, you can determine how the new values compare to the baseline document. Then, when you think there is a problem, you will be able to compare the current statistics against both sets of data to determine if what you are seeing is normal or not. Ideally you would want to run a baseline for a full work day and, if possible, for each day of the week, giving you a baseline of a typical week's activities.

If you graph normal activity on a server, you will see it represented as a continuous stream of high points and low points. Usage on servers is almost always high in the early morning or at the beginning of new shifts when the users log on, check e-mail, or start their Web browsers to read the daily news. There are also specific periods throughout the month that will place an increased demand on the servers. For example, you will notice increased usage on the servers when various departments (finance, operations, and information systems), run applications to perform their end-of-month procedures. These events, although normal, can be taxing on the servers, and will result in some curious spikes in your monitoring graph, especially when compared to the baseline performance.

You should create a new baseline if there is a major change to your system or network, such as adding a new program to the server, or upgrading the old one, or even if the number of users increases significantly on the server. You should recreate the baseline several times per year, at least once every quarter. This ensures that your baseline is always current, even if you have not made any significant changes, and enables you to have a basis for comparison over the course of a year.

Documenting performance

Keeping good documentation not only makes sense, but it will save you a lot of time when you need to find the information. When documenting the system performance, you should record how the server performs under normal conditions and extreme conditions. When documenting performance, you should include:

✦ CPU utilization

✦ Cache buffer utilization

✦ File read and write performance

✦ Disk utilization

✦ Any software that is running

✦ Backup system performance

✦ Backup systems verify performance

✦ Backup systems restore performance

Make sure you keep the baseline documentation in a safe place, such as with your emergency boot disk, at an off-site location, or in a fireproof safe.

Ensure that you update this document any time you make a change to the system by adding additional hardware or software. Create a new baseline, record the results, and compare it to old baseline. It is a good idea to keep the old baseline information on file, so that you can see a trend as you add each additional piece of hardware or software to the system.

Taking a system snapshot

A snapshot, a photograph, is a moment that is permanently frozen in time to be viewed over and over again, but never changed. When you take a system snapshot, you are really just taking an image of the way the system is at that moment, and storing it on some medium to be used later, if necessary. Do not take system snapshots of your production data and call it a backup. The idea behind creating a system snapshot is to record the server's configuration, which may include the following:

✦ Installed software

✦ Drivers, devices, and so on

✦ Server hardware such as RAID level, configurations, partitions

✦ ROM BIOS level

✦ OEM support software

✦ Operating system release levels

✦ Service packs and hot fixes

✦ Third party software (backup and virus software)

You can use your tape backup software to capture the appropriate data, and store it on tape. Don't forget to label and date it the backup tape. You can also use software specifically designed for this application. The big advantage to using specialized software is that most of this software will compress the data into a small image that you can burn to CD and store with the servers. For example, Symantec Ghost 6.5 is a comprehensive solution for most businesses running Windows-based systems. While this software is usually used for making snapshots of PC-based workstations, as opposed to servers, you can use it for taking quick system snapshots. There is a special version that was developed to handle Novell NetWare's complex partitions, thus enabling you to quickly recover an entire NetWare server. However, it is not recommended that you perform this type of snapshot during regular working hours, or at least not during peak hours. Symantec's Ghost software also enables you to create bootable CDs, and it has the ability to write directly to CDR/W devices. For example, once you have your server set up with all the software, drivers, and peripherals attached, you should create the system snapshot using the software utility. Because this software compresses the snapshot by up to 70 percent, you can store this file on a CD-ROM. If for some reason the server fails, or becomes unstable, you can put the disk in the CD drive, turn on the server, and the bootable disk will take care of the rest. Just remember to take a new snapshot after you have updated the server, but only after the update has been qualified.

Measuring and Evaluating Performance

 **4.2** Create a baseline and compare performance

Measuring performance is a good way of initiating proactive, as opposed to reactive, maintenance methods. It is better to find out what is going wrong in your server environment before your users start banging down your door. There are several things that you can do to accomplish this. One is to ensure that you are using some sort of monitoring tool, either the one that came with your operating system, or a third-party tool, to measure the many different performance and troubleshooting metrics available to you. Whatever tool you choose should be able to set thresholds for alerts, log data over an extended period of time, and present the data in chart and report formats.

Throughout this section, I use Windows NT and the NT Performance Monitor utility for examples. Each operating system and third-party utility works slightly differently, but the principles for performance monitoring are the same.

 Cross-Reference   You can look at Chapters 6 and 11 for more information about monitoring performance and what some third-party tools can do for you.

Thresholds

Almost all network devices can be configured for monitoring, and they typically have performance thresholds that you can set. You set a threshold on a device, and when that threshold is met or exceeded, some response is triggered. This could be in the form of sending a message to a network management console, which in turn alerts network administrators via e-mail or pager. Performance monitoring software also includes thresholds that can be set to notify you of potential problems. For example, you could set thresholds for disk space usage, excessive page faults, cache buffers, and so on. If these thresholds are breached, you can be notified, and immediate action can be taken. The idea behind setting thresholds is so that you can react more quickly to issues before they become real problems. Your users never need know that the server almost crashed because the hard disk was 90% consumed.

There are many applications for network devices that can notify administrators of critical events by pager, phone, or e-mail, with the types of notification set through a customizable escalation process. In addition, the application can take advantage of fault isolation capabilities to identify the right person to notify.

The following sections discuss the elements of your system that you should monitor, and gives some suggestions about the thresholds you should set.

Processor

Because the processor is the heart of your system, you need to pay close attention to its performance. How the server is used (file/print server, database server, application server, and so on), will also determine what levels of processor activity you can expect to see. High processor activity is not always a problem. For example, a file/print server may have periodic activity that spikes the processor to 100% CPU utilization, while an application server may consistently place high demand on the processor. To get realistic results that you can form an opinion on, you need to collect data over a period of time, usually about a week for a good set of data. If you performed baseline testing, you can compare this data to the baseline. Some common CPU bottlenecks include CPU-bound applications and drivers, and intense or excessive interrupts that are generated by inadequate or malfunctioning components. Graphics programs, database programs, and Enterprise Resource Planning (ERP) applications are all examples of CPU-bound applications.

The following is a list of the counters you should use to monitor your processor with Windows NT Performance Monitor. These counters may be called something slightly different under different operating systems or performance tools, but the theory is the same.

✦ **% Processor Time:** This counter measures the amount of time that the processor is busy. If the processor usage is consistently running over 80%, there is most likely a bottleneck. You will need to analyze the usage to determine exactly what is causing the excessive processor activity. Processes such as software applications typically cause this activity. If these processes are not to blame, some other resources such as disks, controllers, NICs, or video cards, may be the culprits that make the CPU look like the bottleneck.

✦ **% Privileged Time:** This counter measures the actual time the processor is committed to performing operating system services. This value should be consistently less than 75 percent. If it is not, find the process that is using the processor excessively, and determine if there is anything you can do to fix it. There may be updates to the program, or you may need to consider upgrading or adding another processor if the program is needed.

✦ **% User Time:** This counter measures the actual time that the processor is committed to performing user services, such as running an application. This process should be consistently less than 75 percent. If it is not, you need to figure out which process is causing the excessive use of the processor, and determine how to fix it.

✦ **Interrupts/sec:** This counter measures the number of interrupts the processor is servicing from applications or from the hardware devices. Most servers can handle thousands of interrupts per second, but they do have their limits. If the number of interrupts is consistently above 4000, you may have a hardware error. If you think that one of the devices may be causing the interrupts, you should be able to monitor this using the queue lengths for the devices interfaces, such as disk or network.

✦ **Processor Queue Length:** This counter is found under the System object. This is the number of requests for service (interrupts) the processor has in the queue. Typically, values that are consistently higher than two may indicate a problem.

✦ **Server Work Queues:** The queue length is the number of requests in the queue for the selected processor. A value higher than two can mean there is a problem.

If you think that the processor is causing bottleneck, you may not always necessarily have to replace it or upgrade to a better system. You could change other components in the server, or divert the workload of the server across several other servers. The following list includes some suggestions that may improve performance if the processor is the bottleneck:

✦ Install a faster processor.

✦ Install multiple processors, especially if the server is an application server.

✦ Offload processing to other systems.

✦ Install a higher bandwidth network card.

✦ Schedule processor intensive tasks for non-peak, or non-working hours.

✦ Install a bus-mastering controller.

Memory

The most common problem in a server is memory. In Windows NT systems, RAM is divided into two categories: paged and non-paged.

Paged RAM is *virtual memory,* which is a place on the hard drive called the *pagefile.* This part of the disk is allocated for use by the physical memory. This enables the system to store more data than could be stored in just the physical RAM. Non-paged RAM is data that cannot be written to disk. Data in non-paged RAM always resides in the physical RAM, because it consists of important system data that handle interrupts requests and so on.

This type of memory system is typically referred to as a *pooled system*, and can be the cause in memory bottlenecks. An example is continuous hard page faults. Hard page faults are a result of a program that looks for data that is not found in its portion of the physical memory, or anywhere else in the physical memory. Therefore, the data must be retrieved from disk. Continuous hard page faults of more than five per second can indicate a memory bottleneck.

The following are the memory counters you would use to measure performance in Windows NT.

✦ **Pages/sec:** This counter indicates the number of requested pages that were not available in RAM when it was needed, and had to be processed from the disk, or had to be written to the disk in order to free up space in RAM for other pages. If this counter is consistently over 25 pages per second, you may need to add more RAM.

✦ **Available Bytes:** This counter shows the amount of available physical memory. This figure will normally be low, because Windows NT Disk Cache Manager uses extra memory for caching. However, the cache returns the memory when requests for memory occur. If the value is typically below 4MB, the server may be experiencing excessive paging. The best solution to this problem is to add more RAM.

✦ **Committed Bytes:** This counter shows the amount of virtual memory that has been committed to RAM for storage, or to page file space. You may need to add more RAM to your system if this figure is greater than the actual amount of RAM your system has.

✦ **Pool Non-Paged Bytes:** This counter shows the amount of RAM in the non-paged pool system memory area where space is used by the operating system components as they perform their duties. There may be a process that is causing a memory leak if this value steadily increases without a related increase in activity on the server. Adding more RAM here would only mask the problem temporarily. You need to find the source of the leak, whether it be a driver, service, or an application, and fix it either by removing it or installing an update.

Storage

Monitoring the performance of your disks is an important aspect of measuring the performance of your systems. In a Windows NT scenario, you will need to turn on some switches to make this happen. To turn on these counters, you need to enter the command `diskperf -y` at a command prompt. You must then restart your computer. If you are using a software-based RAID system configured with Windows NT, you also need to turn on the enhanced counters by typing `diskperf -ye` at the prompt and restarting the computer. Remember to turn these counters off when you are finished using them, because they add extensive overhead to the server. It is for this reason that they are left disabled by default. You disable the counters by typing `diskperf -n` at the command prompt and restarting the computer. The following is a list of the counters related to physical and logical disks.

✦ **% Disk Time:** This counter shows the amount of time that the disk drive is busy servicing I/O requests. If this value is regularly near 100%, the disk is being heavily used. You can then monitor some individual processes to figure out what is making all the requests. You should also check to see if it is an application, or a memory problem caused by excessive paging.

✦ **Disk Queue Length:** This counter shows the number of waiting disk I/O requests for the drive. You may have an issue if the number is regularly more than two.

✦ **Avg. Disk Bytes/Transfer:** This counter shows the average number of bytes transferred to or from the disk during input and output operations. The greater the transfer size, the more efficiently the system is running.

✦ **Disk Bytes/sec:** This counter shows the rate at which bytes are transferred. As long as this average is relatively high, then the system should be OK.

If the counters point to a storage bottleneck, you may need to consider upgrading the controller, hard drives, and cabling to something faster. For example, you may need to upgrade the SCSI controller, cabling, and disks to a higher performance SCSI technology, or even fiber. You may need to consider changing your RAID technology, or adding more disks to a RAID 5 system. Even offloading some of the processes to another server may help if you do not have the budget to upgrade the hardware.

Network

The network is a difficult area to monitor, because of the many different devices that it may be made up of, such as servers, routers, bridges, hubs, workstations, and printers, to name a few. However, there are many good third party utilities out there that can assist you greatly when analyzing network packets. This section only discusses the systems that affect the local server, not larger network issues. The following is a list of the counters you would use to monitor performance on Windows NT. To use the Network Interface object and its counters, you must first install the SNMP service on your server.

✦ **Bytes Total/sec:** This counter, which is located under the Server object, measures the number of bytes the server has sent and received over the network. This should give you a good idea of exactly how busy the server is.

✦ **Logon/sec:** This counter, which is located under the Server object, measures the number of logon attempts for local, network, and service authentication in the last second of operations.

✦ **Logon Total:** This counter, which is also located under the Server object, measures the number of combined logon attempts since the server was last started.

✦ **% Network Utilization:** This counter, which is located under the Network Segment object, measures the percentage of the network bandwidth in use for the local network segment. This value should generally be lower than 30 percent.

✦ **Bytes Sent/sec:** This counter, which is located under the Network Interface object, measures the number of bytes sent using the NIC.

✦ **Bytes Total/sec:** This counter, which is located under the Network Interface object, measures the number of bytes both sent and received by the NIC.

If the performance counters indicate that the network is the bottleneck, then there are several things you can do to relieve this problem:

✦ Tweak server settings such as TCP/IP or NIC settings.

✦ Install an additional adapter to share the load.

✦ Install a newer network card that is rated for better performance. For example, you may upgrade from a 10MB to 100MB NIC.

✦ Upgrade your routers, switches, cabling, and bridges.

✦ Add another server to share logon validation, file and print services, or other common network services.

✦ Divide your network into different segments to isolate traffic.

Evaluating Overall Performance

Evaluating performance is not easy because there are so many factors that can affect the performance of the computer. However, once you have gathered all the processor, memory, network, and storage statistics, you can start to evaluate the performance of the machine. The first step in doing this is to compare your results against the system baseline that you took. This will give you a real good idea of how the server is performing now, as compared to how it was performing under normal conditions. You may find that you have a memory issue, network issue, or something else. As I mentioned earlier in the chapter, you should have at least one week worth of data to use as your comparison. To use performance monitoring as part of your proactive maintenance program, conduct this monitoring periodically throughout the year, whether or not there is a problem. Any time you make a change to the system, you should record a new baseline, and store it with the original so that you can track the affects that the changes have on the system.

You may want to consider purchasing some third-party software to help you create these documents, as they usually have a method for tracking trends and creating baselines to compare against. You may also want to consider investing in some benchmarking software, of which many tools are available as free downloads off the Web. Again, this is not the kind of software that you want to run during business hours, as it places a lot of strain on your system. Benchmarking software is designed to let you know how your computer stacks up against its database of comparable computers. It is not really a form of troubleshooting, but a way to see if your server is in the ballpark of some comparable systems.

Documenting Results

All this monitoring will go to waste if you don't document it. This particular document should contain the results of the comparisons that you took, and the baseline that you compared the results to. You could simply create a spreadsheet, or a document that documents your findings. This is a good document to keep in electronic format, because you can easily update it as you perform periodic testing. I find that a spreadsheet program is particularly affective here because you can graph the data. This document should contain any changes that you made as a result of your findings, such as adding processors, RAM, hard drives, and so on. This document need not be complex, but it should be thorough.

If you inherited the server environment because you took a new job, you may not have any documentation on performance statistics. However, if you do some performance monitoring, and things seem to be functioning fine, you can perform a baseline then and start from that point.

Key Point Summary

This chapter we discussed the many aspects of monitoring performance and how you should go about accomplishing such a task. The focus was on proactive techniques as opposed to reacting to a pressing issue. You should perform this type of monitoring regularly and keep documentation of your findings so that you can compare them against your baseline readings and see how your server is working over time. Keep the following points in mind for the exam:

✦ Know what server baselines are and how to create them.

✦ Perform regular backups and document backup performance issues.

✦ Know backup hardware performance considerations such as tape media, SCSI technology, Mirroring , server types, server roles, RAM, and fast Ethernet.

✦ Keep documentation about performance statistics and keep it in a safe place.

✦ Know why you want to perform a system snapshot and what uses it has.

✦ Know how to measure server performance and how to make the necessary adjustments to your system.

✦   ✦   ✦

STUDY GUIDE

The Study Guide section provides you with the opportunity to test your knowledge about proactive maintenance. The Assessment Questions provide practice for the test, and the Scenarios provide practice with real situations. If you get any questions wrong, use the answers to determine the part of the chapter you should review before continuing.

Assessment Questions

1. What is the difference between proactive maintenance and reactive maintenance?

   A. Proactive maintenance is done in a controlled environment, whereas reactive maintenance is done because of a pressing problem that must be resolved.

   B. Proactive maintenance is performed when problems arise, whereas reactive maintenance is done to prevent problems.

   C. They both mean the same thing.

   D. Reactive maintenance is done on a day-to-day bases, whereas proactive maintenance is done on a monthly basis.

2. What is meant by a baseline?

   A. How the system runs when under heavy load.

   B. A compilation of the basic software and drivers needed to make the system run.

   C. The typical activity of your servers when functioning normally.

   D. The typical activity of your server during the company's non-working hours.

3. Users are complaining that the network performance degrades severely in the evening shift between 11:00 p.m. and 1:30 a.m. You suspect that the problem is caused by the backup job that is running during this time frame, but the baseline performance did not show any problems when you took it several months ago. How would you go about determining if the backup job is causing the problem?

   A. Perform a baseline based on the current system configuration.

   B. Monitor performance over the course of a week and analyze the findings.

   C. Take another baseline of the server using the same parameters as the original baseline.

   D. Stop the tape backup from running and see if performance improves.

4. You are setting up your performance monitoring program so that you can take system baseline. What counters should you include?

   A. CPU utilization, Page/sec, Avg. Disk Queue Length, and Network utilization

   B. CPU utilization, Available bytes, Disk bytes/sec, Logon total

   C. Bytes total/sec, Avg. disk bytes/transfer, Pool non-paged bytes, Page/sec

   D. Page/sec, Avg. Disk Queue Length, Network utilization, Pool non-paged bytes

5. A junior technician tells you that she was performing some performance monitoring on the server and noticed a drastic performance degradation on the CPU, memory, network, and disk subsystem, which occurred at the exact same time for approximately 5.5 hours each night over the course of the week. What is most likely the cause of this performance loss?

   A. Nightly jobs running on the server

   B. Virus detection software scanning the local system

   C. Tape backup job (backup and verify)

   D. Malfunctioning hardware

6. You come in one morning to find a system error message on the server terminal. The message is from the backup software, and states that the tape backup job failed because of a hardware error caused by a SCSI Bus Timeout. What might cause this timeout problem?

   A. The SCSI controller is too fast for the tape backup hardware.

   B. The SCSI controller is too slow for the tape backup hardware.

   C. A bad tape.

   D. Power surges.

7. You purchased a new tape backup hardware device, and just finished the physical mounting of the drive and connecting all the cables. You have installed the proper operating system drivers, and it appears that the system recognizes the device. However, when you install the backup software application (which is used on all the backup servers), it will not recognize the device, even though you used the proper drivers that came with the backup software. What should you have checked before purchasing the unit?

A. Vendor's Web site for the latest drivers

B. Backup application's hardware compatibly list

C. Operating system's hardware compatibly list

D. Vendor's Web site for installation guidelines

8. Your company is performing a disaster recovery test at an off site agency. The disaster recovery manager wants you to come in to perform a restore of one of the data from one of the servers, and he needs to know how long it will take. The off-site location is costing the company $5,000.00 per day, and they only have two days to complete the test. You tell the manager that it will only take you 2 hours to complete the restore. Unfortunately, when it comes time to do the test it actually took you 6 hours, therefore, preventing the disaster recovery test from completing properly. What should you have done prior to the test?

A. Record the time it took to do a full backup and estimate the time for a restore.

B. Perform a full restore, or restore a portion of the data to some empty space, and then estimated the restore time based on your results.

C. Consult the backup software manuals for restore times.

D. Explain to the DRP manager that there is no way of knowing the restore time, and that he should be prepared for anything.

9. Your server suddenly crashed when a user tried to copy a large file onto the network drive because the server ran out of space. What could you have done to warn you before this happened?

A. Check the disk space each morning as you logged in, and each evening before leaving.

B. Set policies to prevent users from saving large files on the network.

C. Configure the monitoring software with thresholds that would alert you when the free disk space was less than 15%.

D. Watch the performance monitor for disk activity.

10. What are some common CPU bottlenecks?

    A. Applications and drivers

    B. DLLs and drivers

    C. Backup jobs, and other software applications

    D. CPU-bound applications and drivers, and excessive interrupts

11. You have been monitoring the processor utilization over the course of a week and notice that it is consistently above 80%. The IS department is under a tight budget after recent hardware upgrades. What do you need to do in order to prevent the users from noticing a problem?

    A. Add more RAM.

    B. Upgrade the processor, and offload processes to another server.

    C. Purchase another server.

    D. Upgrade the disk subsystem.

12. In order to properly evaluate performance and compare the results, what will you require?

    A. Two server baselines

    B. A server baseline and current performance statistics

    C. Current performance statistics over one day, one week, and one month

    D. A server baseline, and performance data from the last day of the month

13. You installed a virus defense package on your server, and scheduled it to routinely scan the server and network for viruses every three hours. A couple of weeks later, you monitor the performance of this server over the course of week. When you compare the results to your original baseline, you noticed that the CPU is heavily taxed every few hours for certain periods of time. Although the processor is still operating within reasonable limits, what should you have done after installing the virus software?

    A. Only schedule virus scans for non-peak hours.

    B. Upgrade the processor.

    C. Schedule several virus scan jobs to break up the load on the system.

    D. Perform a new baseline after installing the virus software.

14. Upon checking your performance monitor logs, you notice that the hard page faults are consistently high. What should you do?

   A. Install more RAM.

   B. Upgrade the disk subsystem.

   C. Offload some processes to other servers.

   D. Ignore this, because it really does not mean anything.

15. Upon examining the performance monitor logs, you notice that the Network utilization is consistently high over the 10MB Ethernet network. What should you do?

   A. Install another processor in the server.

   B. Upgrade the NIC to a 100MB Fast Ethernet card.

   C. Upgrade the NIC and switches to 100MB fast Ethernet.

   D. Install additional RAM in the server.

Scenarios

1. A client calls you because he is concerned that his NT SQL Server system was operating slowly. He wants an accurate explanation of why this happened suddenly and why it is not performing as well as before. What steps would you need to have taken prior to this, and what performance counters should you measure?

Answers to Chapter Questions

Chapter pre-test

1. A server baseline defines the typical activity of your network servers. Keeping a baseline document of activity on a server lets you determine when activity is normal and when it is not.

2. You should monitor the processor, memory, network, and storage subsystem.

3. The main reason for performing a regular backup is to provide disaster recovery on network servers for any given operating system, and for the services they provide.

4. Areas of system performance affected by backups are the processor, memory, network, and disk subsystem.

5. Data backups, restore jobs, and verify jobs can all affect performance.

6. Some common backup storage technologies are Travan, DAT, DLT, and AIT.

7. You should include CPU usage, cache buffer usage, file read and write performance, disk usage, any running software, backup performance, and restore performance.

8. A system snapshot is the process of "freezing" the current configuration of the server into an image and then storing it on some sort of medium for later recall in the event of a problem.

9. A threshold is a predetermined limit set on a performance counter. The monitoring program can be configured to notify you via e-mail or page when the threshold is reached.

10. The first step is to compare the results that you have gathered from the performance monitoring software and compare it to your baseline data.

Assessment questions

1. **A.** Proactive maintenance is done in a controlled environment, whereas reactive maintenance is done because of a pressing problem that must be resolved. For more information, see the beginning of the chapter.

2. **C.** A baseline defines the typical activity of your servers when functioning normally. Answer A is incorrect because you do not want to perform a baseline if the server is under an unusually heavy load. Answer B is incorrect for obvious reasons. Answer D is incorrect because it is the exact opposite of what a baseline is meant to record. You want to create a baseline when typical activity is occurring. For more information, see the "Creating a Baseline" section.

3. **C.** You will want to take another baseline using the same set of parameters so that you can compare the results and see where the differences are. Answer A is incorrect because the baseline is always going to be on whatever the current configuration is. Answer B is incorrect because you need the baseline to be the same as the one taken previously, whether it was one day or one month. Answer D is incorrect because you are trying to determine where the degradation is occurring. By comparing baselines, you can accurately see this. For more information, see the "Creating a Baseline" section.

4. **A.** Include the CPU utilization counter, page/sec counter, Avg. disk queue length counter, network utilization counter. Depending on the operating system you are using, these counters may have slightly different names. However, they will be similar in name and in intent. All other answers are incorrect because they are more geared for measuring performance as opposed to trying to create a baseline. For more information, see the "Creating A Baseline" section.

5. **C.** It is most likely that you have a backup and verify job running during this time. A simple check of your documentation would tell you if this is true or not. It can be perfectly normal to see these elements heavily taxed during these operations. Answer A is incorrect because it is unlikely that nightly jobs would affect all four elements. Answer B is incorrect because scanning the local system should not affect the network. Answer D is incorrect because it is

highly unlikely that you're only going to see the performance degradation at exactly the same time, for the same time period. For more information, see the "Performing Regular Backups" section.

6. **A.** The SCSI controller is most likely too fast for the tape backup hardware to handle, and thus generates an error. Answer C is incorrect because the tape backup software should generate an error message that is different from that of a SCSI bus timeout error. Most tape backup packages can determine that the tapes are bad, and will generate an error accordingly. Answer D is incorrect because your UPS should protect your hardware from power surges. However, if you are not using a UPS, the power surges will most likely cause the hardware to fail completely, and act erratically. For more information, see the "Improving backup performance" section.

7. **B.** Always check the backup software's hardware compatibility list before purchasing new backup devices. Answer A is incorrect because this would be done after you purchased the unit, and not prior to purchasing it. Answer C is incorrect because while the tape backup hardware may be compatible with the operating system does not mean it will be compatible with the backup software. Answer D is incorrect because it only tells you how to install the device. For more information, see the "Improving backup performance" section.

8. **B.** If possible, perform a full restore of the data. If this is not possible, restore a subset of the data (2GB) to some empty space on the server. This will give you an idea of how long it would take to restore the rest of the data. Answer A is incorrect because restore processes usually take longer than backups. Answer C is incorrect because the manuals cannot account for your server environment and what data you are restoring. Answer D is incorrect because you can estimate the restore time. For more information, see the "Record it" section.

9. **C.** If you configure the monitoring software thresholds, you can set them to alert you when a potential problem occurs. Answer A may work, but it is not a reliable solution, and leaves out a vital time period during the day. Answer B is incorrect because this defeats the purpose of the network. Answer D is incorrect because watching for disk activity will not tell you if it is reaching capacity or not. For more information, see the "Thresholds" section.

10. **D.** CPU-bound applications and drivers and excessive interrupts caused by malfunctioning hardware are common CPU bottlenecks. Refer to the section titled "Measuring Performance" for more information. For more information, see the "Processor" section.

11. **B.** You may need to upgrade the processor or offload some processes to relieve the processor bottleneck. Answer A is incorrect because memory is not the issue. Answer C would certainly resolve the problem but is not necessarily the right choice because of budget limitations imposed on the IS department. Answer D is incorrect because the issue is not the disk subsystem. For more information, see the "Memory" section.

12. **B.** The first thing you will need to evaluate performance and compare results will be the server baseline, and the current performance statistics. For more information, see the "Creating a Baseline" section.

13. D. Always create a new baseline after making changes to the system. You can never be sure how the changes may affect the performance. You would have known of the performance decrease before you did your monitoring. Answer A is a good idea, but it is better to scan the network regularly. Answer B is incorrect because the processors are not being taxed too heavily, so this would be a waste of money. Answer C is incorrect because it is apparent that the server can handle the load. For more information, see the "Creating a Baseline" section.

14. A. Excessive page faults indicate that the system needs more RAM. Answers B, C, and D are incorrect because the issue revolves around the hard page faults, and the only real solution is to upgrade the memory. Offloading processes may or may not do anything in this situation. It may only be a certain application that is taxing the memory. For more information, see the "Storage" section.

15. C. You should consider upgrading the NIC and switches to 100MB Fast Ethernet to increase performance. Don't forget about the network cables either in case they are not category 5. Answer A is incorrect because installing another processor will not resolve network bandwidth problems. Answer B is incorrect because simply upgrading the NIC and not the rest of the components will only result in more problems. Answer D is incorrect because more RAM will not help with network utilization problems. For more information, see the "Network" section.

Scenarios

1. You should have made a baseline prior to this incident, probably when the server was first installed. You should have included the standard memory, processor, logical disk, and network objects, such as % Processor Time, Pages/sec, Avg. Disk Queue Length, and % Network Utilization. These values represent the system under normal working conditions. Now you can take a new baseline, with the same counters, and compare it against the old baseline. This should help you determine what the problem is. Perhaps the network counter is grossly high, or perhaps processor time is consistently near 100 percent, indicating a need for a new or additional processor. In any event, performing the baseline ahead of time will give you the starting point you need to determine the current problem.

Using Monitoring Agents

CHAPTER PRE-TEST

1. What does SNMP stand for?

2. How many types of SNMP commands are there?

3. What does a Management Information Base consist of?

4. Where is a trap command sent to?

5. Explain the importance of monitoring software applications.

6. Why refer to event logs?

7. What components of a network analyzer would you use to specifically monitor TCP/IP traffic?

8. Why should server hardware be monitored?

9. How can you receive alerts when you are not at the server console?

10. What is the purpose of a network management system console?

✦ Answers to these questions can be found at the end of the chapter. ✦

This chapter describes some of the various tools and strategies you can utilize to measure and optimize the performance of your server. It begins with discussion of the industry standard for network management, Simple Network Management Protocol (SNMP). There are also a number of hardware tools and third party monitoring software at your disposal.

Network management tools are not very helpful if you do not know how to properly use them. Sections on trend analysis, identifying bottlenecks, and network analysis will help you take control of your network monitoring and teach you to perform efficient, logical, server diagnosis.

Monitoring Your Network with SNMP

The Simple Network Management Protocol (SNMP) is a network protocol that enables you to collect and exchange information between devices on a network.

As part of the Transmission Control Protocol/Internet Protocol (TCP/IP), the implementation of SNMP enables you to simplify network management, monitor performance, troubleshoot and diagnose network problems, and aid in capacity planning.

How SNMP works

To function properly, SNMP relies on two main components: an SNMP agent installed on the managed device, and a network management system (NMS) that collects the data.

An SNMP agent can reside on all types of network devices, including routers, switches, hubs, servers, workstations, and printers. Its function is to collect and store management information about that particular device and make that information available to the NMS.

The NMS runs an application that monitors and collects information about the managed devices. It can be run on one single system, but a distributed management system will allow for greater allocation of network resources. Figure 11-1 shows the relationship between the various components that comprise a functioning SNMP system.

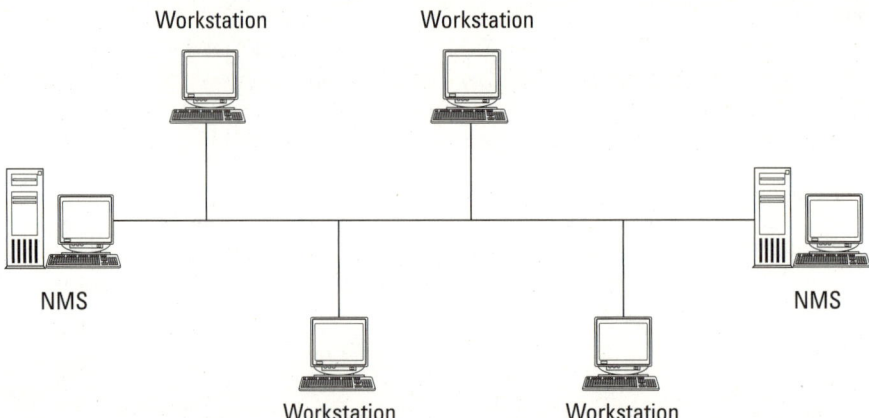

Figure 11-1: A standard SNMP system with the NMS collecting information from the managed devices

SNMP Management Information Base

The Management Information Base (MIB) is a database of information about a managed device. The database consists of *objects,* which describe various functions that can be measured and monitored within that device. For example, there are many different kinds of information you can gather from an end-user workstation. Memory, disk, and CPU usage, network information, user and application information are just some of the different types of information objects you can access.

SNMP commands

There are four basic SNMP operations: read, write, trap, and traversal.

✦ The read operation is used by the NMS to monitor devices and examine the MIB object information hierarchy. An example of a read operation is a `Get` command, which reads an SNMP value from a device.

✦ The write operation is used by the NMS to control devices by changing the object variables of the managed device. An example of a write operation is the `Set` command.

✦ A trap operation is used by the managed devices to relay information and events to the NMS. An alert or event causes a *trap* to be sent to the NMS. The actual SNMP command is `trap`.

✦ Traversal operations are used by the NMS to scan devices for SNMP compatibility and support and gather that information sequentially. An example of a traversal operation is the `GetNext` command.

As a security measure, SNMP uses *community strings.* An SNMP community string is a type of password or identification word that is set for all SNMP operations. Whenever a SNMP management system receives SNMP information, it compares the community string of the incoming SNMP data with its own community string. If they are the same, it accepts the information. If they are different, it discards the request. SNMP software and monitoring programs come with a default community string called *public.* Community strings can be set for different types of SNMP information:

✦ **Read Only:** This type of community string enables a device to only read SNMP information from another device.

✦ **Read-Write:** This type of community string enables a device to both read and write information to and from another device.

✦ **Trap:** A trap community string is used whenever SNMP trap messages are sent from one device to another.

To prevent unauthorized SNMP access to your monitored devices, you should change the default public community string to something different.

Setting SNMP thresholds

 **4.3** Set SNMP Thresholds

All SNMP management programs enable you to set thresholds on MIB objects, and respond with an alert notification when these thresholds have been reached. This provides a way to measure your network against certain baselines, by enabling you to set your thresholds accordingly to what you perceive to be a performance problem.

For SNMP traps to be effective, you must make sure not to set your thresholds too high or too low. If they are set too high, you might be ignoring conditions that are harming your server and network. If they are set too low, you will constantly be notified with false alarms when there is no real performance issue.

For example, you might want to examine server processor load and set a threshold for 75%. This will alert you to any sustained processor activity beyond this point. Setting it too low, at perhaps 50%, will mean you will constantly be getting notifications for processor usage that may be close to normal operating parameters.

 Exam Tip   Although the client SNMP agent is collecting the data, it is at the NMS console where the actual thresholds are set.

Hardware Monitoring Agents

 **4.5** Perform hardware verification

A number of devices are designed specifically for hardware monitoring. Many of these devices, when used appropriately, can help you quickly and systematically determine exactly where network problems are originating.

Hardware monitoring agents vary depending on the application at hand. These agents can be built into software that resides on the server, or they can be special hardware devices that are internal or external to the device.

 Most modern servers come with excellent self-monitoring hardware capabilities installed by the vendor.

Dedicated hardware

In dedicated hardware monitoring, a special hardware device observes the monitored system and detects system errors and events. It performs event detection by probing the system hardware bus, or by connecting physical probes to the processor, memory, ports, and I/O channels. For network activity, hardware devices, such as a network packet sniffer, are plugged directly into the network. These monitoring systems have the advantage of being non-intrusive, because the hardware monitor is usually an external device that has no direct interference with the monitoring application environment. They are also very accurate and efficient because they are dedicated devices that do not lower system performance of the primary system. This type of monitoring is particularly important for real-time systems or when real-time monitoring is required. There are some disadvantages, however, with dedicated hardware monitoring devices:

✦ Some hardware monitoring systems are centralized so that monitoring is restricted to monitor the connected system or object (e.g. network subnet). This limits the scope of the monitoring process and makes it difficult to monitor distributed applications.

✦ Hardware monitoring is more expensive because it requires a special hardware component.

✦ Hardware monitoring is hard to control without a complete software environment, which imposes more expenses and makes the system less flexible.

✦ Hardware monitoring is less portable and often needs an expert to install and maintain, which also makes the system less flexible.

Software monitoring of server hardware

Software-based hardware monitoring agents provide a variety of tools for administrators. Most software monitoring solutions include the following capabilities:

✦ Monitoring the temperature status of the computer

✦ Monitoring all server-related services, including the SNMP MIB

✦ Monitoring the status of the server's disk drives and RAID arrays

✦ Monitoring the network interface card for packets received and transmitted with errors, and packets discarded.

With most monitoring solutions, the administrator can configure the software to send notifications when there are hardware errors, or when certain thresholds are exceeded. Figure 11-2 shows how these signals are sent.

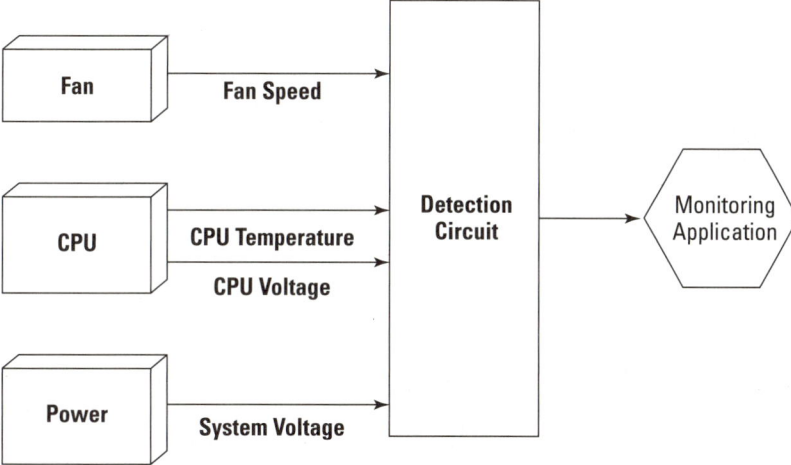

Figure 11-2: Monitoring of hardware environmental factors within the server

Third-Party Agents

Third-party agents provide sophisticated analysis of your server and other devices on your network. These tools help you to diagnose, troubleshoot, and resolve problems quickly. Examples of third-party monitoring programs include HP OpenView, Computer Associates Unicenter TNG, Cabletron Spectrum, and IBM Tivoli.

RMON MIB

The Remote Network Monitoring Management Information Base (RMON MIB) defines the next generation of network monitoring. It uses more comprehensive network fault diagnosis, planning, and performance tuning features than any current monitoring solution. It uses SNMP and its standard MIB design to provide multivendor interoperability between monitoring products and management stations, allowing users to mix and match network monitors and management stations from different vendors.

The RMON MIB enhances the features of typical remote monitoring agents with several new features, such as:

✦ additional packet error counters

✦ more flexible historical trend graphing and statistical analysis

✦ an Ethernet-level traffic matrix

✦ more comprehensive alarms

✦ more powerful filtering to capture and analyze individual packets

RMON MIB software agents can be located on a variety of devices, including network interconnects such as bridges, routers, or hubs; dedicated or non-dedicated hosts; or customized platforms specifically designed as network management instruments. An organization may employ many devices with RMON MIB agents, to monitor one or more network segments, or a WAN link, to further manage its enterprise network.

RMON is not discussed on the exam, but be aware that there are other protocols besides SNMP for monitoring purposes.

In addition to monitoring event logs, services, processes, and performance counters, they can generate alerts when things start to go wrong. You can configure the alerts and event log entries to be forwarded to a central console, which processes the events using notification methods you have defined. Real-time monitoring will help minimize downtime and aid in proactive notification of impending problems. There is nothing worse than your users noticing problems before you do.

Remote viewers included with most third-party agents are used to access the system console from anywhere. Remote viewers can run on most Microsoft Windows systems, and also Unix and NetWare. Remote viewers provide the ability to scan and search event log entries and manage services, processes, and device drivers. It can receive real-time alert messages from any number of consoles.

Distributed system management and real-time monitoring are only half the problem. It is not a simple task to provide definitive information to management about the health and status of your network. Third-party services typically provide a variety of management-style reports that make it simple to provide detailed information about the status, history, and performance of your systems.

In the Real World Many third-party monitoring systems are very large, complex systems involving extremely expensive hardware and software monitoring frameworks. They are used typically in large enterprise environments.

Application Monitoring

In addition to monitoring the health and performance of hardware devices, network administrators must also be able to monitor the performance of mission-critical applications.

There are special software agents that can monitor TCP/IP-based services such as Web servers, POP3/SMTP mail servers, and FTP servers. Other agents can monitor transactional systems such as Oracle and Microsoft SQL server.

With application monitoring, you will be able to proactively monitor your mission-critical applications for any potential problems. For example, you might receive an alert that your mail server is not processing inbound mail. By the time an end user notices that there is no mail coming through, it could be many hours after the initial problem began. Application monitoring alerts you at the time of the problem, and gives you a chance to fix it before it begins to affect end users.

Event Logs

Log files are another invaluable tool in monitoring a system. Certain logs such as system or network messages should be monitored closely, while others can be used only when necessary. For example, you would only use a networking trace log when you're investigating a network problem, but you generally would not constantly monitor and take network traces unless you are having problems. On the other hand, log files for application programs should be monitored closely for application errors that can adversely affect the end users. Log files are used both for diagnostic functions and for predictive or management functions. Events are logged by time and date, giving you the exact time that the problem occurred, and any important error messages or codes that can lead you to the source of the problem.

Exam Tip Event logs should be the very first thing you examine when diagnosing a server problem.

Remote Notification

 **4.6** Establish remote notification

When setting up your monitoring applications, many of them can be configured to notify you through a variety of methods. This is particularly useful if you're off-site. Notifications can be sent through e-mail, console messages, printers, and pagers.

The most common method for the transmission of alerts is through e-mail. Most monitoring programs come with the ability to forward the specific alert to the administrator through the e-mail system. This saves time, because the administrator does not have to continually monitor the application for alerts. This can be very tedious in an enterprise network containing a large number of servers.

Another common method is to configure the monitoring application to send alerts to a pager. This is a bit more complicated, as the computer where the monitoring application resides must have a modem attached to it to dial out to the pager system. The advantages of this system are that the administrator does not have to be on-site to get the alert messages.

Network Analyzers

A network analyzer, sometimes called a *network sniffer,* is used to collect detailed information on network data flow. It can create reports based on statistics like utilization, collision rates, and bottlenecks.

A network analyzer can get down to the packet and frame level of network communications. It can be configured with filters to capture only the types of data you are interested in. For example, you might want to examine all TCP/IP packets between a certain workstation and your server, while ignoring other protocols that are talking on the network.

 **In the Real World** Often, a malfunctioning NIC card can cause a network broadcast storm, in which continuous network messages are sent to the entire network. The clients reply to these messages, and the combined traffic causes the network to be overloaded. A network analyzer can quickly narrow down the culprit using its MAC address.

At the most basic level, you can use a network analyzer to get an accurate snapshot of your network activity, specifically, bandwidth and utilization levels. To get more detailed information about your network activity, you need to use the monitor's built in filters to pick out the information you need. You can filter by protocol, so that on a mixed network of Windows NT and Netware for example, you can specify the network monitor to filter only IPX/SPX traffic so you can diagnose Netware problems. If you believe that a certain workstation is causing too many broadcasts to be sent over the network, you can filter by MAC address to find the exact device. Another useful feature of network analyzers is the ability to record a trace of network activity so that the individual packets and frames can be examined.

Identifying Bottlenecks

 6.3 Identify bottlenecks (e.g., processor, bus transfer, I/O, disk I/O, network I/O, memory)

There are four steps to properly monitoring your server for optimum performance.

1. **Create a baseline.** The first step in performance monitoring should be creating a baseline. A baseline is a measurement of the normal operations of a system, as discussed in Chapter 10. Once the baseline is established, this information can be used to evaluate future monitoring to determine whether your system performance has changed. It is impossible to tell if your system is not operating at normal performance when you haven't measured what that normal performance is.

2. **Monitor your resources.** Once a baseline has been created, you can now modify your monitoring efforts to concentrate on specific components of your system. It is important to measure your system as a whole, because the degradation of one component of your server may be the result of another performance issue. For example, you may notice a large amount of disk utilization, but the actual cause of the problem is that there is not enough RAM in the server, and it is causing an increase in virtual memory swapping to disk.

3. **Analyze the data.** Once you have monitored your components over a period of time, you can now begin to analyze the data to identify any trends. Does performance degradation happen at a certain time, or during a certain application execution? You may be alarmed at a high amount of server activity overnight during the hours of 2 a.m. to 6 a.m., but you know that your network backups happen at that time, which accounts for the high activity. Only after careful analysis of your monitoring data, and comparison to your initial server baseline, can you then proceed to identify your bottlenecks and begin upgrade analysis.

 Exam Tip   It is important that any performance monitoring be done over as large a period of time as possible. This will give you a full scope of server activity in peak and slow periods.

4. **Determine what to upgrade.** When your server bottleneck has been identified, you must now make a choice on an upgrade path. Do you upgrade your RAM? Add another processor? More disk space? Depending on the type of operations your server is performing, it may affect your final decision. Is your server running file/print services? Is it a heavily used database or web server? The bottleneck that you are experiencing is more than likely related to the type of service it is performing.

Key Point Summary

In this chapter, various hardware and software monitoring tools were introduced to aid in diagnosing server problems. Keep the following points in mind for the exam:

✦ Simple Network Management Protocol (SNMP) is a network protocol that allows for the management of collecting and exchange of information between devices on a network. Be sure to know what sort of thresholds to set for devices you are monitoring.

✦ Hardware monitoring agents perform event detection by snooping into the system bus or the network media, or by connecting physical probes to the processor, memory, ports, and I/O channels.

✦ Third-party agents provide sophisticated analysis of your server and other devices on your network. These tools will help the server administrator to quickly diagnose, troubleshoot, and resolve problems. Your current built-in server and network monitoring tools may not be able to handle larger, more complicated problems.

✦   ✦   ✦

STUDY GUIDE

The Study Guide section provides you with the opportunity to test your knowledge about service tools and monitoring systems. The Assessment Questions provide practice for the test, and the Scenarios provide practice with real situations. If you get any questions wrong, use the answers to determine the part of the chapter you should review before continuing.

Assessment Questions

1. When a network device sends an alert to a SNMP network management system (NMS), what type of SNMP operation is this called?

    A. Get

    B. Read

    C. Trap

    D. Traversal

2. To set up your network monitor for pager remote notification, what additional peripheral will be needed?

    A. E-mail

    B. Modem

    C. Tape drive

    D. Keyboard

3. If you are setting up your network analyzer to only monitor TCP/IP on your network, what component will you need to implement?

    A. Filtering

    B. SNMP trap

    C. Sniffer

    D. MAC address

4. The administrator is worried that the company's mission-critical server may be experiencing hardware problems. The technician is asked to take precautionary measures, while keeping costs in mind. The technician should:

    A. Buy a redundant server.

    B. Install a dedicated hardware monitoring device.

    C. Configure remote notification.

    D. Install software-based hardware monitoring agents.

5. Remote notification systems can be configured to send alerts to the following:

    A. System console

    B. Pager

    C. Printer

    D. All of the above

6. During your daily routine of checking each of the servers, you notice a system message on the terminal. What should you check first?

    A. SNMP application log

    B. E-mail

    C. Event logs

    D. Vendor Web site

7. A technician is receiving complaints that the server is slow during the company's midnight shift. The backup system that runs during that time is considered to be the prime suspect. What is the best way to analyze the server to determine if this is true?

    A. Create a baseline of the server during one day shift.

    B. Create a baseline of the server during one night shift.

    C. Create a baseline of the server for a 24-hour period.

    D. Create a baseline of the server on all shifts for one week.

8. A technician notices that a server crashed on the weekend, but no error messages were seen until Monday morning. What can the technician do to prevent further downtime?

    A. Configure remote notification.

    B. Configure SNMP monitor traps.

    C. Hire technicians to monitor the server on weekends.

    D. Configure hardware monitoring.

9. Where would you configure SNMP thresholds?

   A. In the MIB

   B. The packet sniffer

   C. The RMON table

   D. The SNMP NMS monitor

10. Every day at 10 a.m., the company's users complain that the internal Web server is very slow. How would you troubleshoot the server's performance problem?

   A. Upgrade the server processor.

   B. Upgrade the server RAM.

   C. Examine the server logs for any maintenance programs running.

   D. Use a network analyzer to check any network issues.

11. A technician is updating a third-party system monitoring program on a server. What else needs to be done to ensure that the program will work properly?

   A. Increase the server RAM.

   B. Upgrade the client-side agents.

   C. Update the network OS.

   D. Reconfigure SNMP traps.

12. At various times of the day, users are complaining that a particular file server is slow. What should the technician examine first?

   A. Server event logs

   B. Network analyzer traces

   C. MIB database

   D. Performance monitor counters

13. When analyzing a network trace, a technician notices that there is an unusually large amount of packets originating from a particular MAC address. What could this indicate?

   A. The device is a printer.

   B. The device has a malfunctioning NIC card.

   C. The device is a server.

   D. The device is using Token-ring.

14. A technician discovers that his pager has stopped receiving remote alerts from a server. What would most likely be the problem?

   A. SNMP is misconfigured.

   B. The MIB is corrupted.

   C. The event logs are turned off.

   D. The server modem has been disconnected.

15. When examining performance monitor logs, a technician notices a large CPU usage spike everyday at 3 a.m. What could be the source of the problem?

   A. Backups are scheduled at that time.

   B. Someone is logging in remotely overnight.

   C. The SNMP threshold is misconfigured.

   D. The CPU has malfunctioned.

Scenarios

1. You have just installed a new Web server. Your manager is worried about whether the hardware that was purchased will be able to handle the large loads they expect. What steps should you take in monitoring your new server?

2. An article came across the president's desk about how server equipment and network devices can cause problems on a network without the administrator being aware. What solution(s) can you propose?

Answers to Chapter Questions

Chapter pre-test

1. SNMP stands for Simple Network Management Protocol.

2. There are four types of SNMP commands: read, write, trap, and Traversal.

3. An MIB is a hierarchical database of device objects.

4. Trap commands are sent to a Network Management System (NMS).

5. By monitoring critical applications, you will be able to proactively stay ahead of potential problems that could immediately impact end users.

6. Event logs track critical events and errors that can be easily examined.

7. Network analyzers come with filters to aid in packet monitoring.

8. Server hardware can be monitored with software and hardware tools and utilities, to give you advanced warning when a device is not working properly, or is failing. This gives you a chance to replace the part before it fails and causes system downtime.

9. By configuring remote notification using paging or e-mail to receive alerts.

10. The NMS (Network Management System) console is a central computer or device that will collect SNMP and other network management protocol information. When the information is processed, alerts can be sent to notify of an error condition, or data can be collected for reporting functions.

Assessment questions

1. **C.** A trap is an alert sent to the NMS application. Answer A is incorrect because a Get command is a type of Read operation. Answer B is incorrect because a Read operation only retrieves data, it is not a form of alert. Answer D is incorrect because a traversal operation gathers data sequentially from the device's database tables. For more information, see the "SNMP commands" section.

2. **B.** A modem will be needed to dial the pager. Answer A is incorrect because e-mail notification will not be able to send data to a pager. Answer C is incorrect because there is no use for a tape drive in a remote alert system. Answer D is incorrect because the monitoring program does not need any type of keyboard input to send alerts to pagers. For more information, see the "Remote Notification" section.

3. **A.** Filtering enables you to specify only certain criteria to search for. Answer B is incorrect because an SNMP trap is not able to monitor network data. Answer C is incorrect because although you may use a network sniffer or analyzer, you would still need to configure a filter for TCP/IP, so that you would not receive information on other protocols. Answer D is incorrect because a MAC address is the network address of each device, and would still include all protocols. For more information, see the "Network Analyzers" section.

4. **D.** While other solutions are expensive, simply installing software-based monitoring tools can be a cost-effective way to implement hardware monitoring. Answer A is incorrect because adding a redundant server is very expensive. Answer B is incorrect because dedicated hardware monitoring devices are costly. Answer C is incorrect because you will need to set up some type of monitoring tool to monitor the hardware, and then configure it for remote notification in the event of an error condition. For more information, see the "Software monitoring of server hardware" section.

5. **D.** Any of these devices can be used for remote notification. For more information, see the "Remote Notification" section.

6. **C.** Event logs should always be the first thing to check when diagnosing a server problem. Answer A is incorrect because the question did not specify if SNMP was being used. Answer B is incorrect because an e-mail alert will only notify you of the problem, it will not give any specific information that an

event log would. Answer D is incorrect because the information you need is already recorded in the system's event logs, there is no need to go to an outside source. For more information, see the "Event Logs" section.

7. **D.** For best results, a baseline should be taken for a long period of time. Answer A is incorrect because the problem was happening on the night shift, not the day shift. Answer B is incorrect because you should spread out your monitoring efforts over several days to offer more accurate monitoring information. Answer C is incorrect because this will only measure one night shift, and you want to monitor several night shifts to give you a more accurate view of the problem. For more information, see the "Identifying Bottlenecks" section.

8. **A.** With remote notification, the technician can receive error messages while off-site through e-mail, pager, or by other means. Answer B is incorrect because unless the technician is on-site, there is no way to receive the alert. Answer C is incorrect because this is an unnecessary expense when remote notification can be configured. Answer D is incorrect because although the hardware may be monitored, there is no way for the technician to receive the alerts when off-site. For more information, see the "Remote Notification" section.

9. **D.** SNMP thresholds are set from the management application. The NMS will apply these thresholds when it is monitoring devices. Answer A is incorrect because the MIB only holds information specific to that device. Answer B is incorrect because a packet or network sniffer is used to trace networking data. Answer C is incorrect because the thresholds to be set are for SNMP data. For more information, see the "Setting SNMP thresholds" section.

10. **C.** Often, certain applications will run preventative maintenance jobs that consume a lot of CPU time. Consider moving them to an off-hours time slot. Answers A and B are incorrect because you should not immediately upgrade server hardware before examining the origin of the problem. Answer D is incorrect because the server itself should be examined first, before moving on to external items such as the network. For more information, see the "Identifying Bottlenecks" section.

11. **B.** The client agents of a monitoring program should be kept current with the main monitoring application, to ensure compatibility and full functionality. Answer A is incorrect because there is no need to update RAM unless it is a specified minimum requirement for the upgrade. Answer C is incorrect because upgrading the OS may cause the monitoring program to not work properly. Answer D is incorrect because upgrading the monitoring program should not affect any SNMP settings you have already configured. For more information, see the "Third-Party Agents" section.

12. **A.** Examine the event logs to see if any other server events are happening at these times. Answer B is incorrect because you should examine the server first before checking external items such as the network. Answer C is incorrect because examining the SNMP MIB database will not immediately reveal any helpful information, since the data must be processed by a network management system. Answer D is incorrect because the performance has already

been recognized as an issue, and examining the performance monitor will not aid in troubleshooting the problem. For more information, see the "Event Logs" section.

13. **B.** A malfunctioning NIC card will usually broadcast a large amount of packets onto the network. Answer A is incorrect because a printer will not usually send out a large number of network packets. Answer C is incorrect because although a server will generate a lot of network traffic, it should not be anything unusual. Answer D is incorrect because a token ring device would not cause extra network traffic. For more information, see the "Network Analyzers" section.

14. **D.** Without the modem, the server cannot dial the pager to send the alert messages. Answer A is incorrect because this would not stop the pager from receiving remote alerts. Answer B is incorrect because although MIB corruption would only affect a certain device, it would not disable remote notification. Answer C is incorrect because disabling the event logs would only affect local logs on the server, it would not affect remote notification. For more information, see the "Remote Notification" section.

15. **A.** Most off-hours usage spikes are caused by backup operations. This is normal. Answer B is incorrect because a remote user would not cause a big increase in CPU usage. Answer C is incorrect because the setting of the threshold would not cause the CPU spike, it can only measure and detect it. Answer D is incorrect because a CPU malfunction would result in inconsistent behavior. For more information, see the "Identifying Bottlenecks" section.

Scenarios

1. Your first step would be to create a baseline of your current performance. Only until you know at what levels your current system is operating can you measure any changes in performance at a later time.

   Your next step is to monitor your server's performance over a period of time, for example, a seven-day period. When you have the results, you must analyze the data for any changes in performance, especially at different times of the day. Are your backups or scheduled maintenance jobs interfering with performance?

   Finally, if there any issues such as CPU utilization, RAM, or disk performance issues, you must plan for an upgrade of that component depending on the data you have analyzed.

2. Obviously, the management is worried that there could be server problems when the administrator is off-duty or away from the equipment. The first thing you should do is implement a proper monitoring system such as SNMP, or a third-party monitoring program if the software that came with your server will not perform the tasks you need.

Next, you can set thresholds on system parameters that you would like to be alerted to. For example, you may want to receive an alert when CPU usage is too high, or if any hardware has failed. These alerts can appear on the console, or through e-mail.

To ensure that you receive these alerts during off-hours, you must set up remote notification so that the monitoring program will dial your pager with any alerts. That way, they can be dealt with before your users come in to use the system.

Physical
Housekeeping

EXAM OBJECTIVES

4.4 Perform physical housekeeping

CHAPTER PRE-TEST

1. What is the most likely cause of an overheated CPU?

2. What is the difference between a surge protector and a surge suppressor?

3. What is line conditioning?

4. Mechanical sounds coming from a server usually indicate what condition?

5. What is the purpose of server room air conditioning?

6. What do the lights on a NIC card indicate?

7. What sort of physical indicators should you look for when inspecting your server room?

8. Why is server air circulation important?

9. Why is it important to keep a server's doors and panels on during operation?

10. Explain the importance of proper cabling techniques.

✦ Answers to these questions can be found at the end of the chapter. ✦

egularly scheduled physical inspections of your server room are integral to proactive maintenance of your server systems. As part of your daily routine, you should include physical checks of all server status lights, fans, cabling, and environmental issues such as temperature and electrical checks. This chapter stresses the important of using your senses to detect server errors, and details the warning signs of environmental issues that could affect system performance.

Sights, Sounds, and Smells

 **4.4** Perform physical housekeeping

The simplest method of physical server checks is to use your senses to detect any server hardware errors, or environmental issues. Environmental issues such as room temperature are immediately apparent upon entering a server room. If the room feels warmer than usual, it is an indication that at least one or more of your server cabinets or other computer equipment is generating a lot of heat. The worst scenario is that your server room's air conditioning has failed, causing the entire room to heat up to dangerous levels, leading to eventual system failure.

Make a quick, visual scan of your server racks, to look for warning lights or a crimped cable, as part of your everyday routine. Catching a server hardware error at an early stage, such as a failed power supply or hard drive in a redundant system, will give you the time to get replacements parts before the condition results in system downtime.

Another important physical examination you can perform in your server room is to pay attention to sounds. Although servers are mostly electronic circuitry, there are several components that have moving mechanical parts, and are the most likely candidates for failure. Hard drives, tape drives, CPUs, and power supply and ventilation fans are probably the most common types of device to fail. These physical problems often go undetected by hardware monitoring and diagnostic programs, so your senses are the next best tool for proactive monitoring of these items.

Hard drive systems are very sensitive to vibrations, noise, temperature, and electromagnetic interference. The hard drive head is especially susceptible to damage because of its extreme sensitivity. Any vibration can cause it to knock against the hard drive platters and cause damage. Hard drives that have failed, or are failing, can be noted by the sounds that the heads make during operation. Constant clicking or knocking sounds can indicate imminent failure, because one of the mechanical parts is obviously making contact with something else in the hard drive. When you detect any of these strange noises, it is best to immediately backup your data and find a replacement before the unit fails.

Tape drives are also notorious for frequent mechanical failures. A tape drive contains even more mechanical moving parts that load your tapes into the drive, and engage the tape heads for access. Some advanced tape drives and autoloaders come with special mechanical arms that remove your tape from a slot, and automatically insert it into the drive when needed. Because you are typically performing backups daily, these mechanisms can wear out quickly, so you must be wary of strange sounds and other indicators of a mechanical breakdown. When loading tapes, take a moment to listen carefully for any noises such as persistent clicking, or other load sounds that indicate the tape is not being loaded properly. Tape heads must also be cleaned on a regular basis, because of the buildup of dust, dirt, and particles from the tape media themselves.

Cooling and circulation fans are extremely important for maintaining safe temperatures and proper ventilation within the system. Because of their mechanical nature, these fans tend to fail frequently. It is imperative that any fan that has failed, or is not turning properly, be replaced as soon as possible. Any disruption in the ventilation and cooling process can cause an immediate increase in temperature, which results in the overheating of other devices and their possible failure. Take some time to inspect your fans regularly, including CPU, power supply, internal ventilation, and external rack fans, to note any strange motion, or audible clicking and knocking noises. This indicates that the fan is not operating as designed, and could fail at any time.

The most important sounds to listen for are any type of warning sounds such as constant beeping or a constant tone. This indicates that one of your devices has set off an internal alarm. The most common one you will hear is a UPS alarm, which could indicate many conditions such as loss of power, overloading, and power sags and spikes. If your server room loses power, the UPS alarm will sound to indicate that it is currently running on battery. Since UPS batteries are only designed to run for a short period of time, it is important that you begin shutdown of your servers, if auto-shutdown has not been configured through your UPS. Other devices may sound their own type of alarms, so check the manufacturer's documentation to know what they indicate. Smells, such as something that is burning, or has burnt out, are a quick indicator of a device failure such as a power supply, or fan. Power supplies are most notorious for burning out, and are easily identified by the smoke or sparks coming from the unit itself. Keep a fire extinguisher in the server room, in case of the threat of a fire caused by equipment failure.

Checking Status Lights

Most modern servers have many status lights for different server components. System power, hard disk drive health and activity, and network card activity are all aspects of the server that you can easily check by examining their status lights. Many manufacturers include their own self-diagnostic hardware functionality in a system. Check with the vendor manual or Web site to decipher any combinations of flashing lights or error codes.

System power lights

System power lights are relatively simple. Either they are green, indicating the
server is powered on, or they are blank, indicating the server is powered off. Some
manufacturers also have lights that indicate a system stand-by mode, when the
server is receiving power, but has not been actually turned on.

Hardware diagnostic lights

Often, a diagnostic light is located near the power light. Depending on its flashing
sequences or color, it can indicate a hardware error condition. It could be an immediate hardware failure or the indication that some part of the system is showing
signs of failing and should be replaced.

 Exam Tip   Codes differ from manufacturer to manufacturer. Check the manufacturer's manual or Web site to interpret error codes or lights specific to your system.

Hard drive lights

Most hard drives have two lights, one to indicate its status, and another to indicate
activity. The status light typically indicates the current status or health of the drive.
If it is part of a redundant system such as a RAID or mirrored array, it can also indicate the status of the array. Internal hardware diagnostics can determine if a hard
drive is beginning to show signs of a future failure, which is usually displayed as a
yellow status light. This gives you time to order replacement parts, and remove the
drive before an actual failure happens. A red status light indicates immediate failure. If your system is a redundant RAID system, one failed drive should not affect
your system immediately, and will give you time to replace the failed unit.

Server activity can often be measured by your hard drive activity. If the activity
light is continually flashing, and you can hear a grinding sound as the hard drives
operate, your server may be overloaded. You should then consider offloading some
of your applications or services to a separate server. It is also possible that your
server may be low on RAM. If there is little available RAM to properly service
requests, the server will use a virtual memory area on the hard disk. This is called a
swap file, and if the server is very low in RAM, it will make extensive use of this virtual memory area, causing constant disk activity and slower server performance. If
you are also running out of disk space, this will increase the activity to unacceptable levels, because the server will also run out of swap file space. Ensure that you
have enough RAM and disk space for your server to operate efficiently.

Network card lights

NIC cards typically have two to three lights indicating network activity, successful
connection to the network, and a speed or duplex status light. The connection light
is the most important one, indicating that you have a proper connection to the network. A red or blank light indicates that there is no connection, possibly because of

a defective cable, or the simple fact that the cable isn't plugged into a hub or switch at the other end.

The network activity light flashes as packets are sent or received from the network card. There is usually no color for error conditions, as there is either network activity or there is not. This is an excellent indicator to see if your server is talking to the network, even if the connection light is indicating a good connection. If there is no activity, there might be a software issue with the network configuration within the operating system. Sometimes, the connection light and network activity light are combined, so that it will flash to indicate a good connection and network activity.

The connection speed or duplex light indicates the speed that your interface is communicating with the network card. Dual-speed cards, which typically run either 10MB or 100MB connections, use this light to show what speed you are operating at. Often another light will indicate if you are running at half-duplex or full duplex. Network cards are discussed in Chapter 9.

In the Real World   Often, customers misinterpret the flashing lights as error conditions, when they are only indicating network activity.

Tape drive lights

Tape units have a number of status lights to indicate the health and activity of your tape drive. Pay careful attention to these status lights, because any error condition could be interfering with your backups and causing them to fail.

The most-used status light for tape drives indicates when the tape heads need to be cleaned. This condition usually shows up at least once a month, and you should clean the heads right away, or you might find that even though your system logs say the backup was successful, physical errors on the tape render the backup useless.

Various combinations of flashes and error lights can indicate many different conditions for tape drives. Check with the manufacturer's manual or Web site to decipher the error messages.

Temperature and Ventilation

Keeping your server room cool, and providing adequate ventilation, is extremely important in preventing system failures due to the environment. Without proper cooling and air circulation, you risk the danger of overheating, and eventual equipment failure.

Internal air flow

Your first point of failure for server overheating usual involves the server case or chassis itself. The internal vents and fans must all be positioned correctly and functioning properly to provide cooling and air flow. Improper airflow will result in certain components being cooled, while others might be exposed to continuous hot air, and can often quickly raise the internal temperature of the server to dangerous levels. Proper airflow is also integral to keeping the inside of the server clear from dust, which is circulated and pushed outside of the system.

✦ **Chassis covers and panels:** It is a common misconception that taking the cover or side panels off a server will help cool the system. This actually causes the opposite effect, because the air that the internal fans are trying to push is coming from the outside room rather than from around the components. This often causes some components to get hotter, rather than cooler. This also holds true for the front and rear doors on a server cabinet. If they are left off, the airflow will be disrupted, causing most of the hot air to remain within the cabinet.

✦ **Expansion slots:** Cover up any empty expansion slot holes, or any other device bay that has been removed. Any holes in your server will disrupt airflow, and cause hot air to remain inside the case.

✦ **Internal components:** All of your devices, such as hard drives, RAID and SCSI cards, video cards, and other peripherals, should be spaced as far apart as possible to allow the heat radiating from these components to dissipate into the air flow of the case. You may have to make room to add more fans internally to spot-cool certain devices.

External ventilation

To cool the system effectively, it is just as important to have good airflow and ventilation outside of the system. An industrial strength air conditioner is a must, because it will keep your entire server room at a constant, cool temperature. Inspect the air conditioner regularly for any defects in performance, and if it fails, get it fixed as soon as possible to prevent overheating of your servers. As a general rule, keep your room temperatures at an average of approximately 70 degrees F (20 degrees C). Keeping your server room temperature at a constant, cool rate will prevent overheating, and also damage from temperature fluctuations.

After an air conditioning failure, the temperature of a server room can rise dramatically within a very short time. Any failures of your cooling systems must be dealt with immediately to prevent systems from overheating and failing.

Modern server cabinets are built specifically to regulate airflow from the servers and circulate it up and out from the cabinet. Often the cabinet will have its own fans that will perform this function.

Server Fans

Several fans within your server system keep components operating at steady temperatures, and prevent them from overheating. Some of them blow air onto a component to keep it cool; other fans are used primarily for air circulation, to bring hot air away from the system and out through air vents. You should inspect your fans routinely to ensure proper operation. If a fan is sticking, or not operating at all, it can quickly lead to a component failure because of overheating, or it can harm air circulation and cause hot air to remain within your system, causing general temperature overheating.

Chip fan

One of the most important fans in your server and one of the most often overlooked, is the CPU fan. It usually comes bundled with the heat sink and sits on top of the CPU. As the heat sink draws heat away from the CPU, the fan pushes that air away from the CPU, which then circulates out of the chassis through air vents. Other types of fans act as spot-cooling fans by blowing air onto the CPU.

If the fan is installed improperly, even sitting only slightly off the CPU, it can cause the CPU to overheat and malfunction. This often happens after a chip upgrade, when the fan and heat sink are removed to replace the old CPU. When everything is put back in place, check that the fan is sitting properly on top of the CPU and operating normally.

A malfunctioning fan can be indicated by clicking or buzzing sounds, or an odd motion of the fan blades. This indicates some sort of mechanical breakdown, and you should replace the fan immediately.

Exam Tip System freezes or erratic behavior are often caused by a CPU malfunctioning because of overheating.

Power supply fan

Most power supplies contain a fan that is mounted to draw hot air from the inside of a server chassis and push it out through the back of the server. Some newer models also contain an internal fan that blows air onto internal components to keep them cool.

These fans collect a lot of dust as they open out from the back of the server. It is a good idea to regularly clean out the outer fans with a can of compressed air, to remove this dust build-up. Do not spray the air into the power supply from the outside, as this will just push the dust and debris back into the case. Always open up the server chassis, and blow the dust outwards.

Chassis fan

In today's larger servers, especially those with a large number of hard drives for internal RAID systems, extra fans within the server chassis help to cool components and circulate hot air out of the chassis. They are usually mounted in strategic places around the server chassis to regulate proper airflow. Within the server cabinet itself, extra fans in the top of the cabinet take the expelled air from the servers and push them out the top of the cabinet. As with other fan systems, you should check all chassis fans regularly for proper motion, and clean them periodically to prevent dust buildup.

Checking Cabling

Improper cabling techniques can result in a number of unexpected issues. Any type of cable carries information of some sort, whether it is a network cable, a keyboard or mouse cable, or a hard drive or tape drive SCSI cable, and any interruption in service because of careless cabling techniques can be easily avoided with some simple methods.

Network cabling

The most important cables are your Ethernet network cables, which connect your server to the enterprise network. Network cabling laid carelessly across the floor can be easily tripped over, possibly causing an important server to lose its network connection. Cables are often run through the hinges in server cabinet doors, causing them to be pinched or cut every time a door is opened or closed. To protect your network cabling, follow standard practice and run it from the main hubs and switches through either encased conduits in the ceiling or under the floor, or run it along network cable trays high above the server room along the outside walls. This way, the cables cannot be damaged through everyday activity.

Internal cabling

Although issues resulting from internal server cabling are rare, they do happen, most often when something has being upgraded, added, or removed from the server. You will most often replace a component, only to have some other component fail when the server is brought back up because its cable was disturbed during the upgrade. When working internally on the server, remember to check and double-check all cables to make sure they are tightly in their sockets, especially hard drive SCSI and IDE cables, and power connectors.

Keyboard, monitor, and mouse cables

Often, a damaged cable from a keyboard, monitor, or mouse can adversely affect your server. Keyboard errors can easily lock up a system if a damaged cable is causing bad data input to the system. If your server cabinet contains a number of machines hooked up to one monitor, keyboard, and mouse through a KVM switch, be sure to use twist-ties and cable management trays to keep them out of the way and prevent damage. Make sure there is enough slack in the cable to pull your server out of the rack for maintenance, without accidentally pulling the cable connectors out of the rear of the server.

Electrical Issues

Electrical damage to equipment is probably the most common environmental issue affecting server installations. An unexpected power interruption can cause data loss and at its extreme, cause permanent damage to your server.

Every day your server is dealing with electrical fluctuations. In poorly powered sites, electrical surges and brownouts are a daily occurrence. Surges are caused by an overflow of voltage greater than normal, while voltage spikes are short, sharp increases in voltage often caused by lightening storms. Brownouts are caused by voltages fluctuating lower than normal. Any of these conditions can cause a large amount of damage in your electrical equipment. To protect your server from these electrical irregularities, you need some sort of device to provide a barrier between your equipment and the building electrical system.

Surge protection

A surge protector is probably of little use for a critical server system. It basically consists of a power bar with a fuse that breaks the circuit when a voltage surge is detected. For a server system, there can be no room for downtime, and although a surge protector might protect your equipment from being damaged, you will still incur a loss of data if your server loses power.

Surge suppressor

A more advanced solution to surge protection is surge suppression. The circuitry in a surge suppressor is more complicated, and provides a finer detection of dangerous voltages. It is much quicker in reacting to a voltage surge. A surge suppressor still does not solve the problem of loss of power to the server during an outage, however.

Line conditioner

A line conditioner is a device that cleans the input power to your devices. Although it does protect against voltage discrepancies, it can also condition inconsistent power. Inconsistent power is found mostly in older buildings where the electrical systems haven't been updated.

UPS

An uninterruptible power supply (UPS) can combine all the functions of a surge protector, a surge suppressor, and a line conditioner, plus a backup battery to keep your server alive during a power outage. It also comes with special software that will alert your operating system of a power outage, and automatically shut down gracefully.

Cross-Reference UPS devices are discussed in more detail in Chapter 2.

In choosing a UPS, you need to know how many devices will be connected to it, and how much power they will use. Most UPS sizes are measured by VA, or Volts-Amps. This number is the combined VA sizes of all your devices.

The battery on the UPS should keep your systems powered for at least five minutes so they can shut down properly. Most power outages last less than a few minutes, so you want to make sure they at least cover the amount of time it takes to shut down your servers. Depending on how many devices you have hooked up to your UPS, the life of the battery can go up or down accordingly.

A UPS will alert you whenever it is running from battery. This is usually indicated by a beeping sound, or a steady tone. UPS alarms can also indicate other conditions, such as a power spike or sag, or that the UPS is overloaded.

Key Point Summary

In this chapter, several tips for physical housekeeping in your server room were introduced. From simple methods such as using your senses to examine physical lights on your server, or listening for mechanical failures, to more advanced methods for environmental issues, each play a part in your routine preventative maintenance schedule.

Some key points to keep in mind for the exam:

✦ Recognize the physical warning signs of server hardware failure such as status lights, sounds, and smoke.

✦ Remember the importance of keeping the server room cool, including proper techniques for airflow and ventilation.

✦ Remember proper cabling techniques to prevent accidental damage to server cables.

✦ Know the different choices for electrical protection, and the functions of a UPS.

✦   ✦   ✦

STUDY GUIDE

The Study Guide section provides you with the opportunity to test your knowledge about physical housekeeping. The Assessment Questions provide practice for the test, and the Scenarios provide practice with real situations. If you get any questions wrong, use the answers to determine the part of the chapter you should review before continuing.

Assessment Questions

1. Which of the following is usually *not* a server room environment issue?

   A. Temperature

   B. Server Room door unlocked

   C. Brownouts

   D. Power spike

2. A customer is complaining that there is a loud buzzing sound coming from the server. What could be causing the noise?

   A. Malfunctioning CPU fan

   B. Faulty NIC card

   C. Failed RAID controller

   D. Nothing, the noise is normal

3. A new file server is having trouble communicating with the network. What visual check can you perform to help diagnose the problem?

   A. Check the power light.

   B. Listen for hard drive activity.

   C. Check the lights on the NIC card for activity.

   D. Make sure the power supply fan is running.

4. A server that has been installed for a few days is continually freezing up. What is the most likely cause of the problem?

   A. The power supply fan is not working properly.

   B. The CPU fan is not sitting on the chip properly.

   C. The UPS is disconnected.

   D. The server room has improper ventilation.

5. What is *not* a sign of a server malfunction?

   A. Smoke from the power supply

   B. Continuous clicking sounds

   C. Flashing lights on the NIC card

   D. Beeping sounds

6. A technician notices that one of the hard drives in a RAID 5 array has a red light on, and the others are all green. What could be the cause of the red light?

   A. The hard drive has failed.

   B. The hard drive is the parity drive.

   C. The hard drive fan is not working.

   D. The hard drive is currently not in use.

7. A customer currently has four servers attached to a UPS. The UPS load is quite high at 84 percent. What can be done to lower the load on the UPS?

   A. Plug another device into the UPS.

   B. Use a 220V input voltage.

   C. Install a line conditioner.

   D. Buy another UPS to distribute the load.

8. A customer is complaining that their server loses its connection with the network from time to time. What is the most likely cause of the problem?

   A. The OS networking configuration is wrong.

   B. The network cable is being caught in the server cabinet door.

   C. The network cable is not plugged into a hub or switch.

   D. The NIC is only running at 10 MB.

9. What is the most likely cause of CPU overheating?

   A. Improper ventilation

   B. Lack of server room air conditioning

   C. Faulty power supply fan

   D. Malfunctioning CPU fan

10. A server UPS is beeping. What is the most likely cause of the alarm?

   A. The UPS is running from battery.

   B. There has been a power spike.

   C. The server is disconnected.

   D. The UPS software is not configured.

11. A technician is examining a server room to look for the best place to run Ethernet cabling to the servers. What would be the best choice?

    A. Along the floor into the cabinet

    B. Through the front server cabinet door

    C. From a ceiling conduit or under the floor, and into the server cabinet

    D. Through the rear server cabinet door

12. After a recent CPU upgrade, the customer has been complaining that the server frequently exhibits strange and erratic behavior. What could be the cause of the problem?

    A. The CPU is not compatible with the motherboard.

    B. The server's operating system does not allow for dual CPUs.

    C. The CPU fan was not replaced properly, causing it to overheat.

    D. The server needs more memory.

13. A customer is complaining of an odd clicking sound coming from the server. Which of the following is *least* likely to be causing the problem?

    A. Power supply fan

    B. Failing hard disk

    C. CPU fan

    D. Failing NIC card

14. A customer complains that there is a light flashing on the NIC card on the back of the server. What could be the cause of the problem?

    A. Nothing, the light is indicating network activity.

    B. The NIC card is malfunctioning.

    C. The NIC card is running at full duplex.

    D. The NIC card is running at 100MB.

15. A customer has been having a problem with a particular server overheating. The server has been recently upgraded with new memory. What is the most likely cause of the problem?

    A. This CPU fan needs to be replaced.

    B. The server room air conditioning is not running at peak performance.

    C. The server cover was not put back on after the memory upgrade.

    D. The new memory is incompatible and causing the server to overheat.

16. What is *not* a reason for server room air conditioning?

    A. Comfortable environment for technicians

    B. Proper air circulation

    C. Prevent equipment from overheating

    D. Prevent temperature fluctuations

17. A technician walks into a server room, and notices that it is very hot. What is the most likely cause of the problem?

    A. The server room air conditioning unit has failed.

    B. The CPU fan has failed.

    C. The power supply fan has failed.

    D. The server cabinet doors are closed.

18. A technician notices that an Ethernet cable is caught in the cabinet door of a server. What is most likely to happen?

    A. The server will exhibit erratic network connectivity.

    B. The server will overheat and malfunction.

    C. The cabinet door will not shut properly, causing bad air circulation.

    D. The NIC card will only run at 10MB rather than 100MB.

19. A technician is installing a new company e-mail server. What would be the best option to protect the server from electrical power problems?

    A. UPS

    B. Surge suppressor

    C. Surge protector

    D. Power generator

20. A customer has complained that there is a lot of heat being generated from a particular server cabinet. What is the most likely cause of the problem?

    A. Lack of a server room air conditioner

    B. Lack of circulation within the cabinet

    C. The CPU fan is not working.

    D. The server has a large number of hard drives.

Scenarios

1. You have been asked to install three servers into a cabinet. You want to provide proper electrical protection and battery backup. What sort of considerations must you keep in mind when selecting electrical protection?

2. A customer is worried about environmental issues in their server room. What aspects of the server room can you examine to ensure a proper environment?

Answers to Chapter Questions

Chapter pre-test

1. A CPU will overheat if fan is not working, or is improperly positioned.

2. A surge protector is typically just a power bar with a fuse that will only protect your server from a large voltage spike. A surge suppressor contains more specialized circuitry to detect and prevent power spikes and surges from damaging equipment.

3. Line conditioning refers to preventing power fluctuations and bad power quality from harming electrical equipment.

4. Buzzing or clicking sounds usually mean a fan or hard drive is failing.

5. Air conditioning is critical in keeping server room temperatures cool and consistent to prevent equipment overheating.

6. Typically, there are two or three lights. They indicate network connection, network activity, and duplex and speed settings. Sometimes the connection and activity lights are combined. They are useful in diagnosing network connectivity issues.

7. Perform visual inspections, such as checking the status lights on your equipment. Listen for any odd sounds coming from your server, which might indicate a malfunction in a mechanical device. Also check your equipment for abnormally high temperatures.

8. Without proper circulation, any hot air is not flowing out of the server chassis or server cabinet. This will lead to overheating and possible equipment failure.

9. The server chassis and cabinet are manufactured to let air circulate to move hot air out. When the panel or cabinet doors are removed, proper airflow will not occur, which could lead to overheating.

10. Without proper cabling techniques, you increase the possibility of server errors resulting from cabling failures such as Ethernet networking, or loss of input from the keyboard and mouse.

Assessment questions

1. **B.** Having a server room door unlocked is a security issue, not an environmental issue. Answers A, C, and D are incorrect because these are all important server room environmental issues. For more information see the "Temperature and Ventilation" section.

2. **A.** A malfunctioning CPU fan could cause this type of noise if it is not working properly. Answers B and C are incorrect because these cards do not have any moving mechanical parts. Answer D is incorrect because this type of noise is not normal, and indicates some form of mechanical failure. For more information, see the "Chip fan" section.

3. **C.** Most NIC cards have a light that indicates network activity. If it is flashing, the problem might be caused by software rather than hardware. Answer A is incorrect because the power light will not give you any indication of network connectivity. Answer B is incorrect because hard drive activity will have no relevance with the network. Answer D is incorrect because the condition of the power supply fan will not indicate any problems with the network. For more information, see the "Network card lights" section.

4. **B.** Erratic server behavior, including freezing, is most often caused by CPU malfunction as a result of overheating. Answer A is incorrect because the fan failing on the power supply will not cause the CPU to overheat, but it may cause the power supply to fail. Answer C is incorrect because disconnecting the UPS will not cause the server to halt. Answer D is incorrect because this may cause the server room to increase in temperature, but would not directly affect the CPU. For more information, see the "Chip fan" section.

5. **C.** The flashing light on the NIC card indicates network activity, not an error condition. Answers A, C, and D are incorrect because these are all important warning signs of a current or imminent server malfunction. For more information, see the "Network card lights" section.

6. **A.** Any red light is usually an indicator of a failed or malfunctioning device. Answer B is incorrect because there is usually no indicator of which drive is the parity drive in a RAID 5 array. Answer C is incorrect because there are no hard drive fan indicator lights. Answer D is incorrect because if the drive were not in use, there would be no light at all. For more information, see the "Hard drive lights" section.

7. **D.** If the UPS fails, its emergency battery power will be used up too quickly on so many servers. You should also spread the load between several UPS units for multiple systems. Answer A is incorrect because plugging another device in will overload the UPS even further. Answer B is incorrect because different voltages will not affect server load. Answer C is incorrect because the purpose of a line conditioner is to clean up inconsistent power that contains interference; it will not affect UPS load. For more information, see the "UPS" section.

8. **B.** Improper cabling that causes physical damage can cause intermittent communications. Answer A is incorrect because if the configuration was wrong, there would be no connection at all. Answer C is incorrect because there would be no connection at all if the cable was unplugged. Answer D is incorrect because the network speed would not create intermittent communications. For more information see the "Network cabling" section.

9. **D.** A properly functioning CPU fan is integral in keeping the CPU cool. Answer A is incorrect because improper ventilation would heat up the general area around the server, but would not cause the CPU to directly overheat. Answer B is incorrect because a lack of air conditioning would not directly cause the CPU to overheat. Answer C is incorrect because a faulty power supply fan would not cause the CPU to overheat, but it may lead to a power supply failure. For more information, see the "Chip fan" section.

10. **A.** When a UPS loses power, and is using its battery to power connected devices, it will sound a warning to indicate that the battery has been activated. Answer B is incorrect because a sustained beeping would not indicate a momentary surge in power. Answer C is incorrect because there would be no warning sound if the server was disconnected from the UPS. Answer D is incorrect because unconfigured software would not trigger an alarm. For more information, see the "UPS" section.

11. **C.** With this setup, there is little chance of the cables being physically damaged. Answer A is incorrect because the cables are in danger of being stepped on or tripped over, which might pull them free from their connectors. Answer B is incorrect because the cable might get damaged if it is caught in the server cabinet door. Answer D is incorrect because the cable might get damaged if caught in the rear server cabinet door. For more information see the "Network cabling" section.

12. **C.** If the CPU fan is not installed properly, it will not properly cool the CPU. Answer A is incorrect because if this were true, the server would not work at all. Answer B is incorrect because the question did not specify that this was a dual-CPU system, only that is was upgraded. Answer D is incorrect because a lack of memory would cause the server performance to degrade, it would not create erratic behavior. For more information see the "Chip fan" section.

13. **D.** The NIC does not contain any mechanical devices such as a fan that would make such a noise. Answers A, B, and C are incorrect because these devices are mechanical in nature, and prone to mechanical failure. For more information see the "Server Fans" section. For more information see the "Server Fans" section.

14. **A.** Most NIC cards have a light that indicates network activity. It does not indicate an error condition. Answer B is incorrect because there is no error light on the network card. Answer C is incorrect because a duplex light would not flash, it would stay solid. Answer D is incorrect because the speed indicator light would not flash, it would stay solid. For more information see the "Network card lights" section.

15. C. The server's panels and covers must be on for proper air flow and circulation. Answer A is incorrect because a malfunctioning CPU fan would not cause the entire server to overheat, it would only affect the CPU. Answer B is incorrect because the air conditioning unit would have to completely fail to cause the server to overheat. Answer D is incorrect because memory alone would not cause a server to overheat. For more information see the "Internal air flow" section.

16. A. This is not the reason for server room air conditioning. Answers B, C, and D are incorrect because server room air conditioning is integral in keeping temperatures consistent and cool, and to help provide proper air circulation. For more information see the "Temperature and Ventilation" section.

17. A. The failure of a server room air conditioning unit will make the room noticeably warmer. Answers B, C, and D are incorrect because these conditions will only cause individual server overheating. For more information see the "External ventilation" section.

18. A. Any cabling must be properly protected from the possibility of physical damage. A damaged cable will cause intermittent network connectivity. Answer B is incorrect because the cable will not cause the server to overheat. Answer C is incorrect because the server door should shut, but it will damage the cable in the process. Answer D is incorrect because a damaged cable will not affect speed, it will affect network connectivity. For more information see the "Network cabling" section.

19. A. A UPS can offer battery backup in the event of power loss, and built-in surge protection and suppression. Answers B and C are incorrect because a surge suppressor or protector will only prevent large power spikes from affecting equipment, it will not provide battery backup in the event of a power failure. Answer D is incorrect because a power generator will not protect equipment from power spikes, it will only provide backup power in the event of a power outage. For more information see the "UPS" section.

20. B. Without proper air circulation, hot air is trapped within the cabinet or server chassis. Answer A is incorrect because having no air conditioning would cause the entire room to heat up, not just one cabinet. Answer C is incorrect because a malfunctioning CPU fan will only overheat the CPU, not the entire cabinet. Answer D is incorrect because having several hard drives will not increase the temperature of that cabinet noticeably. For more information see the "External ventilation" section.

Scenarios

1. Because a battery backup is needed, a UPS solution is needed, rather than just a surge protector, surge suppressor, or line conditioner. You must calculate how much of a load the three servers will use to come up with a VA rating, and then select a UPS that can protect beyond that rating. The UPS software should be configured for each server's operating system, so that the UPS can shut down the server in the event of a power outage.

2. The most important environmental concern in any server room is temperature. An air conditioning system is integral in keeping the server room operating at a constant, cool temperature. You should also make sure that the room is cabled properly, without any cables cluttering the floor, or in any place where they can be easily damaged.

Each server should be connected to a UPS, to ensure that the power reaching the machines is consistent, with protection for any voltage surges, spikes, or brownouts. The UPS battery should be powerful enough to allow the servers to be brought down gracefully in the event of a power outage.

Examine all the fans operating in the servers to see if they are functioning properly to prevent overheating. Replace any failed units immediately.

Security

The most important part of deployment is planning. It is not possible to plan for security, however, until you have performed a full risk assessment. Security planning involves developing security policies and implementing controls to prevent computer risks from becoming reality. In this Part, physical security issues are discussed, including locks, access control systems, and backup tape security.

This Part also discusses environmental issues within the server room. Understanding the importance of recognizing environmental issues, including temperature, air pollutants, electrical issues, and fire safety is important both on the job and for the exam.

Securing the Environment

CHAPTER PRE-TEST

1. Why should you keep servers in locked rooms?

2. Why should the server room have low visibility?

3. What is the maximum number of doors that a computer room should have?

4. Should a server room have windows?

5. When should the locks to a secure computer room be changed?

6. Who should have access to the server room?

7. What is the best kind of locking device?

8. What is an access control system?

9. Where should backup tapes be kept?

10. What is a biometric system?

✦ Answers to these questions can be found at the end of the chapter. ✦

Security measures have always been available to systems administrators, but are rarely enforced properly. Many networks are very vulnerable to security threats. Many companies spend time and effort to secure their systems from the Internet, but don't do enough to secure them internally.

In a networked environment, you must take the proper measures to secure your systems. This chapter focuses on the physical security issues that administrators can employ to protect the computer environment. It specifically focuses on the center of the networked environment, which is typically the server room. We will look at some of the many things you can do to secure this environment.

Securing the Physical Site

5.1 Recognize and report on physical security issues

The purpose of the server room itself is to ensure the integrity and safety of the equipment inside. All servers should be as secure as possible in keeping with their sensitivity. They should be physically secured in locked rooms, and access to the servers should be restricted to authorized personnel. Ideally, access to the server room should be automatically recorded through the use of an access control system and an electronic lock. Server room walls should extend from floor to ceiling leaving absolutely no space for someone to break in. A highly secure room is useless if all someone has to do is pop open a ceiling tile and climb over the wall. Another important thing to remember is to keep the server console next to the actual server, and all your servers should have key locks. All connection points to the servers should be secured and should require some sort of authentication to enable it. All cabling outside the server room should be completely hidden from public view. Most cabling will run under the floor or above the ceiling tile, and should never be in plain view, where it can be tripped over or damaged. You should also incorporate proper media practices: sensitive information should be encrypted and stored in a secure location. All media such as floppy disks, CD-ROMs, or hard drives should be overwritten to dispose of them.

Server room construction

Server rooms should be located in a central building location away from the building exterior, parking garages, or the top floor. The room should be windowless, lockable, with an access control system that provides some sort of an audit trail of who was last in the room.

Don't attract unnecessary attention to your server room. A secure room should have low visibility; there should not be any signs that point to the location of the room. Consider the following aspects of the room:

✦ **Structural protection:** A secure server room should have full-height walls and fireproof ceilings.

✦ **External access doors:** A computer room should only have one or two doors, and they should be solid, fireproof, lockable, and within view of the staff. Doors to the server room should never be propped open or left unattended.

✦ **External access:** A server room should not have any windows, but if it does, they should be small with locks and alarms.

✦ **Locking devices:** Locking doors can be an effective security measure if appropriate personnel maintain the keys and combinations responsibly. If there is a breach, or an employee leaves or is terminated, the locks should be changed.

You should also make use of other security features such as window bars, anti-theft devices that sound an alarm when any piece of equipment is disconnected from the system, magnetic key cards, and motion detectors.

Server room access

 ✦ Limit access to the server room and backup tapes

Only authorized personnel should have access to the computer room. This usually means that only the information systems department and perhaps the director of operations will have access to this room. No unauthorized personnel should be allowed into the computer room unsupervised, including building service personnel. The type of lock you use for the door will determine how easily you can grant access to employees and repair technicians. For example, swipe cards are excellent because they are typically part of an access control system that enables you to put a time constraint on the card that is issued. You could issue a swipe card for a repair technician that will only work on a specific date, during a specific timeframe.

 Exam Tip   Server room access should only be given to authorized personnel, such as system administrators, data entry supervisors, backup administrators, and database administrators.

Locks

 ✦ Ensure physical locks exist on doors

The location of the computer room may dictate the type of locks you use. The most popular types of locks are key locks, combination locks, and key cards. Biometric systems are discussed later in the chapter.

Key locks are typically considered the least secure because of the inconvenience of using keys, and the fact that they tend to get lost. The other problem with key locks is the fact that duplicates can be made. If an employee leaves, on good or bad terms, you should immediately have the locks replaced. You will probably require a locksmith to come in and install them for you.

Combination locks are quite common, and fairly popular because of their ease of use. The combination is usually easy to remember, and you do not have to worry about losing it. The biggest problem with most combination locks is the inability to track who is going in and out of the room, and the fact that you have to give out the combination to permit service technicians into the room. However, the code is usually easy to change on a combination lock. There is a newer breed of multi-combination locks that eliminates the problems of its predecessors. Some of the more sophisticated electronic doors even offer single-access codes. Many of these are controllable from a PC in real time.

Key card systems are probably the best because they offer multiple levels of security. You can issue an individual card to each person who should have regular continuous access. Typical key card systems are part of an access control system that comes with software that connects to the card system, enabling you to easily track who entered the room and when. The other advantage of using a key card system is the ability to deactivate a user's card when he or she ceases to be employed by the company. You can also issue temporary key cards with these systems that are only valid for a certain date and time.

Access control systems

Access control systems provide protection for people and property by means of a personalized electronic token or key card. Persons can be identified, tracked, located, and granted or denied access into restricted areas based upon their access levels. These systems have central management software that performs various levels of reporting.

These systems enable you to control access to entry and exit points in your server room or other restricted computer areas. Typically, a user will use a magnetic swipe card, a PIN number, or both for verification. These systems can:

   ✦ Establish different access security levels for different locations.

   ✦ Automatically change access requirements to reflect security changes based on the time of day or day of the week.

   ✦ Automatically generate daily or weekly reports.

   ✦ Perform event monitoring.

   ✦ Manage multiple locations.

A typical access control system consists of a central processing unit, which monitors and controls the operations of the system; a control unit device where programmed data is stored and desired access is checked for authorization; and an access control reader, which is the most visible part of the system. The reader converts the physical coding of the identification data carrier or cards into electrical signals and directs them to this control unit.

The identification data carrier or simply the access device (magnetic strip, proximity, chip cards) is how the users identify themselves to the access control system. Proximity systems work by requiring you to pass a small device in front of the access control unit. A card data carrier system looks very much like a credit card, and you do not need to swipe the card but simply pass it in front of the access control unit. A key cap is a small cylindrical object approximately three inches in length and one inch in diameter, and a key ring looks very much like a regular key chain tag. The access control unit can read the card, key cap, or key ring up to 12 inches away. All of these devices contain a chip in them that contains the appropriate security data. Once the card is read and authenticated, access is granted. Chip cards are considered more secure than magnetic swipe cards because it is nearly impossible to replicate the active elements of the card. Different types of coding and data carrier systems provide different access solutions to meet the users needs.

The regulating unit is simply the physical door lock, which keeps the door locked unless access is granted. Different door locks can be used, such as electromagnetic locks, electric strikes, and electric bolts. An electric strike is a door locking device that will unlock the door when electrical power is applied to it. A fail-safe configuration will operated in the reverse manner (normally locked when power is applied, and unlocked when power is interrupted).

Biometric systems

Biometric systems make use of the fact that each person has unique physical traits that distinguish them from anyone else in the world. This technology is used as a front end to a system that requires identification before allowing access. The system could be an access control system that gives users access to a secure room, to an operating system, or even to an application that may typically require a password for access.

 Exam Tip   Biometric systems are one of the most effective methods of restricting access to the server room.

Biometric systems consist of hardware and software. The hardware usually takes a snap shot of the user's unique trait, and the software analyzes the data and determines if it is a match to the one contained in the system's database. In order to add users to the biometric system, you must perform an enrollment process. Each user must get their information stored into the system, and this usually starts with the administrator of the system. For example, a user places his hand into the scanner, and the system examines and takes a snapshot of the appropriate features from the scan, and stores it as a template. The user will then have to repeat the scanning process so that the system can verify that the data is correct, much like changing your password in an operating system.

Once these steps are complete, the user can access the rooms specified in the user's profile. When the user is scanned, the hardware will pass the data onto the software, which checks it against the template, and will either grant or deny access.

The following types of biometric system should be available in most parts of the world.

Fingerprint recognition

The system records the finger print characteristics and saves each user's data in a template. The software refers to the templates each time the users try to gain access. A finger print recognition system analyzes the data scanned and either grants or denies access. Fingerprint systems are accurate, but they can be affected by changes in the fingerprint caused by burns, scarring, dirt, and other factors that may distort the image.

Face recognition

Face recognition software is still in its infancy, because reading and recognizing the various shapes and features of a person's face is very complex. This is accomplished by using a camera to capture the image of a face, and then the software isolates patterns that it can compare with the user templates.

Iris and retina recognition

The iris is the band of tissue that surrounds the pupil of the eye, and it is unique to every person. An iris recognition system uses a video camera to capture the sample, and then uses software to analyze the image.

Retina recognition is the most secure of all the different biometric systems. The retina is the layer of blood vessels located at the back of the eye, which is unique to each person. Capturing a retinal image can be very complex. During the enrollment process, the user focuses on a point while staying very still so that the camera can properly capture the data.

Iris and retina systems offer the best security because of the unique patterns and it is very unlikely that these areas of the eye will change unless there is some sort of permanent damage.

Hand and finger geometry

Hand geometry has been around for several years. The user places his or her hand or finger in a location indicated by guide marks. The system then scans and captures a 3D image of the users fingers and knuckles and stores the data in a template.

With a finger geometry system the user places one or two fingers under the camera. The camera then captures the data and passes the image on to the software, which analyzes the spaces and lengths of areas on the fingers. It then compares it to the user templates.

Palm recognition is very similar to the fingerprint systems, except that the palm reader focuses on the unique characteristic of the person's palm.

Voice recognition

Voice recognition systems record the sound of a speaker's voice and examine the unique patterns that it exhibits. This system has typically been used in telephone-based security systems. Unfortunately, the accuracy is affected by surrounding noise, illness, and even fatigue. Voice recognition systems can also be easily fooled by a taped recording of the user's voice. However, recent advancements have improved the reliability of newer systems. These systems typically require the user to say a longer and more complex phrase, or to say a different phrase each time the user accesses the system.

Signature recognition

Your signature is accepted as proof of who you are in most places. Signature recognition systems go beyond looking at the signature itself. These systems actually look at the unique features in the signature, such as how the user writes the letter *L*. It also looks at the unique features of the signing process, such as: the speed at which the user writes, pen pressure, and when the pen is lifted off the tablet during the signing process. The signature is typically captured using a special pen, or tablet device that compares the data to the user templates. Signatures can vary, so multiple samples are usually required by the system.

Anti-theft devices

✦ Establish anti-theft devices for hardware (lock server racks)

There are a variety of devices for securing servers in the server room. One of the most common and most important is locks for rack systems. If you have several servers in your location, you probably use a rack system. Most rack systems have the ability to lock the servers securely to the system, either by locking the servers directly to the rack, or by locking a door that covers the rack.

Another option for securing servers is a cable lock. A cable lock is simply a strong piece of wire with an adhesive pad that glues to the server at one end, is bolted to a table or wall at the other end. These units are easy enough to break if you have the right tool, but they offer some security for random thievery. A significant step up from the cable lock is the cable alarm. This involves sticking a loop to your server with a small adhesive plate. The loop runs into an electronic alarm box that can be switched on or off with a key. If the server moves, or if the lock is moved, tampered with, or cut, the alarm will be triggered. The loud noise would probably be enough to deter most thieves.

Securing Backup Tapes

 ✦ Limit access to server room and backup tapes

Your organization's confidential information can fall into the wrong hands if unauthorized people have access to the backup tapes. If you keep tapes on-site for any reason, keep them in a locked room or cabinet that only the appropriate personnel have access to. You must also consider what security measures are taken when the tapes are given to an off-site storage agency. For example, some off-site agencies use a sealed deposit bag just as retail stores do for cash.

You must also consider the long-term security of the tape itself. This is usually referred to as the shelf life of the tape, and is often mentioned when tapes are archived. Storage requirements may vary greatly depending on the type of media being used for archive purposes. You should consult the manufacturer's suggested shelf life to determine the maximum amount of time that the media can be stored. Remember that the manufacturer is only estimating the shelf life to the best of their knowledge based on the tests they performed.

To ensure the integrity of the data on the tapes, there are other issues to consider. High humidity shortens shelf life, and dropping the tape can affect the tape's ability to retain the magnetic images. *Bleed-through* is a condition where the magnetic image from one part of the tape is transferred to another part of the tape while it is being wound on the reel. Eventually this can damage the tape enough to render it unusable.

If you are archiving your tapes, you should rewind them at least once per year to prevent bleed-through and to re-tension the tape. Most tape backup software programs have a re-tensioning feature built into the software. This process will run the tape in the tape drive from beginning to end at a fast speed so that the tape winds evenly and runs more smoothly past the tape drive heads. If you need to extend the shelf life of the data on the tapes in your archive, you can transfer the data from the old tape to the new one before the tape's shelf life expiration date.

Fireproof safes

Make sure you use fireproof safes that are specifically designed for magnetic media. Most fireproof safes are intended to keep paper products from burning, and cannot adequately protect your backup media. Magnetic tape, tape cartridges, and other backup media typically melt at a much lower temperature than the flash point of paper. Fireproof safes are usually rated for specific temperatures for specific periods before they lose their ability to protect the contents of the safe. If the fire lasts longer, and as a result burns hotter than what the safe is rated for, your media will most likely be permanently damaged. You should check the manufacturer's suggested guidelines for the melting point of the media, and then choose a safe that goes beyond those guidelines. The other issue with safes is the fact that it could be days or even weeks before the safe can be located and the data restored. This is not a good solution if you are looking for the fastest possible recovery. Fireproof safes are good for storing any media that must remain on-site, but it is better to have a contract with an off-site storage agency.

Off-site storage

Be sure to transfer your backup tapes to an off-site storage facility regularly. This will protect the company's data in the event of a disaster such as a fire or flood. This will also ensure the integrity of the data, and improve the company's ability to quickly resume operations. You should contract with an off-site agency that can meet the strict conditions for media storage. Off-site agencies should meet the following conditions for media storage and retrieval:

✦ The agency should store tapes in a climate-controlled environment.

✦ The agency should pick up tapes on a regular schedule.

✦ Tapes should be stored in a disaster-protected environment.

✦ Rotate the schedule for tape exchanges.

✦ The agency should offer quick response time when you need to restore data.

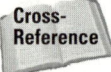 **Cross-Reference** Off-site storage is discussed in more detail in Chapters 17 and 19.

Disposing of Media

In addition to keeping your backups safe, you must ensure that information is properly disposed of. Most users simply throw floppies and CD-ROMs in the garbage and forget about them. Unfortunately, many people will stoop to any level to obtain privileged information. A thief can root through your trash hoping to obtain physical media that may contain private information about your company. The systems department should have a policy for discarding all privileged information whether it is internal or external media. This process is commonly referred to as *sanitization*.

Three techniques are typically used for media sanitization.

✦ Data overwriting

✦ Degaussing

✦ Destruction

Overwriting is very effective for wiping data off magnetic media, and usually is done by a special program that writes a bunch of ones and zeros onto the media. Overwriting is not the same as deleting, because deleting only removes the pointer to the file, and not the actual file.

Tip   A good practice is to overwrite the media 2 or 3 times to ensure it is completely clean.

Degaussing is a method that magnetically erases the data from the media. There are two types of degaussers, strong permanent magnets, and electric degaussers. There are degaussers that cost as little as $150, which may be adequate if speed and depth of erasure are not important factors. These are typically hand-held degaussers that are capable of erasing 20 4mm tapes per hour. There are also much more sophisticated models that can handle large batches of high-density media. These units can range in cost from $500 to $49,000. For example, an eraser designed to process 400 to 500 cassettes per hour is likely to cost $2,000 to $3,000 dollars. These units typically work on a system where the media is placed on a small conveyer and is passed over several eraser coils.

Destruction is usually accomplished through shredding or incineration. If you do not use overwriting or degaussing, you should shred, break, or incinerate the media. This includes CD-ROMs as well. If your company is equipped to do so, it is best to burn the media using an incinerator, but it is unlikely that most companies would own an incinerator. The only way to truly render a CD useless is to remove the pits and lands physically from the polycarbonate. Special CD destruction devices are available for about $8,500, but there are a couple of quick and less expensive ways to make CDs useless. Take it out to the sidewalk and throw it data side down; put your foot on top of it and rub it around for a bit. Tossing it on a belt sander has the same effect. If the data is only moderately sensitive, the reflective portion of the CD can easily be removed by putting duct tape on the data side and peeling it off. This renders the data unreadable for all practical purposes.

Documenting Security Measures

Make a hard copy of the IS operational practices and procedures to help eliminate security breakdowns and oversights. This will give new employees detailed information about the security infrastructure, and provide some quality assurance that operations will be performed in the correct manner.

A security document should include at least the following information:

✦ Contingency plans

✦ Security plans

✦ Security risk analysis

✦ Security policies and procedures

Most of the information, especially anything revolving around risk analysis, must be safeguarded against disclosure to unauthorized personnel. You must keep the document as current as possible, updating it every six months or so. The documentation must also be accessible to all the appropriate staff, both electronically and through hard copy. You should also keep a hard copy of the plan at an off-site location.

Security documentation should be designed to fulfill the needs of the different types of people who will use it. You should divide your security documentation into multiple sections based on who it is intended for. For example, the security procedures manual for the system users would describe how to perform their jobs in a secure manner. The security procedures manual for the systems department would address an array of technical and operations issues in much greater detail. The systems department security information may contain information on what measures are taken to protect data against unauthorized access to software applications and data. It may contain information regarding user login and authentication, workstation security, physical security, Internet security, and security management.

Key Point Summary

The task of security should begin at the server room, which is the life-blood of the information systems infrastructure. Unless the administrator adequately enforces security throughout the network, then all the security products that the company has purchased will be relatively useless. Keep the following points in mind for the exam:

✦ Servers should be physically secured in locked rooms.

✦ Access to the server should be restricted to authorized personnel.

✦ Access to the server room should be recorded through the use of an access control system.

✦ Key locks, combination locks, and key card systems are the most common types of locks for computer rooms. Key card systems tend to be the most secure.

✦ Biometric systems make use of the fact that each person has unique physical traits.

✦ Backup tape should be rotated off-site regularly to ensure maximum security.

✦ If you are archiving tapes, they should be rewound to prevent bleed-through.

✦ Fireproof safes do not necessarily protect magnetic media from a fire because most safes are designed to protect paper products.

✦ Documenting your security plan will help to eliminate security breakdowns and oversights.

✦   ✦   ✦

STUDY GUIDE

The Study Guide section provides you with the opportunity to test your knowledge about physical security. The Assessment Questions provide practice for the test, and the Scenarios provide practice with real situations. If you get any questions wrong, use the answers to determine the part of the chapter you should review before continuing.

Assessment Questions

1. The Director of Operations wants to know what guidelines he should be looking at when deciding where to put the server room. What is the best answer?

   A. In a central location near the parking garage for easy entry

   B. In a central location away from the building exterior, parking garages, or top floor locations

   C. Near the building exterior, not in a central location

   D. In a central location, near the building exterior, but away from parking garages and top floor locations

2. The office supervisor decides to put up signs pointing out all the different office locations. Why might this be a problem?

   A. It will attract unnecessary attention to the server room.

   B. It is not a problem so long as the signs are small, and can only be seen close up.

   C. The signs are a fire hazard if placed near the server room.

   D. It is against company policy.

3. What is the maximum number of doors that a computer room should have?

   A. 4

   B. 1

   C. 3

   D. 2

4. An employee is terminated from the IS department. Your server room makes use of combination locks. What is the first thing you should do?

    A. Change the combination of the locks.

    B. Stand in the room until the employee has left the building.

    C. Ensure the servers are locked.

    D. Back up the servers.

5. Which of the following groups should not have access to the server room?

    A. System administrators

    B. Backup administrator

    C. Users

    D. Database administrators

6. The IS manager has purchased a new Web server and wants you to set it up in a spare office cubicle. What is the primary concern?

    A. Desk space

    B. Proper voltage

    C. Temperature

    D. Proper physical security

7. Why are key locks not the best choice for physical security for the computer room door?

    A. Key locks get lost, and they can be duplicated.

    B. Key locks get lost, and they cannot be duplicated.

    C. Keys regularly break, and they are lent out.

    D. Key locks are affected by power outages.

8. Your boss wants to know the advantages of using a key card system for access to the computer room? What are some advantages?

    A. Individual cards for each person

    B. Ability to issue temporary cards

    C. Ability to track who enters the room and when

    D. Ability to deactivate users permanently, or during certain hours of the day

    E. All of the above

9. Where should backup tapes be kept when in the office?

   A. In the janitor's closet

   B. On your desk where you can see them

   C. In your desk drawer

   D. In the secure computer room

10. If you are archiving backup tapes, what is the minimum number of times per year that the backup tapes should be rewound?

    A. 1

    B. 8

    C. 2

    D. 4

11. Ideally, where should tape backups be stored for maximum security?

    A. Fireproof safe

    B. Off-site agency

    C. Off-site at administrator's house

    D. Locked in the server room

12. What is the problem with most fireproof safes being used for magnetic media? Choose all that apply.

    A. Safes cannot adequately hold all the magnetic media.

    B. Safes were designed for paper products.

    C. After a disaster, it could be weeks before the safe is located.

    D. Some safes degauss magnetic media.

13. Which of the follow is the best biometric security system?

    A. Fingerprint recognition

    B. Face recognition

    C. Iris/Retina recognition

    D. Hand/Finger geometry recognition

14. What are the three techniques commonly used for media sanitization?

    A. Data overwriting, degaussing, encryption

    B. Degaussing, encryption, incineration

    C. Encryption, data overwriting, destruction

    D. Data overwriting, degaussing, destruction

15. What is the minimum amount of times that data should be overwritten?

    A. 2

    B. 3

    C. 12

    D. 1

Scenarios

1. The company is planning to construct a new building to accommodate current and future growth. The entire company will relocate to this new building and the current one will be sold. As the systems administrator you are asked to define specific requirements for the computer room. What are the major requirements for the new server room?

Answers to Chapter Questions

Chapter pre-test

1. Servers should be kept in locked rooms to ensure maximum security.

2. The server room should not be easy for intruders to find.

3. A computer room should not have more than two doors to maintain better control over entry and exit.

4. A server room should not have windows, but if it does, they should be barred, locked, and alarmed.

5. Locks should be changed whenever an employee is terminated or discontinues their employment, or anytime the locks are compromised.

6. Only authorized personnel such as system administrators, backup administrators, and database administrators should have access to the server room. Users should never have access to the server room.

7. A key card is the best kind of locking device because it enables you to track who entered the room and when. Key cards also enable you to impose time restrictions, and to deactivate cards.

8. An access control system is a combination of hardware and software that controls access to secure areas. Persons can be identified, tracked, located, and granted or denied access into restricted areas based upon their access levels. These systems have central management software that performs various functions including reporting.

9. On-site backup tapes should be kept in a locked room, fireproof safe or cabinet. Tapes that go off-site should be kept at a contracted off-site agency.

10. A biometric system makes use of characteristics that differentiate people from each other. Biometric systems are typically fingerprint, face, iris and retina, hand and finger geometry, voice, and signature recognition systems.

Assessment questions

1. **B.** For maximum security, the computer room should be located in a central location, away from the building exterior, parking garage, or top floor locations. For more information see the "Server room construction" section.

2. **A.** You never want to point out the location of your server room. The harder it is to pick out, the better. Any unnecessary advertising is considered a security risk. For more information see the "Server room construction" section.

3. **D.** A computer room should never have more than two doors to ensure maximum security. It is easier to control entry with less access points. For more information see the "Server room construction" section.

4. **A.** You should immediately change the combination code in case the terminated employee attempts to perform malicious acts before leaving the building, or if he or she attempts to gain access on a different day. For more information see the "Server room construction" section.

5. **C.** Only authorized personnel should have access to the server room. System administrators, database administrators, and backup administrators need regular access to the server room to perform their duties. Users do not require this level of access. For more information see the "Server room access" section.

6. **D.** You should be primarily concerned with the physical security of the unit, because you will be unable to lock it in a secured room. For more information see the "Server room access" section.

7. **A.** Key locks are the least effective because the keys are regularly lost, and they are simple to duplicate. For more information see the "Locks" section.

8. **E.** Key cards are one of the best choices for entry systems. They give you the ability to track user access, assign temporary cards, assign time restrictions, and assign individual cards for each user needing access to the computer room. For more information see the "Locks" section.

9. **D.** You obviously do not want to keep your tapes in the janitor's closest, but it is also not a good idea to leave them on your desk or in your desk drawer; you could be distracted for just a second, and the tapes could be stolen. Tape backups should always be kept in a locked cabinet, or room. Ideally the server room should be used for this purpose. For more information see the "Securing Backup Tapes" section.

10. **A.** Backup tapes should be rewound once per year to re-tension the tape, and to stop bleed-through, which can render the tape unusable. For more information see the "Securing Backup Tapes" section.

11. B. Tape backups should be kept at an off-site agency because they can provide the best security and protection for your business. These companies ensure that they meet all the environmental requirements necessary for tape storage. Fireproof safes are not very reliable, and it could be weeks before the safe is located. For more information see the "Off-site storage" section.

12. B and **C.** Fireproof safes cannot adequately protect magnetic media because they are typically designed to protect paper products. Tapes melt much sooner than paper ignites. Even specially designed safes may not work because fires are unpredictable and they may burn longer and hotter than expected. For more information see the "Fireproof safes" section.

13. C. Iris/Retina recognition systems are the best because of the unique patterns in the eye, and it is very unlikely that the patterns will change unless there is permanent eye damage. For more information see the "Biometric systems" section.

14. D. Data overwriting, degaussing, and destruction are the three techniques used in sanitization. For more information see the "Disposing of Media" section.

15. A. Data should be overwritten at least two times, using a special program designed for overwriting, to ensure that the disk is clean. For more information see the "Disposing of Media" section.

Scenarios

1. Server rooms should be located in a central building location away from the building exterior, parking garages, or top floor locations. The server room should be windowless, lockable, with an access control system that provides some sort of an audit trail of who was last in the room. The server room should not be easily visible, and should be constructed with a full-height wall and a fireproof ceiling. There should no more than two doorways, and they should be solid and fireproof. Motion detectors should be considered as part of the design for the computer room. There should not be any windows in the computer room, but if there are, they should be small, barred, locked, and alarmed.

Environmental
Issues

◆ ◆ ◆ ◆

EXAM OBJECTIVES

5.2 Recognize and report on server room environmental issues
(temperature, humidity/ESD/power surges, back-up generator/
fire suppression/flood considerations)

CHAPTER PRE-TEST

1. Why is it important to maintain the proper temperature in a computer room?

2. What is the standard temperature range in a computer room?

3. Why is it important to maintain the proper humidity levels?

4. What is the importance of proper ventilation?

5. Why should all computer rooms be equipped with air conditioning systems?

6. How long should an air conditioning system remain on?

7. Why is it important to control pollutants in the computer room?

8. What are some sources of contaminants in the computer room?

9. What does ESD stand for?

10. Why is fire safety important?

✦ Answers to these questions can be found at the end of the chapter. ✦

Ensuring that the computer room is environmentally sound can sometimes be a monumental task. However, if you take the time to properly plan and implement a few policies, you can ensure that you have a reliable, clean, and safe environment for the computer equipment and the occupants. You need to consider fire suppression systems, proper grounding of power sources, temperature control, and air pollutants. All these and several more issues are discussed in this chapter. While environmental issues are not a big part of the Server+ exam, it is still essential that you know this information to be a successful administrator.

Recognizing Environmental Issues

5.2 Recognize and report on server room environmental issues (temperature, humidity/ESD/power surges, back-up generator/fire suppression/flood considerations)

All computers and networking hardware have operational limitations, guidelines, and thresholds that limit its operational ability. If you read the manufacturers suggested operating guidelines, you will discover how to create an environment best suited for your equipment. This is probably the best and most accurate way of discovering environmental issues in the server room. Good common sense is also fundamental in ensuring a properly configured environment.

Temperature

5.2 Recognize and report on server room environmental issues (temperature, humidity/ESD/power surges, back-up generator/fire suppression/flood considerations)

Electronic equipment has two sets of acceptable temperature ranges. The first is the *power-off temperature range*, or cold temperature range. This range varies from manufacturer to manufacturer, and it states the minimum and maximum temperatures the equipment can reach while not powered on. Whenever a component or piece of hardware is shipped, it should never reach a temperature that falls outside of this range.

If for example, a system is delivered to a loading dock, it should not be left out in the cold, or in direct sunlight for any length of time. You must let the equipment reach the optimal cold start operating temperature of the computer room before you turn it on. Resist the urge to turn on a new server as soon as you get it, and let the equipment reach the proper temperature first. Going beyond the power-off temperature, either above or below, can cause serious, permanent damage to the equipment. Damaged components might fail immediately, or they may cause intermittent failures that can be extremely difficult to diagnose.

The other temperature range to watch carefully is the *operating temperature* of the equipment. This range is always narrower than the non-operating temperature. The operating temperature is actually the ideal ambient temperature at which a particular system can be safely used. A long rack of computers can generate a huge amount of heat, and for this reason, almost all server rooms have some form of cooling or air conditioning. The rule of thumb for computer hardware is not to let the environment exceed 75 degrees F. A typical computer room operating temperature should stay between 70 degrees and 74 degrees F, and if the environment falls out of these constraints, you may be in for some significant problems.

In the Real World

You may find that your servers will actually run at higher temperatures than this. In fact, it is acceptable to see the operating temperature between 50 and 90 degrees F. However, you should still try to keep them within the recommended operating temperatures specified by your hardware documentation. Because your server room will have so many different pieces of equipment, with different acceptable operating temperatures, you may find this task daunting. This is why almost all hardware manufactures try to ensure that they have a median operating temperature that falls somewhere between 70 and 75 degrees F.

Your computer room environment may consist of mainframes and servers, and while PC-based servers are far more tolerant than their high-powered counterparts, they still require a proper operating environment to run optimally. If the room is hot, and the ventilation is less than desirable, the result will be that the server's cooling fans will push hot, dirty air through the chassis. This will only result in premature failure of the electronic components contained in the server.

Many companies shut the air conditioning off over weekends and holidays. This is not recommended for a server room environment, but you may not have a choice if your server room does not have an independent cooling system. If this is the case, make sure that the temperature does not rise dramatically during these periods. You can purchase a monitoring thermometer from most hardware stores, which has the ability to report the high and low temperature milestones seen during a time interval. You can also purchase electronic monitoring equipment that interfaces with a computer that has the ability to send alerts via phone, e-mail or pager. Typically, these computer room monitors have sensors that you place at various locations in the computer room. These sensors can report the temperature, humidity, and power fluctuations, and they will send alerts when the thresholds that you set are breached. This equipment usually isn't very expensive.

Humidity level

Objective

5.2 Recognize and report on server room environmental issues (temperature, humidity/ESD/power surges, back-up generator/fire suppression/flood considerations)

High humidity levels cause corrosion on some metals. This eventually causes a high resistance between connections, leading to equipment failures. High humidity levels can also have an adverse affect on some magnetic tapes and paper media.

Exam Tip   Ambient relative humidity levels between 45 and 50 percent are the most suitable for safe data processing operations.

Low humidity contributes to undesirably high levels of electrostatic charges. This
increases the electrostatic discharge (ESD) voltage potential. ESD can cause component damage during servicing operations. You should always follow proper procedures when working on computer equipment.

Tip   Papers feed problems on high-speed printers are usually encountered in low-
humidity environments.

Ventilation

Server rooms must be properly ventilated, which means you need a way to get air
in from outside, and maintain positive pressure levels. Positive pressurization of
the server room is also an effective means of ensuring contaminants do not enter
the room through small cracks. Positive pressure systems are designed to push air
towards doorways and other access points within the room. You want to have the
air escape the room, rather than letting air enter it, which can bring in particles
harmful to the hardware. In companies that have a data center with multiple rooms,
the most sensitive areas should be the most highly pressurized. The air being used
to positively pressurize the room should not adversely affect the conditions in the
room. Any air introduced from outside the room should be properly filtered and
conditioned before it is introduced into the computer room environment. The conditions for the air entering the room do not need to be as stringent as the desired
optimal conditions for the room itself.

Re-circulating air conditioning systems are used in most computer rooms, and this
means that some sort of ventilation will be necessary in order to introduce fresh air
into the room. Computer rooms typically have very low human population, and the
length of time spent in the room is relatively short. Therefore, air ventilation
requirements will be minimal. In fact, the air that is required to achieve positive
pressurization will exceed the need for ventilation for the occupants. A volume of
15 cubic feet per minute (CFM) outside air per occupant, or per workstation should
adequately accommodate the ventilation needs of the room.

Air conditioning

The cooling capacity of the air conditioning equipment for the computer room
should be enough to counter the equipment heat dissipation, and well as any other
types of heat gain. The air conditioning equipment should include an air filtration
system, cooling or dehumidification, humidification, reheating, air distribution, and
system controls that can adequately maintain the computer room within optimal
temperature ranges. Lighting and personnel must also be factored into the equation.

Caution At altitudes above 10,000 feet (3048 m), the lower air density reduces the cooling capability of air conditioning systems. If your facility is located above this altitude, you need to use other recommended temperature ranges. For each 1000 feet (305 m) increase in altitude over 10,000 feet up to a maximum of 15,000 feet, subtract 1.5 degrees F from the upper limit temperature.

Consider the following factors when designing or upgrading an air conditioning system:

✦ The system should be capable of operating 24 hours a day, 365 days a year.

✦ The system should be independent of other systems in the building.

✦ The system should accommodate expansion of the computer system.

✦ Filters should have a minimum rating of 45 percent atmospheric dust-spot efficiency (ASHRAE Standard 52.1).

✦ The system should only allow enough outside air into the system to meet the needs of the room's occupants, and to maintain positive pressurization.

The following is a list of recommended air conditioning equipment in order of preference:

✦ Complete self-contained package unit with remote condensers. These systems are available with up or down discharge and are typically located in the server room. Up discharge is when the air is forced up through the raised floor air plenum (duct), and down discharge means that the air is forced down through the ceiling ducts.

✦ A chilled water package unit with a remote chilled water plant system. These systems are available with up or down discharge and are typically located in the computer room.

✦ A central station air handling unit with remote refrigeration equipment. Typically, these systems are located outside the server room, as in office environments.

With any air conditioning system, you will need a way to distribute the air. A basic air distribution system includes *supply air,* the air that come out of the vents into the room, and *return air,* the air that leaves the room and flows back to the air handler. In many instances, the type of air conditioning equipment used determines the type of air distribution equipment that is appropriate.

The following is a list of recommended air distribution systems listed in order of preference:

✦ **Under-floor air distribution system:** The downflow air conditioning equipment located on the raised floor of the computer room uses the cavity beneath the raised floor as a plenum for the air supply. Return air from an under-floor distribution system can be room space return air (the air mixes with the air in the room and flows back to the air conditioners for reconditioning), or ducted return air. (the air flows through an air duct to be reconditioned by the air conditioners). Perforated floor panels should be located around the perimeter of the computer equipment. The supply air is emitted through the perforated floor panels, and gets sucked into the cooling vents of the computer equipment.

✦ **Ceiling plenum air distribution systems:** The supply air is ducted into the ceiling plenum for the upflow air conditioning equipment located in the computer room, or from a remote air handling unit. Upflow air systems are typical in most office settings, because they direct cool air or heat from the ceiling, and push it down into the office environment. The ceiling construction must resist air leakage if possible. The perforated panels should be placed around the perimeter of the computer equipment. The supply air is then available to the cooling vents of the computer equipment. The return air should be ducted back to the air conditioning equipment through the return air duct in the ceiling. The return air will pass through several filters before redistribution.

✦ **Above-ceiling ducted air distribution system:** The supply air is ducted into a diffuser system in the ceiling from upflow air conditioning equipment located in the server room or from a remote air handling unit. The return air from an above-ceiling system may be ducted return air above the ceiling, or through a ceiling plenum return air configuration. You should adjust the diffuser system grilles to direct the cool air down around the perimeter of the computer equipment. The cool air is then available to the intake vents of the computer equipment.

The air distribution system should be constructed in such a way that it will deliver adequate air to the cooling intake vents of the computer system equipment, and cabinets. The temperature of the air supply should meet the following guidelines:

✦ Ceiling supply system: from 55 to 60 degrees F (12.8 to 15.6 degrees C)

✦ Floor supply system: At least 60 degrees F (15.6 degrees C)

If a ceiling plenum return air system or a ducted ceiling return air system is used, the return air grille in the ceiling is most effective and is recommended to be placed directly above the computer equipment.

Air Pollutants

Most harmful contaminants are overlooked because they are so small, but their effect on electrical components can be great. Most of these pollutants are less than 10 microns and are typically not visible to the naked eye. These small pollutants can migrate to the computer equipment and cause serious damage, so you must take steps to keep them out of your servers.

Air quality levels

Pollutants such as dust particles and gases can affect the operational quality of computer hardware. Sometimes the effects are intermittent and sometimes they lead to permanent component failure. You should ensure cleanliness in the server room, and keep airborne dusts, gases, and vapors at acceptable levels. Check with your government agency to determine if they have any standards in place for data center or computer room environments. This will help to determine acceptable pollutant levels. As a rule of thumb, you should look at an air filtration system that is capable of filtering out particles that are 0.3 microns or less.

Most standards, however, do not address every environmental issue. Some of the most harmful dust sizes are 0.3 microns and less. These particles are harmful to equipment because they tend to build up and usually aren't caught by internal air filtration systems. Like most particles, they typically accumulate into large masses or absorb corrosive agents that can cause damage to electronic equipment. These particles damage moving parts and sensitive contacts, and cause component corrosion.

Exam Tip   Excessive concentrations of certain gasses can accelerate corrosion and cause failure in electronic components.

Gaseous pollutants are a concern in a computer room because of hardware sensitivity, and because most computer rooms use recirculating air flow systems. Any pollutants are compounded because the air is recirculated.

Sources of contaminants

Contaminants in the server room take many different forms, and can come from many different sources. The way that contaminants are created and the way that they get to the hardware varies greatly. Many activities in the server room can produce dangerous contaminants, or stir up contaminants that have already settled.

To be considered a contaminant, a particle must be able to damage equipment, and must be able to travel to places that can cause damage. Decreasing the potential contaminants in the server room reduces the risk that a potential contaminant will become an actual contaminant and cause damage.

Most contaminants travel through the air. Therefore, measuring airborne contaminants is an excellent means of determining the cleanliness of the server room. Contaminants the size of 1,000 microns or less can become airborne, however, the air filtrations systems filter should snag most of these particles. Contaminants that are 0.3 microns or less can cause serious physical hardware damage. These contaminants are more likely to pass through the filtrations systems filters. The following are some of the major causes of contamination:

✦ **Operator activity:** Human movement is the biggest source of contamination. Dander, hair, or fabric fibers can cause serious problems.

- ✦ **Hardware movement:** Installing or reconfiguring hardware can stir up contaminants and put them back into the air stream.

- ✦ **Outside air:** Unfiltered air from outside the room can introduce many contaminants.

- ✦ **Stored items:** Handling items stored in cardboard boxes can shed fibers into the air.

- ✦ **Cleaning activity:** Chemicals used for normal cleaning can damage computer equipment. Push mops or inadequate vacuums will also stir up contaminants.

Filtration

The filtration systems you use must effectively control contaminants in the server room, and you must keep them properly maintained. The needs and location of the computer room will determine the type of filtration system you need. For example, a computer room located in a manufacturing shop will require a different system than one located in a typical office environment.

The recommended method of controlling the room environment is *room process cooling.* These coolers recycle the air in the room. Air from the equipment zone is passed through the units, where it gets filtered, cooled, and then pushed into the sub-floor plenum. The plenum becomes pressurized, and the air gets forced back into the room through the perforated tiles. The air in a computer room is filtered much more often than typical office environments. The in-room recirculating air conditioning filters should have a minimum efficiency of 40 to 45 percent. You should install prefilters to increase the life of the more expensive primary filters. Any air that is introduced to the server room for ventilation or positive pressurization should pass through the filtration system first. Many layers of prefilters that get changed regularly should guard these expensive primary filters. Prefilters are the first line of defense before the air moves into the primary filters. It is recommended that you use 20 percent efficiency filters for prefilters, and the next filter bank should have pleated filters with efficiencies between 60 percent and 80 percent.

Regular cleaning

All server rooms, no matter how efficient, require regular maintenance. Computer rooms that have design flaws will definitely require more attention to maintain proper conditions. Cleaning the server room regularly will prolong the lifespan of your components. Also, if you keep your server room clean, clients, associates, or business partners who visit your computer room will interpret its appearance as a reflection of how much you care about the vital information that the equipment contains. You need to create and adhere to a regular cleaning schedule to accomplish these goals.

Daily tasks

Daily tasks should consist of trash removal, and the removal of any other items that should not be kept in the computer room. This may included cardboard boxes from newly unpacked equipment. Vacuuming may be required if the computer room is used as a print room, or if there are a lot of people moving through the room.

Weekly tasks

The access floor system should be maintained on a regular weekly basis. The access floor system is simply the type of flooring used in raised room computer environments. A typical raised floor system uses removable panels for access to network cabling, power cables, and so on. You want to ensure this area is clean because the air conditioning system uses it for air distribution. The access floor system should be vacuumed and damp mopped for a good thorough cleaning. All vacuums used in the computer room should be equipped with a HEPA filtration system. Equipment that is not properly filtered will cause small particles to escape the vacuum and drift into the server room environment where they may migrate to your hardware. Make sure that rags and mop-heads are designed not to shed.

Use cleaning solutions that do not pose any kind of threat to the computer hardware. Potentially damaging solutions include phosphate products, bleach products, chlorine products, ammonia products, petro-chemical products, floor strippers, and reconditioners. Use the exact recommended mixtures for cleaning, because over-strengthening the mixture can cause problems.

Quarterly tasks

Only professional computer room cleaning agencies should do the cleaning during this phase of the schedule. This type of cleaning should be done at least three to four times per year depending on the amount of traffic in the server room. All surfaces should be thoroughly cleaned, including racks, shelves, equipment, cupboards, and ledges. Ensure that any high ledges and light fixtures that attract large amounts of contaminants get cleaned thoroughly. If there are any windows, ensure they are thoroughly cleaned. Any doors or glass partitions should also be treated in this phase. Settled contaminants should be cleaned from all exterior hardware surfaces. The computer's air intake and exhaust grilles should be cleaned as well. Using wipes for this type of cleaning is not recommended; a low powered source of compressed air is more suited for this type of cleaning. Keyboards, and other input devices should also be cleaned. Monitors should be cleaned with optical cleansers and static-free wipes or cloths. Be sure that the company uses appropriate cleaning materials. There are special dust cloths treated with particle absorbent materials that are specially designed for this type of application.

Biannual tasks

Based on the condition of the plenum surfaces, and the amount contaminate buildup, the sub-floor area should be cleaned every 18 to 24 months. Even if you perform the weekly cleaning duties, which reduce much of the contamination, some of the dirt will find its way into the sub-floor area. Because the sub-floor is a source for your hardware's air supply plenum in a raised-floor environment, you need to keep this area extremely clean. The people who perform this type of cleaning should have a complete understanding of the process to ensure they can properly assess cable connectivity and priority. All sub-floor activities need to be conducted with proper consideration for the air distribution system and floor loading. The number of tiles that are removed from the floor must be carefully managed in order to ensure the integrity of the access floor. Typically, no more than 24 square feet of tiles should be removed from the flooring at any one time. The access floor's supporting grid system should also be thoroughly cleaned with a vacuum, and then with a damp sponge. Note and report any odd conditions, such as damaged floor suspension, floor tiles, cables, and surfaces within the floor void.

Electrical Issues

 ✦ Recognize and report on server room environmental issues (temperature, humidity/ESD/power surges, back-up generator/fire suppression/flood considerations)

To prevent failures, the power system must be designed to ensure that adequate power is provided to the computer hardware. All power should be distributed from dedicated electrical distribution panels. If computer equipment is subjected to repeated significant power interruptions and fluctuations, components may fail.

Quality of power source

Power quality issues can often be difficult to identify, and are usually even more difficult to fix. The symptoms are often confused with hardware or software problems. The only way to ensure proper power quality is through proper design of the system. A vital part of the system design is to ensure adequate redundancy, and eliminate single points of failure. The following areas should be addressed in the design of the power systems for a computer room.

Multiple feeds

Multiple utility feeds should be provided from separate substations or power grids. This is not essential, but it provides backup and redundancy to the system. The importance of the data on your servers dictates the importance of multiple power feeds.

UPS

A UPS should be installed to carry the full load of the computer hardware for a period that is at least long enough to transfer the equipment to an alternate utility feed or backup generator. The UPS should also be able to accommodate 150 percent of the load for fault overload conditions. Use an on-line UPS that runs continuously as opposed to an off-line unit. Battery backup should be capable of providing at least 15 minutes of power to maintain the critical load of the room, and to allow adequate time to transfer power to a generator.

Cross-Reference   Uninterruptible power supplies are discussed in more detail in Chapters 2 and 10.

Backup generators

Depending on how critical it is to ensure power even during a power failure, you may be able to use a UPS and multiple utility feeds without backup generators. If you decide to use a backup generator, it should be able to carry the fully load of the computer equipment, as well as all the support equipment like air conditioners and lighting.

Maintenance bypass

The power system design should have the ability to bypass and isolate any point of the system so that a technician can perform maintenance, repair, or modifications without interrupting normal system operations. The system must be designed to avoid all single points of failure.

Proper grounding

Proper grounding is essential for all electronic equipment. Grounding design in a computer room environment must address both the electrical service as well as the equipment. Grounding design should comply with your local electrical codes. A properly designed grounding system should have as low an impedance as is practically achievable for the electronics as well as for safety. Impedance is a material's opposition to the flow electric current, and it is measured in ohms. The ground should be continuous from the central grounding point at the origin of the building system. Electronic equipment can be sensitive to stray currents and electronic noise. Therefore, you need to have a continuous, dedicated ground for the entire power system to avoid a ground differential between various grounds. All metallic objects that contain electrical conductors or those that are likely to be charged by electrical currents, such as lightning or electrostatic discharge, should be effectively grounded. This will ensure personnel safety, fire reduction, and protection of the equipment. The common point of ground can be connected to any number of sources at the service entrance: water piping, building steel, or even a driven earth rod. It is recommended that the central point of grounding at the service entrance should be connected to multiple ground sources to ensure redundancy in the event that any one source should become unreliable, for example, if a water pipe bursts.

Electrostatic discharge

Electrostatic discharge (ESD) is perhaps the most common power problem you will encounter. Static can strike anywhere, and at any time. ESD typically does not pose a personal safety threat, but servers can be severally damaged. Electrostatic discharge easily exceeds the acceptable limits of system operation. Even though the discharge lasts no longer than two or three nanoseconds, it is long enough to destroy sensitive circuits. ESD comes from any number of sources: humidity, carpeting, air vents, clothing, office furnishings, and altitude. Anything that moves can generate an electrical field. Simply walking past equipment, or even air movement, can cause ESD. Climate and geographic location play a big factor in static. At sea level in a warm climate, with normal humidity, you may not see much ESD. However, if you are in a high-rise office building, with strong controls determining the air quality, you will most likely see high amounts of static.

Follow these precautions to minimize possible ESD induced failures in the computer room:

✦ Maintain the recommended humidity level and airflow rates in the server room.

✦ Use conductive wax if waxed floors are used.

✦ Use appropriate furniture in the server room that will significantly decrease the chance of ESD because the movement of inappropriate furniture can cause static discharges.

✦ Store spare electronic equipment in antistatic containers.

✦ Install conductive flooring, and be sure a conductive adhesive is used during installation.

✦ Ensure that all equipment and flooring is properly grounded and are connected to the same ground source.

✦ Always use a grounded wrist strap or other method (touching a grounded metal chassis) when handling circuit boards.

Fire Safety

5.2 Recognize and report on server room environmental issues (temperature, humidity/ESD/power surges, back-up generator/fire suppression/flood considerations)

A fire in the server room can have catastrophic effects on the operations of the room and the company. The destructive force of a full-fledged fire can damage electronic equipment and even the building structure beyond repair. The contaminants introduced from a smoldering fire can also damage hardware, and will most likely incur heavy cosmetic costs. Even when a fire is avoided with fire suppression equipment, this too can severally damage the computer hardware. Any sort of fire can have a staggering cost. You must keep off-site backups to ensure a quicker recovery of the computer systems, and a quicker return to regular business operations.

Fire extinguishers

Install manual pull stations at strategic points in the server room. Manual pull stations will activate the fire suppression discharge equipment. If gas is used, there should be a means of manual abort for the suppression system as well. Place portable fire extinguishers throughout the room. These should be unobstructed, and should be clearly marked. Labels should be visible above tall pieces of equipment from anywhere in the room. Appropriate tile lifters should be located at each extinguisher station to provide access to the sub floor void for inspection, or to put out a fire.

Sprinkler systems

A passive suppression system reacts to detected hazards with no manual intervention. The most common forms of passive suppression are sprinkler systems or chemical suppression systems. Sprinkler systems can be flooded (wet pipe) or pre-action (dry pipe). A flooded system uses pipes that are full at all times, enabling the system to discharge immediately upon the detection of a fire. A pre-action system floods the sprinkler pipes upon the initial detection, but has a delay before actual discharge of the fire suppressant. The advantage of a pre-action system is that there is no risk of a pipe bursting and flooding the room with water.

Non-liquid systems

Chemical total flooding systems work by suffocating the fire within the controlled area. The suppression chemical most often found in server rooms is Halon 1301, but this is being eliminated in favor of the more environmentally friendly FM200 or various forms of water suppression. Carbon dioxide systems are also used, but can be a major concern because of operator safety in the event of a discharge. Carbon dioxide is a colorless, heavy gas used for extinguishing flames, but is deadly if breathed in. These systems can be used independently or in combination depending on the exposures in the room.

The ideal system incorporates both a gas system and a pre-action water sprinkler system in the computer room. Gas-suppression systems are better for the hardware in the event of discharge, because hardware can typically be brought back on-line as soon as the room is cleared of the gas. Unfortunately, gas systems are a one-time deal. If a fire is not put out by the discharge, there is no second chance. The gas system cannot be used again until it is recharged. Water systems can continue to address the problem until the fire is brought under control, but often cause irreparable damage to the hardware. Building owners, local laws, and insurance companies often require water suppression systems.

Floods

5.2 Recognize and report on server room environmental issues (temperature, humidity/ESD/power surges, back-up generator/fire suppression/flood considerations)

In recent years, company IT systems have been hit by the worst floods in decades. The companies whose building were flooded had to face the decision of moving back to the damaged building or relocating. Many companies choose to relocate because they do not want to go through the process of trying to rebuild the IT infrastructure again.

Most floods in the computer room are caused by leakage from the cold water pipes in the air conditioning systems. Another common source of flood water is pipes running through the ceiling void above the computer room. Leaks from roofs, especially during a snow melt, are also a big problem where the computer room is in a single-story flat-roofed building. Computer systems in building basements are also at high risk because they are at the lowest point of the building and water always finds the lowest point.

The biggest problem with detecting flood water early is that you do not know where the water ingress will start. However, there are hardware packages that can be purchased to assist in early flood detection. These systems are capable of detecting water at multiple points in the server room. You place as many of these detectors as you want at different areas in the server room. One obvious place to place the detectors is under every air conditioner that is in the room, and near or under critical computer equipment.

There are a few things that you can do regarding the construction of the computer room to protect against floods. Make sure the computer room is higher up in the building and not in a vulnerable basement. You should also ensure that your computer room uses raised flooring so that all critical equipment is off the ground.

Key Point Summary

This chapter focused on the important issues concerning environmental issues in the server room. This chapter represents a very small portion of the goals of the Server+ exam objectives, but it does not mean that it is any less important. A successful administrator must know that environmental issues plague the computer room environment. Keep the following points in mind for the exam:

✦ Electronic equipment have two sets of acceptable temperature ranges: Power off or cold temperature range, and the operating temperature of the equipment

✦ High humidity levels can cause resistance between connections in components, and low humidity levels cause high static buildup

✦ Ventilation is required in computer rooms to introduce a minimal amount of fresh air for operator safety, due to the nature of recirculating air conditioning systems

✦ The cooling capacity of the air conditioning equipment must counter the heat dissipation of the computer equipment

✦ Controlling pollutants in the computer room is important when looking at the computer room environment

✦ Contaminants in the computer room come from many different sources

✦ Filtration systems help to effectively control contaminants in the computer room

✦ Computer rooms must be cleaned regularly to control contaminants

✦ The design of the power system must ensure that adequate power is provided to the computer hardware

✦ Fire suppression systems and equipment such as fire extinguishers, and a sprinkler system must be used to help limit the devastating affects of a fire

✦   ✦   ✦

STUDY GUIDE

The Study Guide section provides you with the opportunity to test your knowledge about hazardous environmental conditions in the server room. The Assessment Questions provide practice for the test, and the Scenarios provide practice with real situations. If you get any questions wrong, use the answers to determine the part of the chapter you should review before continuing.

Assessment Questions

1. A new server has just been delivered to the computer room. The warehouse personnel mentions that it sat in the loading dock for over an hour in 32-degree temperatures. What should you do?

   A. Fire it up immediately.

   B. Wait for the equipment to reach the server room temperature.

   C. Point a space heater at the server to warm it up.

   D. Turn the air conditioner down to cool the room temperature.

2. You notice that the humidity level is low in the computer room. What might result because of this?

   A. ESP

   B. EDI

   C. ESD

   D. Nothing

3. Upon close inspection of the computer room, you notice small gaps around the doorway. What will prevent contaminants from entering through these gaps?

   A. Positive attitude

   B. Silicone

   C. Putting in a new entrance

   D. Positive pressurization

4. What factors should be considered regarding an air conditioning system? Choose all that apply.

  A. Continuous operation for 24 hours and 365 days per year

  B. Independent of other systems in the building

  C. Accommodate expansion

  D. Allow outside air in to the room to accommodate human occupants, and to maintain positive pressurization

  E. All of the above

5. Your boss is looking at replacing the old air conditioning system with a newer one. She would like to know what the best system would be. What would you recommend?

  A. A central station air handling unit

  B. A complete self-contained package unit with remote condensers

  C. A window-mounted air conditioner

  D. A chilled water package unit

6. Contaminants come in many forms, however, some of the most harmful ones are not visible to the naked eye. How small are they?

  A. Less than 10 microns

  B. 1000 microns

  C. 0.3 microns

  D. 100 microns

7. What are the two criteria that must be met in order for a contaminant to be considered harmful?

  A. They must have physical properties that could cause damage to equipment, and they must remain stationary.

  B. They must have physical properties that could cause damage to equipment, and they must have the ability to travel to areas where they can cause damage.

  C. They must have the ability to travel to areas where they can cause damage, and they must not have any physical properties.

  D. None of the above.

8. Your boss asks you to come up with a cleaning schedule for the server room. What should it incorporate?

   A. Daily and yearly tasks

   B. Daily, weekly, and quarterly tasks

   C. Weekly, quarterly, and semi-annual tasks

   D. Daily, weekly, quarterly, and bi-annual tasks

9. What areas should be addressed in the design of a power system?

   A. Multiple feeds, UPS, backup generators, maintenance bypass

   B. Multiple feeds, backup generators, maintenance bypass

   C. Multiple feeds, UPS, backup generators

   D. Multiple feeds, UPS, maintenance bypass

10. To help prevent ESD when working on a server, what precautions can you take? Choose all that apply.

    A. Wear a grounded wrist strap.

    B. Maintain proper humidity levels.

    C. Wear a wool shirt, and polyester pants.

    D. Use conductive furniture.

Scenarios

1. Management wants you to come up with the best possible solution for a fire prevention system to protect the mission-critical systems in the computer room. What would you recommend?

Answers to Chapter Questions

Chapter pre-test

1. Computer systems have an ideal operating temperature range. Temperatures above or below this range can have serious side effects.

2. The standard temperature range is between 70 and 74 degrees F.

3. High humidity levels can cause resistance between connections, and low humidity levels can cause ESD.

4. To allow fresh air to enter the room to ensure occupant safety.

5. To maintain the proper temperature in the room, and to adequately cool the computer hardware.

6. Air conditioning systems should remain operational 24 hours per day, and 365 days per year.

7. Contaminants can cause serious physical damage to electronic equipment.

8. Operator activity, hardware movement, outside air, stored items, and cleaning activities are all sources of contamination.

9. Electrostatic discharge.

10. Fire safety is important because a fire can be catastrophic to a computer room, occupants, and to the successful operations of the company.

Assessment questions

1. **B.** You should always wait for the computer equipment to reach room temperature before turning it on. Turning the equipment on when it is too cold or hot can cause components to fail if they reach the operating temperature to rapidly. For more information, see the "Temperature" section.

2. **C.** ESD can result if humidity levels are too low. ESD can cause damage to electronic components. Answer A is incorrect because it is not a computer term. Answer B is incorrect because this stands for Electronic Data Interchange. Answer D is incorrect because low humidity levels will result in high levels of ESD. For more information, see the "Humidity" section.

3. **D.** Positive pressurization ensures that contaminants cannot enter the room via small cracks or gaps around door ways. Answer A is incorrect because it is irrelevant here. Answer B is incorrect because you cannot possibly fill all the gaps in the room. Answer C is incorrect because putting in a new entrance cannot ensure there will not be small gaps in it. For more information, see the "Ventilation" section.

4. **E.** Air conditioning systems should be able to meet all of these requirements in order to ensure adequate cooling in the computer room, and adequate safety for occupants and equipment. For more information, see the "Air conditioning" section.

5. **B.** A complete self-contained package unit with remote condensers is the best choice for an air conditioning system. They are available with up or down discharge. Answer A is incorrect because central station air handlers are typically used in office environments and not computer rooms. Answer C is incorrect because there should not be any windows in the server room for security reasons, and this type of system does not have the proper environmental controls for server rooms. Answer D is incorrect because a chilled water package is not a complete self-contained unit. For more information, see the "Air conditioning" section.

6. **A.** The most harmful contaminants are less than 10 microns and can bypass air filtration systems. Answer B is incorrect because particles of this size are easily captured by filters. Answer C is incorrect because these particles fall into the category of less than 10 microns, and therefore anything less than this, or greater than but equal to 10 microns are the most harmful. Answer D is incorrect because the air filtration system should be able to capture particles of this size. For more information, see the "Air Pollutants" section.

7. **B.** To be considered dangerous contaminants, particles must have physical properties that could cause damage to equipment, and they must have the ability to travel to areas where they can cause damage. For more information, see the "Sources of contaminants" section.

8. **D.** A proper cleaning schedule should consist of daily, weekly, quarterly, and bi-annual tasks to ensure that the server room meets a high standard of cleanliness. For more information, see the "Regular cleaning" section.

9. **A.** To ensure a high-quality power system, you should incorporate multiple feeds, UPS, backup generators, and maintenance bypass elements. For more information, see the "Electrical Issues" section.

10. **A, B,** and **D.** To prevent ESD when working on a server, you need to ensure that all these conditions were met. If you do not follow these recommendations, you could end up zapping components while handling them. For more information, see the "Electrostatic discharge" section.

Scenarios

1. You need to ensure that you have adequate fire protection by incorporating a manual means of fire suppression in the server room, installing fire extinguishers at strategic locations throughout the room, and using a sprinkler system. Ideally, you should incorporate a dual sprinkler system that makes use of a pre-action water sprinkler system, and gas based sprinkler system using FM 200. This scenario offers the best protection because fire extinguishers and manual suppression equipment will help to control flare-ups while occupants are in the room to control it. The gas system should extinguish the blaze without damaging the hardware. As a last resort, the pre-action water based sprinkler system would run continuously until the fire was extinguished, although it would most likely damage the hardware. However, if it came to that, you would still be able to operate because your tape backups would have been safely stored off-site.

Troubleshooting

Troubleshooting is one of the administrator's main roles on the job. The chapters in this Part provide you with an overall troubleshooting procedure that you can apply to most situations. The first step in this process is determining exactly what the problem is, so there's a chapter devoted exclusively to that step.

There are also many tools and utilities you can use to solve the problem, once you know what it is, and those are described in this Part as well, along with how to use them. Using trouble-shooting resources such as existing server documentation and vendor resources such as the manual to help resolve the issue are also discussed.

Determining the Problem

◆ ◆ ◆ ◆

CHAPTER PRE-TEST

1. What is the key to good troubleshooting?

2. What are two methods of problem determination?

3. What are typical preventative maintenance items?

4. What are two types of network maps?

5. What are some spare components that you should keep on hand?

6. How would you go about gathering information to resolve a computer problem?

7. What are indicator lights on servers or devices?

8. Why should you check cabling?

9. Why should you check software problems first?

10. In a multi-level support system, what would a Level 1 support technician be responsible for?

✦ Answers to these questions can be found at the end of the chapter. ✦

solating the cause of a server problem can be a daunting task. Almost every chapter in this book will help prepare you to troubleshoot and isolate problems. This chapter focuses in detail on the steps in the troubleshooting process. The key to good troubleshooting is having all the available information about the environment, such as network documentation and problem logs. You also need to collect all pertinent information about the problem, and then follow a logical approach to resolving the issue. Staying calm and focused is vital to any good troubleshooter. If you follow the problem through from start to finish and do so with diligence, I can almost guarantee success. Remember that you cannot solve every problem with the snap of your fingers; some things are going to take time.

Isolating the Problem

 6.1 Perform problem determination

Problem isolation is really a science, and an art form. Like a science, it requires that you follow the proper procedures logically and methodically. Like an art form, each person will discover his or her own way to express their skills. This does not mean however, that you can take a haphazard approach to troubleshooting problems.

There are two methods that you can use to resolve a problem:

1. The best guess approach: This approach is based on current knowledge, experience, and a little luck. This method should only be used if you cannot use the logical approach.

2. The logical approach: You follow a step-by-step method of testing to locate and resolve a problem

Troubleshooting methodology

All good troubleshooting needs to start with a few ground rules. These rules can be thought of as a logical troubleshooting methodology. This methodology has six key steps:

1. Keep the servers up to date

2. Eliminate the obvious

3. Gather information about the problem

4. Simplify

5. Perform testing

6. Document what solved the problem

Keep the servers up to date

A large majority of problems with servers have already been resolved by the vendor and are available for download in the form of service packs, hot fixes, patches, and so on. Check the vendor's Web site to find out if the problem has been documented by the vendor, and if there is a fix available. You should also ensure that you use up-to-date drivers for the hardware being used on your server. Use the drivers that are shipped with the operating system, because these drivers are certified, tested, and are made available to you by the vendor. You can also use certified drivers that are released by hardware vendors, because they are usually updates to those provided by the operating system vendor.

Eliminate the obvious

Eliminate any obvious causes for server, network, hardware, software, and device problems. For example it would be wise to check that everything is plugged in and that the power is on before going into too much detail. The following is a list of things you should do to eliminate the obvious:

✦ Check the operating system vendor's knowledgebase for known problems with software and hardware.

✦ Check the hardware and cabling to make sure everything is plugged in, connected, and terminated correctly.

✦ Make sure all hardware is certified by the operating system vendor's hardware compatibility list (HCL).

✦ Make sure that the problem is not a simple user error.

✦ Make sure that the problem does not have to do with permissions problems (rights to folders, files, and so on).

Gather information about the problem

Before you can start troubleshooting, you need information about what the problem is. Make sure that this information is as complete and accurate as possible. The more detailed the information is about the problem, the less work you will need to do later. This will also eliminate the possibility of fixing the wrong problem or creating a new one. You will need to ask questions of the user or technician experiencing the problem to gather this information. You will want to document the following information:

✦ Current date

✦ Name of user experiencing the problem (if applicable)

✦ Contact information of the user (if applicable)

✦ Make, model, age, configuration, peripheral equipment, and operating system of server, or workstation

✦ When the problem first started to occur

✦ Any error messages

✦ Whether or not the error is reproducible

✦ The symptoms of the problem

Simplify

Simplify the system to eliminate as many variables as possible, and to isolate the source of the problem.

✦ Run the server or workstation without loading all the devices, software programs, and drivers. For example, in Windows NT, you can start the workstation in VGA mode, which prevents many drivers from loading.

✦ Remove or stop all nonessential programs, such as performance monitors, network monitors, virus scanners and so on, until the server is using the bare minimum to operate.

✦ Disconnect or remove peripheral devices.

Perform testing

After you have gathered the information, eliminated the obvious, and simplified the system, you can determine what you think is most likely causing the problem. You may come up with several hypotheses during this step. In this event, you need to prorate your hypotheses, by determining which one is the most likely, then the next most likely, and so on. After you have completed your list of hypotheses, test them. Keep the following in mind when doing testing:

✦ Test the most likely hypotheses first, and follow through to the least likely hypotheses. Stop only if one of the hypotheses proves to resolve the problem.

✦ Strip your hypotheses down into smaller sections, and test each one separately. If, for example, you thought the problem was with the network, then you would want to break it down into its smaller sections (Network card, cabling, switches, hubs, and so on).

✦ If you think that a component may be faulty, then replace it with a similar component that you know works. Make sure you only replace one component at a time.

✦ Try removing components from the system that are of course not essential to its operation. This way if the problem still occurs, or does not occur, then you have greatly reduced the number of components that you need to deal with to resolve the problem. If the problem does go away, install each component one at a time, and test to see if the problem occurs after installing the component.

Document what solved the problem

After you resolve any problem, document the solution thoroughly. This information will be extremely helpful should a similar problem occur. Make sure you document any changes made to the servers, workstations, and so on. Also include any hardware and software updates or additions. Record the new version numbers of the updates and any workarounds you had to use to resolve the problem.

These troubleshooting methods established above can be complimented with a few essential things:

✦ Network documentation

✦ Knowledge of networking concepts

✦ Product knowledge

✦ Logic

✦ Intuition

Documentation

Good documentation is often overlooked, which is a mistake, because it can save you hours of time and stress when a problem occurs. Documentation can also show you things that you may not know about your LAN environment. It is also good for new employees, because it can give them a thorough understanding of the server and LAN configurations.

You should also keep records of the problems you encounter, and the resolutions to those problems. Keeping track of what has happened and how it was resolved will save you countless hours when troubleshooting problems.

Network information is fundamental to the overall LAN documentation. It should detail the different aspects of both the physical and logical network. This documentation should include:

✦ Network maps, logical and physical

✦ Device inventory

✦ Update log

✦ Problem log

Maintain network maps

Network maps tell you where devices are located, and how they relate to each other. There are at least two styles of network maps that you should maintain, physical and logical.

Logical maps are typically in the form of topology overviews. They primarily focus on the devices that connect the networks. They should also establish a relationship between the devices and demonstrate the data flow. Logical maps do not give detailed locations of equipment, but serve to help locate potential problems and bottlenecks, and plan for expansion.

Physical maps show where the devices are located. You must update these maps regularly so you can find devices. Most physical maps include blueprints that show room names and locations, wiring diagrams, and cable specifications. Physical maps are often neglected as things change in your LAN. However, the few minutes that it takes to update these maps if a change occurs is minor compared to the time it could save you later.

Inventory everything

An equipment inventory is a fundamental part of the documentation. This document should contain a list of all clients on the network, all the servers on the network, all internetworking devices, and a spare parts inventory.

The client inventory should include how many clients are on the network, types of network cards they have, and the model numbers, and serial numbers of the workstations, network cards, printers, and so on. You can include their locations, and which department uses them, which domain or workgroup they are in, and so on, but this should be laid out in the physical map as well.

The server inventory should include the location of the server, make, model, serial number, operating system, memory, network cards, and any other peripheral devices. It should also detail the purpose of the server (application, database, print, and so on). I recommend that you use a third-party program for this purpose, as they are very good at discovering what is on the server, including software and hardware. A couple of excellent programs for doing this are Track-It by BlueOcean Software Inc, which can be found at `www.blueocean.com`, and Microsoft Systems Management Server, which can be found at `www.microsoft.com/smsmgmt/default.asp`. These programs can save you a lot of time and effort, especially if things change.

The internetworking devices inventory should include a list of all the bridges, routers, gateways, concentrators, and repeaters. This document should also include the vendor name, make, model, serial number, location, and connections.

The spare parts inventory should let you know what is available if something should fail. This is especially important for mission-critical services. Items you should keep as spares are:

✦ Hard disks

✦ Keyboards and mice

✦ Network cards

✦ Disk controllers

✦ I/O ports

✦ System units, and motherboards

✦ Special connectors and adapters

✦ Cables (power cords, serial cables, network cables, and so on)

✦ Concentrators and hubs (perhaps routers, depending on how critical the service is)

If a network card fails in a server, you have the exact spare in your inventory, which makes the problem easy to fix. Your users would be back to work in no time at all. However, if you do not have a spare network card, then you would need to fill out a purchase order and wait for the part to arrive. This could take hours, or even days to get a new network card. This isn't acceptable in most environments.

You should also limit the number of different vendors you user for your servers, as this can keep costs down when purchasing spare components. If each of the servers is made by the same vendor, they probably use similar, or identical components. Therefore, you would not need to keep multiple spares for each server.

If you're thinking about using an old part that has been collecting dust on the top shelf as a spare, forget it. You would only be adding another potential problem to the equation. The money you saved will soon be eaten up by the hours you will have wasted when you have to troubleshoot the problems it will introduce.

Maintain an update log

Maintaining an update log document is absolutely vital for tracking changes. Unfortunately, this is not done in most IS departments. The rule of thumb is that you never leave the office until you have finished recording the changes that occurred, and why they were done. The update log can accomplish the following things:

✦ Show a detail trend of what was done to the servers

✦ Provide accountability for the changes made

✦ Determine if another problem occurred as a result of fixing the first one

An update log should include the following:

✦ **Description of change:** A brief description of the work that was done.

✦ **Who performed the work:** This is not so blame is placed on someone, but a reference of who did the work if you need to get information from this person.

✦ **Why the work was performed:** The reason behind the change or update (resolve a problem, performance tuning).

✦ **Date work began and date it was completed:** Gives a reference point that may help resolve problems that also began within the same time frame.

Problems often occur as a result of changes made to the systems. These issues are not always mistakes; the changes might simply conflict with something else. If you make changes, and soon after other problems start to occur, suspect the changes you made. First, try restoring the old configuration. If the other problem disappears, you know what caused the problem. You can then spend some time trying to figure out exactly why your changes caused the other problem, and how to correct it. With an update log, you can track down exactly when a change occurred, and know what to do to reverse it.

Once you resolve a system problem, record what the problem was, and how you resolved it. You can use that information later to solve similar problems If you do not do this, you will go through the problem discovery and resolution steps again and again. The issue might be a reoccurring problem. If you see a pattern in your log, and notice that a particular problem keeps occurring over and over again, then you will be able to focus on why it keeps reoccurring. This will eventually lead to the resolution of the real problem.

You can use this problem log to store the information from the update log, and also any general troubleshooting information that is relevant to the process, such as detailed instructions or vendor documentation.

Know the network

You should have a good understanding of how things work in theory and in practice, as they are not always the same. Ideally you should know the design capabilities and limits of your network. You should make sure that you are familiar with the network topology you are using, and all the devices that are on it. Much of this information should be contained in the network documentation that was mentioned earlier in the chapter. You should also be familiar with any protocols that you are using in your network environment. I also recommend that you make up a wiring diagram that lists each workstation on the network, and which port on the switch or hub they are plugged into. This information will make it much easier when trying to figure out why a certain user is having network connectivity problems. Without knowing this information, you will have a difficult time resolving certain problems that may occur.

Know the products

Know everything that you can about the software and hardware used in your systems. The best way to do this is to read books (such as this one), including manuals that are supplied by the software or hardware vendor. I would recommend that you know the ins and outs of all the server software in your environment, as you will no doubt have to configure and troubleshoot them.

The book information will give you a basis on how things are supposed to work. However, sometimes the documentation is outdated or inaccurate, so you will need to rely on the vendor Web site or other support forums to get a better understanding of the hardware or software. These sites usually have patches, updates, fixes, or shortcuts to download. The information on these sites changes regularly, so check back often.

Logic and reasoning

There are two general forms of reasoning: deductive and inductive. In deductive reasoning, you solve a problem based on the information that is gathered. Deductive reasoning works best when you have a lot of information at hand. When performing this form of reasoning, it is best to start at one point, and follow it through completely until the end.

Inductive reasoning is when you have a very small amount of information to work with. The nature of inductive reasoning means that you do not have a lot of information available to you to work with. Typically, with this type of reasoning you will eventually need to make an educated guess. Some people have a real gift for taking the information they had to dig up, hypothesize, and make an educated guess based on the collected information. Some people need to work at it. Making educated guesses may be necessary when time constraints are an issue and you need to solve the problem fast. Hopefully, if you followed your troubleshooting techniques, and have maintained all your documentation, you can make a good educated guess.

Ask the right questions

✦ Use questioning techniques to determine what, how, when

Before you can troubleshoot a problem, you need to know exactly what the problem is, or what conditions are occurring. To find that out, you'll need to ask questions of the people affected by the problem. You need to ask specific questions that will provide you with the information you need to analyze the problem.

First, you need to ask questions to determine the scope of the problem. What indicates to you that there is a problem? What are the error messages, indicator lights, or other computer information? Is everyone on the network down? Is it just a group of people, or is it just one person? Is the problem intermittent, or reproducible? Is there a sequence of steps that can be followed to consistently reproduce the problem? If this answer is yes, the problem is reproducible, and if the answer is no, then the problem is intermittent.

Second, you need to question the appropriate people about how the problem occurred, or how it began. Was a change made prior to this problem? What else happened around this time? Did someone trip and knock over a piece of equipment? Third, you will need to determine exactly when the problem began. Did it occur today, yesterday, or did it start 2 weeks ago? Have you noticed other problems? Did these other problems occur around the same time? If computer personnel have been maintaining the problem log, you can see if another issue was fixed in the same time frame. If there is nothing in the problem log, you might still be able to use this information to see if anything else was happening at the same time. Perhaps the server room experienced a temporary power failure at 2:00 p.m., but you find out from the maintenance supervisor that the power system was overloaded, which may have affected the server room.

Be polite and reassuring when asking users or coworkers about the problem. You can start by telling them about how you ran into a similar problem before, and how you learned form that. You want to reassure the user that you are not blaming them. What you want to do is make sure you find out the what, how, and when.

Using Your Senses

✦ Use senses to observe problem (e.g. smell of smoke, observation of unhooked cable, etc.)

Your human senses are an important part of your array of troubleshooting tools. Trust what you see, hear, smell, and feel to help you identify problems. You should use the four S's when they walk into a server room: sight, sound, smell, and sensitivity. The last one encompasses touch, and in general the way things feel (cold or hot).

Sight

When you enter the server room, look at everything you can. Accustom your mind to the way everything looks in the computer room. If you train yourself to do this, eventually it will become second nature, and when things are out of place, you will most likely notice. The following are things you should be looking for when you enter a computer room:

✦ Are any cables out of place, either dangling, or loose on the floor?

✦ Are any cables loose?

✦ Are there any flashing lights, solid lights, or missing lights that should be on?

✦ Are there any messages on server screens from event monitors?

✦ Do you see smoke?

✦ Do you notice a lot of dust or other contaminants?

✦ Are there any trash cans that should not be in the server room, or other garbage lying around?

Sound

Most server rooms have lots of loud noises from air conditioners, cooling fans in servers, and the other equipment in the room. Thus, noise is not typically a major concern when you walk into a computer room. However, you should take note of any noises that are out of the ordinary. The following are things you should listen for when you enter a server room:

✦ Are any fans especially noisy, or are there any that don't sound right?

✦ Are any noises not present that are normally there (cooling fan stopped, air conditioner stopped)?

✦ Are hard drives making unusual noises?

✦ When users dial in, are the modems picking up correctly?

Smell

Just as with your sight and hearing, when you first enter the server room, check to see if you smell anything out of the ordinary. The following are things you should smell for when you enter the server room:

✦ Is anything burning?

✦ Is anything melting?

✦ Are there any funny odors circulating through the air system (gases or chemical odors)?

✦ Does the room smell damp or musty?

Sensitivity

Sensitivity is more of a whole-body experience then anything else. It is how do you feel when you walk into the room. This sense will help you determine if the room is too cold or too hot, or if the room feels moist. The following are things that are typically associated with sensitivity:

✦ How is the temperature? Does it feel too cold, or too hot? Check the thermostat, if it is working, you may have a problem with the cooling system.

✦ How is the humidity? Does the room feel damp or dry? If it is too dry, you will notice lots of static. If it is too damp, the room will feel moist.

✦ Do you have any allergic reactions? This could signal a lot of dust or other contaminants in the room.

Checking Hardware

 6.4 Identify and correct misconfigurations and/or upgrades

6.5 Determine if problem is hardware, software or virus related

When checking server hardware, ensure that everything is plugged in, such as monitors, power cables, network cables, peripheral cables, and so on. Listen for any strange noises coming from the server or other devices. Listen for noises coming from the disks, CD-ROMS, fans, or power supplies. You should be able to identify the noises that don't sound right.

 Exam Tip   One of the top causes of disk failure is excessive vibration.

Checking server components

Open the server cases up and inspect them for excessive contamination (dust or other particles). If you notice a lot of contamination, clean it immediately. You should then get the server room decontaminated, and have a technician check the air filtration system for problems. If you are not careful, the build up of contaminants may end up damaging the components in the server.

In general, check everything that could go wrong inside the server. If you are having problems booting the server, or are experiencing intermittent problems, you may need to open the case and look for loose connections. Most of the chips on the motherboard will be soldered, so don't push on them, or you could damage the chip. Typically, chips that are soldered should never come loose. Some of the chips will be in sockets, and you will be able to push on those. When these chips are exposed to heat, and cold, the metal chip legs tend to expand and shrink. This causes the chip to be come loose in the socket. You may want use some connector cleaner on the chip legs before putting the chips back into the sockets.

If you are experiencing memory problems, you may need to replace the RAM, but first try cleaning it with some connector cleaner designed for RAM. If you do not have connector cleaner, try using an artist's eraser or the eraser on the end of a pencil. Make sure there are no rubber shavings on the connectors after you are done. You should also make sure the RAM is seated properly in the socket by removing it and putting it back in.

Don't forget to check all internal cables as well, and make sure they are secured tightly.

Checking lights

Check the indicator lights on the servers and other devices in the computer room. Devices that may have lights in the server room are:

✦ Servers

✦ Workstations

✦ Printers

✦ Switches

✦ Hubs

✦ Routers

✦ Bridges

✦ Concentrators

✦ Tape backup units

✦ Modems

✦ External drives

All of these devices have indicator lights on them, and if something is wrong, the unit is designed to manipulate the lights in a pattern that you can look up in the hardware manual. It may be as simple as a loose connection, or as complex as a fried component.

The key to troubleshooting when it comes to hardware is isolating the device or component that is causing the problem. The indicator lights and hardware manual should help you to do this.

Checking cabling

First, make sure everything is plugged in. This may sound somewhat simplistic, but it is true. You would be amazed at how many problems can be resolved by simply checking the cables. Things to check with power cables:

✦ Is the server plugged into a surge protector?

✦ Is the surge protector on, or plugged into the wall?

✦ Are there other devices plugged into the surge protector, and are they working?

✦ Are the servers plugged into a wall outlet?

✦ Are there other devices in the wall outlet, and are they working?

You should check the circuit breaker if you are not getting any power to the servers, or particular devices, if other ones in the server room are getting power. If the breaker has tripped, you should find out why, in case you are overloading the circuit. Your server room and devices should be independent of the rest of the building, and the power sources in the server room should be divided into multiple circuits.

The following are tips for organizing cables:

✦ Ensure rack-mounted equipment that slides in or out has enough cable slack so that cables do not bind, pinch, or pull out.

✦ Label all cables at both ends for easy identification.

✦ If multiple sources of power are available, route the cables that supply the cabinets to different sources. If one fails, the others will still operate.

✦ Make sure cables are neat and tidy. Use a cable management system or zip ties. Cables should never be loose in a cabinet configuration.

✦ Make sure all cables are tight and securely attached at either end (screw them down).

✦ Make sure cables cannot be accidentally pulled out; either by getting caught on clothing, or items that move, such as chairs.

✦ Do not plug the power supplies into the same power strip.

Do not forget about internal cables either. If you are experiencing intermittent or complete hardware failures, open the box and check for loose cables. Push them in firmly, but gently. Then reboot and see if the problem disappears.

Examining peripherals

The is the first question you should ask when troubleshooting peripherals is: Are all the peripherals plugged into a power source, and are they plugged into the server? Make sure that the peripheral cables are secured tightly to the server. The pins can bend over time if they are not screwed in securely. Be on the look out for cables that dangle freely, or run across the floor. These tend to take a lot of punishment. All peripheral cables should be tied down in a manner that keeps them from dangling. If you need to run them across the floor, try to place them out of the way of traffic or chairs. Use floor runners designed for cables if necessary.

 Tip   If you are experiencing connectivity issues with peripheral equipment, don't immediately blame the software. Check all the cables first; push them in, and tighten them down. Even if they do not feel loose, there may be that one pin that is not in quite far enough.

Checking Software

 Objective   **6.4** Identify and correct misconfigurations and/or upgrades

6.5 Determine if problem is hardware, software or virus related

Most problems are actually software problems and not hardware problems. Even if it looks like a hardware problem, I recommend that you check the software first. You may find that the software was just configured incorrectly, or the device the program is looking for has been turned off. Besides, it is a easier to dig through the software than it is to go mucking around with your hardware. You may find that you simply need to upgrade or reinstall the misconfigured software to resolve the problem. Check the vendor's Web site for updates, hot fixes, service packs, patches, or upgrades to the software or operating system. More than likely, you find that the problem has been detected and resolved by the vendor. Most software problems result from the operating system or the application software being used.

Software problems are typically disguised as:

✦ Software bugs in applications, or drivers provided by vendors.

✦ Software that does not properly clean out RAM (this happens a lot).

✦ Software that requests hardware that is not connected, or has been turned off, such as backup software that tries to access data from a server that is not on.

✦ Operator error. This is more a problem in the user environment than in the server one. However, computer systems people make errors too.

The most common culprits in software problems are virtual device drivers and
Dynamic Link Libraries (DLLs). Although these files are usually associated with
Windows-based machines, they are actually common among most server operating
systems. However, because Windows is so popular, you tend to see them more in
that environment.

Drivers

Drivers are programs that are written for specific hardware components. These programs act as a layer between the operating system and the hardware. For example,
if you add a new video card to your system, you need the corresponding drivers
that match the operating system you are using. These drivers enable the hardware
to function correctly with the operating system, and any other software that may
use the hardware.

Drivers can sometimes cause serious problems for the stability of the system. This
happens because the operating system is designed by a group of people who work
for the operating system vendor, but the people who write the driver programs
work for a different company. They do not have the privilege of having all the inside
information that the operating system programmers have.

Never try to use drivers that are written for one operating system on another one.
This will definitely lead to more problems, and the hardware will most likely not
function at all, or will function incorrectly.

Exam Tip   Driver programs are the soft spot in the operation of the operating system.

When you install a new driver, if you start to notice problems either with the way
the hardware functions, or the way that the software or operating system responds,
go back to the old drivers and see if the if the problems disappears. I recommend
that you always make a backup copy of the old drivers before installing any new
hardware drivers. You should also ensure that you have system backups, before
adding new hardware, drivers, patches, or updates.

Dynamic Link Libraries

A DLL is a file that contains a bunch of small programs within it. The programs in a
DLL are usually available to any other program that needs it. An example of this
would be a DLL that tells the operating system how it is going to save a file.

This linking is what makes DLLs so useful. If applications did not use DLLs, every
time an application had to save a file, it would have to load the save routine into the
computer's memory. If any other applications also wanted to save a file, they would
have to load the save routine as well. Eventually, because of every application that
needed to save, print, or do another common task, the memory would be come
congested, and errors would occur. By using dynamic linking, a DLL can be linked
over and over again each time an application needs to use it. A program that needs

to link to a particular library file has a command or pointer within its code that tells it what DLL it needs to access. Once that particular DLL is loaded in memory, any other application needing to access the same routines will use that copy of the DLL that is loaded in memory. Therefore, only one copy is ever loaded, saving memory resources on the system.

Sometimes applications do not install correctly, which could be a result of various different issues. Such a program may crash or produce error messages if it cannot find the DLL it needs. This can also happen if the file is corrupt, or missing because someone deleted it. You may also run into this problem if the DLL is replaced by an older or newer version. Although installing updated program releases is usually necessary for program stability, it can have adverse effects.

Software bugs

Sometimes software is just buggy. That is why vendors release service packs for major updates, hot fixes for urgent matters, and patches for obscure problems that not everyone may experience. These bugs usually occur because the programmers did not test for, or anticipate the problem. It is very difficult to write programs for modern, complicated operating systems. It is almost impossible to test for every scenario, or every piece of hardware that someone may try to use. If you find a bug, and you can reproduce it, log your findings and send them to the vendor. They typically welcome bug reports, because they want their program or hardware to function correctly.

Troubleshooting the Operating System

6.4 Identify and correct misconfigurations and/or upgrades

6.5 Determine if problem is hardware, software or virus related

When troubleshooting the operating system, you need to make use of the tools that are built into it. You will need to exam system messages, log files, and check disk space to ensure there is ample room for the programs to perform there operations. Examine the log files on a daily basis or use a software utility to notify you of important events.

System messages

System messages happen all the time, and many of them have very simple solutions. However, whatever message is on the screen, you should take the time to read it thoroughly. Even a simple, and perhaps normal message such as a user being forced off the system because of time restrictions, could mean trouble. Perhaps you know that the user is on vacation for one week, and does not have dial-in rights to the system. This could mean that someone has illegally entered your system as this user.

Sometimes these system messages are vital to system stability. They may inform you of low disk or memory resources. Issues that are severe enough for the operating system to report on demand some sort of immediate attention. If they are important enough, you should log these messages and what you did to resolve them.

Log files

✦ Interpret error logs, operating system errors, health logs, and critical events

Log files are a way for the operating system and applications to record vital software and hardware events. For example, Windows NT has a standard, centralized service for recording events. Applications and the operating system store these occurrences in the Event Log. You then use the Event Viewer program to view these log entries. Windows NT has four types of event log files: application, security, system, and a custom registered log file. You can look through the log files manually, or with a specific application that can scan the logs and look for certain events specified by the administrator. Perhaps you want to know how often a certain user logs on, or a group of users, or maybe you want to see how many times people key in the wrong password. If a specific event is detected, the software can usually be configured to trigger an alert, and the appropriate personal could be notified. Check out SystemGuard for Linux by Disoft. This software can monitor your servers' file systems, daemons, syslog, sulog, system load, and memory. It will send you an email when an event occurs. You can also check out Appmon by Arcanan for Windows NT/2000 for monitoring events.

Critical events, such as a full disk drive or an interrupted power supply, are usually noted in an on-screen display on the server console and in the operating systems error log. Critical events are significant problems, such as loss of data or loss of functions. You can use the error log to get more information about the problem.

Health logs can be daily, weekly, and monthly statistic reports. They will show the overall health of your servers, and network. Health logs will help you to find specific patterns on your servers before they become big problems. These logs will show a trend or pattern over the course of the time period that the log was capturing information. The following items are typically monitored in health logs:

✦ Allocated server processes

✦ Available server processes

✦ CPU utilization for each processor if there is more than one

✦ Connection usage

✦ Available memory

✦ Virtual memory performance

✦ Cache performance

✦ LAN traffic

✦ Available disk space

✦ Disk throughput

There will be other options that you can also include in the health logs depending on the server operating system that you are using.

Mission critical or Enterprise Resource Planning (ERP) applications generally have their own log files. The application scans the log file for certain events, and the appropriate actions are taken if the event occurs. Some log files can be turned on by the software, and these files will log everything that occurs from the point that it is activated; it will only stop logging when you deactivate it. This is very useful when troubleshooting how an application is behaving and why. However, don't forget to turn the logging off, or you may end up consuming most of your hard drive in a short amount of time.

Event logging is extremely useful when trying to resolve resource problems, hardware problems, bad disk sectors, and for information events. Check your log files on a daily basis, because there may be things happening on the server that you are not aware of.

Checking disk space

Checking disk space is very important, and really simple to do. Make sure you regularly check all your servers, and all the usable disks for the amount of free disk space. You would be surprised at how many software issues are a direct result of low disk space on the server or the workstation. Typical applications consume an undetermined amount of disk space while performing certain actions. If the space is not available, the application will crash or the job will fail, and the program will most likely report an error that either points to the problem or obscures it.

There are many programs available that will monitor disk space and generate alerts if the specified threshold is breeched. These programs usually do not cost much; in fact you can find many free programs available on the Internet that will do the job. OpalisRobot by Sunbelt Software can perform all these functions and more. This tool is not free, but is worth every penny. You can download a trial version at `www.sunbeltsoftware.com`. Another excellent utility is Big Brother by BB4 Technologies Incorporated. This tool can monitor NT, Unix, Linux, NetWare, and more. Check it out at `www.bb4.com`. Just make sure you download the programs from a reputable Web site. Windows NT/2000 and Novell NetWare come with their own versions of these programs that will assist you with this task.

Cross-Reference Please see chapter 16 for details on monitoring tools provided by the operating system vendor.

Checking for Viruses

 6.5 Determine if problem is hardware, software or virus related

Do not underestimate the effect a virus can have on a system. Viruses can infect the system's boot sector, floppy disks, and the system area in hard drives. Viruses can infect any type of file that contains executable code. This used to mean that infected files were only those with .exe or .com extensions. These days, with so many programs making use of macros, viruses can disguise themselves in documents. Even HTML documents can spread viruses through JavaScript and VBScript.

The only real way to protect yourself from virus infection is to install and use an anti-virus program from a well-known and reliable company such as Norton or McAfee. One of the best virus programs for Lotus Notes, or Microsoft Exchange server that I have seen, is Antigen, which is created by Sybari. Use the virus program diligently, and absolutely make sure you update the virus definition files regularly. If you take the time to set these programs up correctly, they are almost self-maintaining. You can set them up to scan your servers, and to automatically download updates from the vendor's Web site. Just make sure that you set the virus scanner to scan all program files, and all files that may contain executable code. Once you have the program setup to scan all the files, you can set up a schedule to scan your servers every night, once a week, and so on. Depending on the availability of your servers, you may be able to set up a schedule to scan the servers every night. A good example would be to setup the scan job to take place between 9:00 p.m. and 12:00 a.m. This time period may be when the least amount of people are on the network , and prior to the backup jobs that start at midnight. Many of the server virus software applications come in packages that will also scan your e-mail systems, Web proxies, and more.

The other thing you can do is to check your vendor's home page for any important alerts regarding new viruses. These vendors work hard to get out the code to detect and delete new virus programs, and they typically package them as special updates for your systems.

Maintain high security settings in your operating system and Internet applications and, of course, perform regular backups in the event that a virus erases or corrupts any files. The damage done by some viruses is permanent, meaning that there is no way to repair the damaged files, and the only way to get the data back will be from your tape backups.

Resolving the Problem

 ✦ Identify contact(s) responsible for problem resolution

Depending on your situation, you may have multi-level support in your organization, either internally, or provided by an outside vendor. If this is the case, your company most likely has adopted the three-tier escalation procedures that are commonly used. If not, I suggest that you convince management to implement these procedures immediately, because they will definitely help your company to resolve technical problems more efficiently.

In multi-level support environments there are typically three escalation levels, or three tiers.

✦ **Level 1 Support:** These personnel check to see if all the correct steps were followed by the end-user. They attempt to resolve the issue using standard methodologies. If they cannot resolve the issue, they will classify the type of problem (server, workstation, network, printer), and call a level 2 support person who specializes in that area.

✦ **Level 2 Support:** These technicians typically use standard troubleshooting methodologies and tools that fit their expertise to resolve the problem. This person will also use the problem log to detect trends and fix problems before they affect end-users. If they cannot resolve the problem, then a level 3 support person will be contacted.

✦ **Level 3 Support:** These technicians generally are specialists in a particular field, and each level 3 person only looks at problems within their scope of specialization. These people use complicated tools and techniques to resolve a problem. Level 3 support will also monitor the problem log to detect trends and fix them before they affect end-users or degrade performance.

For example, suppose an end user calls the help desk (Level 1 support), to report a problem gaining access to the network. This particular issue would be handled in the following way:

✦ **Level 1 Support:** This person would run through the problem with the user, and ask questions such as, "What is the exact nature of your problem?" "Does the computer turn on?" "Do you get a logon screen?", and so on. They will use the standard methodologies described earlier in the chapter to resolve the problem. If this person cannot resolve the issue, they will log the problem, and escalate it onto a Level 2 support person.

✦ **Level 2 Support:** This person will provide the support, knowledge, and tools that a Level 1 support person uses to also provide efficient end user help. However, Level 2 support people are more specialized and will use the methodologies discussed earlier. These people are typically on call and, if the need arises, they will meet with end users to resolve the problem. They will work remotely or directly on the user's workstation and analyze the software and error logs. This person would also check the cabling for lose connections or bad cables. They will also check the vendor's Web site for updates, patches, hot fixes, and so on. They will also examine the problem log to see if a similar problem has been logged before, and if the solution can be applied to the current problem.

✦ **Level 3 Support:** These people will typically work directly with Level 2 support people to resolve issues, but do not usually have any direct contact with the end-user. In this instance this person may check the protocol settings on the workstation, or perhaps see if there is a problem with the port on the switch, or hub, and so on. This person may also use cable testers, and other network diagnostic tools to resolve the problem Because these people are experts in a narrow field, they will use the troubleshooting methodologies specific to their area of expertise. They will consult the problem log to see what Level 1 and Level 2 support personnel did in an attempt to fix the problem. If this person cannot resolve the problem with the resources they have, then they will contact the vendor for support. Because this type of support usually has a fee associated with it, these people are typically the only ones authorized to do so.

Keep in mind that no one person can resolve every problem. In a large company, you can escalate the problem to different qualified personnel. In a smaller company, you may need to gain assistance from friends, associates, vendors, or consultants to help resolve the problem. Remember that when you call most hardware are software vendors to report a problem, you typically get passed on to someone who falls into a Level 1 support category. If they cannot resolve it, then it will be escalated to the next level and so on. Paying someone to help resolve an issue that you can't fix yourself is generally worth it.

Key Point Summary

The information in this chapter looked at the steps and information required to perform problem determination, by looking at how to isolate the problem, hardware checking, software checking, and performing problem resolution. Keep the following points in mind for the exam:

✦ Isolate problems using troubleshooting methodologies and multiple forms of documentation.

✦ Ask the appropriate questions to get detailed information about the particular problem.

✦ Make sure you check the software for problems, and check to see if there are any updates or upgrades that may resolve the problem. You may find that the vendor has already detected and corrected the problem.

✦ Make sure you check hardware for loose cables, connectors, or loose peripherals.

✦ Make sure you examine all system messages and log files, as they may give you more detailed information about the problems.

✦ Make sure that you check the system for viruses, as you may find that this is the cause of your problem.

✦ ✦ ✦

STUDY GUIDE

The Study Guide section provides you with the opportunity to test your knowledge about troubleshooting procedures. The Assessment Questions provide practice for the test, and the Scenarios provide practice with real situations. If you get any questions wrong, use the answers to determine the part of the chapter you should review before continuing.

Assessment Questions

1. Building A's computer specialist calls to tell you that their network has stopped responding. Because this network is in high demand, you tell the specialist to reboot the server. Unfortunately this does not correct the problem. What should you do next?

    A. Replace the network card.

    B. Replace the network cable that goes to the server.

    C. Replace the hubs.

    D. Ask the specialist questions, including, what, how, and when.

2. Users in the southeastern branch are complaining that during specific periods of the day, the database system slows down dramatically. How would you go about troubleshooting this problem?

    A. Add another hard disk.

    B. Add another processor.

    C. Check log files to determine if the database system is performing any specific jobs or maintenance.

    D. Add more RAM.

3. You have just been hired as a network administrator at a new company. What will you need to get familiar with network environment?

    A. Topology maps

    B. A list of the servers

    C. Documentation that has been created and maintained by the previous employee

    D. Detailed knowledge of the server operating systems

4. Near the end of day, you decide it is a good time to upgrade the tape backup device drivers. After doing so, you perform a quick test, but the backup software no longer recognizes the device. You confirm that all cables are secure. What should you do next, keeping in mind that the backup begins in 30 minutes?

   A. Consult documentation on the vendor's Web site.

   B. Reinstall the old drivers, and then resolve the issue properly when you have more time.

   C. Pull out all the connections, including the SCSI card, and clean them.

   D. Reinstall the operating system.

5. What are some things you should have on hand before troubleshooting? Choose all that apply.

   A. Documentation

   B. Cable tester

   C. Knowledge of networking concepts

   D. Logic and Reasoning

6. What are the two types of maps that any network documentation should contain?

   A. Logical and physical

   B. Logical and topographical

   C. Hypothetical and real

   D. Physical and location

7. Most physical maps show what? Choose all that apply.

   A. Blueprints showing room names and locations

   B. Topology

   C. Wiring diagrams

   D. Cable specifications

8. You are asked to develop an equipment inventory document. What are some of the things you should include? Choose all that apply.

   A. List of servers and clients

   B. List of internetworking devices

   C. Locations of servers and clients

   D. A spare parts inventory

9. A network card fails in one of the servers. After finding out exactly what type of network card it is, where should you look first for a replacement?

   A. A spare workstation

   B. From your supplier

   C. The spare inventory documentation

   D. Local computer store

10. An end-user calls the help desk to report that she cannot get access to her network resources? What would NOT be an appropriate question to ask?

    A. Do you have access to any network resources?

    B. What did you do wrong?

    C. Are there any error messages when you log in?

    D. When did this problem first occur?

11. Some of your users are reporting that their network connection is down. Upon entering the server room, you notice that the indicator lights on the switch that the users are plugged into looks odd. What should you check first?

    A. Test the network cables to see if they are bad.

    B. Check the network card in the server.

    C. Check the log files on the server.

    D. Consult the hardware documentation to see what the indicator lights mean.

12. One of the servers in the computer room is switching to battery power at roughly the same time each night, and sometimes randomly through out the week. Before leaving you decide to switch off the lights, and at the same time, you hear the UPS kick in. What should you check?

    A. Check the building wiring diagrams.

    B. Turn the light switch back on to see if the wall plug is affected by it.

    C. Contact the building supervisor.

    D. Check the wall plug to see if everything is plugged in.

13. Your tape backup software can no longer detect the backup hardware. What should you do first?

    A. Reinstall the backup software.

    B. Reinstall the tape backup device drivers.

    C. Take off the case and make sure the SCSI card is inserted properly.

    D. Check the peripheral cable at both ends to make sure it is securely attached to the server and the tape backup hardware.

14. What are leading causes of software problems?

   A. DLLs and virtual swap files

   B. Operators not knowing what they are doing

   C. DLLs and virtual device drivers

   D. Power surges and buggy applications

15. Every month, you run a month-end job on one of the server databases, and you never run into any problems. This month you receive an error stating that system resources are low and the job fails. What might be the problem?

   A. Not enough RAM

   B. Bad hard disk

   C. Error in the job configuration

   D. Not enough disk space

Scenarios

1. Your company wants to implement a plan to make use of all the different levels of technical expertise that the information systems department has for troubleshooting and problem resolution. They have asked you to come up with a plan to determine how problems should be resolved and who should resolve them. What type of plan should implement?

Answers to Chapter Questions

Chapter pre-test

1. The key to good troubleshooting is having as much information as possible about the network environment, such as documentation, product knowledge, and problem logs.

2. The two methods are the best-guess approach and the logical approach. The best guess approach is not recommend because of its reliance on experience and luck. The logical approach uses a step-by-step method to locate and resolve problems.

3. Network documentation, knowledge of networking concepts, product knowledge, logic, and intuition or reasoning are typical items that assist you in troubleshooting problems.

4. Two types of network maps are logical and physical. Logical maps show topology overviews, while physical maps include blueprints of rooms and computer locations, wiring diagrams, and cable specifications.

5. Spare components you should keep on hand are:

   • Hard disks

   • Keyboards and mice

   • Network cards

   • Disk controllers

   • I/O ports

   • System units, and motherboards

   • Special connectors and adapters

   • Cables (power cords, serial cables, network cables, and so on)

   • Concentrators and hubs (perhaps even routers, depending on the how critical the service is)

6. Document all the information about the particular problem. Ideally, you would want to document any information pertaining to the hardware and software. You will need to ask several questions to get the root of the problem. Some questions you might ask are: "What indicates to you that there is a problem?" and "When did this problem first occur?"

7. Indicator lights on hardware devices are usually designed to flash a pattern that you can look up in the hardware documentation. This pattern is typically some sort of error code. The documentation should tell you what the problem is and how to fix it.

8. You should check cabling because cables are a leading cause of hardware problems. Connectors can come loose if they are not tightened. If cabling is loose, sometimes it gets caught on people walking by, stepped on, or kicked.

9. You should check software problems first because software problems are usually easier to identify and resolve than hardware problems. The majority of problems are software-related as opposed to hardware issues.

10. A Level 1 support technician would run through the problem with the user, and ask questions to determine the nature of the problem. He or she will attempt to resolve the problem using standard methodologies. If this person is not able to resolve the problem, he or she will log the problem and escalate it to a Level 2 support person.

Assessment questions

1. **D.** Asking the appropriate questions will get you the necessary information to correctly troubleshoot the problem. You can find out if anything changed, when it changed, and how it was changed. The other answers are incorrect because they guess at what the problem might be without gathering the necessary information first. Replacing these items will probably not resolve the problem. For more information, see the "Ask the right questions" section.

2. **C.** The log files for the database software will let you know if any maintenance programs are running at these times, or if any special jobs are running. Adding a disk, a processor, or more RAM will only hide the problem, and will most likely do nothing to resolve it. For more information, see the "Log files" section.

3. **C.** Good documentation is always the best way to get anyone familiar with the computer environment, and is the quickest way to do so. Answer A is incorrect because a topology map alone will not get you familiar with the computer environment. It will only show you what topology the network uses. Answer B is incorrect because a list of all the servers will do nothing more than name each server for you, and will essentially do nothing to make you familiar with the environment. Answer D is incorrect because a detailed knowledge of the operating system does not have anything to do with becoming familiar with the entire computer environment. This will only make it easier for you to do so. For more information, see the "Documentation" section.

4. **B.** Because you have limited time to troubleshoot, you should reinstall the old drivers, because you know they worked before you installed the new ones. When you have more time, you can consult the vendor's Web site for more information. There should not be a problem with the SCSI card, or the operating system because it everything was functioning correctly with the old drivers. For more information, see the "Drivers" section.

5. **A, C,** and **D.** These are all things you should have on hand for troubleshooting. Having these elements in place will make it easier to resolve problems. Answer B is part of your troubleshooting tools, and wouldn't be needed at the beginning of the process. For more information, see the "Isolating the problem" section.

6. **A.** Any network documentation should contain a logical map showing the network topology, and a physical maps showing blueprints for room names and locations, wiring diagrams, and cable specifications. Answer B is incorrect because topographical maps are geographical land maps. Answer C is incorrect because there is technically no such thing as hypothetical and real maps with network documentation. Answer D is incorrect because location is not a type of map. For more information, see the "Documentation" section.

7. **A, C,** and **D.** Physical maps should contain these elements. Answer B is wrong because this is typically part of logical maps. For more information, see the "Maintain network maps" section.

8. **A, B,** and **D.** Equipment inventory documents should at least contain these elements to help you see what equipment you have, and what spares you have. Answer C is wrong because locations are part of network documentation, not inventory. For more information, see the "Inventory everything" section.

9. **C.** You should consult the spare inventory document first to see if you have an identical network card on hand. If not, the document will let you know of other network cards you might be able to use. Answer A is incorrect because you should only take a card from a spare workstation if you absolutely need to use that network card. Answer B is incorrect because it will take a day or two to get a replacement from a supplier. Answer D is incorrect because it is not the quickest solution. You should have spare network cards on hand for each of your servers. For more information, see the "Inventory everything" section.

10. **B.** You do not want to insult the end-user by blaming them for the problem. Answers A, C, and D are incorrect because these are the type of questions that you should ask the end user. For more information, see the "Ask the right questions" section.

11. **D.** The hardware documentation will tell you what the pattern of indicator lights means. Answer A is incorrect because the probability of all the cables being bad in that switch is remote. Answer B is incorrect because only some of the users are having problems, while other users are connecting to that server and using its resources without any problems, so the issue cannot be with the network card in the server. Answer C is wrong because there most likely will not be any errors in the server log files that relate to the switch. For more information, see the "Checking lights" section.

12. **B.** This is the quickest and easiest thing to test. If you turn off the lights and the UPS kicks in, then it is likely that the light switch and power receptacle are on the same circuit. Answer A is incorrect because you are probably not familiar with electrical diagrams, and it would take too long to search through them. Answer C is incorrect because the building supervisor will most likely be unable to help. Answer D is incorrect because the server was working before you turned off the lights, so it must have been plugged in. For more information, see the "Checking cabling" section.

13. **D.** This is the quickest and easiest thing to do, so you should do it first. Loose connections are a leading cause of many hardware and software problems. Answer A is incorrect because it would be time consuming; you could try this after testing other things. Answer B is incorrect because it is not the first step to take. Reinstall the drivers if you think they might be corrupt, or someone updated them. Answer C is also incorrect because this is something that is typically done last. For more information, see the "Examining peripherals" section.

14. C. DLLs and virtual device drivers are the cause of many software problems, especially in Windows environments. Answer A is incorrect because virtual swap files do not exist. Answer B is incorrect, although operators do contribute to a large portion of client software issues. Answer D is incorrect, but these are also factors in software problems. For more information, see the "Checking Software" section.

15. D. A lack of disk space is most likely the problem if the application states it is low on resources. Many applications need to use large portions of hard drive space while performing certain functions. Check this first to see if it is an issue. Answer A is incorrect because RAM is not the easiest to check; however with some testing, you may determine this to be true. Answer B is incorrect because you should notice other problems with the server and in the log files if the hard disk is bad. Answer C is incorrect because the job configuration has not changed. For more information, see the "Checking disk space" section.

Scenarios

1. Because you have the resources, you should implement a three-tier multi-level support plan. There will be three levels of support, and problems would escalate to a higher level until they are resolved. You should also show management how the problems will escalate to each level and what each level is responsible for.

Using Diagnostic Tools

CHAPTER 16

EXAM OBJECTIVES

6.2 Use diagnostic hardware and software tools and utilities

- Identify common diagnostic tools across the following OS: Microsoft Windows NT/2000, Novell NetWare, UNIX, Linux, IBM OS/2

- Select the appropriate tool

- Use the selected tool effectively

- Replace defective hardware components as appropriate

- Identify defective FRU's and replace with correct part

- Use documentation from previous technician successfully

- Locate and effectively use hot tips (e.g., fixes, OS updates, E-support, web pages, CDs)

- Gather resources to get problem solved:

- Identify situations requiring call for assistance

- Acquire appropriate documentation

- Describe how to perform remote troubleshooting for a wake-on-LAN

- Describe how to perform remote troubleshooting for a remote alert

CHAPTER PRE-TEST

1. What are the advantages of having a software maintenance contract?

2. What is the purpose of a POST card?

3. Where is the best place to find current troubleshooting information for your system?

4. Why is it important to keep documentation from previous technicians?

5. What is an FRU?

6. Describe the purpose of wake-on-LAN technology.

7. What information is needed to order proper replacement hardware?

8. In what type of situation would you call a vendor for assistance?

9. What tools do you need to troubleshoot a problem remotely?

10. Why should a solved server problem be documented?

✦ Answers to these questions can be found at the end of the chapter. ✦

Trying to diagnose a hardware or software problem without proper diagnostic tools is often like trying to find a needle in a haystack. Obscure error codes, incomplete documentation, and intermittent symptoms, often make the task of diagnosing a server issue a difficult job. Fortunately, there are many diagnostic tools and resources you can use to diagnose a server problem accurately and efficiently, while minimizing downtime. This chapter first takes a look at various hardware and software diagnostic tools that can help you solve server problems.

If you are off-site, it can be very difficult to troubleshoot a problem without being in front of the failed server, but there are some remote access solutions that can help you fix a server without having to travel on-site. A section on remote troubleshooting details these various tools.

If you are unable to troubleshoot a problem through conventional means, you may need the help of the resources provided by your hardware or software vendor. This chapter takes a look at the different types of support your vendor may offer, and discusses what documentation to use under various circumstances.

Once you have narrowed down the problem, you may have to replace your hardware if it is defective. The chapter details the steps of identifying failed hardware devices, and how to properly and promptly obtain a replacement.

Finally, when your server issue has been fixed, you will need to document your solution, so that if the problem happens again in the future, you can look back and see the steps to take to fix it, while saving a lot of troubleshooting time.

Using the Right Tool

6.2 Use diagnostic hardware and software tools and utilities

- Select the appropriate tool
- Use the selected tool effectively

Depending on the server error you are experiencing, it may be difficult to determine whether the problem is with the hardware or software. For example, a bad memory module may result in several application errors in you network operating system. This may cause you to spend too much time trying to troubleshoot the operating system, when the problem is actually hardware-related.

When you encounter a problem that does not have an obvious origin, it is best to attack it from both ends, examining both your hardware and software until the problem can be narrowed down further.

Exam Tip   For the exam, read the question and answer choices carefully, to verify if the problem is with the hardware or software, and choose an appropriate answer.

To focus on the problem, you must examine the error messages you receive, and both your hardware and software error log files. You may find that the error that is causing your OS to crash is actually coming from the memory, and that your hardware logs contain several error messages that point to the problem.

Hardware diagnostic tools

There are many diagnostic tools dedicated to identifying hardware issues. They can be software programs that scan hardware systems, or actual physical devices that are hooked up directly with the server. They can give very specific and detailed information on the state of your hardware, compared to more general diagnostic tools. The following sections describe some of these tools.

Remote access cards

A *remote access card* is a special expansion board that is installed in an available slot in your server. The card is used to access the server from a remote location, even if the server is in a frozen state, or is powered off. It can be accessed by a direct modem line, or through the network with a LAN connection. Remote access cards are discussed in more detail in the "Remote Troubleshooting" section.

POST card

The power-on self test (POST) is a small diagnostic routine run by the BIOS of a server to check and inventory all critical components before starting the server. If your server fails to start because of a problem in the POST process, it can be very difficult to track down the failed component. Most BIOS vendors use a series of beeps to indicate different types of problems, but often they are difficult to interpret. Another problem with BIOS diagnostic routines is that they will halt on the first error encountered, and there maybe other errors later in the boot process.

Caution   In order for the POST diagnostic card to work properly, it must support your server's BIOS.

A POST card is an advanced hardware diagnostic tool used to help troubleshoot POST errors. To work properly, the card must support the type of BIOS that your server is running. The POST card plugs into an available expansion slot, and gives more advanced information on the boot process. The card will also detect more than one error, and will not halt after the first error is encountered. It displays error codes on an LED display built right on to the card. You can then look up the error code in the manual to determine which component has failed. Some advanced cards can also help troubleshoot IRQ and DMA resource conflicts.

Exam Tip For the exam, know how to use a POST diagnostic card. Remember that it does not need any type of boot disk; it will run on its own when the server starts.

Software diagnostic tools

There are many different software programs available that are used to diagnose hardware problems. Some come with the operating system, and some come from the vendor.

System diagnostic programs

For most operating systems, you can boot the system with a special diagnostic boot disk. The diagnostic program scans all aspects of your hardware. It tests the CPU, RAM, the video subsystem, hard drives, BIOS settings, parallel and serial ports, and many other system components. The program will notify you if there are any problems with the components. The most common problems detected by these types of programs are bad memory and failing hard drives.

Vendor-specific software tools

✦ Identify common diagnostic tools across the following OS: Microsoft Windows NT/2000, Novell NetWare, UNIX, Linux, IBM OS/2

Most hardware vendors have created their own tools created specifically for troubleshooting their own hardware configurations. These tools are either installed by default from the factory, or they may be installed optionally by the end user. I highly recommend that you install these diagnostic tools, because they are specific to your server, and can be extremely useful when diagnosing a hardware problem, or for proactive maintenance purposes.

These tools can monitor all aspects of your server, from internal components such as the motherboard, RAM, and the CPU, to storage systems such as hard disks and RAID arrays. They can warn you if a hardware component is starting to fail, even before the actual component has stopped working. This enables you to obtain a replacement part before the device actually fails, greatly minimizing downtime. The software is detailed enough to bring up the serial number of a component without you having to remove it from the server and physically examine it. This means that if you receive a warning that a hard drive is failing, you will not have to shut down the server to remove the drive, check the serial number and model information, and replace it again.

These tools are usually operating system dependent, so no matter with NOS you are running, you will still have the best diagnostic tools for your particular server Some examples of these types of diagnostic tools include Compaq Insight Manager, and IBM Netfinity Manager.

Troubleshooting Remotely

✦ Describe how to perform remote troubleshooting for a remote alert.

If a server fails during off-hours, it may be inconvenient for the technician to have to come back on-site to fix the problem, especially at 3 a.m. on a Sunday. Although you may have your servers and monitoring systems set up to notify you of any problems by pager, you still will need access to the server to fix the problem. To solve this problem, there are some excellent remote troubleshooting technologies that can be used to examine a server from an off-site location.

Remote access cards

A remote access card is a special server expansion board that enables you to connect to the server from an off-site location through a modem or a Web interface. The board is self-powered, and acts independently from the server hardware and software. The remote access card has several abilities to aid in checking and troubleshooting a remote server:

✦ **Remote access:** Using either a modem connection or using a LAN Web interface, a technician can remotely connect to the remote access card, regardless of the condition of the server. If the server has suffered a software crash or a hardware failure, the remote access card continues to function on its own power and processing capabilities. It is almost like a computer in a computer.

✦ **Alerting and error logs:** The remote access card can be set to handle alerting, by sending a message to a pager, or sending an SNMP trap to a network monitor. The card can also keep its own error log and alert history, which the technician can view at any time to help troubleshoot server issues.

✦ **Remote control and reset:** Using the special remote control and remote reset capabilities, you can get access to the server console to perform tasks just as if you were standing in front of the server. The remote reset ability enables a technician to reset the server. This is a very important and useful feature for when a server's network operating system has locked, and the only way to reset the server is to reboot it.

✦ **Battery backup:** The remote access contains its own battery that keeps it running in the event of a power outage. If a power supply has failed, you can still connect to the remote access card, and analyze hardware error logs to find out what time the server went down. If configured properly, you can also find out the model of the power supply and the part number to order a new one from the vendor without having to be on-site.

Wake-on-LAN

✦ Describe how to perform remote troubleshooting for a wake-on-LAN

A useful feature of new network cards and motherboards is the ability to turn on a computer remotely. Wake-on-LAN technology enables a computer to be powered on remotely by sending a special wake-up packet to the network card. The NIC card is connected to a special connector on the motherboard, which receives this signal and turns the computer on. This would rarely be used on a server, as a server should be on all the time, but if you are pushing software upgrades from a server to its client computers, such as virus signature updates, you don't have to be on-site, because the server can turn on the client computers as needed. The wake-on-LAN service starts the client PC's, performs the update, and shuts them down again. See Figure 16-1 for an example of how Wake-on-LAN works.

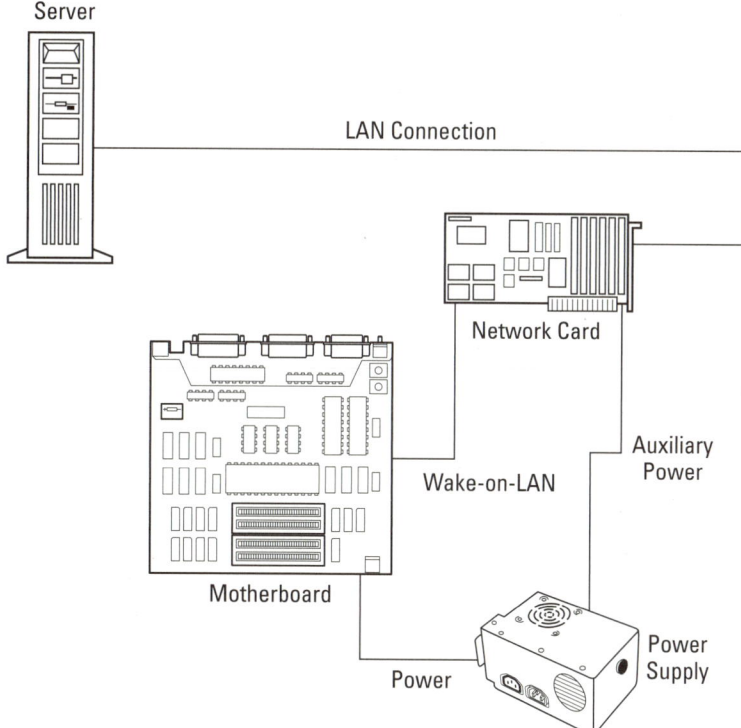

Figure 16-1: A network board is connected to both the motherboard and auxiliary power to enable the Wake-on-LAN service

Exam Tip   A wake-on-LAN card is not something you would use on a server, as your server should be running at all times. A wake-on-LAN card is made for client computers, so that they can be contacted by the server to be powered on for off-hours upgrades and updates.

Troubleshooting Resources

Objective

✦ Gather resources to get problem solved:

- Identify situations requiring call for assistance

- Acquire appropriate documentation

Whenever there is a software or hardware failure, there are a number of different resources you use to troubleshoot your problem. From your own resources, such as server documentation and previous troubleshooting problem reports, to vendor resources such as an online Internet-based knowledge databases, and phone and e-mail support, there is a wealth of information and services to help you fix your problem quickly and efficiently.

Server documentation

Objective

✦ Use documentation from previous technician successfully

You should have current documentation on all of your servers, with a full listing of each server's hardware and software configuration, and an account of any previous problems that have happened to the server. Knowing the current configuration is important, in case a problem with the server changes or deletes your current configuration. If you experience a hardware failure, you will have all the information on that part in your documentation to aid you in getting a replacement.

You should also keep any previous troubleshooting reports concerning server's hardware and software. If the same problem happens again, you can save a lot of troubleshooting time by going back to the documentation and perform the same procedures to fix it.

You have probably inherited old documentation from a previous technician. You must go through and compare the documentation with your current setup, and correct the documentation to reflect any changes.

In the Real World   Often, the documentation for most servers is out of date. You must be sure to update your documentation whenever you install new hardware or software, or change your configuration.

Using vendor resources

 ✦ Locate and effectively use hot tips (e.g., fixes, OS updates, E-support, web pages, CDs)

Most hardware and software vendors provide excellent documentation and troubleshooting tools for their products. The product itself usually comes with a user manual and diskettes on CD-ROM that contain documentation and product-specific troubleshooting tools. For the most current information and support for your product, you should go to the vendor's Web site.

Manual

The manual that comes with your hardware or software is usually the first place to look for troubleshooting information. Most manuals have a troubleshooting section at the end of the book for common problems. It may also list special codes and error messages in the appendices, which can be compared to the error message or code that your server is displaying.

Although there will be a list of common problems and their resolution, they are only as current as when the manual was printed. Any new issues discovered since the printing of the manual, will not be included, although they may sometimes be included separately as errata pages.

CD-ROM

The CD-ROM that comes with your hardware or software may contain important documentation regarding troubleshooting issues. Scan the `readme` files for any troubleshooting tips or pointers to online resources for the product. The CD-ROM may also contain special hardware or software diagnostic tools specific to the product.

The installation CD-ROM is not the best place to find the most up-to-date information. It only contains information up to the point when the CD-ROM was published. For the most current information, you should check the vendor's product Web site.

Web site

The best place to look for current technical support for your products is at the vendor's Web site. Before calling the vendor for technical support, which can be very costly, you should check the Web site for troubleshooting information and issue resolution. Any problems found with the product since its initial release may be detailed on the product support site.

Many vendors use a searchable *knowledgebase*, a database of any issue that has happened in the past and its resolution. This database can be searched by keywords, by product, or by date. A database of downloads is also usually available, so you can search for specific drivers and patches.

By entering a problem description, such as "hard drive failure," you can access technical documents related to hardware failures in your product. Use as many keywords as you can to narrow down your search. Entering too few words will result in hundreds of entries that will take too long sort through.

Exam Tip   The vendor's Web site will usually have the most recent information concerning error codes and problem solutions. The manual and CD-ROM will only have information current at the time the product was released.

Technical support

If you are unable to solve the problem yourself using all the tools at your disposal, you may have to contact the vendor's technical support. Often, you will have to make this call because of time constraints, or because of an emergency situation. For example, if the server in question is your e-mail server, you must get it fixed as soon as possible, because you are hampering your company's users ability to communicate with each other and the outside world. If it cannot be fixed in a reasonable amount of time, you should contact the vendor immediately. Vendors offer varying levels of support, which are discussed in the following sections.

Warranty support

If your equipment is still under warranty, you should have the highest priority support available. Depending on the level of your warranty, you should have at least coverage for one year, and preferably at least three years.

Maintenance contracts

Some companies also sell maintenance contracts, where you pay for a certain amount of support coverage for a varied period of time. For example, a lower-priced support contract may only support problems during normal business hours, and even then, they might only guarantee an answer in 24 hours. Other high priced contracts can cover you at all times, and can have a technician onsite within four hours. The type of contract you purchase for your system will depend on the importance of the server itself. If your server is a database server, supporting an around-the-clock call center, you will need prompt service that can be offered at all times. You would not want to wait 24 hours for a replacement part while your company's call center cannot work.

Tailor your support contract to your needs, and do not forget that both your hardware and your software need support from their respective vendors. If your e-mail server is down because of a software problem, and you only have a maintenance contract with the hardware vendor, you may have to be very high service fees to have the problem fixed.

Software support contacts are also available that offer free upgrades to a product when one is released. For example, you might have a Web application version 3.0, which has just had a major revision release to 3.1. The new version contains many bug fixes and functionality improvements, and will be sent to you automatically because of the maintenance agreement. If you do not have an agreement, you may have to purchase the upgrade, which could be very expensive, depending on the product.

Phone support

If you are unable to solve the problem yourself, or if the problem is an emergency situation, you will need to contact the vendor's technical support phone line. It is also a good idea to phone technical support when you are unsure of a patch or fix that you have obtained by yourself through the vendor's Web site, or through other troubleshooting resources. If the fix that you have implemented is the wrong one for your problem, you may damage your server even further.

Phone support can often be very frustrating, as you may have to wait almost an hour to be able to speak with a vendor technician. It is a good idea to call the vendor's technical support line early in your troubleshooting process, to allow for waiting times, and to get a head start on getting replacement parts if the problem is serious.

As part of your server documentation, you should have the vendor's technical support phone number. With your documentation, you should also keep any other identifying information, such as the hardware or software serial numbers of the product you are calling about. You should also have a customer number or maintenance contract number, if you have purchased such a contract. Having this information on hand will help speed up the call process, because the phone support representative can quickly get your basic company and product information.

Explain to the technician the basics of your problem, and the steps you have already taken to troubleshoot it. This should cut down your phone call time, as most of the basic steps that the technician will ask you to do will be already done. This is important, because you may be charged very high fees per minute while connected to technical phone support lines.

If the problem is very complex, and cannot be solved by the first-level technician, it may be escalated to a more experienced engineer. Take note of the case number for your call, especially if you get disconnected. If you call back with the proper case or ticket number, you can continue the call from where you left off, and you won't have to repeat the entire process. The second-level technician will use more advanced techniques to troubleshoot the problem, including the use of vendor specific diagnostic tools. Diagnostic utilities are important for remote troubleshooting, because they can give the technician a special error to identify a certain failed hardware part or software component.

If the problem still cannot be solved over the phone, the vendor may dispatch a technician to come on-site to examine the problem first-hand. Depending on the nature of the problem, and the suspected cause, the technician may bring spare equipment to perform a replacement. The vendor can only guess what hardware might need replacing, so they can only bring certain items with them. If the on-site technician did not bring the component that needs replacing, you will need to be order it. If the item is in stock, you may receive it within a few hours. If not, there may be a long delay.

E-mail support

Some vendors also offer support through e-mail, with which you can send a message to a technician detailing your problem. This type of communication should only be used for non-critical problems that can wait a few days before a resolution is needed. Typically, you should use this method if you are having configuration issues, or if the problem is very minor. Do not expect a reply back right away, as the mail queues for these types of services will be very long.

Replacing Hardware

✦ Replace defective hardware components as appropriate

✦ Identify defective FRU's and replace with correct part

Depending on the nature and seriousness of your problem, you may need to replace certain hardware parts. If you have already contacted the vendor's phone support about the problem, and they have identified that hardware part, they may ship a replacement part to you to replace yourself, or, depending on the support options you have paid for, a technician may come on-site to perform the replacement.

Some hardware problems can be very obvious, such as a blown power supply, or a failed hard drive. Others can be very hard to trace, such as motherboard components, or memory and processor faults. Once you have identified a failed hardware component as the culprit, you must be able to properly identify the model and serial number before obtaining a replacement.

Some components, such as hard drives, memory, and SCSI cards can look very similar but are completely different internally. Hardware can be identified by three main characteristics: a serial number, a model number, or a vendor part number.

The serial number of the hardware is the most useful method of identification. The serial number is always unique for each type of hardware, and offers a more accurate part referral than the model number. A model number is helpful, but there may be many subcategories of that hardware model that could be different and incompatible with others. For example, a certain model of SCSI card may be an Ultra-Wide controller, but a similar model might be a narrow version. It is possible the vendor has assigned their own part number to the device, which can be matched up with the correct replacement part in their database. These identification numbers will be located somewhere on the device itself, usually on the bottom or the back. You will probably have to remove the part from the server to be able to read the identification information.

A *Field Replacement Unit* (FRU) is a general term a vendor uses to identify hardware parts that can be easily replaced by swapping a failed part out with a new one. They are usually more common types of hardware, such as hard drives, memory, and expansion boards. These items can be easily replaced, because the only step is to remove the old component, and replace it with a new one. More complex hardware, such as a BIOS chip on a motherboard, cannot be replaced so easily without having to replace the entire motherboard. The vendor usually keeps a large stock of FRU components, so that they are available within a short period time to a user with a failed unit.

In the Real World You should double-check the hardware that you order from a vendor for replacement and verify that it is the proper hardware for your system. This is more easily accomplished by giving the vendor the serial number of the component. It is very common to receive the wrong type of part back from a vendor.

Documenting the Problem and Solution

After you have successfully fixed your problem, you should go back and document the problem thoroughly. This information will be invaluable in troubleshooting the problem if it happens again.

When creating your documentation, record the type of symptoms that were occurring as a result of the problem. Was it intermittent? Did it take down your server completely? What is hardware- or software-related? When you search your documentation, you will be looking up similar symptoms to your current problem, so the symptoms are the first information that should be listed on the document.

Detail the steps that were taken to fix the problem. Was it software- or hardware-related? Was it a configuration issue? Was it a hardware failure? What documentation was needed? Did you contact the vendor? You want to be able to easily follow the same steps in the future, so keep the instructions clear and concise.

If the problem was software-related, record the software version at the time of the problem. If you upgrade the program in the future, you will be able to tell if this problem affected an earlier version of the program. Write down any configuration settings for the software, including any changes that you made. If the configuration is wrong, you will be able to go back and know what the correct settings are.

If the problem was with a hardware device failure, take note of the serial number, model number, and vendor number if available. If the same part fails again, you will have all the information handy, without having to remove the device from the server to check the serial numbers.

Keep your notes handy in a folder or special binder. It is a good idea to have a separate binder or folder for each server, so that documentation can be found much quicker than having to search through folders containing items for all servers.

Key Point Summary

This chapter discussed several hardware and diagnostic tools. To aid you in troubleshooting your server issues, several vendor resources were discussed in detail. To fix your problem, various hardware replacement techniques and procedures were outlined. Finally, some advice for documenting your problem and its solution were given.

For the exam, troubleshooting questions often require more common sense and basic troubleshooting skills than anything else. Being aware of the various tools and resources will aid you knowing which one is best depending on the type of problem situation. Keep the following points in mind for the exam:

✦ Know how and when to use remote troubleshooting tools such as remote access cards and wake-on-LAN systems.

✦ Remote access cards operate independently from the server hardware and software, allowing you to connect to the card to perform server diagnostics.

✦ A wake-on-LAN card is not used in a server, but on client computers, so that the server can send them a signal to turn on for a software update.

✦ Know how to properly use a POST diagnostic card.

✦ Know the best place to get error codes for POST diagnostics and vendor diagnostic utilities. If the error is not in the manual, check the vendor's Web site.

✦ Know how to verify hardware information for obtaining a FRU.

✦ Document your problem and solution thoroughly.

✦   ✦   ✦

STUDY GUIDE

The Study Guide section provides you with the opportunity to test your knowledge about using diagnostic tools for troubleshooting. The Assessment Questions provide practice for the test, and the Scenarios provide practice with real situations. If you get any questions wrong, use the answers to determine the part of the chapter you should review before continuing.

Assessment Questions

1. What technology would enable a technician to remotely turn on a client PC?

    A. Modem

    B. RAS

    C. Remote access card

    D. Wake-on-LAN

2. A server will not boot properly. When it starts up, the server beeps twice and goes no further, without booting into the operating system. A technician is using a POST diagnostic adapter to troubleshoot the error, which seems to be POST related. What is the proper procedure for using a POST diagnostic card?

    A. Insert the card into an expansion slot, and boot the server using a diagnostic floppy disk.

    B. Insert the card into an expansion slot, and boot the server. Error codes will display on the POST card.

    C. Connect the POST device to the server's serial port. Information will be saved to a text file on the hard disk.

    D. Insert the card into an expansion slot, and note the error codes displayed on the card while the server is turned off.

3. A technician is using a vendor-specific hardware diagnostic tool to diagnose a problem with the hard drive subsystem. The tool is reporting an error code, but the technician is unable to find the code in the diagnostic tool's manual. What is the best place to check to find information on the error code?

    A. Vendor's Web site

    B. Installation CD-ROM

    C. E-mail the vendor's technical support

    D. Diagnostic tool `readme` file

4. A hardware error is preventing an e-mail server from booting. The error message displayed on the server console cannot be found in the server manual, or on the vendor's Web site. Management needs the server to be operational within one hour. What is the next step in troubleshooting the server?

    A. E-mail the vendor's technical support.

    B. Use a POST diagnostic card.

    C. Call the hardware vendor's technical support number.

    D. Call the NOS vendor's technical support number.

5. A network card is malfunctioning in a server. The card is still under warranty, and the technician is calling the vendor's technical support line to have it replaced. How can the technician verify with technical support that an identical card will be sent as a replacement?

    A. Give technical support the model number.

    B. Give technical support the serial number of the server.

    C. Give technical support the serial number of the network card.

    D. Give technical support the network card's speed and duplex settings.

6. On a Saturday night, a technician's pager goes off, notifying the technician that the file server's OS has crashed, and is in a locked state. The technician dials in to the server's remote access card to troubleshoot the problem. What is the best way to recover the server?

    A. Come on-site to examine the problem.

    B. Remotely reboot the server.

    C. Activate the wake-on-LAN feature.

    D. Connect to the server's console to reboot the server from the OS.

7. An external tape drive is not working properly. A series of lights are flashing on the front console of the drive, but the technician cannot decipher what they mean. Where should the technician first look to begin troubleshooting the problem?

    A. Check for error codes on the bottom of the tape drive.

    B. Install a POST diagnostic card on the server.

    C. Check the error codes on the OS vendor's Web site.

    D. Look up the error code in the tape drive's manual.

8. On a technician's first day with a company, one of the Web servers has crashed with an OS error. What should be the technician's first step in troubleshooting the problem?

    A. Examine the server documentation of the previous technician.

    B. Immediately call the server vendor's phone support.

    C. Examine the manual for the Web server.

    D. E-mail the OS vendor's technical support.

9. During a server's POST routine, a hardware error is observed. What is the best way to determine which Field Replacement Unit (FRU) to replace?

    A. Reboot the sever with a POST diagnostic card.

    B. Check the operating system's event logs.

    C. Find the POST error code in the server's documentation.

    D. Call the OS vendor's technical support line to help find the appropriate part.

10. A new server is being installed to provide an FTP server for a development workgroup. The server isn't needed until next week. The technician has started to install the operating system but is running into problems in its configuration. What should be done to troubleshoot the problem?

    A. Immediately call the OS vendor's support line with a level 1 emergency.

    B. E-mail the OS vendor's technical support with the configuration questions.

    C. Call the hardware vendor for a FRU.

    D. Reinstall the operating system.

11. A user is reporting a strange operating system error on his computer. You are unable to decipher the error message, and it does not appear in the OS manual. What is the next best resource to use to help troubleshoot the problem?

    A. Check the `readme` file on the installation disk.

    B. Enter the error into the vendor's Web knowledgebase.

    C. Call the vendor's technical support line, which charges $3.99 a minute.

    D. Check the manual for the computer's motherboard.

12. A technician wishes to upgrade the virus signatures on all 50 of his company's computers. It has to be done off-hours, to minimize downtime for the users. The technician would like to perform this install remotely, but many users turn their computers off before going home. What tool can best aid the technician in performing the update?

    A. Set the server to automatically update virus signatures using a scheduling program.

    B. The technician will have to be on-site to manually upgrade the computers.

    C. Use the PCs' Wake-on-LAN support to remotely start the PCs, perform the upgrade, and shut them down again.

    D. Set the server's Wake-on-LAN card to automatically start the virus update service.

13. A technician suspects that a server is having problems as a result of bad memory. The technician does not have a POST diagnostic card to test the server. What else can be done to help troubleshoot the problem?

    A. Boot the server with a software diagnostic utility disk.

    B. Run the NOS performance monitor tool.

    C. Examine the OS error event logs.

    D. Reboot the server, and pause the POST routine during the memory check.

14. A technician is logged in remotely to a server's remote access card. The server is having trouble running a Web server as a result of several operating system errors. The remote application log files do not show any hardware errors. What is the next step in troubleshooting the problem?

    A. Check the Web site for the server's hardware vendor.

    B. Examine the OS manual and documentation.

    C. Examine the local application's event logs.

    D. Restart the server remotely.

15. During a phone call to a hardware vendor's technical support line, you are cut off halfway through. What should you do next?

    A. Call the support line back and refer them to your case ticket number.

    B. Call the support line back and start again from the beginning.

    C. Try calling the OS vendor's technical support instead.

    D. Call the support line back and ask to speak to a second level engineer.

16. When looking up an OS software program on a vendor's technical support knowledgebase on Web, you are asked to download a hot fix file. What should be you next step in troubleshooting the problem?

   A. Download and install the hot fix file.

   B. Call the vendor's technical support and verify the hot fix.

   C. Boot the server with the hot fix boot disk.

   D. Look up the software error code in the OS manual.

17. A technician is using a POST diagnostic card to troubleshoot hardware errors during a server startup. However, the error codes displayed on the card do not match any error codes in the POST card's manual. Where should the technician check next to decipher the error code?

   A. Examine the NOS error event logs.

   B. Check the readme file on the diagnostic boot disk.

   C. Call the OS vendor's technical support line.

   D. Check the POST card vendor's Web site.

18. A server manufacturer has installed their own hardware self-diagnostic utilities on your server. While checking the error logs of the utility, the software lists an error code for one of your motherboard components. Where can this error code be checked to find out what it means?

   A. The diagnostic utility's manual

   B. The OS vendor's Web site

   C. The motherboard vendor's technical support phone line

   D. The NOS application logs

19. While off-site, you receive a call from a user that one of the servers has lost power. The server has a remote access card installed, but when you try to dial in by modem, you are unable to connect to the remote access card. What is the most likely cause of the problem?

   A. The card will not answer if no operating system is present.

   B. The remote access card was attached to the same power source as the server.

   C. The battery on the remote access card is dead.

   D. The remote access card is not plugged in to a UPS.

20. A hardware vendor's technical support has sent you a Field Replacement Unit (FRU) for your server's power supply. When you try to install it, you notice that it will not fit into the machine, and the connectors do not match up. What is the most likely cause of the problem?

    A. You need to consult the power supply's manual to install it properly.

    B. The wrong FRU part was delivered.

    C. The vendor sent you a better version of the same power supply.

    D. The motherboard needs to be replaced to support the power supply.

Scenarios

1. A critical database server has suffered a hardware failure. What steps should you take to troubleshoot the problem, keeping in mind that the amount of downtime has to be kept to a minimum?

2. A manager has asked you to take a look at an older server that has not been working for a long time. Because the department's budget has been cut, the manager cannot buy a new server to perform some simple reporting tasks, and would like to get the old server working. The server hangs on the POST routine, but there is no error message except for a single beep. What steps can you take to fix the server?

Answers to Chapter Questions

Chapter pre-test

1. Any software updates, patches, and upgrades will be automatically sent to you at no cost.

2. A POST card plugs into a computer's expansion slot to give detailed POST information during the server's boot-up routine.

3. The most current troubleshooting information for your system can be found at the vendor's Web site.

4. This documentation will help you troubleshoot future problems that might have happened before.

5. FRU stands for Field Replacement Unit, a hardware vendor's term for a hardware component that can be quickly replaced on-site with an identical part.

6. Wake-on-LAN technology enables a client PC to be turned on by signaling the computer's network card.

7. You should know the serial number, model number, and vendor part number before ordering a replacement part.

8. You should call the vendor's technical support when conventional trouble-shooting methods have not fixed a problem, or if the issue is an emergency.

9. You need access to a modem to be able to dial into a server's remote access card.

10. Documenting the solution will aid you in the future if the problem happens again.

Assessment questions

1. **D.** A Wake-on-LAN network card will allow a client PC to be remotely turned on by sending a signal to the network port. Answer A is incorrect because a modem will only let you dial in to a machine that is already turned on. Answer B is incorrect because Remote Access Services (RAS) only enables you to dial in to a machine. Answer C is incorrect because a remote access card cannot turn a server on. For more information, see the "Wake-on-LAN" section.

2. **B.** The POST card needs to be plugged into an available expansion slot, and then the server is rebooted. Errors codes will appear on the card's built-in display. Answer A is incorrect because there is no need for a diagnostic boot disk. Answer C is incorrect because a POST card plugs into an available expansion slot. Answer D is incorrect because the server must be turned on for the diagnostic card to read from the POST routine. For more information, see the "POST card" section.

3. **A.** The vendor's Web site is the best place to get the most current error codes. Answer B is incorrect because the CD-ROM will only have information current up to the release for the product. Answer C is incorrect because you can find the information more quickly by scanning the vendor's website. Answer D is incorrect because the readme file will only be as current as the release of the product. For more information, see the "Using vendor resources" section.

4. **C.** You must contact the hardware phone support line to get the server back on-line as soon as possible. Answer A is incorrect because waiting for an e-mail response might take a few days. Answer B is incorrect because using a diagnostic card will help find the problem, but you must contact the vendor anyway to get a replacement part. Answer D is incorrect because the problem is with the hardware, not the NOS. For more information, see the "Technical Support" section.

5. **C.** The vendor will be able to send an identical card if you give them the network card's serial number. Answer A is incorrect because there might be many different sub-versions of a model of network card. Answer B is incorrect because the serial number of the server will not help identify the right network card. Answer D is incorrect because this is not specific enough information for the vendor to identify the right card. For more information, see the "Replacing Hardware" section.

6. **B.** Because the OS is locked up, there is nothing that can be done other than to reset the server, and see if it boots up properly. Answer A is incorrect because there is no need to go on-site if the server can be remotely rebooted. Answer C is incorrect because a server should not be running a wake-on-LAN, which allows a device to be turned on remotely. Answer D is incorrect because the technician will not be able to connect to the server's console if the OS is locked. For more information, see the "Troubleshooting Remotely" section.

7. **D.** The error codes for the flashing lights can be found in the tape drive's manual. Answer A is incorrect because there is no error information printed on the bottom of a tape drive. Answer B is incorrect because a POST card will not be able to troubleshoot an external device. Answer C is incorrect because the error codes for the hardware device will not be found on the Web site for the OS. For more information, see the "Manual" section.

8. **A.** The previous technician's documentation should be examined to see if the same problem has happened in the past, and a solution was found. Answer B is incorrect because the server vendor will not be able to help with an OS software problem. Answer C is incorrect because the Web server manual will only list errors specific to the Web server software. Answer D is incorrect because it may take some time before receiving a reply from a vendor's e-mail support. For more information, see the "Server documentation" section.

9. **C.** If the POST error code is looked up in the documentation, it will indicate which hardware is malfunctioning. Answer A is incorrect because the hardware error indicated by the internal POST routine is sufficient to track down the problem. Answer B is incorrect because the OS event logs will not help, because the error occurs before the operating system is loaded. Answer D is incorrect because the OS vendor will not be able to help you in troubleshooting a hardware problem. For more information, see the "Hardware diagnostic tools" section.

10. **B.** Because the problem is not urgent, sending an e-mail to the OS vendor's technical support will usually get an answer in a day or two. Answer A is incorrect because this problem is not an emergency, and you may be charged a lot of money for the emergency response. Answer C is incorrect because the problem is with the OS software, not hardware. Answer D is incorrect because reinstalling the OS will not fix the configuration problem. For more information, see the "E-mail support" section.

11. **B.** By entering the error into the vendor's knowledgebase, you should be able to obtain technical documents related to that problem. Answer A is incorrect because the `readme` will only contain error information current at the time of the original release of the OS. Answer C is incorrect because the answer should be found using the free Web knowledgebase. Answer D is incorrect because the motherboard manual will not aid you with OS software errors. For more information, see the "Web site" section.

12. **C.** Using the Wake-on-LAN support on the computers, they can be remotely set to turn on, receive the update, and then shut down again. Answer A is incorrect because the scheduling program will not be able to update

computers that are turned off. Answer B is incorrect because there is no need for the technician to be on-site if the wake-on-LAN technology is used. Answer D is incorrect because the server should not have a wake-on-LAN card; the cards should be on the client computers. For more information, see the "Wake-on-LAN" section.

13. A. The software diagnostic disk will be able to scan the memory modules for errors. Answer B is incorrect because the performance monitoring tool will not be able to scan for hardware errors. Answer C is incorrect because the OS error logs will not show memory errors. Answer D is incorrect because pausing the POST routine during the error check will not aid in diagnosing the problem. For more information, see the "Software diagnostic tools" section.

14. C. The local application logs will contain any OS errors. Answer A is incorrect because the Web site for the hardware vendor will not contain any OS software related information. Answer B is incorrect because the technician will not access to the manuals while off-site. Answer D is incorrect because restarting the server will not permanently fix the OS errors. For more information, see the "Troubleshooting Remotely" section.

15. A. By giving the support staff the case ticket number, you can continue the call from where you left off, without having to start over. Answer B is incorrect because you will waste valuable time if you have to start explaining the problem from the beginning. Answer C is incorrect because the OS vendor will not be able to help you with a hardware problem. Answer D is incorrect because you will still have to explain the problem from the beginning, wasting valuable time. For more information, see the "Phone support" section.

16. B. Before installing any patch or hot fix, you should verify that the problem resolved by the hot fix is the one you are actually experiencing. Answer A is incorrect because the problem might be something else entirely if you haven't investigated further, and installing the hot fix may damage your system. Answer C is incorrect because the hot fix may be for a problem that is not the same as yours, since it wasn't verified with the vendor. Answer D is incorrect because the most current error information will be on the Web site. For more information, see the "Technical support" section.

17. D. The most current error codes will be listed on the vendor's Web site. Answer A is incorrect because the NOS error event logs will not help you with a hardware problem. Answer B is incorrect because there is no diagnostic boot disk with a POST card. Answer C is incorrect because the OS vendor's technical support will not help you solve a hardware problem. For more information, see the "POST card" section.

18. A. The diagnostic utility's manual will contain a listing of all of its error codes. Answer B is incorrect because the OS vendor's Web site will not help you with a hardware problem. Answer C is incorrect because the motherboard vendor will not know the server vendor's specific error codes. Answer D is incorrect because the NOS application logs will not list any hardware problems. For more information, see the "Manual" section.

19. C. The remote access card contains a battery that enables it to remain on during a power failure. Answer A is incorrect because the remote access card operates independently of the operating system. Answer B is incorrect because the remote access card uses its own battery for power. Answer D is incorrect because the remote access card uses its own battery for power. For more information, see the "Remote access cards" section.

20. B. The vendor has sent you the wrong part for your server. Answer A is incorrect because the power supply FRU should be identical to the one you already have. Answer C is incorrect because a FRU is identical to the part that is being replaced. Answer D is incorrect because the FRU should be identical to the original part, and be compatible with the host system. For more information, see the "Replacing Hardware" section.

Scenarios

1. You should reboot the server, so that you can check the POST routine or vendor hardware diagnostic utility for any errors. If you receive an error, check the server's manual to decipher the error code, to identify the failed hardware.

Once you have verified this information, or if you cannot troubleshoot any further, call the hardware vendor's phone support immediately, to help get the problem fixed while minimizing downtime. Depending on the type of maintenance agreement or level of support you have with the vendor, they will either send you a FRU, which will replace your failed component, or they will send a technician to do the replacement.

Depending on your level of support, you will have a replacement part within a few hours or longer, but there is no faster way of getting the problem fixed.

2. If the single beep in the POST routine does not properly identify the problem, even after checking the server manual for POST error messages, you should try booting the server with a POST diagnostic card.

Install the card into an available expansion slot, and reboot the server. The POST card will give more detailed error messages that you can examine in more detail by using the diagnostic utility's manual.

Once you have identified the failed hardware component, you will need to call the server manufacturer to see if they can get you a replacement. Because the server is fairly old, this might not be possible, and other upgrades may be necessary. If you give the vendor's support staff the serial number of the component, they will be able to track it down more easily.

Since the server is probably not under warranty anymore, you should give the server serial number to the vendor to verify this. If not, you will have to get the manager to authorize payment for the replacement part.

Disaster Recovery

As a systems administrator, you must have a disaster recovery documented and tested. How to create an effective disaster recovery plan is discussed in this Part. The uses of hot and cold sites are addressed, along with what you must know to implement a successful recovery if such a disaster occurs that renders your current network inoperable.

Losing the use of your systems for even a few days because of a natural disaster or even vandalism can damage your company's health. A business interruption can cause a company to lose market share, image, and credibility, can reduce customer satisfaction or brand value, and can strain relationships with suppliers and alliance partners. The chapters in this Part will teach you what you need to know to recover quickly if a disaster occurs.

Planning for Disaster Recovery

EXAM OBJECTIVES

7.1 Plan for disaster recovery

- Plan for redundancy (e.g., hard drives, power supplies, fans, NICs, processors, UPS)

- Use the concepts of fault tolerance/fault recovery to crate a disaster recovery plan

- Develop disaster recovery plan

- Confirm and use off site storage for backup

- Document and test disaster recovery plan regularly, and update as needed

7.2 Restoring

- Identify hot and cold sites

- Implement disaster recovery plan

CHAPTER PRE-TEST

1. List the common requirements of any disaster recovery plan.

2. Describe high availability as it relates to the server environment.

3. List some common types of natural disasters.

4. What are the human influences that can lead to a disaster?

5. In order to increase your systems up time and limit the amount of downtime you will want to ensure that your systems have a high rate of _____.

6. What are redundant NICs?

7. What is a hot site?

✦ Answers to these questions can be found at the end of the chapter. ✦

Disaster recovery is perhaps the most important and most challenging aspect of being a systems administrator. After a disaster occurs, you may find yourself in a completely different location, without the tools that you are comfortable with. It can be very difficult to try to restore a company's systems and data without a plan in place. The more accurate your document of the computer environment, the faster you can get the business back up and running. There are specific companies who specialize in providing "hot sites" for companies with mission-critical servers. These hot sites are a separate physical location that your company can use in a time of crisis. This will ensure that your company will have the systems available in the event of a disaster. Being prepared is essential to protecting your company in the event of a systems disaster.

Disasters can be a result of natural disasters such as earthquakes, floods, or hurricanes. More commonly, disasters are a result of human factors such as viruses, system outages, and sabotage by employees and non-employees. Preparation will minimize downtime, and enable the company to resume operations quickly.

Most companies are not prepared for a disaster because of barriers such as a lack of funding, underestimating the importance of disaster planning, and a lack of support from management. Companies need to do an assessment on how a disaster would impact the business.

Forming a Disaster Recovery Plan

7.1 Plan for disaster recovery

- Develop disaster recovery plan

The idea behind the disaster recovery plan (DRP) is to prepare your company for a potential disaster. The finished product is a document outlining the steps to take in the event of a disaster. Most important, you must have a viable backup method, which is discussed later in this chapter, and in Chapter 19, to implement a successful disaster recovery plan. A disaster recovery plan involves several phases before its completion. The following is a common approach to the disaster recovery planning process:

1. Risk analysis

2. Business impact analysis

3. Prioritizing applications

4. Recovery requirements

5. Document production

6. Testing the plan

Before you begin work on any disaster recovery plan, you should ask yourself these questions. Write down your answers, and then work on the weak spots. If your company does not have a plan in place, then review these questions, and use them as checklist.

1. Do you have a plan?

2. Has the plan been fully tested?

3. How did the test turn out?

4. Have you updated the plan since the test?

5. Has a cost analysis been performed to determine the cost of not having a plan in place?

6. Do you keep the plan current?

7. Are backups performed on a regular schedule?

8. Is there a detailed list of what is being backed up, especially mission-critical applications and data?

9. Do you have a service agreement for off-site tape storage?

10. Is the plan understood and supported throughout the various departments in the company?

11. Are the appropriate people committed to the plan?

12. Do you have the proper security in place: server room locked, UPS systems, and so forth?

13. Have you been given management support, and an appropriate budget to fulfill the plan?

14. Does the plan include backup and archive procedures?

Exam Tip   After reviewing your disaster recovery plan, you should be able to identify the weaknesses in the current plan and correct them.

The disaster recovery team

The purpose of the disaster recovery team is to establish and direct plans of action to be followed during an interruption or cessation of computer services caused by a disaster or lesser emergency. The disaster recovery team maintains readiness for emergencies by means of the disaster recovery plan. The team is also responsible for managing the disaster recovery activities following a disaster and can be thought of as the disaster management team. Through the disaster, the team will provide for the safety of personnel, the protection of property, and the continuation of business.

The disaster recovery team consists of a team leader or emergency coordinator, an alternate emergency coordinator, action team leaders, and any other designated individuals. The responsibilities of individuals assigned to the team are in addition to their regular duties and are assigned on the basis of familiarity and competence in their respected areas or specialties. The team leader and the alternate emergency coordinator administer the plan itself. Action teams are used to facilitate the response to various types of emergency situations.

Risk analysis

A risk analysis will incorporate all of the components of your LAN that could be destroyed, whether it is lost connections, computers, or data. In order to find potential threats, you must know what to protect. This usually involves a detailed breakdown of business operations. You begin by analyzing exactly how your company produces its product or service. This seems tedious, but it is vital to analyzing the risk of what a potential catastrophe can do to your business. A risk analysis will bring undesirable outcomes to light, measure the impact on the operations of the company, and estimate any potential loss whether it is in lost revenue or market segment. To aid you in determining the different pieces of computer equipment that are vital to the computer environment, a diagram of all the pieces of your network should be created so that you have an inventory of all the items that you might have to replace after a disaster. This includes all relevant software products as well. Doing an inventory can be much simpler if you invest in software that can analyze your network and automatically inventory the different devices and the software on the servers and workstations. An excellent software package for performing a computerized inventory is Track-It by BlueOcean Software, Inc., which can be found at `www.blueocean.com`. If you miss something in your inventory, you could be looking at a failure when you try to restore your network after a disaster. Do not forget to note the less obvious things like modem cables or network cables; forgetting these pieces could result in unwelcome delays.

Remember that during a disaster, almost anything can go wrong, so you should therefore plan for all possible scenarios. Natural disasters can happen almost anywhere. Flooding can happen from too much rainfall, or when snow melts rapidly, or even from sprinkler systems. These and other disasters are discussed in greater detail later in this chapter. In any event, you must plan for ways to access your network in case you are unable to get into your building for whatever reason. For example, a chemical spill may prevent you from getting to your building, even though it may not be affected by the spill.

The likelihood of a disaster occurring may be greater than you think. However, to accurately assess this you have to take into account your geographic location and the typical weather scenarios that may contribute to a disaster. For example, you may live in a high earthquake zone, or an area that experiences annual flooding. The following list contains the most common types of business outages and the frequency at which they occur:

✦ Power outages account for 28%

✦ Water damage accounts for 27%

✦ Hardware failure accounts for 15%

✦ Earthquakes account for 11%

✦ Fire accounts for 9%

✦ Hurricanes account for 4%

✦ Building damage accounts for 4%

✦ Corrupt data accounts for 2%

Business Impact Analysis

Vital to any plan is understanding which functions of the business are critical to the company's successful operation. In order to understand this you should perform a Business Impact Analysis (BIA). This process will expose your weaknesses and strength, thus allowing you to take corrective measures.

A BIA looks at the loss of revenue, customer service, and legal liabilities. This assessment lets you know exactly what it will cost if your company is non-operational for any length of time. The BIA defines critical, necessary, and non-essential functions for your business. It also identifies techniques that you can use to recover from the disaster. It identifies critical functions, and the priority in which they should be recovered. It also identifies which functions rely on other functions so that you can set a recovery timeline. This will enable you to determine what must be done immediately following a disaster, and what can wait.

A Business Impact Analysis answers the following questions:

1. What is the cost in lost dollars, market share, and customer loyalty you can expect if the company suffers a disaster? Can the company recover their receivables if the accounts receivable records are destroyed?

2. How should you prioritize your recovery options following a disaster (What has to be recovered first, second, and so on)?

3. How soon do you need to get up and running?

4. How much can the company afford in lost revenue?

The disaster recovery team leader's role during the Business Impact Analysis is:

1. Identify organization functions.

2. Identify key personnel for the business functions (Finance, Operations, Marketing, and so on).

3. Define the critical business functions.

4. Involve management to gain support and approval.

5. Coordinate the analysis process.

6. Identify which functions are dependent on other business functions.

7. Define recovery objectives and timelines (recovery times, losses, and critical business function priorities).

8. Identify information requirements.

9. Identify resources needed.

10. Develop the format of the report.

11. Prepare the plan and present it to key management for final approval.

Prioritizing applications

After a disaster, when you are starting to piece your network back together, your need to know which applications to restore first. As mentioned in the previous section, you should restore your mission-critical applications first. Your company may have several applications that fall into this category. Keep in mind that everyone will want their applications restored first, and they will try to convince you that their applications are the most important. If your company uses Enterprise Resource Planning (ERP) software, your task of choosing what should be restored first becomes much clearer. Typically, the individual parts of ERP programs make up one large program, meaning you would have to restore the entire ERP software in order for anything to run. Obviously, this has the benefits of being easier to restore, and the only real drawback is that everyone waits until the entire program is restored. The BIA should determine which particular program comes first. However, if your company did not invest in a BIA, you will need to sit with management and personnel to determine the most logical order in which to restore the applications.

All departments must accept the application prioritization process, and everyone must adhere to the prioritized list of applications. You must ensure that department heads have signed off on the list.

Tip Don't forget the details! This means that printers, fax machines, and e-mail will most likely be a priority for sending and receiving information.

Lay the foundation first

Many administrators set out to re-create their entire network all in one shot, instead of setting a priority as to who needs what first. Just because you had 80 workstations before to the disaster does not mean that you should concentrate your efforts on rebuilding all of them. Rather, what you should do is setup the minimal amount of workstations to get the company functioning. Perhaps one workstation per department or business section is all that is necessary.

An important thing to remember when prioritizing applications is that you do not need to restore the entire server. Only restore what is necessary to get the mission-critical applications running. This will allow you to get the system up and running faster, and will allow you to concentrate on what is really important, getting the applications running. Make sure that department heads inform their employees of this process, so that you do not have to waste time dealing with user requests of this nature.

Know where the data is

In order to restore the priority applications first, you will need to know where all the data is, and any dependencies there might be. There may be system files such as INIs and DLLs that need to be restored in order for the applications to work properly. Make sure you are completely familiar with your backup up system and software or this may become more challenging than it already is. Having the proper media rotation schedule will make this process easier.

Restoring data is the focus of Chapter 19.

Recovery requirements

Recovery requirements are a crucial part of the plan, and you must determine an acceptable and realistic amount of time to recover the systems and the network. As mentioned previously, you need to get the most important applications and systems running first. Some refer to this as the trickle approach, because you only recover exactly what you need to operate, and then recover everything else when your company is at comfortable operation level.

You must give yourself ample time, and not be unrealistic when planning your recovery. It will be extremely difficult to perform your recovery duties if you promise the impossible. People will undoubtedly complain, and the company may lose confidence in your abilities to recover the systems. A good systems administrator will always plan for the worst, and think about potential roadblocks in the recovery. Taking this into account, you can add extra time to your recovery plan. Some experts say that whatever your initial recovery timeline is, double it. If things go smoothly, great, things will be accomplished ahead of schedule. If things do not go as planned, and you accounted for these scenarios, the system will still be recovered within the timeline.

The recovery plan has to be tested to ensure that your goals are met, and are attainable by you and others in the company. In the event that you are unavailable to perform the recovery yourself, some will have to step in and perform the recovery. This is why it is essential that the recovery is fully tested, so that you have real statistics to add to your recovery document.

Management needs to work closely with IS staff to develop the recovery requirements. Do not forget that applications are different in nature, and so are their recovery times. You may have two servers and an AS400 mainframe in your company, and how you prioritized your critical applications will determine the recovery times of each system. For example, suppose the AS400 houses all the data, so it will get restored first. Server One may be the application server that contains the ERP software that connects to the AS400 and the workstations. Server Two might be a file server and e-mail server, so it is recovered last.

Tip While determining the recovery time, include the time it will take to get the tapes from off-site storage facilities. Also include the time it will take to cut purchase orders and receive new equipment.

The disaster recovery document

The disaster recovery document must be so precise and detailed that anyone can follow it. Achieving this will take a large effort on the part of several key people in your organization. The great thing about creating this document is that it provides a comforting reassurance that in the event of a disaster you have the necessary document in place to rebuild the company. It is also a great opportunity to learn the many aspects of your systems.

Exam Tip Have a hard copy of the plan kept both at your location and at an off-site location, because it is probably the most important documentation that you have.

Every disaster recovery document should contain the following information.

✦ Notification lists

✦ Phone numbers of employees, data recovery agencies, and hardware and software vendors

✦ Maps to alternate locations, and their addresses

✦ Purchasing information

✦ Network diagrams

✦ Systems configurations, and tape backups and the methods used

✦ Application priorities

✦ Restoration procedures

You must focus on the priorities you have previously established when responding to a disaster. Time is against you and you must start rebuilding your network as fast as possible, restoring the mission critical applications in the priority that you have previously defined. All personal must be given clear direction and responsibilities. You must also document the relationship between tasks, so you can identify any problems as they arise. Last but not least, you must have detailed operations and tasks showing precise installation and recovery operations. These must be very easy to read and follow so that nothing is overlooked or missed.

Make sure you know how to issue a purchase order as this will save you a lot of time when ordering replacement equipment. Make sure that your inventory list also has the make, model and serial number of all hardware equipment, including phone numbers of the vendors. It is probably best to have copies of the original invoices in your disaster recovery plan. This will make it much easier when trying to order a replacement.

Having up-to-date and accurate network diagrams is obviously very important. Not only will this help you to reconstruct your network, but they will also let you know how much network cable you will need after the disaster, should it be destroyed. This is also an advantage when hiring contractors to lay the cable, because they can look at your wiring diagram to determine what is needed, and will be able to get the job done much quicker than you could.

The disaster recovery team leader is responsible for keeping the plan up to date. This person should periodically review and evaluate the plan to ensure all contingency site procedures have been adequately considered and prepared. This means that this person will be responsible for ensuring that he document is up to date, and includes any new equipment, personnel changes, and so on. The plan should be reviewed semi-annually to ensure its accuracy.

Types of Disasters

Disasters come in many forms, but all can be disruptive to a business. They may only affect a particular person, or they may affect the entire company. Some disasters may even force the company to close its doors forever. Viruses, hackers, hardware or software failures can impair the operations of your systems environment, and even destroy your data. Natural disasters such as tornadoes, earthquakes, flooding, and even hurricanes may completely destroy the company's physical location.

Natural disasters

Natural disasters are usually the most devastating because they not only destroy the LAN environment, but they sometimes also destroy part or all of the building. The most common types of natural disasters are fire, water damage, flooding, earthquakes, tornadoes, and hurricanes. The only way you can truly protect yourself from data loss is to ensure you have a good backup plan, and that the backup media are verified and are stored at a reputable off-site agency. You may choose to use an off-site company in the same city or town as your company, or one that is 50 to 100 miles away. Regardless of this, you must ensure that they provide a safe building to keep your backup media. There is more about choosing an off-site agency later in this chapter. The company can always rebuild or relocate to a new building. They can also purchase new office furniture, equipment, computer hardware, and software, but there is now way to replace the years of customer and financial data. Make sure you secure it properly as this data can sometimes make or break a company.

Human error

Human error can consist of accidental file deletion, crashing a server while adding new hardware, or tripping in the computer room and knocking over one of the servers. These types of incidents are actually quite common, and the only thing that prevents these from being full-blown disasters is the integrity of your backups.

Vandalism and sabotage

Vandalism is particularly devastating because it is senseless, and almost impossible to predict. Typically, vandalism is in the form of a fire or theft. A fire can result in damage on several different levels. First, the fire itself could destroy the entire building, including all the computer hardware, or perhaps just a few of the servers in the computer. Second, the sprinkler systems would more than likely damage any electrical equipping including your users' workstations. If the server room is equipped with regular water-based sprinkler systems instead of a dry sprinkler systems or special fire abatement systems specifically designed for computer rooms, the damage from the water alone would be enough to cripple the computer equipment. Third, the fire department will be using water to extinguish the fire, which will also result in increased water damage.

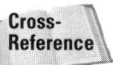

See Chapter 14 for more information about fire and your server room.

Theft can occur either by a person stealing hardware, software, or both. If someone breaks into your computer room and steals your servers, you will have to implement part of your disaster recovery plan to purchase new systems and restore them to their previous working state from the last good backups. Do not underestimate the employees in your company either. Leaving the server room unlocked is sometimes all the incentive a likely thief needs. We recommend that you incorporate the use of combination locks, swipe cards, or keys. Key locks are probably the worst of the three because people tend to lose keys, and they can be duplicated. Combination locks are good only if you do not give the combination out to everyone who wants entry. Electronic swipe cards are probably the best, because you can track who went into the room, and at what time they went in. You can also assign temporary cards for people, such as air conditioning repair technicians who need access to the room on a specific day.

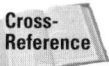

See Chapter 13 for more information about security measures.

Sabotage usually is the result of a disgruntled employee seeking some sort of restitution from the company. These people could delete important company files, corrupt files by inputting false data, or worse. Having proper security, and tape backups can help limit the damage.

Logic bombs are a typical device used by disgruntled employees. Logic bombs are just software programs, and are triggered by a timing device and can cause severe damage to your computer systems. The activation timer is usually a specific date, or perhaps a specific event that occurs on the system. For example, after a specific job runs each night, the logic bomb might be triggered to delete data on your systems.

Hackers

Hackers in the truest sense of the word are a special breed of people who devote all their energy to trying to unlock the proverbial door. Most true hackers follow some sort of ethical code that prevents them from doing any real damage to the systems they break into. In fact, some hackers will even inform you of their discoveries and let you know where you need to improve your system security. Regardless of their ethics, this practice is still considered a crime by most governments. However, there are those that are not so ethical, and when they have accomplished the task of breaking in, they do not stop. They will try to search for important documents and copy them onto their systems. If the information that they steal is valuable enough, they may even fetch a hefty price for it. Do not underestimate your competition's ability to cross the line and hire hackers to get into your systems and steal confidential documents. Some companies will stop at nothing to gain the upper hand, even if it means breaking the law. There are also hackers that enjoy breaking in and wreaking havoc on your computer environment. They will tamper with, erase, and destroy information that is vital to the company, the system operating system, or both. Either way, the damage will definitely result in many hours of work as you restore deleted files, or an entire system.

Most hackers use what is known as the *brute force method*. This method is the art of trying to break into a system by trying different passwords. They will keep trying until they eventually break the password, and eventually it will work. The problem for the hacker is that this can be very time consuming; the problem for the administrator is that most user passwords are easy to figure out.

In the Real World

Recently I downloaded some software that was sold for the purpose of recovering forgotten passwords. However, I doubt that is what most people are using it for, so I tried it on my system. Within minutes, this software had cracked a substantial amount of the user's passwords. About five hours later, it had cracked almost every password on the system except for the administrator's, but eventually this one was cracked as well. Instruct your users on the use of proper passwords, and stay on top of current hacking technologies.

The other method that hackers use is referred to as *social engineering*. This means that the hacker will trick the users into revealing vital information to them. This can be done very easily in large companies when a typical user will not know one systems specialist form the other. For example, a hacker may call a user, pretending to be a systems specialist, and ask the user for his user ID and password. The user assumes that the request is authentic, and provides the information.

The only way you can prevent this form of hacking is to have the proper policies in place prior to the incident. All users should be informed that they are not to give their passwords out to anyone under any circumstances. They should be made aware of the fact that the IS department would not ask a user for his or her password. The technician would temporarily change the user's password, and would notify the user of the change. The user would be required to change his or her password at the next logon.

Hackers commonly use two types of programs that are usually thought of as viruses, but they are actually destructive programs designed to cause damage on your systems: Trojan horses and worms. Many hackers use these programs for various reasons, but it usually just because they want to cause damage to your systems.

Worms are programs that infiltrate your programs and destroy your data. Worms do not replicate themselves like viruses do and, therefore, are not as serious in the sense that you have to worry that every system might be infected. However, just because a worm is not a virus does not mean that it is not destructive. A worm can be designed to tap into your system and destroy all the files. Destroying a worm is typically easier than destroying a virus because you should only have to seek out one copy of the program.

Trojan horses are programs of a very destructive nature that are typically hidden in another piece of software. In fact, other viruses have been discovered inside of Trojan horses. Trojan horses, like worms, do not spread themselves to other computers. The idea behind a Trojan Horse is that the hacker takes an attractive and tempting piece of software and places a malicious program inside of it. The unsuspecting user will download and install the software they wanted, and then the Trojan horse will be unleashed on to the user's system. There have been a variety of uses for Trojan Horses to date, from simple programs that delete files on the users system, to ones that tap into mainframe computers and embezzle money.

Viruses

Computer viruses are programs that typically replicate themselves, attach to other programs, and perform hidden and often malicious actions. The self-replication is what distinguishes viruses from other damaging programs. Viruses can be destructive to productivity as well as data. Some viruses only interrupt users with annoying messages, while others delete information from hard drives. No matter what the virus actually does, it wastes valuable time and money in resources as the I.S. person attempts to clean the infected files. For a virus programmer to consider a virus successful, it needs to be undetected for a sustained period of time. This way it can propagate from one file to the next and typically from one computer to the next. Typical signs that a virus might be present are:

+ Files missing or corrupt

+ Disk space decreases suddenly

+ System is slower

+ Unusual messages keep displaying

Planning for Redundancy

+ Plan for redundancy (e.g., hard drives, power supplies, fans, NICs, processors, UPS)

Redundancy is a key component in making your network stable and reliable. You need to plan your redundancy strategy the same as you plan any other part of disaster recovery. Making your systems reliable is a calumniation of hardware, software, design, and planning. The problem for most administrators is after the initial network is installed, everything after that is not very well planned or documented. This is usually attributed to the time constraints and sometime lack of expertise. An hour of planning can save may hours of aggravation if something goes wrong.

You should ensure that employees are cross-trained on the various systems in your company. In the event that an employee is hurt during a disaster, having other people that are capable of filling in will help reduce the impact of having that person unavailable while trying to recover from the disaster. At a minimum, you should have copies of the manuals and procedures for your mission-critical applications stored at an off-site facility.

Hard drives

Disk drives have become increasingly more reliable, but they still can fail, and you need to be prepared to face that challenge. Disk mirroring, duplexing and RAID are the most common methods of disk fault tolerance. If you have not implemented RAID on your servers, you should. Redundant disk drives enable the system to keep operating if one drive fails. These systems work well, and are relatively inexpensive compared to the time it would take to get a new server up and running if the hard disk failed.

Cross-Reference   RAID is extensively discussed in Chapter 4 and Chapter 18.

External hard drives have bigger advantages over internal drives in a couple of areas. First of all, an external drive system can be moved or replaced without taking apart the server. Secondly, they provide easier server redundancy. If a backup server is configured properly, you can very easily replace a defective server in minutes. You would just need to unplug the disk systems, and plug them in to the backup server. At most, you may lose a little bit of data, but this can be found on your media backups.

You should also keep idle spares to replace a hard drive at moments notice. The idle spare should be the exact same as the original drive, making it easier to set up if you need it.

Along with redundant drives, you may want to use redundant I/O controllers. This is usually referred to as *duplexing*. The extra controller eliminates the server's disk controller as a single failure point. Redundant controllers also increase the disk read performance of the system.

Power supplies

You should always use dual power supplies in servers or other high-end computers, especially if they are critical to the operation of your company. Dual power supplies balance the load by simultaneously supplying power throughout the system. If one of the power supplies fails, the other one will take the full load of the system until you can get a replacement. Before purchasing the server, make sure that one power supply can accommodate the full load of the system on its own, or this feature will be useless. Figure 17-1 shows dual power supplies in action. The system on the right has one power supply connected to the motherboard, and one connected to the hard drive. If either one of these power supplies fails, the system will not work. The system on the left has two power supplies connected to the entire system. Either one can fail, and the backup will run the system until the faulty power supply can be replaced.

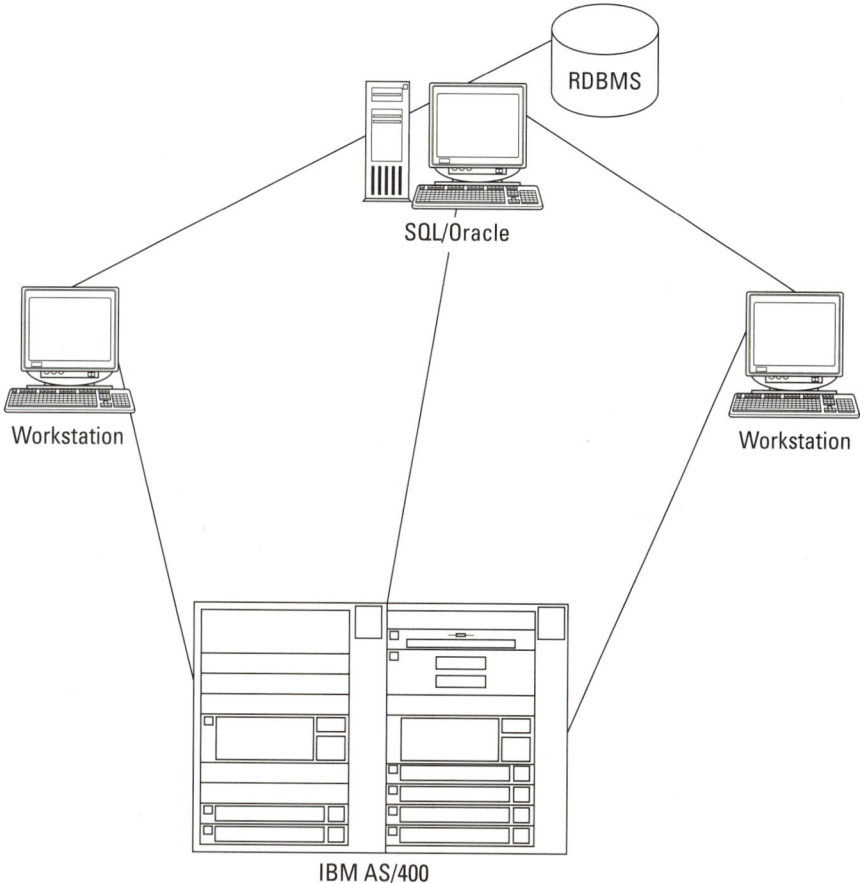

Figure 17-1: On the left, a system with dual power supplies; on the right, a system with two power supplies connected to separate components

Network Interface Cards

Some server operating systems can support redundant network cards (NICs). Having multiple NICs will provide fault tolerance and will load-balance the network traffic. For the fault tolerance to work, each NIC must be connected to a different switch. That way, if one of the switches fails, the server will not lose network access. If you have multiple network cards it is best to connect them to separate switches in the even that one switch fails. You should also use high-speed network cards (typically 100Mbps) to provide the fastest performance for your network. Your switches must also accommodate the same speed in order for this to be useful. You should also keep identical replacement network cards for each server in case one of the network cards in one of your servers should fail. Figure 17-2 shows a server with redundant network cards, each connected to a separate switch.

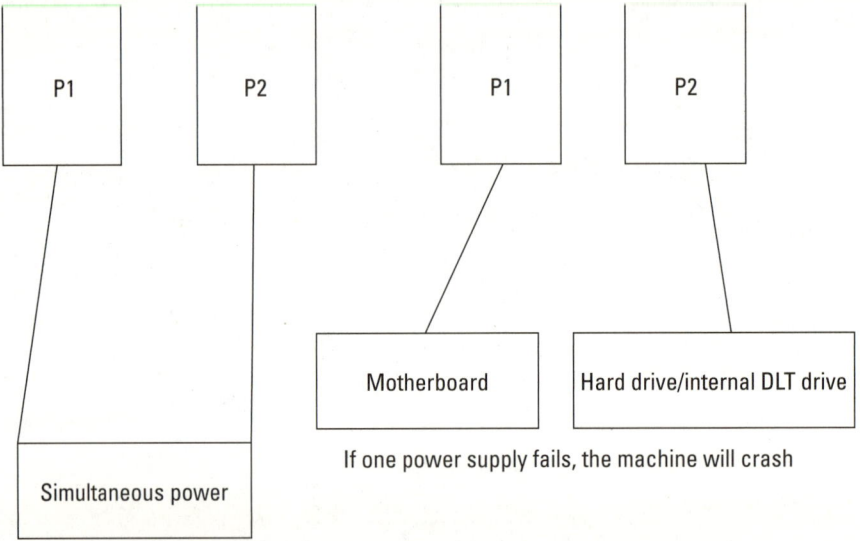

Figure 17-2: Server with two network cards, each on its own switch

Processors

Typically, server processors do not fail, but it can happen. Having redundant processors can save you a lot of time if original one fails. A redundant CPU tracks the operations of the primary CPU, but without interfering. If the primary CPU fails, the secondary CPU should be able to take over the system based on the information tracked in its internal memory.

Symmetric multiprocessing servers use multiple CPUs to divide the work between the processors and provide a degree of fault tolerance. If one CPU fails, the system can run on the other processor. However, multiple CPUs in these situations are more for performance then fault tolerance. This form of multiprocessing relies on the OS to manage memory between tasks running on the processors. A failed CPU can often result in a system crash in this type of setup, because the process that crashed the first CPU will most likely crash the second one.

Asymmetric multiprocessing systems take a different approach to multiprocessing than symmetric. In this design, CPUs have specific tasks assigned to them. In most cases, one CPU will handle I/O operations and the other executes the programs. If either CPU fails in this situation, the system will crash.

Tape backup system

Ensure that you have a working tape backup system, and if possible keep an exact spare system, including cables, SCSI adapters, and device drivers at an off-site location. This will definitely help speed things up should the tape device be damaged as well. If you end up purchasing a new tape backup system, make sure the spare one is updated as well, or it may be incompatible with the new tape media, which would make it absolutely useless. You should also verify that your backups are good by restoring data from backup tapes periodically.

UPS

A UPS is one of the most important pieces of equipment in the server room. If there is a power failure, a UPS can safely keep your servers on-line for an extended period of time. This will also enable you to shut down the servers cleanly, and prevent any damage. The UPS will also protect your systems from brownouts or sags. Brownouts can affect computer systems, causing electrical components to fail after repeated occurrences. To ensure that your UPS can handle the power requirements of your servers, you should first determine the battery capacity that you need in order to meet your power requirements. The best thing to do is to make a list of all the equipment that the UPS will handle, and then determine the power consumption of each. You will then be able to correctly choose the right UPS configuration.

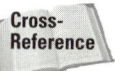
Cross-Reference   UPS systems are discussed in detail in Chapters 1 and 2.

Part of your duties will require you to test the UPS batteries several times per year. Doing this will ensure that the UPS is sustaining a full charge, and that you will not have any surprises should you have a power failure. Most UPS systems come with software that enables you to check system events, and to determine the current condition of the unit. The software also enables you to simulate a power failure so you can test the UPS devices. Be sure to perform these tests when you will not disrupt any of the users on the network.

Ensuring Service

✦ Identify hot and cold sites

If a disaster strikes and your building is destroyed, including all your computer hardware, you can resume business in a relatively short period of time with hot site or cold site services.

Hot site

A *hot site* is a location that offers backup computing resources. Many companies specialize in providing hot site services. A hot site should have the same hardware and network environment that is compatible with your company's computer environment. These sites typically provide an enhanced environment that is protected against most natural disasters and they should have backup power available so that you are not dependent on the power provided by the local utilities company. This will allow you to restore your environment, and set up a temporary network between the hot site and your home site to restore operations. This is the quickest way to restore operations, but it is also the most expensive. Ideally, the hot site is located less than 30 miles away from your company, so that employees can get there easily. It is very important to know exactly what you will need when you establish a hot site contract, because most service providers will not allow you to change your requirements when disaster strikes, well at least not without a hefty fee.

Hot sites are the best choice for insuring availability of your data, and typically offer:

✦ Use of recovery center

✦ Support staff on hand to assist you

✦ Duplicate systems

✦ Configured systems transported to your company's site

✦ Shipping of replacement equipment for anything that has been lost

✦ Work group spaces equipped with furnishings

✦ Workstations and printers

✦ Call management center

✦ WAN links redirected to the hot site

Cold site

A *cold site* has all the appropriate power requirements, network requirements, and floor space to install the hardware and to enable you to recreate your computer environment, but does not provide the actual equipment. Many of the same companies that provide hot sites also provide cold sites. These facilities provided by the companies will be comparable to their hot site facilities, but they will not include the running systems and network equipment. It may be reasonable for your company to consider creating its own cold site if your company has floor space available in a different location from the home site. Cold sites are far less expensive than hot sites, but because you have to purchase or move equipment, and software to recreate your environment, they will require a significantly longer outage before operations can be restored. Most cold site services will include:

✦ Off-site/off-line storage of backup media

✦ Replacement servers for mission critical operations at an added cost

✦ May provide help desk assistance

✦ Alternate location for storage of data

Backup Plan

✦ Confirm and use off site storage for backup

The first part of any backup plan is to ensure you have adequate backups and off-site storage facilities to store the backups. What is backed up, and how often, should be determined by management and the appropriate employees. Minimally, you should backup your servers daily and perform weekly or monthly backups for high end workstations. The methods you employ for performing these backups will be determined based on the time and data constraints you have. These strategies are discussed in greater detail in chapter 19.

One of the most significant factors in a backup plan is where to keep the media. Many smaller companies keep the daily backups at the network administrator's house, hopefully in a fireproof safe. However, this is not realistic for a larger company. Ideally, tapes that cannot be rotated off-site should be locked away in a fireproof safe in a safe part of the building, such as the server room. The weekly and monthly tapes are typically stored at an off-site agency. The off-site agency must ensure that they can protect your vital data, and you should ensure that they have a disaster recovery plan of their own. If they do not, look elsewhere for a reputable company that is qualified to protect you data.

As the administrator, you must ensure that you know where the media is kept, and any hazards that may be encounter during its transit. Look for agencies that do not advertise their business on company vehicles. It would be an easy target for thieves whom could steal the data and sell it to your competitors. You must also ensure that you completely document the backup plan and label all media accordingly.

Testing the Disaster Recovery Plan

   ✦ Document and test disaster recovery plan regularly, and update as needed

  ✦ Implement disaster recovery plan

The final step in creating your disaster recovery plan is to test it. It is almost impossible to simulate a realistic test that will not disrupt the operation of your organization. However, you can perform tests that can give you a reasonable idea of what you can expect under certain circumstances. There are also a wide variety of companies that can help you simulate disaster recovery scenarios. Whatever test you choose, you must establish measurable objectives for the test to be effective. You should try to define exactly what you are trying to accomplish with the test, because if you cannot determine the result, you cannot determine if the test is successful. For example, a good objective would be to determine if you can install the system's operating system, backup software, and hardware, and recover that data at a recovery site.

You must have well-documented, step-by-step procedures in order to accomplish this. If you do not, you will not be able to identify if the testing is going according to plan. You should also keep the tests relatively simple even though and actual disaster could be very complicated. If the test is too complicated, you will not be able to determine what part of test was successful and what was not. It will also make it difficult to determine the causes of various problems you may encounter. If you are testing a complex procedure, make sure you break it down into various parts. You can test each part individually, and determine the success or failure of those parts, and how to correct them.

Record every single detail while you are performing the test. Never wait until after the test is done, because you will forget the important details. Invite various personnel to the tests to observe everything that goes on. They will be able to help you determine if you documentation is easy to follow, and if certain procedures need clarification. This will also help them to refine their own plans. The other added benefit is that more points of view will result in different perspectives on how to solve problems that you would not have noticed. It is a good idea to include people who are involved with the plan but not necessarily with the writing procedures. You will benefit from their viewpoints, and you may discover that things that are obvious to you are not so obvious to other team members.

Once the test is completed, ensure you review and update the Disaster Recovery document accordingly. It will be the team leader's responsibility to make sure that the plan is updated after the testing, and periodically throughout the year. It is also the team leader's responsibility to ensure that the plan is tested at least once per year. The effectiveness of the plan is impacted by changes in the environment that the plan was originally created to protect. Some major factors that will impact the plan are: new equipment, changing the software environment, staff and organizational changes, and new or changing applications. The plan should be reviewed and updated by the team leader twice per year.

Testing is an on-going process, and it is an excellent way of determining if your recovery procedures work. It will also improve your procedures, and familiarize the staff with any new procedures. Testing should also include your emergency repair procedures for servers, and cable testing. Remember that testing is probably the most valuable training tool you will have for your company when planning for a disaster. The more often you practice the more prepared you will be.

Implementing the plan will require the cooperation of the disaster recovery team, and the support of the company as a whole. Ultimately, the implementation of the plan will fall in the hands of the team leader, and this person will have to ensure that each of the various stages of plan are met, before continuing on to the next phase. In order to meet the organization's goal of having its business resume operations quickly in the event of a crisis, the plan must be repeatedly tested, and the key team members must be adequately trained. If the testing becomes routine, adequate feedback will be given to help keep the plan current. This will also make the plan go smoother should it need to be implemented. Testing is vital to the plan implementation, and ultimately to the survival of the business.

Key Point Summary

This chapter focused on the elements that are key to the recovery of a system after a disaster. These elements included the disaster recovery plan, types of disasters, and the backup plan. Keep the following points in mind for the exam:

✦ Conduct business impact analysis.

✦ Assess the risk of particular disasters based on company profile and location.

✦ Select a hot site or a cold site recovery option to ensure service.

✦ Adopt redundancy plans for drives, controllers, power supplies and NICs to ensure high availability of systems.

✦ Test your recovery plan at least once per year.

✦ Verify your backups to ensure they are working properly.

✦ Be aware of the different kinds of natural and man-made disasters.

✦   ✦   ✦

STUDY GUIDE

The Study Guide section provides you with the opportunity to test your knowledge about planning for disaster recovery. The Assessment Questions provide practice for the test, and the Scenarios provide practice with real situations. If you get any questions wrong, use the answers to determine the part of the chapter you should review before continuing.

Assessment Questions

1. Most companies are not ready for a disaster because of which of the following barriers? Choose all that apply.

   A. Lack of knowledge

   B. Little funding

   C. Lack of appreciation by support personnel

   D. Not enough support from management

2. The Disaster Recovery Plan consists of several phases. What are they?

   A. Risk analysis, Business Impact Analysis, prioritizing recovery requirements, producing the document, testing the plan

   B. Risk analysis, Business Impact Analysis, prioritizing applications, recovery requirements, producing the document, testing the plan

   C. Risky business, Cost Impact Assessment, application recovery, analyzing the document, producing the test

   D. None of the above

3. A business impact analysis will perform the following functions for your company? Choose all that apply.

   A. Expose weaknesses and strengths.

   B. Recommend the proper architectural layout for your building.

   C. Define critical, necessary, and non-essential functions of your business.

   D. Completely protect you from disaster.

4. You should keep a hard copy to the DRP document in a minimum of two locations. What are they?

   A. Keep both copies off-site.

   B. Keep both copies on-site; one in the computer room, and one in a safe in your office.

   C. Keep one copy on-site, and one copy at an off-site location.

   D. Keep both copies in a locked safe on-site.

5. During the creation of the DRP document, someone suggests you should have the appropriate purchasing information. Why is this a good idea?

   A. Having the appropriate purchasing information on-hand will reduce the time it takes to issue a purchase order and get new equipment.

   B. It will minimize the effects of a disaster.

   C. All employees should learn how to issue purchase orders so that they can order the new equipment on their own.

   D. It is only necessary for the people in the purchasing department to issue purchase orders.

6. Your boss asks you what steps you have taken to ensure you have a sound tape backup system. How should you respond?

   A. Verify your backups, and purchase a backup unit for the off-site location.

   B. Verify backups, keep an exact spare tape unit, backups, cables, SCSI adapters and device drives at an off-site location.

   C. Keep an additional tape backup unit at your on-site location, so that you can recover even faster.

   D. Rotate the media to an off-site location.

7. Certain types of disasters are more devastating than others, what are they?

   A. Air disasters

   B. Sabotage

   C. Natural disasters

   D. Viruses

8. The insurance agency asks you what precautions you are taking to protect the company from a natural disaster. How should you respond?

   A. Assure them that there are multiple copies of tape backups, and all are kept on-site.

   B. Assure them that you have a sound backup plan, media is stored at a reputable off-site agency, and backups are verified.

   C. Assure them that they have nothing to worry about because you have never received a single error when performing tape backups.

   D. Assure them that you tested your Disaster Recovery Plan two years ago, and updated it immediately after the test.

9. Logic bombs are typically used by whom?

   A. Teenagers

   B. Military experts

   C. Professional hackers

   D. Disgruntled employees

10. Who is responsible for administering the disaster recovery plan?

    A. Team leader and alternate emergency coordinator

    B. President of company and manager of Information Systems

    C. Operations manager and manager of Information Systems

    D. Team leader, and President of the company

11. What are some symptoms that your systems may have been affected by a virus?

    A. System is slower.

    B. Unusual messages keep displaying.

    C. Files are missing or corrupt.

    D. Disk space decreases rapidly.

    E. All of the above

12. What is *not* a component that is typically used for redundancy purposes?

    A. Hard drives

    B. Sound cards

    C. Power supplies

    D. NICs

13. What are some advantages to having a UPS device in the computer room? Choose all that apply.

    A. It will safely keep the server on-line after a power failure until you can shut it down safely.

    B. It will protect systems from brownouts.

    C. It will prevent damage in the event of a fire.

    D. It will keep the system running indefinitely or until power is restored.

14. You boss wants to know the major advantages of using a hot site service. How should you respond?

    A. Use of a recovery center

    B. Staff that knows exactly how to restore your data

    C. Duplicate systems

    D. Call management centers

15. You boss asks you how often you should test the DRP plan. How should you respond?

    A. Every day

    B. Once per year

    C. Once a month

    D. Just before a disaster

Scenarios

1. There is a fire in the computer room that destroys almost all of the equipment in it. What steps should be taken as part of the Disaster Recovery Plan.

Answers to Chapter Questions

Chapter pre-test

1. Risk analysis, business impact analysis, prioritizing applications, recovery requirements, document production, and testing the plan

2. 4mm, 8mm, DLT, DAT, QIC, CD-R, and 3480/3490 are common types of backup media.

3. Natural disasters include such as fire, flooding, earthquakes, tornadoes, and hurricanes.

4. Other potential disasters include human factors such as, viruses, hackers, and sabotage.

5. Availability

6. Redundant NICs are used in servers that need fault tolerance. Having multiple network cards will provide load balancing and fault tolerance.

7. A hot site is a company that specializes in providing servers that will assist your company in a time of disaster. They will provide you with a physical location to relocate your computer environment, including comparable computer and network equipment to your own computer environment.

Assessment questions

1. **B, C,** and **D.** Typically funding, lack of appreciation, and gaining management support are the biggest barriers faced by disaster recovery planners. It is essential to obtain this support for the DRP to be a success. Answer A is incorrect because lack of knowledge is not a problem if you have any sort of involvement with backing up data and taking care of the corporate information systems. For more information see the beginning of the chapter.

2. **B.** This is the common methodology, but certainly not the only one. It is vital that you know what information should be included in a disaster recovery document in order to make it affective and useful. For more information, see the "Forming a Disaster Recovery Plan" section.

3. **A** and **C.** Using a business impact analysis will examine every detail of your company and identify the weaknesses and strengths, and identify critical, necessary, and non-necessary functions. Answer B is incorrect because this typically is not analyzed in a business impact analysis. Answer D is incorrect because unfortunately you cannot completely protect yourself from a disaster; you can only make sure you are prepared for it when it happens. For more information, see the "Business Impact Analysis" section.

4. **C.** Never keep just one hard copy of the disaster recovery plan, because it could get lost or damaged if kept on-site. Also, having only electronic copies is useless if you cannot get to your systems. Answer A is incorrect because you would potentially lose these copies if a disaster occurred. Answer B is incorrect for the same reason as A. Keeping them in a safe on-site is not necessarily any safer. Answer D is also incorrect because keeping both copies on-site is a bad idea. If a disaster strikes, even if they are in a safe, there is no guarantee that the safe won't be damaged. For more information, see the "The disaster recovery document" section.

5. **A.** Every I.S. team member responsible for the DRP should be able to issue a purchase order. Answer B is incorrect, because unfortunately it will not minimize the effects of a disaster. Answer C is incorrect, because you do not want unauthorized employees issuing purchase orders during a non-disaster situation. Answer D is incorrect, because during a disaster, things need to happen quickly, so you will want at least one person from each department to be able to issue a purchase order. For more information, see the "The disaster recovery document " section.

6. B. If you cannot verify your backups, then you really never know if they are good or not. Keeping cables, SCSI adapters, device drives, and a spare unit will save you a lot of time in the recovery process. Answers A and D are incorrect because you also need to include the other items mentioned in the answer. Answer C is incorrect because if a disaster occurs and destroys your company's location, then this unit will be destroyed as well. For more information, see the "The disaster recovery document" section.

7. C. Natural disasters can be the most devastating because they can completely destroy your company's physical location. Answer A is incorrect, because air disasters do not occur that often, and they rarely damage any company locations. Answer B is incorrect because sabotage is not that common. Answer D is incorrect because most companies try to protect themselves from viruses, and complete disasters from them are relatively rare. However, just getting a virus can cost you lots of money, and time. For more information, see the "Types of Disasters" section.

8. B. If tapes are not kept off-site then they could be destroyed in the disaster as well. Verifying backup ensures that they are reliable. For more information, see the "Natural disasters" section.

9. D. Disgruntled employees seeking revenge on the company typically use logic bombs. For more information, see the "Vandalism" section.

10. A. The team leader and alternate emergency coordinator are responsible for administering the plan in the even of a disaster. Answers B, C, and D are incorrect because the President of the company may not be the team leader, nor is the manager of Information Systems necessarily responsible for the implementing the plan. For more information, see the "The disaster recovery team" section.

11. E. All of these are symptoms that a virus may have infected your computer system. For more information, see the "Viruses" section.

12. B. Sound cards are obviously not a necessity in any server system let alone for redundancy purposes. Answers A, B, and D are incorrect, because all these items are usually used for redundancy. For more information, see the "Planning for Redundancy" section.

13. A and **B.** In the event of a power failure, you will be able to keep your systems on-line for an extended period of time, and then perform a clean shutdown. UPS systems also prevent brownouts from damaging components in your systems. Answer C is incorrect because a UPS will not protect you from fire. Answer D is incorrect because a UPS will keep the system running for a set period of time, not indefinitely. For more information, see the "UPS" section.

14. A, C, and **D.** Using a hot site service ensures the maximum protection for your company in the event of a disaster. Answer B is incorrect because you are in charge of restoring your data, not the hot site staff. For more information, see the "Hot site" section.

15. B. Disaster recovery testing should be done on a yearly basis. This is mainly because of the length of time it takes to complete the testing, and the cost of performing the testing. For more information, see the "Testing the Disaster Recovery Plan" section.

Scenarios

1. You should first and foremost call the fire department, and make sure the building is evacuated. After the fire has been extinguished, you will have to assess the damage and notify the disaster recovery team to but the plan into action. As the team leader, it will be your responsibility to notify all personnel, including management. Each member should have a copy of the disaster recovery plan document, so reiterating the information should not be necessary. You will need to follow the document step by step ensuring that each phase is completed, such as contacting the hot or cold site location, notifying the off-site storage company and getting them to deliver the tapes, and so on. This is a huge process, and you do not want to make any mistakes, so proceed with caution and diligence.

Ensuring Fault Tolerance

7.1 Plan for disaster recovery

- Use the technique of hot swap, warm swap, and hot spare to ensure availability

- Use the concepts of fault tolerance/fault recovery to create a disaster recovery plan

CHAPTER PRE-TEST

1. Which RAID level offers no fault tolerance?

2. What is the benefit of a RAID system?

3. How does RAID 5 provide redundancy?

4. What are some causes of disk failures?

5. How does duplexing provide fault tolerance?

6. How do arrays use hot spare systems?

7. What is data regeneration?

8. What are some items that a RAID fault-tolerance document should contain?

9. Why is tape backup important even if you have RAID?

✦ Answers to these questions can be found at the end of the chapter. ✦

Understanding your RAID fault tolerance system is integral to a successful disaster recovery. Chapter 4 discusses RAID systems in detail, and you should read and understand it before reading this chapter. This chapter focuses on of how to recover a RAID system, and what documentation you should keep to ensure a successful RAID system. You should study the RAID controller documentation that you have implemented in your systems, as it will give specifics on how to use the disk array utility to successfully administer, monitor, and recover the system. A RAID system provides you with an excellent method for eliminating downtime should a drive fail, however, backups prevent complete data loss.

Recovering a RAID System

✦ Use the concepts of fault tolerance/fault recovery to create a disaster recovery plan

A RAID system protects your data in the event that a disk fails. If a disk drive fails in RAID system (unless it is RAID level 0), users will never know, because they will be able to continue on with their work as if nothing had ever happened. The benefit is that the RAID system will continue to perform read and write operations, and if you have adopted a hot spare system, it will automatically become part of the array, and the data that was on the failed drive will automatically be recreated on to the new drive in the array. Without a RAID system, especially in critical servers , you can expect lengthy downtime and data loss.

Chapter 4 discusses RAID extensively, so refer to that chapter for information on the RAID levels and their benefits. For the purposes of this chapter, Table 18-1 lists the RAID levels and their redundancy capabilities.

Table 18-1 RAID Levels and Redundancy Capability	
Level	**Redundancy**
RAID Level 0: Data striping	No redundancy. If a drive fails, data is lost.
RAID Level 1: Disk mirroring	A mirrored set of drives is created.
RAID Level 0+1: Data striping with mirroring	A striped array (RAID 0) of mirrored drive pairs (RAID 1) is created. You can sustain more than one drive failure if they are not in the same mirrored set.
RAID Level 3: Data striping with dedicated parity and parallel access	One drive is dedicated for parity. Data is regenerated in the event of drive failure.

Continued

	Table 18-1 *(continued)*	
Level	*Redundancy*
RAID Level 4: Data striping with dedicated parity and independent access	One drive is dedicated for parity. Data is regenerated in the event of a drive failure.
RAID Level 5: Data striping with parity	Parity is distributed across the disks in the array. Data is regenerated in the event of a failure.

Disk failure

Disk failure can strike at any time. Failures can occur for the following reasons:

✦ Defects

✦ Pollutants or contaminants

✦ Vibration

✦ Manufacturer's expected life cycle exceeded

✦ Heat

✦ Static discharge

✦ Power surges

✦ High energy or high frequency bursts on power lines

✦ Power supplies that generate noise or odd voltages when they fail

Duplexing provides excellent data protection by eliminating single points of failure in the disk subsystem. Ideally, one would duplicate all aspects of the hardware in the system configuration including physical disks, power supplies, fans, and cables. Disk duplexing is nothing like disk mirroring. Disk mirroring is a technique where data gets written to two duplicated drives simultaneously. If one of the drives fails, the system can instantly switch to the other disk without loss of data or service.

Most disk arrays can make use of a *hot spare* system. If a drive fails, it can automatically be cycled out of the array, and the hot spare can automatically be cycled in without having to wait for a replacement drive. This can only be implemented on RAID levels that support data redundancy. For example, this cannot be implemented in a RAID 0 system. In capable RAID systems, the data will be rebuilt to the hot spare drive. Unfortunately, during this time, the array is susceptible to a second drive failure. If the second drive failure is not part of the mirrored pair that failed, then the data is safe. However, if the second drive failure is part of the same mirrored pair, the array will fail and data will be lost. The only way to recover the data in this case is from a backup.

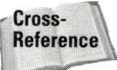

Cross-Reference RAID levels are discussed in great detail in chapter 4.

A disk that is being *rebuilt* is in the process of having the data restored from one or more failed logical drives. The operation that the disk controller performs depends on the RAID level the failed logical drive was configured for:

✦ A RAID 1 or 0+1 rebuild operation copies the mirrored disk.

✦ A RAID 3, 4, or 5 rebuild operation involves multiple read and write operations to reconstruct the data from parity.

✦ RAID 0 drives cannot be rebuilt.

If you are not making use of a hot spare when a disk fails, the rebuild will not take place until the failed drive is removed and replaced. In this situation, a rebuild will either occur manually via the disk array utility or automatically by the array monitor.

Recovering from a disk mirroring failure

In mirrored disk configuration, two drives will contain exactly the same data. If one of the drives fails, the other remains available, so data loss and system interruptions caused by the disk drive failure are basically eliminated.

Failures of one drive in a mirrored pair actually improves the read and write performance, because there is only one drive to write to. Once the failed drive is repaired, it must be rebuilt or re-mirrored with the other drive; the data blocks must be read from the functional drive and copied to the repaired drive. If this is done in the background, that is, the copying only takes place when there is no other disk activity, there is almost no impact on system performance. However, re-mirroring may take a long time, and the disk will have no data protection until the re-mirroring is completed. A hardware RAID array can be instructed to perform foreground, or dedicated, re-mirroring. Background remirroring takes longer but will have less impact on system resources, whereas dedicated is faster, but is harder on the system. Remirroring through software takes longer, even as a dedicated operation.

Recovering from disk failure on a stripe set with parity

A stripe set with parity uses parity to reconstruct data on a failed drive, but distributes the parity information on the data drives. With this type of disk configuration, the system will continue to function without the missing disk by using a parity reconstruction algorithm that creates the missing data from the remaining disks. When a replacement disk is inserted back into the configuration, the RAID system can be repopulated by the RAID controller, which calculates the missing values from the same parity reconstruction algorithm.

If a drive fails, read performance is degraded, but the data remains available. To read the data that resided on the failed drive, all drives have to be read in order for the controller to calculate the data, because the parity data is stored across all the drives. Writes also involve reading from all of the remaining drives, followed by a write to the parity drive. There is no data protection until the array is fully rebuilt.

When a disk fails in an array, and is replaced, the RAID controller rebuilds the data that was on the failed disk by using the parity bits to calculate the lost data and write it to the replacement drive. During the time between when the disk failed and when the new one is regenerated, the controller continues to read data that was on the failed disk by using the parity to calculate and respond to the read request. During this time, the RAID controller performs write operations to the failed drive by temporarily writing the information to another drive and transferring the data to the new drive when the regeneration is complete.

During an automatic rebuild, data is regenerated automatically to a hot stand-by disk if one of the disks fails. Through the configuration utility that accompanied the RAID controller, you can configure how the array should react when a disk drive fails. You can set the software so that it does or does not perform an automatic rebuild. The reason for not performing an automatic rebuild would be primarily because of performance issues. If the server is an application server, and requires all necessary resources at peak performance during business hours, you may not want the controller to rebuild the array automatically. However, you must keep in mind that there will be no redundancy until the array is rebuilt.

RAID drive state conditions

Although most RAID controllers use the same terminology to describe the drive states, there are usually slight variances. Table 18-2 describes the different drive states that the controller should display in the setup utility. However, depending on the manufacture of the controller, it may use slightly different terms.

Table 18-2
Physical Drive States

Drive State	Description
Defunct	A physical drive that was in the hot-spare, online, or rebuild state has become defunct. This means that is does not respond to commands, and the RAID controller cannot communicate with the drive.
Rebuilding	This means that the RAID controller is rebuilding the drive.
Hot spare	Typically, a hot spare is a physical drive that has been defined for automatic use when a drive fails.
Online	This means that the drive is properly functioning and is part of the array.

Drive State	Description
Ready	The drive is recognized by the RAID controller as being ready for definition. The drive is part of the array, but its role hasn't been defined.
Standby hot spare	When an online drive becomes defunct and there are no appropriate hot spare drives available, a standby hot spare drive automatically actives, and enters the rebuild state.

Ensuring High Availability

✦ Use the technique of hot swap, warm swap, and hot spare to ensure availability

To limit the amount of downtime you should ensure that your systems have a high rate of availability. You can do this by implementing hot swap, warm swap, and hot spare technologies.

Hot swapping and hot spares are discussed in detail in Chapter 4.

Hot swap

Hot swapping is the term used when you can remove and insert devices in a RAID system while it is running. In order to prevent a crash while this is happening, RAID systems can handle power surges and bus interruptions. When you insert a new disk into the RAID system, the system will start a rebuild to reconstruct the missing data.

Warm swap

Warm swapping refers to putting the server into suspend mode before initiating a swap. After the swap, the system performs a resume operation.

Hot spare

Hot spares are used in RAID systems for automatic insertion into the array. This is seen mostly in RAID systems with multiple arrays. If a drive fails in any of the arrays, the hot spare will be automatically used to replace the failed drive.

Raid controllers

The controller in the RAID system performs all the disk operations. Consider redundant RAID controllers to ensure high availability in your RAID systems. These controllers provide fault tolerance through redundancy, and improve performance by load balancing.

Documenting Fault Tolerance

As mentioned in other chapters, you should invest some time in documenting your computer environment. This section discusses documenting fault tolerance levels for RAID systems. The things that will affect this documentation are the host operation system, performance requirements, data protection requirements, and capacity. Ideally, you should use this information to document your RAID fault tolerance, and to help you rebuild in case of a disaster.

You will need to include the following information about your systems and its uses to properly document your disk array subsystem:

✦ The operating system and block size

✦ The special needs that certain users have for security, performance, and data protection

✦ Redundancy requirements to protect data

✦ Performance requirements

✦ Storage capacity requirements

✦ Hot spares

The following is a list of the elements that should be included in your RAID documentation.

✦ **Adapter:** Record the number of adapters. Most systems support multiple adapters, but your server may not have enough PCI slots available. Check PCI slot availability before purchasing another adapter.

✦ **Slot selection and boot order:** Record the I/O slot and the boot order of the adapter. The slot you choose for the adapter may affect the boot order of your devices. The boot order will differ between systems so consult your system's documentation to check boot order.

✦ **IRQs and IRQ sharing:** Record the IRQ information. Adapters can share IRQs, so make sure you check your system's and operating system's documentation to determine the affects of IRQ sharing.

✦ **Channels:** Record which physical drives will be on each SCSI channel for the adapter. Record the SCSI ID number and physical capacity of each physical disk.

✦ **External disk enclosures:** Record how many external disk enclosures you may be using. Also write down the cabling requirements.

✦ **Duplexed/Non-duplexed hot swap subsystems:** Record the duplex mode. Most systems can be configured as duplexed or non-duplexed. For example, a server may have two hot swap cages (a box where the hot swap is kept). In a duplex mode, each hot swap cage is typically cabled to a separate SCSI channel, and the same or separate adapters may control these channels.

In non-duplexed mode, both hot swap cages are cabled together on the same SCSI channel of the adapter.

✦ **Arrays and RAID levels:** Record which physical disks are assigned to which arrays. The number of physical disks needed for an array depends on the RAID level chosen. Record the RAID level as well.

✦ **Hot spares:** Record whether any physical disks have been assigned as spares. Most adapters can support multiple hot spares.

✦ **Dedicated or global hot spare:** Hot spares can be dedicated to a specific array or assigned to a global hot spare pool for all arrays controlled by the adapter. Record this information as well.

✦ **Rebuild rate:** Record the rebuild rate for each adapter. The rebuild rate represents the percentage of CPU resources that will be consumed to rebuild the data on the failed disk. A higher rebuild rate will ensure redundancy more quickly, but will affect system performance. A lower rebuild rate will free up system resources, but redundancy will take longer to complete

The following is a list of what you should keep track of regarding the logical disk drive configuration.

✦ **Logical drives:** Record how the array is divided into logical drives. Most adapters support multiple logical drives. There will be at least one logical drive for each array supported by the adapter. Record the logical drives and their parameters.

✦ **RAID level:** Record the RAID level for each logical drive. RAID levels will depend on the *stripe width*. This is the number of physical drives used for a stripe. The rule of thumb is, the wider the stripes, the better the performance.

✦ **Array spanning:** Record whether or not the logical drives are enabled to span arrays. Array spanning is used to enable a logical drive to use more physical disks than allowed by a single array.

✦ **Capacity:** Record the capacity of the logical drives.

✦ **Stripe size:** Record the stripe size for each logical drive. You will get the best performance if you choose a stripe size that is equal to or smaller than the block size used by your operating system.

✦ **Write policy:** Record whether the write policy is Write-through or Write-back. Write-back has better performance, but write-through has better data security. In write-back mode, the controller reports write operations as complete as soon as the data is in the cache. This sequence improves performance, but at the expense of reliability. In write-through mode, the controller will not report a write as complete until it is written to the disk drives. This sequence reduces the performance but gives much higher reliability.

Exam Tip   Write-back should only be used if the adapter has an uninterruptible power supply. Data can be lost from cache memory in a power failure.

✦ **Read policy:** Record whether the read policy is normal, read-ahead, or adaptive read-ahead. It is best to use read ahead for sequential data, and adaptive read ahead or normal for random data.

✦ **Cache policy:** Record the cache policy for each logical drive. This is typically referred to as cached I/O or direct I/O. The cache policy determines how reads are handled with no affect on writes.

You must record all the information described in these two lists to ensure that you and your team have a good understanding of the RAID system. The documentation will also make it easier to reconstruct the system in the event of a disk failure, or a total disaster. Always keep in mind that no matter how many RAID systems you have or what levels you use, there is no substitute for backups.

Key Point Summary

This chapter focused on the fault tolerance features of RAID systems. It covered how to recover a RAID system, disk failures, and documenting fault tolerance. Keep the following points in mind for the exam:

✦ Disk failures can strike at any time and are caused by many things.

✦ Duplexing provides excellent data protection by eliminating a single point of failure.

✦ Hot spares can be automatically rebuilt in the event of a disk failure.

✦ Recovering a mirrored system basically means copying the data from one drive to another.

✦ Recovering a stripe set with parity is more complex and involves using a parity reconstruction algorithm.

✦ When a disk fails in an array, and is replaced, the RAID controller rebuilds the data that was on the failed disk by using parity bits to calculate the lost data.

✦ You should document your fault tolerance RAID levels to ensure everyone understands how the system functions.

✦　✦　✦

STUDY GUIDE

The Study Guide section provides you with the opportunity to test your knowledge about recovering a fault-tolerant system. The Assessment Questions provide practice for the test, and the Scenarios provide practice with real situations. If you get any questions wrong, use the answers to determine the part of the chapter you should review before continuing.

Assessment Questions

1. What can you expect to encounter if you do not implement a RAID system? Choose all that apply.

   A. Employee downtime

   B. Data loss and restoration costs

   C. Continuous backups

   D. Lost customers

2. How does a RAID 1 rebuild work?

   A. This rebuild operation involves multiple read and write operations to reconstruct the data from parity.

   B. RAID 1 systems cannot be rebuilt.

   C. The rebuild operation copies the mirrored disk.

   D. The rebuild operation copies the mirrored disk and reconstructs the data from parity.

3. One of the drives fails in your RAID disk mirroring scheme. How will it be recovered?

   A. Data blocks are copied from the failed drive and copied to the new drive.

   B. The RAID system is repopulated when the RAID controller calculates the missing information from the parity reconstruction algorithm.

   C. The data blocks are read from the functional drive and copied to the replacement drive.

   D. The data is restored from tape backup to the replacement drive.

4. How does a RAID 5 rebuild work?

    A. This rebuild operation involves multiple read and write operations to reconstruct the data from parity.

    B. The rebuild operation copies the mirrored disk.

    C. The rebuild operation copies the mirrored disk and reconstructs the data from parity.

    D. RAID 5 drives cannot be rebuilt.

5. One of the drives fails in your stripe set with parity RAID scheme. How will it be recovered?

    A. The data is restored from tape backup to the replacement drive.

    B. The RAID system is repopulated when the RAID controller calculates the missing information from the parity reconstruction algorithm.

    C. Data blocks are copied from the failed drive and copied to the new drive.

    D. Data blocks are read from the functional drive and copied to the replacement drive.

6. What does a RAID controller use when rebuilding data that was on a failed disk?

    A. Bits and bytes

    B. Reverse parity

    C. Parity bits

    D. Data blocks

7. What reason would you have not to perform an automatic rebuild?

    A. It is good practice to manually initiate the rebuild.

    B. Arrays do not have automatic rebuild options.

    C. You are concerned that system performance will be degraded.

    D. You did not set it up.

8. An alert was triggered by the RAID controller telling you that one of the drives is in a rebuild state. What does this mean?

    A. The RAID controller has removed the drive from the array.

    B. The RAID controller is rebuilding the drive.

    C. The RAID controller is formatting the drive.

    D. The drive is defunct and will not respond to commands.

9. A logical drive failed to report its presence. What should be done?

   A. Contact the vendor.

   B. Correct the problem with the physical drives by reconnecting, replacing, or rebuilding them.

   C. Count the number of physical drives.

   D. Let the controller rebuild the logical drive.

10. The network specialist thinks that the tape backup system should be eliminated because the RAID system is completely fault tolerant. What should you tell the specialist?

    A. Agree, because you have invested a lot of money in the RAID system.

    B. Tell the specialist to purchase a few more hot spares and then stop the tape backup.

    C. Explain to the specialist that the tape backup system is the only thing that can protect the company from disaster, and that disk drives fail fairly frequently.

    D. Tell the specialist that this particular RAID level does not provide enough fault tolerance to warrant eliminating tape backups.

11. How can you ensure high availability in your server systems?

    A. Use hot swap and cold boot devices.

    B. Use warm spare in your RAID systems.

    C. Use hot swap, warm swap, and hot spare devices.

    D. Keep duplicates of every device on your network.

Answers to Chapter Questions

Chapter pre-test

1. RAID level 0 offers no fault tolerance.

2. RAID protects your data in the event disk failure. Users will be unaware that a problem has occurred because the system will continue to perform read and write operations.

3. Parity is distributed across the disks in the array. Data is regenerated in the event of a failure.

4. Causes of disk failures include, but are not limited to defects, pollutants, contaminants, vibration, life cycle exceeded, heat, static discharge, power surges, high energy or high frequency burst on power lines, and power supplies that generate noise or odd voltages when they fail.

5. Duplexing provides fault tolerance by using an additional disk controller, and thereby eliminating single points of failure in the disk subsystem.

6. If a drive fails, it can automatically be cycled out of the array, and the hot spare can automatically be cycled in without having to wait for a replacement drive.

7. When a disk fails in an array, and is replaced, the RAID controller rebuilds the data that was on the failed disk by using parity bits to calculate the lost data and write it to the replacement drive.

8. The RAID fault-tolerance document should include the operating system and block size, the needs of users, redundancy requirements, performance requirements, storage capacity requirements, and hot spares.

9. Tape backup is important because there is no such thing as complete fault tolerance. The only real way to protect the company's data from complete disaster is through tape backups.

Assessment questions

1. **A, B,** and **D.** Employee downtime, data loss, restoration costs, and lost customers can be expected if you do not implement a RAID system, and the drives fail. C is incorrect because continuous backups are always required. For more information, see the "Recovering a RAID System" section.

2. **C.** In RAID 1, the rebuild operation essentially copies the mirrored disk. A is incorrect because this is how RAID 5 systems are rebuilt. B is incorrect because RAID 1 systems can be rebuilt. For more information, see Chapter 4, or the "Recovering from a disk mirroring failure" section.

3. **C.** The data blocks are read from the functional drive and copied to the replacement drive. Answer A is incorrect because once a drive fails, the controller can no longer access it. Answer B is incorrect because this is how a striped set with parity is recovered. Answer D is incorrect because the question refers to a RAID rebuild as compared to restoring data from backup, and you would need to rebuild the RAID before restoring data. For more information, see the "Recovering from a disk mirroring failure" section.

4. **A.** The rebuild operation involves multiple read and write operations to reconstruct the data from parity. Answer B is incorrect because mirrored disks are used in a mirrored set. Answer C is incorrect because RAID 5 does not use a mirrored disk. Answer D is incorrect because RAID 5 can be rebuilt, it is RAID 0 that cannot. For more information, see the "Recovering from a disk failure on a strip set with parity" section.

5. B. The RAID system is repopulated when the RAID controller calculates the missing information from the parity reconstruction algorithm. Answer A is incorrect because the question refers to rebuilding drives in an array and not restoring from backup. Answer C is incorrect because you cannot copy data from a failed drive. Answer D is incorrect because this describes a mirrored set. For more information, see the "Recovering from a disk failure on a strip set with parity" section.

6. C. The RAID controller uses parity bits to rebuild data that was on a failed disk. For more information, see the "Recovering from a disk failure on strip set with parity" section.

7. C. An automatic rebuild can greatly affect the performance of the system. A rebuild will use the available CPU resources to complete its task, and depending on what the rebuild rate is set to, this may make the system unusable to the users. B is incorrect because the arrays do have automatic rebuild options. D is incorrect because automatic rebuild is on by default. For more information, see the "Recovering from a disk failure on strip set with parity" section.

8. B. An alert that a drive is in a rebuild state typically only means one thing, and that is that the RAID controller is rebuilding the drive. A is incorrect because the drive is being rebuilt, not being removed. C is incorrect because RAID controllers cannot format drives. D is incorrect because if it was defunct, an appropriate alert would have been generated telling you that the drive was defunct. For more information, see the "RAID drive state conditions" section.

9. B. Try to correct the problem with the physical drives by reconnecting, replacing, or rebuilding them. Answer A is incorrect simple because you want to resolve the problem as fast as possible, so you should try to correct the problem yourself first, and then contact the vendor. Answer C should have been done as part of your documentation, and really won't help in this situation. Answer D is incorrect, because the logical drive has failed because several physical drives have failed. For more information, see the "Disk failure" section.

10. C. This is the only possible answer, because without tape backup you have no protection against failure. RAID only provides a means of data redundancy and protection against downtime. However, if the RAID fails then your data is gone. For more information, see the "Disk Failure" section.

11. C. Using a combination of hot swap, warm swap, and hot spare devices will maximize your system up-time. A is incorrect because cold boot devices is a made-up term. B is incorrect because warm swapping refers to putting the server into suspend mode before initiating a swap. D is also incorrect because keeping duplicates of every device, such as printers, or fax servers, would be unrealistic and not necessary. For more information, see the "Ensuring High Availability" section.

Backing Up and Restoring

CHAPTER PRE-TEST

1. Why should a system administrator perform a backup?

2. Define a full backup.

3. Define a differential backup.

4. Define an incremental backup.

5. Why would an administrator want to use media rotation schedules?

6. List some common media rotation methods.

7. What are some disadvantages of the son media rotation method?

8. What are the benefits of the grandfather-father-son media rotation method?

9. What does DLT stand for?

10. What does DAT stand for?

✦ Answers to these questions can be found at the end of the chapter. ✦

Backing up data on your servers is perhaps the most important thing you can do as an administrator. A sound backup strategy is crucial to any business, and not having one could lead to disaster. A backup plan that isn't well thought out could cost a company thousands or millions of dollars in lost data, and lost productivity time. The company may be unable to recover from such a loss.

In this chapter you learn about the different types of backups available to you, and the various kinds of media rotation methods in use today. More importantly, you will learn to take the necessary steps to confidently and securely protect your company's data.

To effectively back up and maintain your system's data, you need to use a combination of hardware and software. Make sure you choose a reputable vendor. If your backup hardware malfunctions, you must be confident that the vendor will be able to repair it, or get you replacement parts in a timely manner. You should also ensure that the vendor will not be out of business a week after you purchase the hardware or software.

Planning the Backup

The first step in establishing a good backup system is to create a plan. The plan should take into account the importance of the data, the time you have in which to back up, and the budget for your department. The following are some questions to consider when beginning to create your backup plan:

✦ How critical is the data that needs to be backed up? Can some data be skipped?

✦ How often the system be backed up?

✦ How much storage media will be needed?

✦ Which devices will you back up?

✦ How will backup information be documented?

How critical is the data

You need to decide how essential is it to back up all the data on the servers. For example, you may find it a waste a space to back up folders that simply store applications that get installed on user workstations (Microsoft Office, Lotus Smart Suite, CorelDraw, and so on). In case of disaster, this data could simply be copied from the CD media they originally came on into the folder on the server. This would save space on the tape, and save time during a backup or restore.

You should also determine what data is most critical to back up. This would have to be done with the help of several personnel throughout the company, in order to determine the importance of the data.

How often to back up the system

There is no requirement on how often you should backup your data; however, you should consider the cost of recreating the data that has been added or modified since the last backup was performed. You should then calculate the lost time, sales, and productivity, and any other costs that might be incurred as a direct result of recreating the data. If a file server fails right before the backup, and the system and data are not recoverable, then you must determine what that would cost. If the cost is high, the strategy to protect that data must have a high priority.

For example, the cost would be very high to recreate a SQL database server that is updated with transactions continuously, and contains the company's mission-critical data. On the other end of the spectrum, the cost to recreate one user's system would be much less. In this situation, the administrator would ensure that the database is backed up several times per day, if possible, and that the users system would be backed up on a daily basis or less. Most administrators have their network users store their files on a file server, which would normally be backed up on a daily basis, thus eliminating the need to backup each workstation in the company. However, if this workstation is vital to the company, such as a CAD station or a graphics station, you will want to ensure that it is backed up as well.

Ideally, you would perform a full backup on workstations every day, and servers even more often. Important data files may need to be backed up several times per day. However, because media and time constraints, this may not be feasible. To compensate for this, administrators must develop a schedule that includes full, incremental, and differential backups. These types of backups are discussed later in the chapter.

Exam Tip   Always perform a full backup before adding new applications or hardware, or changing the server configuration.

How much data to back up

The amount of data to be backed up is key factor in determining the media rotation method. If you back up large amounts of data that must be retained for a long period of time, you need to choose the correct strategy. There is no right or wrong amount of data that can be backed up, just make sure that the *correct* data is backed up. The constraints that typically affect your decision are, time, cost, and size of the media.

How long to store data

The length of time for data storage is directly related to the media rotation method. For example, if you use seven media for Monday through Sunday, then your back-ups are never more than one day old.

Storage media are relatively inexpensive compared to the data that is on them. Administrators should back up systems on extra media that is not in the media rotation schedule, and store this off-site as well. Some choose to do this weekly, monthly, yearly, or a combination of all three.

Exam Tip   Perform full backups in duplicate. Keep one off-site and one on-site.

The administrator should have quick access to the following backups to perform a restore at any time.

✦ Three daily backups

✦ One week-old full backup

✦ One month-old Full backup

Which devices to back up

There is a lot to consider when trying to determine which devices will be included in the backup strategy and which devices will be excluded. To help you should come up with a plan that weighs the importance of the devices. Does the high-end CAD workstation need to be included, or does the workstation with the locally installed financial reporting software? As the administrator, you should request that all staff submit a summary on what they use their workstations for, and what data is local to workstation. You can then determine if the data can be stored on the server, and if not, whether it should be backed up. Obviously all data should be stored to the server when ever feasible, because this will ensure the protection of the users data, and it will simplify the backup strategy. However, this sometime is not possible because the large size of some CAD files, and thus this data may have to be backed up off the workstation. It is wise to hold a meeting with management to discuss what should be done, based on your findings.

In addition to determining what should be backed up, you will also need to deter-mine if you should create one job for all devices, or a job for each device.

Having one backup job for each device that is being backed up means that each separate device has its own schedule and its own media. The advantages of this system are:

✦ You will know which device was not backed up if the job fails.

✦ Backups of other devices are not affected if a device is turned off, or moved.

✦ You can easily set up new jobs as you add devices to your network.

The disadvantages of this system are:

✦ There are more jobs to keep track of. If you have 25 devices, you may have to examine all 25 log files to determine the problem.

✦ It is much more complex when scheduling.

Having multiple devices backed up in each job means that all these devices will be backed up simultaneously, and all will be backed up to one media. The advantages of this system are:

✦ You can use the same name for the media and the job if you choose the over-write option when setting up the job.

✦ You will know the order in which the data is backed up.

✦ You will have fewer jobs to keep track of.

The disadvantage of this system is:

✦ The job will result in a non-completion status if any one of the devices is moved, turned off, or simply unavailable.

✦ If the job fails, you will not be able to tell which devices were not backed up.

Types of Backup Hardware and Media

 ✦ Identify types of backup hardware

As I mentioned already in this chapter, having good backups is crucial for surviving a disaster and getting your systems back on-line. The quality of the backup depends on the hardware and backup media you choose. This section discusses the various types of hardware and media you can choose from to fit your needs and your budget.

Backup media

Backup media come in many forms. These include 4mm, 8mm, DLT, AIT, QIC, Travan, and CD-R. You are certainly not limited to these formats, but they are the most widely used types in the computer industry. Choosing which media type you will choose depends on a number of factors such as, cost, speed, data integrity, shelf life for archiving, ease of operation, and so on. The following sections discuss some of the common media types.

4mm media

The 4mm digital audio tape (DAT) is a type of magnetic tape that uses a scheme called *helical scan* to record data. This is the same type of recording that is used in common video-tape recorders and is somewhat slower than the DLT type. It is for this reason that most applications for 4mm DAT tapes are in environments requiring large data backups.

The helical scan system is pulled from a two-reel cartridge and wrapped halfway around a drum containing two read heads, and two write heads. The read heads verify the data that is written by the write heads. When a read head verifies the data, and if errors are present, the data is rewritten, otherwise the controller buffer is emptied and is ready for more data. The second write head writes data at a 40-degree angle compared to the first one. The first and second writes overlap but use different polarities, and this ensures that they will only be read by the correct read head. This design allows more data to be stored on the tape, and enables helical scan systems to gain higher data densities.

When restoring the data from backup, the backup software reads the entire directory of the tape's contents, and then winds the tape to the location of the data. It then reads the data and stores it in the controllers buffer. The controller uses the cyclic redundancy check code to ensure the data is correct. If an error is detected, the error correction code will be used to correct these errors. The data is then verified, and if it is correct, the contents of the controller's buffer are placed into the systems memory and then restored to the hard disk.

There are two formats for DAT tapes, DDS, and DataDAT. Table 19-1 shows the Digital Data Storage (DDS), which is the most common and seen in several formats. All DDS formats are backward-compatible with older DDS formats.

Table 19-1 DAT Formats		
Type	**Capacity (Normal/Compression)**	**Data Transfer Rate**
DDS	2GB	55K/sec
DDS-1	2/4GB	1.1MB/sec
DDS-2	4/8GB	1.1MB/sec
DDS-3	12/24GB	2.2MB/sec
DDS-4	20/40GB	4.8MB/sec

8mm media

8mm technology was derived from videotape recorders, and the original purpose was to transfer high-quality color images to tape for storage and retrieval. Exabyte Corporation created the 8mm tape and drives for data backup. The 8mm technology is very reliable and is capable of storing large amounts of data. It is very similar to DAT, and it also uses the helical scan system, but 8mm can store much more data.

Tip

A weakness in the helical scan system is that the tape path is very complex, and because the tape must be pulled from a cartridge and wrapped tightly around the spinning read/write cylinder, a great deal of stress is placed on the tape.

There are two popular formats that use different compression schemes and drive technologies. Exabyte Corporation uses the standard 8mm format, and Mammoth, Sony, and Seagate adopted the new technology, which is known as Advanced Intelligent Tape (AIT). Table 19-2 lists the key elements of the 8mm standards.

Table 19-2 8mm Standards			
Type	**Capacity (Normal/Compressed)**	**Interface**	**Data Transfer Rate**
8mm	3.5/7GB	SCSI	32MB/min
8mm	5/10GB	SCSI	60MB/min
8mm	7/14GB	SCSI	60MB/min
8mm	7/14GB	SCSI	120MB/min
Mammoth	20/40GB	SCSI	360MB/min
AIT-1	25/50GB	SCSI	360MB/min
AIT-2	50/100GB	SCSI	360MB/min

The Advanced intelligent tape (AIT) is targeted at the midrange server market that has anywhere from 2 to 150 users. AIT has excellent data integrity, capacity and speed, which was possible because of major breakthroughs such as thinner media, stronger media, stability, and new head technologies. This tape drive system has low error rates, and is being utilized in tape libraries and robotic applications. AIT also incorporates the ALDC compression technology, and this helps to provide high performance and high capacity. The end result is a search speed that is up to 150 times faster than the typical read/write speed of the drive.

Quarter-inch cartridge

The quarter-inch tape cartridge (QIC) is the same width tape that has been used for years in the audio recording industry. The technology is very stable and well-established. QIC cartridges look much like audio tape cassettes, with two reels inside, one with tape and the other for take-up. QIC uses a linear recording system where the data is written to parallel tracks that run along the length of the tape. The number of tracks are what determine the capacity of the media. There are two types of cartridges, the DC600 and the more popular DC2000 minicartridge.

Table 19-3 lists the capacities for the most common QIC formats. These capacities are doubled when compression is used.

Table 19-3 Common QIC Formats				
Type	*Tracks*	*0.25inch width*	*Longer tape*	*0.315-inch width*
QIC-80	28/36	From 80MB	To 400MB	To 500MB
QIC-3010	40/50	340MB	-	420MB
QIC-3020	40/50	670MB	-	840MB
QIC-3080	60/72	1.2GB	1.6GB	2GB
QIC-3095	72	-	4GB	2GB

Travan

Travan is a magnetic tape technology, developed by the 3M corporation, that provides higher data densities. Travan has been standardized by the QIC consortium, and is compatible with older QIC standards. Essentially this means that Travan tape drives can read and write older QIC tapes, as well as the newer high-capacity Travan tapes. Table 19-4 depicts the newer Travan Formats.

Table 19-4 Travan Formats				
	Capacity (Normal/ Compressed)	*Data Transfer Rate*	*Tracks*	*Compatibility*
TR-1	400MB/800MB	125 KBps	36	QIC 80, QIC 40 (Read-only)
TR-2	800MB/1.6GB	125KBps	50	QIC-3010, QIC-80 (Read-only)
TR-3	1.6GB/3.2GB	250KBps	50	QIC-3010/3020, QIC-80 (Read-only)
TR-4	4GB/8GB	70MB/min	72	QIC-3080/3095, QIC-3020 (Read-only)
TR-5	10GB/20GB	110MB/min	108	QIC-3220, TR-4/QIC-3095 (Read-only)

Digital linear tape

Digital linear tape (DLT) uses a serpentine technology tape system developed by Digital Equipment Corporation that was originally used on MicroVAX systems. The tape itself is a half-inch in width, and is made out of a sturdy, hard plastic cartridge that can withstand a lot of punishment. A number of companies have now licensed the use of this technology. DLT tapes are roughly 60% wider than 8mm tapes, and are the widest tapes available for data backup. The serpentine system uses parallel tracks that are grouped into pairs, and each track extends the entire length of the tape. The first set of tracks are recorded on the entire length of the tape, and when the end of the tape is reached, the heads get repositioned to record a new set of tracks. The data then is recorded for the entire length of the tape in the reverse direction. This continues until the tape is completely used. Today's drives record 128 or 208 tracks.

DLT uses a unique guide system that helps to reduce tape wear, and stress. DLT tapes have a head life of approximately 30,000 hours, which is far greater than the 2,000 hours reached by 8mm helical scan systems.

DLT devices minimize file seek time through a file mark index located at the logical end of the tape. The index lists the tape segment address of each file on the tape, the drive then hops to the track containing the file, and does a high-speed search for the file. The average 20GB DLT system can find a file in less than one minute.

DLT is very popular because of the benefits that the technology has, such as higher data transfer rates, increased reliability, and greater storage capacity. However, having said that, DLT is sometimes not useful for some companies because of the increased cost of the hardware and media. Table 19-5 lists the different types of DLT formats.

Table 19-5 **DLT Formats**			
Type	*Capacity (Normal/Compressed)*	*Interface*	*Data Transfer Rate*
DLT2000	15/30GB	SCSI	2.5MBps
DLT4000	20/40GB	SCSI	3MBps
DLT7000	35/70GB	SCSI	20MBps

3480/3490

3480 and 3490 are the IBM designation for families of half-inch magnetic tape drives typically used on mainframes and AS/400s. The 3480 drives use 18-track cartridges at 38000 bpi (bytes per inch)to for at total of 200MB. The 3490 uses built-in compression to obtain 400MB, while the 3490e records to 36 tracks and uses longer tape to hold a capacity of 800MB. Tape libraries are available that hold from fewer than a dozen cartridges to thousands of cartridges. The 3490 drives provide transfer rates of 3MB per second. There are drives available that utilize Fast SCSI-2 interface to reach speeds of up to 20MB/sec.

Optical media

Optical media are storage media that are read and written with lasers. Optical disks can store much more data than most portable magnetic media, up to 6GB. Optical media are based on interpreting the reflections of laser light off the surface of the media. This type of media is more reliable than tape because the media is static compared to the rigors that tape endures as it gets wrapped around spools and moved through tape transports. However, optical media is much more challenging to write to then tape, because of the many different formats available, and the cost associated with the devices and media.

CD-R

CD-R is short for Compact Disk-Recordable drive, a technology based on a smooth, clear surface platter with a dyed background that can be changed with a laser to signify the difference between bits. CD-R technology is rapidly dropping in price, and a single high quality unit can be purchased for less than $150. These devices are capable of reaching speeds of 3.6MBps. The media itself is very inexpensive and is capable of storing 650MB of data. Table 19-6 shows a summary of transfer rates of different types of drives.

Table 19-6 CD-R Transfer Rates		
Drive	*Minimum Transfer Rate*	*Maximum Transfer Rate*
1×	150KB/sec	150KB/sec
2×	300KB/sec	600KB/sec
4×	600KB/sec	600KB/sec
6×	900KB/sec	900KB/sec
8×	1200KB/sec	1200KB/sec
10×	1500KB/sec	1500KB/sec
12×	1800KB/sec	1800KB/sec
16×	930KB/sec	2400KB/sec
20×	1170KB/sec	3000KB/sec
24×	1400KB/sec	3600KB/sec
12×/20×	1800KB/sec	3000KB/sec

Backup hardware

There are also many different kinds of backup hardware. You can choose tape stackers, libraries and autoloaders, and jukeboxes. Each of these types of backup hardware has a different purpose, and function. The sections that follow discuss some of the hardware types that you can choose from.

Tape stackers

A tape stacker is a sequential access device that uses tapes in the order they are loaded in the changer. If an operation exceeds the limits of a tape, the stacker continues the operation onto the next tape, and so on, until all the data is backed up. You must have the tapes inserted in the correct order, or you run into problems. Stackers work best in a single-system backup, where there is less confusion about the order of the tapes. They are less suitable for certain restore operations, such as those where files may be restored at random. Stackers are very common in mainframe applications.

Libraries and autoloaders

Tape libraries and autoloaders are more complex and more sophisticated than stackers. A library device will allow any one of the tapes to be loaded into the drive. Most library devices use multiple drives for parallel reading and writing operations. Because these devices are based on a random-access principle, you can load the tapes in any order that you want, as the device will make the necessary adjustments and ensure the media is used correctly. Libraries also make it easier to access files for restoration, as any one of the media can be easily accessed. Some library systems enable end users to perform medial tasks such as restoring files that they accidentally deleted. This type of machines can also be set up for automated tape cleaning. When the tape-cleaning cartridge is loaded into the drive, the cleaning will be automatically triggered. However, remember to replace these tapes based on the tape manufactures suggested capabilities.

Jukeboxes

Jukeboxes are typically used in conjunction with optical media. Jukeboxes are like libraries in the sense that they use the same random-access methodology. Jukeboxes can read and restore data far faster than their tape counterparts, and this reason makes them invaluable to many companies. Jukeboxes are excellent choices for near-line storage components used in archival schemes.

 Exam Tip   *Near-line storage* is used by data warehouses as an inexpensive, scalable way to store large volumes of data. Near-line storage devices include DAT, DLT tapes (sequential access), CD-ROMs, DVD-ROMs, DVD-RAMs, and Magneto-Optical (random access) devices. Retrieval of data can be slow, but the type of data (archives, past records, etc.) dictates that the information will not be accessed often.

Maintenance

To achieve peak performance for your tape drive, you must follow the manufactures suggested schedule for cleaning. If you cannot find the manufacturer's specifications, the general rule is to clean the tape after every 30 hours of use. If you can't keep track of the hours each tape has been used, you should try to do this three or four times per month. The tape heads act like a magnet, and airborne particles get attached to the heads. This greatly reduces the drive's efficiency and reliability, which could result in read/write errors when trying to perform a backup or restore operation. The other problem is that the tapes themselves can flake off dirt particles onto the heads. Simply reading and writing tapes makes the drive heads dirty.

You may start to get an increase in tape head errors from the tape backup system if the heads are badly damaged or dirty. If this happens, try cleaning the heads several times, and then use a brand-new tape for the next backup. If you still see the errors, you may need to replace the tape heads. This is often an expensive procedure, and hopefully the warranty is still in effect. If not, you may opt to purchase a new unit.

If you have tapes that sit around for extended periods of time, you should exercise the tape at least once per year. Most backup systems have a procedure for doing this, but it is a simply procedure of reading data to the end of the tape and then rewinding it. This will ensure that the tape remains flexible and reliable.

Types of Backups

 ✦ Identify types of backup and restoration schemes

Part of forming your backup strategy is deciding what to back up. Sometimes you need to back up all the data on a certain device. However, if only ten percent of the files on that device have changed since the last time it was backed up, backing up all the files is a waste of time. In this case, you would only want to back up the files that have changed. The following sections detail several methods to help you achieve an efficient backup plan.

Each file has a special bit called the archive bit. When a file is changed, the archive bit is set to indicate that the file has been changed, and should be backed up. Some types of backups reset the archive bit, indicating that the file has been backed up, and is safe until the next time the file is changed.

Full backup

In a *full backup,* you back up all the files on all the selected devices. It would be ideal to perform a full backup every time. However, because of the size of a typical full backup, and the time required to execute one, it may be impractical to do so. A full backup resets the archive bit on every file that is backed up.

The advantages of a full backup are:

✦ A full backup contains all the system's data on the media.

✦ If you must restore a full volume, the recovery time is shorter.

✦ Files are easier to locate because backups include all the data contained on the device.

The disadvantages of this method are:

✦ Backups become redundant because the majority of files rarely change.

✦ Full backups take longer and can require more media. This increases as more devices are added.

Incremental backup

An *incremental backup* captures all the files that have changed since last full or incremental backup The *archive bit* is switched off so the files will appear to the system as having been backed up. To restore the full volume, you must first restore from the last full backup, and then apply each of the incremental backups. To execute this effectively, you should plan to have current full backups on hand that go with the incremental ones. Suppose, you perform a full backup on Saturday, and incremental backup on Monday through Friday. If the system fails on Thursday morning, you will need Saturdays' full backup, and the incremental backups from Monday, Tuesday, and Wednesday to fully restore the system. Be sure you label the media appropriately, so you know which incremental backups go with which full backup.

The advantages of a differential backup are:

✦ The backup takes less time to perform because not all files are being backed up.

✦ Fewer media are required because not as much data is being backed up.

The disadvantages of this method are:

✦ Media must be restored in the correct order to bring the system back to its previous state.

✦ Backups are spread across multiple media. This can cause recovery to take longer.

Differential backup

Differential backups capture all the files that have changed since the last *full* backup. The archive bit is left on so the files will appear to the system as not having been backed up. This is different from incremental backups, because incremental backups include the files that have changed since the last *full* or *incremental* backup. Monday's differential backup captures all the changes since the full backup on the weekend. Tuesday's differential backup captures all the changes that occurred on Monday and Tuesday, and so on. If a file is changed on Monday, it will be backed up on *both* Monday and Tuesday, because the archive bit isn't reset. Therefore, each differential backup replaces the previous one. This makes restoring easier, because you only need the most recent full backup, and the most recent differential backup. However, more data is backed up than with an incremental backup, which takes longer.

The advantages of this method are:

✦ Restore the files requires only a full backup and the most recent differential.

✦ Restoring files is faster then with an incremental backup because only two backups are needed. This is a big advantage in disaster recovery.

✦ Files are easier to find because only two backups are required.

The disadvantages of this method are:

✦ Backups are redundant because all the files that were created or modified since the last differential backup are included.

✦ Backups are more time consuming because differential backups done later in the week will take more time than incremental backups.

Daily backup

Daily backup can be performed in addition to the media rotation schedule that you are using. This method backs up all the files on your devices with today's date. Essentially what this means is that a daily backup grabs all files that are created or changed today. The daily backup method does not reset the archive bit.

Media Rotation Methods

Another important factor in your backup plan is to determine how long each copy of a file needs to be kept. If you do not choose a media rotation method, each time the media becomes full, you have to archive it and purchase another one. Obviously, this is not practical in the sense that not all files need to be kept permanently, especially if they do not change regularly. The following sections discuss the most common methods for rotating your media. These methods are called *son, father,* and *grandfather,* because the "son" backup is the most recent. These methods can be combined into more complex systems.

Son rotation method

The son strategy involves doing a full backup every day, using the same media each time. This method typically only requires one tape (or other media). This is not the most effective method to implement even though it is easy to administer. Be cautious if you choose this strategy because the media you are using will eventually wear out after repeated use, and the data available only extends to your last backup. Figure 19-1 shows the backup rotation with the son method.

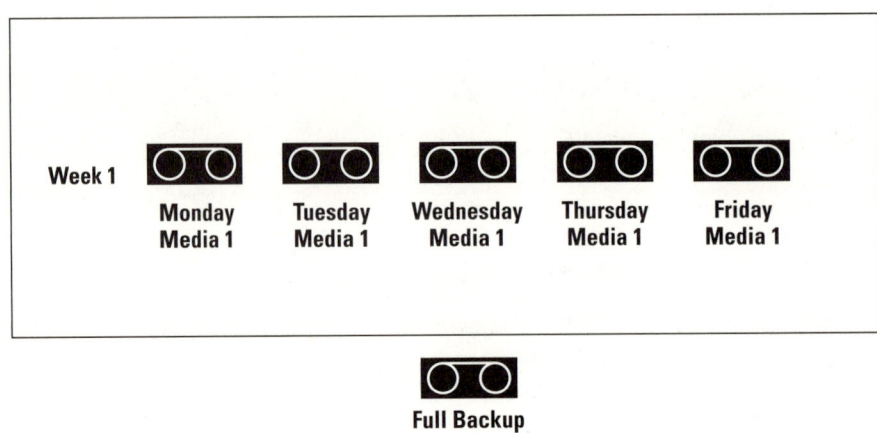

Figure 19-1: Son rotation method

Father-son rotation method

The father-son media rotation method uses a combination of full and differential or incremental backups for a two-week schedule, as shown in Figure 19-2.

There are four media used Monday through Thursday, for differential or incremental backups. The Friday media contain full backups and are rotated out and usually stored off-site each week. This method requires six different tapes, and provides a two-week backup history.

You are not limited to this scenario for a father-son strategy, although this is a very common one. For example, you could perform two full backups per week on Tuesday and Thursday, with incremental backups on Monday, Wednesday, and Friday. This scenario will definitely increase the security of the data, but it will take more time to do the full backups. Keeping three weeks of history would then require a minimum of eight tapes.

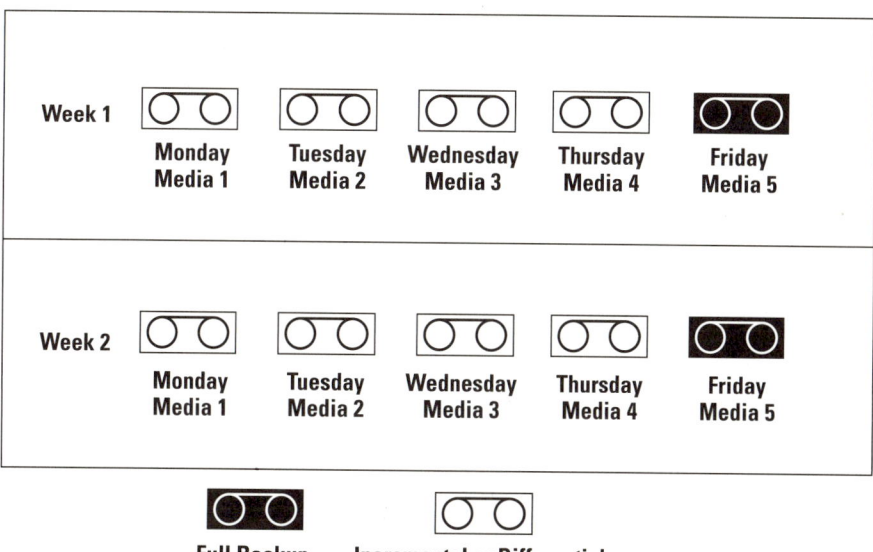

Figure 19-2: Father-son rotation method

Grandfather rotation method

The grandfather method is one of the most popular media rotation methods, because it is fairly simple to administer, yet it is comprehensive enough to easily locate files for restoration. See Figure 19-3 for an example.

There are four media used Monday through Thursday for differential and incremental backups; these are reused every week. An additional three media are used every Friday for full backups; these are used only once a month, and are reused each month. Twelve additional media are used, one each month, for monthly full backups. These aren't reused, and should be kept off-site. This strategy offers excellent storage life for the number of media used. Four daily tapes, three weekly tapes, and the twelve tapes for monthly backups are a total of nineteen tapes for one year. This way, your backup history extends for one full year.

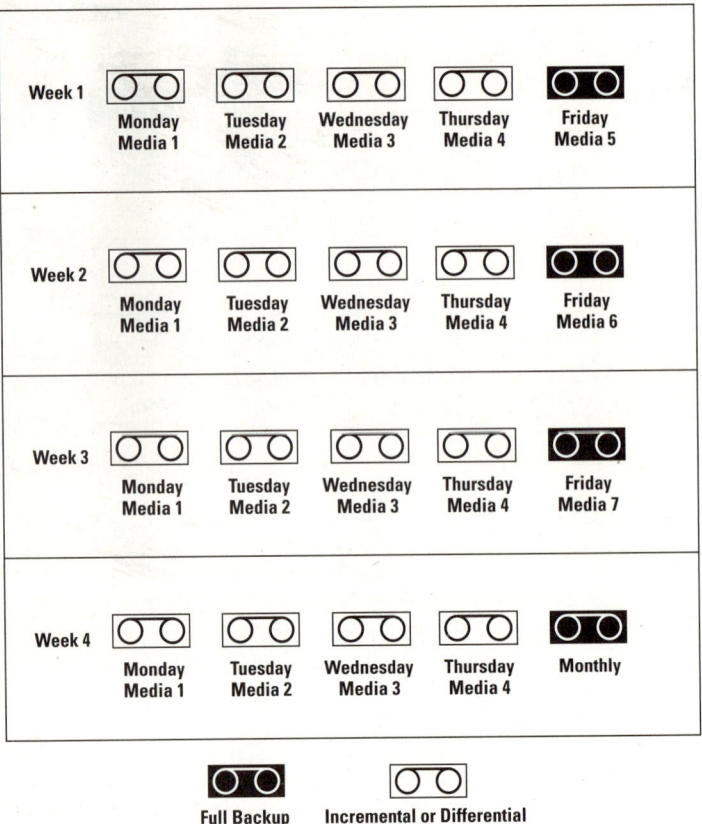

Figure 19-3: Grandfather rotation method

Grandfather-father-son rotation method

The grandfather-father-son method reduces the wear on the media, but the history is reduced to a 12-week period. In the Father-Son method, you will notice that the same four media are used over and over again in order to perform differential or incremental backups. The grandfather-father-son method eliminates this problem by rotating the media in such a way that allows all the media to be used equally over a 40-week period Figure 19-4 shows an example.

The grandfather-father-son cycle begins with a full backup. After that, incremental or differential backups are performed Monday through Thursday. Each Friday, a full backup is performed, and the media are rotated, as in the grandfather method. On the fourth Friday of each month, a full backup is performed and should be stored off site. This method is divided into 10 four-week intervals. The same four media are used Monday through Thursday throughout the 12-week period, but are rotated at the start of the next quarter.

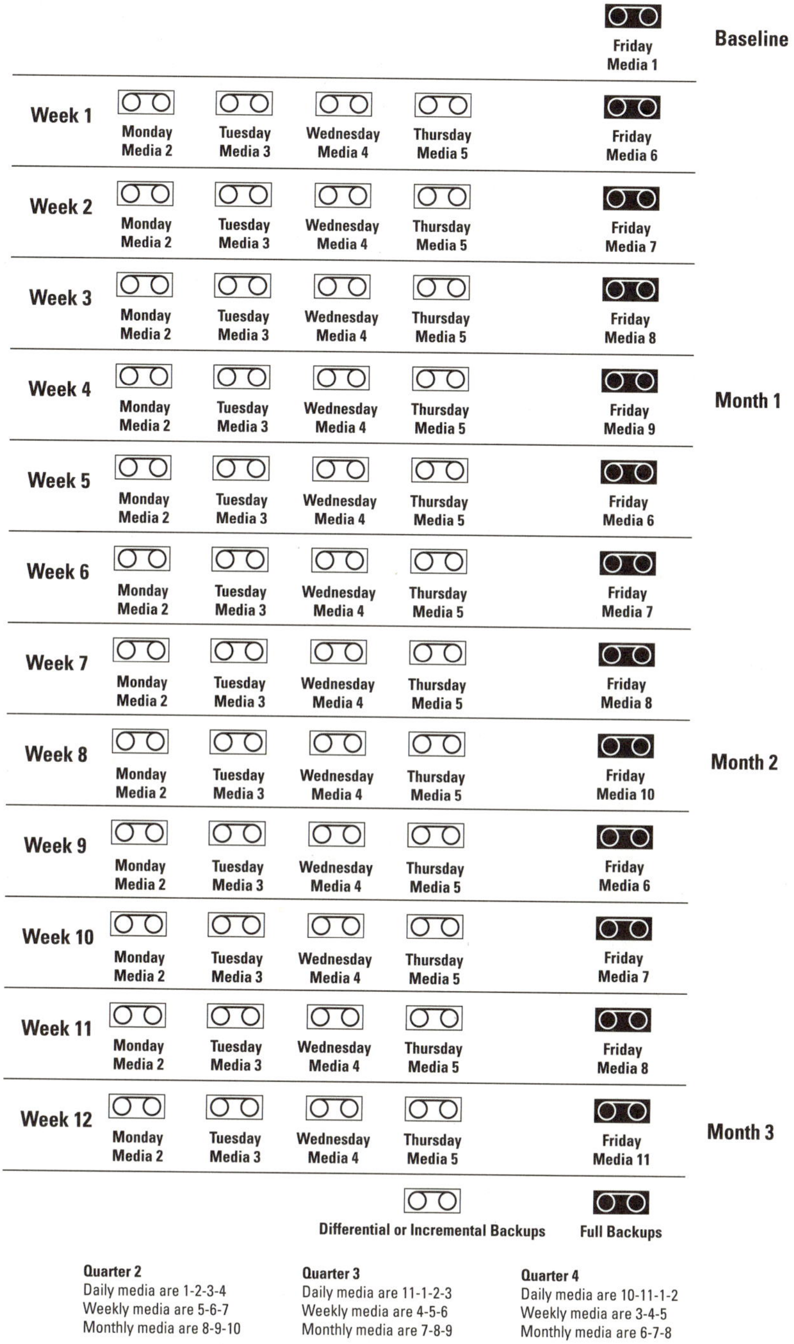

Figure 19-4: Grandfather-Father-Son Media Rotation Method

You must:

✦ Perform a full backup on Media 10 when you start this strategy

✦ Start with media 2 on Monday

Performing the above suggestions will ensure four-week old data at the end of the first four week cycle.

Exam Tip   Restoring data from a particular week or month using the grandfather-father-son method only requires one backup set.

The advantages to this method are that all media are used equally, so the wear on the tapes is distributed, and it only requires 11 media, which is fewer than the grandfather method. However, keeping track of the rotation schedule makes this method more difficult to administer, and your backup history is only 12 weeks long. If you want to increase the number of months in your history, use more monthly tapes.

Documenting Backup and Restoration Procedures

Objective   **7.2** Restoring

Preparing a backup and restoration plan is an integral part of accessing the company's protection level. The first step is to have documentation that lists the hardware and software environments. In short, you should keep track of the following items, although you are not limited to this list:

✦ Type of computer

✦ Add-on hardware (drives, printers, etc)

✦ Storage media

✦ Network connections

✦ Devices

✦ Model numbers

✦ Serial numbers

✦ Upgrade levels or service pack levels

✦ Software installed and its purpose

Many system administrators opt to purchase special software designed to automatically detect your hardware, software, and other devices, and it maintains them in a database. The big advantage to this is the reduced time it takes to catalog your environment and the ability to easily track new devices as they are added. However, this is not necessary as you can use a word processor or design you own database to perform the same task.

The second step in the backup plan is to plan your off-site media rotation. This means having the proper software installed, and having the ability to know how to use these tools. This also means having your media transported off site by company personal, or hiring a company that specializes in off-site tape storage. The big advantage to hiring a company is that they also keep detailed records of each tape that you give them, and each piece of media they return. You also do not have to worry about the employee being sick, or losing the tape. These companies should guarantee a high level of service, and have any number of employees to deliver the media upon your request. Hopefully, there is a reputable company that performs this service in your immediate area, because the closer they are, the less time you have to wait in the event of an emergency.

Third, you should perform mock backup and restoration tests. Using the methods described in Chapter 17, you should use an off-site facility to accomplish this. Document everything that happens during the backup and restoration procedures, and the time it takes to accomplish each task. This includes the time it takes to install the operating system to the time it takes to restore all the necessary data. If you come across a problem during the backup, decide how will it affect your restoration.

You will also need to ensure that you can restore the devices to their most recent states. This means that you will have to restore from the most recent full backup, and the subsequent incremental or differential backups based on the media rotation method you adopted. Make sure that you have correctly labeled all your media physically and electronically.

For greater control and security, all backups should go off-site on a nightly basis. Disasters such as fires, flooding, earthquakes, tornadoes, and hurricanes, happen more often than one might expect. Don't forget about your user workstations either, as some may have important files stored locally on their systems. Most backup software has agents that specialize in backing up and restoring workstations. You should treat this data with the same respect as your centralized server data.

Key Point Summary

This chapter presents various aspects of performing backups and restorations as part of your disaster recovery plan. You should now be able to describe various backup types, and the media rotation methods that are used in conjunction with them.

✦ Your backup plan should include which data to back up, how often, and on which storage media.

✦ Know the various types of media and backup hardware available.

✦ A full backup stores all the files on all the selected devices.

✦ Incremental backups capture all the files that have changed since the last full or incremental backup.

✦ Differential backups capture all the files that have changed since the last full backup.

✦ There are various media rotation methods; the most common are:

  • Son

  • Father-son

  • Grandfather

  • Grandfather-father-son

✦ Document your backup and restoration as part of your disaster recovery plan.

✦   ✦   ✦

STUDY GUIDE

The Study Guide section provides you with the opportunity to test your knowledge about backing up and restoring. The Assessment Questions provide practice for the test, and the Scenarios provide practice with real situations. If you get any questions wrong, use the answers to determine the part of the chapter you should review before continuing.

Assessment Questions

1. The system administrator is having difficulty determining how often to back up the devices on the network. How should this be done? Choose all that apply.

   A. Consider the cost of recreating the data.

   B. Contact an agency to determine this.

   C. Calculate the lost time, lost sales, and employee time required to re-create the data.

   D. Consult with your network users and management to help formulate a plan.

2. On Monday morning, a user asks you to restore a file that they created on Wednesday of last week, but accidentally deleted on Friday evening of that same week. They need the file for a meeting that is scheduled 30 minutes from now. Unfortunately, you keep all the backup tapes from last week at home, and you only have Monday's and Friday's tape with you. How could you prevent this from happening again?

   A. Keep one daily backup, and one week-old full backup on hand.

   B. Keep one week-old full backup on hand, and one month-old full backup on hand.

   C. Keep three daily backups, one week-old full backup, and one month-old full backup on hand.

   D. Keep all backup media on hand.

3. You come in on Monday morning and check your e-mail. You notice that you have a message from your backup software stating that the last backup was not completed. What are the possible causes for this? Choose all that apply.

   A. You forgot to schedule the job for Saturday night.

   B. One of your systems has been turned off.

   C. The software is wrong and everything is fine, so you should ignore the error.

   D. The device has been moved to a different location, and is no longer part of your backup domain.

4. You come to work on Wednesday morning and discover an error message on your file server. It reads, "Disk Failure! Unable to access operating system!" You have incorporated an incremental backup plan. How will you restore the system based on your backup media?

   A. Restore from the weekend full backup and restart the system.

   B. Restore from the weekend full backup and Monday's and Tuesday's incremental backups.

   C. Restore from Tuesday's backup.

   D. Restore from the weekend backup and Tuesday's backup.

5. You come to work on Wednesday morning and discover an error message on your file server. It reads, "Disk Failure! Unable to access operating system!" You have incorporated a differential backup plan. How will you restore the system based on your backup media?

   A. Restore from Tuesday's backup.

   B. Restore from the weekend backup and Monday's backup.

   C. Restore from the weekend backup and Monday and Tuesday's backup.

   D. Restore from the weekend backup and Tuesday's backup.

6. Your boss asks you to determine a backup type that is best suited for your company. He asks you to keep in mind that backup time is limited, and the restoration should be as quick as possible. What is the main reason(s) for choosing differential backup over incremental backup?

   A. Only one backup is needed for differential.

   B. Differential is less time-consuming than an incremental because only two backups are needed.

   C. Differential backups make it easier to find files.

   D. Backups are not redundant, thus time is not wasted backing up the same information later in the week.

7. What is the typical number of media used in the son rotation method?

    A. 8

    B. 4

    C. 1

    D. 19

8. Why is the son strategy not the most effective one? Choose all that apply.

    A. It involves doing a full backup on weekends and incremental or differential backups during the week.

    B. It will eventually wear out the tapes after repeated use.

    C. It is difficult to administer.

    D. The data available only spans back to your last backup.

9. You have just been hired as the new systems administrator, and part of your duties includes data backup. Your boss was unsure of the current backup strategy, and needs to know the history of data that is available for restoration. With a little research, you discover that the previous administrator adopted the father-son media rotation method. What are you going to tell your boss?

    A. The backup history is only as recent as the last backup.

    B. The backup history available is 12 weeks.

    C. Based on the current media rotation method, you have two weeks of history available for restoration.

    D. You could not determine the backup history available for restoration.

10. Currently, your father-son media rotation strategy makes use of six media. The Monday through Thursday backups use four incremental media. There are two media used for the Friday backup, because one is stored off-site each week. Based on this scenario, only two weeks of history are available, and your boss has just requested you increase it to three weeks of history that must be stored off-site. How many tapes will need to be added in order to keep three weeks of history off-site?

    A. 7

    B. 8

    C. 9

    D. 10

11. The grandfather method is the most comprehensive media rotation method because:

   A. The backup history extends to six months.

   B. The backup history extends to nine months.

   C. The backup history is twelve weeks.

   D. The backup history is one year.

12. You have been given a new budget to purchase new media for your disaster recovery backup plan. You have implemented the grandfather media rotation method. How many media will you require in order to backup your system?

   A. 52

   B. 19

   C. 21

   D. 20

13. What are some of the advantages of the grandfather-father-son media rotation method? Choose all that apply.

   A. It is less difficult to administer than other methods.

   B. All media are used equally.

   C. It has a longer backup history than the grandfather method.

   D. Fewer media are required than the grandfather method.

14. As the system administrator, you need to determine an off-site storage plan. What is the best solution for having a secure system, and also having media readily available in the event of an emergency?

   A. Keep copies at an off-site storage agency only.

   B. Keep copies at an off-site storage agency, and some in the computer room.

   C. Keep all copies in your office cabinet.

   D. Keep copies at an off-site storage agency, have copies at home in a fire safe, and keep copies in your desk.

15. What is not a common type of backup media?

   A. 4mm

   B. 9mm

   C. 8mm

   D. DLT

   E. DAT

16. You have 30GB of data to backup from your database server. You have a DAT backup system. What tape format will you most likely be using?

    A. DDS-1

    B. DDS-2

    C. DDS-3

    D. DDS-4

17. You are using a DLT system that is backing up 55GB of data. What type of DLT system are you using?

    A. DLT2000

    B. DLT4000

    C. DLT6000

    D. DLT7000

Scenarios

1. You're employed by a medium-sized manufacturing facility that has several servers and network nodes. Through analysis, you have determined that a total of 8GB needs to be backed up. However, the organization has three shifts running six days per week. Your ability to restore the data is obviously crucial but you only have a small window on Sunday in which to a full backup, and a few hours each weeknight to do the rest of the backups. Three to four weeks of backup history is acceptable. You are told that you are to use the father-son media rotation method. Why might you opt for an eight-tape rotation schedule?

2. You get a call from the operations manager telling you that there has been a fire in the building, and everything appears to have been destroyed. You are sick with the idea of how much work it is going to be to get the company back in shape, but you are confident that your disaster recovery plan will enable you to get the computer systems back up and running in a short period of time. What steps should you have taken regarding your backup plan?

Answers to Chapter Questions

Chapter pre-test

1. Backing up data on your servers is perhaps the most important thing you can do as an administrator. Backing up data will help to ensure that company's data is secure, and will prevent extensive downtime and costs in the event of disaster.

2. A full backup is when you back up all the files on all the selected devices.

3. An incremental backup captures all the files that have changed since last full or incremental backup.

4. Differential backups capture all the files that have changed since the last full backup.

5. Using media rotation methods will help to reduce the wear on your media, and provide for a comfortable history period between rotation cycles.

6. Son, father-son, grandfather, grandfather-father-son.

7. The media will eventually wear out from repeated use, and the data available for restoration only extends to your last successful backup.

8. The grandfather-father-son strategy reduces wear on the media, and fewer media are required than the grandfather method.

9. Digital Linear Tape

10. Digital Audio Tape

Assessment questions

1. **A** and **C.** In order to effectively determine this answer, you need to know how much it is going to cost you to recreate the data that was lost. To correctly determine everything that needs to be backed up, you will need to meet with various people in your company. For more information, see the "Planning the Backup" section.

2. **C.** To be better prepared for these common types of requests, you should keep a minimum of three daily backups, one week-old full backup, and one month-old full backup on hand. The other answers are incorrect because there is too much guess work as to which media you will keep on hand, and you cannot safely keep all you media on location. For more information, see the "How long to store data" section.

3. **B** and **D.** Most backup software will report a non-complete status message if it could not access all the information selected in the backup job. The most common causes of this are usually the device being turned off, or being moved to a different location. Answer A is incorrect because you would not

receive an error message if you forgot to schedule the job. Answer C is incorrect because the software is most likely not wrong, and you should never ignore errors regarding backups. For more information, see the "Which devices to back up" section.

4. **B.** Incremental backups require the last successful full backup and all incremental backups. Because this is Wednesday, you will require the full weekend backup, and Monday's and Tuesday's incremental backups. For more information, see the "Incremental backup" section.

5. **D.** Differential backups require the last successful full backup, and one differential backup. In this case, you need the full backup from the weekend and the most recent differential backup from Tuesday. For more information, see the "Differential backup" section.

6. **B** and **C.** Differential backups are less time consuming than incremental backups to restore because they only require two backups. They are the last full backup, and one differential backup. This also makes it much easier to find files since fewer media are required to search through. Answer A is incorrect because a differential backup requires two backups. Answer D is incorrect because the backups are redundant. For more information, see the "Differential backup" section.

7. **C.** The son rotation media uses the same media for full backup every day; therefore, you only have a history of your most recent successful backup. For more information, see the "Son rotation method" section.

8. **B** and **D.** The media will eventually wear out, and the data available only spans back to the last backup. Answer A is incorrect because this is how incremental or differential backups work, although the full backup does not necessarily have to be on the weekend. You could do differential and incremental backups from Monday through Thursday, and full backups on Friday. Answer C is incorrect because the son strategy is the easiest to administer. For more information, see the "Son rotation method" section.

9. **C.** Typical father-son rotation methods incorporate the use of six media. Four are used for differential or incremental backups through the week, and two Friday media are rotated and stored off-site. Therefore, at most you have a two-week backup history based on the Friday media. For more information, see the "Father-son rotation method" section.

10. **B.** In order to ensure that three weeks of history can be maintained at an off-site location, you will need to use eight media. Adding two more media to the Friday rotation does this. You would then, at any given time, have three weeks of data stored off-site. For more information, see the "Father-son rotation method" section.

11. **D.** The grandfather strategy is the most comprehensive because it offers the longest history for the number of media. Depending on your situation, this is typically 19 media. For more information, see the "Grandfather rotation method" section.

12. **B.** You will need to purchase 19 media for a standard rotation strategy. Four media will be used Monday through Thursday for the differential or incremental backups. An additional three media are used every Friday for full backups, and 12 media are used for the monthly full backups. For more information, see the "Grandfather rotation method" section.

13. **B** and **D.** This strategy ensures that the media is used equally over a 40-week cycle, and it uses less media than the grandfather method. Answer A is incorrect because this method is much harder to administer than the other methods. Answer C is incorrect because the backup history is 12 weeks, where the grandfather history is one year. For more information, see the "Grandfather-father-son rotation method" section.

14. **B.** You should keep one copy off-site to ensure that it is safe and secure in the event of disaster at your location. The other tape should be kept on-site in case you need to quickly recover the system. For example, a virus might damage the server on Tuesday, and you know through checking that the virus was also received that day. You could use the Monday tape you have on-site to restore the data quickly. Answer A is incorrect because this would not provide for a quick recovery. Answer C is incorrect because this not secure, and the data is not protected from a disaster at your location. Answer D is incorrect because keeping the tape at home still makes it difficult to get the tape for quick recovery. If you take tapes home, bring them in each morning. Keeping another copy in your desk is not very secure. For more information, see the "Documenting Backup and Restoration Procedures" section.

15. **B.** The common types of backup media are, 4mm, 8mm, DLT, and DAT For more information, see the "Backup Media" section.

16. **D.** DDS-4 is capable of backing up 40GB of data with compression turned on. For more information, see the "Backup Media" section.

17. **D.** DLT7000 is capable of backing up 70GB of data with compression turned on. For more information, see the "Backup Media" section.

Scenarios

1. The eight-tape father-son rotation schedule gives you the three to four weeks of backup history, while enabling you to effectively back up all the required data. You will use a differential or incremental backup for the Monday through Thursday media. Four media will be used for the Friday full backups, and they will be rotated and stored off-site. During week one, media 1 through 5 are used. Week two will see the usage of media 1 through 4, and media 6 for the full backup. This continues until media number eight is used.

2. Document the hardware and software environments. Maintain a database of all the devices and software programs being backed up. Use off-Site media rotation for weekly and monthly data. Maintain backup and recovery documentation from the testing you performed. Clearly label all the media both physically and electronically to ensure that you can restore the system to its most recent state. Store the nightly backups in a safe location such as your house.

Exam Objective Mapping

In this appendix, you'll find the table listing the exam objectives for the Server+ certification exam. The table is an exhaustive cross-reference chart that links every exam objective to the section in this book where the subject matter is covered.

Table A-1
Exam SKO-001 — Server+ Certification Objectives

Exam Objective	Chapter	Section
1.0 Installation		
1.1 Conduct pre-installation planning activities	Chapter 1	Installation planning
Plan the installation	Chapter 1	Installation planning
Verify the installation plan	Chapter 1	Installation planning
Verify hardware compatibility with operating system	Chapter 1	Verifying OS Hardware Compatibility
Verify power sources, space, UPS and network availability	Chapter 1	Verifying Power Sources and UPS Installation
		Verifying Rack Space
		Network Cabling and Connectors
Verify that all correct components and cables have been delivered	Chapter 1	Verifying Components
1.2 Install hardware using ESD best practices (boards, drives, processors, memory, internal cable, etc.)	Chapter 3	Installing Hardware
Mount the rack installation	Chapter 2	Server Rack Installation
Cut and crimp network cabling	Chapter 2	Making the cable
Install UPS	Chapter 2	Installing the UPS
Verify SCSI ID configuration and termination	Chapter 3	Verifying SCSI IDs and Termination
Install external devices (e.g. keyboards, monitors, subsystems, modem rack, etc.)	Chapter 3	Installing external devices
Verify power-on via power-on sequence	Chapter 3	Monitoring the Power-On Sequence
2.0 Configuration		
2.1 Check/upgrade BIOS/firmware levels (system board, RAID, controller, hard drive, etc.)	Chapter 3	BIOS and Firmware Levels
2.2 Configure RAID	Chapter 4	RAID Levels

Exam Objective	Chapter	Section
2.3 Install NOS	Chapter 5	Installing the NOS
Configure network and verify network connectivity	Chapter 5	Configuring and Verifying Network Connectivity
Verify network connectivity	Chapter 5	Verifying Network Configuration
2.4 Configure external peripherals (UPS, external drive subsystems, etc.)	Chapter 3	Peripherals
2.5 Install NOS updates to design specifications	Chapter 5	Applying Patches and Service Packs
2.6 Update manufacturer specific drivers	Chapter 5	Hardware driver support
2.7 Install service tools (SNMP, backup software, system monitoring agents, event logs, etc.)	Chapter 6	Using Tools and Services
2.8 Perform Server baseline	Chapter 6	Performing a Server Baseline
2.9 Document the configuration	Chapter 6	Documenting the Configurations
3.0 Upgrading		
3.1 Perform full backup	Chapter 7	Backing up Before Upgrading
Verify backup	Chapter 7	Backing up Before Upgrading
3.2 Add Processors	Chapter 7	Installing a CPU
On single processor upgrade, verify compatibility	Chapter 7	Installing a CPU
Verify N 1 stepping	Chapter 7	Installing a CPU
Verify speed and cache matching	Chapter 7	Installing a CPU
Perform BIOS upgrade	Chapter 7	Installing a CPU
Perform OS upgrade to support multiprocessors	Chapter 7	Installing a CPU
Perform upgrade checklist, including: locate/obtain latest test drivers, OS updates, software, etc.; review FAQs, instruction, facts and issues; test and pilot; schedule downtime; implement ESD best practices; confirm that upgrade has been recognized; review and baseline; document upgrade.	Chapter 7	Perform upgrade checklist

Continued

Table A-1 *(continued)*

Exam Objective	Chapter	Section
3.3 Add hard drives		
Verify that drives are the appropriate type	Chapter 8	IDE/ATA standards SCSI standards and technologies
Confirm termination and cabling	Chapter 8	Termination
For ATA/IDE drives, confirm cabling, master/slave and potential cross-brand compatibility	Chapter 8	IDE configuration
Upgrade mass storage	Chapter 8	Upgrading SCSI RAID Systems
Add drives to array	Chapter 8	Upgrading SCSI RAID Systems
Replace existing drives	Chapter 8	Installing SCSI drives
Integrate into storage solution and make it available to the operating system	Chapter 8	Configuring the OS to Recognize New Hard Disks
Perform upgrade checklist, including: locate and obtain latest test drivers, OS updates,software, etc.; review FAQs, instructions, facts and issues; test and pilot; schedule downtime; implement using ESD best practices; confirm that the upgrade has been recognized; review and baseline; document the upgrade.	Chapter 7	Performing an Upgrade Checklist
3.4 Increase memory	Chapter 7	Installing Memory
Verify hardware and OS support for capacity increase	Chapter 7	Installing Memory
Verify memory is on hardware/vendor compatibility list	Chapter 7	Installing Memory
Verify memory compatibility (e.g. speed, brand, capacity, EDO, ECC/non-ECC, SDRAM/RDRAM)	Chapter 7	Installing Memory
Perform upgrade checklist including: locate and obtain latest test drivers, OS updates, software, etc.; review FAQs, instructions, facts and issues; test and pilot; schedule downtime; implement using ESD best practices; confirm that the upgrade has been recognized; review and baseline; document the upgrade	Chapter 7	Performing an Upgrade Checklist

Exam Objective	Chapter	Section
Verify that server and OS recognize the added memory	Chapter 7	Installing Memory
Perform server optimization to make use of additional RAM	Chapter 7	Installing Memory
3.5 Upgrade BIOS/firmware	Chapter 7	Upgrading BIOS and Firmware
Perform upgrade checklist including: locate and obtain latest test drivers, OS updates, software, etc.; review FAQs, instructions, facts and issues; test and pilot; schedule downtime; implement using ESD best practices; confirm that the upgrade has been recognized; review and baseline; document the upgrade	Chapter 7	Performing an Upgrade Checklist
3.6 Upgrade adapters (e.g., NICs, SCSI cards, RAID, etc.)	Chapter 9	Upgrading Network Interface Cards
Perform upgrade checklist including: locate and obtain latest test drivers, OS updates, software, etc.; review FAQs, instructions, facts and issues; test and pilot; schedule downtime; implement using ESD best practices; confirm that the upgrade has been recognized; review and baseline; document the upgrade	Chapter 7	Performing an Upgrade Checklist
3.7 Upgrade peripheral devices, internal and external	Chapter 9	Upgrading Peripheral Cards
Verify appropriate system resources (e.g., expansion slots, IRQ, DMA, etc.)	Chapter 9	System Resources
Perform upgrade checklist including: locate and obtain latest test drivers, OS updates, software, etc.; review FAQs, instructions, facts and issues; test and pilot; schedule downtime; implement using ESD best practices; confirm that the upgrade hasbeen recognized; review and baseline; document the upgrade	Chapter 7	Performing an Upgrade Checklist

Continued

Table A-1 *(continued)*

Exam Objective	Chapter	Section
3.8 Upgrade system monitoring agents	Chapter 9	Upgrading System Monitoring Tools
Perform upgrade checklist including: locate and obtain latest test drivers, OS updates, software, etc.; review FAQs, instructions, facts and issues; test and pilot; schedule downtime; implement using ESD best practices; confirm that the upgrade has been recognized; review and baseline; document the upgrade	Chapter 7	Performing an Upgrade Checklist
3.9 Upgrade service tools (e.g., diagnostic tools, EISA configuration, diagnostic partition, SSU, etc.)	Chapter 9	Upgrading Diagnostic Tools and Utilities
Perform upgrade checklist including: locate and obtain latest test drivers, OS updates, software, etc.; review FAQs, instructions, facts and issues; test and pilot; schedule downtime; implement using ESD best practices; confirm that the upgrade has been recognized; review and baseline; document the upgrade	Chapter 7	Performing an Upgrade Checklist
3.10 Upgrade UPS	Chapter 9	Upgrading UPS
Perform upgrade checklist including: locate and obtain latest test drivers, OS updates, software, etc.; review FAQs, instructions, facts and issues; test and pilot; schedule downtime; implement using ESD best practices; confirm that the upgrade has been recognized; review and baseline; document the upgrade	Chapter 7	Performing an Upgrade Checklist

4.0 Proactive Maintenance

4.1 Perform regular backup	Chapter 10	Performing Regular Backups
4.2 Create baseline and compare performance	Chapter 10	Creating a Baseline
4.3 Set SNMP thresholds	Chapter 11	Setting SNMP thresholds

Exam Objective	Chapter	Section
4.4 Perform physical housekeeping	Chapter 12	Entire chapter
4.5 Perform hardware verification	Chapter 11	Hardware Monitoring Agents
4.6 Establish remote notification	Chapter 11	Remote Notification
5.0 Environment		
5.1 Recognize and report on physical security issues	Chapter 13	Securing the Physical Site
Limit access to server room and backup tapes	Chapter 13	Server room access Securing Backup Tapes
Ensure physical locks exist on doors	Chapter 13	Locks
Establish anti-theft devices for hardware (lock server racks)	Chapter 13	Anti-theft devices
5.2 Recognize and report on server room environmental issues (temperature, humidity/ESD/power surges, back-up generator/fire suppression/flood considerations)	Chapter 14	Entire chapter
6.0 Troubleshooting and Problem Determination		
6.1 Perform problem determination	Chapter 15	Isolating the Problem
Use questioning techniques to determine what, how, when.	Chapter 15	Ask the right questions
Identify contact(s) responsible for problem resolution	Chapter 15	Resolving the problem
Use senses to observe problem (e.g., smell of smoke, observation of unhooked cable, etc.)	Chapter 15	Using Your Senses
6.2 Use diagnostic hardware and software tools and utilities	Chapter 16	Using the Right Tool
Identify common diagnostic tools across the following OS: Microsoft Windows NT/2000, Novell NetWare, UNIX, Linux, IBM OS/2	Chapter 16	Vendor-specific software tools
Perform shut down across the following OS: Microsoft Windows NT/2000, Novell NetWare, UNIX, Linux, IBM OS/2	Chapter 5	Shutting Down the Operating System
Select the appropriate tool	Chapter 16	Using the Right Tool

Continued

Table A-1 *(continued)*

Exam Objective	Chapter	Section
Use the selected tool effectively	Chapter 16	Using the Right Tool
Replace defective hardware components as appropriate	Chapter 16	Replacing Hardware
Identify defective FRUs and replace with correct part	Chapter 16	Replacing Hardware
Interpret error logs, operating system errors, health logs, and critical events	Chapter 15	Log files
Use documentation from previous technician successfully	Chapter 16	Server documentation
Locate and effectively use hot tips (e.g., fixes, OS updates, E-support, web pages, CDs)	Chapter 16	Using vendor resources
Gather resources to get problem solved: Identify situations requiring call for assistance, Acquire appropriate documentation	Chapter 16	Troubleshooting Resources
Describe how to perform remote troubleshooting for a wake-on-LAN	Chapter 16	Wake-on-LAN
Describe how to perform remote troubleshooting for a remote alert	Chapter 16	Troubleshooting Remotely
6.3 Identify bottlenecks (e.g., processor, bus transfer, I/O, disk I/O, network I/O, memory)	Chapter 11	Identifying Bottlenecks
6.4 Identify and correct misconfigurations and/or upgrades	Chapter 15	Checking Hardware Checking Software Troubleshooting the OS
6.5 Determine if problem is hardware, software or virus related	Chapter 15	Checking Hardware Checking Software Troubleshooting the OS Checking for Viruses

Exam Objective	Chapter	Section
7.0 Disaster Recovery		
7.1 Plan for disaster recovery	Chapter 17	Forming a Disaster Recovery Plan
Plan for redundancy (e.g., hard drives, power supplies, fans, NICs, processors, UPS)	Chapter 17	Planning for Redundancy
Use the technique of hot swap, warm swap and hot spare to ensure availability	Chapter 18	Ensuring High Availability
Use the concepts of fault tolerance/ fault recovery to create a disaster recovery plan	Chapter 18	Recovering a RAID System
Develop disaster recovery plan	Chapter 17	Forming a Disaster Recovery Plan
Identify types of backup hardware	Chapter 19	Types of Backup Hardware and Media
Identify types of backup and restoration schemes	Chapter 19	Types of Backups
Confirm and use off site storage for backup	Chapter 17	Backup Plan
Document and test disaster recovery plan regularly, and update as needed	Chapter 17	Testing the Disaster Recovery Plan
7.2 Restoring	Chapter 19	Documenting Backup and Restoration Procedures
Identify hardware replacements	Chapter 8	Adding Hard Drives
Identify hot and cold sites	Chapter 17	Ensuring Service
Implement disaster recovery plan	Chapter 17	Testing the Disaster Recovery Plan

✦   ✦   ✦

Practice Exam

This appendix contains a complete practice exam with questions similar to those that you can expect to see on the CompTIA Server+ exam. The answers to the questions, with detailed explanations, are found at the end of the exam.

Test Questions

1. Before performing a BIOS and firmware upgrade on a newly installed server, what is the best resource for acquiring the most recent BIOS and firmware?

    A. The vendor's Web site

    B. The network OS Web site

    C. The CD-ROM that came with the new server

    D. A list server resource

2. A technician is looking for the best place to confirm current hardware compatibility with the Network OS's hardware compatibility list. Which of the following is the best resource to confirm current hardware compatibility?

    A. The network OS installation media

    B. The network OS Web site

    C. The HCL diagnostic utility

    D. The `readme.txt` file

3. A new hardware monitoring agent has been installed and configured in a server. After the installation, the monitoring program does not detect the systems BIOS settings. What is the most likely cause of the problem?

    A. The network OS needs to be patched.

    B. The BIOS needs to be upgraded.

    C. The special BIOS driver needs to be loaded.

    D. The BIOS is damaged.

4. A company wants to install a new server beside an existing server. The technician has already verified power availability and environmental requirements. Which of the following should be checked next?

    A. Cable lengths to the switch

    B. The version of the NOS

    C. Firewall location

    D. Network connectivity

5. A company has recently installed a new database server. After six months the number of users connecting to the server has grown to the point where the company must invest in adding a new processor for the server to keep up with demand. When the new processor arrives, what should the technician verify to make sure that the processors will operate together correctly?

    A. Serial number

    B. Stepping

    C. Voltage

    D. Cache

6. To begin a SCSI RAID-5 array upgrade for a customer, a technician has ordered a SCSI RAID card, SCSI cables, and five10GB, 40-pin hard drives. What component will not be compatible once all the parts have been delivered?

    A. The SCSI cables.

    B. The hard drives, because you need a minimum 20GB drive for SCSI RAID-5.

    C. The hard drives, because they are 40-pin IDE drives, not SCSI.

    D. The SCSI RAID card.

7. A new SCSI hard drive system has been installed with four hard drives. After the server is powered up, the system exhibits erratic behavior, with drives disappearing and data loss. After a reboot, the server runs fine for a short time before the problems begin again. What is the most likely cause of the problem?

    A. One of the SCSI devices is defective.

    B. The technician did not upgrade the BIOS.

    C. The devices were not properly terminated.

    D. The SCSI adapters' firmware needs upgrading.

8. From the list below, what will a technician NOT find on the back of a UPS?

    A. Surge-suppression protected outlet

    B. RS-232 connector

    C. SCSI connector

    D. Battery-protected outlet

9. A company would like to connect 20 hard drives to their five database servers. What is the best technology to use for this configuration?

   A. Fast SCSI

   B. UltraWide SCSI

   C. UDMA

   D. Fibre Channel

10. A technician is installing a new NIC into an existing server. The server already has a serial mouse on COM 1, a Modem on COM 2, and a sound card that is configured to use IRQ 5. The technician manually sets the IRQ for the NIC to 3. What device will the NIC have a conflict with?

    A. The sound card

    B. The modem

    C. The mouse

    D. The keyboard

11. Why would a technician perform a backup of the system files before flashing the system BIOS?

    A. To make sure the BIOS is clear of old data.

    B. To move the data to another server.

    C. To ensure data can be recovered if the update corrupts the server.

    D. There is no need to back up before a BIOS update.

12. How many controllers are needed for disk duplexing?

    A. 3

    B. 5

    C. 2

    D. 1

13. What is the minimum number of drives need for RAID 5?

    A. 3

    B. 4

    C. 2

    D. 6

14. A customer has had a hard drive failure on their file server and lost all of their data. The customer asks for a new fault-tolerant solution that will support multiple hard drives with room for expansion. What RAID level should be implemented?

    A. RAID 5

    B. RAID 0

    C. RAID 1

    D. RAID 2

15. A technician is verifying the network configuration on a Microsoft Windows NT server. Which of the following commands should be used to accomplish this?

    A. `config`

    B. `ifconfig`

    C. `netstat`

    D. `ipconfig`

16. A technician has just updated the network OS on an e-mail server. The technician notices that after the upgrade, some hardware on the system is no longer operating. Which of the following will fix the problem?

    A. Replace the hardware that does not work.

    B. Test the hardware in another system.

    C. Check for new drivers specific to the Network OS.

    D. Reinstall the operating system.

17. When a technician is adding new hardware to a server, what is the most important step to be performed prior to the upgrade?

    A. Back up the BIOS.

    B. Flash the BIOS with the most current version.

    C. E-mail a message to everyone stating the server will be going down.

    D. Perform a full backup.

18. A technician has just completed a full backup of a critical file server. Where is the best place for the technician to store the backup tapes?

    A. In a locked desk drawer

    B. In the fire-proof safe beside the server room

    C. At a location off-site

    D. On top of the backup tape unit

19. Which backup method will clear the archive bit?

    A. Daily

    B. Incremental

    C. Differential

    D. Random

20. What is a disadvantage of using incremental backups?

    A. Not all files are being backed up, so it is faster than a full backup.

    B. Not all files are being backed up, so fewer tape media are required.

    C. Backups are spread across multiple media, which can cause recovery to take longer.

    D. All files are being backed up, therefore it will take longer than a full backup.

21. Which of the following is a recognized backup media rotation method?

    A. The grandfather-father-son media rotation method

    B. The grandfather-cousin-son media rotation method

    C. The full-last-differential media rotation method

    D. The grandmother-father-son media rotation method

22. For a father-son media rotation method, what is the typical number of media used?

    A. 19

    B. 6

    C. 1

    D. 11

23. What should NOT be done during a BIOS upgrade?

    A. Install other software while the BIOS upgrade is performed.

    B. Power down or reboot the system.

    C. Perform a backup of the system.

    D. Upgrade the Network OS.

24. What RAID level provides the least fault tolerance?

    A. RAID 1

    B. RAID 3

    C. RAID 0

    D. RAID 5

25. What RAID level uses disk mirroring?

   A. RAID 5

   B. RAID 0

   C. RAID 1

   D. RAID 2

26. What is the cable length of a SCSI-1?

   A. 6 meters

   B. 3 meters

   C. 1.5 meters

   D. 12 meters

27. What is RAID 10 also known as?

   A. RAID 1

   B. RAID 0+1

   C. RAID 0+5

   D. RAID 0+10

28. While attempting to download a software patch, you notice that there is no network connectivity. What visual check can you perform to diagnose the problem?

   A. Check the power cord.

   B. Check the NIC card for link light activity.

   C. Replace the network cable with a new one.

   D. Reboot the system.

29. What does DLT stand for?

   A. Dynamic Linear Tape

   B. Digital Linear Tape

   C. Diagnostic Line Tester

   D. Direct Line Telephone

30. You are configuring a new UPS for a single server. The UPS software has been installed, and the signal cable has been connected to the server's parallel port. When you pull the power plug to test the configuration, the UPS runs for fifteen minutes, and then the UPS and the server immediately shut down. What is the most likely cause of the problem?

    A. The battery was not charged.

    B. The UPS software was not correctly configured.

    C. There is too much of a load on the UPS.

    D. The signal cable should be connected to the serial port.

31. You have just received an 8-port network hub that is to be daisy-chained off of a 24-port switch. Neither of the devices has an uplink port. What type of cable is needed to connect the hub and switch together?

    A. UTP cable

    B. Rollover cable

    C. Crossover cable

    D. Straight through cable

32. A technician would like to add memory to an existing server. Which of the following is the most important item to check before purchasing memory?

    A. Check POST for memory errors.

    B. Verify compatibility with existing memory.

    C. Verify the availability of a memory slot.

    D. Verify compatibility with the network OS.

33. What command would you use in Microsoft Windows NT to test end-to-end connectivity?

    A. `ping`

    B. `netstat`

    C. `ifconfig`

    D. `config`

34. What should a technician verify before upgrading a third-party system monitoring agent?

    A. The system meets the minimum requirements for the agent.

    B. The agent's SNMP traps are configured on the system.

    C. The agent is in stand-by mode.

    D. The network OS HCL lists the agent.

35. Where are SNMP thresholds set?

    A. SNMP service layer

    B. SNMP monitor

    C. IP table

    D. ACL

36. A technician is creating a list of people who should have access to the secure server room. Who would be least likely to be recommended for having access to the server room?

    A. System administrators

    B. Accounting users

    C. Unix administrator

    D. Database administrators

37. You want to ensure that a memory upgrade package that has arrived is compatible with the server's motherboard. Where is the best place to find the information?

    A. The motherboard manual

    B. The OS manual

    C. The CPU manufacturer

    D. The RAM manufacturer

38. Which of the following is considered a server room environmental issue?

    A. Temperature

    B. Noise

    C. Loose cables across the floor

    D. The server cabinet is unlocked

39. What does KVM stand for?

    A. Keyboard/Vector/Monitoring

    B. Key/Vender/Mounting

    C. Keyboard/Video/Mouse

    D. Kernel/Vector/Memory

40. A technician notices that one of the servers is making a very loud buzzing noise. Which of the following is least likely to be the problem?

    A. Network card

    B. CPU fan

    C. Power supply

    D. Hard drive

41. When a new server technician is hired, which of the following would be the quickest way to get the new technician knowledgeable about the IT environment?

    A. Take the new technician out for lunch and tell him how the network functions over a cup of tea and a sandwich.

    B. Make the new technician aware of the corporate dress code and proper instructions on how to not spill his coffee on the new carpet.

    C. Show the new technician where all the print servers are in the building.

    D. Use the documentation from the former employee.

42. A technician must remove a failed hard drive that is in a hot-plug slot in a RAID 5 array. What does the technician have to do before removing the drive?

    A. Power down the server.

    B. Put the server in standby mode.

    C. Shut down the operating system.

    D. Nothing

43. After a technician has performed a full backup and has stored the tapes off-site, what else should the technician store off-site with the backup tapes to help facilitate the recovery of data?

    A. Spare backup tapes

    B. Spare Network OS CD-ROM

    C. Spare tape drive and cables

    D. Remote notification pager

44. At what stage of a server installation should a disaster recovery plan be prepared?

    A. Before deployment

    B. After deployment

    C. Before the installation of the SCSI devices

    D. Immediately after the first full backup has been verified

45. What is the maximum length of a 10Base5 Ethernet segment?

    A. 200 meters

    B. 500 meters

    C. 500 feet

    D. 10 meters

46. What does DAT stand for?

    A. Diagnostic Audio Transceiver

    B. Digital Audio Tape

    C. Digital Analog Tape

    D. Diagnostic Analog Tap

47. When adding memory to a server, what should be the first item to check before ordering additional RAM?

    A. Make sure it is the same brand as the current RAM.

    B. Check for an available memory slot.

    C. Upgrade the system BIOS.

    D. Run a memory check on the current RAM.

48. To gain maximum performance from your backup tape drive, which of the following can a technician do?

    A. Use a cleaning tape regularly

    B. Use DAT tapes

    C. Use a toothbrush to clean the heads of the tape drive

    D. Replace the tape drive every 12 months

49. What is SNMP?

    A. A video bus technology

    B. The method of using dual processors in a system

    C. A network protocol for routing information

    D. A protocol used to measure various system attributes

50. After a new server is installed, the technician notices that the NIC on the newly installed server is not functioning properly. What is the most likely cause of the problem?

    A. The technician did not verify hardware requirements.

    B. The technician did not get the latest drivers from the manufacturer.

    C. The technician did not flash the BIOS to recognize the NIC.

    D. The technician forgot to enable plug-and-play capabilities on the new server.

51. What does the term *multiprocessing* mean?

    A. Running a system that has two or more database files installed.

    B. A database can be updated by several users at the same time.

    C. Running a system with more than one processor.

    D. Able to connect two or more monitors to the server.

52. What are the two types of multiprocessing?

    A. Symmetric and asymmetric

    B. Stepping and cache

    C. Pentium II and Pentium III

    D. RAID 5 and RAID 3

53. A technician has to connect two 100MB Ethernet switches. Which of the following cable types would the technician use?

    A. 10BaseT

    B. Crossover cable

    C. PS/2 cable

    D. Serial cable

54. Using a crossover cable, which of the following would a technician be able to connect?

    A. Server NIC to a server NIC

    B. Server NIC to a hub

    C. Server NIC to a standard port on a switch

    D. Server serial port to a UPS

55. What is the correct command to shut down a Unix server?

    A. `shutdown`

    B. `down`

    C. `off /s`

    D. `down it`

56. What should always be done before monitoring a server's performance?

    A. Perform a full backup.

    B. Upgrade the BIOS.

    C. Restart the server.

    D. Create a baseline of current performance.

57. Which backup method enables you to make one full weekly backup, and then only back up files that have changed since that backup?

    A. Daily

    B. Incremental

    C. Differential

    D. Full

58. Which of the following uses an RJ-45 connector?

    A. Fiber-optic

    B. Coaxial

    C. 10BaseT

    D. 10Base2

59. What Network OS would you be using if you had to refer to a HCL?

    A. Novell NetWare

    B. Unix

    C. IBM OS/2

    D. Microsoft Windows NT

60. Which of the following has the MOST impact on your server security?

    A. Password lock on the application server

    B. Keeping the server room door locked at all times

    C. Changing the administration password every seven days

    D. Only granting administrators and users access to the server room

61. A technician is attempting to do a full restore onto a server from backup tapes. After the technician has put in the second backup tape, the restore stops. The technician tries the backup again, and the restore stops on the second backup tape again. Which of the following is the most likely cause of the failed restore?

    A. The technician is using a DLT tape and not a DAT tape.

    B. The restore was complete.

    C. The second tape in the restore is corrupt.

    D. For a full restore, the technician should only need one tape

62. A manager calls you to report that no one can access the network anymore. Which of the following would be the first thing you should do to diagnose the problem?

    A. Get all the users to reboot their systems.

    B. Reboot the server and ask the users to log in again. If all the users can log in to the network, examine the server logs for errors.

    C. Ask more specific questions to determine the source of the problem.

    D. Escalate the problem to the OS vendor.

63. A technician has just installed Microsoft Windows NT on a new server. When you log into the server, you receive a message that not all the services have started. Which of the following should the technician do next?

    A. Check to see if the server's NIC has a link light.

    B. Reboot the server and see if the message reappears.

    C. Check the event logs.

    D. Check to see if the server is in the proper domain.

64. Which hard disk interface is most commonly used in a desktop computer?

    A. IDE/ATA

    B. SCSI

    C. PCMCIA

    D. RAID

65. What command do you use to shut down a Novell NetWare 5.*x* server?

    A. Down

    B. Root Down

    C. Shutdown

    D. Shutdown now

66. A technician is using 24 GB DAT tapes for backing up a file server. What industry standard is being used?

    A. DDS-1

    B. DDS-2

    C. DDS-3

    D. DDS-24

67. HVD is a type of voltage signaling for what technology?

    A. IDE/ATA

    B. SCSI

    C. EIDE

    D. HCL

68. What two backup methods do NOT clear the archive bit of the files being backed up?

    A. Full

    B. Differential

    C. Incremental

    D. Daily

69. Disk mirroring requires a minimum of how many hard drives and how many disk controllers?

   A. 2 hard drives and 2 disk controllers

   B. 2 hard drives and 1 disk controller

   C. 3 hard drives and 2 disk controllers

   D. 1 hard drive and 2 disk controllers

70. A Microsoft Windows NT server can be configured for what categories of software RAID?

   A. 0, 3, 5

   B. 0, 1, 5

   C. 1, 3, 5

   D. 1, 2, 5

71. A technician needs to install a new NIC in an existing server. What type of NIC should the technician get that would offer the best performance?

   A. PCI

   B. ISA

   C. EISA

   D. AGP

72. How many pins are on a standard IDE interface?

   A. 50

   B. 68

   C. 20

   D. 40

73. You have just replaced a video card in a server. When you reboot the server, the network OS loads, but the screen turns blank at the logon screen. What is the most likely cause of the problem?

   A. The video driver needs to be updated.

   B. The card is conflicting with another device.

   C. The monitor is not compatible with the OS.

   D. The BIOS needs to be upgraded.

74. A company suffered a major power loss and all the systems were down for 15 minutes. Many server disk drives were corrupted, and some had to be restored from backup tapes. What could have prevented the server problems?

   A. Line conditioner

   B. Uninterruptible Power supply

C. Power surge protector

D. More frequent backup schedule

75. A technician installs a new SCSI controller and network adapter into an existing Microsoft Windows NT server. After the technician restarts the system, the technician receives message that says, "The logon service failed to start." Where would the technician first look to diagnose the problem?

A. Network card documentation

B. Error logs

C. Disk administrator

D. Performance Monitor

76. Using a disk administration utility, a technician is creating a stripe set with parity. The system is using four 9GB hard disks. How much total space will the technician have available for data storage?

A. 27GB

B. 36GB

C. 18GB

D. 9GB

77. A technician discovers that one disk in a mirrored set has failed. The technician already has a replacement disk ready. What should the technician's next step be in fixing the problem?

A. Break the mirror.

B. Implement RAID 1+0.

C. Replace the controller.

D. Erase the entire set and restore from backup.

78. Which of the following would be considered an important environmental issue?

A. Security cameras not functioning

B. An air conditioning unit with no filter installed

C. Server doors unlocked

D. Ethernet cables run across the floor

79. A customer would like a server to be installed with disk striping but with no parity, because they want to conserve their current disk space. What RAID level should the technician recommend?

A. RAID 0

B. RAID 1

C. RAID 5

D. Disk duplexing

80. Which of the following is considered a Hybrid RAID level?

   A. RAID 0

   B. RAID 1

   C. RAID 1+0

   D. RAID 5

81. How many pins would you find on a narrow SCSI connector?

   A. 50

   B. 40

   C. 68

   D. 80

82. How many devices can be attached to a SCSI chain?

   A. 4

   B. 6

   C. 7

   D. 8

83. You have just upgraded a server's NIC card from a 10 Mbps card to a 100 Mbps card. The company uses Category 3 UTP cabling, with RJ-45 connectors. When the server is rebooted, the network card does not connect to the network. What is the most likely cause of the problem?

   A. The Ethernet switch only supports 10/100 network cards.

   B. The connectors should be RG-59.

   C. The network cable is defective.

   D. The cabling must be Category 5 to support 100 Mbps.

84. A technician wants to protect the company's servers from erratic power and blackouts. What device would best protect the servers?

   A. A surge protector

   B. UPS

   C. A line conditioner

   D. Extra electrical outlets

85. What is the special characteristic of ECC memory?

   A. It is the fastest memory available.

   B. It will only work in ECC-compatible motherboards.

   C. It must be installed in pairs.

   D. It contains built-in error-checking and correction.

86. Baseline performance data can be compiled through which of the following sources?

    A. Audit logs

    B. Event logs

    C. Performance monitors

    D. Observation

87. Of the following items, which one should always be properly documented?

    A. Disaster recovery plan

    B. Administrative tasks

    C. Administrator e-mail addresses

    D. User passwords

88. A technician has successfully installed a new NOS onto a new server. What should the technician do next?

    A. Perform a baseline of the installation.

    B. Install OS patches.

    C. Document installation procedure.

    D. Examine compatibility lists.

89. Which of the following is not a valid backup strategy?

    A. Incremental backup

    B. Full backup

    C. Differential backup

    D. Random backup

90. When a technician begins to diagnose a problem with a NIC, the technician should first:

    A. Reboot the system.

    B. Replace the bad NIC.

    C. Gather information.

    D. Call the NIC vendor.

91. Which of the following are least likely to be contaminated with a virus?

    A. Floppy disk

    B. E-mail attachment

    C. Downloaded files from Internet

    D. BIOS flash update

92. A customer is worried about a flashing light on the back of a network card. What is the most likely cause of the condition?

    A. It indicates the device is powered on.

    B. It indicates an error.

    C. It indicates network activity.

    D. It indicates 100MB full duplex mode.

93. Which of the following sources of information should you consult when you are installing a new device?

    A. Device documentation

    B. Vendor's telephone support

    C. The vendor's Web site

    D. None of the above

94. Which of the following is the best method for establishing a baseline?

    A. Document the information at 8 a.m. every day for six months.

    B. Document the information every day for two weeks.

    C. Document the information every few hours for two weeks.

    D. Document the information once a month.

95. What should a technician do after performing a full backup?

    A. Lock the media used for the full backup in a fire-proof safe off-site.

    B. Lock the tape in a safe on-site for future use.

    C. Verify the full backup.

    D. Clean the heads of the tape backup unit.

96. A technician comes into work in the morning and notices a server is not responding to network requests. How can the technician determine when the problem occurred?

    A. Check the link lights on the NIC.

    B. Check the error logs.

    C. Find out who was the first user to log on to the network.

    D. Reboot the server and watch for error messages.

97. How does disk duplexing offer more fault tolerance?

    A. Two disks are mirrored and use different controllers

    B. With disk duplexing, three controllers are used

    C. Disk duplexing uses a minimum of three hard drives

    D. Two disk are mirrored and use the same controller

98. A technician is installing two new IDE drives in a new e-mail server. How should the new IDE drives be set to work properly together?

    A. Primary/Secondary

    B. Master/Slave

    C. Master/Servant

    D. First/Second

99. How often should a technician replace the battery of a UPS?

    A. Every month

    B. Every year

    C. Every three to five years

    D. Every week

100. Which locations would be a poor choice for a network server?

    A. Ventilated wiring closet

    B. Non-ventilated wiring closet

    C. In front of a window

    D. Ventilated wiring closet with no air conditioning

Answers

1. A. The vendor's Web site will almost always have the latest BIOS and firmware revisions for their hardware. Answer B is incorrect because the OS vendor will not have hardware-related patches. Answer C is incorrect because the updates on a CD that came with the system could be out of date. Answer D is incorrect because it is always best to use the primary vendor's resources rather than third-party information.

2. B. The Network OS Web site should be the best resource to confirm current hardware compatibility. Answer A is incorrect because the installation media will only have the current drivers released at the time of the product. Answer C is incorrect because there is no such thing as a HCL diagnostic utility. Answer D is incorrect because the readme.txt file will give you the latest information, but not a hardware compatibility confirmation list.

3. B. The BIOS needs to be updated to take advantage of the monitoring system's capabilities. Any type of hardware monitoring system will be dependent on the BIOS for certain types of hardware information. If the BIOS is not up to date, the program may not recognize it at all if it uses newer technology than the BIOS can handle. Answer A is incorrect because the OS software will not have anything to do with the BIOS. Answer C is incorrect because there is no need for a special driver. Answer D is incorrect because if the BIOS were damaged, the server would not be able to start.

4. D. Verifying network connectivity verifies that there is a proper connection to the network available. Answer A is incorrect because at this time cable lengths are not an issue. Answer B is incorrect because the version of the OS should have been verified before the installation. Answer C is incorrect because the firewall location has nothing to do with the current server at this time.

5. B. The processor stepping versions must be the same, or the dual-processor system will not work properly. Answers A, C, and D are incorrect because in general the CPU should be identical to the current one, but the stepping version is the critical item to check.

6. C. The hard drives that have been ordered are IDE drives, not SCSI. SCSI drives come in 50-pin Narrow, 68-pin Wide, and 80-pin SCA configurations.

7. C. Improper termination will result in irregular performance and often failure of the SCSI bus. Answer A is incorrect because all the drives were available initially. Answers B and D are incorrect, although it is always best to update the BIOS and firmware levels of the system board and SCSI controller cards to their latest version.

8. C. There is no need for a SCSI connector on a UPS. The protected outlets are for connecting to the serial port of server so the UPS can communicate with the server and shut it down in the event of a power outage.

9. D. Fibre Channel will offer the best performance for such a large environment that needs the fastest technology available. Answers A and B are incorrect because they are older, slower SCSI protocols. Answer C is incorrect because UDMA is based on IDE, and cannot support that many hard drives.

10. B. The newly installed NIC will conflict with the modem. IRQ 3 is the default assigned IRQ for COM 2. No two devices can share the same IRQ. Answer A is incorrect because the sound card is assigned to IRQ 5, which does not conflict with IRQ 3. Answer C is incorrect because the mouse is installed on COM 1, and the default IRQ for COM 1 is 4. Answer D is incorrect because the keyboard is assigned to IRQ 1 by default.

11. C. If the BIOS update gets interrupted, or does not work, it could render the server inoperable. Answer A is incorrect because you do not clear the BIOS before updating. Answer B is incorrect because there is no need to move data elsewhere. Answer D is incorrect because you should back up your data before doing any kind of update to the server.

12. C. A minimum of two controllers are needed for disk duplexing. If one controller fails, the other can take over.

13. A. For RAID 5 you need a minimum of three drives for proper parity using striping.

14. A. RAID will provide a fault-tolerant solution by providing parity striped over many disks. It can also be easily expanded with more drives. Answer B is incorrect because RAID 0 does not provide fault tolerance. Answer C is incorrect because RAID 1 will not provide for easy expansion. Answer D is incorrect because RAID 2 is not a proper current standard.

15. D. `ipconfig` is the proper command to examine network information on an NT server. Answer A is incorrect because there is no `config` command in Windows NT. Answer B is incorrect because the `ifconfig` command is used for Unix. Answer C is incorrect because `netstat` is used by Windows machines for examining routing tables.

16. C. A new driver that came with the updated OS is not working. Install a better driver that enables your hardware under the new operating system. Answers A and B are incorrect because the problem is software, not hardware. Answer D is incorrect because a reinstall of the OS will not fix the problem.

17. D. Before any type of upgrade, you should perform a full backup of your system in case the upgrade renders the system inoperable. Answer A is incorrect because there is no way to back up the BIOS. Answer B is incorrect, although it is important to keep the system BIOS current to support new hardware. Answer C is incorrect, but it is a good idea to have users log off of the system before performing an upgrade.

18. C. The safest location is off-site. In the event of a disaster in the building, the tapes are safe at another location. Answer A is incorrect because the tapes are still vulnerable to natural disasters. Answer B is incorrect, although a fire-proof safe would be a good place to store non-critical backups. Answer D is incorrect because the tapes can be easily misplaced, or overwritten by another employee.

19. B. An incremental backup will clear the archive bit. Answers A and D are incorrect because a Daily backup does not clear the archive bit and Random is not a correct backup scheme.. Answer C is incorrect because a differential backup will back up changes since the last full backup; therefore, the archive bit will remain.

20. C. Incremental backups take longer to restore if a full restore is needed because data is spread across multiple tapes. Answers A and B are incorrect because these are advantages of an incremental backup. Answer D is incorrect because not all files are backed up in an incremental backup.

21. A. The grandfather-father-son method uses daily, weekly, and monthly backups.

22. B. The typical number of media used for a father-son rotation is 5. Answer A is incorrect because 19 media are generally used for the grandfather media rotation method. Answer C is incorrect because only one media is used for the son media rotation method. Answer D is incorrect because 11 media are used for the grandfather-father-son rotation method.

23. B. Powering down or rebooting a server during a BIOS upgrade could render the system inoperable. Answer A is incorrect because you cannot install software during a BIOS upgrade. Answer C is incorrect because backup of the system should be performed before the upgrade. Answer D is incorrect because there is no need to upgrade the OS for a BIOS upgrade.

24. C. RAID 0 uses striping without parity, and does not provide any fault tolerance. Answer A is incorrect because RAID 1 mirroring is fault-tolerant. Answers B and D are incorrect because they use parity for fault tolerance.

25. C. RAID 1 uses disk mirroring. Answers A and B are incorrect because RAID 5 and RAID 0 use disk striping. Answer D is incorrect because RAID 2 does not use mirroring.

26. A. 6 meters is the standard length for a SCSI-1 type cable. Answer B is incorrect because the Fast SCSI-2, Wide SCSI-2, and Fast Wide SCSI-2 types use cables that are 3 meters long. Answer C is incorrect because the Ultra SCSI-3 8 bit and 16 bit types use cables that are 1.5 meters long. Answer D is incorrect because the Ultra-2 SCSI, Wide Ultra-2 SCSI, and the Ultra-3 SCSI types use cables that are 12 meters long.

27. B. RAID 0+1 is also known as RAID 10.

28. B. The link and activity lights on a NIC card can be visually examined to determine proper network connectivity. The light usually flashes to indicate network data being sent and received from the card. This is a good, quick check to indicate proper network activity. Answer A is incorrect because the power cord will have nothing to do with network activity. Answer C is incorrect because the problem has not been traced to the cabling in these initial stages. Answer D is incorrect because rebooting the server is not a visual examination.

29. B. DLT stands for Digital Linear Tape, a high-capacity magnetic tape used to backup large amounts of data in an enterprise.

30. D. The signal cable is designed to be attached to the server's serial COM port. This is to allow communications between the UPS and the server. During a power failure, the UPS will signal the server of the power loss, and then the OS will begin a shutdown of the system. Answer A is incorrect because the UPS ran for a required amount of time before shutting down, so the battery was charged properly. Answer B is incorrect because the software was configured properly, but the signal cable was not properly connected. Answer C is incorrect because a single server on a UPS should not overload it.

31. C. A crossover cable will be needed to reverse the transmit and receive wires. An uplink port would automatically do this, but the devices do not have one, therefore, a crossover cable is needed to reverse the wires. Answer A is incorrect because a regular UTP cable will not work in the case. This is used to connect a server to a switch, or a switch to another switch with an uplink port. Answer B is incorrect because a rollover cable is used to for special console access on network devices. Answer D is incorrect because a regular straight-through cable is the same thing as a regular UTP cable.

32. C. You must have extra memory slots to add any additional memory to a server. If no slots are available, you must replace the existing memory with larger capacity memory chips. Answer A is incorrect, although it should be done after the new memory is installed to ensure it is functional. Answer C is incorrect because compatibility should be examined after verifying the additional slot. Answer D is incorrect because any OS should work with any type of memory.

33. A. The `ping` command is used to test end-to-end connectivity on a Microsoft Windows NT system. Answer B is incorrect because `netstat` is used on a Windows system to view listening ports. Answer C is incorrect because `ifconfig` is used on Unix and Linux systems to view network statistics. Answer D is incorrect because the `config` command is used on a Novell NetWare system to view network statistics.

34. A. You must ensure that your system is compatible with the new agent, or it may not function properly. Answer B is incorrect because your trap settings will have nothing to do with the upgrade. Answer C is incorrect because there is no stand-by mode. Answer D is incorrect because a software agent would not be listed on a Hardware Compatibility List.

35. B. The thresholds are set on the SNMP monitoring device, where the captured data is compared. Answer A is incorrect because there are no thresholds for SNMP services. Answer C is incorrect because the IP table has nothing to do with SNMP functions. Answer D is incorrect because the ACL is an access control list for OS security.

36. B. Users have no reason to be in the server room. Answers A, C, and D, are incorrect because all these people need access to the server equipment.

37. A. The motherboard manual will contain the appropriate information for what types of RAM can be installed. RAM must be inspected carefully for its type, the number of pins, and its speed, so that is it compatible with the motherboard. Answer B is incorrect because the OS manual will not have any type of hardware compatibility information. Answer C is incorrect because the CPU is not relevant to memory compatibility with the motherboard. Answer D is incorrect because the RAM manufacturer will only have information on its own product, not the motherboard where the memory will be installed.

38. A. Temperature is the most important environmental issue affecting server rooms. Answer B is incorrect because noise will not harm the servers. Answer C is incorrect, although it is a physical concern for the server room. Answer D is incorrect because this is a security issue.

39. C. KVM is short for keyboard/video/mouse, used to describe switches that enable you to control multiple servers with one keyboard, monitor, and mouse.

40. A. The network card does not have any moving parts that cause such a condition. Answers B, C, and D are incorrect because all these components contain mechanical parts and fans that could make noises when not working properly.

41. D. Answer D is the only correct answer. When a new server technician is hired, the quickest way to get the new technician knowledgeable about the IT environment within the company is to provide the new technician with existing documentation. Answers A, B, and C are all incorrect because these methods do not help the new technician gain knowledge about the IT environment within the company. **Note from the Author:** Answers A, B, and C are true accounts of my experience on a contract position I held during the writing of this book.

42. D. The hot-plug system enables you to remove and replace hard drives without powering down the system. In this case, the RAID array will rebuild itself automatically with the new drive. Answers A and B are incorrect because the hot-plug capability eliminates the need to power off or suspend the server. Answer C is incorrect because the hot plug RAID system allows drives to be removed and replaced without interrupting normal operations.

43. C. In the event of a disaster, having a spare tape drive off-site, along with your backup tapes, can reduce the time it takes to recover. Answers A, B, and D are incorrect because none of the items will aid in data recovery.

44. A. A disaster recovery plan should be prepared and in place before the equipment is installed. Answer B is incorrect, because in between the time you have installed your system, and a recovery plan is being prepared, a disaster could happen. Answer C is incorrect because the SCSI devices are irrelevant. Answer D is incorrect because your plan should already be in place before your backups begin.

45. B. 500 meters is the maximum length for a 10Base5 segment. Using more than the maximum length will lead to inconsistent network performance and data loss.

46. B. Digital Audio Tapes are used for backup up of small to medium size servers.

47. B. You must have available memory slots to be able to install additional memory. If you do not have any slots available, you must remove your current memory modules and upgrade them to a larger size. Answer A is incorrect because the brand name of the memory is irrelevant. Answer C is incorrect because the BIOS does not have to be upgraded before installing RAM. Answer D is incorrect because there is no need to run a memory check on current RAM; a check is performed by the POST routine whenever a server is powered on.

48. A. Regular cleaning will ensure that the tape heads will not get dirty and corrupt backups. Answer B is incorrect because a DAT tape refers only to the size and compression technology of the tape. Answer C is incorrect because you should never use an abrasive tool or substance on a tape drive head. Answer D is incorrect because replacing the drive every 12 months is both unnecessary and impractical.

49. D. SNMP is Simple Network Management Protocol, which is used to monitor system performance through various software and hardware attributes. Answer A is incorrect, and SNMP does not describe a video bus technology. Answer B is incorrect because a multiple processor system is referred to as SMP, symmetric multi-processor. Answer C is incorrect because SNMP is not used for network routing information.

50. B. It is always important to get the most recent drivers for your device cards. Answer A is incorrect because this is more likely a software problem than hardware. Answer C is incorrect because a BIOS is rarely needed for network card installation. Answer D is incorrect because plug-and play is typically enabled by default.

51. C. Multiprocessing is defined as using more than one processor in a system. Answer A is incorrect because any system can have more than one database running. Answer B is incorrect because this refers to file locking and multi-user capabilities of database programs. Answer D is incorrect because you would rarely connect more than one monitor to a server, and has nothing to do with server processing.

52. A. Symmetric and asymmetric are two types of multiprocessing, which refer to the processors working in tandem or independently. Answer B is incorrect because stepping and caching refer to individual characteristics of a single processor. Answer C is incorrect because these are two different generations of a CPU chip. Answer D is incorrect because RAID levels refer to storage fault tolerance.

53. B. Connecting two Ethernet switches together requires the use of a crossover cable. Answer A is incorrect because a 10BaseT cable would not work, because it is only capable of 10MB and the wires are not connected as a crossover. Answer C is incorrect because a PS/2 cable is used for keyboard and mouse connections. Answer D is incorrect because a serial cable on a switch is typically for the switch configuration.

54. A. To connect two servers together using their network cards, a crossover Ethernet cable is needed. Answers B and C are incorrect because a standard connection between a server and a hub or a switch requires a standard Ethernet cable. Answer D is incorrect because a connection to a UPS from the serial port would require a serial cable.

55. A. To shut down a Unix server, the proper command is `shutdown`. Answer B is incorrect because the command `down` is for a Novell NetWare server. Answers C and D are both fake commands.

56. D. A baseline of current performance should be created so that you can compare it to the new monitoring data for any changes. There is no use in measuring the performance of a server if you have no data to compare it to. Answer A is incorrect because there is no danger in monitoring a server, it will not affect your data. Answer B is incorrect because there is no need to upgrade the BIOS before measuring server performance. Answer C is incorrect because there is no need to restart the server before monitoring performance. With some operating systems, it may be a good idea to restart the server to refresh system memory and resources before beginning a monitoring program.

57. C. A differential backup will back up all files that have changed since the last full backup. Answer A is incorrect because a daily backup is only a simple designation for the frequency of backups. Answer B is incorrect because incremental backups will only back up files that have changed since the last regular backup. Answer D is incorrect because this designates a type of backup where all files are backed up.

58. C. 10BaseT uses the RJ-45 connector to terminate twisted-pair wiring. Answer A is incorrect because fiber-optic cables use special optical connectors. Answers B and D are incorrect because coaxial 10Base2 cables use RG-58 BNC connectors.

59. D. Microsoft Windows NT refers to its hardware compatibility documentation as the HCL, or hardware compatibility list. Answers A, B, and C are incorrect, although each system has its own hardware compatibility documentation.

60. B. Keeping the server door locked will keep unauthorized users from entering the server room. Answers A and C are incorrect because passwords do not prevent intruders from gaining physical access to the server room. Answer D is incorrect because users should not be given access to the server room.

61. C. There is something wrong with the second tape and, therefore, not all the files from the full backup can be restored. Answer A is incorrect because the technician should be using the same type of tapes, which would be compatible with the tape drive. Answer B is incorrect because the restore failed on the second tape. Answer D is incorrect because a full restore can take any number of tapes to fully restore all of the data.

62. C. You should probe more to find out if there are any error messages that happen when users try to log in or access the network. Answer A is incorrect because the problem might be a server issue, and having everyone reboot their systems will be too inconvenient. Answer B is incorrect because you should only reboot the server if the problem has been investigated and determined to be a server issue that can only be resolved by a reboot. Answer D is incorrect because the problem could be hardware-related, and you should investigate further before calling the OS vendor.

63. C. The first thing to check would be the event logs, where important system information and messages will help you diagnose why the services did not start. Answer A is incorrect because the problem has not been narrowed down to a network issue at this stage. Answer B is incorrect because the issue will probably appear again. Answer D is incorrect because the issue has not been narrowed down to a domain issue.

64. A. IDE/ATA interfaces are normally used in desktop computers, as there is usually no need for fault tolerance or expansion capabilities. Answer B is incorrect because SCSI is typically used in server installations. Answer C is incorrect because PCMCIA is used for laptop peripherals. Answer D is incorrect because RAID is used for fault-tolerant server installations.

65. A. Down is the proper command to shut down a NetWare server. Answer B is incorrect because the command does not exist. Answers C and D are used for Unix and OS/2 systems.

66. B. DDS-3 defines the DAT tape standard of a maximum 24GB compressed capacity. Answer A is incorrect because DDS-1 type tapes have a maximum capacity of 4GB compressed. Answer B is incorrect because DDS-2 has a maximum capacity of 8GB compressed. Answer D is incorrect because DDS-24 does not exist.

67. B. High voltage differential is a type of signaling method used in early SCSI devices. Answers A and C are incorrect because IDE/EIDE/ATA drives do not use voltage signaling. Answer D is incorrect because HCL refers to a hardware compatibility list.

68. B and **D.** The differential and daily backup methods do not clear the archive bit of the files being backed up. Answers A and C are incorrect because the full and incremental backup methods do clear the archive bit of the files being backed up.

69. B. Disk mirroring requires a minimum of one disk controller and two hard drives. Answer A is incorrect because two controllers are used in disk duplexing. Answers C and D are incorrect because you need an even number of hard drives for disk mirroring.

70. B. Windows NT software RAID only supports level 0, 1, and 5.

71. A. PCI cards come in a data bus width of 32 and 64 bits, and are as fast as the speed of the processor. Answer B is incorrect because ISA only has a max speed of 8 MHz, and only a 16 bit data bus width. Answer C is incorrect because EISA only has a maximum speed of 8 MHz and a 32 bit data bus width. Answer D is incorrect because AGP is for video cards only.

72. D. A standard IDE drive uses 40 pins. Answer A is incorrect because 50 pins normally define a narrow SCSI device. Answer B is incorrect because 68 pins typically define a wide SCSI device. Answer C is incorrect because a 20-pin interface does not exist.

73. A. The video card driver needs to be updated within the network OS to make it work. If there is no driver available beforehand, you may risk losing your display after the operating system is loaded. Without a display, it is very difficult to properly shut down the server. Answer B is incorrect because the other conflicting device would have failed as well. Answer C is incorrect because the monitor worked before, using a different video card with the same operating system. Answer D is incorrect because the display worked up until the point of the OS load, so the video card is compatible with the current BIOS.

74. B. A UPS would have sensed the power disruption and powered the servers by battery so that they could be automatically shut down gracefully. Answer A is incorrect because a line conditioner does not provide battery backup in case of power loss. Answer C is incorrect because a surge protector would not provide battery backup in the event of a power loss. Answer D is incorrect because more frequent backups would not have prevented the data loss in the first place.

75. B. The error logs should always be the first place to look to help diagnose a problem. Answer A is incorrect because the problem could be with the SCSI controller. Answer C is incorrect because the problem might not have anything to do with the disk subsystem. Answer D is incorrect because Performance Monitor will only give you data on current working systems.

76. A. A stripe set with parity will reserve the equivalent of one drive for parity operations, so the total will be 27GB. Answer B is incorrect because the parity operations will take up part of the total size of the array. Answer C is incorrect because the drives are not mirrored. Answer D is incorrect because this is the equivalent of only one drive.

77. A. Before replacing the drive, the mirror should be broken. Next, replace the drive, and then recreate the mirror. Answer B is incorrect because there is no need to redefine the RAID configuration. Answer C is incorrect because there is no need to replace the controller; it is only the drive that has failed. Answer D is incorrect because there is no need to erase the entire array.

78. B. A filter should be used to remove airborne dust from the air. Answers A and C are incorrect because they are server room security issues. Answer D is incorrect because this is a physical housekeeping issue.

79. A. RAID 0 defines a striped disk array, with no parity. Answer B is incorrect because RAID 1 defines mirroring. Answer C is incorrect because RAID 5 defines striping with parity. Answer D is incorrect because disk duplexing is another configuration of RAID 1 mirroring.

80. C. RAID 1+0 is considered a Hybrid RAID level because it is the combination of RAID-0 and RAID-1. Answers A, B, and D are all incorrect because they are all standard RAID levels.

81. A. A narrow SCSI connector has 50 pins. Answer B is incorrect because 40 pins is typically a standard IDE drive. Answer C is incorrect because 68 pins define a wide SCSI connector. Answer D is incorrect because 80 pins usually define a SCA SCSI connector.

82. C. Up to seven devices can be daisy-chained to a SCSI controller, each with a unique ID number.

83. D. You need a minimum of Category 5 cable to support 100Mpbs. Category 3 cabling will only support up to 10Mbps speed. Answer A is incorrect because a dual-speed switch will support both 10 and 100 Mbps. Answer B is incorrect because RG-59 connectors are designed for coaxial cabling. Answer C is incorrect because the same network cable worked properly before the upgrade.

84. B. An uninterruptible power supply (UPS) contains a battery backup to provide power to the server during power interruptions and blackouts. Answer A is incorrect because a surge protector only protects the server from surges and not blackouts. Answer C is incorrect because a line conditioner does not protect the server from blackouts. Answer D is incorrect because having an extra electrical outlet will not help during erratic power issues and blackouts.

85. D. ECC memory is able to check for and correct errors internally. Answer A is incorrect because ECC memory tends to be a bit slower than regular memory,. Answer B is incorrect because ECC memory can be used in most motherboards. Answer C is incorrect because having to install memory in pairs is a restriction of older SIMM-type memory.

86. C. Performance monitors can compile data over a period of time so that it can be analyzed against current performance. Answers A and B are incorrect because audit and event logs will not give you the proper information for measurement. Answer D is incorrect because the only way to get quantitative data on server performance is through the use of special monitors.

87. A. Your disaster recovery plan should always be properly documented to ensure quick recovery of your systems in the event of a disaster. Answer B is incorrect because your daily tasks are not as critical as disaster recovery documentation. Answer C is incorrect because in the event of a disaster, you might not have access to e-mail. Answer D is incorrect because hard or soft copies of password lists should never be available.

88. B. It is important to install all OS and security patches before using the network OS to ensure it is running the most stable and secure version. Answer A is incorrect because you have not installed any applications to warrant measuring a baseline. Answer C is incorrect because the entire procedure is not yet finished until you install patches. Answer D is incorrect because compatibility lists should have been consulted before the installation.

89. D. There is no such strategy as a random backup. Answers A, B, and C are all standard backup strategies.

90. C. The technician must gather the information first because gathering information will determine where the problem lies. Answer A is incorrect because rebooting the system is a drastic action to take before the technician even knows what the problem really is. Answer B is incorrect because if the technician does not gather the proper information about the problem, replacing the NIC will not determine what the problem actually is. Answer D is incorrect because the vendor will ask the technician questions, and if the technician did not gather the proper information first, the vendor will not be able to help.

91. D. It is very unlikely that a virus would be contained in a vendor BIOS update. Answers A, B, and C are all common ways of receiving a virus.

92. C. The network activity light flashes to signal that packets are being sent and received from the NIC card. Answer A is incorrect because there is no power light on a network card. Answer B is incorrect because the light does not indicate an error. Answer D is incorrect because the light that signals the speed and mode of the NIC card would be off, or would be solid without flashing.

93. A. The documentation that came with the device should be consulted first for any installation or compatibility issues. Answer B is incorrect because you should not need to call the vendor's support line unless you have a problem. Answer C is incorrect, although you may need to check the Web site for updated drivers for the device.

94. B. To record a proper baseline, you need to measure performance at all times for a period of a few weeks to account for all usage and performance statistics. Answers A and C are incorrect because you would be only taking a snapshot of a certain time of day. Answer D is incorrect because you need to collect information on the server continuously for several weeks, not just on one particular day of the month.

95. C. It is extremely important to test your backups to ensure that files are being backed up properly. Answers A, B, and D are incorrect, but are also very important in managing your backup system.

96. B. The error logs should reveal at what time the errors began. Answer A is incorrect because checking the lights on the NIC card will only give you your current connection conditions. Answer C is incorrect because this will not tell you when the problem started. Answer D is incorrect because any error message should already be in your log files.

97. A. Disk duplexing uses more than one controller, to remove the controller as a point of failure in a mirrored disk system. Answer B is incorrect because only a minimum of two controllers are needed. Answer C is incorrect because only a minimum of two hard drives are needed. Answer D is incorrect because this system is not duplexed. Answer A single controller can be a point of failure.

98. B. When you have two IDE hard drives, one will have to be set as the master and one as the slave to work properly. Answers A, C, and D are all incorrect designations.

99. C. It is recommended that you replace the battery of a UPS every three to five years.

100. B, C, and **D.** When choosing a location for a new server, make sure there is proper ventilation, so answer B is incorrect. Answer C is incorrect because keeping a server by a window would be a bad choice because of direct sunlight. Answer D is incorrect because air conditioning is also very important when choosing a location for a network server. If the temperature is too hot, damage will occur.

✦   ✦   ✦

Test Taking Tips

The CompTIA Server+ exam is *not* easy, and requires a great deal of preparation. The exam questions measure real-world skills. Your ability to answer these questions correctly will be enhanced by as much hands-on experience with the product as you can get.

About the Exam

An important aspect of passing the Server+ Exam is understanding the big picture. This includes understanding how the exams are developed and scored.

Every job function requires different levels of cognitive skills, from memorization of facts and definitions to the comprehensive ability to analyze scenarios, design solutions, and evaluate options. To make the exams relevant in the real world, the Server+ exam tests the specific cognitive skills needed for the job functions being tested. These exams go beyond testing rote knowledge — you need to *apply* your knowledge, analyze technical solutions, solve problems, and make decisions — just like you would on the job.

Server+ certification exam items and scoring

The CompTIA Server+ Certification exam consists of 80 questions. You must have a passing score of 70% and you have 90 minutes to complete the exam. The certification test is administered on a computer at a Prometric or VUE authorized testing center, in an easy-to-use format. The format of the test looks very much like other multiple-choice examinations you have taken before. The difference is, this examination is taken on a desktop computer connected into a testing network, where all the data is stored centrally and securely. Directions for using the testing software are displayed on the screen. A tutorial is provided, as well as the assistance of a nearby proctor. On-screen help is also available, including information at the bottom of the screen that lets you know how to enter your answer, move forward in the test, mark a question for answering later, or review a previous question.

Usually each question has one correct response. However, there are some that have multiple correct responses. When there are multiple correct answers, a message at the bottom of the screen prompts you to "choose all that apply." Be sure to read the messages.

Exam formats

The CompTIA Server+ exam is based on a how-to approach. Thus, it is recommended that you have some hands on experience before actually taking the test. CompTIA recommends that you have been working in a related field for at least 18 to 24 months.

The exam is straight multiple-choice, not adaptive. There are 80 questions, with a few figures.

Preparing for the Server+ Exam

The best way to prepare for an exam is to study, learn, and master the job functions on which you'll be tested. For any certification exam, you should follow these important preparation steps:

1. Identify the objectives on which you'll be tested.

2. Assess your current mastery of those objectives.

3. Practice tasks and study the areas you haven't mastered.

If you visit the CompTIA Web site at `www.comptia.org`, you will find relevant information about the Server + certification exam. CompTIA has information that will help you locate a test center in your area and any fees that are involved. They also have links to help you find study resources and hands-on training centers in your area.

The CompTIA web site also has the exam blueprint in an adobe acrobat format. This blueprint will help you to determine what areas need to be covered to pass the exam. However, you will find that this book covers all the objectives listed on the blue print.

Taking the Server+ Exam

This section contains information about registering for and taking an exam, including what to expect when you arrive at the testing center to take the exam.

How to register for an exam

CompTIA testing and certification is administered by the worldwide networks of Prometric and VUE. You can find a testing center in your area by following the links from the CompTIA Web site. You can choose which testing center you would like to use.

If you visit the Web sites of Prometric (www.prometric.com) and VUE (www.vue.com), you will find the necessary information on how to register for an exam and what to expect when you get there. Both Web sites offer electronic registration for the CompTIA exams to help speed up the testing process.

What to expect at the testing center

As you prepare for your certification exam, it may be helpful to know what to expect when you arrive at the testing center on the day of your exam. The following information gives you a preview of the general procedure you'll go through at the testing center:

✦ You will be asked to sign the log book upon arrival and departure.

✦ You will be required to show two forms of identification, including one photo ID (such as a driver's license or company security ID), before you may take the exam.

✦ The test administrator will give you a Testing Center Regulations form that explains the rules you will be expected to comply with during the test. You will be asked to sign the form, indicating that you understand the regulations and will comply.

✦ The test administrator will show you to your test computer and will handle any preparations necessary to start the testing tool and display the exam on the computer.

✦ You will be provided a set amount of scratch paper for use during the exam. All scratch paper will be collected from you at the end of the exam.

✦ The exams are all closed-book. You may not use a laptop computer or have any notes or printed material with you during the exam session.

✦ Some exams may include additional materials or exhibits. If any exhibits are required for your exam, the test administrator will provide you with them before you begin the exam and collect them from you at the end of the exam.

✦ Before you begin the exam, the test administrator will tell you what to do when you complete the exam. If the test administrator doesn't explain this to you, or if you are unclear about what you should do, ask the administrator before beginning the exam.

Because you'll be given a specific amount of time to complete the exam once you begin, if you have any questions or concerns, don't hesitate to ask the test administrator before the exam begins.

As an exam candidate, you are entitled to the best support and environment possible for your exam. In particular, you are entitled to following:

✦ A quiet, uncluttered test environment

✦ Scratch paper

✦ The tutorial for using the online testing tool, and time to take the tutorial

✦ A knowledgeable and professional test administrator

✦ The opportunity to submit comments about the testing center and staff, or the test itself

The Certification Development Team will investigate any problems or issues you raise and make every effort to resolve them quickly.

Your exam results

As soon as you finish the test, you receive the final score. You will see the results immediately on the computer screen. In addition, a hard copy of the score report is provided at the testing center.

The score report shows whether or not you passed the test. You can also see how you did on each section of the test and on each technology. Please retain this score report as it contains your unique ID number, which is also your certification number. It can be used to verify your certification until your certificate arrives.

If you pass the examination, a certificate will be mailed to you within a few weeks. Should you not receive your certificate and information packet within five weeks of passing your exam, contact CompTIA at fulfillment@comptia.org or 630-268-1818 and ask for the fulfillment department.

Certification indicates that you have completed the steps and have the knowledge required to perform at a specified level and prove to your employer and clients that your expertise is attested to by a recognized industry organization. Today, virtually every technology professional can benefit by pursuing a well-chosen certification. Becoming certified can increase your salary, enhance your skill set, and make your job more satisfying.

If you don't receive a passing score

If you do not pass a certification exam, you may call the testing center to schedule a time to retake the exam. Before retaking the exam, you should review this book and focus additional study on the topic areas where your exam results could be improved. Please note that you must pay again for each time you retake the exam.

One way to determine areas where additional study may be helpful is to review your individual section scores carefully. The section titles in your score report generally correlate to specific groups of exam objectives.

Here are some specific ways you can prepare to retake an exam:

✦ Go over the section-by-section scores on your exam results, noting objective areas where your score could be improved.

✦ Review the objectives for the exam, with a special focus on the tasks and objective areas that correspond to the exam sections where your score could be improved.

✦ Increase your real-world, hands-on experience and practice performing the listed job tasks with the relevant products and technologies.

For More Information

VUE has teamed with Self Test software, which is a world leader in certification practice tests. These practice exams will help to prepare you for the actual test. Visit their Web site for more information at www.vue.com. VUE lists several resources that can help you pass the CompTIA Exams.

The Prometric Web site (www.prometric.com) also contains information about how to pass the CompTIA exams. They offer many ideas on resources you should acquire to pass the exam. The also offer practice exams for a fee.

Visit www.cramsession.com for other useful information about the CompTIA Server+ exam. This Web site offers free sample exams and study resources.

✦   ✦   ✦

What's on the CD-ROM

This appendix provides you with information on the contents of the CD-ROM that accompanies this book. There are thirteen programs included on this CD-ROM:

- ✦ *Hungry Minds* Test Engine
- ✦ PC-cillin 2000
- ✦ Network View 1.2
- ✦ Qcheck
- ✦ Lan-Watcher 1.0
- ✦ ipPulse 1.4
- ✦ SNMPc Enterprise Edition
- ✦ NetStat Live 2.11
- ✦ CommView 2.4
- ✦ AdRem Secure Remote Console 3.0
- ✦ AdRem Server Manager 4.4
- ✦ AdRem Free Remote Console 3.3

Also included is an electronic, searchable version of the book that can be viewed with Adobe Acrobat Reader.

System Requirements

Make sure that your computer meets the minimum system requirements listed in this section. If your computer doesn't match up to most of these requirements, you may have a problem using the contents of the CD.

For Microsoft Windows 9*x* or Windows NT/2000:

✦ PC with a Pentium processor running at 120 MHz or faster

✦ At least 32MB of RAM

✦ At least 50MB of free hard drive space

✦ Ethernet network interface card (NIC) or modem with a speed of at least 28,800 bps

✦ A CD-ROM drive — double-speed (2x) or faster

For the SNMPc 5.0 Network Manager program the minimum requirements are:

✦ Microsoft Windows 98 or Windows NT/2000

✦ PC with a Pentium II processor running at 266 MHz

✦ 64MB of RAM (128MB recommended)

✦ 500MB of available hard drive space

✦ Ethernet network interface card (NIC)

✦ A CD-ROM drive — double-speed (2x) or faster

Using the CD with Microsoft Windows

To install the items from the CD to your hard drive, follow these steps:

1. Insert the CD into your computer's CD-ROM drive.

2. Click Start ➪ Run.

3. When the Run dialog box appears, choose Browse and locate your CD-ROM drive. Double-click your CD-ROM drive to view the contents of the CD-ROM.

4. Double-click the folder of the software you would like to install and then choose `setup.exe`.

5. Click OK.

6. In the Run dialog box you should see the path of the software you wish to install, click the OK button.

CD-ROM Contents

The CD-ROM contains some great applications that I think you will enjoy. Also included on the CD-ROM is the *Hungry Minds* Test Engine and the electronic version of the book in Adobe PDF format. The following is a summary of the contents of the CD-ROM arranged by category.

Hungry Minds Test Engine

The version of the Hungry Minds test engine software included on the CD gives you the opportunity to test your knowledge with simulated exam questions. The Hungry Minds test engine product includes:

✦ Features study sessions, standard exams, and adaptive exams

✦ New exam every time

✦ Historical analysis

Follow these steps to install the Hungry Minds test engine software:

1. Place the Server+ Certification Bible CD-ROM in your CD-ROM drive. Wait for the Autorun program to start. After a moment, the Welcome screen appears containing the following options: PDFs, Install, Browse, and Exit.

2. Click Install to start the Boson HMI Tests Installation wizard. Read the splash screen and click Next. The End User License Agreement appears.

3. Read through the End User License Agreement for details about the acceptable uses of the Hungry Minds Test Engine software. Click Next to continue to the Hungry Minds Trademark and Disclaimer page.

4. Read through the information about trademarks and disclaimers about the Hungry Minds test engine. Click Next after you finish.

5. Choose a destination for the files to install to. You can accept the default by clicking Next.

6. The installer begins and installs the test engine on your hard drive. A screen appears to tell you that installation was successful.

7. You can start the test engine by choosing Start ➪ Hungry Minds ➪ Server+ Certification Bible.

Network monitoring applications

The following network monitoring applications are on the CD-ROM. Every program on the CD-ROM is located in the folder name associated with the Software name.

LAN-Watcher 1.0

I created this program to be a simple but efficient network-monitoring program. It will enable you to monitor the status of any server connected to a LAN. This includes print servers, routers, mail servers, AS/400, fax servers, and any other device connected to your LAN that has a workstation name or an IP address. All monitoring is done in real time to allow constant and extremely accurate monitoring. This program is provided as an unregistered trial version.

NetStat Live 2.11

NetStat Live, from AnalogX, is a freeware TCP/IP protocol monitor, which can be used to see your exact throughput on both incoming and outgoing data. This program also lets you see how quickly your data goes from your computer to another computer on the Internet and even will tell you how many other computers your data must go through to get there.

SNMPc 5.0 Network Manager

SNMPc 5.0 Network Manager, from Castle Rock Computing, Inc., is a scalable, distributed management suite for managing small- to large-sized networks. This evaluation version employs multiple components running on different computers, and uses distributed database technology to provide a high-performance platform regardless of the size or configuration of the network.

Network View 1.2

Network View 1.2, from Network View Software will discover all your TCP/IP nodes and their routes using DNS, SNMP, and TCP Ports information. Even with a database of more than 5,000 SNMP enterprises and devices, it can be run from a floppy disk. In a few seconds, you produce a high quality map of a network, print it, or save it to a floppy, and modify it as you like.

ipPulse 1.4

The 30-day trial of ipPulse, from Northwest Performance Software, Inc., is a remote status monitoring tool. Use ipPulse to monitor the up/down status of IP connected devices (nodes) on any IP connected network. ipPulse uses a variety of methods, including `ping`, TCP connects, and SNMP to poll and check the network connectivity of a list of user-defined nodes. ipPulse alerts you to failures using a variety of techniques ranging from audible messages to email and pager notification. You can even control ipPulse remotely by logging into Remote Control using any Telnet application.

CommView 2.4

CommView, from TamoSoft, Inc., is a program for monitoring network activity capable of capturing and analyzing packets on any Ethernet network. It gathers information about data flowing on a LAN and decodes the analyzed data. With CommView you can see the list of network connections, vital IP statistics, and examine individual packets. IP packets are decoded down to the lowest layer with full analysis of the main IP protocols: TCP, UDP, and ICMP. Full access to raw data is also provided. Captured packets can be saved to log files for future analysis. A flexible system of filters makes it possible to drop packets you don't need or capture only those packets that you wish to capture. This is a 30-day trial version.

Remote console applications

The following remote console applications are included.

AdRem Secure Remote Console 3.0

This evaluation version of Remote Console for Windows environment, from AdRem Software, enables remote access to the NetWare server console. Its key benefits include easy logging on to the server and switching between console screens. The connection is safe thanks to authorization by NDS and 128-bit encryption.

AdRem Free Remote Console 3.3

Free Remote Console, also from AdRem Software, is an extremely efficient solution, enabling remote operation on the server. The program offers security for network operations thanks to NDS authentication. Remote Console operates in LAN and WAN environments using the IPX and TCP/IP protocols. It connects with servers with secure NCP connections, automatically using the right network protocol.

Server manager application

The following server manager application is included.

AdRem Server Manager 4.4

Server Manger, from AdRem Software, operating in a Windows environment ensures easy access to information about the state and configuration of every NetWare server in your network. It combines the features of many other programs into one solution, which is easy to use, inexpensive, and secure. Server Manager is an indispensable tool for administrators and it makes your everyday work substantially easier. While helping maintain your network integrity, it improves the efficiency of the whole company. Check out this great evaluation version.

Virus protection

The following virus protection program is included.

PC-cillin 2000

This is my favorite antivirus software I have ever used. I am proud to have the opportunity to include a 30-day evaluation copy of PC-cillin 2000 antivirus software, from Trend Micro, Inc., on the CD-ROM for you to evaluate. This software provides complete Internet-era antivirus protection for your home computer. PC-cillin 2000 handles updates quickly and efficiently and uses an incremental update procedure to update only the virus patterns that have changed since the last release

Electronic version of *Server+ Certification Bible*

The complete (and searchable) text of this book is on the CD-ROM in Adobe's Portable Document Format (PDF), readable with the Adobe Acrobat Reader (also included). For more information on Adobe Acrobat Reader, go to www.adobe.com.

Troubleshooting

If you have difficulty installing or using the CD-ROM programs, try the following solutions:

- ✦ **Turn off any anti-virus software that you may have running.** Installers sometimes mimic virus activity and can make your computer incorrectly believe that it is being infected by a virus. (Be sure to turn the anti-virus software back on later.)

- ✦ **Close all running programs.** The more programs you're running, the less memory is available to other programs. Installers also typically update files and programs; if you keep other programs running, installation may not work properly.

If you still have trouble with the CD, please call the Hungry Minds Customer Care department at: (800) 762-2974. Outside the United States, call (317) 572-3993. Hungry Minds will provide technical support only for installation and other general quality control items; for technical support on the applications themselves, consult the program's vendor or author.

✦   ✦   ✦

Glossary

10baseT A type of network cable. 10BaseT Ethernet networks run at 10 MB/s, and have a maximum segment length of 100 meters.

100baseT A type of network cable also referred to as Fast Ethernet. 100BaseT runs at 100 MB/s, and the maximum segment length is 100 meters.

1000baseT A type of network cable also referred to as Gigabit Ethernet. 1000BaseT runs at 1 Gbps, and the maximum segment length is 100 meters.

Accelerated Graphics Port (AGP) A special port that provides a video controller card with a dedicated path to the CPU.

Access Control List (ACL) A list of rights an object has to resources in the network in Microsoft Windows NT and Windows 2000.

ACL See Access Control List.

adaptive teaming Two or more network interface cards brought together in a team. If one network interface card fails, the other one will take over.

AGP See Accelerated Graphics Port.

Antivirus software A category of software that uses various methods to eliminate viruses in a computer. It typically also protects against future infections.

application log A Windows NT Log file, viewable in Event Viewer, used to keep track of events for network services and applications.

application server Any server that acts as a middle tier in a multi-tiered application that involves using transactional database data, and processing client requests to use that data.

AT Attachment Packet Interface (ATAPI) A protocol created to enable non-hard disk devices to also use the IDE channel on a computer system. Using a special ATAPI driver that is loaded into system memory, devices such as CD-ROMS, tape drives, and optical drives, can plug into the IDE interface, and can also be configured as master or slave, by themselves, or in conjunction with a hard drive.

ATAPI See AT Attachment Packet Interface.

Attachment Unit Interface (AUI) An interface that is typically used on coaxial-based network cards. The AUI interface includes a transceiver that connects a coaxial cable with a 15-pin connector.

AUI See Attachment Unit Interface.

bandwidth In network communications, the amount of data that can be sent across a wire in a given time. Each communication that passes along the wire decreases the amount of available bandwidth.

baseband A network technology that uses a single-carrier frequency and is used for short-distance transmission. The complete bandwidth of the channel is used.

baseline A snapshot of the system under normal operating conditions and used as a yardstick to measure future abnormalities.

Basic Input-Output System (BIOS) A set of detailed instructions for system startup that are usually stored in ROM on the system board.

Biometric system Technology, such as fingerprint or retinal scanners, that makes use of the fact that each person has unique physical traits. Used as a front end to a system that requires identification before allowing access.

BIOS See Basic Input-Output System.

BNC connector See British Naval Connector.

boot sector virus A virus that overwrites the boot sector, making it appear as if there is no pointer to the operating system. When this happens, you will see a "Missing operating system" or "Hard disk not found" error message on power-up.

bottleneck An area that can slow down a computer's performance by creating a queue where processes or functions must wait to be processed or executed.

bridge A network device that separates a single network into logical segments, but lets two segments appear to be one network to higher layer protocols.

British Naval Connector (BNC Connector) Also known as barrel connector, this connector type is used in 10base2 (Thinnet) networks to connect two cable segments.

broadband A network transmission method in which a single transmission medium is divided so that multiple signals can travel across the same medium simultaneously.

Business Impact Analysis (BIA) A Business Impact Analysis is an evaluation of the strengths and weaknesses of your company's disaster preparedness and the impact an interruption would have on your business.

cable A physical transmission medium that has a central conductor of wire or fiber surrounded by a plastic jacket.

Central Processing Unit (CPU) The main chip on a motherboard where instructions are executed.

Client/server A network architecture in which all resources are stored on a file server. Processing power is distributed among workstations and the file server.

coaxial A type of cable used in Ethernet networks.

Cold site A prepared network environment that is wired and air-conditioned, and can be used to house people and replacement equipment if the main network site is down due to a disaster.

Compact Disk-Recordable (CD-R) A storage medium that uses a smooth, clear surface platter with a dyed background that can be changed to signify the difference between bits. The laser is capable of changing the dye and, therefore, is able to write data to the disk.

Complementary Metal Oxide Semiconductor (CMOS) The type of chip commonly used to store the BIOS for a PC. It is usually backed up with a small battery for times when the PC's power is off.

CPU See Central Processing Unit.

crossover cable A network cable that has its transmit and receive pins reversed on one end. A crossover cable is used to connect two server together through their network ports, or two hubs that do no have uplink ports.

DAT See Digital Audio Tape.

Database server A server that stores structured data in a filing system that can be retrieved by multiple users simultaneously.

DHCP Server A server that runs the Dynamic Host Configuration Protocol, which assigns network IP addresses to a client as the client starts up on the network. With this configuration, each client workstation does not need to be set up with a static IP address.

Differential backup A backup routine that backs up data that has changed since the last full backup.

Digital Audio Tape (DAT) A type of magnetic tape that uses a scheme called helical scan to record data. This is the same type of recording that is used in common video-tape recorders and is somewhat slower than linear tape.

Digital Linear Tape (DLT) A type of magnetic tape cartridge that is used to back up data.

DIMM See Dual In-Line Memory Module.

Direct Memory Access (DMA) A method by which a peripheral can communicate directly with RAM, without intervention by the CPU.

Disaster recovery plan A plan that is created and tested to ensure network availability if a disaster occurs that renders the network inoperable.

disk duplexing The practice of using two hard drives with identical data, each on a separate controller. If one of the disks or controllers fails, the other can continue to provide data.

disk errors Hard drives can contain defects in the surface magnetic media that result in loss of the data that the operating system attempts to store there.

disk mirroring A system that consists of one controller and two hard drives. Disk mirroring provides redundancy by mirroring data from one hard drive to another. Also known as RAID 1.

disk striping A technique in which data is spread evenly across a number of physical drives to create a large, logical volume. The data is divided into stripes, which are written across the drive array within a defined block size. Also known as RAID 0, the most basic form of RAID.

DLL See Dynamic Link Library.

DLT See Digital Linear Tape.

DMA See Direct Memory Access.

DNS server A server that runs the Domain Name Service (DNS), and keeps a database of tables that translate fully qualified Internet domain names to their respective IP address.

downtime Time wasted as a result of a malfunctioning computer or network.

Dual In-Line Memory Module A small plug-in circuit board that contains memory chips. Similar to a SIMM.

Dynamic Link Library (DLL) Small pieces of executable Windows code that Windows programmers use so they don't have to write commonly used routines into each program.

ECC See error correcting code.

EDO See extended data output.

EEPROM See Electrically Erasable Programmable Read-Only Memory.

EISA See Extended Industry Standard Architecture.

Electrically Erasable Programmable Read-Only Memory A type of memory that holds data without power. It can be erased and overwritten from within the computer or externally.

electrostatic discharge (ESD) A release of electrical energy when two items with dissimilar static electrical charges are brought together. It can damage computer components.

error correcting code (ECC) A type of memory that tests for memory errors, which it corrects automatically.

ESD See electrostatic discharge.

Ethernet A networking technology defined by the Institute for Electrical and Electronic Engineers (IEEE) as IEEE standard 802.3. Ethernet networks use coaxial, twisted-pair wiring or fiber-optic cable to connect stations. Ethernet networks can transmit data at 10 Mbps, 100 Mbps, and even 1,000 Mbps.

event logs Log files containing the system, security, and application events.

expansion slot A slot on the computer's bus. Expansion cards, such as NIC cards are plugged into these slots to expand the functionality of the computer.

Extended Data Output (EDO) A type of memory that approaches the speed of static RAM by overlapping internal operations.

Extended Industry Standard Architecture (EISA) A type of SCSI architecture that expands the 16 bit ISA bus to 32 bits and provides bus mastering.

fail over In a mirrored system, when one of the disk drives crashes, the system will transfer operations to the mirrored drive until the original drive is replaced. Also used to describe when a RAID system uses an online hot spare to rebuild a new drive.

Fast Ethernet An Ethernet topology using category 5 twisted-pair cable to transmit at 100 Mbps.

Fast Page Mode RAM (FPM RAM) The traditional RAM used in PC's for many years. It came in modules of 2 to 32MB. It is considered too slow for fast, modern system memory buses.

father-son A backup media rotation method that uses a combination of full and differential or incremental backups for a two-week schedule.

fax server A server that enables clients to be able to fax documents directly from their computer.

fiber-optic cable Extremely high-speed network cable that consists of glass fibers that carry light signals instead of electrical signals. Fiber-optic cable is best used for transmission over long distances.

file and print server A server that provides file storage and printing services to clients. Client files are stored on the server, then they are centralized in a common place that can be more easily backed up.

File Transfer Protocol (FTP) The protocol used to download files from an FTP server to a client computer.

firewall Software that prevents unauthorized traffic between two networks by examining the IP packets that travel on both networks.

firmware Coded instructions for hardware that are stored in read-only memory.

flash memory Non-volatile storage device similar to EEPROM, but where erasing can only be done in blocks or the entire chip.

FPM See Fast Page Mode RAM.

FTP See File Transfer Protocol.

FTP server A server that stores files for download via the FTP protocol.

full backup A backup method that backs up all the files on all the selected devices.

full duplex A communication channel that enables data to travel in both directions at once.

gateway server A type of server that acts as a link between different types of networks.

grandfather A type of backup method that provides one year of backup history and typically uses 19 tapes.

grandfather-father-son A type of backup method that reduces wear on backup tapes and provides 12 weeks of backup history.

hacker A malicious intruder who tries to discover sensitive information, or destroy information by breaking into networks from a remote system.

half duplex A communication channel that limits data to traveling only in one direction at a time.

host adapter Within SCSI technology, a device that facilitates communications between the PC bus and the devices on the SCSI bus. You must choose a host adapter that will be compatible with the SCSI technology you wish to use.

hot plug Term used to describe hard drives that can be installed and removed from the host system without interrupting its regular operation. This is very important for production servers where downtime often isn't an option.

hot site A remote location is one that offers computing resources in the event that a disaster has made the company's main site inoperative. Ideally, the hot site is located less than 30 miles away from your company.

hot spare A drive in a RAID system that is automatically used to replace a failed drive.

hot swap A term used to describe devices that can be inserted or removed from a RAID system while it is running.

hub A device that connects several computers or several networks together. A passive hub may simply forward messages. An active hub, or repeater, amplifies or refreshes the stream of data, which otherwise would deteriorate over a long distance.

IDE See Integrated Drive Electronics.

incremental backup A type of backup that backs up data that has changed since the last full or incremental backup.

Industry Standard Architecture (ISA) An expansion bus commonly used on PCs.

Input/Output (I/O) addresses Addresses represent locations in system memory that are reserved for a particular device.

Integrated Drive Electronics (IDE) A popular hardware interface used to connect hard drives to a PC.

Interrupt request (IRQ) A hardware interrupt generated by a device that requires service from the CPU.

IRQ See Interrupt request.

ISA See Industry Standard Architecture.

jumper A device used to accomplish manual hardware configuration. Jumpers are made of two separate components: a row of metal pins on the hardware itself and a small plastic cap that has a metal insert inside of it. The two parts together form a circuit that sets the configuration.

LAN See Local Area Network.

line conditioner Device that cleans the input power to your devices. Although it does protect against voltage discrepancies, it can also condition power that is inconsistent.

link light A small LED found on a NIC or a hub. It is usually green to indicate a successful connection and yellow to indicate no connection.

Linux An open-source implementation of Unix, created by Linus Torvalds, that runs on many different hardware platforms.

Local Area Network (LAN) A network composed of two or more computers in a limited geographic area, linked by high-performance cables so that users can exchange information, share peripheral devices, or access a common server.

log file A file that keeps a running list of all errors and notices, the time and date they occurred, and any other pertinent information.

mail server A type of server that stores e-mail. Clients connect to the mail server by supplying their mail account information, with which they can send and receive e-mail.

Management Information Base (MIB) A database of information concerning a managed device. It consists of objects, which describe various functions that can be measured and monitored within that device.

MCA See Micro Channel Architecture Bus.

memory bank A slot on a motherboard that a memory card fits into.

memory interleaving A process used by high-end motherboards to increase performance. Memory interleaving allows simultaneous access to more than one area of memory. This improves performance because the processor can access more data in the same amount of time.

MIB See Management Information Base.

Micro Channel Architecture Bus (MCA) A bus created in 1987 by IBM as a rival to the ISA bus. It boasted 32-bit bus width, a bus mastering system for greater bus efficiency, and a plug-and-play system that predated modern plug-and-play technology by many years.

multiprocessing The practice of running a system with more than one processor. In order for this to work, multiprocessing must be supported by both your hardware and your software.

NetWare The network operating system made by Novell.

network analyzer Hardware or software that is used to collect detailed information on network data flow. Sometimes called a *network sniffer.*

Network Interface Card (NIC) A physical device that connects computers and other network equipment to the transmission media.

network media The physical cables that link computers in a network; also known as physical media.

Network Operating System (NOS) The software that runs on a network server and offers file, print, application, and other services to clients.

NIC See Network Interface Card.

non-paged RAM A type of memory that cannot be written to disk. Data in non-swapped RAM must reside in RAM constantly, because it is made up of vital system data information.

NOS See Network Operating System.

off-site storage A method of storing backup media in a location other than the company's premises. This protects the company's data in the event of a disaster such as a fire or flood in the main building.

operating system A set of computer instruction codes whose purpose is to define input and output device connections, and provide instructions for the computer's processor to operate on to retrieve and display data.

optical media A storage medium on which data is written by lasers. Optical disks can store much more data than most portable magnetic media, up to 6GB. Optical media is based on interpreting the reflections of laser light off the surface of the media.

OS See operating system.

OS/2 A network operating system created by IBM.

packet The basic division of data sent over a network.

paged RAM A virtual memory space allocated on the hard disk that is mapped to physical memory.

parity A technique used to store data information that will enable you to rebuild a failed disk drive from other drives.

partition A section of the storage area on a computer's hard disk.

patch Software that fixes a problem with an existing program or operating system.

patch cable Any cable that connects one network device to the main cable or to a patch panel that in turn connects to the main cable run.

PCI See Peripheral Component Interconnect.

Peer PCI A technology that was created to alleviate the negative characteristics of having several PCI buses being daisy-chained through a bridge controller. Multiple Peer PCI buses are directly connected to the host bus, enabling the CPU to access each bus directly.

Peripheral Component Interconnect A popular expansion bus that provides a high-speed data path between the CPU and peripherals.

physical media See network media.

plug-and-play An Intel standard that enables a PC to automatically configure components when they are connected. The standard requires support from the BIOS, the expansion card, and the operating system.

POST See power-on self-test.

power-on self-test (POST) A series of built-in tests that are performed at system startup.

power spike An event that occurs when the power level rises above normal and drops back to normal for less than a second. This can damage computer components.

power surge An event that occurs when the power level rises above normal and stays there for longer than a second or two. This can damage computer components.

proxy server A proxy server forwards network requests on behalf of another client or server. A proxy server is typically configured to facilitate Internet web server requests between a client and a web server.

RAID A configuration of multiple hard disks used to provide fault tolerance should a disk fail. Different levels of RAID exist, depending on the amount and type of fault tolerance provided. Stands for "redundant array of independent (or inexpensive) disks."

RAM See Random Access Memory.

Rambus Direct RAM (RDRAM) A new RAM type created by a company named Rambus, partnered with Intel. It contains an intelligent micro-channel memory bus, which can run at a very high clock speed.

Rambus Inline Memory Module Memory modules for RDRAM, which contain 184 pins. Because RDRAM works in channels, any empty sockets have to be filled with a blank memory module called a Continuity Rambus Inline Memory Module.

Random Access Memory The system's main memory system. Data stored in RAM can be accessed directly without having to read information stored before or after the desired data.

RAS Server See remote access server.

RDRAM See Rambus Direct RAM.

readme file A text file that comes with some software and gives information on the program, often additional information not in the manual.

Read-Only Memory (ROM) A type of memory that cannot be written to. Its information is static. When power is disconnected from and reconnected, the information stored in ROM is retained. Most commonly used in system BIOS chips.

remote access server A computer that has one or more modems installed to enable remote users to connect to the network.

Remote Network Monitoring Management Information Base (RMON MIB) A monitoring system that uses comprehensive network fault diagnosis, planning, and performance tuning features. It uses SNMP and its standard MIB design to provide multivendor interoperability between monitoring products and management stations.

remote notification An alert method that sends remote messages to a technician if a problem occurs with the network while the technician is off-site.

RIMM See Rambus Inline Memory Module.

risk analysis A survey of all the components of your system to enable you to calculate the cost of replacing these items in a disaster.

RJ-45 connector A cable connector used by telephone and data systems. The RJ-45 connector is modular by design to provide a quick way of connecting and disconnecting circuits. It uses an eight-wire (four-pair) system.

RMON MIB See Remote Network Monitoring Management Information Base.

ROM See Read-Only Memory.

router A device that connects two networks and enables packets to be transmitted and received between them. A router determines the best path for data packets from source to destination.

SCA Adapters See Single Connector Attachment adapter.

SCSI See Small Computer System Interface.

Serial Presence Detect (SPD) A small EEPROM that resides on newer fast RAM DIMMS. When a computer system boots up, it detects the configuration of the memory modules in order to run properly.

SIMM See Single Inline Memory Module.

Simple Network Management Protocol (SNMP) A management protocol created for sending information about the health of the network to network management consoles.

Single Connector Attachment (SCA) adapter Connectors that allow all signaling and power to be fed through one connector that the hard drive plugs right into without any cabling. Used in RAID systems with many SCSI hard disks.

Single Inline Memory Module (SIMM) A narrow printed circuit board that holds memory chips. The connector is integrated into the edge of the board so it can easily be added to sockets on the system board.

Small Computer System Interface (SCSI) A hardware interface that allows the connection of up to seven devices.

SNA server See System Network Architecture server.

SNMP See Simple Network Management Protocol.

son A backup method that involves doing a full backup every day.

SPD See Serial Presence Detect.

SRAM See Static RAM.

Static RAM A type of RAM requires power to hold content but does not need refreshing like other types of RAM. SRAM is very fast.

stepping A number that indicates design or manufacturing revision data for production microprocessors.

surge protector An electrical device that protects a computer from spikes and surges in the power line. All computers have some surge protection built in, but this protection is not always enough. External surge protectors come in the form of a unit that plugs into the wall, with outlets for several electrical plugs.

System Network Architecture (SNA) server A server that acts as a gateway between the client computer and the mainframe computer.

tape drives A device that holds magnetic tape, and enables the computer to read from and write to it.

TCP/IP TCP/IP is a protocol suite running the Transmission Control Protocol (TCP) on top of the Internet Protocol (IP).These protocols were developed by DARPA to enable communication between different types of computers and computer networks. The Internet Protocol is a connectionless protocol that provides packet routing. TCP is connection-oriented and provides reliable communication and multiplexing.

terminator A device that prevents a signal from bouncing off the end of the network cable, which causes interference with other signals.

third-party A term that refers to manufacturers other than the manufacturer of the specific application or hardware.

topology The configuration of a network, or the pattern in which the computers are interconnected. Common network topologies are the star, bus, and Token-ring.

transceiver The part of any network interface that transmits and receives network signals.

Uninterruptible Power Supply (UPS) A device that provides backup power when the main power fails or moves to an unacceptable level.

Unix A 32-bit, multitasking operating system developed in the 1960s for use on mainframes and minicomputers.

UPS See Uninterruptible Power Supply.

virus A program that infects a computer by attaching itself to another program and propagating itself when that program is executed. A computer can become infected by files downloaded over a network, or by the installation of new software or floppy disks that are infected with viruses.

Web server A server that delivers Internet Web pages to client computers. The client runs a Web browser, which makes a request for an HTML Web page from the server. The server receives that request and sends the desired page, which is displayed in the client's Web browser.

Windows NT A network operating system developed by Microsoft.

Windows 2000 A network operating system developed by Microsoft, a revision of Windows NT.

WINS Server A special Windows NT server that runs the Windows Internet Naming Service (WINS). It allows clients to resolve Windows NetBIOS names to standard Internet domain naming conventions.

Index

Symbols & Numerics

A

Continued

Hungry Minds, Inc.
End-User License Agreement

READ THIS. You should carefully read these terms and conditions before opening the software packet(s) included with this book ("Book"). This is a license agreement ("Agreement") between you and Hungry Minds, Inc. ("HMI"). By opening the accompanying software packet(s), you acknowledge that you have read and accept the following terms and conditions. If you do not agree and do not want to be bound by such terms and conditions, promptly return the Book and the unopened software packet(s) to the place you obtained them for a full refund.

1. **License Grant.** HMI grants to you (either an individual or entity) a nonexclusive license to use one copy of the enclosed software program(s) (collectively, the "Software") solely for your own personal or business purposes on a single computer (whether a standard computer or a workstation component of a multi-hyuser network). The Software is in use on a computer when it is loaded into temporary memory (RAM) or installed into permanent memory (hard disk, CD-ROM, or other storage device). HMI reserves all rights not expressly granted herein.

2. **Ownership.** HMI is the owner of all right, title, and interest, including copyright, in and to the compilation of the Software recorded on the disk(s) or CD-ROM ("Software Media"). Copyright to the individual programs recorded on the Software Media is owned by the author or other authorized copyright owner of each program. Ownership of the Software and all proprietary rights relating thereto remain with HMI and its licensers.

3. **Restrictions On Use and Transfer.**

   (a) You may only (i) make one copy of the Software for backup or archival purposes, or (ii) transfer the Software to a single hard disk, provided that you keep the original for backup or archival purposes. You may not (i) rent or lease the Software, (ii) copy or reproduce the Software through a LAN or other network system or through any computer subscriber system or bulletin-board system, or (iii) modify, adapt, or create derivative works based on the Software.

   (b) You may not reverse engineer, decompile, or disassemble the Software. You may transfer the Software and user documentation on a permanent basis, provided that the transferee agrees to accept the terms and conditions of this Agreement and you retain no copies. If the Software is an update or has been updated, any transfer must include the most recent update and all prior versions.

4. **Restrictions on Use of Individual Programs.** You must follow the individual requirements and restrictions detailed for each individual program in Appendix A of this Book. These limitations are also contained in the individual license agreements recorded on the Software Media. These limitations may include a requirement that after using the program for a specified period of time, the user must pay a registration fee or discontinue use. By opening the Software packet(s), you will be agreeing to abide by the licenses and restrictions for these individual programs that are detailed in Appendix A and on the Software Media. Except as expressly provided herein, none of the material on this Software Media or listed in this Book may ever be redistributed, in original or modified form, for commercial purposes.

5. Limited Warranty.

(a) HMI warrants that the Software and Software Media are free from defects in materials and workmanship under normal use for a period of sixty (60) days from the date of purchase of this Book. If HMI receives notification within the warranty period of defects in materials or workmanship, HMI will replace the defective Software Media.

(b) **HMI AND THE AUTHOR OF THE BOOK DISCLAIM ALL OTHER WARRANTIES, EXPRESS OR IMPLIED, INCLUDING WITHOUT LIMITATION IMPLIED WARRANTIES OF MERCHANTABILITY AND FITNESS FOR A PARTICULAR PURPOSE, WITH RESPECT TO THE SOFTWARE, THE PROGRAMS, THE SOURCE CODE CONTAINED THEREIN, AND/OR THE TECHNIQUES DESCRIBED IN THIS BOOK. HMI DOES NOT WARRANT THAT THE FUNCTIONS CONTAINED IN THE SOFTWARE WILL MEET YOUR REQUIREMENTS OR THAT THE OPERATION OF THE SOFTWARE WILL BE ERROR FREE.**

(c) This limited warranty gives you specific legal rights, and you may have other rights that vary from jurisdiction to jurisdiction.

6. Remedies.

(a) HMI's entire liability and your exclusive remedy for defects in materials and workmanship shall be limited to replacement of the Software Media, which may be returned to HMI with a copy of your receipt at the following address: Software Media Fulfillment Department, Attn.: *Server+ Certification Bible,* Hungry Minds, Inc., 10475 Crosspoint Blvd., Indianapolis, IN 46256, or call 1-800-762-2974. Please allow four to six weeks for delivery. This Limited Warranty is void if failure of the Software Media has resulted from accident, abuse, or misapplication. Any replacement Software Media will be warranted for the remainder of the original warranty period or thirty (30) days, whichever is longer.

(b) In no event shall HMI or the author be liable for any damages whatsoever (including without limitation damages for loss of business profits, business interruption, loss of business information, or any other pecuniary loss) arising from the use of or inability to use the Book or the Software, even if HMI has been advised of the possibility of such damages.

(c) Because some jurisdictions do not allow the exclusion or limitation of liability for consequential or incidental damages, the above limitation or exclusion may not apply to you.

7. U.S. Government Restricted Rights. Use, duplication, or disclosure of the Software for or on behalf of the United States of America, its agencies and/or instrumentalities (the "U.S. Government") is subject to restrictions as stated in paragraph (c)(1)(ii) of the Rights in Technical Data and Computer Software clause of DFARS 252.227-7013, or subparagraphs (c) (1) and (2) of the Commercial Computer Software - Restricted Rights clause at FAR 52.227-19, and in similar clauses in the NASA FAR supplement, as applicable.

8. General. This Agreement constitutes the entire understanding of the parties and revokes and supersedes all prior agreements, oral or written, between them and may not be modified or amended except in a writing signed by both parties hereto that specifically refers to this Agreement. This Agreement shall take precedence over any other documents that may be in conflict herewith. If any one or more provisions contained in this Agreement are held by any court or tribunal to be invalid, illegal, or otherwise unenforceable, each and every other provision shall remain in full force and effect.

CD-ROM Installation Instructions

Each software item on the *Server+ Certification Bible* CD-ROM is located in its own folder. To install a particular piece of software, open its folder with My Computer or Internet Explorer. What you do next depends on what you find in the software's folder:

1. First, look for a `ReadMe.txt` file or a `.doc` or `.htm` document. If this is present, it should contain installation instructions and other useful information.

2. If the folder contains an executable (`.exe`) file, this is usually an installation program. Often it will be called `Setup.exe` or `Install.exe`, but in some cases the filename reflects an abbreviated version of the software's name and version number. Run the `.exe` file to start the installation process.

The `ReadMe.txt` file in the CD-ROM's root directory may contain additional installation information, so be sure to check it.

For a listing of the software on the CD-ROM, see Appendix D.